LET'S GO: GREECE

is the best book for anyone traveling on a budget. Here's why:

No other guidebook has as many budget listings.

In Athens we list dozens of places offering bed and breakfast for less than $15 per night; in the countryside, we found hundreds more for much less. We tell you how to get there the cheapest way, whether by bus, plane, or thumb, and where to get an inexpensive and satisfying meal once you've arrived. There are hundreds of money-saving tips for everyone plus lots of information on special student discounts.

LET'S GO researchers have to make it on their own.

No expense accounts, no free hotel rooms. Our student researchers travel on budgets as limited as your own.

LET'S GO is completely revised every year.

We don't just update the prices, we go back to the places. If a charming restaurant has become an overpriced tourist trap, we'll replace it with a new and better listing.

No other budget guidebook includes all this:

Coverage of both the cities and the countryside; in-depth information on culture, history, and the people; distinctive features like rail, city, and regional maps; tips on work, study, hiking and biking, nightlife and special splurges; and much, much more.

LET'S GO is for anyone who wants to see the real Greece on an inflation-fighting budget.

LET'S GO:

The Budget Guide to GREECE

1984

Ted Osius, Editor

Written by Harvard Student Agencies, Inc.

ST. MARTIN'S PRESS
NEW YORK

Distributed in the United Kingdom by Columbus Books,
Devonshire House, Bromley, Kent BR1 1LT, England

Distributed throughout the rest of the world by Fleetbooks
S.A., 100 Park Avenue, New York, New York 10017

ISBN: 0-312-48220-5

First Edition
10   8 7 6 5 4 3 2 1

Let's Go: Greece is written by Harvard Student Agencies,
Harvard University, Thayer Hall-B, Cambridge, Mass. 02138.

Editor: Ted Osius
Assistant Editor: Susan B. Whitlock
Managing Editor: Linda Haverty
Assistant Managing Editor: Steven Parkey
Advertising Representatives: James Heideman, Jean Huang
Advertising Manager: Richard Foote
Assistant Advertising Manager: Pamela Stedman
Researcher/Writers:

    Scott Campbell: *Athens, Crete, Cyprus*
    Jim Conant, Juliet Floyd: *Turkish Coast*
    Amy Gluckman: *Dodecanese, Northeastern Islands*
    Vlad Jenkins: *Northern Greece*
    Greg Mansfield: *Ionian Islands, Epirus*
    Jim Millward: *Cyclades, Central Greece, Sporades,*
        Northern Greece
    Gideon Schor: *Saronic Gulf Islands, Peloponnese, Cen-*
        tral Greece, Cyclades

Staff Assistants: Miriam Roberts, Michael Della Rocca, Phuong Pham, Jenny Wittner
Proofreaders: John Caldwell, Scott Campbell, Natalie Carley, Lee Carr, Deborah Fickling, Debbie Friedmann, Martha Hodes, Deb Iles, Jenn Kapuscik, Diane Klein, Joan Kocsis, Jim Kralik, Matthew Krauss, Michael Loo, Tom Looney, Steven Parkey, Susan Peisner, Debbie Roth, Gayle Sato, Janet Savage, Gideon Schor, Stephanie Seminara, Bennett Singer, Rick Wertheim, Brent Whitman
Maps: Jeanne Abboud
Legal Counsel: Harold Rosenwald

Acknowledgements

The nine *Let's Go* travel guides that emerged this year are the products of immense amounts of dedication, enthusiasm, and sheer hard work. The results are no more due to the skill of this season's staff than they are a tribute to the high standards set by researchers, writers, and editors of years past. I salute the *Let's Go* tradition of excellence, and thank our predecessors for the fine examples provided over the last two decades.

To my superb assistant editor, Susan Whitlock, I owe the greatest debt of gratitude; her unparalleled competence and perseverance, and uncanny ability to make sense out of nonsense made her the best thing that could have happened to this book. Linda Haverty, our tireless leader and confidante throughout the long and heated summer, was a constant source of inspiration, and always the first to help in times of desperation; I'm proud to call her a friend.

Abundant thanks go to Jim Conant, my own *Let's Go* mentor; I'm honored that he asked me to edit this first edition of the book he envisioned, and thankful for his patience and expertise in preparing itineraries. He and Juliet Floyd provided comprehensive coverage of the Turkish coast, which appears here for the first time. My heartfelt thanks, although insufficient, go to the dedicated researchers who braved hotel proprietors and NTOG officials during the ferociously hot Mediterranean summer. Scott Campbell's meticulous research exposed the stones left unturned by his predecessor, me; he doesn't let me forget it. Gideon Schor refused to succumb to the ravages of the Peloponnesian climate or populace, and sent copy which invariably gleamed with wit and intelligence. Amy Gluckman, whose "vacation" in Greece proved far more arduous than anyone expected, met the challenge without a complaint, and even added new territory to the regional coverage. Despite amorous pursuers and bewildering boat schedules, Jim Millward always managed to send brilliant and amusing copy. Vlad Jenkins and Greg Mansfield also deserve accolades: Vlad survived gassing on a train and went on to hike the mountains and gorges of Northern Greece; Greg persisted in his research of the Ionian islands on crutches after a debilitating motorcycle accident.

On the home front, Steve Parkey, Miriam Roberts, Steve Harris, Mike Della Rocca, and Jenny Wittner performed yeoman's service by typing and preparing the manuscripts for the publisher. Chris Caldwell, Rachel Conrad, and Mark Fishbein, the other Europe editors, provided a core of support; I enjoyed their camaraderie during the difficult hiring process and in the wee hours all summer long. Thanks go to Maura Gorman of HSA for providing money, encouragement, and a place to put the typewriters. Joseph Walton provided generous and cheerful assistance for the chapter on the Turkish coast, and George Selimis, director of the NTOG in New York, contributed to the General Introduction.

I also wish to thank my sister Meg, whose hospitality made possible a productive business trip to the Big Apple, and my housemates, Andy, Maja, Jenny, Linus, Daniel, Scott, and Mr. Lobster, for their patience. Finally, thanks go to my parents for their enduring love, for their wisdom in letting me choose which roads to travel, and for guiding me with gentle hands whenever a guide was needed.

—T.O.

CONTENTS

8 Contents

10   Contents

LET'S GO: GREECE, including Cyprus and Turkish Coast

$1 U.S. = 94.55 dr.   **100 dr. = $1.06**

As seductive as Circe, Greece welcomes hordes of tourists to its shores each year, yet somehow manages to retain its allure. It is easy to understand the country's popularity; with plenty of sunny weather, beautiful beaches, magnificent ancient ruins, exciting nightlife, and the lowest prices in Europe, Greece is quite simply a budget vacationer's paradise.

Greece abounds in striking natural scenery, ranging from the mountains of Thessaly to the grottoes of southern Crete. In the countryside, ancient temples stand in stony silence upon their rocky promontories, while enormous monasteries cling precariously to sheer cliff walls. And, of course, there are the islands, infinite in their variety; some offer the bustling crowds and fast-paced nightlife of a ritzy resort, others the peace and solitude of a secluded retreat.

The Greece of today is rapidly becoming a modernized, industrialized nation. Unfortunately, this means that some of the larger cities, like Athens, Volos, and Thessaloniki, are somewhat ugly and modern, an unappealing mixture of bland new buildings and decaying old structures. But the Greeks continue to cherish their ancient traditions. If Apollo blessed Greece with the warmth of the sun, then Dionysus infused its people with a spirit of celebration. Even the remotest village stages some kind of festival or pageant each year; for the traveler, these events are an invitation to the timeless.

Timelessness need not leave you penniless, and that's where *Let's Go* is designed to help. Our researchers, traveling on a shoestring, share your concerns: how to eat, drink, get around, see the sights, and sleep in the least expensive and most enjoyable way possible.

Most tourists who flock to the Greek islands in search of sun and surf ignore other equally beautiful parts of the country. *Let's Go* tries to take you off the beaten track. We cover everything from the wilds of Macedonia to the southern coast of the Peloponnese, from untouched islands in the Dodecanese to the mountain villages of Crete. In addition, we include a chapter on Cyprus and, for the first time, a chapter on the Aegean and Mediterranean Coast of Turkey. Easily accessible from the eastern Greek islands, this handsome, winding coastline represents a bridge between Europe and the Orient, and features some of the finest ruins in the Mediterranean.

Let's Go will also help guide you through some of the tasks that you need to do before you go. We provide cost-cutting practical information that will help you decide what kind of trip you'll want to take, and a valuable introduction to life in Greece. And our regional introductions try to give the flavor of the areas you might choose to visit.

Once you're there, *Let's Go* tells you some of what there is to see and do in Greece. The orientation and practical information sections in the larger cities and regions help you get settled more easily, if you want to stay. Our sights sections help you explore the pagan temples, Byzantine churches, bustling marketplaces, and golden beaches of glorious Greece. Check special write-ups on entertainment for the festivals and concerts you might otherwise have missed, and nightlife sections for some of the best clubs and most active neighborhoods.

A word of warning: healthy skepticism will serve you better than blind faith in using any guidebook. This book was researched in the summer of 1983, and since then the world has not stood still: prices have changed, hostels have moved, and restaurants have closed. Perhaps the most important advice we can give you is to put *Let's Go* aside occasionally and explore on your own. The most memorable discoveries will be those you make yourself.

Planning Your Trip

Before you go, it's a good idea to decide on a tentative itinerary, even if you discard it as soon as you arrive. Where you go often depends on how long you plan to stay and how much you plan to spend, but there's a lot to be said for following your impulses. Most novice travelers try to see as much as they can in as short a time as possible. But after twenty towns in twenty days, you'll be lucky if you can still distinguish countries. For the sake of your tranquility, let alone money and health, be more selective initially and then spend more time in the places you do visit.

A good practice when planning your trip is to vary the kinds of days you spend. Don't visit too many ancient ruins, churches, or museums consecutively. Think about taking a "day off" from sightseeing to relax in an obscure hill town or on the beach. Take the time to sit back and watch the people walk by, and enjoy your freedom.

Traveling with a companion can be rewarding. A friend can share your experiences and make discoveries that you might have missed. And a companion can shield against isolation, boost your morale, and provide security and protection that might prove valuable in a pinch.

On the other hand, traveling alone affords greater independence. You won't have to argue over itineraries or where to eat. Meeting other people will be much easier, especially if you stay in hostels. And going solo can be a test of your resilience and affability. Language will be the greatest problem, since English is not widely spoken in Greece. But natives always appreciate attempts by visitors to use their language; and if all else fails, it's usually easy to find other English-speaking travelers to provide you with temporary companionship. Even if you travel with a friend, make a point of splitting up occasionally, both to preserve your equilibrium and to gain a new appreciation of your missing partner in adversity.

Off-Season Travel

Summer is the high tourist season in Greece; be prepared to meet fellow travelers almost everywhere you go if you visit between late May and early

September. If you feel stifled by crowds or taxed by the frantic pace of summer travel, seriously consider traveling in the off-season. From September to May there are fewer tourists, prices are lower, and life is more equable. You will find the local residents more receptive and interested in you and the weather even more pleasant, especially in May or September. Even in the chilly winter months, some areas continue to be mild—in southern Crete, swimming is still possible. But Greece also has winter sports, with ski areas at Parnassos, Mt. Pelion, Metsovo, and elsewhere. An extra bonus of off-season travel is that inexpensive airfares are much easier to obtain.

Starting in 1983, the Greek government will subsidize some hotels during the winter, in an effort to encourage off-season tourism—you shouldn't have much trouble finding places to stay. While museums may have shorter hours, don't get the idea that nothing goes on in the off-season. Wherever possible, we try to give an idea of what off-season travel is like in Greece; in particular, we provide some off-season rates for accommodations and travel.

Useful Organizations

Although other sections of the Introduction contain much valuable information for planning your trip to Greece, you may want to do some extra research from this side. The organizations listed below offer both general and specific information on budget travel in Greece.

National Tourist Organization of Greece (NTOG). USA: 645 Fifth Ave., New York, NY 10022 (tel. (212) 421-5777); 611 West Sixth St., Los Angeles, CA 90017 (tel. (213) 626-6996); 168 North Michigan Ave., Chicago, IL 60601 (tel. (312) 782-1084). Canada: 1233 de la Montague, Montreal Q.C., Quebec H36 1Z2 (tel. (514) 871-1535). Australia: 51-57, Pitt. Str., Sydney, N.S.W. 2000. Great Britain: 195-197, Regent St., London W1R 8DR. General information, including pamphlets on different regions and other tourist literature. Ask for the booklet "General information about Greece."

Greek Press and Information Office, 601 Fifth Ave., New York, NY 10017 (tel. (212) 751-8788) and 870 Market St., #849, San Francisco, CA 94102 (tel. (415) 398-1513). Information on work and study opportunities in Greece, as well as other cultural information.

Council on International Educational Exchange (CIEE): 205 East 42nd St., New York, NY 10017 (tel. (212) 661-1450). This is the main office for inquiries by mail and telephone. For in-person inquiries, visit the New York Student Center, 356 West 34th St., New York, NY, or any of the branch offices in San Francisco, Los Angeles, Berkeley, San Diego, Seattle, Miami, and Boston. CIEE is one of the broadest ranging student travel services. Ask for information on low cost travel, educational, and work opportunities. All the usual discount travel cards are available from CIEE, as is the **International Student Identity Card.** They will send you the annual Student Travel Catalog for $1, or you can pick it up free at most student travel offices.

Travel CUTS (Canadian Universities Travel Service): 44 St. George St., Toronto, Ontario M5S 2E4 (tel. (416) 979-2406). Other offices in Victoria, Vancouver, Edmonton, Saskatoon, Ottawa, Montreal, and Halifax. The Canadian representatives to the International Student Travel Conference, Travel CUTS offers discounted transatlantic flights from Canadian cities, sells the ISIC and discount travel passes. Their magazine, *The Canadian Student Traveller,* is available free at all offices.

Harvard Student Agencies (Travel Division): Thayer Hall-B, Harvard University, Cambridge, MA 02138. International Student ID Cards, Eurailpasses, etc. Write for their informative travel packet.

Educational Travel Centre (ETC): 438 N. Frances St., Madison, WI 53703 (tel. (608) 256-5551). ISIC, flight information. If you mention that you are a *Let's Go* reader, ETC will send you a free copy of their travel newspaper *Taking Off*.

Nomadic Books: P.O. 454, Athens, GA 30603. Kevin Kelly publishes a useful free catalogue listing the most recent guidebooks to *all* parts of the world. Good if you're planning to extend the boundaries of your European trip.

Below is a partial list of Greek embassies and consulates in the U.S. and Canada, for technical advice:

Embassy of Greece, 2211 Massachusetts Ave., N.W., Washington, DC 20008 (tel. (202) 667-3168).

Embassy of Greece, 80 MacLaren St., Ottawa, Ontario K2P OK6 (tel. (613) 232-6796).

Consulates:

Illinois, 168 N. Michigan Ave., Chicago, IL 60601 (tel. (312) 372-5356).

California, 2441 Gough St., San Francisco, CA 94123 (tel. (415) 775-2102).

SEND US A POSTCARD

**We'd like to hear your reaction.
Did you make any discoveries?
Did we steer you wrong?**

Let us know.

Massachusetts, Park Square Bldg., 31 St. James Ave., Boston, MA 02116 (tel. (617) 542-3240).

Louisiana, 2318 International Trade Mart Bldg., New Orleans, LA 70130 (tel. (504) 523-1167).

New York, 69 East 79th St., New York, NY 10021 (tel. (212) 988-5500).

Quebec, 1010 Sherbrooke St. West, Suite 204, Montreal PQ, Quebec H3A 2R7 (tel. (514) 845-8127).

Ontario, 100 University Ave., Suite 1004, Toronto, Ontario M5G 1V6.

Vancouver, 890 One Bentall Center, 505 Burrard St., Vancouver, British Columbia.

Documents and Formalities

Passports

You need a valid passport to enter Greece, and to reenter the United States or Canada. If you are 18 or older, you can get a U.S. passport good for ten years at any Passport Agency, clerk of court, or post office. To locate the nearest agency, check the phone book under "U.S. Government, Department of State," or call your local post office. If this is your first passport, if your current passport is more than eight years old, or if it was issued before your eighteenth birthday, you must apply in person—otherwise, you can apply by mail. You must submit a completed application (available from above offices), proof of U.S. citizenship (a birth certificate or naturalization papers), identification (such as a driver's license), and two identical photographs (two inches square on a plain white background). The cost is $35 for a first ten-year passport, $20 for a five-year passport (issued to persons under 18); both types have a $7 execution fee. Renewal by mail is also $35, but there is no execution fee. Processing the application usually takes from two to three weeks. If you have to leave within 48 hours, the Passport Agency provides a "rush" service while you wait, but you must have valid proof of your departure date. For more details, check with your local Passport Agency, or write to the Office of Passport Services, Department of State, Washington, DC 20524 for their free pamphlet *Your Trip Abroad.*

If you lose your passport abroad, notify the U.S. consulate and local police immediately. The U.S. consulate can issue you a new passport, usually within two hours of application. In an emergency ask for an immediate temporary passport.

Canadian passports can be obtained from the Passport Office, Department of External Affairs, Ottawa, Ontario K1A 0G3, or in person at regional passport offices, which are listed in the phone book. You'll need a completed application (available at passport offices, post offices, and travel agencies), evidence of Canadian citizenship, two photos, and $21 cash or certified check. Passports will usually be issued within three to five days after receipt of the application. Canadian passports are valid for five years only. More complete information can be found in the booklet, *How to Obtain a Canadian Passport,* available free from the Passport Office.

It is a good idea to carry a second proof of your citizenship (in the form of a birth certificate, driver's license, etc.) when traveling abroad, and to keep it separate from your passport. That way, if your passport is lost or stolen, you will be able to speed up the processing of a new passport by the nearest consular office. Canadians *must* be able to prove their citizenship with a document or they will not be issued a new passport.

Visas

A visa is essentially written permission granted by a government to allow foreigners to enter a country. You do not need to obtain a visa ahead of time to visit Greece; a valid passport will allow you to stay in Greece for three months. A transit visa, valid for four days, can be obtained from any Greek consulate if you wish to stay in Greece on your way to another country. Once in Greece, you can apply to stay longer at the **Aliens Bureau** in Athens at 9 Halkokondili St., 1st floor (tel. 36 28 301). Other branches of the Alien's Bureau are in Piraeus and Thessaloniki; outside these cities you should contact the local police authorities.

Customs

Upon entering Greece, you must declare certain items including cameras, typewriters, portable radios, and musical instruments. These may be brought in duty-free as long as they will be in use and will be taken with you upon departure. Upon reentering your own country, you must declare all articles acquired abroad. Keep all receipts. Under the new U.S. laws, you can bring in $400 worth of goods duty-free; you pay 10% on the next $1000 worth. The duty-free goods must be for your personal or household use and cannot include more than 100 cigars, 200 cigarettes (one carton), or one liter of wine or liquor (you must be 21 or older to bring liquor into the U.S.). All items included must accompany you; you cannot have them shipped separately.

While in Europe, you can mail unsolicited gifts duty-free if they're worth less than $50. However, you may not mail liquor, tobacco, or perfume into the U.S. If you mail home personal goods of U.S. origin, mark the package "American goods returned." Spot checks are occasionally made on parcels, so it is best to mark the accurate price and nature of the gift on the package. If you send back parcels worth over $50, the Postal Service will collect the duty plus a handling charge when it is delivered.

Canadian customs regulations are different from their American counterparts. Once every calendar quarter you can bring in goods up to the value of $50. Once every calendar year you're allowed $150. These two allowances can't both be claimed on the same trip. Anything above the duty-free allowance is taxed at 25% on the first $150, and at varying rates afterwards. You can send gifts up to a value of $15 duty-free, but again, you cannot mail alcohol or tobacco.

American or Canadian, you have to declare any items that you bought at duty-free shops abroad with your other purchases, and you may have to pay duty on them if they exceed your allowance. Remember, "duty-free" means only that you didn't pay taxes in the country of purchase. When you return from abroad, you may also run into trouble with clothing or jewelry of foreign make that you originally purchased in North America. You must be able to indicate their origin with purchase receipts or identifying marks.

According to the U.S. Customs Service official brochure, *Know Before You Go,* available from the Department of the Treasury, U.S. Customs Service, Washington, DC 20229, "A vital part of Customs' role is screening out items injurious to the well-being of our nation." Among these are non-prescription drugs and narcotics, obscene publications, lottery tickets, liquor-filled candies, and most plants. To avoid problems when carrying prescription drugs, make sure the bottles are clearly marked and have the prescription ready to show the customs officer.

Student Identification

There is no single piece of identification so widely honored for procuring discounts and services as the **International Student Identity Card (ISIC)**. This card is essential if you plan to use student flights, trains, or clubs, and can get you discounts on museum admission, theater tickets, local transportation, and more. In Greece, the ISIC can be used for discounts on admission to archeological sites and certain festivals—sometimes it can even secure you half-price drinks at local discos. In addition, the ISIC can be used for discounts on local transportation, including ferry travel and Student Air Travel Association flights. Olympic Airways offers some student discounts for flights within Greece and between Greece and Europe. For the $8 fee and the time spent applying, the rewards the ISIC brings are considerable. The fee also provides you with medical insurance coverage of up to $1500, plus $100 a day up to sixty days for in-hospital illness.

No application form is necessary, but you must supply all of the following information, whether you apply in person or by mail: 1) current dated proof of student status (a photocopy of your school ID showing this year's date, a letter on school stationery signed and sealed by the registrar, or a photocopied grade report); 2) a vending-machine-size photo with your name printed on the back; 3) your birthdate and nationality (xerox of birth certificate). The card is good until the end of the calendar year in which you bought it. Unfortunately for those taking a year off from school, a new card cannot be purchased in January unless you were in school during the fall semester. If you have just graduated, you may still obtain an ISIC during the year in which you graduated. If you don't qualify for the ISIC and are under 26 years of age, do not hesitate to ask about youth discounts wherever you go—your passport will be the best proof of your age.

Non-students under 26 years of age should consider buying a Federation of International Youth Travel Organization or FIYTO card. It will be good for discounts on ferry transportation and various sightseeing tours within Greece, and on ferry travel between Greece and Italy, Israel, or Egypt. If you plan to travel to Greece overland from northern Europe, the FIYTO card will give you discounts on train travel.

Among the student travel offices which issue the ISIC are the Council on International Educational Exchange (CIEE), Harvard Student Agencies, and Canadian Universities Travel Services (all addresses are listed in the Useful Organizations section above). In addition, over 375 travel offices in universities around the United States issue the ISIC. The FIYTO card is issued by CIEE and by agencies within Europe. See the Student Travel Offices section for addresses in Greece.

Money

Few things cause more headaches than money, even when you have it. Carrying large amounts of cash, even in money belts, is too much of a risk—and leaving your wallet unattended invites disaster. A little forethought can prevent money nightmares from becoming realities.

Travelers checks are still the safest way to carry money abroad. They're sold by several agencies and most major banks, usually at face value plus a 1% commission charge. Your best choice will be a widely-known check; some American banks offer their own checks, which may not be honored in Greece. **American Express** travelers checks are usually considered the most widely recognized and the easiest to replace if lost or stolen, though other major checks are sold, exchanged, cashed and refunded throughout Europe just as easily. American Express provides five services free of charge to travelers whose checks have been lost or stolen. Local American Express offices will cash personal checks up to $200 (including foreign checks), have stolen credit cards canceled, arrange to obtain a temporary ID, help change airline, hotel, and car rental reservations, and send a Western Union mailgram or international cable to one individual. **Citicorp** travelers checks are sold in financial institutions throughout the U.S. and Europe, and can be easily replaced if lost or stolen. For refund information and assistance in the U.S., dial toll-free (800) 632-6388. **BankAmerica** travelers checks can be obtained and refunded at numerous banks throughout the States and in Europe. For claims and refunds outside the U.S., call either the San Francisco or London BankAmerica Customer Service Center collect. (San Francisco: (415) 622-3800; London: 01/629 7466.) **Barclay's,** a British bank with branches in major U.S. cities at local offices of the American Automobile Association (AAA), sells Barclay's Visa checks without a commission, as does **Thomas Cook,** another British firm. Thomas Cook checks may also be purchased at AAA offices. Finally, **Deak-Perera,** a foreign exchange with offices throughout the U.S. and Canada, offers Thomas Cook and Visa travelers checks commission-free in dollars and a number of foreign currencies.

Buy at least some of your checks in small denominations, $10 or $20, to minimize losses if you need cash fast and have to deal with a lousy exchange rate. To lower losses another way, avoid keeping all your currency in the same place: split it up among pockets and bags or, better yet, use a money belt. Try to stash away a small amount of currency in case you stay for several days in a small town with no exchange service.

Credit cards can be used in place of travelers checks for cash advances up to your credit limit. With Visa or MasterCard, you can get a cash advance at any institution that supplies the card (a transaction fee is always charged). American Express offices give out travelers checks instead of cash, but will cash a personal check for cardholders in the local currency (up to $1000 in any 21-day period). An advantage of the American Express card is that it allows you to use Amex offices as mailing addresses for free. (Otherwise you may have to pay to pick up your mail.) The Amex cards are the most difficult to get, but if your parents or a relative is willing to sign a guarantee form, Amex will issue an extra card for $25. But Visa, MasterCard, and American Express are mostly a form of extra insurance for the budget traveler. Most places you visit will deal strictly in cash.

Sending Money

It's a good idea to visit your bank before you leave to get a list of its corresponding banks in Greece. That way, if you need to have money sent, your bank knows where to send it and you know where to look for it. You can even arrange in advance for your bank to send money from your account at home to foreign banks on specific dates.

Cable transfer is the fastest way to receive money; you should have it within 48 hours if you're in a major city, or a bit longer if you're in a less central location. You pay cabling costs plus the commission charged by your bank. A cheaper but slower method of receiving money is by bank draft; you pay $3-5 commission on the draft plus the cost of sending it air mail (preferably registered). Or, an American Express cardholder at home can cable you up to $500 in travelers checks. The process takes one to three days, depending on where you are. Whichever method you use, make sure that both you and the sender know the exact name and address of the bank to which the money is being

sent. The sending bank requires the telephone number of the recipient as well, so try to find it out in advance.

Finally, if you are stranded in Greece with no money and no apparent way to procure any, a consulate will wire home for you and deduct the cost from what you receive. They're often less than gracious about performing this service, so you should turn to them only as a last resort. If all else falls through and you need money immediately, consider selling some of your belongings. Merchants in the marketplace, people you meet, or even other travelers will consider buying some things you have to offer.

Health

The simplest prescription for health while traveling is to keep your body and anything you put into it clean. Eat well, and try not to overextend yourself physically. Cutting out nutritious food to economize and introducing radical shifts into your meal schedule can become criminally easy while on the road. Remember that you're moving around more than usual, so your body needs fuel. Treat it kindly and it will more than return the favor. As always, common sense and restraint remain the best preventive medicines.

The self-assembled traveler's kit should include soap (both mild and antiseptic), an extra pair of eyeglasses, multiple vitamins (plus iron for women), aspirin, sunscreen, a thermometer in a rigid case, something for diarrhea (like Lomotil with Neomiacin), something for motion sickness, and bandages. When you visit archeological sites, the dust of centuries might trigger allergic reactions you've never experienced before; bringing some basic antihistamine is a good idea.

Although no special immunizations are necessary for travel to Greece, you should check your medical records to see that your innoculations are up-to-date: typhoid shots remain good for three years, tetanus for ten.

If you know that you will require medication while you travel, obtain a full supply before you leave; matching your prescription with a foreign equivalent is not always easy or even possible. You should always carry up-to-date prescriptions and/or a statement from your doctor, especially if you will be carrying insulin, a syringe, or any narcotic drugs. Distribute all medicines between carry-on and checked baggage to minimize loss. Travelers with a medical problem or condition that cannot be easily recognized (e.g. diabetes, allergies to antibiotics, epilepsy, heart conditions) should seriously consider obtaining a **Medic Alert identification tag.** This internationally recognized emblem communicates vital information in emergency situations. In addition to indicating the nature of the medical problem, the tag provides the number of the Medic Alert's 24-hour hotline, through which attending medical personnel can obtain information about the member's medical history. Membership is $15; write to Medic Alert Foundation International, P.O. Box 1009, Turlock, CA 95381, or call (209) 668-3333.

Of course, even the hardiest traveler may meet with an unexpected mishap while on the road. Before you leave, find out whether your current health insurance covers costs incurred abroad. Although emergency care is provided free of charge in Greece, you must pay for any scheduled visits or check-ups. Most major companies will cover these costs on a "short-term" or regular basis. Many university health plans also apply abroad, while Medicare (except for limited coverage in Canada and Mexico) does not. If your insurance does apply, you still have to pay in cash for treatment and be reimbursed later. You must keep all receipts and statements from your doctors and file an out-of-country claim with your insurance company; try to have all receipts written in English. If you find that your insurance covers only domestic health costs, we strongly advise you to acquire coverage for the length of your stay. Remem-

ber, the ISIC carries accident and sickness insurance (see Student Identification section). CIEE has a low-cost plan, as does the American Automobile Association (AAA). Or you can contact any insurance agency or your student travel office.

The best place to find a good doctor (and the psychological balm of an English-speaking one) may well be the emergency room of a university hospital. Otherwise, your best bet is to go to as large a city as possible, and hope that someone at the hospital will speak English. *Let's Go* lists hospitals in most cities; we try to note where you can find English-speaking doctors. American, Canadian, and British embassies and consulates, American Express offices, and the local police can also help you find English-speaking doctors in Greece.

The hot climate of Greece requires some special preparation. If you plan to do much hiking, carry a canteen filled with water, and wear a hat to guard against the possibility of sunstroke. If you have a light complexion, use some sort of sunscreen to prevent sunburn. Perspiration carries away a lot of salt, which must be replaced. However, you should *not* bring along salt tablets. The high concentration will upset your body's balance and accelerate the dehydration process. Salting your food should be adequate. Finally, it may be a good idea to carry antidiarrhetic pills or other intestinal medications with you (Lomotil is effective in most mild cases), as your diet in Greece will be much different from what you've encountered in North America or other parts of Europe.

Packing

First, and most importantly, pack lightly. A good rule of thumb is to settle on all the items you might need to bring with you, and take only half of them.

Since you'll have to carry your belongings from the station or ferry to a youth hostel, hotel, or campground more often than you may realize, walk a mile or so with your loaded pack before you leave to see how easily it carries. If you can't manage comfortably, unload some things—the convenience of an easily transportable pack, suitcase, or duffel bag far outweighs any disadvantages of a limited wardrobe. And the more luggage you carry, the more you'll look and be treated like a tourist. Besides, you'll need room for any gifts or other purchases you bring back.

Whether or not you use a backpack depends on the kind of traveling you'll be doing. If you intend to visit mostly cities and towns, you might want to consider a light suitcase. If you're going to be covering a lot of ground or camping out, it's more efficient to carry a backpack. A small daypack will come in handy for carrying a lunch and poncho; for unobtrusive travel choose a large shoulder bag that zips or closes securely.

The hot summer weather in Greece demands that you wear light clothing. Because of the heat, bring lightweight shirts and pants, and plenty of cotton underwear. Laundry service can be expensive, so take permanent press or wrinkle-free clothes. Best of all, do as the locals have done for centuries—wear long, pale, gauzy things, whether shirts or skirts, in preference to typically American bright, tight T-shirts, tank tops, or shorts. Not only will you avoid offending local standards of modesty (which might otherwise prevent your admission to places of worship), but you'll be cooler and more comfortable. Footwear is the crucial item on your packing list. An oft-worn pair of sturdy lace-up, rubber-soled walking shoes or well-cushioned running shoes will do for longer hikes, but you'll want a pair of lighter shoes, such as sandals or espadrilles, for everyday wear. Bring along a few pairs of socks and a can of foot powder—both will keep your feet fresh and prevent blisters.

To avoid being robbed and left with nothing, don't pack everything in the same large bag. Instead, you should have some kind of pouch or money belt to hold your money, passport, and the articles you'll want with you at all times. A small notebook for writing down addresses, phrases, directions, or whatever else you discover or need during the perambulations of your day, for example, will prove useful.

In addition to the hat, sunscreen, and canteen already suggested in the Health section, you should also include a flashlight, toilet paper, first-aid kit, petroleum jelly, needle and thread, and a portable alarm clock. A rain poncho and sweater are also a good idea, whether for off-season travel or the occasional cool night. Rubber bands and plastic bags serve a myriad of purposes while on the road. You don't have to pack a summer's worth of toiletries such as aspirin, razor blades, or tampons, but make sure you're adequately stocked before exploring less populated areas of Greece.

If you decide to bring a camera, be sure to register it with U.S. customs at the airport before leaving or you might have trouble bringing it back. You can protect your film from airport x-rays by buying a special leadlined bag from any photo shop. If you don't mind the extra bulk, buy all your film before you go—it's much more expensive abroad.

The standard electrical outlet in Greece produces 220 volts AC; in a few areas it is still 110 DC. North American appliances are usually designed for 110 volts AC. If you want to use your own appliances in these countries, they must be dual-voltage appliances, or else you will need both a converter and an adapter. (An adapter alone changes only the shape of the plug—in most areas they're three-prong; in the U.S., the norm is two-prong.) You can get adapters in department and hardware stores. Converters cost about $26. To order a converter by mail, write to Franzus Company, 352 Park Ave. South, New York, NY 10010. Ask for a copy of their pamphlet, *Foreign Electricity Is No Deep Dark Secret.*

Drugs

In Greece, as in other European countries, possession of drugs is a serious offence. If you're lucky, you'll be kicked out of the country—otherwise, you could find yourself conducting extensive research on Eastern Mediterranean penal codes and prisons. Avoid buying drugs unless you know the seller, since he may be a police informer.

Never bring anything across borders. International express trains are not as safe as they might seem: you and your belongings may be searched thoroughly while on board. The assistance available from the U.S. consulates to anyone arrested is minimal. Consular officers can visit the prisoner, provide a list of attorneys, and inform family and friends. They cannot obtain any more lenient treatment than that dictated by Greek law, no matter how innocently you may have become entangled in drug trafficking.

Security

The theft of one's belongings while abroad is one of the greatest potential setbacks of a trip. A significant loss can often force a bitter, premature return. Thieves who prey on backpackers are exceedingly clever; the techniques employed are variegated, and crowded youth hostels and overnight trains are favorite hangouts for petty criminals. While you sleep or see the sights, a local pilferer may be rifling through your things.

Prevention is far more effective than mistrust, and a healthy, cautious attitude should carry you safely through your travels. Always keep your money and valuables with you, preferably in a money belt, and especially while sleeping. If you plan to sleep outside, try to store your gear in a safe place at a train or bus station.

The following firms offer insurance against theft or loss of luggage:

Tour Master Travel Insurance, c/o the Edmund A. Cocco Agency, 75 Federal St., Suite 1012, Boston, MA 02110 (tel. (617) 426-0652). Offers the cheapest baggage-only protection, as little as $1 per day for $1000 worth of coverage.

The Travelers Insurance Co., 1 Tower Square, Hartford, CT 06115 (tel. (203) 277-0111). Also has baggage-only policies, but at steeper rates.

Tripmaster Insurance, c/o CNA Insurance, 100 Newport Ave. Extension, Quincy, MA 02171 (tel. (800) 343-5601) or CNA Plaza, Chicago, IL 60685 (tel. (312) 822-5000), also has baggage-only protection.

Carefree Travel Insurance, c/o Arm Coverage, Inc., P.O. Box 247, Providence, RI 02901. Offers more comprehensive travel insurance which includes loss of luggage. Over $2 per day for coverage which includes $1000 worth of baggage coverage.

TravelSafe, Inc., 300 71st St., Suite 520, Miami, FL 33141 (tel. (800) 327-9966 or (305) 866-7233). Similar coverage to that of Carefree at nearly $3 per day.

No firms cover loss of travel documents (passport, plane ticket, railpass, etc.), and claims can only be filed upon return to the United States. Claims must be accompanied by a police report of the incident.

Special Travelers

Women

Visiting Greece often poses difficulties for women traveling alone. If you look like a foreigner, especially if you're fair in a land where everyone else is dark, you'll almost certainly be harassed somewhat by over-zealous and un-wanted admirers; many of these men assume that all American women are willing targets. However, common sense and sensitivity to the culture you are visiting can often prevent threatening situations from arising. It may be a good idea to imitate the dress and behavior of local women, if you can do so com-fortably—women wearing T-shirts, halter tops, and not wearing bras will at-tract particular attention (and may be denied admission to sacred sites). Avoid riding alone in train compartments, especially at night. Though it may be difficult, remember that not all interested males are dangerous. Southern Euro-peans of both sexes tend to be warmer and more physical than their North American counterparts; this is no reason to ignore them. If a man starts to bother you, your best answer is no answer, since any kind of response may be interpreted as an encouragement. Of course, you should not hesitate to be rude if the situation becomes threatening. A harsh scolding in any language, espe-cially in the presence of onlookers, should cool the pursuit. In real emergen-cies, scream for help. *Let's Go* lists emergency, police, and consulate phone numbers in every city.

For those who dislike the attitudes and behavior of the Greeks, a warning: you can't hope to change an entire culture in one short visit, and you shouldn't spend your time trying. Most men won't even understand your annoyance at their wolf-whistles and propositions; obnoxious as it may seem to you, to them it is only a game. If it will make life easier, find a traveling companion. Above all, try not to let unfamiliar social norms and your reactions to them spoil your trip.

Disabled Travelers

Greece is just beginning to respond to the needs of disabled travelers. In Thessaloniki one travel agency advises handicapped travelers and organizes tours; plans have been made to open up another such agency in Athens. But advance research is particularly important. The following organizations can provide you with information:

Mobility International, founded to promote travel exchange among the disabled and the able-bodied, has contacts in 25 countries and offers advice and assistance to would-be visitors. For information on travel programs, accommodations, ac-cess guides and organized tours, write to Mobility International USA, P.O. Box 3551, Eugene, OR 97403.

Moss Rehabilitation Hospital provides free help in planning trips and obtaining information about particular countries and cities. Write to Travel Information Center, Moss Rehabilitation Hospital, Twelfth St. and Taher Rd., Philadelphia, PA 19141 (tel. (215) 329-5715).

Rehabilitation International USA (RIUSA) is a federation of national and interna-tional organizations providing information and services for the disabled in more than 130 countries. Write to the Travel Survey Dept., Rehabilitation USA, 1123 Broadway, Suite 704, New York, NY 10010 (tel. (212) 620-4040).

Language

Despite the annual summer influx of American, Canadian, and British tour-ists, English has never been widely spoken in Greece. Tourist officials often have a working knowledge of English, but you should try to master a few essential Greek phrases; Greeks will certainly appreciate any efforts you make. Take along Berlitz' *Greek for Travelers;* it provides key phrases in a simple and comprehensible format. As you learn, get someone who knows the language to explain the pronunciation to you. Only use the phrases when you're sure the person you're speaking to will understand. Above all, *don't* use Greek if you get into an argument, unless you're fluent. They'll think you're only pretending not to understand when they make their points. Below are some useful words:

> *NEH:* yes.
> *OH-khee:* no
> *pah-rah-kah-LOW:* please/you're welcome
> *ef-hah-ris-STOW:* thank you
> *ef-hah-ris-STOW-po-LEE:* thank you very much
> *sig-NO-mee:* excuse me
> *YAH-sas:* hello/goodbye/gesundheit (polite form)
> *YAH-soo:* (same as above but familiar)
> *kah-lee-MEH-rah:* good morning
> *kah-lee-SPEH-rah:* good evening
> *kah-lee-NIK-tah:* good night
> *DA-ksee:* OK
> *pov-EE-neh. . . ?:* where is. . . ?
> *PO-so ko-NEE?:* how much?

See what kind of a response you get from these: *O gaidaros mou theli kenouyo bouzi* (My donkey needs a new spark plug). *Afto to raki me ekane san piomeno papaglo* (This raki has got me as drunk as a parrot). *Mipos borona paro tin Katsika sas ya volta?* (May I take your goat for a walk?).

Even if you don't know any spoken Greek, you *must* know the Greek alphabet. Although it is very different from the Roman alphabet used in English, French, Spanish, and Italian, it's just similar enough to be doubly confusing. Some road signs, some street names, and certain bus timetables may be transliterated (spelled out as they would be pronounced in English), but many are not, and at best, transliteration is an inaccurate business. You'll sometimes find three separate words representing the same name. For example, Patra, Patras, and Patrai all refer to the same place. We have provided a table of Greek letters to help you decipher signs.

If you're really stuck, try to find someone of high-school age; English has recently replaced French as the compulsory language of schools, so most young Greeks speak at least some English.

Finally, be warned that body language also differs from country to country. To indicate a negative, the Greeks silently close their eyes and lift their heads. If you ask them what they mean, they often grow highly impatient. Likewise, they wave their hand up and down in a gesture that seems to mean "Stay there"; it actually means "come." And be careful when waving goodbye; if you do so palm forward, the gesture may be interpreted as an insult. Try to be alert to the signals used by native Greeks.

The alphabet

Here are the characters which comprise the Greek alphabet. The column at left shows the printed capital and small letters, while written letters are shown in the center column. The column at right gives you the name of these letters as pronounced by Greeks.

Printed		Written		Name
A	α	A	a	**ah**lfah
B	β	B	ʎ	**vee**tah
Γ	γ	Γ	γ	**ghah**mah
Δ	δ	Δ	δ	**dheh**ltah
E	ε	E	ε	**eh**pseelon
Z	ζ	Z	ʒ	**zee**tah
H	η	H	π	**ee**tah
Θ	θ	θ	ϕ	**thee**tah
I	ι	I	ι	**yee**otah
K	κ	K	u	**kah**pah
Λ	λ	Λ	ɔ	**lahm**dhah
M	μ	M	μ	mee
N	ν	N	ν	nee
Ξ	ξ	Ξ	ʒ	ksee
O	ο	O	ο	o**mee**kron
Π	π	Π	ω	pee
P	ρ	P	ρ	ro
Σ	σ ς	Σ	ε ς	**seegh**mah
T	τ	T	τ	tahf
Y	υ	Y	υ	**eep**seelon
Φ	φ	Φ	φ	fee
X	χ	X	ɹ	khee
Ψ	ψ	Ψ	x	psee
Ω	ω	Ω	ω	o**mehgh**ah

From the Berlitz phrase book "Greek for Travellers", by permission of Editions Berlitz.

To and From Greece

Travel to Europe has been a booming business for as long as the New World has been settled, but in recent years, due to the strength of the dollar abroad, transatlantic tourism has increased at a feverish pace. Burgeoning new companies and cut-rate offers have insured steep fare competition, so with a little effort and advance planning, you can find economical ways to get to Greece. As we go to press, it is impossible to predict 1984 rates, or even to say with certainty what types of inexpensive flights will be available. We can, however, offer valuable suggestions about the sort of transatlantic packages that will be worth investigating during 1984-85.

Some general rules are good to keep in mind. Off-season travelers will enjoy lower fares and face much less competition for inexpensive seats, but you don't have to travel in the dead of winter to save. Peak-season rates are generally set on either May 15 or June 1 (departure) and run until about September 15 (return). If you can arrange to leave in May and return in late September, you can travel in summer and still save. The budget travel options outlined below differ from one another in economy, flexibility, and security. The simplest and surest way to decide among them is to find a travel agent who keeps abreast of the chaos in airfares and who is committed to saving you money. Don't hesitate to shop around—travel agents are by no means the same. Commissions are smaller on cheaper flights, so some agents are less than eager to help you find the best deal. The travel section of the Sunday *New York Times* or another major newspaper is a good place to start looking for bargain fares, but be sure to read the fine print on restrictions and cancellation procedures. Start looking early; some popular bargain fares are fully booked by April.

Direct Flights

The days when you had to travel to New York City for a cheap flight are over, although it can still be more economical to change planes in New York, particularly for those flying from Canada and the west coast. Reasonably direct flights to Greece are available from nearly twenty gateway cities across the U.S. Inexpensive flights are also available from some major Canadian cities; Canadian students should be sure to consult **Travel CUTS** (see Useful Organizations section for address).

Charter flights have expanded tremendously this year and should continue to be the most economical option for a transatlantic crossing. Rules governing charters have been liberalized, so you can often book up to the last minute, although most flights fill up well in advance of the departure date. Regular charter tickets do not permit flexibility; you must choose your departure and return dates when you book your flight. Some companies will allow you to book a one-way flight, but most do not. If you cancel your one-way or roundtrip ticket within three weeks of your departure date, you lose most or all of your money. With some companies, however, you can alter the ticket (date of return, etc.) by paying a $50-$75 penalty fee. In addition, charter companies reserve the right to change the dates of your flight, cancel the flight, and add fuel surcharges after you have made your final payment. Beware of fares that sound too good to be true, as not all charter companies are entirely honest or reliable. Even some of the most well-known charter groups, such as CIEE, have inconvenienced passengers with mechanical failures (remember, charter companies do not have back-up planes—you're stuck on the one they've got). Flight changes and delays are the rule rather than the exception. A good travel agent can help you choose a charter wisely, but remember that once you sign the charter contract, no one can offer you full protection against a cancelled flight or a last-minute change of date.

In 1983, **Tourlite** (tel. (800) 223-7605) offered seasonal (April-December), twice-weekly flights from New York to Athens, ranging from $529-$559 (high season) and from $499-$539 (off-season). One-way fares were lowest at $299 (April) and highest at $369 (July). **Homeric Tours** (tel. (800) 223-5570) had similar prices, with high season roundtrip at $599, off-season $549, and one-way fares ranging from $249-$399.

The **Advanced Booking Excursion Fare (APEX)** is the most flexible of the reduced fares—it provides you with confirmed reservations and is not as restrictive as charters in terms of cancellation penalties and adjusted travel dates. The "open-jaw APEX" will even allow you to return from a different city than the one into which you originally flew. However, APEX does have drawbacks: you must fly back within a specified period of time, usually 7-60 or 22-45 days after leaving; payment is due three to five weeks in advance; and APEX fares are considerably higher in peak-season. In 1983, the high season APEX fare from New York to Athens on major carriers was $589. Somewhat cheaper "super-APEX fares," available on some routes, work in the same way. A $50 cancellation fee applies for both APEX and super-APEX. Book APEX flights early; by early June you may have difficulty getting your desired departure date.

Another option is to investigate unusual airlines that try to undercut the major carriers by offering special bargains on regularly scheduled flights—and to watch for those major carriers who fight back by offering special bargains of their own. Most of these special fares are in effect for short periods only, so watch for advertisements in the pages of the major national newspapers. And, as with charters, be wary of the truly incredible fares; the dubious dealings of some companies could make you painfully aware of the risks of economizing too far.

From Within Europe

By Air

If you cannot find an economical direct flight to Athens, you might want to fly into Northern Europe, and from there on to Greece. Fares to London can be very cheap—in 1983, **People's Express** offered a one-way ticket for only $149. **Capitol Airways, Metro International,** and **Icelandic** traditionally offer cheap fares from New York to the Continent, but check with a travel agent for the current bargains. Since the demise of the original Laker Airlines (the newer version is a regular charter), **standby** fares have risen substantially, and some carriers no longer offer the service. But you can still save some money and retain your flexibility by buying a standby ticket on those lines that sell them.

Once you're in Europe, there are plenty of flights to Athens and Thessaloniki from major cities. Although the number of student flights within Europe is rapidly decreasing due to so-called "camping flights," a new form of roundtrip charter, the London-Athens connection remains popular. In 1983, the one-way ticket for students under 30 cost approximately $150; tickets for **Student Air Travel Association (SATA)** flights can be obtained from CIEE or from student travel offices in Europe. **Olympic Airways** offers discounted fares to students with ISIC for flights between Europe and Greece, as do other national carriers. Watch also for special package fares offered by travel agents or advertised in newspapers. From London and Amsterdam, these packages may be the least expensive intra-European flights available, even if the fare includes a few nights in a hotel.

Overland

Greece is also served by a number of international train routes, which connect Athens, Thessaloniki, and Larissa to most European cities. You should count on at least a three-day journey from Trieste or Vienna to Athens so if you board a train which has no available compartment space, seriously consider getting off and waiting for the next one—three days in an aisle crowded with local travelers and livestock can be a nightmare. If you're in no great hurry to get to Greece and are going overland, you might consider traversing Yugoslavia by way of the coast using local buses or ferries rather than taking the train through the far less scenic urban centers of the interior. If you plan to hitchhike to Greece, however, by all means do not get off the main Zagreb-Belgrade highway. Hitching in Yugoslavia is already difficult enough; using back roads, you may never get to Greece at all.

There are several companies that offer reduced fares from European cities (particularly London) to Athens. **Eurotrain,** a group of nine student organizations in Europe, offers 15-30% reductions on point-to-point rail tickets (reduction rates depend on the distance traveled). You buy a ticket for a certain route, and can stop off at any point along the way, resuming your trip when you wish from the same point or another on the route. Eurotrain tickets are available if you're under 26, and can be purchased at local travel offices in Britain or from Eurotrain, 52 Grosvenor Sq., London W1 (tel. 01/730 6525). For tickets and information in Athens, see the Orientation section below. **Transalpino** offers reduced second-class rail fares in Europe, including Greece and Turkey, to anyone under 26. Tickets are generally valid for two months. Transalpino offices are distributed throughout Europe; the head office is at 15 Greycoat Place, London SW1P 1SB (tel. 01/222 9521). Travel CUTS (see Useful Organizations for address) sells vouchers for both Transalpino and Eurotrain passes. In the U.S., you can get a voucher for Eurotrain tickets only from the International Study and Travel Center, 300 Washington Ave. SE, 44 Kauffman Memorial Union, University of Minnesota, Minneapolis, MN 55455 (tel. (612) 373-0180). (One warning: though you can often save time and money by taking overnight trains, there have been sporadic instances of train compartments being gassed, especially along the route south through Yugoslavia. You could wake up from a deep sleep to find your money—or worse, all your belongings—gone.)

Another inexpensive overland possibility is **Magic Bus.** As we go to press, the status of Magic Bus is uncertain. It went out of business for some time in 1983, but may revive. It formerly offered rides almost daily to Athens and Thessaloniki from London, Amsterdam, and other cities. Magic Bus has a reputation for being rather erratic—you may find yourself on an incredibly quick bus or one that perpetually breaks down, requiring days to reach your destination or even forcing you to transfer to local transportation. You just have to take your chances. Magic Bus had offices all over Europe, including London at 67-69 New Oxford St., WC1 (tel. 01/836 7799) and Athens at 20 Filellinon St. (tel. 32 37 471).

Numerous other long distance bus services offer inexpensive rides from all over Europe. Check local student newspapers and entertainment magazines for fares, addresses and phone numbers of the various companies. Many of these companies are unreliable, but they generally offer slightly lower fares than the more widely-known Magic Bus. Expect to pay roughly $70 to travel from London to Athens in the high season, or $40-$60 from Northern and Central European cities.

By Ferry

Certainly the most popular way of getting to Greece from Europe is by ferry. Boats travel primarily from **Brindisi** on the southeastern coast of Italy to **Corfu, Igoumenitsa,** and **Patras.** The trip to Corfu takes eight hours, to Igoumenitsa nine to ten hours, and to Patras eighteen hours. From Patras, buses leave for Athens every 45 minutes (four hours, 510dr). With a ticket to Patras, you can stop over in Corfu, provided you indicate your intention prior to embarkation (they must write "S.O. Corfu" on the ticket). You'll have to pay a port tax of 200dr when you reboard. No stopovers are permitted on tickets to Igoumenitsa.

If you plan to travel from Brindisi in the summer, expect long waits and large crowds. In high season (July 1-August 20), you must reserve before you get to Brindisi to be sure of getting a ticket. It's important to arrive at the port well before your departure time. Allow yourself plenty of time for late trains and the 1km walk from the train station to the maritime station (you may prefer to take a taxi). If you don't check in at least three hours ahead of time, you stand to lose your reservation and possibly your ticket. When you check in at the main office of the line you are using (see below), they will give you an embarkation pass. You must take the pass to the police station on the second floor of the maritime station to have it stamped. Then, upon entering the boat, you must present your passport to the Greek officials.

Rates vary only slightly from company to company, so unless your destination is one few boats serve, shopping around won't be necessary. Most lines offer reduced fares to ISIC cardholders under 30 and IYHF or FIYTO cardholders under 26. Youth discounts are generally only 5-10%. Eurail pass holders travel free on boats operated by Hellenic Mediterranean and Adriatica Lines. However, only deck passage is free (seats cost extra), and between June 10 and September 30, pass holders must also pay a £19,000 ($12) supplement. Moreover, they often delay entry to the ferry for pass holders, favoring paying passengers. On some lines, InterRail pass holders receive discounts of 30% (slightly more than the regular youth discount). Often, however, the reduction is offered only if the ticket is bought in Brindisi, a risky option. Finally, on some lines it is possible to arrange "group rates" through certain travel agents. Makeshift groups can secure a 10-15% discount per person, with a free trip for the enterprising leader. No matter what ticket you end up purchasing, you must pay a £4000 port tax in Brindisi before embarkation. A general note: you needn't spend the money on anything more than deck class to take advantage of the hot showers on board—while technically not allowed, you'll rarely be hassled.

The main ferry line in Brindisi is **Adriatica-Hellenic Mediterranean Lines,** Staz. Marittima, 2nd floor (tel. 23 82 5). In 1983, regular high season fares ran $75 for deck class to Patras, $65 to Corfu or Igoumenitsa. Pullman berths cost $100 and $85, respectively. Student fares were $64 to Patras and $59 to Corfu deck class, $85 and $75 respectively for Pullman berths. Ships run daily at 10:30pm and, in high season, at 8pm (Brindisi-Patras only). The return trips leave Athens at 1:30pm (by coach) and depart from Patras at 10pm (summer express to Brindisi departs 5pm). As on other lines, bicycles travel free, and motorcycles cost approximately $36 extra. Other lines include the following: **Fragline,** c/o Il Globo, corso Garibaldi, 97 (tel. (0831) 29 98 9 or 27 68 4), with a daily ferry to Corfu, Igoumenitsa, and Patras from July-Sept. (less frequent service year round); **Libra Maritime,** c/o Libra Mare, corso Garibaldi, 73-75 (tel. 23 51 4), with year-round service to Patras daily Wed.-Mon.; and **Strintzis**

Lines, c/o Discovery, corso Garibaldi, 62 (tel. 27 66 7), with departures every other day June-Sept. for Corfu, Igoumenitsa, Cephalonia, and Patras. **Ionian Lines,** c/o Italmar S.N.C., corso Garibaldi, 96/98 (tel. 29 77 2), has departures every other day June-Sept. for Corfu, Paxos, Ithaca, Cephalonia, and Patras. You can make one stopover in the Ionian Islands, but you must pay embarkation and disembarkation fees. Always buy your ticket from an accredited ticket office, not from so-called "representatives" hanging around the waterfront. Try to avoid Sunny Cruises, although they advertise the cheapest fares; they're less than reputable.

Brindisi is not the only Italian city with ferry service to Greece. Boats also sail from **Bari** to Corfu, Igoumenitsa, and Patras. **Stability Lines** runs boats on alternate days with student high season rates of approximately $35 to Patras and $32 to Corfu and Igoumenitsa; non-student fares are $42 and $36. **Roana Lines** sails daily from **Otranto** to Corfu and Igoumenitsa for around $20 in high season. Two ferry lines connect **Ancona** with Igoumenitsa and Patras. **Strintzis Lines** runs twice a week May-Oct.; in high season a seat to Patras costs $54 (student fare $48). To Igoumenitsa fares are slightly lower. **Minoan Lines** also leaves twice weekly. Finally, those with a bit of extra cash can travel to Piraeus from Venice on Adriatica Lines' luxurious car ferry. The boat leaves Venice once a week in high season on Friday at 10pm, and arrives in Piraeus between 4 and 10pm on Sunday. E-class cabins (three berths) cost $140 in high season, $125 low season ($120 and $110 for students). The boat continues on to Alexandria, Egypt; student fare from Alexandria to Piraeus is $145 high season, $130 low season.

Greece is also accessible from the other Mediterranean countries. Several companies run boats between two or more. The *Odysseus Elitis* plies a route between Piraeus, Rhodes, Limassol (Cyprus) and Alexandria once a week. Fare Alexandria-Piraeus is $148 in high season, $128 in low season, deck class $92. **Stability Lines** travels between Haifa, Israel, and Greece once a week March-Dec.; student fare from Haifa to both Athens and Crete is $60. There is frequent service from Limassol, Cyprus, to Rhodes, Iraklion, and Piraeus (see Cyprus chapter for details).

Finally, it is possible to catch ferries from **Dubrovnik, Rijeka,** and **Split,** Yugoslavia to various points in Greece. From Dubrovnik to Corfu, ferries take twelve hours and cost around $35. The **Black Sea Shipping Co.** runs twice-monthly boats (May-Oct.) from Odessa, USSR, stopping in Bulgaria, Istanbul, and Piraeus. Aside from this, there are relatively few connections from Istanbul to Piraeus, though there are frequent runs from Piraeus to Istanbul. For information on ferries between the Greek islands and the Turkish Coast, refer to the Turkish Coast chapter or to the sections on specific islands.

To the East

Ranking with London and Amsterdam, Athens has become one of the cheapest travel centers in Europe. From Athens you can take student flights at surprisingly low cost to many points around the world, especially in Africa and Asia. Though Magic Bus still goes from Istanbul to New Delhi for only $140, (see note in Overland travel section), obtaining an Iranian visa is impossible for Americans, and very time-consuming (six to eight weeks) for other nationals. Thus flying has become the most practical way to travel east, and airline price wars have made Athens one of the most popular gateways.

The budget travel offices which line Nikis and Filellinon Sts. in Athens offer student and youth fares to all five continents, as well as round-the-world stopover tickets to North America. Bombay ($250) and Bangkok ($300) are the cheapest ports of entry for India and Southeast Asia, respectively. Nairobi, in

Central Africa, can be reached for as little as $350, and a stopover ticket to Los Angeles can be had for $900. Though all travel agents have access to these fares, we suggest you shop around, since not all are aware of the ultra-bargain flights. Addresses for some of the offices are listed below, in the Orientation section.

Orientation

Tourism

Tourism is the Greeks' bread and butter; they are understandably reluctant to bite the hand that feeds them. As a result, they have designed one of the most eager and polished tourism systems in Europe: first, to attract visitors (you'll notice that official books, posters, and brochures are produced with taste and care); and then to protect them (hotels, restaurants, and camping facilities are strictly regulated and maintained, and proprietors are severely punished for trying to take advantage of visitors). Thus, except in Athens, where a large number of hostels and pseudo-hostels have cropped up, the range of accommodations and restaurants available is generally the same for all of Greece. This does not prevent some proprietors from tiptoeing around the law to claim substantial profits, especially in the most popular areas; but on paper at least, the facilities and prices of two places of the same class should be identical, and only the service or location will differ.

Tourism in Greece is managed by two nationwide organizations: the **National Tourist Organization of Greece** (NTOG) and the **Tourist Police** (*Touristiki Astinomia*). The NTOG has only a few branches, but they tend to be modern and efficient, and can supply general information about sights and accommodations all over the country. The Tourist Police deal with more local and immediate problems—where to find a room, a dentist, what the bus schedule is, or what to do when you've lost your passport. They are open long hours and are always willing to help, although their English is often limited. The NTOG offices in the U.S. and other countries are listed in the Useful Organizations section above; in Athens, the Head Office is at 2 Amerikis St., Athens (tel. 32 23 111).

Student Travel Offices

Nikis and Filellinon Sts. in Athens are lined with agencies and organizations geared specifically for student travelers. Included among them are the following:

Athens Student Travel Service, 1 Filellinon St. (tel. 32 25 165 or 32 30 483). Helpful advice on discount plane, bus, and boat tickets as well as the best information in town on travel to the far east. ISIC and FIYTO cards available.

Student Travel Service Ltd., also at 1 Filellinon St. (tel. 32 27 993 or 32 47 433). Representatives for ISSTA in Israel and CIEE in the U.S., they offer student charters to points throughout Europe. The best place to book tickets. ISIC and FIYTO cards.

ISTYS, 11 Nikis St., 2nd floor (tel. 32 33 767 or 32 21 267). Also sells ISIC and FIYTO cards.

Transalpino Travel, 28 Nikis St. (tel. 32 20 503). Helpful for economic overland travel to Northern Europe. Information on discounts for boat and plane tickets.

Magic Bus, 20 Filellinon St. (tel. 32 37 471). Cheap but erratic bus service to Europe and flights to the Mideast and Asia. Don't rely on their service to India; the twice-monthly buses are run-down and the drivers reputedly maniacal.

For the many technical issues of international travel, contact the Greek embassy of your country (see Useful Organizations). If you are confronted with a lost passport or need a lawyer, contact your country's embassy in Athens (address in the Athens section).

Currency and Exchange

The drachma is the legal tender of Greece. It is issued in both paper notes (50, 100, 500, 1000dr) and coins (1, 2, 5, 10, and 20dr). It is often difficult to get change for notes of 500dr or more. When entering the country, you can bring up to 1500dr (in banknotes only) and an unlimited amount of foreign currency. However, if you are carrying more than $500 in cash, you must declare it upon entry in order to re-export it legally. All banks in Greece are authorized to convert foreign currency at official rates; branches of the National Bank of Greece are located in major towns throughout the country. Banks are generally open Mon.-Fri. 8am-2pm, although hours at local branches may vary. Money exchange counters are open later, mainly as a convenience for tourists; check with the NTOG for a list of banks having longer hours. We have also listed travel agencies, restaurants, and hotels (especially in smaller towns that have no banks) that provide currency exchange in off hours as well as regular business hours, but may offer you a rate about 10% lower than the official one. All establishments charge a 20-50dr commission for changing travelers checks. If you're coming by ferry and scheduled to arrive in Greece at night, you should consider changing currency before you leave or on the boat coming over (many boats provide some exchange service) so you won't be stranded without money the first night, but expect to receive far fewer drachmas for the dollar anywhere outside Greece. It is also advisable to change your drachmas back into dollars while still in Greece since you'll find they're not worth the paper they're printed on once you leave. Remember, though, that no more than $100 worth of drachmas can be changed back into dollars during any one stay.

A special note on prices: inflation in Greece hovers around 25%, and since all of our prices were researched in the summer of 1983, you must add 20-30% to each price listed in this book. Fortunately, the exchange rate of the U.S. dollar relative to the drachma is increasing at roughly the same rate as Greek inflation which serves to cancel out any price increases.

Business Hours and Holidays

In Greece, shops are closed on Sundays, with only restaurants, cafes, dairy shops, and bakeries remaining open. During the week business hours vary, but most places close after 2pm for an afternoon break and reopen at about 6pm. Banks are open Mon.-Thurs. 8am-2pm, Fri. 7:45am-2pm. Shops and pharmacies are open Monday, Wednesday, and Saturday 8am-2:30pm and Tuesday, Thursday and Friday 8am-1pm and 5-8:30pm. Foodstores have slightly longer hours: Monday, Wednesday, and Saturday 8am-3:30pm and Tuesday, Thursday and Friday 8am-2pm and 5:30-8:30pm. Many gift shops are open straight through from 8am-11pm. Museums and archeological sites close on Tuesdays, and have slightly shorter hours from mid-October to mid-May. We try to list them when appropriate.

All banks and shops close on holidays. The major holidays are New Year's Day, Epiphany (January 6), Shrove Monday (February), National Holidays

(March 25 and October 28), Good Friday, Pashka (Easter) Sunday and Monday, the Feast of the Dormition of the Virgin Mary (August 15), and Christmas and Boxing Day (December 25 and 26).

Telephones, Telegrams, and Mail

Long-distance phone calls and telegrams should be placed at the **OTE (the Greek Telephone Organization)** offices that are found in nearly every village. Hours vary from place to place; in small villages, they are usually 7:30am-3pm, in towns 7:30am-10pm, (shorter hours or closed on weekends), and in larger cities 24 hours a day. If you visit one of the latter in the middle of the night, the door may be locked, but ring and they'll let you in. Long-distance calls take a while to get through because lines are usually jammed: for collect calls, you'll have to wait in the office itself (bring a good book). Try, if at all possible, to call early in the morning. To make a direct call to the United States, dial 001 and then the area code and number. For assistance, ask the attendant at the OTE or dial 162 for an English-speaking operator. Person-to-person long distance phone calls to the US cost about $15 for the first three minutes and $3 for each additional minute. Direct calls cost about $11 for the first three minutes. If you're going to talk for a while, dial your number in the U.S. and ask to be called right back. Rates from the U.S. are cheaper and the call will be charged the U.S. rate (and billed in U.S. dollars). If you call the U.S. collect, you'll be charged the U.S. person-to-person rate; in most cases, you'll still save money over the expensive hotel surcharges. There is no surcharge if you go to an OTE. Remember the time difference when calling North America: subtract seven hours (Eastern Standard Time), eight hours (Central), nine hours (Mountain), or ten hours (Pacific), depending where you call. In other words, if it's 5pm in Athens, it's 10am in New York and 7am in Los Angeles. Telegrams cost about $1 a word. Public phones, located in most kiosks, take 5dr coins for local calls.

It's generally safe to assume that Post Offices are open Mon.-Fri. 7:30am-2:30pm, although services (such as parcels) may close early; occasionally, you'll find a large office that keeps longer hours. For registering a letter, ask for *systemeno*, for express, *epeegon*. Both services are fairly inexpensive, and surface mail is exceptionally cheap. *Poste Restante* functions here as elsewhere, but you have to bully tellers mercilessly to get your mail; ask them to check under both first name and surname, and, if possible, check yourself.

Getting Around

Bus

If you plan to spend an extended period of time in Greece, you'll probably want to travel by bus. Service is extensive and frequent, fares are very reasonable, and the drivers are skillful. On major highways, buses tend to be more modern and efficient than in the mountainous areas of the Peloponnese or Northern Greece. No matter where you want to go, you can probably find a bus that goes there.

Nevertheless, you should be aware of certain potential hazards. Always ask an official when a bus is scheduled to leave (posted schedules are often out of date, and all services are radically curtailed on Sundays), and try to arrive at least ten minutes early (Greek buses have a habit of leaving early). You must also make sure that you know where the buses leave from. In major cities, KTEL bus lines have different stations for the different destinations—the bus for Patras may leave on the other side of town from the bus for Athens. In villages, a cafe usually serves as the bus station and you can only find out schedules by asking the proprietor. Always ask the conductor before entering the bus whether it's going to your destination (the signs on the front are often irrelevant or outdated), and make sure he knows where you want to get off. If the bus whizzes past your stop, just stand up and shout "Stassis!" If you are on the road, you can flag down an inter-city bus at any point, but it's best to stand near a "Stassis" sign.

For long-distance rides, generally in Pullmans, you should buy your ticket beforehand in the office—it will specify a reserved seat (if you don't do so, you may have to stand throughout the journey). For shorter trips, just grab a seat and pay the conductor when he comes around. Fares are very inexpensive—no more than a second-class train ticket. The fare from Patras to Athens is about 500dr. On Crete and some of the larger islands, fares tend to be more expensive for comparable distances. Some lines offer return (roundtrip) fares with a 20% discount. As with other forms of transportation, long-distance fares are often lower in the off-season. In towns and cities local buses and trolleys charge around 20dr for a ride. You must stand at the stop and flag them down, or the driver will ignore you.

Train

Greek trains are still inferior to the sleek, modernistic lines in Northern Europe, and only service major cities. Service to some areas is painfully slow, and no lines run to the western coast. Trains are not very useful for traveling to remote areas or to many archeological sites—the rugged, mountainous terrain is far more easily and quickly traversed by bus or car. Trains travel daily between Athens and Thessaloniki (eight hours), continuing on to Alexandroupolis and Turkey or north to Yugoslavia and the rest of Europe. Lines also extend into the Peloponnese to Corinth, Patras, Olympia, and Kalamata.

Eurail and InterRail passes are both valid on Greek trains, though occasionally a conductor will give you a dull stare when you present them. In addition, the **Hellenic Railways Organization** offers a 20% rebate on all roundtrip fares. They also sell Touring Cards that offer unlimited travel for ten, twenty, or thirty days. For more information write to Hellenic Railways Organization (OSE) at 1-3 Karolou St., Athens (tel. 52 22 491). If you want to call for schedules and prices in Greece, dial 145 or 147.

Boat

Every summer, visitors to the Greek islands envision sunning leisurely on spacious ferry decks while being smoothly conveyed from isle to isle; every summer, the same visitors get turned off by the bewildering ticket schedules and crowded boats inherent in island-hopping. But to see the islands, you will have to take the boats. The tips below should help keep you afloat.

First, don't worry about planning an itinerary far in advance, unless you are traveling in the off-season. During the summer months, boat connections between major islands are extremely frequent. However, you often have to change several times to get a destination off the main route. Direct connections are less expensive than longer routes (the more stops, the higher the price), but they tend to be less frequent. Second, do not assume that the most direct way to get to between distant islands—e.g., Samos and Sifnos—is the shortest in nautical miles (i.e., via Paros). Returning to Piraeus can be quicker, because it gives you access to a much wider range of sailings. In the off-season, boats from Piraeus continue regularly, while boats between islands cut back their service.

Ferry rates are carefully regulated by the government: it costs around 200-

250dr one-way to take a ferry between neighboring islands, 400-550dr to go between islands a couple of islands apart, and 935dr to go from Piraeus to Crete. For a given route all ferries must charge the same price, except for the small excursion boats that do package daytrips; shopping around for price isn't necessary. On the other hand, you must visit several different agencies to get a full list of departures. Each office will only inform you about its own ferries, and may even deny that others exist. The Tourist Police can sometimes help you sort out the mess and the harbor police (*Limenarchion*) always have a master plan of sailings.

Once you have found the appropriate boat, wait until the last minute to buy your ticket: exchanges and refunds are difficult to obtain and, needless to say, one company will not honor another's ticket to a given island. Recheck every connection you intend to make once you reach an island, and again a few hours before departure, with the boat company or the agency selling tickets. Since boat schedules often change at the last minute, it's advisable to let your plans do so as well. Some boats will sell you tickets on board (at 20% above the agency price); others won't let you board without a ticket.

When you depart from Piraeus, the same ferry-chasing isn't necessary. The NTOG (see the Athens section) prints a schedule of all ferries each week. Remember that the boat itineraries do not necessarily run on daily or weekly cycles, so you cannot rely on outdated schedules.

In general, the boats come in three types: large car ferries, small passenger boats, and smaller excursion boats. Which one you get depends on the distance involved and the popularity of your destination. The Saronic Gulf Islands and the Cyclades are closest to Piraeus and are serviced by hydrofoil; the trips are much faster and more frequent, but also more expensive than on the regular ferry routes. If you have a choice of several different vessels, bear in mind that the passenger boats give more of a sense of sailing the Aegean, but this intimacy can cause trouble in rough weather. Seasickness is a more common problem than Greece's idyllic waters may lead you to believe, and the strong *melitima* winds buck up waves that toss small boats like corks. Smaller boats and hydrofoils don't sail unless the seas are calm. It's a good idea to bring some Dramamine—even if you don't use it, it will make you a lot of friends. If the seas look rough, don't eat before, during, or immediately after your voyage, but do drink (avoid coffee).

To and from Piraeus, all passengers must pay a 47dr embarkation tax. Third class fares from Piraeus to: Iraklion (1038dr), Hania (933dr), Agios Nikolaos (1543dr), Mykonos (711dr), Santorini (911dr), Paros (643dr), Naxos (739dr), Ios (911dr), Syros (640dr), Tinos (711dr), Rhodes (1288dr), Patmos (924dr), Kos (1300dr), Samos (1040dr), Chios (827dr). Children under 4 years travel free, ages 4-10 pay half fare. Passenger insurance fees are minimal.

A warning: boat crews throughout the Aegean occasionally call strikes during the summer months. Though the strikes are usually brief, they can cause problems, particularly if you need to make an infrequent connection. Keep your ears open: the strikes are often announced a few days in advance.

Motorcycle

Motorcycling is a popular way of touring Greece, especially the islands. Bikes rent more cheaply than cars, and offer much more freedom than buses, particularly if you wish to visit more remote areas. You'll see plenty of places offering scooters or mopeds for rent, but the quality of the bikes, speed of service in case of breakdown, and prices for longer periods may vary drastically. Nearly all agencies are open to bargaining. Expect to pay 500dr for a moped or mobilet, 700-800dr per day for a 50cc scooter, the cheapest bike able to tackle the steep Greek mountain roads. 150cc and 200cc motorbikes cost 20% and 30% more, respectively, but require a motorcycle license. (Many establishments will lease the bikes without a license, but in the event of an accident you'll be in trouble.) For week-long rentals, most shops charge as if for five days. If the agency provides a full tank, they're apt to add 200dr to the daily bill. If you're buying gas, you can expect to spend 1dr per kilometer. Many agencies request your passport as a deposit, but this practice is illegal.

While most places offer insurance at about 140dr per day, it is usually third-party liability insurance, which pays only for damage to anything you hit. It never covers damage to your machine or yourself. Full insurance coverage is not available in Greece; the best you can do is to purchase insurance with a hefty 16,000dr deductible. It costs about 80-140dr more per day, and is not always available. In any case, before you rent a scooter or motorcycle, demand to know the details of the coverage. Ride a bike down the block before you take it, and insist on a helmet. Finally, be sure that you are leasing from the bike company itself, and not from a commission-seeking agent.

Most importantly, ride carefully—never famed for safety, motorcycles are particularly dangerous on rocky and rough Greek roads. Wear a helmet and do not carry a heavy pack on your back. Motorcycles have other drawbacks: they need retuning frequently, they can't carry much luggage, and long trips are tiresome. Don't use motorcycles unless you're already comfortable with them.

Hitching

It's hard to generalize about hitching in Greece. You may find hitching difficult in very popular tourist areas because the Greeks are not eager to pick up foreigners. You may also find it difficult to hitch through sparsely-populated areas because there is simply no traffic. By and large, most of Greece falls between these two extremes and hitching is an adequate way of getting around. Make sure your destination is clear and unambiguous. It helps to write your destination on a sign, in both Greek and English letters, if possible. Moreover, try to hitch from turn-offs rather than along long stretches of straight road (the driver will have a better idea of your ultimate destination).

Most of your rides will come from truck drivers. Women will probably be safe hitching alone, but a companion can be extra insurance: the best combination is a man and a woman. Private cars are usually full, since they are used mostly for family excursions. Two or three people hitching together with large backpacks should try to split up to get rides more easily.

Car

If you want to see as much of Greece as possible, have a bit of spare cash, and can get together four or five people, driving can be the ideal way to tour. Rentals with unlimited mileage and insurance start at 15,500dr per week in the off-season, and 17,500dr in summer; gasoline is 56dr per liter and going up. Agencies quote low daily rates, but these prices exclude the 18% tax and CDW insurance. (CDW stands for Collision Damage Waver. Without CDW insurance the driver is responsible for the first 70,000dr worth of damage, more for vans.) Some places quote even lower rates, but charge you for 100km even if you never leave their driveway. Check the small print with care. Despite its expense, however, a car gives you an unparalleled chance to explore the beaten and unbeaten tracks for about $70 per person per week.

Most of the rental agencies are based in Athens, though you can probably find one in any major town. The cheapest and largest are **Just, InterRent** and **Retca,** with offices in Athens, Crete and several of the islands as well as numerous mainland cities. The Just main office is at 43 Singrou Ave., Athens (tel. 92 39 104 or 92 33 389), InterRent is at 4 Singrou Ave. (tel. 92 15 788/9 or 92 33 452), and Retca is at 20 Kalisperi St. (tel. 92 14 373 or 92 24 998). Another inexpensive agency is **Herodian,** at 11 Mitseon and Madjihristou Streets in Athens (tel. 92 32 318 or 92 32 415). **Avis** and **Hertz** also operate all over Greece, but their rates are far steeper. Minimum required ages for rental vary between 21 and 25 depending upon the rental agency.

Foreign drivers are required to have an international driver's license to drive in Greece. To get the license in Greece, you should present your national driver's license, passport, a photograph, and 600dr fee to the **Greek Automobile and Touring Club (ELPA).** Their main office is at 2 Messogian St., Athens (tel. 77 91 615); there are other offices in most major cities. To enter the country with a car, you need a "Carnet de Passage en Douanes," available from the American Automobile Association, though you may be allowed in for a short period of time without it. The ELPA provides tourists with any assistance and information they may require. They have an emergency repair service (tel. 104) and a 24-hour information line (tel. 174).

Greece has 4100km of asphalt roads. Superhighways connect the major cities, while smaller roads service more remote areas. The roads in the mountains tend to be particularly narrow and tricky, though taxi drivers seem to think otherwise. Driving in Greece is on the right side of the road.

One eerie note: the miniature church-like boxes that appear on the sides of the roads every few hundred yards or so are offerings of gratitude by people who survived car accidents on the same spot. (Just to keep you on your toes.)

Accommodations

Although hotels and guesthouses have become considerably more expensive in the past few years, it is still relatively easy to find cheap accommodations. In addition to the usual budget hotels and student hostels, most Greek towns have inexpensive rooms to let and some camping facilities. The real saving grace is Greece's warm, sunny climate—if all else fails, you can always unfurl your sleeping bag in some secluded field or deserted beach.

Hostels

Greek youth hostels are an excellent alternative to hotels. The accommodations are quite good and the cost is very reasonable (180dr per night). Unfortunately, hostels are relatively scarce; they turn up in places you'd least expect them and not in places you most need them. At present Greece has over 25 official youth hostels, ranging from the big complexes in Athens and Corfu to the smaller, more rustic lodges in the Thessaly mountain range.

The Greek youth hostels generally have fewer restrictions than those in Northern Europe. They are open all year round and have midnight or 1am curfews. They are open in summer from 6-10am and 1pm-midnight (shorter hours in winter). The large hostels offer breakfast at 60-70dr. The hostels have a maximum stay of five days. It is advisable to book in advance in the summer at some of the more popular hostels, i.e., Athens, Thira, Nafplion.

You'll usually need an IYHF card to stay at Greek youth hostels. The card is available from the **International Youth Hostel Federation** at **American Youth Hostels,** 1332 I Street, N.W., Suite 800, Washington, DC 20005 (tel. (202) 783-6161). In Canada, write to the **Canadian Hostelling Association,** Place Vanier, Tower A, 333 River Road, Vanier City, Ottawa, Ontario K1L 8H9. If you arrive in Greece without an IYHF card, you can purchase an International Guest Card from the **Greek Association of Youth Hostels,** 4 Dragatsaniou St., Athens (tel. 32 34 107), or from the hostels directly.

Camping

The National Tourist Organization of Greece (NTOG) is the primary organization responsible for campgrounds in Greece. If you write to them at 2 Amerikis St., Athens 133 (tel. 32 23 111), or at one of their foreign offices (see Useful Organizations), they will send you a list of all their campgrounds in Greece. Most of the official NTOG campgrounds have good facilities, and many are located in areas of outstanding natural beauty. The Hellenic Touring Club also runs a number of campgrounds, most of which are less expensive than the NTOG campgrounds. In addition, Greece has many campgrounds run by private organizations. These vary widely in quality and price.

The prices charged at campgrounds vary according to the facilities; most campgrounds charge 100-130dr per person, plus 100-130dr per tent, car, or camper. NTOG campgrounds tend to be ritzier and most expensive (140dr).

More often than not, you can discover unofficial campgrounds on the outskirts of town or along quiet shores. On many of the Greek islands, campers will simply take to the beaches. Camping outside of campgrounds is technically illegal, though most people ignore the rules. Freelance camping is outlawed to avoid littering and fires, but if the local police think you will avoid either of these unpleasantries, especially during the off-season, they will not disturb you. The more likely reason for the prohibition is to give the hotels and campgrounds business. If you sleep on a famous beach in front of some empty hotel during the off-season, there is a good chance that one of the hotel owners will report you to the police, who are then obliged to act. During July and August, when hotels and pensions are booked solid, sleeping outdoors becomes commonplace and no one will object since you are no longer hurting business. The most that ever happens if you are caught camping illegally is that your passport is confiscated temporarily and sold back for several hundred drachma; often, you may just be told to move.

Hotels

In the past, all hotels in Greece were legally regulated for price and quality. Hotels, rated from A to E, were required to observe the fixed prices for each category. But the Socialist government has recently deregulated the hotels; the rating system remains, but the categories are only useful now as very vague guidelines. In some places, the sky's the limit for prices. Moreover, proprietors are privy to every trick in the book: they are entitled, and therefore inclined, to charge 10% extra for stays of less than three nights (hence their first obvious question always concerns how long you plan to stay) and 20% extra in high season, from July 1-Sept. 15. Beyond that, though, they may only offer you the most expensive rooms available, may compel you to buy breakfast, may squeeze three people into a hostel-like triple and charge each for a single, or may quote you a price for a room with breakfast and private shower and hope that you bite. Showers are usually 50dr extra, but can cost as much as 100dr. They're usually located off the hall for communal use, and unfortunately, the hot water needs to run anywhere from ten minutes to half an hour before there's enough for a shower.

The advantage of variability in hotel facilities is that you can, and should, barter. If they offer you a room that seems unreasonably expensive, stress that you don't want luxuries and, perhaps grudgingly, they'll tell you of a cheaper option. Late at night, in the off-season, or in a large town where there are plenty of options, it's a buyer's market, and a proprietor will almost always agree to go below the quoted prices or offer free showers. Most hoteliers will ask for your passport and return it when you leave—just make sure the one you gave is the one you receive. Most hotels will let you leave your luggage in the reception area during the afternoon, though checkout is at 11am or noon. Above all, remember that the Tourist Police are on your side: if the hotel flagrantly violates the prices shown by law at the registration desk, or if you think that you've been exploited in any way, threaten to report the hotel to the Tourist Police; the threat alone will often resolve "misunderstandings." We list almost exclusively D- and E-class hotels, ranging in price from 400dr for a single to 700dr and beyond for a double (prices may be at least 100dr less in the off-season). If we say a hotel has no singles, you may still be put in a room by yourself; just remember to haggle over the price *before* you accept the room.

	Single		Double		Triple		2-bed	3-bed
Class	with bath	w/o	with bath	w/o	with bath	w/o	Price per bed	
C	750	600	900	800	1100	1000		
D	600	500	800	700	1000	900	350	300
E	500	400	650	600	750	700	300	240

Rooms to Let

Wherever there are tourists, you'll see lots of private homes with signs offering "rooms to let." Indeed, the owners of these houses often crowd around all incoming boats or buses in order to solicit customers. If you don't see them, just ask at a cafe where you can find rooms. Needless to say, this is a much easier, cheaper, and more attractive option if you speak Greek; but even if you don't, the rooms are often very cheap (300dr for a single, 400dr for a double) and perfectly dependable. There may not be locks, towels, or telephones, but there may be warm offers of coffee at night and friendly conversations. Prices here are especially variable, so make sure that you're paying no more than you would at a D-class hotel. If in doubt, ask the Tourist Police: they will usually set you up with a room and conduct all the negotiations themselves.

If you're really strapped for money, you might consider asking proprietors to let you sleep on the roof. In many cases, they will let you and charge you only a few drachmas. Alternatively, in Athens many proprietors hire young students to seek out prospective boarders. In return, the students are allowed to stay at the hotel free of charge. Be careful; some proprietors might charge you anyway.

Work

Work is extremely hard to find in Greece. Job opportunities are scarce and the Greek government makes every attempt to restrict employment to Greek citizens. If you desire long-term employment you must first secure a work permit from your employer, the **Ministry of Labor,** 45 Piraeus St., Athens or the **Aliens Bureau,** 9 Halkokondili St., Athens (tel. 36 28 301).

Your best bet is to secure a job with an American or Canadian firm, but this usually requires fluency in Greek and some specialized skill. Furthermore, regulations permit foreign firms to employ only 10% non-Greek citizens. All arrangements and negotiations should be made before you leave home. For a list of American firms, subsidiaries, and affiliates operating in Greece, write to the **American Hellenic Chamber of Commerce,** 17 Valaoritou St., 2nd floor, Athens 134 (tel. 36 18 385). The list costs $40, including postage. They can also offer advice about finding temporary or permanent employment in Greece (open Mon.-Fri. 9am-2pm).

Other opportunities for work are limited; check the nearest university library for ideas. Archeological fieldwork is sometimes available, but most excavations require experienced volunteers and pay little or no wages. For information on archeological field work opportunities write to the **Archeological Institute of America**, 15 Park Row, New York, NY. If you've read *The Magus* by John Fowles, you might have the impression that a lot of young people teach English in Greek private schools. Unfortunately, teaching jobs are scarce, but holders of valid U.S. teaching certificates can obtain a list of schools in Greece that employ American teachers. The **Institute of International Education (IIE)**, 809 United Nations Plaza, New York, NY 10017 (tel. (212) 883-8470) puts out an excellent publication called *Teaching Abroad,* which lists sources of information on teaching opportunities. In addition, the U.S. government sponsors a teacher exchange program. The commitment is generally for one academic year and you must be fluent in Greek. Write to the U.S. Department of Education for more information. Finally, the **International Association for the Exchange of Students for Technical Experience (IAESTE)** supports on-the-job training for undergraduates and graduates in Greece. The ability of the IAESTE program to secure places in other countries depends on the number of openings offered, so you will have to locate prospective American employers. For more information, write or call IAESTE Trainee Program, c/o AIPT, 217 American City Bldg., Columbia, MD 21044 (tel. (301) 997-2200).

During the summer, many young Westerners find casual employment in hotels, bars, restaurants, and as tour guides for proprietors who need English-speaking employees. Pay, however, is very low by American standards. Waitresses can expect to earn only 500-1000dr per eight-hour shift. Hotel clerks receive about 2000dr per week, plus free room and board, for a forty to fifty hour work-week. Working conditions vary greatly. Though jobs are usually easier to find for women than for men, sexual harassment is a serious threat. To find jobs, check the bulletin boards of many of the budget hostels in Athens and the classifieds ads in the Athens Daily News. Or contact **Working Holidays** at 11 Nikis St. in Athens (tel. 32 24 321). They will take applications from overseas, but require prepayment of the $40 registration fee. A final possibility is to work as a farm laborer—the Peloponnese and Crete are good places to look for farm work.

Study

If you have a strong interest in Greek classics, a love of the modern land, or a desire to learn the Greek language, you might consider studying in Greece. Many American students come to Greece on programs run by American universities and organizations, or on independent study projects financed by universities. These projects range from a whole semester of language instruction to a three-week whirlwind tour of classical sights. If your college has an office that gives advice on study abroad, talk to a counselor or use their library for a start. The **Institute of International Education** publishes several reference books on study abroad, which you should be able to find at your college: *U.S. College-Sponsored Programs Abroad: Academic Year* is a catalog of undergraduate and graduate-level programs run by U.S. colleges and universities; *Vacation Study Abroad* serves the same function for summer programs. If you cannot find either of these books, you can order them directly—each volume costs $9.95. In addition, IIE's New York office will answer written or phone inquiries, and has a reference library that is open by appointment (see Work section for address).

College Year in Athens, Inc. runs a two-semester program in Greek civilization open to undergraduates (usually juniors), which includes travel to important sites as well as classroom instruction. The program has its own faculty, but will issue a transcript to your home university. The program, including field trip travel expenses, costs $8,000; some scholarship money is available. For more information, contact the American Representative at 1702 South High St., Bloomington, IN 47401 or the Director, College Year in Athens, P.O. Box 17176, 100 24 Athens, Greece.

For the short-term student, the **Hellenic Language School** and the **Athens Centre** both offer intensive Greek language courses. The Hellenic Language School is located at 4 Zalogou St., Athens (tel. 36 27 560). The Athens Centre, which also has dance and yoga classes and a special on-site summer course on Classical and Byzantine Greece, is at 48 Archimidous St., Pangrati, Athens (tel. 70 12 268), and is open Mon.-Fri. 9am-2pm and 5-8:30pm.

More information on educational programs in Greece can be obtained from the Greek Press and Information Office, 601 Fifth Ave., New York, NY 10017 (tel. (212) 751-8788) or 089 MacLaren St., Ottawa, Ontario K2P OK6 (tel. (613) 232-6796).

Life in Greece

Food

Greek food seems to have been inspired by Hermes, the god of invention. Showing particular ingenuity in discovering nearly unlimited usages for the plentiful native product of olive oil, the Greeks combine it with herbs and spices in a cuisine that satisfies everyone from the gourmet to the ordinary fisherman broiling the catch of the day.

Breakfast is a light meal, often just a pastry or bread with *marmelada* or *meli* (honey) with some coffee or tea. Lunch is similarly light, though you can order most of the same dishes served in the evening. If you go to a taverna for lunch, try a *choriatiki*, a "Greek" or "peasant's" salad containing olives, tomatoes, onions, and cucumbers, with a hefty slab of feta cheese on top. These usually cost between 60 and 80dr, and since they're chaperoned by a basket of bread, provide a quite filling meal for about $1. Otherwise you can stop at a cafe or snack bar and see whether they have *souvlaki pita*, a wondrous conglomeration of skewered lamb, tomatoes, sauce and french fries wrapped in pita bread, that costs about 20dr. There is also *bifteki pita*, which differs from souvlaki pita only in that it has a hamburger patty instead of lamb meat. More expensive is the *gyros pita* variety; the meat for this is carved from a huge leg of lamb turning on a barbeque spit. Straight *souvlaki* (essentially, *shish kebab*), is one of the most popular snacks, sold at most places for around 30dr per stick. Your third option is to visit a market to stock up on the wonderful fruit that's available all summer, or on some indigenous cheeses, like *feta* (a semi-soft, salty white cheese made from goat's milk), *kasseri* (a creamy, mild type), or *manouri* (an unsalted, soft white cheese).

Dinner is the main meal of the day, a leisurely and late affair that's part social occasion and part gluttony (some restaurants don't even open until 9pm). Most dinners start with a salad (*salata*), followed by a meat entree and dessert. The main dishes usually feature *moskari* (veal), *arni* (lamb), or *katapoulo* (chicken), with french fries (*patates*) or beans (*fasolakia*). Chicken is always the cheapest item on the menu and usually tasty, though small. Uniquely Greek dishes include *moussaka* (chopped meat and eggplant mixed with a cheese and tomato paste) and grape leaves stuffed with rice and small packages of minced meat (called *dolmades* when served hot with egg and lemon sauce, *dolmadaki* when served plain). Moussaka is also quite inexpensive (at 100dr). Many menus also feature *souvlaki*, a large skewer of steak, generally pork or lamb (very different from the snack). Be warned that pizzas in Greece are as costly as they are cheap in Italy.

For dessert, Greeks like to eat *karpouzi* (big, delicious slices of watermelon) or *peponi* (yellow melon), or to nibble at pastries. Try either *baklava*, honeyed strudel filled with chopped nuts, or *kataifi*, strands of dough wrapped around nuts and cinnamon.

Greek coffee is the most popular beverage, though you may wonder why. A legacy of Turkish rule, it is exceedingly strong and hideously sweet. Ask for *metrio* and you'll get a cup with half the regular amount of sugar, but that still means several spoonfuls of the white drug. *Sketto* will get an entirely sugarless cup. Greek coffee is usually served, drunk, and tempered with a glass of water. Fortunately, regular coffee (called *Nescafe*) is usually also available; specify *zesto* (warm). If you ask for *frappé*, you'll get a tall glass of iced coffee, shaken up so it's frothy. Greek cookies are surprisingly good, and pasteli (a healthy sesame and honey biscuit) makes a filling snack.

Another favorite snack combination is *ouzo* with *mezes*, tidbits of cheese, sausage, cakes, and octopus. Ouzo itself is a distilled spirit (raki) to which anise is added, giving it a licorice taste. Most people drink it as an aperitif, all afternoon long, though some have it after dinner as a liqueur. It's certainly worth a try. You may even develop a taste for it—mixed with water it's sweet but not overwhelming, though slightly reminiscent of paregoric.

If you have trouble deciphering a menu or deciding whether to eat at a particular restaurant, you might want to browse through the kitchen. It's an accepted practice in many places. This technique will allow you to sample the fancier dishes, but may land you with a bill of 350-400dr or more. All restaurant prices are strictly regulated by the Tourist Police. Menus always have the same format; each restaurant merely writes on the prices of the meals they serve. Since most places have only a few of the fixed-price dishes available at any one time, if you choose a restaurant for a particular dish on the menu, make sure they have it before you sit down. Unfortunately, you may find that not only do the prices not vary widely, but the taste doesn't either. Differences in the way dishes are prepared is minimal, and dining in restaurants can become very monotonous.

Wine

One of the most creative arts in Greece is wine-making. Long ago the Greeks discovered that when wine was stored in pitch pine-sealed goatskins it developed a fresh sappy flavor. After some studious deduction, they discovered they could achieve the same effect by adding pine resin in varying amounts to wine during fermentation. The result was an unusual tasting product called *Retsina*. Resinated wines now come in three varieties: light white, rose, and red. There are also a number of non-resinated wines, including white (*aspro*), red (*kokkino*), sweet (*gleko*), and semi-sweet (*imigleko*). Greek wines can be classified in two basic groups: ordinary wines, which are one to three years old, and special wines, which are three to nine years old.

Festivals

The Dionysian spirit is alive and well in Greece. Festivals and artistic events abound, and even the most remote Greek village holds some sort of annual fair. The Greek penchant for celebrating is particularly infectious; visitors are welcome and easily swept up in the festivities.

Major holidays are the principal cause for festivals in Greece. Most Greek towns and cities hold a celebration on Christmas, Epiphany (January 6), Easter, and St. John the Baptist's Day (June 24). In addition, many towns honor their own patron saint with special festivals.

The main artistic events in Greece take place at the amphitheater of **Herod Atticus,** below the Acropolis, from May through September, and at the outdoor theater of **Epidavros** during July and August. The program for the **Athens Festival** features international concerts, opera, and ballet, as well as classical drama. But the ancient plays are more impressive on the circular Epidavrian stage, surrounded by a wooded grove rather than a jagged cityscape. Don't worry about the language barrier; it won't detract from the ominous choreography of the Furies' chorus which, in the time of the ancient tragedian Aeschylus, made "boys die of fright and women have miscarriages." Tickets and programs for both series are available at the **Athens Festival Box Office,** 4 Stadiou St. (inside the arcade, tel. 32 21 459); while you're there, ask about the **Dora Stratou Folk Dances.** But stop by several days before a performance and expect a line shortly after the 8:30am opening time. There are a number of annual local wine festivals throughout Greece. The largest of these are at Daphni, Rethymnon, and Alexandroupolis; all run from July to the end of August or early September. Hours are 7pm-1am. The 65dr admission gives you a jar and glass and unlimited "tasting." On Crete, Rethymnon's popular festival runs the last two weeks of July.

Here is a list of some of the more important celebrations:

Carnival. Three weeks of feasting and dancing before the Lenten fast. The first week fatted pigs are slaughtered, the second week villagers feast on meat, and the third week villagers feast on cheese. The most notable celebrations occur in Patras and Cephalonia, the first three weeks in February.

St. George's Day (April 23). Celebration in Arachova in honor of the "knight on the white horse." Festivities include races, wrestling matches, and dancing.

Easter Celebration at Tripolis. Roast lambs in the central square. Visitors are offered wine, red eggs, and a bit of lamb.

May Day (May 1). Festival of spring celebrated in many towns and villages.

Anastenaria (usually May 21 or 23). The most important feast day, it honors Constantine the Great. Includes the religious ritual of walking on burning charcoal. Celebrated in Agia Eleni, Thessaloniki, and Veria.

International Festival of Crete (late May). Dancing performances in the various villages of Hania.

St. Charalambs' Day (June). A calf is sacrificed in honor of the patron saint. Horseracing, dancing, and music. In the village of Napi on the island of Lesvos.

St. John the Baptist Feast (June 24). Lighting of bonfires, masquerades, and parades in Greek villages.

Wine Festival at Alexandroupolis (mid-July to early August). Boogie.

Wine Festival at Rethymnon (late July). Drink and be merry.

Peasant Weddings (August). Reenactment of traditional ceremony at Pelion and Kitsa on the island of Crete.

Ohi ("No") Day (October 28). Each year Greeks celebrate the day on which, in 1940, Mussolini received a resounding Greek *No* to the entrance of Italian troops into Greece from Albania.

For more information on festivals, artistic events, and religious fairs, contact the NTOG or the local Tourist Police.

Art and Architecture

Although Greek armies have rarely ventured far beyond their country's borders, the influence of Greek culture has been felt worldwide. Every serious student of art dreams of a trip to Greece, the storehouse of magnificent ancient works. The layman, however, may find that the bewildering array of archeological sites, museums, and exhibits tests his patience and taxes his energy. If you don't know Doric from Ionic, and want to make sense of all those stones and rocks that make up ancient Greek ruins, you should make an attempt to learn something about Greek architecture.

To simplify matters, think of ancient Greek art as divided into a number of different periods: the Metal Age cultures, the Geometric Period, the Archaic Period, the Classical Period, the Hellenistic Period, and the Byzantine Period. Of course, many of these divisions are superficial and somewhat arbitrary, but they represent major periods of artistic development and should make it easier for you to distinguish between the many archeological sites and ruins.

The earliest Greek artists were heavily influenced by ancient Egyptian art and inherited its concern with pleasing the gods. But in time, the Greeks moved away from the stiff, stilted forms of the Egyptians and developed a bolder, more expressive art. Above all, ancient Greek art was a humanistic art; it placed a greater emphasis on man as a subject and treated divine subjects in terms of human behavior.

The earliest Greek societies consisted mainly of warrior tribes that spread across the Peloponnese and Crete. These societies developed the craft of metalwork. Many sculptures remain from this period, during which two important civilizations emerged. The first, the Minoans, flourished on the island of Crete from 2000 to 1600 B.C. The Minoan kings built many grand palaces, but all were destroyed by an earthquake in 1450 B.C. The second major civilization emerged from the city of Mycenae. Many ruins and artifacts survive from the Mycenean civilization that dominated mainland Greece from 1600 to 1100 B.C. The Myceneans had a fondness for monumental sculpture. One of the best examples is the Lion Gate at Mycenae, a magnificent structure that is remarkably well preserved.

The **Geometric Period** (900-700 B.C.) saw the development of new artistic techniques and styles, and greater freedom of expression in sculpture and painting. The city-states that grew up at this time helped to promote the works of painters, sculptors, and architects. Vases from this period, which can be seen in the National Archeological Museum in Athens, display a greater interest in action and complete scenes than previous works; narrative becomes the dominant element.

During the Geometric Period, architects continued to build simple structures. The most prevalent form was the one-room temple or cult-building, such as the Temple of Zeus at Olympia, with columned porches and raised altar. Many examples of Geometric architecture can be found in Olympia.

The **Archaic Period** (700-480 B.C.) marked an important transition from the simple forms of the Geometric Period to the more elaborate forms of the Classical Period. Architects developed two new column forms: the Doric, a plain, cylindrical column, and the Ionic, a fluted column. The classic Doric temple was a massive rectangular structure with rows of columns around the outside and two interior rooms, the cella and the pronaus. Sculptors in the Archaic Period turned increasingly to kouroi or free-standing statues of naked human beings, many examples of which are housed in the National Archeological Museum. Finally, vase painting proliferated; artists developed an iconography for gestures, figures, and composition, thus improving the techniques for narrative painting.

None of these periods matches the magnificence of the **Classical Period** (480-

323 B.C.), during which Athens reached the pinnacle of its cultural, military, and economic power under Pericles, and the arts flourished. Although some relics from this era (in particular, the Elgin Marbles from the Parthenon) have found their way to British museums, many outstanding statues, ruins, and vases remain in Greece. Sculptors concentrated on the heroic nude form, with Praxiteles and Scopas as the main practitioners. They introduced the technique of counterpoise, in which a free-standing figure has legs spread apart, one seeming to bear weight and the other not, thus suggesting motion. The statue of Hermes holding the baby Dionysus by Praxiteles and the statue of Niki (Winged Victory) by Paionius are two excellent examples of Classical sculpture (they can be viewed in the Olympia museum).

Architecture underwent a tremendous boom in the Classical Period. The great Greek leader Pericles ordered the construction of the Parthenon and the Agora in Athens. Under the watchful eye of the architect Iktinos, these constructions, like many other Classical buildings, showed a greater spaciousness, fluidity, and gracefulness than the massive temples of the Archaic Period.

When Alexander the Great led Greek armies south toward Egypt, Greek civilization spread far beyond its present borders. The **Hellenistic Period** (323-first century B.C.), as this period was called, saw the addition of new styles. In architecture, the Corinthian column, a fluted column with a multi-leaved top (shaped somewhat like an inverted bell), was introduced in many buildings. The Monument of Lysicrates in Athens is a fine example. Several amphitheaters were built at this time also, most notably those at Epidavros and Argos. The magnificent acoustics of these constructions mystify architects today, and stand as testaments to the creative genius of their Greek designers.

From the first century B.C. to 500 A.D., the Romans controlled Greece, but they adopted much of the Hellenistic style. One of the more interesting examples of Greco-Roman architecture is Hadrian's Arch in Athens, built by the Emperor Hadrian in the second century A.D. In 395 A.D., the Roman Empire split into two parts; the Western and the Eastern, or Byzantine, Empire. The Greeks fell under the latter, and the new political arrangement gave Greeks the opportunity to exercise more political control. Since the Roman Emperor Constantine commanded the Christianization of the empire in 313 A.D., Greek artists had begun to devote their work to the glorification of Christianity. During the **Byzantine Period** (500-1200 A.D.), many churches were built and a religious iconography developed.

The most notable examples of Byzantine art in Greece are the monasteries built at Ossios Loukas, Daphni, Mt. Athos, and Meteora. The churches here were built in a cruciform style; they followed the form of a Greek cross (a cross with arms of equal length). A narthex or small chamber was added at one end and an apse or half dome at the other. The transept or intersection of the two lengths of the church was capped by a domed ceiling.

Byzantine artists produced ornate but beautiful icons and mosaics to decorate their churches. A mosaic of the Christ Pantocrater was almost always placed in the dome or apse. Mosaics were composed of fragments of hard stone, irregularly cut to catch the light.

History

It's tempting to think of Greece as simply the land of Plato and Aristotle, of Homer and Herodotus, of Pericles and Alexander, but that would be a grave misconception. Recorded Greek history spans nearly thirty centuries, from the Dorian invasion in 900 B.C. to the present republican government.

Ancient Greek history is not simply a series of starts and stops, but a relay race with each civilization passing the baton of its cultural heritage on to the succeeding civilization. Although recorded history dates back to only 900

B.C., archeological evidence suggests that migratory tribes inhabited the Hellenic peninsula as far back as 4000 B.C. The introduction of metalwork from the east during the Bronze Age (2000 B.C.) enabled these tribes to develop great cities and powerful navies. Three great civilizations arose at this time— the Cycladic, the Minoan, and the Mycenean.

The Minoans (1900-1500 B.C.) are of interest for the magnificent palaces they built at Knossos and other sites on Crete. Minoan influence reached far into the Peloponnese and sowed the seeds of the greatest prehistoric civilization, the Mycenean (1400-900 B.C.). Mycenean society dominated the Aegean world for several centuries with its powerful navies; Homer recounts in *The Iliad* the famed Trojan expedition of the Myceneans led by the ill-fated King Agamemnon.

Powerful as they were, the Myceneans could not withstand the forces of historical change. The mass migration of four Hellenic tribes to the Greek mainland in 900 B.C., known as the Dorian invasion, laid the foundation for a pan-Hellenic society that superseded the Myceneans. This marked the beginning of the Geometric Period (900-700 B.C.), the first period of recorded history. During this time, the various tribes developed a common alphabet and religious system, and a uniform though separate form of government. The cultural unity was further enhanced by the establishment of the Olympic Games in 776 B.C., an athletic event involving all the tribes, and the institution of pan-Hellenic sanctuaries.

In the Archaic Period (700-480 B.C.), this cultural integration progressed, though the tribes continued to divide politically into separate city-states. The two greatest city-states were Sparta and Athens. Much has been written about these two societies, and their great rivalry: Sparta essentially developed a totalitarian society with a rigid military code based on territorial conquest, while Athens developed a more loosely-ordered and democratic society that encouraged cooperation between city-states and cultivation of the fine arts. But the two city-states united against a foreign enemy during the Persian Wars, which lasted from the battle of Marathon in 490 B.C. to the battle at Plataea in 479 B.C.

The Classical Period (480-323 B.C.) marked the height of Greek cultural development. As the leader of an alliance between the main city-states called the Delian confederacy, Athens flourished both economically and culturally. The wealth accumulated from shipping and trading enabled the Athenians to build great temples and theaters. Under the leader Pericles, the architects constructed the Parthenon and the Agora. In the cultural sphere, philosophers, historians, and artists produced some of the greatest works of art and literature—this was the time of the playwrights Aeschylus, Sophocles, Euripides, the sculptor Mnesicles, and the historian Herodotus.

The Spartans became jealous of the Athenian cultural and political hegemony; their attempt to conquer Athens in the fifth century resulted in the 27-year Peloponnesian War. Athens never regained its former military strength, but Athenian cultural life continued to prosper: from 400-300 B.C., Socrates, Plato, and Aristotle, the holy trinity of philosophy, made tremendous contributions to human thought while sculptors such as Scopas and Praxiteles experimented with new forms of artistic expression.

While Athens and Sparta struggled for military supremacy, a new, more powerful political force began to emerge in Macedonia. During the Hellenistic Period (323-146 B.C.), the Macedonians under King Philip II conquered most of the Greek cities and built a powerful Hellenic confederacy. The illustrious Alexander, son of Philip, embarked in 336 B.C. on a historic expedition to conquer the vast empire of the Persians. In only thirteen years, he subdued the mighty foe, and extended Hellenic influence far into Africa and Asia. Alexander's achievement marked the height of Hellenic military power. After his death, internecine squabbles made the Greek city-states vulnerable to invasion. In 146 B.C. Roman legions conquered Greece, although as Herodotus noted much earlier, the Greeks in general did not become slavish subjects. Greece had a profound impact on Roman culture for the next four centuries.

The Christianization of the Roman Empire in 398 A.D. launched Greece along a different path. The Byzantine Period (500-1200 A.D.) saw Greeks abandon paganism and adopt Christianity. There was a magnificent flowering of Byzantine art, mostly in the form of monastic frescoes and a new iconography (Christian symbols replaced the mythological figures). The fall of Constantinople to the Ottoman Empire in 1453 A.D. propelled Greece into its darkest period; Turks ruled Greece with a cruel and ruthless hand throughout much of the Middle Ages. Persecuted Christians fled to remote monasteries, such as Meteora, or to the West.

Uprisings against the Turks occurred sporadically throughout the Middle Ages, but it was not until the early nineteenth century that the modern Greek state came into existence. In 1821, a revolutionary army composed of guerillas from the Peloponnese and the Aegean Islands began to battle the Turkish armies. Although both sides scored successes, the conflict soon reached a stalemate, thus creating the opportunity for intervention by the three great Western powers, France, England, and Russia, on the side of the Greek insurgents. The final military solution came in the Battle of Navarino in which the British, French, and Russian navies decimated a joint Turkish-Egyptian fleet, and broke the Turkish hold in Greece.

During the twentieth century, Greek politics became a high-level chess game of moves and countermoves, coups and uprisings, wars and treaties. In 1909, the great Greek leader Eleftherias Venezelos managed to oust the monarchy that had ruled Greece for almost a century and install a republican government, but in 1930, the army returned the monarchy to Greece and kicked out Venezelos for his democratic sympathies.

During World War II the Greeks fought valiantly on the side of the Allies. Greek resistance fighters, led by the communist-backed ELAS, held off the Germans for several months and greatly aided the Allied effort. Shortly after the war, the communist forces attempted to take over the government, but were defeated by British forces and the monarchists. In 1949, with substantial American aid, the Greek government defeated another attempt by the communists to take over the government.

From 1952-1963, Greece was governed by a coalition of conservative parties under a republican government led by Constantine Karmanalis. In 1963, the center Union party took over the conservatives but was unable to maintain firm control on the government. This inability to form a stable coalition and a latent fear of communism convinced junior military officers to stage a coup d'etat on April 21, 1967, instituting a military dictatorship. The junta, led by General Papadopolous, was criticized for repressing speech and intimidating political opponents through torture and imprisonment. Many Greeks left the country, including actress Melina Mercouri and Karmanalis; movies such as Z publicized the oppressive and undemocratic nature of the junta.

The downfall of the dictatorship came in 1974 when General Ioannide seized power from Papadopolous and decided to overthrow Archbishop Makarios, the President of Cyprus, and install a client regime. Ioannide's move provoked the Turkish invasion of Cyprus which almost led to war between Turkey and Greece. Afraid of a loss of public confidence and the possibility of a disastrous war, senior military officers requested the return of Karmanalis, who had lived in self-imposed exile for several years. As the designated prime minister, Karmanalis headed a coalition government and skillfully orchestrated parliamentary elections and organized a referendum to determine the fate of the monarchy. The monarchy was defeated by a two-thirds vote and a constitution for a republican government was drawn up in 1975.

The current political scene is relatively stable. The Pan-Hellenic Socialist Party is in power under Papandreou, but two other parties, the NDA and KKE, together make up a strong opposition and are well represented in parliament. Among the tasks facing Greece now are adjusting to life in the Common Market and improving relations with Turkey. Rapid industrialization in the past few years has improved Greece's economic strength, but at the expense of the standards of living; some of the country's major cities suffer terrible overcrowding, pollution, and noise. Another hot issue, and one on which the KKE and the KNE, Greece's two communist parties, campaign, is that of American bases in Greece. The KKE and the KNE are both vehemently opposed to the American presence. You're sure to see the spray-painted slogans: *Kato to Pasok* (down with the pasok) and *Exo oi vaseis* (out with the bases). The Greeks are among the most politically-minded people of Europe—perhaps that's why their cafe conversation is so spirited—and often talk politics, not weather, to break the ice. Ask them what they think of Papandreou, or Reagan, for that matter, and you're bound to get an earful.

Literature

So many people have had so many classical texts stuffed down their throats for so long that it's hard to read the works of ancient Greece with innocent eyes and recognize them as urgent, archetypal, and often very beautiful. But they are—and a visit to Greece presents a fine opportunity for using some of the heavies as colorful and original guides to the sights. In the Ionian Islands, for example, you can still visit the places and hear the names chanted in Homer's *Odyssey*. To this day, captains can sail their ships from isle to isle following the directions given by Homer, and visitors will find children called Telemachos, caves corresponding to the home of the Cyclops, islands that may have belonged to Kalypso, and palaces ruled by Odysseus' colleagues. Read the poem in Robert Fitzgerald's lovely lyrical translation unless you can handle the ancient Greek original, whose lines magically reproduce the sound of water lapping against a boat.

If you're seeing a play at Epidavros, go back to one of the famous dramatists: Aeschylus, whose *Orestian Trilogy* burns with a terrible and thunderous independence; Sophocles, whose plays are mystical enough to give Oedipus a bad name through history; or Euripides, whose sensibility is more modern—guarded, skeptical, ironic, and who takes the great myths and heroes of Ancient Greece and quietly dismantles or discredits them (his version of *Helen* weirdly mocks all the grandiloquent stories and suggests that the long, famous, brutal Trojan War was fought over a phantom). In Aristophanes are the seeds of a hundred situation comedies and slapstick routines, as well as a healthy dose of topical barbs and bawdy pricks.

For better or for worse, Greek writers immortalized their culture's values in art. Some probed myths ancient even to themselves; others—the historians—examined events of recent memory. And what events! The fifth century B.C. stank of two great cultural conflicts: Greeks toppled Persians in the first and each other in the second. Herodotus preserves the monumental battles and personalities of the Greco-Persian conflict. He traveled widely to gather information and in describing the little-known, remote rituals he witnessed, from Egyptian urination to Scythian burial, he created a poignant metaphor for the war's size. Thucydides grimly exposes man stripped of his intellectual clothing by war; "war," he writes, "is a violent teacher." His analysis of the Peloponnesian War, in which Athens and Sparta slugged each other to a Hellenic pulp, remains a great anthropological study on par with Herodotus'. And the description of historic sites in their works is a boon to any visitor.

Greek literature began with such titans, but it by no means ended with them. Many forget that in the last two decades alone Greek poets have claimed two Nobel prizes. George Seferis' poems deal with the overwhelming legacy of the Greek past, so try to fit them into a modern context. By contrast, Odysseus Elytis (winner in 1978) writes visceral, almost surreal poems that celebrate a nature charged with mystical presences and erotic forces. More famous than either, ironically, is C.B. Cavafy, whose dry, rational poems earlier this century have a huge underground following and deeply influenced such writers as E.M Forster, W.H. Auden, and Lawrence Durrell. Everyone knows the music, and probably the movie, of *Zorba the Greek.* Kazantzakis' other books (including a version of the *Odyssey* and novels about Jesus and St. Francis of Assisi) are, if anything, more serious and better. And one outstanding modern Greek novel, written in English and published recently to great acclaim in America, is *When The Tree Sings,* by Stratis Haviaris, which tells in short fragments the story of World War II as seen by a young boy.

Accounts of Greece in English are, of course, manifold, since the country has had devotees and pilgrims since people were doodling on papyrus. The best among them include Lawrence Durrell's numerous novels, coffee table productions, and guide books (*In Prospero's Cell* is about Corfu, *Mante Venus* is about Rhodes); Henry Miller's typically exuberant *The Colossus of Maroussi;* all books by Patrick Leigh-Fermor (especially *Mani: Travels in the Southern Peloponnese*); and *An Affair of the Heart* by Dilys Powell. Also recommended are almost anything by Mary Renault, Leonard Cottrell's *The Bull of Minos,* plays by Aeschylus, Sophocles, Euripides, or Aristophanes, Edith Hamilton's *Mythology,* and Robert Graves' *The Greek Myths.*

In addition to narrative works, there is a long tradition of tour guides to Greece. The first writer to approach the problem of sorting archeological fact from myth was Pausanias, whose *Description of Greece* (Penguin Books; two vols.) explores sites throughout Greece. Pausanias lived around 150 A.D.; his vantage point was a little closer to the history he discusses that ours is. Though the text is rather dry, it contains fascinating anecdotes relating to many of the areas covered. A more modern account of the archeological and historical backgrounds to Greece's numerous sights is the Benn's *Blue Guide,* the most comprehensive guide to Greece in English (though it doesn't cater to budget travelers). Buy it in North America ($15), where it costs about $10 less than in Greece. The *Blue Guide* also publishes a separate volume on Crete, and this or John Bowman's thorough *Traveler's Guide to Crete* is a must for anyone planning a lengthy stay on the island. In addition, the locally published *Greece: History, Museums, Monuments* (200dr) provides good orientation for sight-seers.

Helping Let's Go

Each year hundreds of readers send us suggestions and corrections—from two-word postcards to ten-page letters. These invaluable suggestions are often used in our next edition. To share your discoveries with our readers, and to help us improve *Let's Go,* please send the tear-out postcard in the back of the book (or a letter) by December 31, 1984. Mail it to *Let's Go* Staff, Harvard Student Agencies, Thayer Hall-B, Harvard University, Cambridge, MA 02138.

Athens

1 Funicular
2 University
3 Moussion Ethnikon Archeologikon
4 Post Offices
5 American Express
6 Parliament
7 Akropolis
8 Olympion

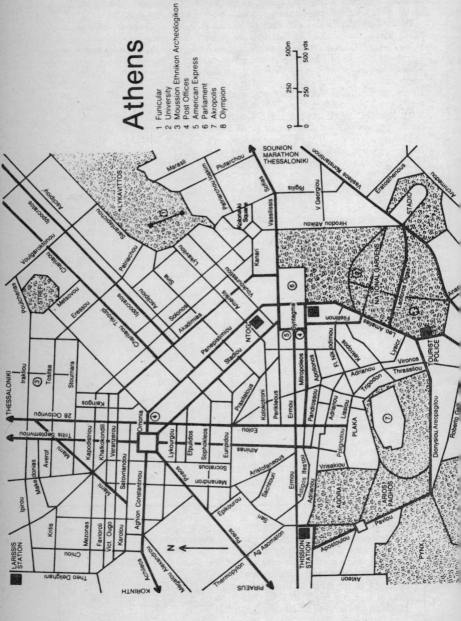

ATHENS

Elegant, serene, immaculate—Athens is none of these. It is a rare example of an unabashedly modern city (with all the accompanying noise and crowds) growing up amid two and a half thousand years of history. The combination may drive you crazy: you may wish that the ruins stood alone, as in Pompeii, or that the modern buildings adhered to ancient designs and materials, as in Jerusalem. But Athens does have a singular, special beat. Its originality emerges like the sun from behind the clouds when you suddenly discover a Byzantine church in the middle of a crowded intersection or a Roman wall next to a snack bar. Athens' beauty and dignity have been marred since the fifth century B.C., when it was the cultural and political center of the Western world, but some of its grandeur still remains.

According to Greek mythology, Athens received its name when the gods Poseidon and Athena vied to rule the city. The Gods of Olympus decided that whoever bestowed the most beneficial gift on the city would become its protector. Poseidon struck the rock of the Acropolis with his trident, causing salt water to gush forth. But Athena won the contest when she caused an olive tree to grow out of the same rock, and the city was thereafter named in her honor.

Ancient Greek civilization reached its zenith in the fifth century B.C. In that glorious century, Iktinos designed the Parthenon, Aeschylus and Sophocles brought drama to new heights with their tragedies, and Herodotus and Thucydides wrote historical tracts which still form the basis of much of our knowledge of Greek civilization. This splendid age came to an end when the rival state of Sparta defeated Athens in the Peloponnesian War (431 to 404 B.C.).

The city never fully recovered from its defeat. As late as 1800, Athens served only as a minor outpost of the Ottoman Empre. Today, rapid growth has fostered a rash of problems. The order and beauty of Hellenic architecture have given way to disordered rows of squat, ugly concrete structures. Public transportation remains primitive and overcrowded, while pollution envelops the city in summer, worsening the effects of the often oppressive heat. Rather than deal with these problems, wealthy Athenians have fled the city for some of the more cosmopolitan and developed cities of Western Europe. The rest of the country, meanwhile, pours into Athens: holding over 30% of the Greek populace, it is noted as the noisiest city in the world.

A word of advice: don't sacrifice time spent on the coast of Crete or the mountains of the Peloponnese for the concrete jungle of Athens. But while you're there, enjoy what both the ancient and the modern city have to offer. Brave the crowds and climb the **Acropolis** or stroll through the winding alleys of the **Plaka.** Visit the **National Archeological** and **Benaki Museums,** and escape the heat for the shaded paths of the lush **National Garden.** Become attuned to the creative, artistic life of this bristling metropolis. Revel in the evenings, when the city truly comes alive. Only then will you discover that Athens is much more than a faceless, noisy, sweltering city.

Orientation

You can get a free map of Athens from the Tourist Police at the airport or railway stations, or at the main branch of the **National Tourist Organization of Greece,** in the National Bank of Greece on Syntagma Square. If you plan to spend much time in Athens, consider purchasing an indexed map of the city, available at most newsstands (50dr).

For most tourists, the center of Athens is **Syntagma** (Constitution) **Square,** an acre-large plaza covered with trees, stairways, and over-priced outdoor cafes. The avenues surrounding it feature the **Parliament** (Vouli), the **Tomb of the Unknown Warrior,** and the **National Garden,** as well as an American Express office, leading banks, the main branch of the National Tourist Organization, top hotels, and numerous restaurants. To get to Syntagma from Athens' East Terminal, which serves all foreign airlines and charter flights, take the yellow bus which leaves every twenty minutes for Amalias St. from the *stasis* to the left as you leave the airport's main entrance. Bus #133 leaves the West Terminal, which serves all Olympic Airways flights, every fifteen minutes for Othonos St. (20dr). From the train station, take trolley #1 to Filellinon St; from the port of Piraeus take the subway from Rousvelt St. to the Monastiraki stop and walk east (the Acropolis should be on your right) on Ermou St., or take green bus #40 from Vassileos Konstandinou, across from the Public Theater *(Demotikon Theatron)* to the last stop. Between Syntagma and the Acropolis is the **Plaka,** the oldest section of Athens still in use. It's a warren of little streets brimming with cafes, restaurants, clubs, discos, and a few inexpensive hotels.

Most of the major arteries of Athens extend from Syntagma. **Leoforos Amalias** leads past the National Garden and the **Temple of Zeus** to the Acropolis. Ermou and Mitropoleos Streets lead to the **Monastiraki** (Monastery) section, which has the closest subway station to Syntagma, as well as the **Athens Flea Market.** Adjacent to the Flea Market is the **Agora,** the ruins of the ancient Greek and Roman marketplace. Walk along **Stadiou Street** or **Eleftherias Venizelou (Panepistimiou)** from Syntagma to reach Omonia Square—a noisy and aggressively urban downtown area of little interest to tourists. From Omonia, however, a stroll up **28 Oktovriou Street (Patission)** brings you to the **National Archeological Museum** and **Areos Park,** the larger of Athens' two state parks. Athens has two bus stations which provide long distance service to all major Greek cities on the mainland. For all of the Peloponnese and major urban centers in the northeast and northwest (Thessaloniki, Volos, Ioannina, Igoumenitsa), take bus #51 from the corner of Vilara and Menandrou Streets near Omonia Square to the station at 100 Kifisou St. (tel. 51 24 910). The other station, at 260 Liossin St. (tel. 83 17 096), serves Delphi and a number of other cities in Central Greece. To reach it, take bus #24 from Tritis Septemvriou St. near the Omonia Hotel. City buses in Athens are frequent, far-reaching, and cheap—only 20dr. Taxis are likewise inexpensive, and are actually cheaper than buses for short journeys if the fare is split by three or more people.

There are two invaluable publications for finding useful addresses, phone numbers, and opening hours for businesses, museums, and the like. *This Week in Athens* is free and is available at the tourist office, hotel lobbies, and at a few kiosks. The *Athens News* (30dr) is an English-language newspaper and is sold at all newsstands. Also of use, if you can find a copy (check the OTE offices or the lobby of a major hotel), are the blue pages of the Athens telephone book, which list businesses, hotels, and other organizations in English. In general, summer business hours are 8am-2:30pm on Monday, Wednesday, and Saturday, and 8am-1:30pm and 5-7:30pm on Tuesday, Thursday, and Friday.

When hitching to Patras or the Peloponnese, take bus #853 to the last stop. For Northern Greece, take the subway to the last stop. Be advised, however, that hitching out of Athens is almost impossible. Your best bet is to go to the truck parks near the cargo wharves in Piraeus. If you look respectable and carry a sign, you will probably be able to get out of town in a truck.

Practical Information

National Tourist Organization of Greece (NTOG): Head Office, 2 Amerikis St. (tel. 32 23 111), open Mon.-Fri. 11am-1:30pm. Information desk in the National Bank of Greece at 2 Karageorgi Servias in Syntagma Square (tel. 32 22 545), open Mon.-Sat. 8am-8pm. This office has an accommodation-finding service, but does not handle E-class hotels or the IYHF hostel. Also at the East Terminal of the airport, where the information desk and nearby banks are open 24 hrs.

Tourist Police: (tel. 171, someone always speaks English). Headquarters at 7 Singrou St. (tel. 92 39 224). Open daily 8am-9pm. Office at train station (tel. 82 13 574) open 7am-11pm. Airport office (tel. 98 14 093) open 24 hrs.

Student Travel Offices; ISIC/FIYTO purchase: see Useful Organizations in the Introduction. Most are on Nikis and Filellinon Streets off Syntagma Square.

American Express: 2 Ermou St., Syntagma Square (tel. 32 44 975). Open Mon.-Fri. 8:30am-5:30pm, Sat. 8:30am-1:30pm. Bank open Mon.-Fri. 8:30am-3pm, Sat. 8:30am-1pm. Holds mail and provides all banking services.

Central Post Office: 100 Eolou St., in Omonia Square. Also in Syntagma Square. Both offices open 7:30am-8:30pm. Parcel post at 4 Stadiou St.

OTE Offices: 28 Oktovriou St. #85. Open 24 hrs. Also at Omonia Square, and at 15 Stadiou St. Both offices open daily 7am-midnight. A fourth office is located at the train station, open Mon.-Sat. 7:30am-10pm. To make a collect call overseas, you must use the offices at 15 Stadiou St. or 28 Oktovriou St. #85. Information for overseas calls (tel. 162), directory assistance (tel. 131).

Greek Youth Hostel Association: 4 Dragatsaniou St., 7th floor (tel. 32 34 107). Open Mon., Tues., Thurs., Fri. 9am-2pm and 6-8pm, Wed. 9am-2pm. Sells the **International Youth Hostel Card** for 1050dr. Bring two photos. You can get photos underneath Omonia Square for 100dr.

Emergency Police: (tel. 100).

Emergency Medical Care: (tel. 166).

Red Cross First Aid Center: 21 Tritis Septemvriou St. (tel. 150).

U.S. Embassy: 91 Vassilissis Sofias (tel. 72 12 951 or 72 18 400) Open Mon.-Fri. 8:30am-5pm.

Canadian Embassy: 4 Ioannou Genadiou St. (tel. 72 39 511). Open Mon.-Fri. 8:30am-5pm.

Australian Embassy: 15 Messogheion Ave. (tel. 36 04 611). Open Mon., Wed., Fri. 8am-2:30pm, Tues., Thurs. 8am-1pm and 2-5pm.

British Embassy: 1 Ploutarchou St., at Ypsilandou St. (tel. 72 36 211). Open Mon.-Fri. 8am-1:30pm.

New Zealand Embassy: 15-17 An-Tsoha St. (tel. 64 10 311). Open Mon., Thurs. 8am-1pm and 2-5:30pm, Tues., Wed., Fri. 8am-2:30pm.

Egyptian Embassy, Visa Section: 3 Vassilissis Sofias, visa window on Zalokosta St. Open Mon.-Fri. 9:30-11:30am. Bring one photo. The **Egyptian State Tourist Office** is nearby at 10 Amerikis St. (tel. 36 06 906), but is not very helpful.

English Bookstores: The best for new and used books is at 4 Nikis St. Also at 33 Nikis St., 11 Amerikis St., 23 Amerikis St., and on Kapsali St. in Kolonaki

Square. All open Mon., Wed., Sat. 8:50am-2:30pm, Tues., Thurs., Fri. 8:50am-1:30pm and 5:30-8:30pm.

American Library: 22 Massalias St., 4th floor, behind the University (tel. 36 37 740). Open Mon.-Thurs. 9:30am-2pm and 5:30-8:30pm, Fri. 9:30am-2pm. A wonderful air-conditioned oasis where you can read current issues of the *Herald Tribune* and American magazines. The Hellenic American Union on the seventh floor has a large collection of English books on Greece. The **British Council** in Kolonaki Square also has English reading material, and sponsors cultural events.

Self-Service Laundries: 24 Kidathineon St. 115dr for washing, 60dr for drying, 25dr for soap. Also at the corner of Lisikratous and Frinihou Sts. 120dr for washing, 20dr for 10 mins. drying, no soap available. Both open Mon.-Sat. 8am-4pm.

Telephone Code: 01.

Accommodations

Gone are the days when Athens was a mecca for that all-too-rare European commodity: the inexpensive pension or hotel. In an effort to improve Athens' image and attract wealthier visitors, the Tourist Police have closed almost all of the unlicensed (and inexpensive) hotels which formerly graced the Plaka. Unfortunately, this yen for "the right people" has also infected many hotel proprietors. Longhairs, North Africans, other minorities, and even Greeks may be subtly turned away from all but the dirtiest and most rundown flea-bag joints. These unlicensed and/or undiscriminating establishments are easy to find; most are near the train station or the Monastiraki and Thissio subway stops. Remember that in these unofficial places, bargaining is quite feasible, since prices are not set by the government.

If you arrive late at night on the train from Patras, be wary of the swarms of hotel hawkers who will greet you at the station. Some are honest, but too often backpack-laden travelers are lured to some obscure corner of the city—only to find much higher prices than advertised and abysmal conditions. Try to choose carefully before you go. Have the salesman show you the location on a large map of the city, and be certain to agree firmly on a price. Don't be bullied into agreeing on anything if you're unsure of its reliability.

In the warm summer months, many hotels and hostels allow guests to sleep on the roof for 150-200dr a night. The roof is always cooler than the rooms after dark, but it has its disadvantages: your posterior will suffer, rain is a threat midsummer, and the scalding Athenian sun will prevent you from taking the traditional Greek afternoon nap.

Finally, if at all possible, try to arrive in the morning. In July and August, the beds and even the roofs fill up by early afternoon. If you do arrive late, the further you venture from Syntagma Square and the Plaka, the greater your chances of locating a room. One warning: avoid sleeping in any of the city's parks. Like most other major metropolises, Athens is crime-ridden and thieves are forever on the prowl for money-laden tourists.

John's Place, 5 Patrou St. (tel. 32 29 719). Take a left off Mitropoleos from Syntagma. In his mixture of English and pantomime, John is an enchanting host. Ask him for some war stories; if you're lucky, he'll even show you his pictures of the U.S. Singles 500dr, doubles 670dr, triples 1150dr. Showers are 70dr extra, but John provides free "special" coffee in the morning.

Clare's House, 24 Sorvolou St. (tel. 92 22 288). Take trolley #2 or 12 from in front of American Express in Syntagma Square to the stop just beyond Hadrian's Arch.

Continue around the square to the street with the stairs. Sorvolou is quite steep, so you may consider taking a taxi. Floors here are clean enough to eat on. 625dr per person (including breakfast) in a single, double, or triple. 100dr more for a room with a private hot shower. In a quiet neighborhood; perfect for families.

Hotel Kouros, 11 Kodrou St. (tel. 32 27 431). Turn left from Mitropoleos onto Voulis. Not outrageously clean, but in a convenient location. Singles 450dr, doubles 800dr, triples 1050dr.

Tony's Pension, 26 Zaharitsa St. (tel. 92 36 370 or 92 30 561). Take trolley #1 or #5 to the Zini stop, or Tony, the engaging manager, will pick you up from Syntagma. Arguably the finest budget lodging in Athens, but women should be aware that we have received complaints of harassment. 500dr per person in a double or triple, 450dr in a quad. Ask Tony about the nearby *souvelaki* stand.

Hotel Phaedra, 16 Herefondos St. (tel. 32 27 795). From Filellinon, go right on Kidathineon. At the first *plateia,* go left on Farmaki, then right on Herefondos. Enchanting location in a quieter part of the Plaka, overlooking a recently-excavated park. Doubles 800dr, triples 1000dr, quads 1200dr, but the owner can be bargained down if the Plaka isn't too crowded. Roof space 200dr.

Festos, 18 Filellinon St. (tel. 32 32 455). About three blocks out from Syntagma. Dingy rooms and depressing bathrooms, but a lively travelers' atmosphere. On a noisy street, staffed entirely by an interesting crew of expatriates. 350dr per person in a double or triple, 300dr in a quad, 250dr in a crowded dorm room. Check-out at 9am. Fills fast.

Acropolis House, 6-8 Kodrou St. (tel. 32 22 344). Four blocks left from Mitropoleos at the end of Voulis St. Staff speaks good English and French. Singles 1231dr, doubles 1354dr, triples 1853dr. Cheaper for longer stays and rooms without private showers. Worth the extra money.

Hotel Cleo, 3 Patrou St. (tel. 32 29 053 or 32 46 344). Next to John's Place off Mitropoleos. Doubles 961dr, triples 1166dr, quads 1400dr. Most rooms have private facilities.

Hotel Tempi, 29 Eolou St. (tel. 32 13 175). Take Ermou from Syntagma or Monastiraki and turn away from the Acropolis on Eolou St. Some rooms are oppressive and stuffy, others have nice balconies. Kostas, the amicable owner, has another hotel a few blocks away where he will find beds for the overflow at a higher price. Singles 400dr, doubles 650dr (780dr with private bathrooms), triples 800dr, roof 150dr. Includes a small but well-stocked bar. 2am curfew.

Hotel Ideal, 39 Eolou St. and 2 Voreou St. (tel. 32 13 195). Two short blocks north of Ermou St. (50 yards from the Hotel Tempi). Rooms well-furnished but grimy. Singles 463dr, doubles 653dr, triples 891dr, but try bargaining. Likely to have space for late ferry arrivals.

Joseph's House, 13 Markou Moussouri St. (tel. 92 31 204). Walk along Amalias from Syntagma, turn left on Olgas and then right on Arditou to Markou Moussouri, or take trolley #2 or 12 to the stop just beyond Hadrian's Arch. A psychedelic experience. Guests here have been all over the world. 350dr for a single, 250dr for a place in a 3-4 bed dorm, 150dr on the roof. Cooking and washing facilities. Clean for the price.

Hotel Krist, 11 Appolonos St. (tel. 32 34 581). Take Mitropoleos to Nikis St., turn left, and Appolonos will be the first street on your right. Has clean rooms in a convenient location. Inexpensive cafe downstairs, but count your change. 650dr singles, 900dr doubles, 1200dr triples.

Youth Hostel #1 (IYHF), 57 Kypselis St. (tel. 82 25 860). Take trolley #2 from Syntagma Sq. or Omonia Sq. (To get to either Square from the train station, take trolley #1.) A large, crowded hostel. Has cooking facilities. A pauper's delight at only 200dr per night in a room with 6-10 beds (20dr extra for sheets). Closed 10am-1pm, 1am curfew. Unless you love hostels, this one is too far out to be worth the trip. Will hold mail.

XEN (YWCA), 11 Amerikis St. (tel. 36 24 294). Take Stadiou St. from Syntagma, turn right on Amerikis. Clean and impersonal, for women and married couples only. Staff speaks English but is not particularly helpful. Singles 580dr, doubles 580dr per person with private bath (440dr without), triples 394dr per person. 100dr cheaper after the first night. Breakfast included. Cafeteria upstairs open to all. 1am curfew. Ask for a room away from the noisy street.

XAN (YMCA), 28 Omirou St. (tel. 36 26 970). From Syntagma, take Venizelou, turn right on Omirou. Large and clean, but unbearable traffic noise. Used mainly by Greek students. Closed in 1983 for renovation, but should be open by 1984.

Hotel Eva, 31 Victoros Ougo St. (tel. 52 23 079). From the train station, go right on Deligiani to Victoros Ougo, the second left after the road curves. Clean for this neighborhood. The best of the train station dives. Singles 550dr, doubles 750dr, triples 900dr, all with private shower. Good for late arrivals.

San Remo Hostel, 8 Nisyrou St. (no telephone). Walk along Deligiani from the train station; Nisyrou is four blocks up on the left. Rooms and bathrooms reek of disinfectant, but dirt cheap, at 300dr per person in a double, 270dr in a triple, 250dr in a quad. 2am curfew, but knock and someone should answer.

Thisseus Inn, 10 Thiseos St. (no telephone). Walk down Karageorgi Servias from Syntagma to Thiseos St., the third right. New, and not too grimy. Eager staff speaks good English. 200-250dr for a dorm bed. Singles, doubles, and triples all 700dr. Has bar and occasional hot showers.

Athens Connection Hotel, 20 Ioulianou St. (tel. 82 13 940 or 82 24 592). From the train station, take Filadelfias St., which becomes Livaniou St. and then Ioulianou St. From Syntagma, take trolley #2 or 12 from in front of the National Garden. Also accessible via the subway (Viktorias Square station). Large and crowded. A raucous atmosphere, good for meeting other travelers. Doubles 800dr, triples 1050dr, quads 1120dr, 230dr per person in a dorm with 6-8 beds, 150dr on the roof. Will usually make space if you're desperate.

Joy's Hotel, 38 Ferron St. (tel. 82 31 012). From the train station, take Filadelfias St. (which becomes Livaniou) to Aharnon St., turn left, then right on Ferron St. The bathrooms are not for those with a weak stomach, but the place is inexpensive. 400dr per person in a double, 350dr in a triple, 300dr in a quad, 200dr in a dorm, 150dr on the roof. Has a small, drab cafe on the first floor.

Student's Inn, 16 Kidathineon St. (tel. 32 44 808). Take Filellinon from Syntagma, turn right on Kidathineon. Great location, but the owner tends to hassle women. Dirty and loud below at night. Singles 500dr, doubles 700dr, 300dr per person in 3-4 bed rooms. Outdoor snack bar. 1:30am curfew.

Annabel Hotel, 28 Koumoundourou St. (tel. 52 43 454). From the train station, follow Deligiani around to Victoros Ougo. Turn left, and Koumoundourou is the fourth street on the right. From Omonia Sq., Koumoundourou is the third right off Agiou Konstandinou. In a bad neighborhood, and not very clean, but cheap and likely to have space. Doubles 700dr, triples 900dr, quads 880dr, 150dr on the roof. Can be bargained down. 3am curfew.

Camping: See Sounion and the Apollo Coast in the **Near Athens** sections.

Food

Although Athens does not rank highly among the world's culinary capitals, you will be able to eat both reasonably well and inexpensively here. As in the rest of Greece, breakfast and lunch are light while dinner is large and late. Most places in the Plaka serve early but outside the touristed quarters, few restaurants open before 8:30pm.

You can eat very cheaply in Athens: two eggs go for about 40dr. *Souvlaki*, either beef or lamb, is a bargain at 35dr, and locally brewed beers—Fix, Amstel, Henniger, Löwenbräu—usually run about 50dr for a half-liter bottle in any taverna. Spinach or cheese *tyropit*, served hot, sells for 35dr, and Athens' excellent *baklava* or ice cream cones will satisfy any sweet tooth for 30-35dr. One warning: when buying bottles of soda to quench your inevitable thirst, remember that there is a deposit on them—drink them on the spot.

Before ordering a meal in any restaurant, check the prices and look around both in the kitchen and on other people's plates. If you don't know the word for what you want, point. The price for a meal without entertainment should be between 200 and 300dr per person. Be adventurous and have a bottle of *ouzo* for 50dr. Service is always included, but it is customary and polite always to leave 5-10% of the bill as a small tip.

If you're careful not to get hustled into buying a meal with *bouzouki* entertainment, folk dances, or outrageous prices, the best place to eat is the Plaka. Although tourists abound, the outdoor tavernas and roof gardens are extremely pleasant and great for people-watching. And even if you're serious about cutting costs, there are a number of greasy spoons where a filling meal can be had for less than 200dr.

Below are listed some of the better restaurants outside of the Plaka:

Socrates Prison, 20 Mitseon St., near the entrance to the Acropolis, off Dionissiou Aeropagitou. A traditional taverna with Greek specialties. Try the chicken (170dr), and the fantastic mixed salad (90dr).

Taverna Strofi, 25 Rovertou Galli, at Propileon St. A bit expensive (300-400dr for a meat dish), but worth it for the fine roof-top view of the Acropolis. Try the roast veal with okra and eggplant salad.

E Rouga (sign is in Greek). Take the first left off Kapsali St. from Kolonaki Sq. One of Athens' best kept secrets. Small and quiet, most entrees under 300dr.

To Skalakia, 32 Eginitou St., one block from the Holiday Inn off Vassilissis Sofias. Specializes in grilled meats. Also try the pickled red peppers and the fried zucchini. A bit of a hike, but still highly recommended. Several courses and wine for under 350dr.

16th Century Restaurant, 5 Kidathineon St. On the edge of the Plaka. Inexpensive and filling "traveler's specials." Conveniently located. 250-350dr. Good for breakfast, too.

Eden Vegetarian Restaurant, 3 Flessa St., in the Plaka. Traditional Greek food without the meat; unfortunately not very imaginative, but the only one of its kind. Also serves seafood. Lovely roof-top garden.

To Fanari, Eratoshenos St. in Plastira Sq. You'll find no tourists here—go to the kitchen and point. Entrees 100-150dr.

Sindrivani, 5 Filellinon St. A large garden restaurant specializing in traditional Greek food—*moshari stifado* (veal and onions in a wine sauce), *moussaka*, and various stews. Most dishes in the 250-300dr range.

Costoyanis, 37 Zaimi St., near Areos Park. Visit the kitchen before you order. Not as good a value as it used to be, but still recommended. Entrees 250-350dr.

Sights

Athens was first settled in Neolithic times. Because of its commanding position overlooking the Aegean Sea and the Attic Plain, the **Acropolis,** or "high city," was always at the center of Athenian life. During the Neolithic Age, its nearly inapproachable location made it the residential center of the area. The Mycenaean Period (1600-1100 B.C.) saw the construction of Cyclopean walls to protect the royal palaces on the site. The Acropolis continued to be the political center of the city after the abolition of the monarchy in 682 B.C., but when the tyrants were themselves overthrown in 510 B.C., the old Mycenaean walls were torn down, and the center of civic activity was shifted to the nearby Agora. During the sixth century B.C., numerous temples were built on the site, but they were destroyed when the Persians sacked the city in 480 B.C.

Athens quickly recovered from this defeat, and under Pericles (the city's leader during the Golden Age) the temples of the Acropolis were built. Since that time, the four buildings remaining on the site—the Parthenon, the Propylae, the Temple of Athena Nike, and the Erectheum—have influenced the Western conception of architectural beauty.

The Acropolis continued to be fortified, embellished, and fought over through the Hellenistic and Roman periods. Under the Byzantines, it was converted into a Christian place of worship. The Parthenon, for example, was transformed into the Church of St. Sophia—interesting because "Sophia," like Athena, to whom the Parthenon was originally dedicated, signifies "wisdom." Later, the Acropolis served as a palace, a fort, and as the headquarters for the Frankish prince. In the fifteenth century, the Turks made the Parthenon into a mosque, and the Erectheum into the headquarters for the Turkish commander's harem. In 1822, the Greeks once again occupied the Acropolis, and apart from a six-year occupation by the Turks from 1827-1833, and the brief Nazi occupation of this century, the Acropolis has been in Greek hands ever since this 1822 occupation.

In classical times a straight ramp led to the Acropolis, but today the visitor enters through the **Beule Gate** (added by the Romans). One then passes through the **Propylae,** built by Mnesicles between 437 and 432 B.C. The structure was one of the most ambitious Greek architectural projects ever, because the rapid rise of the ground necessitated a multi-level building. Behind and to the right is the tiny **Temple of Athena Nike,** built in the last third of the fifth century B.C. Entirely reconstructed, the Temple shows the least deterioration on the Acropolis.

In front and to the left as you enter is the **Erectheum.** This was the last of the Golden Age temples to be completed and incorporated the oldest cults in Athens, those of Poseidon and Athena. It is known best for sculptured **caryatids,** or columns in the shape of women. Because of the ravages of air pollution, the originals have been removed to the Acropolis Museum and replaced by plaster copies. The Temple itself is now being entirely rebuilt and was under scaffolding for all of 1983.

In front and to the right looms the **Parthenon.** It was the first building completed under Pericles' plan and housed the legendary gold and ivory statue of Athena Parthenus (Athena the Maiden) of Pheidias. Whatever your expectations, witnessing the monumental size, lightness of construction, and harmony of proportions of the Parthenon is an extraordinary experience. One of the miracles of the Parthenon's design is its almost total reliance on curves rather than straight lines or corners; the rectilinear effect is a credit to the genius of its architects, Iktios and Callicrates. A significant portion of the Parthenon was tragically destroyed in the seventeenth century, during the Venetian siege of the city. Ammunition stored inside the building was somehow ignited during the attack. Further damage was caused during the War of Independence in the 1820s. But the Parthenon still stands in majestic ruins today, despite the ravages of time, wars, earthquakes, and twentieth-century pollution.

Also on the Acropolis is the **Acropolis Museum,** which contains a superb collection of sculpture from the site, including the caryatids of the Erectheum. Only a few pieces from the magnificent pediments of the Parthenon are displayed here. Rather, most of the sculptures were removed to London in the early nineteenth century, and are now on display in the British Museum. The Acropolis is open Mon.-Sat. 7:30am-7:15pm, Sun. 8am-4:45pm. The Museum is open daily except Tuesday, 9am-3pm. The 150dr admission fee (80dr for students, free on Sundays) includes entrance to both the site and the Museum. Try to visit the Acropolis early in the morning. By 10am, the place is mobbed with telephoto-toting tour groups.

From the southwest corner of the Acropolis, look down upon the reconstructed **Odeon of Herod Atticus** (a functioning amphitheater). To the left are the ruins of the **Theater of Dionysis.** All of the great Greek tragedies were performed on these two stages. For a closer look, walk down to the entrance on Dionissiou Aeropagitou St. The theater and the adjacent **Asclepium** and **Stoa of Eumenes** are open to visitors Mon.-Sat. 8am-4pm., Sun. 10am-4pm. Admission 50dr, 30dr for students, free on Sundays.

The **Athenian Agora,** at the foot of the Acropolis, was the administrative center and marketplace of Athens from the sixth century B.C. (the time of Solon the Lawgiver) through the late Roman period of the fifth and sixth centuries A.D. The decline of the Agora accompanied the decline of Athens itself, as both city and square were buffeted by barbarian and Roman attacks, beginning in 267 B.C. and climaxing in 580 A.D. It was in the Agora, along with Pynx Hill (a kilometer to the south), that Athenian democracy was born and flourished. Socrates walked here, as did Aristotle, Demosthenes, Xenophon, and St. Paul. Plato says that Socrates's preliminary hearing was at the (recently discovered) Royal Stoa.

The sprawling archeological site features two particularly brilliant constructions. The **Temple of Hephaistos,** on a hill in the northwest corner, may be the best-preserved classical temple in Greece. It was built around 440 B.C., and today is especially notable for its friezes of the labors of Hercules and the adventures of Theseus. The **Stoa of Attalos** (a multi-purpose building for shops, shelter, and informal gatherings) to the south was rebuilt with new materials in 1953-56 and today houses the **Agora Museum.** The original structure, built in the second century B.C., was given to Athens by Attalos II, King of Pergam, in gratitude to the city where he received his education. The Museum contains a number of relics from the site; upstairs are miniature models of both the Acropolis and the Agora. The Agora and the Agora Museum are open Mon.-Sat. 7:30am-7:15pm, Sun. 8am-5pm (in the off-season, Mon.-Sat. 9am-3pm, Sun. 9am-2pm). Admission to both is free. There are several entrances to the Agora. The most commonly used is the gate near the Acropolis entrance (turn right as you leave the Acropolis).

The two most recent excavations of the American School of Classical Studies are visible as you leave the Agora and cross the railroad tracks. On the left is the **Royal Stoa** (excavated in the 1970s); on the right are the current excavations.

The buildings of the Acropolis give a glimpse of the glory of the Golden Age, but for an understanding of the development of Greek culture and a view of how the Greeks lived, go the the **National Archeological Museum** on 28 Oktovriou St. (take trolley #2 or 12 from Syntagma). The collection contains an embarrassment of riches; pieces that would dazzle elsewhere can here be passed by as insignificant. In order not to be overwhelmed, see the collection slowly, returning to each room several times, or tag along with a guided tour group.

When you enter the Museum, the room directly in front of you contains Schliemann's discoveries from Mycenae, including the "Mask of Agamemnon" (in fact that of a king who lived at least four centuries earlier), as well as jewelry, pottery, and other trinkets from Mycenae.

Perhaps the most interesting thing to do here is to look carefully at the vase painting and sculpture for some clues as to how the Greeks lived, dressed, and fought. As you move through the exhibits, arranged roughly sequentially from the left to the right side of the building, look in particular for the increasing freedom of experimentation with equipoise and leg positions. In earlier works, legs held stiffly together signify a tendency to think of sculpture as a "heavier," more substantial painting. In the later works the limbs assume a less stylized position, so you can look through the sculpture rather than just at it. The climax of this great trend is, of course, the bronze statue of Poseidon from the fifth century B.C., famous for its spread legs, pointed beard, and meticulously crafted male musculature.

Before leaving, be sure to visit the two exhibits upstairs, the Santorini Frescoes and the Numismatic Collection. The latter requires an additional admission fee.

The museum is open Tues.-Sat. 9am-3:15pm, Sun. 9am-3pm; admission 150dr, 80dr for students, free Sundays. 150dr extra for cameras.

Often overlooked, the **Temple of Olympian Zeus** deserves a visit. Fifteen majestic columns are all that remains of the largest temple ever built in Greece. Seven hundred years of labor went into constructing this shrine to the king of the Greek gods. Now in the middle of downtown Athens and suffering from the ravages of air pollution, the Corinthian columns are a visible reminder of the glory of ancient Greece. Nearby, just off Amalias St., is **Hadrian's Arch**, built in the second century A.D. as the symbolic gateway from ancient Athens to the new Roman city. The Temple of Zeus is open Mon.-Sat. 9am-3pm, Sun. 9am-2pm; admission 30dr, 20dr for students.

The two heritages which form the basis of modern Greek culture are the Classical and the Byzantine. Nowhere is the contrast between the two more clearly shown than in a comparison of their religious architecture. There are a handful of tiny eleventh-century Byzantine churches scattered through the city and you should try to visit some of them. The **Church Kapnikaria,** on the corner of Eolou and Ermou Streets, illustrates the Byzantine style most clearly. In place of the soaring lightness of the Parthenon, one sees a squat building, dimly lit, and filled with somber icons depicting suffering saints. Notice the votive offerings hanging on the icons and the mosaic over the door, added in modern times. If at all possible, dress properly and try to attend Sunday liturgy here. The chants and incense give the church a uniquely Oriental feeling. Other Byzantine churches include the **Agia Apostili,** on Vrissakiou St. on the eastern edge of the Agora, **Metamorphosis,** in the Plaka near Pritaniou St., **Agios Nikodimos,** on Filellinon St. a few blocks from Syntagma, and **Panagia Gorgoepikoös,** next to the **Mitropoli Cathedral** on Mitropoleos St. Most of these churches are open in the morning and for services, and require proper dress.

The **Byzantine Museum,** housed in an elegant Florentine building at 22 Vassilissis Sofias, has a large and excellent collection of Christian art from the sixth through the eighteenth centuries. The first floor of the main building contains sculptures from early Byzantine times. Upstairs, the museum's icon collection includes works from the entire Byzantine period. Also displayed here are a number of superb reliefs done in bronze, silver, and gold. One wing of the building features an array of unattributed but well-preserved frescoes and mosaics. The exhibits are poorly labeled, however, so consider buying the catalog (200dr) before you go. Open Tues.-Sat. 9am-3pm, Sun. 9am-2pm; admission 100dr, 50dr for students.

The **Benaki Museum,** down the street from the Byzantine Museum toward Syntagma at the corner of Koumbari and Vas. Sofias, houses the tremendously diverse collections of Anthony Benaki. Islamic art, Chinese pottery, early Bronze Age Greek relics and Byzantine icons are housed in this lovely, uncrowded, 19th century home-turned-museum. Be sure to visit the Greek Folk Art exhibition downstairs; the Greek costumes on display are a far cry from those worn by the dancers in the Plaka. Open daily except Tues. 8:30am-2pm; admission 70dr, students 35dr, free on Sunday.

An amusing tourist attraction is the changing of the guard in front of the **Parliament** building on Syntagma Square. It's not Buckingham Palace, but every hour on the hour two sets of stern-faced guards kick their heels about and fall backwards into symmetrical little guard houses on either side of the **Tomb of the Unknown Warrior.** If you're lucky, you may catch a whole herd of them kicking their way down the street in pursuit of their fluffy-heeled commander.

There is no better way to escape the mid-day heat than by venturing into the lush **National Garden** (open sunrise to sunset). For a fantastic view of Athens at night, take the funicular (60dr round trip) to the top of **Lykavitos Hill.** The station is at the end of Ploutarchou St., and operates until midnight. (Or burn off dinner by walking up the hill). The cafe is hopelessly expensive, but the panorama of the city at night is worthwhile. For a cheaper date, climb the rocks near the Acropolis entrance which overlook the Agora and most of Athens.

On your way to the Acropolis, wander through the narrow, steep streets and stairways between Thespidos St. and Dioskouron St. As you climb higher, the tourist shops and tavernas dissipate, giving way to a warren of tiny residences. Have no fear—any path you take through this area will eventually lead to the path to the Acropolis.

There are two markets of interest to tourists in Athens. The **Athens Flea Market,** adjacent to Monastraki Square along Ifestou, Adrianou, and Pandrossou Sts., contains some colorful and relatively inexpensive shops. A huge outdoor-indoor market lines the sides of Athinis St. between Evripidou and Sofokleous Sts., where you can buy fruits, vegetables, fish, meat, cheese, nuts, and almost anything else edible. Open the same hours as the regular food stores, although it's smart to go early for meat and fish.

There is a synagogue and **Jewish Museum** at 8 Melindoris St. To get there, walk down Ermou from Syntagma, past Monastiraki, turn left on Asomation St. and left again on Melindoris. Open Sun. 9am-1pm, Wed. 1-5pm, and by appointment (tel. 32 52 875).

Nightlife

The **Plaka** is Athens' liveliest nightspot, but the quality within varies greatly. In general, it is a good idea to ascertain the price of everything before you sit down. Be especially wary of places offering *bouzouki* entertainment. Men traveling alone or in pairs should be careful if they enter a bar and are approached by women habituées, or they may end up paying a two weeks' bar bill. With these precautions in mind, nightlife in Athens is excellent.

The Plaka has two main squares. The one formed by Filomoussou Eterias, Angelou Geronta, and Kidathineon and Farmaki Sts. has at least seven outdoor cafes and is a popular hangout for tourists. The other main square, formed by Adrianou and Eolou Sts., is taken up entirely by the **Poseidon Cafe,** which has good pastries and an ambience classy enough to be almost worth the cost.

The most popular disco (and one of the best) in the area is **Pinocchio's** at 117 Adrianou St. Open 10pm-2am; admission 350dr, but most drinks are free. The **Mad Club** on Lissiou St. is a great New Wave club. Open 10pm-2am. Admission is free Mon.-Fri., but drinks are expensive. On Saturday, there's a steep cover charge, but the first drink is included.

For a quieter, more refined (read: more expensive) evening, go to one of the many sidewalk cafes in **Kolonaki Sq.**

Before the junta, (1967-1974) the **National Garden** was one of the most popular places to gather in the evening. Since the junta's collapse, the park has experienced something of a revival. Every evening the cafes near the **Zappeion** present (mostly second-rate) singers, comedians, and acrobats at an outdoor stage. Free if you stand, as most people do; otherwise, get a table at one of the expensive cafes. The outdoor cinema in the Zappeion generally has the most enlightened selection of English-language films in Athens. Check the *Athens News* for complete addresses and timetables of all the Athens moviehouses.

In the summer there are about six performances a week in the **Odeon of Herod Atticus,** ranging from drama to orchestral concerts to opera. The **Athens Festival Office** at 4 Stadiou St. has information and tickets—student prices of 100dr are a real bargain. Even if you're not wild about the program, it's worth seeing something in the restored amphitheater near the Acropolis.

If you've had a bit (or a lot) to drink, the hokey 9pm **Sound and Light Show** on Philopappou Hill (also near the Acropolis) can be quite entertaining. Admission 150dr, 75dr for students. The nearby **Greek Dances,** which follow the light show at 10:15pm, are entertaining if less absorbing. Admission 360dr or 310dr, 250dr or 130dr with Student ID.

Near Athens

Piraeus

Blessed with a safe natural harbor, Piraeus has been Athens' port since ancient times. If you are going to the islands, your boat will probably leave from here, but the town itself is worth a brief visit, especially if you're a landlubber. The **Archaeological Museum** of Piraeus is beautifully and spaciously laid out, and (rarity of rarities in Greece) its collection is well-labeled. Consisting mostly of large pieces dredged out of the harbor, the Museum is the best place to kill a few hours. Especially interesting is the group of "mass-produced" plaques from the first century A.D., which were made for the undiscriminating Roman market. The Museum is at 31 Har. Tricoupi St. and is open Mon.-Sat. 9am-3pm, Sun. 10am-2pm, closed Tues. Admission 50dr, 30dr for students, free on Sunday.

If the Museum is closed, walk across to either **Zea Marina** or the **Mikrolimano.** The former is Piraeus' main pleasure craft harbor (and its busiest), and is lined with inexpensive restaurants. The latter is a perfect place for a slow, elegant promenade followed by an endless seafood dinner in one of the fairly expensive waterfront restaurants. If you still have time, or if you prefer

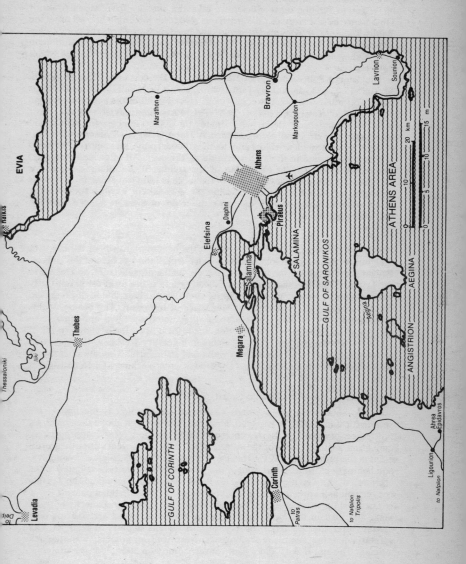

to stay closer to the wharves, there is a shady park on II Merarchias St. three blocks from Akti Miaouli.

To get to Piraeus most efficiently, take the subway from Monastiraki or Omonia to the last stop, or take green bus #40 from Filellinon St., get off at the Public Theater *(Demotikon Theatron)*, and head right, towards the port. Long-distance trains for Patras and the Peloponnese leave daily from the station on Akti Kalimassiati. Once in Piraeus, ask one of the many travel agents where your boat docks.

The **Tourist Police,** at 87 Akti Miaouli St., on the corner of Mavrokordatou St. (tel. 45 23 670, open daily 7am-10pm), have a list of all the D- and E-class hotels in Piraeus. Be selective, however, since not all of the accommodations are reputable. **Hotel Enos** (tel. 41 74 879) at 14 Anadistoseos St. near the wharf is relatively safe and clean, with singles for 400dr, doubles for 600dr, and triples for 1000dr. Also recommended is **Hotel Galaxy,** 18 Sahtouri St. (tel. 45 12 973), with singles (450dr) and doubles (600dr) only. Inexpensive fast-food restaurants abound in the area surrounding the port. All offer mediocre food for similar prices. At **The Posidinion,** II Merarchias St. #8, filling meals go for 150-250dr. A few doors away is one of the more helpful travel agents, **Lycoudis Brothers** (tel. 45 20 822), at II Merarchias St. #2. Ask for Vasilios Nanopoulos. They will hold luggage while you prowl the town, or even for a few days while you visit the islands.

Kesariani

Perhaps the most pleasant way to beat the heat and crowds of Athens is to take bus #224 to Kesariani (20 mins., 20dr). Board the bus behind the University on Akadimias St. (the farthest *stasis* up, on the outside lane), and take it to the last stop. Follow the road uphill, bearing left at the fork, for about thirty minutes, and you will be rewarded by the lush grounds and well-preserved buildings of the eleventh-century **Monastery of Kesariani.** The beauty of this area at the foot of Mt. Hymettus was first noted by Ovid and, thanks to extensive landscape restoration, this is the best spot for a picnic in all of Attica. Visit the chapel, with its eighteenth-century frescoes, the eleventh-century refectory, and the monks' cells and bathhouse. The site is crowded with Athenians on weekends, so try to visit on a weekday. Open daily 9am-2pm; admission free.

Cape Sounion and the Apollo Coast

A two-hour drive from Athens (70km), Cape Sounion is the impressive setting for the **Temple of Poseidon.** On a promontory high above the coastline, this place of worship to the ancient Greek sea god offers, appropriately enough, a beautiful view of the Aegean Sea. Built a few years after the Parthenon in the fifth century B.C., this Doric temple shares its balance, symmetry, and lightness of form. The design of the Temple of Poseidon is attributed to the architect of the Temple of Hephaistos in the Athenian Agora, and the Temple is every bit as impressive as, if less complete than, its Athenian cousin.

The ideal time to view this tribute to Poseidon is at sunrise. Otherwise, try to make the visit in the morning, before the tour buses start arriving, or near sunset, after they've left. The last bus to Athens departs at 8:30pm. The cafeteria near the Temple is shamelessly overpriced, so you may want to pack a lunch. The site is open daily 9am-sunset; admission 50dr, 30dr for students, free on Sunday.

For swimming, head for the magnificent waters at the base of the site. There are several paths leading down to the ocean from the inland side of the Temple, or, if you're especially agile, the cliff on the ocean side of the promontory can be negotiated. Several sandy beaches are situated at the base of the hill, but the rocks below the Temple are more interesting, less crowded, and free of charge.

Because of their proximity to Athens, nearly all of the beaches along the 70km Apollo Coast between Athens and Sounion take on a crowded, touristy, carnival atmosphere, especially on summer weekends. The farther you venture from Athens, the better the beaches. Most strands are privately (hotel) owned, with admission ranging from 20-50dr, but each town usually has a free public beach.

There are two campsites on the Apollo Coast. Both are large, crowded, well-maintained, and on the ocean. The site at **Voula** (tel. 89 52 712) charges 180dr per tent plus 130dr per person, and is accessible via bus #122 from the Zappeion station. **Camping Varkiza** (tel. 89 73 613) charges 110dr per tent and 140dr per person. Take bus #115, 116, or 117 from Zappeion. Prices do not include 5% tax. In Sounion, try **Sounion Beach and Camping,** about 5km beyond the Temple of Poseidon, or nearby **Camp Bacchus.**

To reach Cape Sounion and all points on the Apollo Coast, take the yellow bus leaving every hour on the half hour from the Mavromateon St. stop in the square opposite Areos Park. The fare is 170dr one-way. Two buses serve Sounion—be sure to catch the one traveling the coastal route. The bus can also be picked up on Filellinon St., at Xenofondos St., twenty minutes before the hour, but your chances of getting a seat are better if you catch it at Mavromateon St. Don't be surprised if you're forced to change buses just before Sounion. The new coach is usually waiting, and is free.

Marathon

The 42km (26-mile) road from Athens to the town of Marathon follows the original path of the Olympic Marathon. If you've brought your running shoes, trace the route of the Athenian soldier bearing tidings of the stunning Greek victory over the Persians on the Plain of Marathon. 5km from town is the **Tomb of the Plataeans,** the ancient burial mound built as a tribute to the allies from the north who died in the Battle of Marathon in 490 B.C. The **Archeological Museum** a few hundred meters away contains a wide variety of artifacts retrieved from the Cave of Pan and nearby burial grounds. The eclectic collection includes pieces from the Neolithic, Geometric, Helladic, and Classical Periods. Only a few pieces are labeled, however, and no guidebook is available. Open Mon., Wed.-Fri. 9am-6pm, Sun. and Tues. 9am-3pm; admission 50dr, 30dr for students.

Four kilometers from the museum, on the road back to Athens, is the **Marathon Tomb,** a larger burial mound erected in tribute to the two hundred or so Athenians who were killed in the historic battle. Only the most avid historians will want to make the 45-minute walk, however. Open Mon., Wed., Thurs., Fri. 9am-6pm, Sun. and Tues. 9am-3pm; admission 50dr, 30dr for students.

Eight kilometers past the town is beautiful **Lake Marathon,** which, until World War II, was the sole source of Athens' water supply, with its huge marble dam. Thirty kilometers to the northwest is the important archeological site of **Amphiareaion,** the sanctuary built to worship the healing god Amphiaoros. The ruins, which feature a very good museum, slumber peacefully in the lush green foliage of Attica, well removed from the tourist circuit.

For non-Olympians, the bus for Marathon leaves from Mavromateon St. by Areos Park (100dr one-way). Ask the driver to let you off at Mousseion Marathonas, or watch for the sign 3km before the town. The walk to the museum is 2km long, and takes about twenty minutes. To get to the Marathon

Tomb or nearby beach, walk or hitch back towards Athens. The Tomb is on the left, 1½km from the turn-off for the museum. Lake Marathon and Amphiaraeion are only accessible by hitching or private automobile.

Daphni

The suburb of Daphni, 10km west of Athens, deserves a visit for three reasons: the monastery, the wine festival, and the campsite. The **Monastery of Daphni,** a splendid eleventh-century structure, contains the finest mosaics in Greece. With the exception of Agia Sophia in Istanbul, its dome is the largest of any Byzantine church in the world. The mosaic lining the inside of the dome is considered by some art historians to be the most beautiful in the world. It depicts the great bust of the **Pantocrator** (Christ the Almighty). Believed to have been made in the eleventh century, these mosaics are in remarkably good condition. Although some experts claim that the mosaics have been over-restored, for the layman it is a pleasant change to see at last a Byzantine church displaying some of its original brilliance. (The monastery was closed for repairs in the summer of 1983 so check for reopening, new times, and admission charges with the local tourist office.)

Daphni's second major attraction is the **wine festival** that takes place on the grounds next to the monastery between mid-July and mid-September. Admission to the grounds is 100dr, which includes all the wine you can drink. Greeks and tourists alike stroll from stand to stand sampling the numerous varieties of local wine and watching or participating in the festivities. Bring your own glass or you'll have to buy one at 20dr. The food is overpriced and not very good on the grounds, so bring a picnic dinner to consume with the wine. Next to the grounds of the wine festival is the third principal attraction in Daphni: a large campground, in front of which is the bus stop. To get to Daphni take bus #818, 853 or 862 from Pl. Eleftherias at the end of Euripidou St.

Elefsina (Eleusis)

About 15km from Athens, and well worth a morning's excursion, is Elefsina. Buses #818, 853, and 862 run frequently from Pl. Eleftherias. Get off the bus at the second stop in Elefsina and continue across the square until you see a blue sign. The modern road from Athens to Elefsina follows much the same route as the ancient sacred way, which tens of thousands of pilgrims used to reach the Eleusinian Mysteries, the largest pan-Hellenic event in ancient times besides the Olympic Games. The mysteries were enacted in Elefsina from roughly the eighth century B.C. until the fourth century A.D., when the sanctuary was closed by Roman Emperor Theodosius.

The origin of the annual ritual is associated with the myth about the Rape of Persephone. Briefly: Persephone, the daughter of the corn goddess, Demeter, was abducted by Hades, Lord of the Underworld, while playing with some friends. Stricken with grief, Demeter retired from her duties, allowing the earth to lie barren. Mankind was threatened with extinction, while Demeter disguised herself as a wet nurse, and suckled the child of a leading citizen of Elefsina. When the goddess' identity was discovered she ordered the Eleusinians to build a temple for her, and to enact certain "mysteries" there once a year. The Mysteries initiated men into the secrets of the underworld. Participants were sworn to secrecy, and although tens of thousands attended each year, no trace of the secret has been found. All those who participated left with the unshakable faith that they no longer had any need to fear death. Incidentally, Zeus eventually struck a bargain with Hades on Demeter's behalf, returning Persephone, and thereby fertility, to the human world for two-thirds of the year.

Those who come to Elefsina without an appreciation of the Mysteries and simply with the expectation of enjoying another famous site are apt to be disappointed, for though the ruins are impressive, very little of what is left of the ancient sanctuary stands above waist level. The remains of Elefsina, however, are extremely interesting insofar as they contain fragments from a wide variety of historical periods, a veritable architectural goulash. If you feel the need to find a little method in this madness, head first for the museum, where you will find a model of the original layout of the sanctuary. Externally it resembled a fortress more than a place of worship, being surrounded on all sides by heavily fortified walls to keep the curious outside. The interior of the site was dominated by the huge, windowless hall of the **Telesterion**, the sanctuary of the Mysteries, where the actual initiation process took place. The remains of the **Anaktoron**, the holiest of the buildings in the complex, which could only be entered by the high priest, can also be seen. From the top of the hill overlooking the ruins, you can see across the Saronic Gulf to the island of Salamis. Open Mon.-Sat. 9am-3:30pm, Sun. 10am-2pm; admission 50dr, 30dr for students. The museum at Elefsina was closed in 1983, but may reopen by 1984—check with the local tourist office.

Brauron (Vravrona)

On the east coast of Attica, 40km from Athens, Brauron is the isolated setting for the two thousand-year-old **Sanctuary of Artemis.** Though poorly maintained, the site contains the recently-uncovered **Temple of Artemis** and the adjacent **Chapel of Agia Giorgiou,** whose interior is decorated with rapidly-decaying frescoes from the late fifteenth century.

Follow the road around to the other side of the hill to reach the excellent **Brauron Museum,** which contains pottery, sculpted heads and figures discovered at the Brauron site. Vases and funerary reliefs unearthed at nearby **Meranda,** dating from the Geometric, Archaic, and Classical periods, are displayed in Room 4. Room 5, behind the courtyard, is filled with Geometric-period pottery found at Anavyssos and Mesogea.

To get to Brauron, take bus #304 from the Thissio subway station to the last stop. Walk along the road for several kilometers, and turn left on the first paved road. The ruins are open Mon.-Sat. 9am-3pm, Sun. 9am-2pm, closed Tues.; admission 50dr, 30dr with student ID.

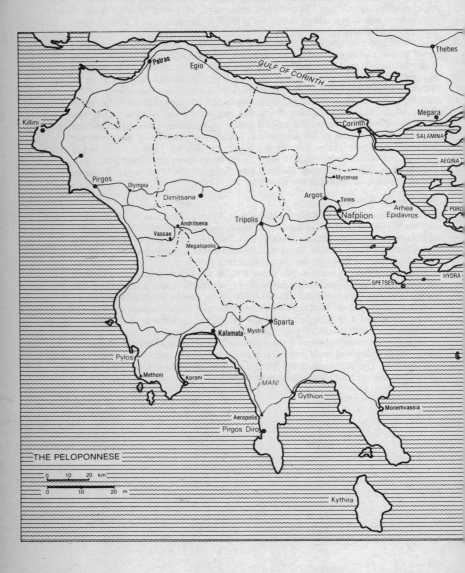

THE PELOPONNESE

PELOPONNESE

If you have only a week or two to spend in Greece, the Peloponnese is a good place to begin. A peninsula now separated from mainland Greece by the Corinth Canal, the region's big attraction for visitors is the 3500 years of history archeologists have unearthed from its ground. The classical sites at Mycenae, Corinth, Epidavros, and Olympia, and the Byzantine ruins at Mystra are among the most extensive and impressive in Greece, a visible testament to the area's unsurpassed importance in Greek civilization. But the Peloponnese also has some of Greece's most beautiful beaches and mountainsides; so if you don't have time for the islands, you can at least get a taste of what you're missing right here.

The mountain ranges that dramatically cover most of the Peloponnese have kept many parts of it isolated and traditional—when donkeys are the only means of transportation, news travels slowly. Of course, the easiest way to manage the Peloponnese is by car, supplemented by feet. But those without the means to support the car habit need not despair: buses reach most towns in the Peloponnese, they run pretty much on schedule, baggage always seems to end up in the right place, and drivers are helpful and kind to (if a bit bemused by) bewildered non-Greek-speaking visitors. Unfortunately, the further you get from heavily-touristed areas, the less frequent service tends to be. To explore areas like the Mani, southern Messenia, or the mountain villages of the central Peloponnese by bus, you need time and patience—they usually run only once a day, thus requiring an extra day for each stop you want to make unless you feel like taking the local village taxis whose fares are often quite reasonable. Hitching is pretty good in the summer, but the number of cars drops dramatically in off-season.

When planning a route through the Peloponnese, a couple of things are worth keeping in mind. Most of its large cities don't merit more than a day's attention, although areas like the Argolid, southern Messenia, and the Mani can be conveniently toured using the one city as a base. Unless you are strongly partial to nightlife, you may find it a relief to stay in smaller villages or at beaches near the cities, at least for an occasional change.

There are a number of places from which to enter and leave the Peloponnese. The heavily-used ferry connection from Brindisi, Italy lands at Patras in the northwest corner of the Peloponnese, and boats for Crete and Piraeus leave from Gythion and Monemvassia in the south. From Athens you can enter through Corinth by bus, or through port towns on the Argolid by ferry. As a result, you can cover the entire area without retracing your steps.

One final note on the Tourist Police. It is rarely a waste of effort to stop in at their office when you arrive in a town (in smaller towns, the regular police serve this function)—you can usually get a partial list of accommodations and find out about bus connections. But their degree of helpfulness varies considerably, often in direct proportion to your knowledge of Greek. In this respect, at least, things will look much better when you head for the islands.

Corinthia and Argolis

Ancient writers frequently mention a grotesque yet immensely powerful monster that was feared by all. Its huge body covered with round eyes, the beast occasionally entered the lower regions of the Peloponnese to subdue an unruly stray bull or satyr on the rampage. The creature's name was Argos, and although this doesn't tell us exactly how much fact lies in myth, the castles, might, and campaigns of the Argive empire curiously mirror the beast's eyes, strength, and wanderings. This correspondence should come as no surprise. Any city that could dominate such a strategically key peninsula, become over-lord of the strongholds at **Mycenae, Tiryns, Nafplion,** and **Assini,** and give its name to the entire region would inevitably be memoralized in the imaginative realm of Greek storytelling. If you're still skeptical, a visit to any of the 3000-year-old sights—Mycenae and Tiryns are the best examples—will erase all doubts. Myth and history are closer than we think.

Historically, Corinthia was united with its southern neighbor, Argolis. In the 1940s, officials separated the two regions and redrew the boundaries. Corinithia's major city **Corinth** never fell to the Argives, but allied with Sparta against Argolis and Athens in the Peloponnesian War (fifth to fourth centuries B.C.). Because it controlled the **Isthmus,** the only land connection between the Peloponnese and the rest of mainland Greece, Corinth became a wealthy com-mercial center—so wealthy, in fact, that St. Paul journeyed there to halt the inhabitants' moral slide, which their prosperity had encouraged. Judging from the ruins of **Ancient Corinth** and the earthquakes that have demolished **New Corinth** in the past century, you'll agree the Corinthians should have heeded the apostle's words and avoided the earthshaker's wrath.

For the connoisseur of astonishingly beautiful scenery, three different bus routes will lead you through equally stunning terrain to Argolis and Corinthia. From Athens, when the last stretch of industrial outlets and gas stations ends, the road gives way to glowing green sea on the left and precipitous cliffs of rock on the right as the bus skirts the jagged shore. From Porto Heli or Kosta, if you're coming from the Saronic Gulf Islands, the bus heads straight inland, following deserted and dusty asphalt roads that snake through the dry moun-tains and groves of sere olive trees—with no sea in sight. The mountains seem ready to tumble down at any moment, perhaps to reveal some wonder of the ancient world lost for centuries beneath a monstrous heap of stones. In the more fertile ground of the eastern coast, the sanctuary of Asklepios and thea-ter at **Epidavros** will reassure you that these usually intractable boulders can be tamed and refined to display the symmetry and arresting proportions of a work of art. Finally, if you ride into the region from Arcadia (the central Pelopon-nese), you'll cross green, cloud-capped mountains, which separate the upland Arcadian plain from the Argive.

New Corinth

The first stop for most tourists visiting the Peloponnese from Athens is Corinth (Corinthos), immediately to the west of Corinth Canal. What most locals know as Corinth—New Corinth to us—dates from only 1858, when the ancient site was destroyed by an earthquake. Residents moved 3km to the east in the hopes of avoiding another disaster, but to no avail. In 1928, the new city was levelled by another quake, and the town was rebuilt with squat, colorless, but earthquake-proof structures. The result is a town safe from natural disaster but artificial in layout. If you like grids and midget palms, you'll love New Corinth.

Corinth faces the **Bay of Corinth,** and swimming is excellent towards the west. But, except for the seafront and the tree-lined park in the center of town, Corinth offers little besides lots of nocturnal mosquitoes—and lots of noctur-nal mosquito bites. The main reason for coming here is to see the ruins at Old

Corinth, a 7km bus ride away. While some people stay in New Corinth and see the archeological site as a day trip, it is better to head directly for the ruins and spend the night at Nafplion, a beautiful city only an hour's bus ride away.

Practical Information

You'll probably arrive in New Corinth in either the train station or one of the two bus stations. To orient yourself, go straight to the park, near which you can find anything you need. One bus station, on the corner of Ermou and Koliatsou Sts., is right on the park; just stay put. From the other station, make a left onto Ethnikis Antistasis St. (formerly Vas. Konstantinou St.), and the park will be a block away. If you arrive by train, follow Agiou Nikolaou St. for one block, head left on Antistasis Anaxartesias St. (formerly Vas. Georgiou St.) for four blocks, then take a right onto Koliatsou until you reach the flower gardens and shade. The **Tourist Police** (tel. 23 28 2) will help quite cheerfully with accommodations and other information. Follow Koliatsou toward the water and make a right on Periandrou St. Open Mon.-Sat. 7am-1:30pm and 6-8:30pm, they share quarters with the regular **police,** open 24 hours a day seven days a week. By 1984, the Tourist Police will probably have moved to Ermou St., next door to the bus station. The **Post Office** (open 7:30am-2:30pm) and **bank** are both on Adimandou St. at the eastern edge of the park. A very small **OTE** on Koliatsou St. sits one block from Ethnikis Antistasis and the park; you'll see it on the way to the police. **Albani bookstore,** across from the Hotel Akti, sells English newspapers, books, and a dated and unnecessary map of New Corinth (30dr). In the other direction on Ethnikis Antistasis St. you'll find a **laundry** and a **rent-a-Vespa** shop (1000dr per day). The **telephone code** for Corinth is 0741.

For those planning to stay in New Corinth, the **Hotel Apollon,** at 18 Pirinis St. (tel. 22 58 7), is a stone's throw from the train station, with singles for a steep 700dr and doubles for 900dr. Near the bus stations is **Hotel Akti** (tel. 23 33 7), which offers singles for 506dr, doubles for 619dr, and triples for 844dr; showers 70dr extra. It's the last building on Ethnikis Antistasis St. before the wharf. A campground (tel. 33 30 2), 2km west of town (near a great beach) charges 120dr per tent and 120dr per person.

If you happen to be in Corinth long enough to eat, head for one of the coffee shops in the town square for coffee, toast and shade, or down to the water-front. Avoid the overrated and overpriced Pantheon restaurant on the corner of Damaskinou and Ethnikis Antistasis. You'll be better off taking a left and continuing along the water until you see the **Taverna Anaxagoras,** where you will get an excellent meal for almost nothing. You can also head right, where you'll find the slightly more costly **Kantina.** Other than these two, Corinth has little in the way of eateries besides numerous spaghetti and pizza stands.

Buses leave Athens for Corinth every half hour, 6am-9pm, from the station at 100 Kifissou St. (200dr). From New Corinth to Old Corinth, buses leave the station at Koliatsou and Ermou Sts. every hour on the hour and return hourly on the half hour, 7am-9pm. The fare is 25dr for the twenty-minute ride. The same station also dispatches buses to Isthmia six times a day, returning about fifteen minutes later (25dr), to Loutraki and returning to Corinth every half hour 6am-10pm (34dr), and to Nemea six times a day (105dr). The other bus station, on the corner of Ethnikis Antistasis and Aratou Sts., is the place to catch buses for Sparta (eight times a day, 410dr), Tripolis (nine times a day, 260dr), Kalamata (eight times a day, 475dr), and Nafplion (150dr), Argos (120dr), and Mycenae (95dr). The same bus goes to the last three, and leaves every hour on the half hour, 7:30am-10pm. (Note: the bus to Mycenae will leave you at Fichtia, a 1½km walk from Mycenae—see the section on Mycenae.) To go to Patras by bus you have to go first to Loutraki, where you'll change for your final destination. The train runs directly to Patras (240dr). Trains run to Athens from Corinth less frequently than buses, but also more cheaply at 165dr.

Ancient Corinth

Corinth figures prominently in both Greek mythology and ancient history. In the beginning, Apollo and Poseidon struggled for control of Corinth and finally compromised, Poseidon taking the Isthmus and Apollo the Acrocorinth. Oedipus, the son of Laius and Jocasta of Thebes, grew up in Corinth with his adopted parents, Polybus and Merope. Neither told the little tyke, or the proud adolescent, that his parentage was uncertain, leaving him to find out the hard way.

In the realm of recorded history, Corinth was a center of commerce and one of the wealthiest cities in the region under Greek and later Macedonian rule. When Philip and his son Alexander the Great had a stranglehold on their neighbors to the south, the Greeks met in Corinth to approve by a formal vote the *de facto* Macedonian control. The city's free population during this era (300,000) blanches in comparison to its slave population—over 450,000. Destroyed by a Roman in 146 B.C. and rebuilt by another one—Julius Caesar—in 44 B.C., Corinth gradually acquired a reputation for indolence and debauchery: the residents worshipped Aphrodite before all other deities. The unabashed enjoyment of luxury and sensuality attracted the attention of the Apostle Paul, who attacked this way of life in I-II Corinthians.

The remains of the ancient city now stand on a plateau near the base of the **Acrocorinth,** the huge mountain of rock that was the key to the military control of the entire Peloponnese. Excavations of the city, which are still underway, have uncovered the ruins of the Roman settlement. From the museum at the site, go left and down the stone stairs to enter the spacious **forum,** a complex of shops and meeting places similar to the Greek agora. To the left, the **northwest shops** contained by the **northwest stoa** still have an impressive arch remaining. Across the forum, to your right, the **south stoa** was one of the largest buildings of its era. In the middle of the row of central shops contained by the south stoa, you'll see the **bema,** a raised platform for general announcements and official proclamations. Sensibly placed in the busy forum, the bema assured any speaker a large audience. At the far end of the forum, just before the **Julian basilica,** you can make out a **race track** with more than a dozen lanes. It may not have been very long, but in this case victory took precedence over achievement. Turning left out of the forum, you'll pass through the **propylaea,** a great gateway now replaced by shade trees, and proceed down some worn steps onto a stone pathway known as the **Lechaion Road.** If you listen closely, you can hear the gushing of the well-preserved **Fountain of Peirene,** the first structure on your right. Named after a woman who wept so profusely over the death of her son, slain by Artemis, that the gods transformed her into a fountain, the complex was rebuilt generation after generation. The layers of external architectural embellishments, however, have not altered the cool, dark, and muddy interior, a refreshing shelter from the ferocious midday sun. Unfortunately, without a flashlight you won't even begin to see any of the enticingly noisy flow.

Further on to the right of the Lechaion Rd., the **Peribolos of Apollo** provided Corinthians and others with an open air court surrounded by columns, some of which now stand restored. But if you really want to know how the Romans did it, don't ask St. Paul and don't spend any time in open air courts. Instead, look at the **public latrine** just past the peribolos. Some of the thrones are still in place, providing you with a humorously illuminating peek into the private lives of the ancient Corinthians. On the other side of the Lechaion Road stand more shops. But the greatest attraction of the ruins is the **Temple of Apollo.** All that survived the Roman sacking of the original Greek city was the temple's seven monolithic columns, once part of one of the oldest and most important temples on the Greek mainland. Erected in 550 B.C., it replaced a seventh-century B.C. temple on the same site. From the Lechaion Road, you'll have to double back through the forum or climb up through the shops to reach it. Next to the museum the ornate columns belong to **Temple E,** a Roman edifice of the first century which stood to the southwest of the museum. The **museum** itself (included in the admission fee) is filled with sarcophagi, glassware of Greek, Roman, and Byzantine times, friezes (some of dancing maenads and heroes), Roman mosaic floors, and various sculptures, all the impressive yield of the excavations. The building itself offers welcome relief from the sun, and its inner courtyard, decorated with friezes of Amazons and Herculean labors from the theater across the road, offers a perfect spot for a picnic lunch. Just off the courtyard, the **Asclepion room** houses offerings by the sick to the god of medicine, usually a cast of the affected body part. Generally feet, some privates. Ask the guard to let you in. The whole site is open Mon.-Sat. 9am-3:30pm, Sun. 9:30am-4:30pm, museum closed Tues.; admission 100dr, 50dr for students.

Atop the **Acrocorinth,** overlooking the site, are the imposing ruins of a gigantic fortress. Built on the lower of the two summits, the fortress has foundations dating to ancient times, although most of what you'll see—walls, towers, gates—was erected during successive captures by the Byzantines, Franks, Venetians, and Turks. The upper summit originally held a **Temple to Aphrodite,** which, historians have noted, was served by one thousand "sacred courtesans" who initiated disciples into the "mysteries of love." Time has destroyed all of this and subsequent structures on the site, but has done nothing to alter the magnificent view. On a clear day you can see, if not forever, at least far enough to verify your map-maker's rendition of the northeast Peloponnese and the Corinth and Saronic Gulfs that bound it.

The Acrocorinth is open 24 hours a day, since there isn't exactly any way to lock up a mountain, and people have been known to carry up sleeping bags and spend the night (one ancient building on the grounds can provide semi-shelter). You'll be on your own at the site, except for a refreshment stand open during the summer, 8am-10pm.

The ascent as far as the lower summit can be traversed by car along a dirt road. There is no bus service, but you can get a taxi in town for 500dr round trip (the driver will wait an hour for you at the end of the road), or hitch fairly easily during tourist season. But the best way to do it is on foot. Try to go early in the morning or at sunset to avoid the brutal summer sun at midday, and wear good shoes. It's a long, arduous hike (one and a half hours to the lower summit, a half hour more to the top), but the panoramic views definitely make it worthwhile.

The current residents of Old Corinth occupy a small village flanking the ruins. The town's main street, which runs right in front of the site, is lined with cafes and souvenir shops. The only hotel in town, the **Xenia** (tel. 31 20 8), is expensive at 2000dr for a double (including breakfast and a shower), but try the handful of pensions on the side streets. Most have signs in front which advertise rooms, but if you have trouble finding one cheap enough, ask a local cafe or shop owner for directions.

Near Corinth

Isthmia and Nemea

The ancient Greeks celebrated two important athletic festivals in the vicinity of Corinth, the Isthmian and the Nemean games, both of which the poet Pindar has preserved to some extent in his odes honoring the winners. The bus from Corinth to **Isthmia** makes several stops in the tiny village and you should ask to be let out at the **museum** *(moussion)*, which houses reconstructions of the Temple of Poseidon and the Isthmian games, handweights released by jumpers in mid-flight for greater distance *(haltares)*, fishhooks, mason's tools, and panels of Homer and Plato found at nearby Kenchreae. Open Mon.-Sat. 8:45am-3pm, Sun. 8am-4pm, closed Tues.; admission free. Behind the museum lie the actual ruins of the **Temple of Poseidon,** to the right of which is a **starting device** (reconstructed in the museum). About 50m behind and to the right of the Temple is the **theater,** from which the emperor Nero proclaimed the specious freedom of the Greeks, as had other Romans before him. The Greeks were pawns easily moved by any Roman proclamation of freedom, and the Romans took full advantage.

To get a good view of the **Corinth Canal,** walk down towards the mouth of the canal from the Isthmia museum to a quaint taverna, the **Dioriga,** next to a one-car ferry. Then walk up the road which roughly parallels the canal until you get to the bridge (2km). Over four miles long, the canal's dramatic razor-smooth sides, thirty yards apart, were cut into rock over 270 ft. high. Of course, many people will be sharing the view since the bridge is a popular rest-stop for buses.

If ancient ingenuity intrigues you, some parts of the **diolkos** still remain at the western mouth of the canal. Since no time-saving canal existed in ancient times, boats were hoisted onto a pathway (the diolkos) across the narrowest point of the isthmus and were rolled across on logs to the other side. The emperor Nero tried to cut a canal but failed miserably.

At **Nemea,** where Herakles slew the Nemean lion, Greeks from ancient times sought to emulate the hero by taking part in their own contrived struggles. The ruins include the **Temple of Nemean Zeus,** the **stadium,** which has a starting line and an entrance tunnel with the fans' graffiti, and also a **palaestra** and **baths.**

Loutraki

To play a few games of your own, head for Loutraki. Known for its hot mineral springs and beautifully clear drinking water, this seaside resort town is no secret to tourists, Greek or international. Its long beach of small smooth rocks, flanked by a white stone boardwalk, attracts quite a few sunworshippers and bathers—hence the scores of hotels lining the waterfront. Of course the crowds and commerce don't really detract from the beauty of the emerald green sea and the imposing Yerania mountains, which keep watch over the town and bay. But you might try to reach the beach before the high season for added enjoyment and peace of mind. To orient yourself, stay on the bus until the last stop at a sort of triangle, where the bus station is located, across from the Hotel Mizithra. Walk down El. Venizelou, the main drag, with the water to your left. The **Post Office** is on Iras St., a few blocks down and to the right. On El. Venizelou in the same area, the **Tourist Police** (tel. 42 25 8) will provide you with information on lodgings and sights from 8am to 2pm every day. At 10 El. Venizelou, across from the Tourist Police, is the **OTE,** open Mon.-Fri. 7:30am-10pm. Most cheap hotels are close to the Tourist Police station. If you continue down El. Venizelou and bear left on G. Lekka St., you'll find the **Hotel**

Kanadas (tel. 48 01 1) at #6 on your right, which has singles for 563dr and doubles for 788dr; showers 90dr extra. Also nearby, with comparable prices, are the **Hotel Gallia,** (tel. 42 21 3), **Hotel Iraion** (tel. 42 37 8), and **Hotel Karadani** (tel. 42 32 2). Across from the Hotel Kanadas, a well-planned park provides welcome shade. Buses leave Loutraki for the town of **Perahora,** which has the best view of the bay of Corinth and some archaic remains to boot, on the hour 6am-8pm and return on the half hour 6:30am-8:30pm. Buses leave for Athens six times a day and for Corinth every half hour. If you wish to get to Loutraki from Isthmia, cross the canal bridge. The bus stop for Loutraki is next to a railroad station sign, behind a billboard for Italian car ferries. From there to Loutraki the fare is 25dr.

Mycenae (Mikines)

No city figures as largely in Greek mythology and legend as Mycenae. The focal point of Mycenean civilization (1660-1120 B.C.), the city was founded by the hero Perseus. Later, at its height, Mycenae was ruled by the ill-fated House of Atreus, whose scion, Agamemnon, served as commander-in-chief of the Greek armies during the Trojan war. The family's passions formed the subject of many Greek tragedies—Agamemnon was murdered by his wife Clytemnestra and her lover, and they, in turn, were murdered by her son Orestes.

From a more historical perspective, Mycenae presents not only tragedy but two still unresolved mysteries: how Mycenean civilization began and how it ended. The site was occupied as early as the Middle Helladic period (1900-1660 B.C.), when it was home for a primitive tribe related to the Minoans of Crete. During the seventeenth century B.C., the burial rituals of the inhabitants changed suddenly: gold and metalwork began to accompany the corpses in their tombs. Since death ceremonies played a large role in most ancient cultures, and in many modern ones too, this drastic change has puzzled scholars.

Two centuries after its first appearance, the new civilization (called Mycenean) dominated Greece politically and its culture had taken root in lands as distant as Italy and Syria. All we know of the Myceneans is that they spoke an early form of Greek; this much is clear from the deciphering of stone tablets (found in the palace) by Michael Ventris, who, as the story goes, resolved to crack the code when a mere schoolboy. (This script is called "Linear B"; others, like the Cretan "Linear A," still defeat would-be translators.)

After two more centuries, the Mycenean civilization declined as inexplicably and rapidly as it had risen. In the thirteenth century B.C. many citadels in the Argolis, not just that of Mycenae, built secret cisterns to ensure an especially impregnable water supply, as if some fearsome external threat prompted the construction of this new defense. But it was all in vain. An unknown group attacked Mycenae in the twelfth century and, though the city recovered once, it was attacked again and finally burned. Tragically, the destruction coincided with the peak of the Mycenean civilization, which produced magnificent works of architecture—*tholos* (beehive) tombs and monumental palaces—as well as expert metalcraft. The Dorian invasion, and the Greek Dark Ages, followed closely on the heels of the devastation.

The well-preserved ruins of the ancient city rank as one of the most celebrated archeological discoveries in modern history. In summer, hordes of tourists swarm to the site, but if you visit early in the morning or late in the afternoon, you can bypass the mobs. Although most travelers make Mycenae a day trip from either Athens, Argos, or Nafplion, you can spend the night in the adjacent modern village.

Practical Information

The only direct bus connection to Mycenae is from Nafplion and Argos. Buses run four times daily from Nafplion through Argos, stopping both in the town of Mycenae and at the ruins (a fifteen-minute uphill walk from the village). Alternatively, you can take a train or a bus to Fichtia, and walk 1½km to Mycenae. There are also tour buses from Nafplion, which cost 300-1100dr.

Accommodations and Food

Although tourists crowd the town by day, it becomes pleasantly quiet in the evening when the tour buses have departed. Mycenae has a fairly wide choice of accommodations for its modest size, but most of them are immodestly priced. If you do decide to stay, consider one of the camping sites that offers cheap rooms for the tentless in high season. All accommodations are located along the main road and are easy to find.

IYHF Youth Hostel, in the restaurant Iphigenia (tel. 66 28 5). No showers, and you have to use the restaurant's toilets. Only 20 beds, 10 for each sex, 400dr per bed. Dirty and currently under construction—it may improve by 1984, but then it couldn't get much worse.

Belle Helene Hotel, on the main road (tel. 66 22 5), also functions as the bus stop for Nafplion. The rooms are clean and spacious; the register display on the wall claims that Virginia Woolf and Debussy slept here. Nice but very expensive: singles 850dr, doubles negotiable.

Camping: Mycenae has two excellent campgrounds. The more luxurious one is Camping Atreus (tel. 66 22 1), at the bottom of the hill. It offers a TV room, kitchen, cafeteria/bar, and, in case of rain, rooms for the tentless in high season. Fees are 100dr if you don't have a tent and 50dr if you do. Prices include hot showers. Camping Mycenae (tel. 66 24 7) is smaller and friendlier, and set amidst orange and lemon trees. There is also a bar/restaurant and a kitchen, where a gracious owner will prepare homemade and inexpensive fare. 100dr per person, plus 50dr per tent. Hot showers included.

All of the restaurants in town are overpriced due to the demands of the tourist trade; even groceries are expensive. Since there are no real bargains, try the Achilles on the main road—at least they're friendly.

Sights

The excavated site of Mycenae sprawls over a large tract of rough and steep terrain, tucked in between Mt. Ayios Ilias to the north and Mt. Zara to the south. The site is enclosed by Cyclopean walls forty feet high and twenty feet thick. Archeologists have found evidence that the ancient city was settled as early as 3000 B.C. The bulk of ruins standing today, however, date from 1280 B.C., when the city was the center of the famed Mycenean civilization.

It was here that Homer, and the later Greek tragedians following his cue, located the House of Atreus. How far Homer the poet was playing historian as well had long been debated when the amateur archeologist, Heinrich Schliemann, convinced of the authenticity of Homer's account, set off to prove him right. He began digging just inside the citadel walls at the spot where (according to his interpretation of several ancient authors) the royal graves were located. Discovering fifteen skeletons which he described as being "literally covered with gold and jewels," Schliemann became convinced he had disinterred Agamemnon and his followers, but later archeologists have dated the tombs to four centuries before the Trojan War. One skull was covered with a golden death mask still referred to as "Agamemnon's mask"; it is now exhibited in the Athens museum.

Before you visit you might consider obtaining a map of the site, and, if possible, a flashlight. The bus will take you to the end of the asphalt road; on your right the ruins stand, waiting for explanation. The imposing **Lion's Gate,** named for the two lionesses carved in relief above the lintel, is the portal into ancient Mycenae and perhaps the finest relic of Mycenean culture we possess today. These beasts were symbols of the mythical house of Atreus and their heads (now missing) had eyes of precious gems. The **Gate** and the **Cyclopean Walls** of the Citadel date from the thirteenth century B.C. Schliemann made most of his findings (now exhibited in the Mycenean Room of the Athens Museum), including Agamemnon's mask, in **Grave Circle A,** to the right of the entrance. These shaft graves have been dated around the sixteenth century B.C., and were originally located outside of the city walls. They were later incorporated when the city was expanded.

Following the ramp upward to the highest part of the citadel, you reach the palace and the royal apartments. At the far end of the city is the underground cistern which was used to store water in time of siege. Use your flashlight to explore the cold, slimy passage down, but be careful, since the steps are worn and slippery. Turning left out of the cistern and following the hill around, you'll find a "back door," thought to be the exit taken by Orestes after he killed his mother, Clytemnestra.

Just outside the Lion's Gate (down and to your left as you leave the city, between the walls and the road) are two of the excavated tholos (beehive) tombs, used for noble burials. The one closer to the city was reputedly the **tomb of Aegisthus** and the other the **tomb of Clytemnestra.** If you follow the asphalt road for 150m back towards the town of Mycenae you'll find just to the right of the road the **Treasury of Atreus,** the largest and most impressive tholos, which Schliemann also unearthed. It is also called the **tomb of Agamemnon,** which many believe it to be. The tomb is entered through a 115-foot passage called the **Dromos,** cut into the mortar. The site is open Mon.-Sat. 8:30am-6pm and Sun. 10am-6pm, off-season 9:30am-3:30pm. Admission for both the citadel and Agamemnon's tomb is 100dr, 50dr for students. Be sure to hang on to your ticket or you will have to pay admission twice.

Argos

In his play *The Flies,* Jean-Paul Sartre paints a rather bleak picture of the ancient city of Argos. His description applies just as aptly to the modern city that stands in its place. Argos is an unattractive industrial metropolis where swarms of cars and trucks from all directions converge on the main square, leaving all bystanders with the unpleasant memory of exhaust fumes, churning gears, and screaming drivers. Only for a brief spell in the afternoon does the chaos let up, and even then the pace is anything but peaceful. However, for those planning to take advantage of its proximity to Tiryns, Mycenae, Epidavros, and Nafplion, Argos is entirely bearable, and it even has a few impressive ruins of its own.

Argos has two bus stations. Buses to Tripolis (140dr) leave nine times a day from the station on the corner of Nikitara St. and the Platia (Danaou St.). At the other station, just across from the lower end of the square, you can catch buses to Athens (320dr) every hour on the half hour (5:30am-8pm), to Nafplion (30dr) every half hour, to Nemea (75dr) three times a day, and to Mycenae (30dr) six times a day.

Accommodations and Practical Information

Since Argos does not attract as many tourists as Mycenae or Nafplion, its accommodations tend to be slightly cheaper. Several inexpensive hotels all lie close to the square: the **Apollo Inn**, at 15 Korai St. (tel. 28 01 2; take Nikitara St. off the square), which has doubles for 500dr, showers 50dr extra; **Hotel Hermes,** on Vas. Konstantinou St. (tel. 27 51 0) at the higher end of the square, whose affable proprietor charges 500dr for singles, 700dr for doubles, showers 60dr extra; **Hotel Theoxenia** (tel. 27 37 0), also on Vas. Konstantinou St. near the square, offering doubles for 700dr, showers 50dr extra; **Hotel Palladion** (tel. 27 34 6), at the top of the square where Danaou St. ends, which has singles for 500dr, doubles for 700dr, showers 50dr extra; and **Hotel Pseloritis** (tel. 28 08 4), on Tzokri St. (go left on Vas. Konstantinou St. until you come to the arches, to the left of which is the hotel), which has comparable prices. Even if you decide not to stay, you'll probably pass through Argos, since it is a major transfer point for buses to Mycenae, Epidavros, Nafplion, Tiryns, and points in the central Peloponnese.

Because so few visitors make it to Argos, the city has no Tourist Police (the Nafplion Tourist Police cover Argos), but the regular **police** (tel. 27 22 2) will help in emergencies and are open every day 24 hours. From the top of the square take the road to Athens, turn on Agelou Bobou St. and the police will be at #10, on your right. On Danaou St. past the bottom of the square you'll find a **laundry,** the "Star," at #13, and further down the **Post Office,** open Mon.-Fri. 7:30am-2:30pm. If you follow Nikitara St. off the side of the square and bear right you'll find the **OTE** at #8, open every day 6am-midnight (one of the few open on weekends). There's a **supermarket** next door to the Hotel Hermes, a left onto Vas. Konstantinou St. off the top of the square. The **telephone code** for Argos is 0751.

Sights

Archeological findings indicate that the plain of Argos has been inhabited since 3000 B.C. According to Homer, it was the kingdom of the hero Diomedes, to whom even the powerful king Agamemnon acknowledged subservience. Not a major center of Mycenean civilization, Argos was captured by the invading Dorians in the twelfth century B.C., around the same time as the fall of Mycenae, and the conquerors used it as their base for controlling the Argolid peninsula. Through the seventh century B.C., Argos remained the most powerful state in the Peloponnese, and even defeated Sparta, its growing rival—but this was the last of the glories. By the fifth century B.C., Argos was no match for the invincible Spartan war-machine, which in one famous battle, under the leadership of Cleomenes, defeated Argos though it failed to penetrate the city walls thanks to courageous defensive action by the poetess Telesilla. Thenceforth, Argos lost any claim to political or military preeminence, though culturally, the city stayed in the forefront because of its advanced school of sculpture. In 272 B.C. the great general Pyrrhus died in an Argive street where, after he attacked the city, a female inhabitant let a heavy roof tile fall directly onto his head. Pyrrhus (whose name gives us our phrase "Pyrrhic victory" in reference to a terribly costly military triumph) commented, "Another victory like this and we shall be lost." Such was the crushing end of a clever leader. In medieval times, Franks, Venetians, and Turks all captured and ruled Argos in turn, leaving behind many examples of defensive architecture, such as the fortress on top of Larissa, the great hill behind the city. If you've been to the Palamidi in Nafplion, this one probably isn't worth the climb. Since the 1820s, when Greeks convened the first national assembly here, Argos has had little importance, strategic or political.

Archeologists hoped to uncover a large part of the ancient city, but most of it lies underneath the modern town. The principal excavations have occurred on the western edge of town on the road to Tripolis (off Theatron St.). The present archeological site is small, but usually uncrowded and quite interesting. To reach it go left out of the museum, make another left onto the road just before the flea market, follow it to the end and make a right onto Theatron St. The ancient **theater,** built in the fourth century B.C., is the main attraction at the site. Although some of the theater has crumbled away, it retains much of its former magnificence. It was large, with a seating capacity of twenty thousand, though it is not nearly as well preserved as its famous counterpart in Epidavros. Perhaps more interesting is the **Roman bath** complex next to the theater. Look for the ancient pipes and the mosaic floors. A bit further on is the **Roman Odeion** (indoor theater) and, across the road, the **agora,** which has blue and white mosaics still in place. Past the Odeion are the remains of a **smaller theater.** The site is open Mon.-Sat. 8:30am-2:30pm, Sun. 10am-3pm, closed Tues.; admission free.

The small but excellent **museum** just off the main square is highly recommended. It contains mostly Mycenean and pre-Mycenean finds dating as far back as 3000 B.C. Make sure to visit the famous fifth-century Roman mosaics displayed in the interior courtyard. Ask a guard to sponge them down, for they only reveal their true brilliance when wet. Open the same hours as the site; admission 50dr, 30dr for students. For another set of ruins, follow Tzokri St. off the square (where it is Vas. Konstantinou St.) for several blocks and continue up a hill, to the right of which is **Aspis,** the main ancient citadel. **Larissa,** an alternative citadel and site of the Venetian fortress, will be on your left. Just to the right of the road at the top you'll find the **Temple of Apollo and Athena,** and below it a series of **Mycenean graves.**

Near Argos

Just 8km from Argos on the road to Nafplion lie the impressive Mycenean ruins of Tiryns (or Tirintha), also the birthplace of Hercules. The finest prehistoric site outside of Mycenae, Tiryns was reputed, during ancient times, to be one of the most impregnable cities ever constructed, until finally it was captured by Argos and destroyed in the fifth century B.C.

Although parts of the ancient stronghold date as far back as 2600 B.C., most of what you see today was built one thousand years later, during Mycenean times. The massive walls that presently surround the site indicate the immensity of the original fortifications. Standing about 25 feet in both height and width, the "Cyclopean" walls were so named by the ancient Greeks because they believed that the stones composing the walls could only have been lifted by the Cyclops, a race of giants from Asia Minor with superhuman strength. It remains a mystery to modern historians how the stones were moved. On the eastern and southern slopes of the ancient acropolis, the walls reach a width of almost sixty feet. Inside these massive structures are vaulted galleries. The remnants of the palace at the top of the acropolis contain impressively decorated floors, but the frescoes which once adorned its walls are now on display in the National Museum in Athens. The site is open Mon.-Sat. 9am-3:30pm and Sun. 10am-4:30pm; admission 50dr, 30dr for students. The site is easily reached; just take the bus that runs between Nafplion and Argos (25dr).

Hera was the main deity of the Argives and the temple of her cult, the **Argive Heraion,** is a short bus ride north of Argos (two buses a day in the afternoon for 25dr). The complex contains a pair of **temples,** a **stoa,** and **baths,** among other things. The amateur archeologist, however, will want to venture out to **Prosimni,** several kilometers northeast of Argos and past the Heraion, to find a whole series of prehistoric graves. A few miles east of Agias Trias lie the remains of the city of **Dendra,** whose tombs yielded the completely preserved suit of bronze armor now on exhibit in the Nafplion museum.

Nafplion

With its beaches, castles and excellent bus connections, Nafplion is the ideal base for exploring the **Argolid.** According to ancient legend, Poseidon's son, Nauplius (also named Palamedes), founded the city, and Hera took her yearly bath on the outskirts of town at the Kanathos springs to restore her virginity (now the Agia Moni convent). In more recent times, Nafplion served as the first capital of independent Greece between 1829 and 1834, hosting the swearing-in ceremonies of Kapodistrias, the Greek republic's first governor. Now, resting peacefully beneath a magnificent Venetian fortress, the **Palamidi,** Nafplion, the capital of the Argolid, conducts a modest export trade in currants and tobacco, with a booming import trade in tourists.

Practical Information

Buy the maps of Nafplion and Tolo (50dr) in one of the tourist shops where the bus stops. (If you're one of the few who reach the city by water, the shops on the dock sell them as well.) The bus terminal, on Singrou St., sits near the front of Palamidi fortress, which you'll see to the right facing inland and crowning the hill. To reach the statue of Kapodistrias, roughly the center of town, turn left out of the bus terminal and walk one block toward the water. Continuing down Singrou to the harbor and then turning left on Bouboulinas St., you'll find many shops and tavernas, behind which are four good hotels (Acropol, Tiryns, Epidavros, and Tryfon). Again from Kapodistrias' statue, follow Vas. Konstadinou St., with the harbor on your right, for about six blocks until you reach Syntagma Square, also called Platia Syntagmatos. There you will find several good tavernas, the bank, and the museum. Two blocks behind the museum is the King Otto Hotel.

On the other side of Kapodistrias' statue—the part to his back—is the newer section of town. Follow Singrou again to the water, but this time make a right on Bouboulinas. If you have a heavy backpack, the Tourist Police and anything else on the road to Argos may be too far to reach without an occasional rest stop. To get to the beach, take the road between the Palamidi and the Akronafplion.

Bus Terminal: Singrou St. off the Platia Kapodistrias (tel. 27 32 3). Buses leave from here to all relevant points: hourly to Corinth (150dr) and Athens (350dr), 5am-8pm; every half hour to Argos (30dr) and Tiryns (25dr), 6am-10pm; three times daily to Epidavros (75dr), and four times daily to Mycenae (65dr). Buses also leave hourly for Tolo and Assini (30dr), 7am-7pm, three times daily for Galatas and Methana (210dr), and three times daily for Kranidi (200dr).

Tourist Police: Praxitelous St. (tel. 27 77 6). Keep asking questions; you'll find out what you want to know sooner or later. A long hike along 25 Martiou St. from the Bus Terminal.

Post Office: two blocks behind the Bus Terminal.

OTE Office: two blocks in front of the Bus Terminal.

Bank: in Syntagma Square.

Laundry: Sik Laundry Service, 14 Vas. Konstadinou St.

English Bookstore: Odyssey, in Syntagma Square.

Rent-a-Vespa or Bicycle: on Sofroni St., one block from the dock.

Telephone code: 0752.

Accommodations

Don't be surprised to find the prices 100-150dr more than what we list. Ever since the deregulation of hotel categories, owners tend to raise their prices at the drop of a hat. The Tourist Police will also help you find private rooms and pensions, both of which vary greatly in price.

IYHF Youth Hostel: Neon Vyzantion St. (tel. 24 72 0). From the bus terminal, walk down 25 Martiou and take a left on the road to Argos. After a few blocks, you will come to Argonaeton St. on your right. The hostel is at the end of this street. The hostel is big, not very clean, but easygoing. 200dr a night, breakfast 75dr, midnight curfew.

Hotel Emporiko: 31 Plapouta St. (tel. 27 33 9). Right near the bus station. Small, but bargaining may get prices even lower. Singles 500dr, doubles 675dr.

Hotel Epidavros: Ipsiladou St. (tel. 27 54 1). From Singrou St., make a left on Amalias St., a right on Kotsonopoulou St., and a right onto Ipsiladou. Has a variety of rooms, some singles for as little as 500dr, and doubles for 800dr; these are in an older, more run-down building down the street but are still clean and have showers.

Hotel Tryfon: 17 Argous St. (tel. 27 64 3). On the road to Argos. Singles 450dr, doubles 675dr, triples 1013dr. Shower 50dr extra. Run by a kind woman with a mothering instinct.

Hotel Amymoni: Off Syntagma, and near Hotel Otto (tel. 27 21 9). Good location, clean rooms. Singles 675dr, doubles 1013dr. Shower 50dr extra.

Hotel Tiryns: On Ferreou St. off Othonos (tel. 28 10 4). Also near the water, offers singles with shower for 563dr and doubles with shower for 1013dr. Doubles without shower 810dr, but you can add one for 75dr. Optional breakfast 110dr.

Hotel King Otto: 3 Farmakopolou St. (tel. 27 58 5). A beautiful old house with a spiral staircase, near the water, and off the town square. Breakfast is served in a garden underneath lemon and orange trees. Singles 619dr, doubles 788dr, triples 1103dr. Shower 75dr, breakfast 150dr. If they have no room they'll send you to Hotel Leto.

Hotel Leto: 28 Zigomala St. (tel. 28 09 3). At the top of Farmakopolou St., up two flights of steep stone steps. Run by the owner of Hotel King Otto. Singles 788dr, doubles 1125dr.

Hotel Akropol: 7 Vas. Olgas St. (tel. 27 79 6). From Singrou St. go left on Amalias, right on Sofroni, and left on Vas. Olgas. Singles 563dr, doubles 698dr.

Hotel Rex: On Bouboulinas St., in the new part of town (tel. 28 09 4). Singles 718dr, doubles 1050dr, but the owner is reluctant to rent the former. He has cheaper rooms in **Hotel Annex,** which is right next door.

On the road to Argos:

Hotel Artemis: 17 Argous St. (tel. 27 86 2). Singles 596dr, doubles 821dr, triples 900dr, all without shower. With shower, singles 675dr, doubles 900dr, triples 1069dr.

Hotel Argolis: 26 Argous St. (tel. 27 72 1). Singles 800dr, doubles 985dr, triples 1200dr, all including shower. Across the street from Hotel Artemis.

Hotel Semiramis: 28 Argous St. (tel. 27 32 1). Clean and tidy. Singles 700dr, doubles 900dr.

Camping: Nafplion Camping is within walking distance of town off the road to Argos. 150dr per person, 200dr per tent or car. There are 7 campgrounds on the route from Nafplion to Tolo (buses leave the terminal every half hour).

Food and Nightlife

Most meals will cost 250-350dr depending on what you order; the difference is in the setting. Nafplion is a terrific place to sample fresh seafood at reasonable prices.

On the water: go down Sofroni St. from the center of town till you come to the water, then make a left onto Bouboulinas. Here and further on past the Platia Iatrou are many good restaurants, especially **T'Anapli, Hundalas, Nauplion House restaurant,** and **Kanaris.**

In Syntagma Square: **Noufara** and **Ellas** restaurants will serve you out on the peaceful square, which is closed to traffic.

On Plapouta St., which becomes Staikopoulou St.: **Ta Fanaria, Kelari** (which has a lovely garden), **To Koutouki, O Khelmos,** and the **Staikopoulou Taverna** (further down the street) are all small and cozy.

In Kapodistrias Square: Pines, palms, and Palamidi are all in full view from **Dionysus** at #3 and the more expensive **Matsikas,** two doors down.

On 25 Martiou St.: A few blocks before the Tourist Police is the **Three Brothers** restaurant. Stop in only if you're in that part of Nafplion and need food before you return to the old town.

For dancing you can try two sorts: traditional Greek and disco. On the corner of Bouboulinas St. and Sofroni is **Sirena,** where you can learn the *Syrtaki* to live traditional Greek music every night beginning at 9:30pm. You can find a similar program nearby on Bouboulinas at the **Boite Lichnari.** As for more up-to-date movements, try **Disco Idol** on Singrou St. near the water. Up on the hill past the Tourist Police is the outdoor **Disco Kirki.**

Sights

Nafplion is a dream town for fortification fanatics. The **Palamidi Fortress,** built by the Venetians in the eighteenth century, is one of the most amazing defensive buildings in Greece. The nine hundred and ninety-nine steps that once provided the only access to the fortress have been superceded by a 3km road; taxis up cost about 100dr, but purists can still make the assault by foot. If you opt for the steps, bring along some water and climb in the morning when the sun is blocked by the hill. At the top, you can walk around the intricate and well-preserved walls and enjoy the absolutely spectacular view, both of the town below and of much of the Argolid. The fortress is open Mon.-Sat. 10am-4:30pm, Sun. and holidays 10am-3pm; admission 50dr, 30dr for students, free on Sundays.

One of Nafplion's most unusual sights is the huge **Bavarian Lion.** Ludwig I, King of Bavaria, after seeing many of his men die in an epidemic in 1833-34, had a lion carved out of a monstrous rock as a memorial. Today there is a small park in front of it. Instead of turning right onto Praxitelous St. to go to the Tourist Police, make a left onto Mikh. Iatrou St. and walk for two hundred meters. The lion will be on your right.

The small island of **Bourtzi** was fortified (compactly and elegantly) at the end of the fourteenth century. Caiques run back and forth constantly (25dr). Unless you love ruined walls, skip the medieval **Akronaplion Fortress.**

Finally, Nafplion has two fascinating museums. The **Folk Art Museum** displays very comprehensively the styles and construction techniques of ancient, medieval, and eighteenth-century Greek clothing. Open 9am-1pm and 5-8pm, closed Tues. and February; admission free. The **Archeological Museum,** housed in a Venetian palace on Syntagma Square, has a small but choice collection of pottery, displayed by historical period. open Mon.-Sat. 9am-3:30pm, Sun. 10am-3pm, closed Tues.; admission free.

Near Nafplion

The beach resorts of **Tolo** and **Assini** offer delightful respites from the monotony of exploring archeological ruins. Although Tolo has become heavily touristed, and its shores are lined with luxury hotels, its beach is still quite beautiful. A better choice, however, is to visit Assini located nearer to Nafplion. It was a prehistoric city mentioned by Homer and excavations within the town have uncovered fortifications, chamber tombs, and pottery. In addition it has a beautiful beach which is less crowded and less pricey than the one at Tolo. Both Assini and Tolo can be reached easily by bus from Nafplion.

Epidavros

"At Epidavros I felt a stillness so intense that for a fraction of a second I heard the great heart of the world beat and I understood the meaning of pain and sorrow."

Henry Miller, *The Colossus of Maroussi*

When Henry Miller visited Epidavros, he did not encounter legions of tour buses to mar the transcendency of his experience. While the ancient theatre at Epidavros attracts almost as many tourists as Mycenae, don't let the hordes deter you—there is nothing quite like it in all of Greece. Whereas the other key sights in the Argolid, such as Mycenae, Nafplion, and Tiryns, were built as fortified cities, Epidavros was designed as a sanctuary for healing. Its atmosphere, with pines, flowers, and herbs, is still soothing.

The spot was originally dedicated to a local healing god, Maleatas, who, by the pre-Classical period, was eclipsed and replaced by the god Apollo. In the fourth century B.C., about the time of a major cholera epidemic, the cult of Asclepius (a healer with miraculous curative powers) gained popularity throughout Greece. Asclepius seems to have been an actual person who had great success in curing people in Northern Greece. Despite his success, however, Asclepius incurred the wrath of Zeus by disrupting the balance between the living and the dead. In the end, Zeus struck him down with a thunderbolt. Asclepius was first revered as a hero, and later worshipped as a god.

Excavations at the site have uncovered the foundations of a **temple to Asclepius,** a *tholos,* **temples to Artemis** and **Aphrodite,** as well as a gymnasium and several buildings used to house the hundreds waiting to be cured. Amidst the ruins of the sacred hospital grounds, you can see the ancient marble bathtubs in which patients used to bathe in the firm belief that the waters possessed magical powers. Since most tourists skip the ruins and see only the theater and museum, you will have the ancient sanctuary practically to yourself. The museum displays surgical instruments, casts of sculptures, testimonies of cures, and a reconstruction of the site.

The prime attraction, however, is the theater constructed toward the end of the fourth century B.C. It has miraculously remained in almost perfect condition, and still has a seating capacity of 14,000. Cut into the side of a hill in the middle of a pine grove, the theater is completly hidden from view until you have climbed nearly to its level. Then, in a huge clearing, its 55 stone tiers arch into the air, utterly serene and timeless. The structure's true immensity can only be appreciated from above, so climb up the steps for the view from the top.

At midday with the sun beating down and the seats empty the theater is an impressive relic. To appreciate its full grandeur, however, and to test its amazing acoustics, you must visit Epidavros on Saturday or Sunday nights from June 26 through September 11. The National Theater of Greece and visiting companies perform plays from the classical Greek canon. Performances are at 9pm and tickets can be purchased at the theater four hours before show time, or in advance at the Athens Box Office of the National Theater at the corner of Agio Konstantinou and Mandrou Sts. (tel. 52 48 600), or at the Athens Festival Box Office (4 Stadium St.; tel. 32 21 459). Since all performances are in modern Greek, you might also want to pick up a translation to follow along. All the relevant plays are available in English translation at the bookstore in Nafplion, as are various books about Epidavros. The site at Epidavros is open in summer, daily 9am-7pm, Sun. and holidays 10am-6pm; admission 100dr, 50dr for students. Hold on to your ticket stub: it gets you into the museum, which is closed Tues. There is an extremely expensive hotel near the site (the **Xenia**). Cheaper accommodations can be found in the village of **Ligouri,** but most people make Epidavros a daytrip from Nafplion or from Athens. The bus fare from Nafplion is 75dr. Tour buses from Nafplion cost anywhere from 300 to 1100dr.

Elis and Achaïa (Northwestern Peloponnese)

Déja vu should hit you like a sandbag when you cover ground in the northwest Peloponnese. Once you leave the divinely beautiful groves and streams of Olympia and start traveling between Pirgos and Patras, the respective (and dingy) capitals of Elis and Achaïa, you'll see tassled corn stalks reaching toward the sun, plains flat as a tabletop, and farmland as far as the eye can reach. If you still can't guess where it is you've seen this before, then pack your bags and head home—you've been away too long. The plains of this region resemble the American heartland to a striking degree. Like America's midwest, this area—especially Elis—was blessed with flat fertile ground, a universe of open space that lends itself not only to agriculture but also to horse-breeding, and since antiquity, generations of fillies and colts have taken their first strides and matured into powerful mares and stallions on this soil. True, the bus rides through the Peloponnesian mountain passes excite most travelers, but the unique nostalgia of crossing these plains will be exhilarating in ways you never expected.

A less pleasant surprise, especially for readers of the *Iliad*, is Achaïa. Alas! The great Achaïa, once a synonym for Greece itself, the land of the warriors of yore who journeyed to retrieve Helen from Troy, now huddles within its narrow confines, a shadow of its former size and greatness. The main city, Patras, would give Homer nothing to sing about and the ride along the Bay of Corinth, though a few sandy beaches dot the coast, is generally unspectacular. What's more, the name that meant the whole of Hellas to Homer and Greece-south-of-Thessaly to Rome now represents only a small political subdivision in the northern tip of the Peloponnese. At this rate it may soon disappear completely—perhaps the most compelling argument for a visit.

Patras

With its homogeneous high-rises cowering beneath a shroud of smog, the busy port city of Patras is a huge blemish on the otherwise serene Peloponnesian coast. To many Greeks this western gate to the center of the country symbolizes the nation's growing economy in modern times. Almost everyone coming to Greece by boat ultimately sets foot in Patras, but since there is little of interest to the tourist here, the wisest move is to leave as soon as possible.

Orientation and Practical Information

If you're coming by boat from Brindisi and Corfu with the rest of the hordes, you can reach the center of town by turning right as you leave the customs house on to Iroon Polytechniou St. (at the customs house is a **National Tourist Office** open 7:30am-2:30pm and 4-10pm in summer; OTE telephones and money exchange open when the boats come in). Three and a half blocks further down on the waterfront is the main **KTEL bus station,** with buses leaving for Athens every 45 minutes (four hours, 510dr), for Killini, Kalamata, and other towns near Patras. KTEL buses for some places (Lefkas, for example) leave from the bus stop on Favierou St. across town, so be sure to check beforehand at the information booths in the bus station. Government-owned buses also leave for Athens and other major cities from the **train station,** which is just a block-and-a-half past the bus station on the right. Prices for KTEL and government buses are comparable, but the schedules are different. If you're pressed for time, check the schedules of both lines. Neither company will give you information about the other, so you'll have to do some walking. On your way from the bus station to the train station the road curves and the name changes to Othonos Amalias St. **Trains** leave seven times a day for Athens (six in low season for 325dr (compared to 510dr for a bus), but be warned: the bus stops only once in Corinth, while the train stops in every town along the way and may take up to twice as long (seven to eight hours at least). There are several trains a day to Kalamata (375dr), Olympia (225dr), and Pirgos (180dr). The station is also a good place to leave **luggage** (24dr per day). Even if you have a railpass, you should reserve a seat at the ticket window before taking a train. Just across the street, at 40 Othonas Amalias, the **Tourist Police** are open 24 hours every day (tel. 22 09 02/03) and can help you find a cheap hotel or a room in a private home. Since each bus station and boat company supplies information for its own services only, check first with the Tourist Police for timetables.

Just past the station is the **Platia Trion Simahon,** a large square with palm trees, cafes, kiosks, and a large clock set in the side of an embankment with flowers planted to form the face and numerals. The **National Bank,** one block past Platia Trion Simahon along the waterfront, changes money Mon.-Fri. 7:30am-2pm and 5:30-8:30pm, Sat. and Sun. 9am-1pm. For medical emergencies there are English-speaking doctors and interns from Patras University at the Hospital (22 28 12). The telephone code for Patras is 061.

If you are coming to Patras by road from the north, the ferry between Rio and Anterio operates every twenty minutes from 6am-11pm and every half hour from 11pm-6am (25dr per person, 232dr per car). The last bus from Rio to Patras leaves at 11:10pm (32dr) from a station four blocks up the hill from the main bus station; the ride takes 25-30 minutes. If you're heading to Athens by car the quickest way is to take the scenic route along the northern border of the Peloponnese. Take the National Road Street which is the new expressway and runs along the Gulf of Corinth, featuring views across the water of the white-capped Mt. Parnassos. Old Road Street follows essentially the same route, but you must grind to a halt as you pass through every town on the way. For travel arrangements out of Patras try **Med-Link** at 36 Iroon Polytechniou St. (turn left as you leave the port; open every day 8:30am-2pm and 4-9:30pm). George Martikas, the director, will also change money. If you're going to Brindisi you can get a better boat fare here than in Igoumenitsa or Corfu. With a Eurail pass deck fare is 165dr. With InterRail (or if you're under thirty) deck is 2,380dr; over thirty or without train passes the price for deck is 2,900dr. The trip takes nineteen hours and leaves each night at 10pm, arriving in Brindisi the next day at 5pm. Everyone pays the port tax of 200dr. Inglessis Bros. at 12 Othonas Amalias St. (tel. 27 76 76), has all the information you'll need for a ferry to Corfu. Tourist (student) class fares begin at 989dr. Connections to **Cephalonia** and **Ithaca** can be made at Tsimaras Agency, 12/14 Iroon Polytechniou St. Ferries leave daily at 2pm from June 15 through September 15 and sporadically at other times. Cost for the four-hour trip to Sami (Cephalonia) is 600dr, low season 575dr; add another hour and 210dr for the trip to Vathi (Ithaca).

Accommodations and Food

The cheapest place to stay in Patras is the **IYHF Youth Hostel** at 68 Iroon Polytechniou St. (tel. 42 72 78). Turn left as you leave the ferry and walk nine hundred meters. This turn-of-the-century mansion sat empty for forty years after it was used as German officers' headquarters in World War II. Although the managers, Thodoros and Spiros, have been working on renovation since July 1980, it still lacks adequate shower facilities and is a bit cramped with 8 beds to a small room. But it offers a convenient location (and a view of the harbor), a washing machine for 100dr a load, no curfew, and cut-rate meal prices. The 180dr per person includes hot showers. **Camping** is also available on the premises for 100dr per person. Thodoros is also the Head Scout Master for the Greater Patras area and on any weekday afternoon about forty uni-formed Cub Scouts may descend on the hostel for a pack meeting, and travel-ers may be asked for a song or two.

Other inexpensive accommodations can be found in the tangle of shabby buildings on Agiou Andreou St., one block from the waterfront, running along the main square. At #63 is the **Hotel Delphi** (tel. 27 30 50), with singles for 625dr, doubles for 937dr, triples for 1311dr, and baths 100dr extra. You can have a room with a view of the harbor, but you'll have to contend with the noise and traffic of the busy main street. At #95 is **Hotel Brettania** (tel. 27 34 21), a spacious hotel that is clean and well-kept and offers singles for 562dr, doubles for 937dr, and triples for 1249dr, with showers 100dr extra. At the same prices is the quieter and more pleasant **Hotel Parthenon** (tel. 27 34 21) at 25 Erman St. (off Agiou Andreou one block south of Platia Trion Simahon). The manager doesn't speak English but is friendly and enjoys a good game of charades with English-speaking tourists. **Hotel Splendid,** at 37 Othonas Amalias St. (tel. 27 65 51/52), is not really splendid, but it is cheap with singles at 500dr, doubles at 700dr, and triples at 1000dr, all including showers.

There are plenty of cheap, stand-up fast food joints along Agiou Andreou St. where you can get a toasted sandwich and fries for around 85dr. There are several good *souvlaki* bars near Platia Olgas on Kolokotrani St. (three streets in from the waterfront). Beware of the little shops and cafes along the water-front which cater to tourists: they are definite rip-offs and won't hesitate to part fools from their money.

Sights

St. Andrew lived and died in Patras, and the largest Orthodox cathedral in Greece, **Agios Andreas,** is located here to commemorate him. St. Andrew was a martyr who was crucified on an X-shaped cross because he said he was not worthy to die on the same kind of cross as Jesus. When we write "xoxox" for hugs and kisses on a letter it is a custom from ancient times, when one placed an "X" on a document to recall the faithfulness of St. Andrew and then kissed the mark as a pledge of one's own faithfulness. In time St. Andrew was forgotten and the "X" associated only with the kiss. A little over ten years ago the Catholic Church in Rome presented the Bishop of Patras with the disciple's head, which is enshrined in an ornate gold and silver reliquary in the church. The cathedral is open to tourists 9am till dusk (except during services), and the rules against halters, shorts, etc. are strictly enforced. To get there, follow the water all the way to the western end of town (about a mile from the port).

Dominating the city is the Venetian **Kastro** (medieval castle) and surrounding park. The thirteenth-century fortress was built on the ruins of the ancient Acropolis on the site where the temple of the Panachaian Athena once stood. Parts of the walls are still in good condition, and from the battlements one finds a superb view of the city and the Peloponnesian coastline. Nine kilometers southeast of town is the **Achaia Clauss** winery (open 9am-1pm and 4-6:30pm, admission free). The tour is dull, but the winetasting and very inexpensive *ouzo* and wine could make the trip worthwhile. Try the sweet *Mavrodaphne* ("Mavro" is Greek for "dark"), which made Achaia Clauss famous. According to legend, the winery's founder, German Baron von Clauss, lusted after a Greek girl named Daphne and when she died he used black grapes to make a dark wine to remind himself of her.

About 1 km from Achaia Clauss there's a picnic spot overlooking the village of Saravali near the **Church of St. Constantine,** where the Byzantine Emperor Constantine Paleologus lived in 1425. During the summer months the **Roman Odeon** (ancient theater) features plays, dances, and pageants beginning at 8 or 9pm. Ask at the Tourist Office for performance information and tickets. For those who missed the ferry to Corfu or have other frustrations to vent, Patras has a bumper car rink on Agiou Andreou St., one block east of the park (50dr for ten minutes). You can also while away the hours there playing Pac-Man and Donkey Kong for 10dr a game, if you're so inclined.

Killini

Since most travelers come to Killini in order to catch the ferry to Zakinthos, layovers here are usually unplanned—but they are also unusually pleasant. One of the reasons is the broad beach, whose smooth and abundant sands are bathed by the warm waters of the sea. There's so much sand, in fact, from the ribbed bottom beneath the waves to the main road along the shore, that shopowners give the streets a hosedown every day (after their afternoon nap) in order to subdue the inevitable dust storm. The few tourists who spend time here—mostly French and Italian—have neither spoiled the town's uncommercial air nor rushed its leisurely tempo. And nearby are the perfectly Frankish **Chlemoutsi Castle** and the mineral springs of **Loutra Killinis,** a well-manicured resort maintained by the NTOG.

To get to Killini, catch one of the two daily buses from Pirgos or one of the few buses from Patras (185dr—check with the KTEL office in Patras for the details about the latter trip, since you may have to transfer at Lehena). A train leaves five times daily from Patras, changing at Kavassila (155dr, 2½ hours).

Killini's one pension, the **Pandohion,** has only quads and no hot water, but at least one room is usually empty so that a lone traveler can stay. Inquire at the Mobil station across from the train tracks—the affable owner will charge about 700dr for two people. The pension itself is on Glaretzas St. before the Glaretzas Hotel. Go right at the Mobil station and take your first left. On the same corner are the **OTE** and **Post Office** (both open Mon.-Fri. 7:20am-2:30pm), above which is the **police** department (tel. 92 20 2), open 7:30am-8pm. A right instead of a left will lead you to a cheap **restaurant**. Killini also has two C-class hotels, the **Glaretzas** and the cheaper **Ionion;** the latter will reduce its prices—after heavy bargaining—to 1100dr for a double and 750dr for a single. You can also camp on the beach, along with everyone else, without difficulty from the police, who will nonetheless tell you it's illegal.

Getting to Loutra Killinis and the castle is difficult unless you have your own transportation, or are willing to pay a taxi driver 350dr (to the castle) or 550dr (to Loutra). To get there by public transportation, take the train to Vartholomio (22dr one way, 36dr round trip; twenty minutes), a bus from there to Loutra (25dr) and then another bus to the castle (called the Kastro). Trains leave Killini for Vartholomio from the end of the tracks seven times a day. (If you get on at Killini, buy your ticket at the Killini station, a few minutes down the tracks; otherwise buy it at the Vartholomio station.) Take a right out of the Vartholomio train station and continue down this road for a kilometer, until you reach a square with a fountain. From here, buses to Loutra depart eight times a day. Halfway between Vartholomio's train and bus stations is the **Hotel Ilida,** which has singles for 500dr and doubles for 800dr. The bus to Loutra can leave you at one of three places: the turn-off to Kastro, the mineral springs, or the excellent **camping** area, which is close to the sea. Buses leave Loutra for Kastro three times a day; wait at the turn-off, where you can hitch while you're standing.

Ferries from Killini to Zakinthos depart seven times a day; deck fare is 250dr (boats run only three times a day in winter). Boats also leave Killini for Cephalonia (315dr) twice a day.

Pirgos

Pirgos is a dump, but you're almost certain to pass through here on the way to Pylos or Olympia. There is only one thing anyone in his right mind could possibly want to know: how to get from the train to the bus station. When exiting the former, walk straight until you get to the Hotel Olympus, and then veer slightly to the left as the street goes up the hill. After about fifty meters, turn right (at the supermarket) on Manolopoulou Street; the **bus station** is on the left. The **Tourist Police** are on Karkavitsa St. (tel. 23 68 5), left just before the Hotel Olympus (open Mon.-Fri: 8am-1:30pm and 6-8pm, irregular hours on weekends). For the unfortunate or the masochistic, the way between the train and bus stations is littered with cheap and empty hotels. The **Hotel Kantron** is near the train station and charges 650dr for doubles (tel. 22 73 3). For a meal, the **O Morias** is better than most, but there really is no excuse for staying here. Trains leave four times daily to Olympia (40dr), and buses almost every hour (55dr); in either case the trip takes about 45 minutes. Buses leave twice a day for Killini (140dr); four times a day for Kiparissia (150dr); twice a day for Kalamata (320dr); and three times a day for Tripolis (360dr). Ten buses a day go to Athens (730dr) and to Patras (250dr).

Near Pirgos are the sulphur springs at **Kaïpha,** named for Jesus' friend the high priest Caiaphas.

Modern Olympia

Whenever the ancient games were held in Olympia, they were chaperoned by a huge tent city, where vendors hawked wares and entrepreneurs seduced crowds with all kinds of diversions. Little has changed over the centuries; the modern town of Olympia, about half a kilometer from the ruins, is a slick reincarnation of the same old scam. And yet, if the ruins are less imposing than you'd wish, the town is more agreeable than you'd expect. Yes, it's merely a compound of hotels and tourist shops; yes, many places are unduly expensive and some cafes charge twice as much as their neighbors; yes, it's inauthentic. But the place isn't tawdry, tacky, or tasteless. Its shops are stylish and interesting; you can browse for hours around smart jeweler's stores and places selling English books, as there is none of the hectic hucksterism that sours some of the islands.

Practical Information

The town essentially consists of one long street—walk along it towards the Hotel Spap and you'll come to the Old Museum (currently closed), and a little further down the road, across the river, the **archeological site** and the **New Museum.** Buses stop near the Hotel Hereon. They run at least every hour to Pirgos (55dr), though less frequently in the evening. There are three departures a day for Tripolis (340dr). To reach Andritsena, go to Pirgos and change. Hitching, at least to Tripolis, is terrible. There are also five trains daily to Pirgos, leaving every three hours, with the first one at 7:25am (40dr). One of these is an express linking Olympia directly with Patras (three hours; rail pass holders must pay a supplement of 35dr).

The **Tourist Police** (tel. 22 55 0), friendly and fluent in English, are open every day 24 hours, and are located down a sidestreet off the center of the main road. The **national bank** on the main street is open Mon.-Fri. 8am-2pm. The **Post Office,** up a side street at the end of town closest to the Hotel Spap, is open Mon.-Fri. 7:30am-8:30pm, though a few services close at 2:30pm. Nearby but on the main street, the **OTE** is open Mon.-Fri. 7:30am-10pm, weekends 7:30am-3pm. For medical emergencies, call the **hospital** (tel. 22 59 1). The **telephone code** for Olympia is 0624.

A word on tourist shops. Most open late (10:30am) and close late (10:30pm). Most, too, are run by honest people, though a few rip off unsuspecting customers from time to time. The best strategy for shopping is to make a list of the goods you've got your eye on and then quickly and methodically comparison shop by stopping at every shop on the strip. You'll weed out the overpriced and you won't waste time trying to remember which store sells the cheapest tassled caps.

Accommodations and Food

If you want a bed for the night and care only about price, then head for the Youth Hostel. Otherwise, you can pick from four superb D-class hotels, most of which offer private baths, balconies, and immaculate modern rooms for a fraction of their price elsewhere. Between these two extremes, private rooms in Olympia all go for about the same price and the bulk of them line the road parallel to and one block up from the main street—just start knocking on doors.

IYHF Youth Hostel, on the main road at #18 (tel. 22 58 0). Cards rarely requested. All the facilities are clean. A bed in a single-sex bedroom for 4-6 people costs 180dr. Sheets 50dr extra. Breakfast 90dr. Cool showers are free. Midnight curfew, lockout 10am-1pm.

Hotel Praxiteles, 7 Spiliopoulou St. (tel. 22 59 2), parallel and above the main street. The bargain of the century—a B-class hotel with D-class prices. Spotless, modern, and quiet, with balconies, private baths, and round-the-clock hot water. Singles 550dr, doubles 850dr.

Hotel Hereon, on the main street, where buses stop (tel. 22 54 9). Clean singles 560dr, doubles 790dr; showers 100dr extra.

Hotel Alexandros (tel. 22 53 6). Right next door to Praxiteles and of similar quality, but less of a bargain. One day the management will realize its neighbor is under-cutting it, but until then you should remind them. About 150dr more than Prax-iteles.

Hotel Pelops, 2 Varela St. (tel. 22 54 3), off the main street at the end farthest from the Hotel Spap. Gleamingly modern but as expensive as Hotel Alexandros.

Camping: First try **Olympia Camping** (tel. 22 74 5), on the main road in the direction of Pirgos, which has shady sites under orange trees for 180dr per person and 150dr per tent or car. Hot showers noon-2pm. If this is full, try **Diana Camping** (tel. 22 31 4), just up the hill off the main avenue.

Be careful when you spend money on food—or in shops for that matter. One establishment may ask twice what an identical neighbor would charge. The two best restaurants are down the side street across the main road from Pete's Den (not recommended). The taverna across from the Tourist Police is quiet, but its offerings are less varied. Otherwise try **O Manos** near the Hereon. For snacks, go to the **Strouka** pastry shop, on the road to the Museum of the Olympic games. The presence of beaming locals fully attests to the divinity of their cakes.

Ancient Olympia

Not only is the area divinely verdant and tranquil, but the customs and legends consecrating the tradition of the Olympic games are remarkably com-pelling. Unfortunately, the array of stones littering the area has not been restored for the most part, though their quantity hints at the size of the now-ruined structures. You'll find the site especially interesting if you buy the historically informative guidebook (150dr). Once you can put names and func-tions to the tattered columns, the site no longer looks like a featureless set of meaningless stones.

For over a thousand years, starting in 776 B.C., young men from all the cities in Greece (and later Rome too) gathered in Olympia for the quadrennial festival of Zeus and the athletic competition that accompanied it. Beginning with a simple footrace and wrestling match, both completed in one day, the games grew in diversity and prestige. By 472 B.C., the games spanned five days and included the following events: six different kinds of races (races of one-, two- and 24-stadium lengths, and horse, chariot, and full armor races), boxing, all's fair wrestling (gulp) called the *pankration,* regular wrestling, and the pentathlon (wrestling, discus toss, javelin throw, long jump, and one-stadium length race). With all of the competition, a victory was considered the consummate honor that could be bestowed on an individual and the city he represented. The games themselves commanded respect; the Olympic Truce declared for the duration of the games was strictly observed by the otherwise perpetually warring Greek cities. Besides Homer and the main oracles, the games were the only truly pan-Hellenic institution reminding citizens of the different city-states that they were all Greeks. Only two violations of the Truce were ever recorded in the entire history of the games.

According to myth, the **sanctuary** on the Peloponnese was originally founded by King Pelops. After his death, the site was gradually taken over by the cult of Zeus, and by the classical era (circa fifth-fourth century B.C.) Olympia had become the chief sanctuary of Zeus in all of Greece. All the festivities, including the games, were conducted in honor of this "father of gods and men," as Homer called him. The trees surrounding the site are even said to have been planted by Hercules to mark off the boundaries of his father's territory.

The ancient town of Olympia was considered sacred by the Greeks and never actually inhabited except by officials connected with the games. The center was reserved for the **Altis,** or sacred grove of Zeus. On the far east side of it stood the stadium in which the competitions were held (it can still be seen). Just before the stadium stood the **echo stoa,** said to have had a seven-fold echo. Surrounding the Altis on the other three sides, buildings were gradually added for the competitors to train and eat in, and to accommodate the staff of administrators, high priests, doctors, and flute players. Over the centuries, council houses, treasuries, and a variety of monuments were added to the site—most of these last to victors, numbering 3000 at the peak. The Olympic games were discontinued by Christian Emperor Theodosius in 393 A.D. because he felt the festival was too intimately connected with the worship of Zeus. In 426 A.D., his son Theodosius II called for the destruction of the pagan sanctuary.

On the right as you enter the main gate are the remains of the **gymnasium,** the extremely well-preserved columns of the **palaestra** (wrestling school) and the **theokoleon** (official residence of the priests). Next to the latter is a small building that was the workshop of Phidias, the famous artist (supposedly the creator of the lost Gold Statue of Athena) who was commissioned to produce a sculpture for the site. His tools, terracotta moulds, and a cup bearing his name were found during excavations, and are all on display in the old museum. On the northern edge of the Altis are the remains of the **Temple to Hera** (seventh century B.C.), the oldest and best preserved building on the site, and the oldest Doric temple in Greece. Originally built for both Zeus and Hera, it was devoted entirely to the goddess after a separate temple for Zeus was built to the south. To this day, the Olympic flame is lit here and borne to the site of the modern games. Adjacent stood the **Philippeum,** built by Philip II of Macedon.

Only the base remains of the **Temple of Zeus,** one of the largest temples in mainland Greece during ancient times. The Temple, a colossal edifice standing in the center of Olympia, dominated the entire complex. Now all that remains is a huge platform with fragments of the original structure. The scattered piles of enormous capitals and cylindrical cross-sections of pillars indicate that the massive edifice was toppled by human hands—or earthquakes. Some of the original mosaic floor can still be seen on the Temple base. The nave of the Temple once housed a forty-foot statue of Zeus by Phidias, which was reckoned by the Greeks to be one of the seven wonders of the ancient world. Emperor Theodosius ordered that the gold and ivory statue be brought to Constantinople, where it was destroyed in a fire in 475 A.D.

The **stadium** can be reached through the archway on the east end of the Altis. As originally constructed, its artificial banks accommodated forty thousand spectators. The judges' stand, a paved area on the south side, is still in place, as are the starting and finishing lines; you can even discern the grooves in which the runners placed their toes for the start. The sole stone seat on the northern side of the stadium was reserved for the priestess of Demeter, the only woman allowed to see the games (remember, competition was conducted in the nude). Beyond the stadium flows the Alpheus river, said to flow underground all the way to Sicily and fabled to have helped Hercules clean the Augean stables.

Perhaps Greece's best museum outside of the national archeological museum in Athens, the gleaming modern **New Museum** is across the street from the site and really brings the place to life. On the right as you enter, for example, are stones with highly evocative inscriptions (be sure to read the captions). One bids farewell to a boxer who died while sparring, after pledging himself to victory or death; another is a 315 lb. boulder which a competitor raised above his head with one hand (!). The Museum also has a fine model of the site as it probably looked in its prime. But the star attraction here is the famous **statue of Hermes** attributed to the fourth-century B.C. sculptor Prax-iteles. The statue originally stood in the interior of the Temple of Hera and was protected by mudbrick walls; when the sanctuary was flooded, the master-piece was comfortably buried in the mud. In another gallery, the life-like messenger playing babysitter to Dionysus without losing a shred of his dignity is one of the greatest masterpieces to survive the classical period.

The site is open Mon.-Sat. 7:30am-7:30pm, Sun. 8am-6pm; admission 100dr, 50dr for students. The New Museum has the same admission prices and hours, except for Tues., when it is open noon-6pm. Olympia is one of the most touristed sites in the Peloponnese—try to arrive by 7:30am to enjoy an hour's peace before the tour groups arrive. In the town, drop in at the **Museum of the Olympic Games,** open Mon.-Sat. 8am-2:30pm, Sun. 9am-1:15pm; admission 100dr. This houses lots of medals, stamps, and paraphernalia commemorating the modern games.

Arcadia (Central Peloponnese)

When the modern Greek republic redrew its internal boundaries Arcadia received a long stretch of badly needed coastline. Not that it has ever suffered from the ring of mountains that almost lock it into the Central Peloponnese. On the contrary, the two main plateaus where the Arcadians have dwelt receive fertile mountain run-off, the magic soil that has enabled these pastoral peoples to prosper. But the mountains or the plains or the near-isolation or maybe even the prosperity once produced a people with unusual and bizarre beliefs. Zeus, they say, was not only born here, but suckled by an Arcadian goat. He then sired Arcas (for whom Arcadia was named) by a figure named Callisto, whose father Lycaeon chopped Arcas into bite-sized pieces and served him to Zeus for dinner—just to see if he would notice. As observant as Lycaeon was demented, Zeus turned the murderer into a wolf and gave Arcas new life. In the form of a bear, the grown Arcas one day chased his mother to Zeus's holy precinct atop Mt. Lycaeon (just west of Andritsena), where he raped her repeatedly. Zeus afterwards turned them both into constellations. It is thus not surprising that Pan, that licentious, part-human part-goatish deity, was an Arcadian god.

The Arcas story explains the swift execution of any who crossed the thresh-hold of the sacred spot on Mt. Lycaeon, accidental offenders incurring not the usual penalty of stoning but rather the more suspenseful one of unexpected slaughter within a year's time. The same mountain site was used for human sacrifice; whoever ate any part of the victim became, like Arcas's grandfather, a wolf, condemned to roaming the region in lonely hunger. One Arcadian ritual, however, deserves a renaissance, especially on the coast. At Aliphera, also near Andritsena, residents sacrificed to the minor god Myiagros, who supposedly drove all flies from the area in return. Not a bad trade at all, especially since the sacrifice wasn't human. These days, butchers, were-wolves, and cannibals aren't all that common in Arcadia, so don't come ex-pecting the like. But journeying west from the capital **Tripolis** through the

surrounding fruited plains of **Tegea** and **Mantinea** and out to the more mountainous areas of **Lagadia** and **Dimitsana, Megalopolis** (actually in a plain of its
own) and **Andritsena**, you'll get a rewarding eyeful of the untouristed land with
the multi-faceted myths.

Tripolis

With plenty of spacious squares and a lush, almost tropical park, Tripolis
isn't a bad place to spend time. A town with four bus stations, it's the transportation hub for those trying to reach one corner of the Peloponnese from
another. If you come at Easter, your visit will coincide with its celebrated
festival, and if archeology interests you, the remains of three ancient cities—
Tegea, Mantinea, and Orchomenos—are all nearby. Tripolis itself, though,
dates only to 1467, after which the Turkish pashas ruled the Peloponnese from
here. One of them, Ibrahim Pasha, destroyed the town in 1825 after Greeks,
who held it briefly, slaughtered the Turks living in it.

Practical Information

Buses are the first order of business in Tripolis. The main station, in the
square dominated by the Arcadia Hotel, sends nine buses daily to Argos
(140dr), Corinth (260dr), and Athens (450dr). Each bus stops at all three cities
and additional express buses run directly to Athens twice each day. Only one
bus a week (on Tuesday) runs to Patras (445dr), leaving at 6:45am from the
main station. The main station also sends buses daily to six other cities: to
Andritsena twice daily (200dr), to Megalopolis eight times a day (85dr), to
Dimitsana twice daily (165dr), to Olympia (310dr) and to Pirgos (360dr) three
times a day, and to Kalamata once a day (220dr). (There are more buses to
Kalamata from another station; see below.)

If your destination is Sparta, or points accessible from Sparta, you must
leave the main station and turn left on Vas. Olgas St. You'll very soon see a
sign on your right—"**Stathmos Lakonias**"—below which is the cafe/ticket
office/departure point for buses to Sparta. Buses leave four times a day
(100dr). For buses to Areopolis, Gythion, and Monemvassia, inquire at the
cafe if any buses to Sparta will go on directly or where and when you have to
change.

For buses to Kalamata and other points in Messenia, leave the main station,
cross the square, and take Georgion St. (just to the left of the Arcadia Hotel)
past the Hotel Alex until you reach an even larger square, Plateia Georgion.
On the opposite side in the left corner, the Stavropoulos Cafe dispatches buses
to Messenia. Buses to Kalamata (205dr) leave nine times a day. Buses to
Kiparissia (240dr) and to Pylos (325dr) leave twice daily. One bus leaves for
modern Messini (210dr) and for Koroni (325dr). For Petalidio (270dr) change at
Kalamata. For points in Messenia other than Kalamata, go to Kalamata and
then take a bus from there.

Finally, for buses to Tegea and Mantinea, and usually Orchomenos, go from
the Plateia Georgion onto Konstantinou IB St. The first square, Theod. Pet-
rinou Sq., is where you can catch local buses which shouldn't cost more than
30 or 35dr. Buses to Tegea leave every hour on the half hour and return hourly on
the half hour, while buses to Mantinea leave infrequently and irregularly.
Check at the cafe on the far side of the square or with one of the conductors.

If you can find your way from one bus station to another, the rest of the town
will fall to rather neatly. (Maps of Tripolis do exist but for some reason they
can only be bought in Kalamata.) In the Plateia Georgion, dominated by the
Church of St. Basil, you'll find a **bank** to change your money (open Mon.-Fri.
8am-2pm), the **Tourist Police** (not very helpful), **English newspaper** stores,

plenty of cafes, and a restaurant. For the **Post Office** (open 7:30am-2:30pm, poste restante till 4pm), cross the square, take Vas. Pavlou St., and turn right onto Io. Metaxa St. (called Nikitara St. by locals). If you follow Ouasikton St., you'll come to a large open air **market,** open every morning. The **OTE** is located a short distance away from the Plateia Georgion on Konstantinou IB St. If you follow Konstantinou IB St. farther down you'll come to several large squares and a beautifully verdant park. The **telephone code** for Tripolis is 071.

At 26 Georgion St., near the main bus station, is the centrally located **Hotel Alex** (tel. 22 34 65), with singles for 650dr and doubles for 950dr, showers 50dr extra. Right across the street is a flophouse, the **Averof** (tel. 22 21 35), which has doubles for 600dr. Had it fleas or bugs we'd call it a fleabag; but the bathroom walls have scum. Fortunately, the beds are clean and the flopping old men, who by all odds have sleeping sickness, won't harm anyone. As you walk down Georgion St., just before you arrive at the Plateia Georgion, a street on your left will take you to the similarly scruffy **Hotel Byron** on Byronos St. There's no hot water and only one dark toilet for seven rooms, so it may not be worth it—singles 550dr, doubles 750dr, showers 70dr extra. **Hotel Neon** (tel. 22 28 43) behind the bus station (take a right off El. Venizelou St. onto Lagopati St.) has singles for 600dr and doubles for 850dr. Just off the main square, on Petropoulou St., is a refreshingly good restaurant, **To Kanake.** There's no outdoor seating, but the interior is unusually smart and clean, the service attentive, and the souvlaki and fries delicious.

Near Tripolis

For several hundred years before the birth of Christ, the cities of **Tegea** and **Mantinea** maintained a fierce rivalry. Some say it began over water; others trace it to the inevitable sparring caused by the rivalry of Sparta and Athens. Tegea, south of Tripolis, took Sparta's part, while Mantinea, to the north, sided with Athens, and though the two cities no longer exist, the rivalry still continues. Now, however, it is not their inhabitants but their ruins that compete; they vie for the prize of most interesting. The bus company believes Tegea to be the winner, since it sends three times as many buses there every day. If you can't get out to Mantinea, you're missing some well-constructed city walls standing smack in the middle of a plain—not in the usual position on top of a hill or mountain. Tegea has a bit more to offer than this, though. Your first stop there will be the **museum,** which contains marble thrones of honor from the Tegean theater, large sculpted heads of Herakles and Asclepios, dramatic friezes of lions, and sculpted remains of the Temple of Athena Alea. The museum is open Mon.-Sat. 8:30am-2:45pm, Sun. and holidays 9am-2pm, closed Tues.; admission 50dr, 30dr for students. Going left out of the museum, a 100m winding road takes you to the site of the **Temple of Athena Alea.** The base of the huge building remains almost fully intact, and though weather and vegetation have discolored the stones considerably, they remain their original imposing size. Huge slices of the columns litter the site, some on their side, others balancing precariously on a pile of rubble. Named for King Aleus, who founded Tegea in the ninth or eighth century B.C., the temple often gave refuge in ancient times to exiled Spartan leaders.

. If you leave the site and continue down the road to **Palaia Episkopi** (1 km), you'll realize why Atalanta, one of the swiftest runners in Greek mythology, hails from Tegea. This is the famous plain of Tegea, a flat, fertile stretch of land that makes perfect running territory. Today, irrigation and modern farming methods have rendered it even more productive, and your walk will take you through groves of pear, apple, and cherry trees. At the end of the road sits the site, where a church, tavernas, and chirping birds all share the park's tranquil shade. Following the signs that read "Palaio-Christianiki Psiphidota," you'll find a small building with many windows, through which you can see the sheltered and quite expansive ancient mosaic floor. Also in the park is a monument to Greek Olympic runners, the heirs of Atalanta. If you need more antiquities, venture to ancient **Orchomenos**, whose temples, theater, and acropolis preside over a magnificent view of Tegea.

Megalopolis

The small, modern town which currently bears the name Megalopolis (from the Greek, *megale polis,* or "large city") inherited its grandiose title from the ancient city whose ruins lie 1km to the north. The original Megalopolis sprang full grown from the brain of Epaminondas of Thebes, who hoped to appease the surrounding cities, all contending to be capital of the new confederation of Arcadia, by inventing a completely new city to fill the office. The northern cities welcomed the idea in the hope that Megalopolis would provide them with some insulation from the belligerent city-state of Sparta to the south. Megalopolis was built in 371-368 B.C., and was stocked with people borrowed from neighboring communities. At its height, the city had 200,000 inhabitants within walls 5km in circumference. But the plan, not surprisingly, was a tremendous failure, and after a century of desertion and treason by its reluctantly naturalized citizens, the city was finally destroyed in 223 B.C.

Excavations carried out in the 1890s unearthed a theater that was at one time the largest in ancient Greece, seating over 20,000 people in its 59 rows. Only the first six rows have been dug out, but you can easily detect the remainder in the rippled slope of the curved hillside. To appreciate the theater's original dimensions, you should gaze down at it from above. The theater lacks the imposing grandeur of the fully excavated and restored theater at Epidavros, and if you go with that comparison in mind, you are sure to be disappointed. But in its own more modest and pastoral way, it is quite as beautiful. Its shape is perfectly maintained and not the least of its charms is that few people believe their guidebooks and actually visit the site. To reach the theater, walk 1km north on Gortinias St., which runs beside the main square in the center of town, one block from the bus station. Continue straight out of town for ten minutes, then turn left at the sign for "Ancient Theater." The theater, invisible from the road, is just over the hill before you. You can enter directly from the right, but you'll get a more impressive first view by climbing the hill to the left. The site is open Mon.-Sat. 8am-3pm, Sun. and holidays 9am-3pm; admission free.

There's nothing else to do in Megalopolis, so it's best to visit the city as a daytrip. When you arrive, leave your luggage in the bus station, spend maybe two hours wandering to the site and around town, and then jump on the next bus out of town. Buses leave every couple of hours for Tripolis (last at 8:30pm); nine buses a day make the five-hour trip to Athens (530dr); and buses leave less frequently for Andritsena. The cheapest and most convenient accommodations are at the **Hotel Paris** (tel. 22 41 0), right next door to the bus station, where singles are 500dr, doubles 750dr, and showers an exorbitant 100dr. Since the tourist business is slow, you should try bargaining (offer about 550dr for a double). For a somewhat nicer place, leave the main square down the street by the bank; you'll see the sign for the **Hotel Achilleon**, 61 Sabatakaki (tel. 22 31 1). Singles are 500dr without shower and 600dr with, doubles 850dr without shower and 1200dr with. The **Post Office** is one block north from the square on Gortinias St. and is open Mon.-Fri. 7:30am-2:30pm. **OTE** telephones are in the same building (open Mon.-Fri. 7:30am-10pm). The **telephone code** for Megalopolis is 0791.

Andritsena

West of Megalopolis the road climbs into the mountains once again and passes the charming medieval village of **Karytena,** dramatically perched on a high slope with a breathtaking view over the ravine of the Alfios River. The medieval fortress overlooking the village from the top of the mountain exemplifies the thirteenth-century Frankish architecture. One and a half hours (and 115dr) west of Megalopolis, or two hours (and 200dr) east of Pirgos is Andritsena. Buses from Pirgos (leaving daily at 6am and 1pm) lurch across unsteady, often unpaved roads, and scramble up slopes towards this wonderful village, crouched impressively against the hillside. Andritsena is touched, but hardly affected by the handful of tourists who pass through here (most on their way to Vassae). Its three hotels and half-dozen taxis do not disturb the village's dusty, sleepy tranquility. Protected by its own remoteness, the inaccessibility of Vassae, and the unsteadiness of nearby roads, Andritsena is a good place for escaping tourists. Most of the townsmen hang out in the cafe next to the square, sipping coffee and taking life easy. To the east is a wonderful view of the surrounding mountains—on a clear day you can see towering snow-capped peaks. If the town, with its ramshackle mountainside houses, tends toward picturesque poverty, it may well come as a relief from the distinctly unpicturesque version found in many low-lying towns of the Peloponnese.

Infrequent bus connections usually force the carless to stay overnight in Andritsena. The first hotel you'll see is probably the **Vassae** (tel. 22 27 3) in the main square. Incredibly, it is as dingy as its appearance suggests—the rooms are grungy, the bathrooms are filthy, and there are no showers. Posted prices are 400dr for singles, 550dr for doubles (the owner will ask you for more, but you should be absolutely adamant—start by offering 50dr less). The **Hotel Theoxenia** (tel. 22 21 9), on the edge of town nearest Megalopolis, has very comfortable singles for 1600dr and doubles for 2650dr, but the slightest mention of the Hotel Vassae will send the prices plummeting—bargaining may get the price of a double down to 1000dr. Breakfast and another meal are supposed to be obligatory (and included in the price), but the proprietors are so desperate that you can virtually name your conditions and price. The plush B-class facilities are in a state of woeful disrepair, but if you've ever wanted a luxury hotel to yourself, here's your chance. Of a lower category, but actually nicer, the **Hotel Pan** (tel. 22 21 3), on the other end of town near the Shell station, has beautiful doubles with private bathrooms for 820dr. None of the local restaurants are very pleasant, but the best place for a coffee is the cafe next to the church, on the Megalopolis side of the main square. The **bank** and **post office** are near the Hotel Pan. Across the street is the cafe that doubles as the **bus station,** run by the friendly Mr. George Kostopoulos. Buses to Pirgos (change there for Olympia) and to Megalopolis leave twice daily. Hitchhiking is eminently absurd. **OTE** telephones are off the main street towards the Xenia. The **telephone code** for Andritsena is 0626.

Vassae

If you're in Andritsena, either you're lost or you've come to see the **Temple of Epicurus Apollo** at Vassae. From the town, the road snakes up along cliffs for about 14km. The Greeks picked a fitting place to worship the sun god—the temple is spectacularly set on a rocky plateau, surrounded for miles by mountains scored with ravines.

To get to Vassae (there is no bus), you must either hitch (the turn-off is just outside Andritsena on the road to Pirgos), or round up some people and take a taxi from Andritsena. Don't call them, they'll call you—the minute you step off the bus. The going rate round trip is 750dr per car (no matter how many people); with a little dickering between the half dozen drivers in the square you should be able to get it down to 550dr (look bored and let the word "autostop" fall from your lips a few times). Make it clear from the start that the rate is for the group; some may attempt to charge by the individual. Pay nothing until you are safely back in Andritsena. Ignore threats to abandon you or charge more if you take too long—they'll stay close to you until they get their money. You may wish to walk the fourteen kilometers back to town (it takes three and a half hours over the hills). Since vegetation is sparse and low, every point along the way affords an exhilarating view of distant mountains. Except for the occasional sound of a car, the road is remarkably still; on these lonesome slopes even sheep and donkeys are few and far between.

Dimitsana

If inaccessible mountain villages attract you, head west out of Tripolis for Dimitsana. Built into the slopes of a verdant, rugged mountain, completely remote from tourists and their transatlantic culture, Dimitsana oozes that indigenous culture you've been seeking. The older men congregate in one of the three cafes to play cards with macho flair, the women are never seen, and the children walk the hilly streets hand-in-hand, shouting songs. The donkeys plod under balanced loads of firewood and the roosters tamely march about like overgrown pigeons. There's even a town weaver (whose immortal cloths sell for quite a pretty penny). But only hardy travelers will enjoy a lengthy sojourn. The combination of boredom and climate—the altitude chills the air even at midday, and the near daily cloud cover often gives the town a cold shower—will sooner or later send you on your way.

After a ride through rising mountains interspersed with unusually fertile plateaus, you'll reach a group of peaks covered with towering pines; just beyond these lies Dimitsana. The bus will drop you off in front of a cafe next to the **Post Office.** To the left is the Plateia Pesonton, under which is the only eatery, the **Vlahos restaurant,** which is surprisingly inexpensive. If you continue up Labardopoulou St., the main road, and turn left onto Nikolaou Makris St., you'll come to the helpful **police** (tel. 31 20 5), open 24 hours every day. Further up on the right, behind a marble memorial, the immaculate **Xenodohio Ipnou** offers the only cheap lodgings (beds 470dr). Unfortunately its five beds (three in one room, two in another) are all you have to choose from, unless you want to pay the nearby **Hotel Dimitsana** (tel.31 51 8) 860dr for a single or 1160dr for a double. At the top of the hill, also on the right, are the **museum** and the **library.** Because so few distractions interrupt a Dimitsanian pupil's thought, the town has been a center of education over the last three hundred years, and these two institutions memorialize its scholarly achievements. Returning to the main road and continuing, you'll reach the OTE (open Mon.-Fri. 7:30am-3pm) at 402 Labardopoulou St., and just past it the **bank** at #406 (open Mon.-Fri. 8am-2pm). Further down toward the Hotel Dimitsana on the right is the weaver's shop, complete with strung looms and warm colors. Two buses daily leave Tripolis for the two-hour ride to Dimitsana; two buses daily leave Dimitsana for Olympia (185dr, 2½ hours), and one a day leaves Dimitsana for Tripolis. On the way to Olympia, you'll pass through the smaller town of **Lagadia,** which like Dimitsana looks out over a ravine created by plunging mountainsides.

Messenia

The westernmost of the Peloponnese's four peninsulas is rarely visited by Americans, though local residents and a handful of Europeans have long appreciated its charms. The interior of Messenia, like the rest of the Peloponnese, is mountainous and largely unsettled. Its irregular and rocky coastline is dotted with small towns, and the parts of it accessible by foot offer some of the most beautiful (and deserted) beaches around.

During the fourth and third centuries B.C., the Spartans dominated Messenia until there was nothing left to dominate. The Messenians moved to the greener pastures of Messenia in Italy, and Sparta repopulated the area with their own version of slaves ("Helots"). Today, most people congregate around the large and ugly town of **Kalamata**, or around **Pylos**, which acts as a base for visiting Nestor's Palace to the north (near Hora) and the coastal villages to the south. But you'll leave those crowds behind if you plunge further south, where you'll find three particularly lovely spots. The twin cities of **Methoni** and **Koroni**, known in medieval times as the "two eyes of Venice," are each guarded by their own Venetian fortresses and graceful sandy beaches. Sandwiched between them is the secluded village of **Finikous**.

Pylos

Although a small and picturesque port famous since antiquity, Pylos now feels like an island town—it's expensive and thickly touristed. Geographically, Pylos has always been protected from the open sea (if not the open season for tourists) by the long, thin, uninhabited island of Sfakteria. Also known as Navarino, the town is best remembered for the battle of the same name in 1827, when the allied forces of England, Russia, and France tried to bring peace to warring Turks and Greeks. The Turks resented the intrusion, a shot rang out from no one knows where, and a blood bath ensued. When the smoke cleared, the allies had an unexpected and somewhat awkward victory and Greece was considerably closer to independence.

Flanked on either side by medieval fortresses that guard the Bay, the town beach is tiny and, moreover, stained with tar (the result of the 1980 oil spill is still visible on rocks and on the bottoms of many fishing boats). If you arrive in Pylos in the afternoon during the high season, you'll find hardly a room in town available, which might force you to go (where you should go anyway) 12km south to the emptier beaches and lower prices of beautiful Methoni. Pylos is, however, a good base for making the trip to Nestor's Palace (see Near Pylos section), and if you do stay, you can drink in the heady aroma of the *daphriis* on Kalamatis Street.

Practical Information

Buses arrive in Pylos at the main square on the waterfront. Buses to Kalamata leave nine times a day (125dr), and make the 3½ hour trek from Pylos to Pirgos four times a day with buses that leave for Kiparissia (150dr), Nestor's Palace (40dr) and Hora (50dr). To continue to Pirgos, change at Kiparissia, where at least two buses a day further the journey. One bus daily leaves for Tripolis (355dr), continuing to Athens (800dr). Buses for Methoni and Finikous leave four times a day (25dr). From Finikous to Koroni there is no direct bus: walk, hitch, or take a taxi all the way to Koroni or, if not, to Yamia, where bus service to Koroni begins.

Pylos has no Tourist Police, but the regular **police** are on the lefthand side of the harbor as you face the water. The **Post Office** (open Mon.-Fri. 7:30am-

2:30pm) is up Nileos St. on the left. To get to the **OTE,** go up Filellinon St. on the left side of the harbor, take the second left, and walk one block. The **telephone code** for Pylos is 0723.

If you walk past the police station and turn left along the water, you'll come to the green **Hotel Navarino** (tel. 22 29 1). Doubles here are 700dr, singles 510dr; showers are on the second floor, and a good restaurant is right next door. The **Hotel Trion Navarkon** (tel. 22 20 6) is right on the main square near the bus station; look for the sign that says "Hotel Ipnou." Same prices as the Navarino, the rooms are noisier, but the proprietor is friendlier. Nicer and quieter is the **Astir Hotel** (tel. 22 20 4), with the same prices, up the hill from the right-hand side of the harbor as you face the water. You will also see several rooms to let signs near the Astir that have doubles for 650dr. In low season these places are forbidden to operate, so you should be able to knock off 150dr. People also camp on the wooded hill across from the expensive Castle Hotel, apparently without any trouble from the town police.

Near Pylos

The *Odyssey* vaguely mentions that the Palace of Nestor (Odysseus' old friend whom Telemachus goes to consult) is somewhere in the southwestern corner of the Peloponnese; to make matters worse, Homer also describes three places called Pylos. However, archeologists are confident that their excavations 4km south of Hora have actually uncovered the real thing, **Nestor's Palace.** Evidence indicates that the palace was built in the late Mycenean period (1300 B.C.) and, after a short term of use, was destroyed about 1200 B.C. All the rooms are clearly marked—and everything, incidentally, is shaded by a large roof—but don't miss the guard towers, the *megaron* (the throne and hearth room), the bathroom, and the stairway leading up to the second story. It does take a bit of imagination on the part of the modern visitor to envision the present ruins in their former glory, and the watercolor reconstructions at the Hora museum provide much needed aid in this respect. But the site is of great interest archeologically and is impeccably excavated, almost sanitized. Fittingly, the bathroom is one of the best preserved items. There is a conspicuous absence of tourists at Nestor's Palace, a good view of the surrounding countryside, and a tholos tomb. The tomb, off to the edge of the site, is well-preserved and dates back to Mycenean times. The site is open Mon.-Sat. 9:15am-3:30pm, Sun. and holidays 9am-2pm; admission 50dr, 30dr for students. The tomb is free (although you shouldn't limit yourself to this cheaper feature).

A few kilometers from Nestor's Palace is **Hora,** a village whose fine archeological museum has a good collection of Mycenean art, principally artifacts found at the nearby Palace of Nestor (see above), including a whole case full of gold cups and chips, Linear-B tablets, fragments of frescoes from the palace walls, and, best of all, watercolor reconstructions of the artwork, which most Greek museums sorely lack. The museum is open Mon.-Sat. 9am-3:30pm, Sun. and holidays 10am-4:30pm, closed Tues. Admission is 50dr, 30dr for students. Buses between Pylos and points north stop at Hora; from the bus stop it is a short walk up Marinatou St. to the museum.

Buses go from Pirgos to Nestor's Palace (40dr) and to Hora (50dr) five times a day.

Further north, the town of **Marathopolis** offers miles of rocky beach, a couple of little pensions, and a superb chance to get away from other tourists. Near **Filiatra,** a beautiful eleventh-century church can be found in the town of **Hristiano.** In **Kiparissia,** a coastal town with its own mountain fortress, the train tracks come to an end and buses, after some reshuffling, continue north or south. A stop here, in fact, is almost inevitable, whichever direction you're headed. The friendly, well-informed train station manager, Georgios Constantopoulos, can provide you with a double for 350dr. There is also wonderful camping here, if cheap pensions don't thrill you. Four buses a day run to Kiparissia from Pylos (150dr), or from Pirgos to Kiparissia (150dr).

Methoni

Methoni is a jewel of a town set into the coast and stunningly appointed with a huge and majestic fortress and a long, sandy, uncrowded beach. Whether or not Cervantes was here, you can see why Agamemnon offered this priceless treasure to Achilles as a gift to placate the warrior's rage.

The town's two main streets form a Y at the billiard hall where the buses stop (ask inside for bus information). Shops are on the upper fork to the right, the beach and fortress down to the left. Above both is an intricate network of narrow streets where the townspeople live. Flowers overflow from porches, windows, and garden walls everywhere, and the area is worth exploring. Despite the signs in English, Methoni is characterized much more powerfully by its locals than its foreign visitors; if you want even more solitude, head further south to Finikous (buses run four times a day).

As you walk towards the beach, you'll pass on your left an unlikely combination of Elbyn gas station and National Bank of Greece. Despite the oil cans in the office, they'll change your travelers checks from 7am-9pm every day (though they close for lunch around 1-2pm). Almost next door is the **Post Office** (open Mon.-Fri. 7:30am-2:30pm) and the **OTE** telephones (open Mon.-Fri. 7:30am-3pm). On the other side of the street is a very friendly young man who plays excellent music on his stereo and rents bicycles at exorbitant prices (150dr for an hour, 350dr for a half day, 700dr for a day). Next door is a pint-sized outdoor movie house, a drive-in with chairs instead of cars. If you follow this street almost all the way to the end, you'll see a large, beautiful garden with banana trees on the right. Here, **Dionysus N. Psilolihnos** (tel. 31 31 7) rents good doubles for 600dr and triples for 800dr (no bath, no singles). The surrounding streets are absolutely jammed with rooms to let places at similar prices. The cheapest place to stay in town is halfway down the upper road from the cafe on the left, amidst a number of shops. It is run jointly with the restaurant **I Kali Kardya** ("the Good Heart"); go into the restaurant to get a room. Rates are about 250dr for singles, 450dr for doubles. The old man will probably be offended if you don't also eat in his restaurant, so give it a try—it's a good deal. Near the beach is the **Hotel Galini** (tel. 31 46 7), which asks 756dr for singles, 1080dr for doubles, and 1300dr for triples, but will bargain. The **Hotel Iladision** (tel. 31 22 5), has beautiful rooms next to the fortress moat and is located about two blocks from the beach. Singles are 490dr, doubles 710dr, triples 980dr; showers 70dr extra.

The **telephone code** for Methoni is 0723.

Sights

Even if you are totally disenchanted with Venetian fortresses (after all, they're all over Greece and most are nothing but broken walls), you will be happy to spend an hour wandering around this radiantly photogenic mini-city, as large as the village of Methoni and studded with treasures.

Wait until the sky is cloudless, then cross over the moat bridge and turn left. You will soon come to a huge clearing; here you can climb up onto the wall and walk along the outside of the stronghold. The walls look magnificently out upon the sea; when you're half way around the circumference, you come to a small, perfectly preserved town sitting on the sea on its own tiny island. Walk out and clamber up the stairs at its center. Come back, and continue the circuit. In the midst of the fortress is a vast field, peppered with underground chambers and mysterious cellars. There is also at its heart a simple, exquisite church: at one end, the stucco is painted blue like the sea, and a simple cross hangs against it. The fortress is free and open Mon.-Sat. 8:30am-7pm, Sun. 10am-4:30pm.

Finikous (Finikunda)

Halfway between Methoni and Koroni is the less impressive, but more secluded village Finikous and a beach that rivals any in southern Messenia. Finikous (also known as Finikunda), set on a beautiful, tranquil cove, is accessible only by dirt road, and is a teeming metropolis of less than 600 people. Beyond the rock jetty to the east is a more deserted cove backed by cliffs. Since the oil from the Pylos spill did not make it around the corner of the peninsula, the water here is still transparent. Because there is no dock to speak of, the sponge fishermen bring their boats right up to the beach. If you like to swim and sit in cafes on the beach, you'll probably want to stay here a week—if you don't you should be warned that that's all there is to do, and bring plenty of drachmas, since there is no bank.

Most of the restaurants either rent rooms or know of people who do, but they are invariably overpriced (doubles 800dr), as are most places on the water. As you walk east on the street along the beach, at #38 you will see a place with a green gate, a garden, and cardboard sign that says "English spoken" (absolutely false). If you bargain, the old man will let you have a double room for 500dr, including a cold shower. Places on streets away from the water have similar prices. The whitewashed **Sophia Tsoni** at the eastern end of the beach (the last house) has very nice doubles overlooking the sea for 700dr, including shower. Of course, the beach, Greece's universal hotel, is just over the hill.

The best way to get to Finikous is from Methoni, where buses depart four times daily (last one at 6:45pm). Leaving Finikous is more difficult. Two buses run daily to Methoni (7am and 3pm). There's no bus to Koroni so you have to hitch, walk, or take a taxi to Yamia and take a bus from there.

Koroni

Koroni is a seductive little town by the sea, blessed with small clean houses, narrow streets, and steep white staircases climbing the hills behind the waterfront. The entire town is dramatically overlooked by a majestic, medieval Venetian fortress which leads down to a long crescent of pebbled beach, and affords depthless views of the emerald sea. European and Greek tourists congregate here, but Koroni still seems unperturbed by the influx of foreigners.

Buses travel to and from Kalamata (two hours, 125dr) up to nine times a day, stopping at the small main square near the church (since there's no official KTEL depot, ask at any cafe around the square for departure times). In the same square, you'll find the **Post Office** (open Mon.-Fri. 7:30am-2:30pm) and a **bank** (open Mon.-Fri. 8am-2pm). Just off the square, the town's least expensive hotel, the **Diana** (tel. 22 31 2) has singles for 550dr, doubles for 750dr, and triples for 1134dr (all including shower). Bargaining can be productive here. The **Parthenon Restaurant** opposite the Diana also has rooms overlooking the sea with private bath for 700dr. There are several less expensive rooms in the streets further away from the water. If you are coming from Harokopi, you will see one just at the edge of town that has doubles for 600dr or less if tourists are scarce. Most of the restaurants on the water are overpriced; the **Parthenon,** however, offers a large and very tasty Greek salad for only 40dr, and other dishes from fresh fish and lobster to more common Greek specialties, at very reasonable prices. You can also follow the street that leads to the little beach on the far left-hand side of the harbor (as you face the water); at the end of the street is an eatery with reasonable prices, huge portions, and great pork chops. They serve homemade red wine at 65dr a liter that tastes a little like retsina.

Aside from the spectacular view of the rocky coastline, the fortress has several underground rooms that are worth exploring. For this you are going to need the help of one of the locals, as they are hard to find. Especially worth seeing is the huge room with a pillar to which the Turks used to chain their prisoners. To get to the fort, walk along the waterfront until it ends in a small plaza, just before the pier. Walk down Ang. Kambyses St. (at the bottom right-hand corner of the square as you face the water) for one block, then turn left and follow the street up a long staircase to the stronghold. In the evenings, sit on the pier and watch the gliding fishing boats use bright gas lamps to stun fish, which they then spear with long tridents.

Kalamata

A large, dirty port with too many video jockeys, pizza parlors, and neon lights, Kalamata has one redeeming feature—a large, bright square which at midday will let you know you're close to the equator. With such beautiful places as Mystra to the north, Methoni and Koroni to the west, and Mani to the southeast, there's little reason to stay in Kalamata, though it's almost impossible not to pass through (five highways converge at this point). Fortunately, you'll probably not have to stay here very long.

Practical Information

Flights leave daily for Athens. Buses for Athens (660dr), which stop at Megalopolis (135dr), Tripolis (225dr), Argos (345dr), and Corinth (475dr) leave eight times a day. For Pylos (125dr) buses depart ten times a day. If Koroni's seclusion is what you're after, buses leave nine times a day, four times on Sunday (125dr). Two buses leave daily for Sparta (160dr) and for Patras (550dr). For the trips to Patras and Athens, round-trip fares are 900dr and 1170dr respectively. To get to Areopolis, take the twice-daily bus to Itilo (185dr), and then make the speedy connection to Areopolis (another 30dr). There's also an evening bus to Itilo with no connection; you'll have to spend the night. Trains also leave Kalamata five times daily for Athens (535dr) with stops at Argos (320dr), Corinth (405dr), and Piraeus (535dr). Trains leave three times a day for Patras (375dr) and from there to Athens. To get to the train station, go down Aristomenous St. (see below) toward the water, turn right on Frantzi St. at the end of the square, and walk a few blocks.

Unfortunately, too, Kalamata is rather large; the bus station and slightly tawdry area nearby are 3km away from the beach located in another slightly tawdry area. When exiting the bus station, turn right, then immediately left across the bridge to Plateia 23 Martiou. The first street on your right is the main drag, Aristomenous St., which leads in about four blocks to the central Plateia Georgion, site of most of the city's amenities. You can buy English newspapers at the corner of Aristomenous and Plateia 23 Martiou. **Liberopoulos bookseller,** 2 Aristomenous St., sells a map (75dr) that has the whole Peloponnese in detail on one side and maps of Kalamata, Nafplion, Corinth, Tripolis, Sparta, Patras, Epidavros, Olympia, Mycenae, Tiryns, and Old Corinth on the other.

Around the outstretched rectangle of Plateia Georgion you'll find all that you need. At its northern (bus station) end is the **National Bank.** Opposite are the **OTE** telephones (open 24 hours every day). From the southern end of the square, a right onto Iatropolou Street brings you to the **Post Office** (open Mon.-Fri. 7:30am-2:30pm). South of the main square on Aristomenous Street are the **Tourist Police** at #46 (tel. 23 18 7). On the second floor, they're open every day 8am-10pm.

At the other end of town on the waterfront is an extremely helpful **Tourist Information Center** (open daily 8:30am-1:30pm and 5:30-8pm), next to the Valassis Hotel. They will try to help you as much as possible, and can reserve hotel rooms anywhere in Messinia. Nearby is a bike rental place that seems absurdly expensive (1300dr for a single day on a Vespa). The beachfront is somewhat depressing, and the sand itself crowded and grubby, although it improves the farther east you walk.

Accommodations and Food

If you're only spending a night here, it's probably best to stay in one of the many cheap hotels around Aristomenous near the bus station. Clean, classy, and cheap, the **Vasilikon** (tel. 22 70 3) is at the second left off Aristomenous—singles 470dr, doubles 630dr, triples 910dr; showers 70dr extra. The **Hotel Acropolis** (tel. 22 04 2) has slightly higher prices and is located at the third right off Aristomenous. In emergencies try the buggy **Hotel Gallia** (tel. 23 02 9) facing you on the first left off Aristomenous. It has the same prices as the Vasilikon, though it's a quarter of the value. Across the dry riverbed from the bus station is the well-stocked **Houliara** restaurant. While in Kalamata be sure to sample the figs and the olives, its two major products.

If you want not just to endure, but to enjoy Kalamata, take bus #1 from Plateia 23 Martiou to the waterfront (buses leave every 10 minutes and cost 20dr), and get off as soon as the bus begins traveling next to the sea (ask the conductor for Faron St.). There are several inexpensive pensions on somewhat rundown Santa Rosa St., parallel to the water and one block in. Try one of the following:

Hotel Nevada, 9 Santa Rosa St. (tel. 28 02 9). Friendly, cheap, and clean, it even has a kitchen. Doubles 756dr.

Avra, 10 Santa Rosa (tel. 82 75 9), across the street, charges 800dr for doubles and 1200dr for triples; showers 50dr extra.

Hotel Elpis, 202 Faron St. (tel. 26 05 0), around the corner, has similar prices and rooms.

Camping: 2km east along the water. Take the #1 bus to the end and walk two blocks (150dr per person, 150dr per tent). Other, nicer campgrounds are found on the beach even farther to the east. For these, walk or take #1 special buses marked "Motel Philoxenia," which run every half hour until 11:30pm.

Near Kalamata

The road from Koroni to Kalamata hugs the eastern coast of the Messenian peninsula. Between Harokopi and the very pleasant coastal town of **Petalidio** is a long string of sandy beaches. Petalidio itself features a good campground and one of the best beaches in Messenia.

If you're hungry for more antiquities, take the bus to **Mavrommati** (twice daily, no bus Sunday), where you'll find the well-preserved remains of ancient Messene (not the same as modern Messini) on Mt. Ithomi. The ancient Messenians continually fought off Spartan incursions into the area and succeeded as long as they controlled the acropolis (Mt. Ithomi). The most striking part of the site is the fourth-century B.C. **walls,** which epitomize the period's defensive architecture. An **agora,** a **theater,** and a **temple to Artemis** also remain. If you continue up the road, you'll come to the fallen doorpost of the monstrous **Arcadian gate,** designed by Epaminondas, the architect of the city of Megalopolis to the north. Also nearby is the sixteenth-century **Monastery of the Voulcanos,** containing some outstanding frescoes. The Doric columns at the foundations of the church indicate that the structure rests upon the ruins of Ithomi, an ancient sanctuary dedicated to Zeus. The only difficulty with the trip is timing. The bus takes you to the site (look for the sign at the end of the village of Mavrommati), continues up to the hamlet of Petralona and then returns past the site to Kalamata. If you get off and look at the site while the bus is in Petralona, you'll have about fifteen minutes of exploration time before the bus picks you up. The alternative is to catch the morning bus out there and return on the post-Petralona leg of the afternoon bus. Hitching on these deserted roads is very difficult.

From Kalamata to Areopolis

Just south of Kalamata, the bus to Areopolis winds through the spectacular and surprisingly lush Taygetos mountains, which soar to 7,900 feet at their highest point. There's really no place to get off; just sit back and enjoy the view. The first major stop comes at the enchanting coastal village of **Kardamili.** One glimpse of the somber stone houses, the elegant spire of the church of St. Spyridon, the sparkling waterfront overlooking a tiny wooded island, and you will surely fall in love with this place. There are a few rooms to let and the restaurant on the beach serves good, cheap food. There is one good hotel, the **Dioscouri** (tel. 73 49 7). Nearby are several secluded caves with pebble beaches and excellent swimming. About 5km to the south is the secluded village of **Agio Nikolaos,** which also has rooms to rent (the beaches here are not as nice as those in Kardamili) and one hotel, the **Mani** (tel. 94 23 8), with singles for 400dr, doubles for 600dr, and triples for 750dr. If you have a car or are up to hitching, the four little villages of Platsa, Nomitsis, Thalomes, and Lagada south of here all have great little Byzantine churches with fine frescoes and carvings. Hitching down the coastal road is quite good in tourist season.

If you're bound for Areopolis, change buses in the village of **Itilo** immediately upon arrival—the bus leaves promptly. If you are seeking solitude, this is the place, but be warned that the pension just off the main square (#69, with the blue shutters) will try to extort 800dr for a double. Bargain hard and indicate that you're prepared to camp out. The town itself is a study in stone: the beautiful stone houses, the medieval fortress on the neighboring hill, and the brilliant frescoes in the Monastery of Dekoulou reflect a variety of architectural styles. The entertainment quarter consists of two cafes off the little square, and a restaurant where you can enjoy an inexpensive meal if you don't mind being stared at by the villagers. To camp or swim, take a 3km hike down to the sandy beach next to the tiny village of Neon Itilon, or New Itilo. The beach is set on an idyllic cove which cuts so deeply into the coast that it could almost be mistaken for a lake. From New Itilo the road continues to wind along the Gulf of Messenia to the old harbor of Areopolis, Limeni. The tiny port features the **Castle of Potrombei** and a very lovely beach. For information on **Areopolis,** see Laconia section.

Laconia

Ever wonder where the word "laconic" comes from? You won't need the impetus of unsatisfied curiosity to figure it out. In the tenth century B.C., a tribe of Dorians from the north invaded the southwest Peloponnese and drove out its Mycenean inhabitants. Famed mainly for slaughtering their enemies, the region's new masters also distinguished themselves by their style of speaking—cramming mountains of meaning into the tiniest speck of a phrase. While the northern orators argued in long, flowery sentences that were a drachma a dozen, Laconians often dispatched their opponents with a single, caustically witty phrase, like a rapier slicing a lit candle and leaving it seemingly intact. Thus, those antipathetic to prolix epideictica accordingly received the appellation of the people similarly disposed—in short, the reticent are "laconic."

Though time has considerably preserved the ancient Laconian qualities, it has devilishly scattered them in the oddest corners of the modern region. It's almost as if Zeus spun a balled-up mass of the old ways until it flew apart and each fragment of personality landed in a different place. With its symmetry, gleaming buildings, and arrow-straight main road, **Sparta** obviously received the neat precision of Laconian speech, though ironically the city used to be the center of the war machine and an elite ruling class. The piece containing immense, rugged strength landed in **Monemvassia,** that monstrous island rock that presides over the eastern coast. And while the strange island of **Kythira** got a share of Spartan elitism, the **Mani** ended up with a double dose of fierceness and belligerence—'nuff said. But for all its interests, Laconia attracts remarkably few tourists. Except for the Byzantine ruins at **Mystra** and the astonishing stalactite caves at **Pirgos Dirou,** it is the part of the Peloponnese to see if you want to escape the crowds without escaping the fun.

Sparta

The Spartans are always portrayed as the Bad Guys of the classical world—crude, severe, savage hawks always provoking and pestering the democratic doves of civilized Athens. Much of this reputation is well earned. Around 700 B.C., Sparta barely subdued a revolt of the Messenians, its subject neighbors, and so the leader Lycurgus instituted wide-ranging reforms that turned Sparta into a war machine. For the next three and a half centuries, it dominated the entire central Peloponnese with its invincible armies and primitively austere society. Needless to say, outside of war, it made no contribution to Greek culture—no philosophy, no poetry, no art, no architecture—and for hundreds of years remained exactly as it was in 700 B.C. Suspicious of Athenian expansion and jealous of Athenian success, Sparta attacked its rival to start the thirty-year Peloponnesian War and, after triumphing in 404 B.C., emerged the supreme military power in the Hellenic world. The Spartans relished their strength (they didn't even bother to build protective walls around their city) as much as they despised all forms of weakness (small or deformed children were left to die in nearby ravines). Although the city's decline was in part due to the temptations that always accompany the spoils of conquest, only the combined efforts of earthquakes, depopulation, and the united resistance of its neighbors broke Sparta's hegemony.

A young Spartan's training for the life of war began early—before speech, before birth, even before conception. Lycurgus believed that two fit parents produce stronger offspring, so he ordered all Spartan women to undergo rigorous physical training, just as the men did. He separated newlyweds, permitting only an occasional procreational tryst, on the grounds that the heightened desire of the parents would help produce more robust children. What's more, by a famous Lycurgean law the young wife of a tired old man could choose a suitable young male to service her and to provide the old man with healthy children by him.

If they survived the first few years, boys began a program of toughening practices. Remember that, though brutal by our standards, the regimen was foisted upon the young when they were too small to object, and they grew up accustomed to and wholly supportive of the system. The Spartans entrusted the education of their boys to a leading Spartan citizen—elsewhere in Greece only mild slaves taught—who often used whips to increase obedience. The young were forced to walk barefoot to toughen their feet and wore only a simple piece of clothing in winter and summer to inure them to drastic weather changes. Moreover, since fat foods were said to stunt growth, and delicacies to harm health, young Spartans ate the simplest foods, and these only sparingly. Why sparingly if the goal was a strong, healthy body? Hunger made them steal food, and theft developed the resourcefulness and survival skills that come in handy during a war. In fact, those who were caught received severe punishments—for ineptness rather than for theft.

After childhood, the routine intensified. Adolescence to the Spartans was the period of life most fraught with danger, when the young men required most guarding because of their vulnerability to new temptations. Forced to look down at the ground virtually every waking minute, the adolescents grew so modest that Xenophon wrote, "You would be more likely to hear a stone statue speak than them, more likely to catch a wandering glance from a bronze figure." Some fun. And in adulthood, too, much was forbidden. For example, a popular diversion of other Greek men, pederasty, was ruled off limits—the Spartan man had to leave the boys behind. Lycurgus also instituted competitions designed to make friends scuffle and beat one another so they wouldn't become soft, and he permitted men to drink only to quench thirst. In fact, Spartans were forbidden to sleep where they ate so that they welcomed sobriety, which let them walk home in the dark without stumbling drunkenly and cracking their heads open. Like drinking, the pursuit of wealth was roundly criticized, and thorough searches discouraged misers, capitalists, and their ilk. Only the aged had it easy. They didn't face as much physical abuse and were alone eligible for seats in the esteemed council of government. This latter fact Xenophon uses to conclude that the Spartans valued nobility of character above fitness of body. But could anything redeem a city that approved of long hair because it made the wearer look bigger and fiercer? Did you know certain apes do the same thing?

Fortunately, the prosperous and pleasant modern city of Sparta retains little resemblance to the mighty and fearsome warrior city-state that bore the same name. With its wide promenades, abundant parks, and spacious plazas, the town is indeed a pleasant place to visit; even the somber, craggy mountains that preside over the town only add to its beauty. However, ancient Sparta was less careful of its treasures than the other city-states, and almost no ruins remain. As Thucydides predicted, "Suppose the city of Sparta to be deserted and nothing left but the temples and the ground plan, distant ages would be very unwilling to believe that their power was equal to their fame." History has proved him right.

Orientation and Practical Information

To get to the main intersection in town, turn left out of the bus station and go left onto the broad main street, Palaeologou, until you reach Lykourgou St. At the intersection you'll find a **bank,** open Mon.-Fri. 8am-2pm. Follow Lykour-gou across Palaeologou, where it becomes Daphni, to reach the helpful **Tourist Police,** at 8 Hilonos St. (tel. 28 70 1), open every day 7am-1:30pm and Tues. and Thurs. also 6-8:30pm. If you go down Kleombrotou St., one block from Lykourgou and Palaeologou, you'll reach the OTE, open seven days a week 6am-midnight, and the **Post Office,** open Mon.-Fri. 7:30am-2:30pm. **Foreign periodicals** are at 54 Palaeologou and a **laundry** is at #81. The **telephone code** for Sparta is 0731.

The main **bus station** is on Brasidou St., off Palaeologou. Buses leave eight times a day for Athens (600dr), stopping at Argos (290dr) and Corinth (410dr). Buses leave four times a day for Tripolis (145dr, one hour). To get to Nafplion, go to Argos and change. To get to Patras, go to Corinth or Tripolis and change there. Buses leave the main station five times a day (115dr); for Kalamata twice a day (two hours; 85dr to Artemisia, where you change, and 60dr from Artemisia to Kalamata); for Areopolis three times a day (175dr); for Pirgos Dirou (205dr) and Gerolomin (250dr) twice a day; and for Monemvassia twice a day (260dr, with a change at Molaï). **Note:** if you get stuck in Molaï, there are two cheap hotels in the square up the hill from the bus station. **Hotel Gregory** (tel. 22 04 2) has singles for 389dr and doubles for 562dr; **Hotel Kentri-kon** (tel. 22 43 6) has singles for 486dr, doubles for 670dr, and triples for 810dr, with showers 80dr extra. Sparta is located 60km from both Tripolis and Kalamata, and if you enjoy beautiful bus rides, head for Kalamata. The bus crawls past deep gorges, huge mountains, and little settlements teetering on the edge of precipitous cliffs.

Another bus station, on the corner of Lykourgou and Agisilaos, handles buses to Mystra (25dr, fifteen minutes). The schedule is posted in a florist's window, the second door on the right down Agisilaos. Twelve buses leave Mon.-Fri. between 6:10am and 8:40pm, returning from Mystra fifteen minutes after they leave. On weekends, there are six buses a day 9am-8:40pm.

Accommodations and Food

To get to most of the budget hotels from the bus station, turn left onto Palaeologou and take the second right onto Lykourgou. Continue past the large square on your left. If you take a right on the side street marked "Mystra bus station," you'll see the **Hotel Sparti** on Agisilaos St. (tel. 28 59 1). The proprietors are unusually warm and good-natured, and charge 630dr for dou-bles, 750dr for triples, and 50dr extra for showers. No singles, but you can get a bed in a triple room for 350dr. If you continue up Lykourgou, you'll pass the **Hotel Anessis** (tel. 23 13 3), run by a kind woman who loves students. Singles 506dr, doubles 731dr, triples 900dr; showers 75dr extra. However, you might not want to stop until you reach the **Hotel Cyprus** (tel. 26 59 0), just off Lykourgou at 72 Loridou St. It offers very clean doubles for 610dr and triples for 800dr. The friendly manager, Mr. H. Starogionis, speaks English and will give you lots of information about Sparta. On Palaeologou St., just past Ly-kourgou, is the **Hotel Panellinion** (tel. 28 03 1), complete with indoor gardens and canaries. Doubles 787dr, triples 1012dr. Be warned that the rooms on Palaeologou are noisy. Five blocks in the other direction on Palaeologou (north) is the **Hotel Cecil** (tel. 24 98 0), with singles for 530dr, doubles for 780dr, and triples for 1060dr. Prices for all hotels are 100-150dr cheaper in the off-season. About 3km away on the road to Mystra is a **camping** area (Camping Mystra). To get there, take the regular Mystra bus and ask the conductor to let you off at the camping site.

Restaurants near the main square are outrageously expensive. You'll do better to walk down to Palaeologou Street and turn right. Alternatively, **E Kale Kardia** at 39 Agisilaos St., opposite the Hotel Sparti, is an interesting place with friendly service, generous portions, and acceptable prices. After dinner, go to one of the cafes around the main square to watch the promenade and pick-up.

Sights

By comparison with the other great cities of ancient Greece, little remains of ancient Sparta. Its austere and disciplined code of life scorned unnecessary luxuries of any sort, including superfluously elaborate buildings. Despite its enormously wide sphere of influence, the city itself was of such modest construction that it prompted Thucydides to remark "their city is not regularly built, and has no splendid temples or public buildings: it rather resembles a straggling village and would make a poor show." Hence the modern visitor is apt to be disappointed if he expects to find a southern counterpart to the Parthenon. The ruins consist of the outlines of an ancient theater and some fragments of the acropolis (1km from the main square at the northern edge of the modern city). Around the corner, at the end of Palaeologou St., stands a statue of the famous warrior **Leonidas.** A short walk east on the banks of the Eurotas River brings you to the sanctuary of **Orthia Artemis,** dedicated to the goddess Aphrodite. A gruesome ritual was conducted here, in which Spartan youths were called upon to prove their courage by unflinchingly enduring a public flogging. The local **museum** on Daphni St., which turns into Lykourgou on the other side of Palaeologou, is open Mon.-Fri. 8:30am-2:45pm, Sun. and holidays 9am-2pm, closed Tues. The 50dr admission will get you a look at pottery, masks, and mosaics, and the museum itself sits to one side of a beautiful park, with swaying palms and towering pines.

Mystra

About 6km west of Sparta is Mystra, an extraordinary site that some regard as the finest in Greece. It's an entire mined Byzantine city, staggered on three tiers along a steep hillside. The whole complex is a marvel. The frescoes in the **church of Perivleptos,** located in a pine grove, are perhaps the site's most stunning relic—every inch of the church is covered with paintings. Above the door you can see a fresco of Doubting Thomas and on the dome the figure of the Pantocrator. Also in the Lower Town is the **Metropolis,** now a museum, and the **Pantanassa,** whose buildings are still inhabited by nuns. Among the many frescoes inside, look for those of Jerusalem and Lazarus. In the Upper Town you can visit the **grand hall,** the **Palace of the Despots,** and the fine **church of Agia Sofia.** Finally, you should climb up to the **Kastro,** the fortress which was the first building in Mystra (as the town developed, its layers moved down the hill), built by William Villehardouin in 1249 A.D. The Castle commands an exceptional view of mountains on one side, thickly forested hills on another, and the Spartan plain on a third. The castle isn't quite as far as it looks—you can get there in about an hour if you walk directly up from the Main Gate. The site is open in summer Mon.-Sat. 9am-3:30pm, Sun. and holidays 10am-4:30pm; admission 100dr, 50dr for students. You can enter either by the Fortress Gate (higher up, it allows you to ascend to the Castle quickly, then saunter down) or the Main Gate (near the bottom of the hill and close to most of the interesting sights). Although tramping around the hillside in mid-summer can be murderously hot, men should at least carry a shirt, since respectful dress is sometimes requested in the nunnery and churches. Everyone should bring some fairly tough shoes since paths are rocky, and, like many Greek sites, Mystra makes much more sense if you bring a small guidebook. Even a cursory inspection of the site, including the long climb to the summit, requires at least three hours. On the bus from Sparta, don't get off until the last stop—

the site is about 1½km beyond the town of Mystra. For the schedule of buses back, it's best to ask at the **Xenia Restaurant,** next to the parking lot from which they leave. These buses sometimes depart ten minutes early, but they're fairly frequent throughout the day. The Xenia itself is predictably expensive, though you may not care if the site makes you desperately thirsty. You can also leave backpacks here—you certainly won't want to be dragging them up and down the hill.

Gythion

The capital of the Mani, Gythion is also the first major stop on the road from Sparta and one of the nicest port towns in the Peloponnese. Built on the side of a hill that descends into the Laconic Gulf, Gythion is laced by narrow, terraced streets, perfect for an afternoon of meandering about. The most picturesque part of the town is the harbor; the brightly colored cafes and shops reflect off the water, their images framed between graceful wooden fishing boats. But Gythion does have its funky side. In addition to its numerous retired sea dogs, this comely little port also seems to be a convention center for all the chic chicks, shaven-headed punks, muscular bikers, and mellow Bohemians who float around the Peloponnese. The streets are often lined with languid hipsters wearing peasant shirts and distant expressions. Best of all, although the frayed brigade is primarily German and French, everyone speaks a good-natured English.

Orientation

As you approach Gythion from Areopolis (forty minutes and 95dr by bus), you'll pass a turn-off for the tiny coastal town of Ageranos, and the nearby Temple of Aphrodite (about 5km out of Gythion). Closer still are a series of beautiful and often deserted swimming coves intermittently accessible from the cliffs above. Your first glimpse of the town itself will be a wooded island, seductively furnished with a lighthouse and a bright white church, linked to the mainland by a thin causeway. It was here, some say, that Paris wooed Helen and changed the destiny of a thousand ships and the entire ancient world. Passing the island, as the bus follows the water and turns a corner, you'll be deposited in a small main square. From here, the waterfront extends further, and then splits: one side curbs around a park, hugging the sea, while the other leads onto a triangular plaza. Off this plaza are the less touristed and cheaper shops of Gythion.

Practical Information

Boats from Gythion leave twice a week for Kythira and Crete at midnight on Mondays and 11pm on Thursdays, and once a week for Kythira, Neapolis, Monemvassia, and Athens on Fridays at 3pm. Deck fare is 216dr to Kythira (three hours), 372dr to Neapolis, 527dr to Monemvassia, 875dr to Crete (seven hours), and 1030dr to Athens. One boat a week leaves Crete for Gythion on Fridays at 8am, and one leaves Crete for Kythira, Neapolis, Elafonissos, Monemvassia, and Piraeus on Tuesdays at 8am. For up-to-date information on prices, times, and tickets, contact the very friendly and helpful **Theodore V. Rozakis Travel Agency** on the waterfront (tel. 22 22 9 or 22 20 7), open Mon.-Sat. 8:30am-1pm and 4-9pm.

Three buses a day leave for Athens (710dr), five for Sparta (115dr, change at Sparta for Tripolis), five for Areopolis (65dr), one for the caves at Pirgos Dirou (95dr), two for Gerolimin (135dr), two for Itilo (115dr), and at least two a day for Monemvassia. To reach Monemvassia, take an early bus to Tarapsa (50dr);

you'll be let off at a Mobil station in the middle of nowhere. Cross to the side of the road opposite the station, and a bus marked "Neapolis" will pick you up in about half an hour. This bus will take you to Molaï, where you'll change for Monemvassia after about an hour's wait. The trip from Tarapsa to Monemvassia costs 200dr and is a lot less complicated but a lot more tedious than it sounds.

The **police** are located on the waterfront, but they aren't very helpful. Walk along the harbor to the triangular plaza and you'll find various **banks** open Mon.-Fri. 8am-2pm. One block down Herakles St. is the friendly and efficient **OTE** office, open Mon.-Fri. 7:30am-10pm. Walk down another block on Herakles and turn left to find the **Post Office,** open Mon.-Fri. 7:30am-4pm, parcels until 2:30pm. To get to a beautifully preserved ancient theater, turn left off Herakles onto Ermou St., then take a right off Ermou onto Archaia Theatrou St. to the end. The **museum,** usually closed, is located in a small, pristine alley across from the Laryssion Hotel, which is on the other side of the triangular plaza. Just to the left of the triangle, on Basileus Pavlou St., is **Ladopoulou Books,** where you can buy English newspapers. There's also a small beach just past the triangle. The **telephone code** for Gythion is 0733.

Accommodations and Food

There are two surprisingly inexpensive hotels right on the waterfront near the Tourist Police. The **Kranai** (tel. 22 24 9) is the cheapest, with singles for 510dr, doubles for 700dr; showers 60dr extra. Although it's slightly seedy, there are plenty of rooms and a friendly proprietor who speaks excellent English. It's also used as a part-time bordello. Nearby is the more comfortable **Aktaion** (tel. 22 29 4), with 560dr singles, 900dr doubles, 1180dr triples, and showers 80dr extra—some of the rooms overlook the harbor. Near the causeway, and also on Izannibei Grigoraki (which runs up the hill from the bus station and then parallel to the waterfront) are lots of rooms to let, many with balconies overlooking the harbor. You shouldn't have to pay more than 400dr for a single or 550dr for a double (with shower). Avoid the temptation to camp out on the wooded island. Seedy characters frequent it at night. Try the base of the cliffs further south, or the very nice campground on the beach 6km south of town.

The restaurants along the waterfront, like the grocery stores around the main square, are absolutely exorbitant (the **Cork House,** just on the Areopolis side of the main square is your best bet). For provisions, you should walk to the triangular plaza, and bear left along Leoforos Basileos Georgiou (look for the British flag on the top of a building). You'll find lots of good supermarkets here. At #45, you'll see a small cafe with **Psetopoleion** written on it; here you can get Japanese as well as Greek food (170dr will get you Omoo Rice, an omelette stuffed with rice, herbs, and peppers). Just off the main square on Izannibei Grigoraki you can have *souvlaki* for dinner at the friendly **Kali Kardi.**

Veronica, next to the Hotel Panthean, will supply you with *Italiante* ice creams for 30dr per scoop and sundaes and splits for 130dr or more.

Mani

Most visitors to the Peloponnese head for the archeological sites and never make it as far south as Mani, the middle of three peninsulas in the southern coast. You'll be glad they don't; the savage beauty of this region has remained completely unspoiled. Tall, unbelievably barren mountains soar up in the interior; steep, rocky cliffs on the coast are punctuated by an occasional pebble beach. Life here is very hard; without the thousands of stone walls that crisscross the hills to prevent erosion, not a single olive tree could survive.

The harshness of the land answers for the ferocity of its people. Even today, Mani contributes a disproportionate number of men to the armed forces, including several generals. In ancient times, the Mani people tenaciously held out against domination by the Spartans and Romans; later, the Turks had to give up trying to conquer the region, allowing the people to pay a tax instead. In the Second World War even the Germans failed to subdue this proud and obstinate peninsula.

Most revealing of all is the area's bizarre history of family blood feuds which raged here from at least the ninth century B.C. until only thirty years ago! The spirit of the land and its people immediately recalls Homer's description of the land of the Cyclops: "These people have no institutions, no meetings for counsels, rather they make their habitations in caverns hollowed among the peaks of the high mountains, and each one is the land for his own wives and children, and cares nothing about the others." The landscape south of Areopolis is dotted with hundreds of medieval tower houses which families built to protect themselves from mortal enemies often no further than the tower next door. The height of the tower supposedly reflected the social status of the family who built it. As is often true in such cases, actual origins of the feuds were lost in the distant past. Conflicts were often sparked by disputes over land, since trespassing was considered an offense against family honor and grounds for murder. The offense committed was often either imagined or non-existent; several men of a family would ambush the leader of another family and kill him without warning. The obligation to avenge such a murder then passed on to the family of the victim. In this manner, feuds could continue for generations.

If this sounds terrifying, relax. The inhabitants have become considerably more docile in recent decades—tamed, perhaps, by the advent of television. But traveling in these parts is not without its feudal side. For one thing, there are no banks; the closest ones are in Gythion and Kalamata. Another problem is that sights are scattered and transportation is infrequent. Generally, any afternoon stop you make commits you to a night's stay. As usual, you can catch the bus anywhere along the way at signs marked *stassis*. However, there are no posted bus schedules—if you ask the authorities when the next bus leaves, you'll receive three different answers, probably all wrong. Play it safe, or take a chance, but be prepared to improvise. From Gerolimin, you will have to return the way you came; the road around to the eastern coast is a figment of the NTOG's imagination. To get to the east coast, there is one bus a day from Areopolis, stopping at the secluded beach towns of Kotronas, Soloteri, and Kiprianos. Inquire about rooms to rent or just sleep on the beach.

Areopolis

A small, quiet village on a rocky ledge above the coast, Areopolis has nothing in particular to recommend it, but it isn't a bad place to spend the night. In any case, if you're traveling by bus, you'll have little choice, since it is the transportation junction for the region. It's a two-hour trip from Kalamata to Itilo (185dr) and then twenty minutes and 30dr from there to Areopolis. Buses leave three times a day from Areopolis for Gythion (65dr). To get to the coves at Pirgos Dirou, take the bus at 11am (it's the only one), which returns at 1:30pm (30dr).

An inconspicuous pension in the main square where the bus stops has singles for 350dr, and doubles for 550dr, though they'll initially ask for much more. Two other places offer even cheaper accommodations. Follow Kapetan Matapan St. off the main square until you see the sign on the left-hand side. Singles 300dr, doubles 500dr. Or you can take the same street, turn right at the tiny stone church, and go to #28, marked "Rooms," which has the same prices. If you can't find rooms and don't mind losing an arm and a leg, find your way to the **Hotel Mani** (tel. 51 26 9), a comfortable and outrageously expensive C-class hotel that may change travelers checks if the bus station can't. Next door and just as steeply priced is the **Kapetanakos** guesthouse (tel. 51 23 3).

Areopolis has more restaurants and grocery stores than anywhere else in the Mani, but that's not saying much. Next to the bus station is a taverna with a cheap interior and food to match. For variety, the neighboring establishment sells filling pizzas and refreshing drinks. The **bank** in the main square remains closed almost continuously. If you need to change travelers checks, the bus station will oblige you with a great deal of difficulty. The little road beside the bank will take you to the **police,** but they aren't very well informed. Just off the main square, on Kapetan Matapan St., you'll find the **Post Office,** open Mon.-Fri. 7:30am-2:30pm, and the **OTE,** open Mon.-Fri. 8am-10pm, though opening hours are interpreted extremely liberally. To reach the heights over the sea, where billowy clouds rest on mountain tops and where you'll see the tower houses and town tower, goats, and donkeys, follow Kapetan Matapan St. off the main square until you reach Andreakou St., which leads to the cliffs.

Pirgos Dirou

Continuing south from Areopolis, you will soon reach the little village of Pirgos. Besides its proximity to the famous caves, the town is a pleasant place to spend the night. For the most reasonable accommodations, walk about 50m past the turn-off to the caves on the main road south to the green cafe **Ta Spillia** with a yellow "rooms to let" sign. Singles 350dr, doubles 500dr, including shower. The restaurant below is mediocre; try the place a few doors down back towards the center of town instead. The **Tourist Police** are at the turn-off to the caves.

The caves, known as Spillia Dirou or Pirgos Dirou, are one of the most splendid and remarkable attractions in Greece, but the process of seeing them is complicated and frustrating. Although the organization of the site is absolutely miserable, amazingly the caves are just wonderful enough to make most people exit with a smile of forgiveness.

Getting to them initially is a somewhat chancy business. If you don't constantly ask the people in the bus station as well as the conductor for the "spillia," you may be directed to get on the bus for Pirgos town, 4km away— hitch or walk from there. Usually, however, the bus will drop you off at the entrance. Since the caves are immensely popular and the little rowboats taking you around them only hold eight people, you should count on spending four or five hours at the site, although the trip itself only lasts fifty minutes. The caves are open May-Sept. daily 8am-7:10pm, Oct.-April daily 8am-2:30pm. If you get there in high season, you may have to wait. Fortunately, or perhaps unfortunately, a sign at the ticket booth alerts you to the approximate waiting time. If the tourists have invaded, don't come after 2pm—you won't get in. There's an **NTOG office** here (tel. 52 20 0), but they won't help you much. At the entrance to the site, you pay a 25dr entrance fee, which entitles you to use the beach nearby; you then buy a 230dr ticket, which entitles you to a spectacular boat ride through the caves with a dry land exploration to match. It's a bit expensive, but truly worthwhile. Another option is to buy a cheaper ticket for just the land exploration of the caves, though they're not always available. But the boat ride makes the exploration a hundred times more exciting. The serial number of your ticket is your entrance number, which will be called when it's time for you to enter. Ticket safely in hand, walk down the hill; turn left at the hairpin turn and you'll see the entrance to the caves ahead, next to the restaurant. On your right is a pleasant beach, where you can swim or sunbathe for a couple of hours until your number is called (there's also a small church where, presumably, you can pray that you don't miss your number). Be sure not to miss your number, however; exasperatingly, the numbers are called only in Greek and the men at the entrance will refuse to answer your questions. The place is usually crowded with bewildered and enraged customers not knowing what is going on.

Once inside, all your frustrations vanish. It's not just the quality but the quantity of the stalactite and stalagmite formations that takes your breath away. You climb into a small lifeboat with seven others, the ferryman sends the boat into the water by grabbing a stalactite, which is how he propels and guides the boat, and the trip begins. Overhead, and sometimes straight ahead, are the astounding formations; beneath is the pristine spring water. Listen to the water lapping against the wall of the cave and dripping from the projections. These are the sounds that continued for ages, unbroken and unheard. As you ride deeper and deeper, a chill fills the air and your breath begins to thicken, rising into the spiked darkness. Fortunately, only the innermost recesses are dark; most of the caverns are illuminated by floating lamps, framed by undulating rings of light. When the ride ends, you leave the caves overwhelmed and enter the boring sunlit world crying for more of the cold damp dark. You might even make the whole trip again.

South of Pirgos Dirou

South of Pirgos, the countryside begins to get rugged and life more traditional. This is the Mani of bandits and blood feuds. From the road, you can see the hundreds of tower houses, with tiny deep-set windows. Many of the villages in the region see hardly any tourists. By far the best way to see the area is to latch on to Europeans touring it by car.

Besides the tower houses, many of the villages have tiny "barrel-vaulted" churches, some constructed as early as the ninth century. A good place to stop is the village of **Maina** (Mina), just off the main road to the left about halfway to Gerolimin from Pirgos. From the main road, you wind past olive groves and perfect stone walls built without mortar. Besides tower houses, the town has a tiny church probably smaller than your living room. It is hard to believe, but members of the leading family were recognized by the Turks as the chieftains of the entire peninsula. If you have the time and energy, there are a few villages further up the hill worth exploring.

At the end of both the good road and the bus line (forty minutes, 80dr from Areopolis) is the rocky little port of **Gerolimin** ("old port"). The little houses here hug the jagged shore of a large cove. There is no sandy beach, but diving with a mask off the rocks in the harbor is very good and the town is a feasible place to spend the night. The **Hotel Akrogioli** is right in the center of town and has clean if cramped doubles for 850dr, triples for 1300dr. The restaurant downstairs is also quite reasonable. By the left-hand side of the harbor as you face the water, the **Hotel Akrotainaritis** is several steps down in cleanliness and price: very drab doubles 650dr, triples 900dr. Inquire here about bus schedules. Usually buses leave twice a day for Athens (850dr), with stops at Areopolis (80dr), Kalamata (250dr), and Tripolis (260dr). Schedules are notoriously untrustworthy, so be sure to ask several times. There is no bank here, but the **Post Office** is open Mon.-Fri. 7:30am-2:30pm. Eerily set in the hills 11km south of Gerolimin is **Vathia,** one of the most famous of the tower-house towns. The town is not equipped for visitors (in fact, most of the houses are uninhabited), so you'll have to make it a daytrip. No buses travel over the rugged dirt road (really a jeep trail) from Gerolimin; even if you have a car you should think twice about driving it here. However, the NTOG is in the process of converting these gray buildings into guesthouses, so the place may become much more accessible in the next few years. Unfortunately, they may be as costly as they are fancy. At present, you'll have to hitch or take a taxi from Gerolimin (500dr). Also of interest for their tower houses, castles, and churches are the villages of Kittz and Nomia.

Monemvassia

Undoubtedly one of the most striking and unique cities in Greece, Monemvassia is, with Mystra, the architectural treasure of the southern Peloponnese. Nestled at the foot of a mammoth rock formation that rises straight up out of the sea, forming a strange-looking island that is as high as it is wide, Monemvassia is surrounded by sloping fortified walls—the walls even border the whole length of the zig-zagging staircase that climbs the sheer cliff face of the one thousand-foot promontory. At the top of the rock face are the ruins of an entire Byzantine city, which was besieged by the Frankish armies for three long years before it finally fell in 1248. The only surviving structure is the graceful thirteenth-century church of **Agia Sofia,** modeled after the famous monastery at Daphne near Athens. Some of the original frescoes that once covered the entire interior of the church are still in remarkably good condition.

Passed around among the Turks, the Vatican, and Venice after having been conquered by the Franks, Monemvassia has had a checkered history. Most of the fortifications that remain, including the Kastro (citadel) at the top of the mountain, were constructed by Venetians in the sixteenth century. The inhabited part of the old city lies at the base of the huge rock, amidst more ruins. With its weathered stone houses and narrow, winding passageways, the extremely well preserved medieval village is one of the most delightful towns in the Peloponnese. No wonder the NTOG has been vigorously promoting the city. The peaceful village is gradually becoming a private target for Greek tourists mostly on daytrip tours from Athens, and can become unpleasantly crowded on weekends during the summer.

A narrow causeway connects the island to the mainland and the modern town of Monemvassia. This unusual arrangement of the two parts of the city has helped to preserve the old town's peaceful splendor. The modern town across the water houses the hotels, restaurants, and gift shops, and absorbs all the business from the tourist traffic. This has allowed the medieval village to retain its original character to an extraordinary degree; the only commercial intrusions are a few small restaurants near the entrance to the ancient city.

Practical Information

The problem with Monemvassia is getting there. From Sparta, take one of the two daily buses and change at Molaï—the change sometimes requires an hour's wait. The trip costs 260dr. From Gythion, take either of the two daily buses to Tarapsa (50dr), where it'll be just you, the Mobil station, and a long stretch of road. Cross to the side of the road opposite the station and wait until a bus marked "Neapolis" picks you up a half hour later. The trip from Tarapsa to Monemvassia costs 200dr, and you have to change at Molaï, where again you may wait as long as an hour. Buses leave Monemvassia for Athens (860dr) twice a day and for Sparta (260dr) at the same times. For Sparta, change at Molaï where—would you believe it?—you'll have to wait an hour. To reach Monemvassia by boat, you can take the once-a-week boat from Gythion on Friday at 3pm (527dr). The same boat continues on to Athens. There's also a hydrofoil from Piraeus to Monemvassia every day, which takes three hours and costs 1556dr. In Monemvassia itself, buy tickets from the souvenir stand across from the Hotel Likineion. Given all the complexities of the bus travel, you may get stuck in Molaï. If so, there are two cheap hotels in the square up from the bus station: **Hotel Gregory** (tel. 22 04 2), with singles for 389dr and doubles for 562dr, and **Hotel Kentrikon** (tel. 22 43 6), with singles for 486dr, doubles for 670dr, and triples for 810dr; showers 80dr extra. In the nearby village of Plitra, you can see some excavated mosaics, and, when the tide is out, the ruined foundations of the ancient city. Best of all, the coastline here is beautiful and absolutely empty. The nearby island of Elafonissi, accessible from Neapolis, is similarly deserted.

There are no banks in Monemvassia, but the Cypros restaurant on the waterfront changes travelers checks. For good swimming, go halfway up the road to the medieval village—there's a pleasant cove to the right.

Accommodations and Food

There are three ways to stay in Monemvassia. The first is simply to look around the island for a likely spot to pitch your tent. The police don't seem to mind, though you might, since it can be windy and rainy even in summer. At the other end of the price scale, it is occasionally possible to stay in the medieval village, but cheap rooms (800dr for a double) are few and far between. It's best to ask at the tourist shop on the right side of the old village path. If you arrive in the middle of the week with several people, it's within range for a splurge; a bit of bargaining may bring triples down to 1100dr. Places aren't marked, so ask directions at the good restaurant next to the pottery studio. Since both these options are very chancy, the third option, staying in the modern town, is your best bet. The **Hotel Likineion** (tel. 61 20 9 or 61 22 4), right on the waterfront above the more expensive Hotel Minoa, and the **Hotel Akrogiali** (tel. 61 20 2), just up the street, both charge 567dr for a single and 810dr for a double. The latter is often full so it's best to phone in advance. Slightly more expensive but well worth it is the **Hotel Aktaion**, also called Hotel Sapountzakis (tel. 61 23 4). Here you'll get modern rooms with balconies overlooking the island and screens to keep out the bugs. Singles 600dr, doubles 850dr; showers 50dr extra. Solar panels produce the hot water, so take your showers in the late afternoon, preferably on sunny days. For a friendly pension, walk to the edge of town on the road going north until you get to the police station. The pension here has doubles of 600dr with shower, but no singles (tel. 61 30 7).

There are four very good, moderately priced restaurants in the new town, but unfortunately all close in the afternoon and don't reopen until 7pm. The **Cypros restaurant** has tables on its porch, which has a superb view of the island. The restaurant in the **Hotel Aktaion** has a similar set-up, with glass windows to boot, and about as wide a variety of dishes as you'll find in a cheap Greek restaurant. There's another **taverna** down the street from the Cypros, run by a lovely Greek woman who speaks English with an impeccable Australian accent. Across from the Hotel Aktaion is the **Dionysos** restaurant, serving decent food in a calm atmosphere.

Kythira

Kythira is a rocky and barren island, definitely not designed for tourists (which is probably the main reason why you've decided to come here). The only regular boats serving the island leave from a small and obscure port in the middle of nowhere (Neapolis), and, of the four ferries each week from the more accessible town of Gythion, two deposit you here at 2am. And there your problems just begin; though it's a large and quite populous island, Kythira does not have a single hotel and its buses are at best sporadic. The schedule for each week is chalked up on a blackboard in every town, but on a given day perhaps only two of the island's various towns will be connected.

In every way, the island is bizarre. Officially, it's one of the seven Ionian Islands, but the other six are located hundreds of miles away on the other side of the Peloponnese. Its capital town, Kythira, is not a port (which is what you'd expect on an island), but is atop a hill. All the main shops and facilities are in another town. Although there are few boats connecting the island with mainland Greece, strangely enough in summer there are two flights daily between the island and Athens. But that's not all: although the island has no tourist facilities, there are plenty of tourists, and contrary to what you might expect, most aren't frugal young backpackers living off the land and enjoying indigenous Greek culture, but rather tycoons and yachting jet-setters. The most common strategy for visiting Kythira seems to involve waiting for a rich relative to buy a villa here, and then dropping in.

For the record, boats from Neapolis leave several times a day in summer (there is also a daily hydrofoil, taking four hours), and will take you to Agia Pelagia, located on the northern part of the island. Boats from Gythion (see Gythion section) also stop at Kapsali in the south, which is less a town than a collection of sweeping white villas dotted majestically around the cliffs. Kapsali exudes hideaway chic. You can eat here at the **Kapsi Kamales,** one of the few places in Greece with an elegant stucco interior and an attractive American style menu. The prices, as the quality, are both lower then you'd expect, and the trendy atmosphere allows you to watch the Beautiful/Ugly People without expense. Beside the harbor is a beach, half sandy half rocky, where you can sleep if the rooms in the town's restaurants are full. A steep walk up from Kapsali will take you to Kythira Town, site of a Venetian fortress and some five vistas over the irregular curves of the harbor below. The island's main road (mostly dirt) will take you from Kythira to **Potamos** (60dr, one hour by bus). Potamos is the island's biggest town, and a post office, OTE office, bank, police department, and Olympic airways office are all arranged around its main square. From here, you can either hitch west to the nudist beach of Ag. Eleftherion or north to the nicest spot on the isle, Ag. Pelagia. If something is very wrong, you might even find a bus to take you there.

CENTRAL GREECE

Delphi

Legend has it that when Zeus wished to discover the earth's center, he sent forth two eagles from the opposite ends of the earth. They met at Delphi, where the *omphalos,* or navel stone, marks the exact spot of the mythological rendezvous. Delphi may not be the "navel of the earth," but, as the home of the Temple and Oracle of Apollo, it was considered the hub of the civilized universe throughout ancient Greek history.

Orientation

Like most touristy areas, Delphi Town exists not for beauty but for business. Yet somehow it has retained a certain charm—its several main avenues are cut like terraces along the side of the mountain, with passageways of stone steps leading from one to the next. Though the main drag, Pavlou & Frederikis St., is unattractively lined with a long string of hotels and souvenir shops, Delphi is for the most part quite tastefully arranged. It has few modern buildings, and the large, ugly hotels hug the cliff wall below the town, invisible from the streets. Best of all, the view is unbeatable.

At 25 Pavlou & Frederikis St. you'll find the friendly **Tourist Police** (tel. 82 22 0), open every day 8am-10pm. Two doors up is the **Post Office,** open Mon.-Fri. 7:30am-7:30pm. Across the street and closer to the ruins is the **OTE,** open Mon.-Fri. 7:30am-9pm. Delphi is well-serviced by bus. To reach Delphi from Athens, take the Amfissa bus from the station at 260 Liossion St. (look behind the hardware store), which has five departures daily but fills up fast. The trip lasts three and a half hours and costs 420dr; if you have a railpass, you can save 230dr by taking the train to **Levadia** and catching the Delphi bus from there (115dr). Buses depart for Athens seven times a day in summer; buy your ticket in advance so you can reserve a place on the usually jammed bus. Buses also leave for Itea nine times a day (45dr) and for Arachova seven times a day (25dr). Buses depart for Navpaktos four times a day (275dr), and for Levadia six times a day (115dr). To reach Ossios Loukas, ask at the bus station; you have to take a bus to Levadia and get off at the branch to Distomo, but you have to find out when buses go from Distomo to the monastery.

Accommodations and Food

The cheapest beds are found at the **IYHF Youth Hostel** at 29 Apollonos St. (tel. 82 26 8). Run by a Greek man and his gracious wife from New Zealand, the hostel charges 200dr for a dormitory bed; curfew is 11pm and the doors aren't open until 2:30pm, so don't count on catching the earliest bus out of Delphi. The hostel has one hundred beds, but when they are full the wardens let people sleep on the roof for 140dr. Down Isaia St. is the cheapest alternative, the **Pension Odysseus** (tel. 82 23 5), which charges 529dr for a single, 698dr for a double, and 838dr for a triple; showers 60dr extra.

Delphi's least expensive hotels are all D-class, equally comfortable, and, except where noted, right on the main drag. If you stay more than a couple of nights, prices drop by 10%, and in the off-season rates drop by 20%. For rooms with private bath, try the **Sibylla** (tel. 82 33 5), singles 675dr and doubles 844dr, or the **Lefas** (tel. 82 32 4), singles 732dr and doubles 1067dr. The

119

Dionysos (tel. 82 25 7) charges 602dr for a single and 750dr for a double; the **Kotopuli**, 34 Apollonos St. (tel. 82 24 7), charges 507dr for a single and 732dr for a double. Both hotels charge 60dr extra for a shower. The **Athena** (tel. 82 23 9) has singles with shower for 620dr, doubles without for 698dr plus 60dr for a shower. Finally, the **Phoebus** (tel. 82 31 9) offers singles for 563dr, doubles for 732dr, and doubles with shower for 957dr. Remember that prices come down when business is slow or a number of people plan to stay.

Taverna Vakhos, adjacent to the Youth Hostel, serves the cheapest meals in town on its spectacular terrace. Otherwise try the more poorly situated **Pan** or **Omphalos,** both on Isaia St. above the kiosk that sells English newspapers.

Sights

Anyone who has visited the temples at Cape Sounion or at Vassae knows that the beauty of a temple's natural surroundings meant as much to the ancient Greeks as the beauty of the temple itself. The **Delphic Oracle** is no exception: it is situated at the foot of **Mt. Parnassos,** flanked by a towering cliff on one side and the 600m deep Pleistos ravine on the other. Yet isn't it odd that the Greeks chose such an inaccessible and narrow slice of mountainside as the site for their most important religious sanctuary? The explanation is that the gods picked it, not their human subjects. According to legend, a goatherd searching for a missing goat in the area found the animal seized by a fit of hysteria, and he, too, soon fell into a frenzy. All who subsequently visited the spot were supposed to be similarly affected. The ancient Greeks concluded that the gods had chosen this secluded mountain ledge as the site for a divine oracle, where gods communicated directly with men.

All of the ancient Mediterranean world hastened to Delphi to consult the Oracle. From private citizens seeking marital advice to rulers wanting guidance for entire nations, everyone clamored for the Oracle's response—delivered by the priests of the sanctuary. Proof of the widespread devotion to Delphi can be seen in its numerous treasuries, which housed the priceless gifts brought by pilgrims to propitiate Apollo, and, perhaps more crucially, to gain the attention of Apollo's priests. At its peak, Delphi was so busy that three oracles had to be employed to meet the demand.

The legend of the Delphic Oracle began when Apollo slew the dragon Python, from which the god Pythius emerged. **Pythius** served as Apollo's mouthpiece by speaking through an intermediary, a priestess called the **Pythia,** who was an elderly woman seen only by the priests. She sat on the *adyton,* or oracular tripod (believed also to have been the throne of Apollo), and declared her visions, which were brought on by chewing laurel leaves and inhaling the vapors rising from the earth around her. The Pythia's crazed, semi-coherent prophecies were recorded and interpreted by the priests for their audience. The Oracle owed its enduring success and long-lived popularity to these shrewd and knowledgeable priests, who dealt with ministers from all parts of the ancient world. In mythology, the prophecies of the Oracle are usually presented as clear and forthright, but in truth they were often ambiguous. Consider the case of poor Croesus, the Greek king who was told that if he waged war on the Persians he would destroy a great power; unfortunately for him, he didn't realize that the great power he destroyed would be his own.

The Delphic Oracle maintained its popularity among Greeks from the seventh century B.C. until after the Christianization of the Roman Empire. Seen throughout most of its history as the spiritual center of the Hellenic world, it became an important arbiter between the city-states and greatly influenced the major Greek political decisions. During its heyday, those who doubted the Oracle's authenticity were tried and usually condemned to death. Delphi's popularity even survived a great blunder—its recommendation that the Greeks surrender to the Persians in the sixth century B.C. (The Oracle's advice was wisely ignored, and eventually the Persians were defeated at the Battle of Salamis.) Beginning with the Roman occupation in 146 B.C., Delphi was gradually robbed of many of its treasures, and the oracular cult was eventually banned in 399 A.D. by the Roman Emperor Theodosius the Great, when he undertook to purge the world of pagan religions. The site was largely forgotten until French archeologists excavated it in the last century.

Today Delphi is one of the most impressive historic sites in Greece, both for the fascination of the ruins and for the breathtaking views across the mountains to the Gulf of Corinth. The principal set of ruins at Delphi, known collectively as the **Pythian Sanctuary,** lies 400m before the town. The **Treasury of Sifnos** lies to your left as you ascend the Sacred Way, the main route through the sanctuary. Because the island of Sifnos had several gold mines, the Sifniotes were able to build one of the most beautiful of Delphi's numerous treasure houses. The frieze that once adorned the structure is now exhibited in the archeological museum. Around the corner is the **Athenian Treasury,** a beautifully restored building of polished white marble supported by two Doric columns. The remaining columns of the fourth-century B.C. **Sanctuary of Apollo** dominate the site. The priests would utter the pronouncements of the Pythia to an anxious audience of visitors in the middle of this enormous Doric Temple. The massive walls of the Temple were once inscribed with famous maxims of Greek philosophers such as "know thyself" and "nothing to excess." The **Theater of Apollo** overlooks the sanctuary. At the top of the mountain and well worth the climb are the excellently preserved remains of the **Stadium,** where the Pythian Games (musical and poetic contests) were held. Open in summer Mon.-Sat. 8am-2:45pm, Sun. 9am-4:15pm, 9am-3:30pm in the off-season; admission 100dr, 50dr for students.

The **Archeological Museum** at Delphi, located just before the Pythian Sanctuary as you come from town, is one of the finest in Greece, after Athens' National Archeological Museum and Olympia's New Museum. The museum contains two masterpieces of ancient Greek art. The magnificent **Frieze of the Sifnian Treasury,** which depicts the battle between the gods and the giants, is housed in a room to the right of the entrance, along with the elegant winged sphinx of the Naxiens. The graceful bronze **Charioteer of Delphi** is located on the opposite side of the museum in its own room. Open Mon.-Sat. 8am-6:30pm, Sun. 10am-4:30pm, closed Tues., off-season 9am-3pm; admission 100dr, 50dr with student ID.

You don't really have to worry about closing hours or an admission charge when you visit the unfenced ruins of the **Temple of Pronaia Athena.** Open in daylight, they are located on the right side of the road going away from town, about eighty yards past the main set of ruins. Commanding a spectacular panorama of the surrounding mountains, the three remaining Doric columns of the unusual **circular tholos** of the sanctuary of Athena are the most elegant and most photographed of the ruins at Delphi. Next to the tholos lies the **Treasury of Marseilles;** this treasure from France indicates the extent of the Oracle's prestige. The perfect time to visit the tholos is at either dawn or dusk, when you can enjoy the ruins at Delphi without the company of busloads of tourists.

If you visit the tholos first and then head back towards the main site, you will see on the right side of the road the famous **Castelian Spring.** If, after glancing at the remains of the fountain, you drink from the crystal clear water before continuing on to the rest of the ruins, you'll be following the practice of ancient pilgrims, who cleansed themselves here both physically and spiritually before calling upon the Oracle.

Near Delphi

Fifteen winding kilometers southwest of Delphi is the small resort town of **Itea,** most notable for its cooling beach on the Gulf of Corinth. The cheapest hotel in Itea is the **Parnassos** (tel. 32 34 7), with singles for 450dr and doubles for 700dr. The hotel also runs a pension which costs about 100dr more because it's near the water and has baths. A cleaner and less-touristed beach can be found at **Kira,** located only 2km from Itea—walk, hitch or take a local bus.

The serene port of **Galaxidi,** with its pastel-colored houses, is located 18km further west along the coast. Unfortunately, bus service from Delphi is slow and infrequent (75dr, take the Navpaktos bus), but the trip is worth it if you have the time. Galaxidi had been a shipping community from the first century B.C. to the Greek War of Independence, when it was demolished by the Turks. If you can rouse yourself from the beach, visit the ruins of the ancient castle, or the thirteenth-century **Monastery of Transformation.** Many travelers continue on to **Navpaktos,** close to the mouth of the Gulf of Corinth and the ferry crossing at Antirion over the Peloponnese. The harbor of Navpaktos is flanked by medieval fortifications and surrounded by a peaceful modern town. If you are traveling from Patras to Delphi, you'll have to catch a bus from the dock at Antirion to Navpaktos (26dr) and then catch one of the four daily buses to Delphi (298dr), with stops at Galaxidi and Itea. Be warned that the last bus sometimes goes no further than Itea. If you want or have to stay in Navpaktos, head for the **Aegli** (tel. 27 27 1), with singles for 500dr, doubles for 800dr.

Just 10km east of Delphi, stacked onto the slopes of Mt. Parnassos, is the "Alpine" Greek village of **Arachova.** While the main street where the bus lets you off has a comparatively appealing array of tourist shops selling local woolens and handicrafts, if you climb the hill a bit you'll find an even more tempting unspoiled labyrinth of alleyways. The best approach leads straight up the steps from the main square to the **Church of St. George** and then meanders down the side streets. The plaza surrounding the church contains a stone clock tower and offers spectacular views of the surrounding mountains. Below, you can see an even older stone clock tower perched on a natural rock pedestal which juts above a cluster of houses and is Arachova's most noticeable landmark. Behind the church is a huge wash-stand supplied by a natural spring, whose waters cascade down Arachova's streets in bubbling gutters. This embarrassing wealth of water keeps Arachova green and full of flowers all summer, preserving its Tyrolean appearance despite the scorching sun.

You can climb up from Arachova to the Corcyrian Grotto; from there a three-hour hike will bring you to the top of **Mt. Parnassos.** At almost 7500 feet, it is not the tallest mountain in Greece, but it is one of the more accessible. Recently a ski center opened on the upper ridge. The nearest lodgings are to be found in Itea, Delphi, and Arachova. There are two cheap hotels in Arachova, right next to each other on the main road west of the town square. The **Apollon** (tel. 31 42 7) has singles for 600dr and doubles for 850dr, both including shower. The **Parnassos** (tel. 31 30 7) charges 550dr for a single and 850dr for a double, also including shower. Both give a 10% discount for stays longer than two days. The best restaurant in town is the little taverna (it has no name) on the main street opposite the fountain in the square.

Eighty kilometers north of Delphi, the pass of **Thermopylae,** guarding the eastern flank of Athens against land attack from the north, will always be associated with the heroism of King Leonidas and his three hundred Spartans. Herodotus claims that Leonidas held off Xerxes's Persian army of over five million in 480 B.C., yet even the more conservative modern estimates of three hundred thousand cannot detract from the courage of the three hundred. Today the Athens-Volos highway traverses this once strategic pass just before the turn-off to Lamia. The site, with an imposing statue of a fierce Leonidas casting a spear, requires a leap of the imagination to conjure the great battle. Unless you're driving, the site isn't really worth a stop.

Ossios Loukas

Second in Greece only to Daphni for the quality of its mosaics, and perhaps second to none for the beauty of its stone exterior, the monastery at Ossios Loukas seems divinely inspired. The secluded monastery complex, situated 1700m above sea level, commands a magnificent view of the neighboring mountains. Located only 12km west of Arachova, Ossios Loukas makes an excellent daytrip from either Delphi or Athens.

The main building in the complex, the **Church of St. Luke,** is in fact dedicated to a local hermit named Luke who managed to attain sainthood, and not to the evangelist who wrote the third Gospel. The large narthex providing entrance to the eleventh-century church is adorned with Byzantine mosaics, easily examined because of the low ceiling and the natural lighting from the door. The most notable scenes show *Doubting Thomas* inserting his finger in Christ's wound, *Christ Washing the Apostles' Feet,* the *Crucifixion,* and the *Resurrection.* Outside the nave is a rectangle, but the interior has been modified to a Greek cross by the placement of alcoves in the four corners. The original dome collapsed during an earthquake and, upon being reconstructed, the mosaic that had filled the dome was replaced by a fresco of Christ Pantocrator. The fresco sustained a few bullet holes during the Greek war of independence in the nineteenth century when Turkish soldiers shot into the eyes of the Christ image in an attempt to discourage the monks of the monastery from participating in the Greek resistance. The most beautiful mosaics that survived are tucked in the squinches that support the dome—the *Nativity, Presentation at the Temple,* and *Baptism.* The last mosaic, showing Christ standing in a cleft of rock covered by stylized ripples of water, is so similar in composition to such scenes in the Byzantine churches of Daphni and Sicily that it seems the same group of artists traveled throughout the Mediterranean.

Although not as famous as the mosaics in the upper church, the eleventh-century frescoes that cover almost the entire interior of the crypt are every bit as beautiful. Most tourists pass the crypt by, since its entrance is on the side of the building and is not well-lit. Having been concealed from daylight for the last nine hundred years, these frescoes are extraordinarily well-preserved. They can only be viewed with the aid of a flashlight, so be sure to bring one with you. The oldest part of the monastery is the tenth-century **Church of St. Mary** adjoining the larger church. With the exception of the exquisitely carved Byzantine capitals and lintel over the altar, all of the interior decoration has been destroyed, either by earthquakes or by Turks, who converted the structure into a mosque. The building is still used daily by the five monks who live at the monastery for religious services and ceremonies. (Admission to the Church of St. Luke is 50dr, 35dr for students. Admission to the monastery, crypt, and Church of St. Mary is free. Open daily 8am-6pm.) The easiest, and naturally the most expensive, way to reach Ossios Loukas is to catch a taxi from Arachova or Levadia. Intrepid bargaining should get the price down to about 1000dr. Getting to the monastery from Levadia is tricky—the one daily bus (85dr) is rather unreliable. Try hitching if it doesn't show up. Buses leave Distomo for Levadia about every two hours.

Should you wish to stay the night, a small hotel (tel. (0267) 22 22 8) next to the monastery offers double rooms without bath for 600dr. Inquire at the refreshment stand.

Levadia

The only redeeming feature of Levadia is its proximity to the ruins at **Orhomenos.** The ancient city was the capital of the Minyans, a very powerful Mycenean people. A **theater** and a **tholos** or **beehive tomb** remain, like those at Mycenae. The bus station in Levadia for Orhomenos is located near the Pallas theater, down the street from the police station. Buses leave and return every half hour (34dr each way). You'll be let off in a square and from the main street, Minyou, you'll see some white stone gates about 200m away. To the right of these is a church built in part from a temple's column bases. Across from the gates is a little theater. Turn left at the theater and you'll reach the tomb, open Mon.-Sat. 9am-3:15pm, Sun. 9am-2pm; admission free.

If you must stay in Levadia, try the malodorous **Hotel Erkyna** at 6 I. Lappa St. (tel. 28 22 7), with singles for 400dr and doubles for 530dr, or the equally grim **Hotel Viotia** across the street (tel. 28 35 0). Cheap eats are to be found at the **Helicon restaurant.** Buses go seven times a day to Delphi (115dr) from Plateia Katsoni, and hourly on the hour for Athens 6am-8pm (320dr) with a stop at Thebes (110dr). One bus a day goes to Ossios Loukas (85dr), or you can take a bus to Distomo and take a taxi or hitch from there. Buses for Athens and Ossios Loukas depart from behind the Helicon.

Thebes

Thebes once ranked among the most important of ancient Greek cities, but seems never to have recovered since Alexander razed it in the fourth century B.C. Today it is a noisy, unattractive town, worth visiting only for its **museum.** Housed in only five rooms, the collection's strength lies in the uniqueness of its pieces. The room opposite the entrance displays Mycenean *larnakes* or clay coffins decorated with paintings of funerary rites that yield some rare insights into Mycenean ritual. The only such pieces found on mainland Greece, they were unearthed near Tanagara, halfway between Thebes and Chalkis. Other items worth noting are the black stone stelae incised with fine white line figures in the adjacent room and the peculiar reliefs depicting birds on the museum's garden wall. Open Mon., Wed.-Sat. 9am-3pm, Sun. and holidays 9am-2pm; admission 50dr, 35dr with student ID, free on Sunday.

Also of interest are the remains of the **House of Cadmus,** a Mycenean palace dating from the fourteenth century B.C. (opposite the Central Bank of Greece at #82 Pindari Street). From the evidence of the palace at Thebes, along with that of other palaces at Mycenae, Tiryns, and Pylos, archeologists have determined that by 1300 B.C. the Mycenean civilization had spread throughout the Aegean area, and was ruled by a powerful central authority. A trace of the former Mycenean strength is detectable in a few blocks of remaining cyclopean walls that once girded the House of Cadmus.

If you plan to stay in Thebes, try the **Niovi** (tel. 27 60), two blocks up from the bus station at 61 Epaminoude St., with singles for 500dr and doubles for 800dr without private bath. Most other hotels clustered nearby are similarly priced but not quite as clean and bright. Although Thebes does not warrant a separate excursion, you may have to change buses here for Chalkis, especially if you're going to Evia or the Sporades. Buses for Chalkis leave from Thebes every two hours, and buses for Thebes leave frequently from Levadia and from the bus terminal at 260 Liossin St. in Athens (see Athens Orientation). Often you must take a bus that is specifically bound for Thebes, since the city lies slightly off the main highway.

Evia

The long, green island of Evia (Euboea) embraces the mainland coastline north of Athens. Severed from the mainland in ancient times by an earthquake (or, if you prefer the mythical interpretation, by Poseidon's trident), Evia is now connected by a swingbridge at Chalkis. Nevertheless, with frequent bus service from Thebes and Athens, Evia remains in heart and spirit very much part of the mainland. Indeed, most of its visitors are Athenians on weekend outings. Evia has recently been trying to exploit its status as a Greek island to attract foreign tourists, who have taken over the coast near Eretria on the southern coast, but little else. Fortunately, the most beautiful part of Evia, its interior, dominated by lush Dirfis mountains, is still untouched. If it's beaches you're after, head to the town of Kimi where you can catch ferries to the Sporades Islands, or make for the coastal towns on Evia's northwestern and southern shores.

Chalkis, the ugly and undistinguished capital of Evia, is the transportation hub for the island, and visitors inevitably wind up spending a few hours here. The **bus station** is in the center of town, up the hill from the water. But if you have taken the train from Athens (130dr) you will find yourself on the mainland, not the island of Evia when you disembark. Simply walk across the bridge to get to the busier section of Chalkis. Four blocks up from the waterfront, on the third floor at 32 Venizelou St., are the **Tourist Police** (tel. 24 66 2). Unfortunately, they close up for a long afternoon siesta from 2-6pm, the time when most visitors arrive in the city. A few doors up, the **OTE** is open daily 6am-midnight. Across the street from the Tourist Police is the **Archeological Museum,** which was under renovation in 1983 but may have reopened by 1984. If not, try the **folklore museum,** around the corner from the bus station in a section of the Venetian Kastro. The museum is open to the public Wed. and Fri. 6-8pm, Sun. 10am-1pm.

Nearby, on Kotzou Street, a marble fountain inscribed in Arabic stands overgrown with shrubbery across the street from an old Turkish mosque. Chalkis is a regional headquarters for Greece's two major out-parties, the N.D.A. and K.K.E., so don't be surprised if in your wanders you hear competing loudspeakers trumpeting music and political slogans. The best part of the city for enjoying the sunshine is the waterfront. But since the hotels are expensive and the town has little to offer, you should probably take the first bus out. If you are reduced to staying in Chalkis, the **Iris Hotel** is less expensive than the neighboring ritzy hotels and conveniently located amidst a press of tavernas by the drawbridge. Singles 418dr in off-season, 488dr in high season; doubles 594-693dr; triples 830-969dr. Showers 75dr.

Southern Evia

Most tourists head for the crowded beaches and overpriced hotels around **Marmari** on the southern coast, or the other major resort area, **Eretria.** In addition to its shore, Eretria is also noted for archeological sites providing evidence of the region's wealth during its heyday as a shipping and colonial power between the eighth and fourth centuries B.C. The city's **ancient theater** and the **temple of Daphinphoros Apollo** are the most impressive monuments.

Sixteen buses per day run from Chalkis to Eretria; the last goes at 10pm.

The three-hour bus ride from Chalkis to Karistos winds over mountainous roads, revealing a spectacular southern coast lined with gnarled olive trees. Three buses make the trip daily (400dr). Buses run more frequently to **Aliveri,** a town one-third of the way to Karistos. But since the only buses linking Aliveri to Karistos are the three which originate in Chalkis, don't get off in Aliveri first unless you plan to try hitching south from there (it's possible, but probably as slow as waiting for the bus).

Although **Karistos** is the largest village in southern Evia and a growing resort, it attracts few foreign tourists. In town, the coastal fort of **Bourdzi** resembles the crusader castle in Rhodes, but consists of only a tower; the extensive walls are lacking. Karistos' **Post Office,** open Mon.-Fri. 7:30am-2pm, and **bank,** open Mon.-Fri. 8am-2pm, are both on Theochari Kotsika St., above the Melissa. The **OTE** is above the square, around the corner to the east.

Near the fort is the long sandy beach of **Psili Ammos,** a good place to sleep if the hotels are full. The cheapest hotel in Karistos is the **Louloudi** (tel. 22 33 7) on the waterfront: singles 596dr in off-season, 787dr in high season; doubles 900-1125dr; triples 1400dr, all with private bath. A few private rooms in town are less costly, particularly if you are traveling alone; they start at 300-400dr per person. The waterfront restaurants tend to be expensive, but a good place to watch the fishermen haul in their catch and hang the octopus up to dry. The **Melissa** restaurant on Theochari Kotsika St. (up from the port) serves the best seafood in town. While its interior is far from elegant, the food is reasonably priced and it is a favorite among the local fishermen. **Peroulakis Restaurant** on the port, serves good food in large portions.

Karistos and Marmari are both connected to the mainland by twice-daily ferries to Rafina. Take the orange-and-white striped bus from the corner of Mavromateon St., just off Leoforos Alexandras in Athens. Buses leave every hour on the hour for Rafina; fare is 65dr. Boat fare to Marmari is 255dr, to Karistos 363dr.

If you have a free morning, explore the villages north of Karistos. Follow Aiolou St. (one block east of the square) out of town; continuing straight at the crossroads will take you to **Palaio Chora,** a village sprawled among lemon and olive groves. Turn right at a sign reading "metamorphosis" and you will find a shaded stone path up to an old church. For a more interesting but also more strenuous trek, turn right at the crossroads outside of Karistos towards the village of **Mili.** The road ascends sharply and follows a clear stream up to the village, where the water has been diverted to flow from the mouths of three lions in a small roadside fountain. From Mili, a twenty-minute hike up the hill on the left will bring you to **Kokkino Kastro,** a thirteenth-century Venetian castle, named for its reddish stones. The castle wall commands a fine view of Karistos' harbor and the ocean beyond; it is easy to see why the Venetians considered the hill to be of great strategic importance.

From Mili, the road continues to twist up the valley along the stream bed, past several more fountains. Because it is so well watered, this lush valley supports a large variety of plant life, including eucalyptus as well as the ubiquitous olive trees. Finally, about a half hour beyond Mili, the road ends in a small square where stone benches surround a spring: the source of the stream. A donkey path leads up to a pass and much drier country above.

If you wish to do more extensive hiking in the region, climb **Mt. Ochi** (1898m). The second highest mountain on Evia, it is located in the heart of this unspoiled southern area and the landscape is still relatively untouched. There is a stone refuge hut on the mountain; if you want to stay here, ask for the key at City Hall in Karistos. A large structure of unmortared stone blocks was built during the Pelasgian period on the summit of Mt. Ochi; it is believed to have been either a temple to Hera or a signal tower. The ruin is known as the "dragon's house" today, and since the Greeks think the place is haunted, you will have it all to yourself.

The most breathtaking stretch of road on Evia winds northwards through the mountains, starting from the village of **Lepoura.** The scenery improves with each twist and bend in the road, and each mountain village somehow seems more picturesque than the one before. Here the road follows the slopes of the magnificent Mt. Dirfis and ends at Kimi.

Kimi

Dubbed "the balcony of the Aegean" because of its perch 250m over the water, Kimi is a delightful village that today receives even fewer visitors than it once did. The construction of a road connecting the harbor of Paralia Kimi directly to the Chalkis road a few miles before Kimi itself means that travelers heading to the Sporades no longer pass through the town. This suits the townsfolk fine; as a community of ship captains and officers' families, their trade is more dependent on visitors to the Sporades than to their home town. In addition to two boats daily to Skyros, four boats a week go from Kimi to Alonissos, Skopelos, and Skiathos. Once a week, you may sail from Kimi to the islands of Agios Efstratios and Limnos, and then on to the mainland at the Macedonian city of Kavala. Buses run seven times a day from Chalkis to Kimi (200dr); from Karistos, take the bus to Lepoura (110dr) and change for Kimi (90dr).

Kimi has one major street which sprawls out to form a plaza around the cathedral. This area is the "balcony of Kimi" and fills during the evenings with townspeople enjoying its cool sea breezes. Tucked in a corner to the right of the church is a statue of Georgios Papanicolaou, a famous Kimian known for his development of the Pap smear. A small whitewashed seaman's chapel and the ruins of a windmill are perched on the hill behind town. A climb to either offers excellent views of Kimi and the sea beyond. Elderly Greeks go to the spring at **Choneftico,** north of Kimi, to take the waters—this may not interest you, but the twenty-minute walk along the road from Kimi towards the spring is delightful, especially if you turn off on one of the dirt tracks leading off the road and ramble up in the hills. On a good day, one may glimpse, in theory at least, the shores of Macedonia, Thrace, and Asia Minor from the majestically situated **Monastery of the Savior,** 6km from Kimi. Back in town, the **Folklore Museum** on the road descending to Paralia offers three floors of Evian crafts: mostly clothing, needlework, and furnishings. The collection, housed in a wooden building with wrought-iron balconies and fences, is open 10am-1pm and 6-9pm on weekdays.

Kimi's indifference to tourism is indicated by the scarcity of tourist accommodations. The cheapest rooms available in Kimi are in a wooden building, the quaint, narrow **pension** linked to the church plaza by a bridge that spans the street below. Singles are 380dr, doubles 530dr, without bath. If you can, get a room on the second floor with a view of the sea.

Hotel Krinon (tel. 22 28 7) in the main square, is slightly more expensive but has a spacious, flower-filled balcony; singles 300dr in off season, 400dr in high season, doubles 600-700dr. The **Kimi Hotel,** on the road south of town (tel. 22 40 8), has singles for 400dr, doubles 740-800dr, with bath 925-1025dr. For a great meal, try the unnamed **taverna** in the plaza behind the church where you'll spend 350-400dr per person. The less expensive establishment down the street, **Markos,** will suffice to fill you up; the management speaks French, but the food is unmistakably Greek.

Buses run down the twisting 52 turns to Paralia Kimi and back roughly every two hours. If you don't catch one in time to make your ferry, the local taxi drivers may try to capitalize on your predicament, so make sure to know which bus you are counting on when you buy your ticket. Since there is virtually nothing to do in Paralia Kimi except sit in one of the cafes and wait for the ferry, your time could be better spent exploring the village and its sylvan environs, even if it means the cost of a taxi back to Paralia Kimi (150dr).

Northern Evia

If you have time, venture to Evia's northern coast. Although the fishing village **Limni** is a beaming tourist resort, it has maintained a lazy, relaxed quality and probably will continue to be a place where there is little to do but nobody minds. A long pebble beach fringed by pine trees stretches from Limni 8km north to the village of **Rouvies.** Many Greek families get up tents along the northern end of this beach; if you choose to sleep further south, you will be alone. Within Limni, the **Ilion,** 2 Ossiou Christodoulou St. (tel. 31 76 8) is the cheapest hotel, with singles for 400dr, doubles for 700dr. Have dinner at the **Pouemplo** taverna on the water where variety is wide, portions large, and prices moderate. This is a good spot to watch the Greek *volta,* when the people of Limni meander up and down the waterfront, chatting, and greeting each other from 8-10pm every evening. There is one bus daily to Limni from Chalkis, leaving at around midday (210dr). North of Limni is the village of **Loutra Edipsou,** one of the biggest resorts in Evia. Stay instead at **Pefki,** further north and less touristed, with a quiet secluded beach. There are no hotels here, but a number of places offering rooms to let. **Epidos,** praised by Herodotus, Aristophanes and Aristotle for its healing sulfurous waters, attracts older tourists suffering from arthritis and rheumatism.

NORTHERN GREECE

The wild and unexplored parts of Greece are its northern provinces. Tourists hear little about the area, but Northern Greece has as much to offer as any other part of the country, with the added advantages that it is cheaper and unspoiled. The mountains of Northern Greece abound in spectacular scenery, with snow-capped peaks, picturesque mountain villages, roaring waterfalls, precipitious gorges, bizarre rock formations, and plenty of good hiking trails. Archeology buffs will find a number of excellent archeological sites, including Dodoni, Vergina, Pella, and Philipi. The student of Byzantine art will find more of interest in the North than anywhere in Greece, particularly in the monasteries located at Mount Athos and Meteora. Above all, the North invites the adventurous and inquisitive traveler. Since almost all of the larger cities are, for the most part, modern and unattractive, what there is of interest to the traveler is invariably off the beaten track, hidden away in more secluded villages scattered across the dramatic landscape.

Northern Greece consists of four provinces. The largest of them by far is **Macedonia,** in the north central part of the country. Thessaloniki, Greece's second largest city, sits in its center, and the peninsulas of Haldiki extend along its eastern edge. The most beautiful of the provinces is **Epirus,** with its scenic coast facing the Ionian Isles and lush, waterfed interior. More modern and industrialized, but not without a number of interesting sights is the province of **Thessaly.** Finally, the least touristed of the four, in the northwest corner of the country bordering Turkey, is **Thrace.**

Thessaly

While the major cities of Thessaly are modern, industrialized, and unattractive, the countryside is mountainous, unspoiled, and filled with enchanting villages and beautiful monasteries. A vast green plain surrounded by the gorges and ravines of Mount Olympos and Mount Ossa, Thessaly stretches from the fascinating monasteries of Meteora in the west to the traditional mountain hamlets on Mount Pelion in the east.

Volos

Jason and the Argonauts set off on their quest for the Golden Fleece from the site of modern-day Volos, which is on the northern coast of the Pagassitikos Bay. If these adventurers could see the sprawling modern city that occupies their departure point today, they probably wouldn't even need the quest to justify leaving. Volos, geographically, culturally and in every other sense in the armpit of Pelion, is possibly the most oppressive city you could visit in Greece. Buses for the beautiful villages of Mount Pelion and ferries for the Sporades Islands originate in Volos, but otherwise there is little to attract the tourist.

The only place of interest in town is the **Archeological Museum** at the eastern edge of the city located in a small park off Tsitsilianou St. (tel. 28 56 3). Open Mon.-Fri. 8am-2:15pm, Sat., Sun. 9am-2pm, closed Tues.; admission 50dr, 25dr with student ID. (The museum was closed for renovations in 1983, so call or check at the NTOG before walking all the way out there.) The museum contains a variety of pieces spanning the entire historical spectrum from the latter part of the Paleolithic era to the Roman period. The collection includes findings from the site of the Homeric Iolkos, which is located on the other side of town off Feron St. Don't waste your time trying to find the ruin: it has been lost to mankind once more, re-interred somewhere beneath the railroad station and a barrel factory. The area from the museum to the other park at Plateia Georgiou is the least offensive section of Volos. Not only is the museum courtyard cool and shady, but the residential streets surrounding it are lined with orange trees whose fruit (slightly seedy but refreshing) is ripe in late July and August.

The **NTOG office** (tel. 36 23 3 or 23 50 0) provides maps of the city and the Mount Pelion region, and posts bus and ferry schedules. If you are coming from the ferry, turn left as you get off and continue down Argonauton St. along the waterfront; from the train station, walk down Papadiamandi towards the water and turn left on Dimitriados by the square; from the bus station, walk towards the water and turn right on Dimitriados. The NTOG is open Mon.-Sat. 7am-2:30pm, 5:30-7:30pm; although nominally closed on Sundays, there is often someone inside. The **Tourist Police** (tel. 27 09 4) are at 87 Hatziargyri St., off the corner of Kartali St. several blocks up from the waterfront. There are two cheap hotels on Korai St. a few blocks from where the ferry stops. At #18 is the **Hotel Europa** (tel. 23 62 4) with single beds in a large room for 350dr, double rooms for 700dr, including showers. At #45 is the **Hotel Acropolis** (tel. 25 98 4) with doubles for 800dr, triples for 1137dr. Since the manager of the Acropolis has a habit of tacking an extra 50dr on the price for foreign guests, be prepared to bargain. **Hotel Iasson** (tel. 26 07 5 or 24 34 7) at #1 Mela St., even closer to the ferry stop, has singles for 641dr, doubles for 776dr, and triples for 990dr. As the "No Camping" signs (in English) indicate, some people do sleep in Plateia Georgiou park.

The tavernas and cafes along the harbor in Volos are quite expensive; you can generally judge just how expensive by the quality of the chairs and tables out front. Avoid the cushiony vinyl marshmallows by the eastern end and look for plastic and wickerwork to the west if you want to save money and eat just as well. The **Bosporus Ouzeri,** in between the two extremes, is clean, comfortable, and reasonably priced. Back up in town on Korai St. (across the street from the Europa), the Kavouras Ouzeri has a good selection of seafood. Try the marinated octopus for starters. You can rent bicycles at any of the bike repair shops in Volos, but make sure you get one that works—that's the best you can hope for. The bicycles rented by the shop on the corner of Koutarelia and Iasonos (a few blocks from the port) are less clunky than those available elsewhere.

The bus terminal, located on the corner of Ermou and Metamorfosseos Streets, should probably be your first and last destination in Volos. There are reasonably frequent connections to Athens, Trikala, Larissa, and Thessaloniki, as well as buses for points in Pelion. If you want to spend a night in the area, a far wiser move would be to stay in the lovely village of Makrinitsa (see below); buses leave every ninety minutes or so until 8:45pm.

For those who are hungry for ruins, the remains of the ancient city of Demetrias, named after Demetrios Poliorcetes, who founded the city in 293 B.C., lie 5km south of Volos. The most interesting part of the small site is the well-preserved, small, ancient theater. With a little searching, you'll find the surprisingly large archeological site of Pagassae outside of the modern village of Nees Pagasses, a kilometer or so further south of Demetrias.

In Volos' defense, it should be said that its nightlife is lively in the truest Greek sense. The long promenade along the waterfront overflows with people enjoying the cafes, restaurants, and each other, from 9pm to 1am. Moreover, the town itself has recognized the need to do something about Volos in the summer, and hosts a municipal festival in late July and August, with concerts, dance, and exhibits in the Riga Fereou Park. Later in August, the Pazari, held just outside of town, is a fair featuring Balkan handicrafts and a small amusement park.

Makrinitsa

Probably the most beautiful of the Mt. Pelion villages is Makrinitsa. Its shady maple and plane trees, stone houses with stained wooden trim and slate roofs, and cobblestone streets seem more characteristic of an Alpine hamlet than a Greek village. The occasional woman in traditional dark dress riding side-saddle through the village on a donkey, or the breathtaking view of Volos against the deep blue background of the Pagassitikos Bay, however, reveal that you could only be in Greece.

The NTOG has declared Makrinitsa a "traditional settlement," thus signifying an effort to preserve the many old houses and prevent the construction of modern homes that would blemish the village's appearance. They are also renovating three of the more exquisite villas—the **Xiradakis, Sissilianou,** and **Mousli** mansions—and converting them into guesthouses. They are, without a doubt, gorgeous, but with prices starting at 1760dr for a double without bath and 1985dr with, you might want to wait for your honeymoon (or second honeymoon, as the case may be). Presiding over the town square, the charming little church of **Agios Ioannis** contains some fine examples of woodcarving, as do many of the houses around it. Also of interest are the austere monastery of **Agios Gerasimou,** with its tall clock-tower and resident peacock and the seventeenth-century **Monastery of Sourvias** (a five-hour hike to the northwest).

The cheapest place to stay in town is the **Achilles Pension** (tel. 99 17 7), just below the town square, with balconies and a spectacular view. Doubles are 1050dr, triples 1260dr. The **Pilioritico Spiti** (tel. 99 23 1) is a new building, but built to resemble the old mansions. Doubles 1125dr; open May 1-Dec. 31 (the mansions themselves are open all year). Less expensive rooms may be found along the road which runs between Makrinitsa and Portaria, the next village down the hill. Makrinitsa has no post office, but you can buy stamps in the kiosk and mail letters in the post box. To change money, you must go to Portaria. While in Makrinitsa, be sure to sample the *spetsophai,* a stew made with sausage and local spices. The **Pantheon** restaurant in the square is a good place to do this, since the plaza commands a wonderful view, but the prices are lofty as well. The balcony of the **Galini** restaurant, above the square, is the next best thing. The town has a major festival on the 1st of May, re-enacting an ancient festival of Dionysus. While the celebration used to last eight days and nights, it is now considerably shorter.

If there is no more room in Makrinitsa, accommodations may be easier to find in Portaria, which is somewhat larger, though not as splendid as Makrinitsa. Portaria has a number of pensions and two noteworthy churches: the fourteenth-century **Panagia** of Portaria and the church of **Agios Nikolaos.** Buses leave ten times a day from the bus terminal in Volos for Makrinitsa and Portaria (last bus is at 8:45pm). If you are driving, follow Venizelou St. out of Volos to the north. Makrinitsa is only 17km from Volos but the ride, almost straight uphill, takes 45 minutes.

Mount Pelion Area

The Mt. Pelion peninsula was the home of the mythological centaurs, and it is easy to imagine how much the half-man, half-horse mischief-makers must have enjoyed frolicking on its misty green slopes. Natural springs and a moist climate keep Pelion lush and cool year round, a delightful change if you are feeling a bit singed by Greece's summer sun. Man has complemented nature here by building some twenty villages out of the local materials, rock and trees. The stonework of the Pelion mansions is so finely hewn that mortar almost seems superfluous and the wood decoration at times matches Tyrol's. Even the balconies delight, offering spectacular panoramas of the surrounding coastline.

If you want to explore some of the villages around the Volos area, there are two ways you can go: either across the peninsula and along the Aegean coast or along the coast of the Pagassitic Bay. Both are rewarding, but if you take public transportation, it can be difficult to get around since most villages are only serviced by two or three buses a day and the first buses often leave at 6am. You might consider renting a car or a bicycle in Volos to explore the area. Unfortunately, motor-bikes are not available for hire, unless you find someone who will rent privately. Although riding a bike on Pelion's mountainous roads under the blazing Greek sun can be exhausting, it is not entirely impractical; there are enough small pick-up trucks motoring about that you can often get a ride along uphill stretches of your journey. Likewise, if you catch them at a bus stop (as opposed to along the highway) and they have room in their luggage compartments for your bike, bus drivers should give you a ride at the regular rate. But hitching may be the best alternative, though it can be slow going in less traveled areas and on the outskirts of Volos.

Regardless of your mode of transportation, if you opt for the Aegean route, after Makrinitsa (see above) the first place of interest will be the Ski Area of Hania, only 26km from Volos, where you can see both sides of the Pelion peninsula. There is a **Youth Hostel** in the village (tel. 39 54 2). The road forks 14km east of Hania. One route goes north to **Zagora**, the largest of the Pelion villages, with a view of the sea and excellent beaches only 8km away at **Horefto**. The bus runs to Hania, Zagora and Horefto only four times a day, so walking or hitching are the most flexible means of transportation. If you get stuck here for the night, sleep on the beach or at the **Hotel Katerina** (tel. 22 77 2) with doubles for 1500dr. The other fork follows a delightful route through the richest cherry and apple orchards in Greece, tended by residents of the picturesque hamlets of **Anilio** and **Makrirahi**. This stretch makes a great hike and the bus schedule encourages you to try it as well. After 8km you come to a turn-off down to **Agios Ioanis**, a pleasant little beach resort frequented by Greeks and slowly being discovered by foreigners. This is a delightful place to relax and spend the night, with inexpensive tavernas and hotels. Try the **Avra** (tel. 31 22 4) with doubles for 750dr, or the **Anessis** (tel. 31 22 3) with doubles at 800dr; bargaining can help lower the price at either establishment if they are not crowded. The telephone code for the area is 0426.

If you want a beach to yourself, take the path over the footbridge and up the hill at the end of town. Three-quarters of an hour later you'll be in **Damouhari cove**, accompanied by local fishermen and a few hardy tourists. There are two small white pebble beaches here, the remains of a Venetian castle, and a peaceful olive grove. If you're looking for solitude, this is an ideal place. Buses run to Agios Ioanis from Volos at 4:45am, 8am, and 1:30pm.

The road heads south then forks to **Kissos**, the highest of the villages on the eastern slope, where you will find the eighteenth-century basilica of **Agia**

Marina. Continuing down the main road you arrive in **Tsangarada,** which has a palm tree in front of its church reputed to be a thousand years old and mansions that rival those of Makrinitsa. Eight kilometers downhill from Tsangarada, more good beaches can be found at **Milopotamos,** but buses only run to the beach in July and August. There are no inexpensive hotels in Tsangarada, but a number of rooms to let. Buses for Kissos and Tsangarada leave Volos four times daily, between 5am and 6pm. At 7:45am, there is a bus which goes all the way to Milopotamus.

The alternative route from Volos leads first to **Agria,** a lively resort town with many good seafood tavernas where the locals dine boisterously until late every evening, oblivious to the traffic whizzing by on the coastal highway. Inside Agria is the turnoff for **Drakia,** only 19km from Volos, a good place to head if you want to get out of the city and spend a night on the mountain. Of its many fine Pelion-style houses, the most noteworthy is the **Mansion of Triandafylou.** Buses for Drakia go to and from Volos three times a day. Except for three pleasant campgrounds in the quiet olive groves around **Gatzea** (approximately 120dr per person, 60dr per tent), little proves inviting about the coast between Agria and Afissos. Heading inland at Kala Nera, however, will bring you to two rustic villages perched on Pelion's mountainous spine. From the cool plaza of the first, **Milies,** you can look down to the still blue Pagassitikos Bay below. The frescoes in the **Church of the Taxiarches,** also on the plaza, are in good condition. Three kilometers north and uphill from Milies, the town of **Vizitsa** lies in sedate splendor like a carved wooden heirloom. The NTOG is restoring some of the mansions in this old village as well, but it remains quieter and less-visited than Makrinitsa. The stillness is richest during the afternoon, when the only sound is the splash of innumerable springs and fountains and the wind rustling through the poplars and maples that shade the village. You'll find a cafe in the center of Vizitsa, and rooms to let nearby. You can sit like an aristocrat and sip coffee while surrounded by cool wood and stone in a smaller and more elegant cafe above the town to the right, in the courtyard of one of the old houses. Buses run to Milies and Vizitsa six times a day between 6am and 7:30pm.

Farther down the main road, 3km after Kala Nera, a turn-off leads to the beach town of **Afissos,** a resort popular among Greek tourists, and graced with Pelion-style houses (with rooms to rent) overlooking the water. The cheapest hotel in town, the **Irene** (tel. 33 20 9) is hardly cheap; doubles 1250dr with private bath. However, a pleasant campground is in the woods, near Afissos. Seven buses run to Afissos per day, between 6am and 8:30pm, last return 9:30pm. After Afissos, the road turns inland and winds south through hilly orchard country; if you are taking the bus either north or south, you may be asked to get out and wait for an hour at **Promirio** before continuing. This is a true village of old Pelion, with stone houses, stained wood, and steep paths. At the same time, it seems rundown and flyspecked.

The farthest you can go by bus and paved road is to **Platania,** a peaceful town with a few good beaches and tavernas, and little else. Because many Greek tourists spend their whole summer here, year after year, the village community is close-knit even during holiday season and it's hard to find a room. If you want to try, call the town's one phone number, 0423 54 24 8, and ask about rooms in the **Platania Hotel.** Buses service Platania three times per day, in the early morning, at midday, and the early afternoon. Unless you specifically want to mingle with Greek society on holiday (not hard for Americans to do, especially if you speak Greek), the best reason to come to Platania is to step off for Skiathos; excursion caïques embark from the pier in Platania for **Koukounares Beach** in Skiathos two or three times each morning, depending on demand, and return in the evening (200dr one way). Usually, people get to Skiathos from Volos, but this route lets you see Pelion as well, for about the same price as a boat ticket from the larger city. You can also persuade one of the local captains to take you to the secluded hamlet of **Trikeri** or the still more isolated island of **Palio Trikeri,** which curves around like a finger in the mouth of the Pagassitikos. Both stops have deserted beaches way away from it all. Trikeri is also accessible by caïque, by a long walk on a dirt road from Milina, up the coast, and by weekly boats from Volos.

Trikala

In the heart of northern Greece, Trikala offers good bus connections and little else. Should you have to switch buses here, try to arrive before 6:30pm, when the last buses leave. The bus from Athens' 260 Liossion St. Station takes five hours; the trip from Thessaloniki takes two hours. The civic **Police Station** at 93 Larisis St. (tel. 27 40 1), the **Post Office** on Vas. Konstantinous St., and the **OTE.** on 25th Martiou St. are all in the neighborhood around Platia Politechniou, just across the river from the hotels. Trikala offers neither Tourist Police nor tourist offices.

Should you become stranded here, stay in one of Trikala's hotels which lie in the bustling cafe district, one block upriver from the Bus Station and to the left. The **Hotel Panhellinion** at 6 Vas. Olgas St. (tel. 27 68 4) offers lofty ceilings, porcelain bathtubs (hot water), and large, clean rooms at only 375dr for a single, 625dr for a double. Around the corner at 3 Asclepius St. is the **Hotel Pindos** (tel. 20 88 6). Cramped, lacking in hot water, it's still Trikala's least expensive accommodation (350dr for singles and 475 for doubles). The **Hotel Palladion** at 7 Vyronos St. (tel. 28 09 1; singles 375dr, doubles 640dr) is also slightly cramped, but it is much cleaner than the Pindos and its spiral staircase is always fun.

There is a bright side to this city on the Lethaios River: the old section of town on the northwestern corner of the modern city has delightful old houses and winding streets and contains a variety of interesting sights. The most conspicuous of Trikala's attractions is the restored **Fortress of Trikala** with its elegant, turreted clock tower visible upriver from the cafe district. The public garden in front of the Fortress has a fountain, a nice view of the valley, and an expensive restaurant built into the Fortress walls which lives off the tour buses that stop there on the way to Meteora. Trikala is believed to have been the birthplace of the superhuman physician Asclepius, so it comes as no surprise that Trikala contains the remains of an Asclepion, the oldest of the sanctuaries to the healing god, near the Fortress. All these sites are in the old quarter of town, an excellent place for a stroll, graced as it is with brightly-painted stone churches such as Agios Stephanos, Agios Dimitrios, Agia Paraskevi, Agia Episcopi, and the Panagia Phaneromeni (which contains a small museum). Also worth seeing is the **Cathedral of St. Nikolas** on Vas. Konstantinou St. The southwestern part of the city has the **Koursoum Mosque,** next to the church of Agios Konstantinos. It was built under Turkish domination when Trikala was the capital of Thessaly.

Pyli

The small thirteenth-century church of **Porta Panagia** is a convenient excuse to visit this charming town at the base of a river valley 20km west of Trikala. From the center of town, a kilometer's walk over a long, new footbridge upriver and to the left, the church has a small, beautiful yard with protective cypress trees and a meter-wide moat that is now empty. To get inside, go to the low building with green trim on the hillside and an old woman will lug over a huge key. Look for the beautifully preserved mosaics of Christ and the Madonna and Child on either side of the altar. The church also contains a few column heads from the Roman ruins excavated in the area. Upstream another kilometer is a large, sturdy Roman bridge that still provides a steep passage over the river, which doubtlessly was much deeper in earlier times.

As you get off the bus in Pyli, you'll find the town's only hotel, **Hotel Babanara** (tel. 22 32 5) with singles costing 520dr, and doubles 870dr, both with showers. Across the street, there is the usual line of cafes, and a couple of places where you can buy the delicious, slightly sour local yogurt. Twelve buses leave daily for the half-hour trip to Pyli from behind the Trikala Station between 6:15am and 7:30pm.

Kalambaka

Kalambaka thrives on its proximity to the weird rock formations and exquisite monasteries of Meteora. Running essentially north-south, one main avenue (Trikalon St.) with a village square at each end bisects Kalambaka. German and French tourists filling the restaurants and souvenir shops along this main drag leave intact the more authentically rural life on the quaint narrow streets and in the small enclosures filled with vegetable gardens and animals. From either of the two main squares you can head uphill toward the towering cliffs. If you can see past the effects of tourism, then Kalambaka is a good place to spend a night or two.

The least costly way to get to Kalambaka from Athens is to take one of three daily trains. The ride, however, is very rough, takes seven hours, and requires a change at Paleo Farsalos. Trains also run five times daily to and from Volos and Thessaloniki. To reach the Kalambaka **Train Station,** follow the large signs from the southwest corner of Platia Riga Fereo (just south of the triangular plaza). The bus trips from Athens and Thessaloniki are more pleasant than those by train; you must come via Trikala and then make the half-hour trip to Kalambaka (19 departures daily). The **Bus Station** is one block west on K. Oikonomou St. from the triangular plaza. Buses depart for Volos four times daily, for Metsovo and Ioannina twice a day, and for Meteora four times a day during high season and less often at other times (24dr). The **Tourist Police** (tel. 22 81 3) have an office in the regular Police Station at 33 Rammidi St. several blocks south of the rectangular square. The **OTE.** (open Mon.-Fri. 7:30am-10pm, Sat. 7:20am-3pm) and the **Post Office** (open Mon.-Fri. 7:30am-4:20pm) share the building a short distance down Ioanninon St., which starts at the northern tip of the triangular plaza.

Accommodations and Food

The **Hotel Meteora,** an amazingly comfortable and well-kept establishment on 13 Ploutarchou St. (tel. 22 36 7), charges 450dr for a single and 650dr for a double. If you stay more than one night, some hard bargaining might take 50dr off the price. To get there, head north, in the direction of Meteora, and look for the steep alley three blocks past the square with the Bus Station. Next to the Post Office on Ioanninon St. is the **Hotel Epirotikon** (tel. 22 43 0) with a friendly management but slightly dingy rooms; singles for 450dr and doubles for 550dr. You can also stay in one of the larger four- of five-bed rooms for 250dr per person. Less expensive alternatives include sleeping on the roof of the **Hotel Aeolic Star,** or heading for the Train Station, where **Hotel Atlantis** and **Hotel Astoria** each offer some beds for 300dr (the former is more pleasant). There are also five campgrounds near Kalambaka, three of which are slightly closer to Meteora (see Meteora section).

The **Kentrikon Restaurant** and **Nikosi Tavern,** both on the north side of Platia

Riga Fereo and the **Astoria,** around the corner from the Bus Station are good and inexpensive. For fresh fruits and vegetables, stroll up G. Kondyli on the way to the church.

Sights

Kalambaka's foremost sight is the Byzantine **Church of the Dormition of the Virgin** (open 9am-noon and 5:30-7pm; modest dress is strictly required). To get to the church, walk up G. Kondyli St. at the northeastern corner of Platia Riga Fereo. Turn right at the corner just before the sign for the Greek Tavern Meteora onto Eith Vlakhava St. and then left at a large, gray modern church. Proceed and you will soon see the graceful bell tower of the old church. A stork's nest, usually occupied, crowns the tower.

Built in the eleventh century on the ruins of a fifth-century basilica, the main structure was remodeled in 1573. Unfortunately, the interior frescoes painted by the Cretan monk Neofytos have been badly blackened by centuries of flickering candles and incense, making the massive sculpted marble pulpit the central feature. To enjoy an expansive view of Kalambaka from above, head down the road from the church on Mitropolios St. about a hundred yards and ascend the steps to the right.

Meteora

Unquestionably the premier tourist attraction in Northern Greece, and deservedly so, is Meteora. The name means "rocks in the air;" the Greeks could not have coined a more appropriate description for the tremendous, misshapen pillars of rock that rise straight up from the plain just north of Kalambaka. Legend has it that the mammoth rocks were dropped from the heavens for the sole purpose of providing a haven for pious Christians. Appropriately, the secluded summits of these unearthly formations were selected by monks in the eleventh century as the ideal setting for a life devoted to God.

Orientation and Practical Information

Before you begin to tour the area, be sure to stop off at the Hotel Aeolic Star, just off the triangular plaza in Kalambaka, to pick up the excellent free map of Meteora (printed on the back of the hotel's business cards). Two kilometers from Kalambaka is the hamlet of **Kastraki.** Kastraki contains three campgrounds that, listed in order of closeness to Meteora, are **Camping Vrachas Kastraki** (tel. 22 29 5), **Camping Meteora** (tel. 22 28 5), and **Camping Spilia** (tel. 22 28 9). All three charge 150dr per person, and 80dr per car and/or tent. Vrachas is the only one open November through April. In addition to camping, Kastraki also has one cheap hotel, aptly named **Hotel Kastraki** (tel. 22 28 6), with singles for 600dr and doubles for 800dr during the high season. Although Kastraki is more bucolic than Kalambaka, it's not much closer to Mete$ra. Unless you camp out, staying at Kalambaka, which offers ample accommodations and places to eat, is a better idea.

You will need a full day at the very least to see all the monasteries. If you lack a car, buses make the twenty-minute drive from Kalambaka to the Grand Meteoron four times a day during the summer from the main square above the bus station—check the schedule in Kalambaka. The bus can be flagged down anywhere along its way. Hitching should be quite easy given the large number of tourist cars, but these are generally packed, and the drivers less friendly than in less crowded areas. Even if you have to walk all the way to the **Grand Meteoron,** it should take no more than an hour and a half; you will also be able to savor the fantastic view at a slower pace. Notice, for instance, the gypsy settlements in the grottoes around Kastraki. If you bring along a light lunch you can spend the day pleasantly taking an early bus up to Grand Meteoron and Varlaam in the morning, eat on the mountainside above Roussanou at midday when the monasteries are closed, and then hitch to Agios Stephanos, Agios Triados, and Agios Nikolas in the afternoon. From the bottom of Agios Nikolas it is only a 2½km walk back to Kalambaka. As a second alternative, visit Agios Nikolas in the morning before the Grand Meteoron to allow for the more time-consuming hitching to Agios Triados and Agios Stephanos in the afternoon.

History

In the eleventh century, hermits and ascetics first began to occupy the pinnacles and crevices of Meteora. As religious persecution at the hands of foreign invaders increased in the twelfth century, Christians were attracted by the almost ideal refuge offered by the summits of these inaccessible, towering columns of rock. The first of many monastic communities was officially founded here in 1336. In the late Byzantine period when Greece suffered under Turkish domination, Meteora became one of the foremost strongholds of the Christian faith. The first of the surviving monasteries, however, was not built until the Serbian occupation of Thessaly during the fourteenth century. Meteora gradually flourished into a powerful community of 24 monasteries, all decorated by the finest artists and craftsmen of the day. Ironically, their wealth turned out to be their own undoing. Bitter quarrels over acquired riches led to neglect and consequent deterioration of many of the monasteries during the sixteenth century. Today only five of the monasteries are still active; the Transfiguration, Varlaam, St. Nicolas, Holy Trinity, and St. Stephen (now a nunnery). The Roussanou monastery is intact but uninhabited; of the others, only occasional ruins remain.

In modern times, as a result of the well-paved road and easy access to the summits, Meteora is no longer the secluded religious haven it once was. Hordes of tourists flock to the monasteries every day, especially to Grand Meteoron and Varlaam. The few remaining monks there devote much of their time to managing the rush of visitors. In the smaller, less accessible monasteries, however, solemn and austerely serene monastic life prevails.

The first ascetics scaled the sheer cliff faces by wedging timbers into the rock crevices, thereby constructing small platforms. In the caves and along the ripples of the rock walls you can occasionally see traces of wooden scaffolding. After the monasteries were completed, they were usually reached by extremely long ladders which could be pulled up at any time, rendering the summit virtually inaccessible. People could also be hoisted up in rope-nets. In 1922, steps were carved into the rocks and bridges built between the pillars, so the ascent is no longer the terrifying affair it once was. A word of caution: women wearing pants or skirts above the knees or men wearing shorts are forbidden to enter. Since women are required to cover their arms as well as their legs, you should bring a light, long-sleeved shirt to put on as you enter each monastery.

All of the monasteries have interesting features and artistic motifs to watch for. Large wooden slabs or bent scraps of iron suspended by two chains from the ceiling, for instance, serve as "bells" sounded with large wooden mallets by the monks at 6am and 6pm to signal the beginning and the end of the monastic day. The wooden seats lining the monastery churches are of one traditional form consisting of very small compartments with hinged seats. The seats fold back so that the monks can either stand or sit during prayers without moving from the compartments. The six-sided star or "star of David" which appears repeatedly in these churches was as much a Byzantine symbol then as it is a Jewish one today. Finally, the ubiquitous pair of eagles with elongated necks represent the Byzantine concept of the unity of church and state. They also stand for Constantinople itself, the religious and political center of the Empire.

The Monasteries

The **Monastery of the Transfiguration** *(Metamorphosos),* more commonly known as the **Grand Meteoron,** is the oldest and largest of the monasteries. Built on *Platylithos* (flat rock, the most massive of the occupied stone columns), the complex of buildings towers about 500m above the Thessalian plain. Founded by Athanasius, a monk from Mt. Athos, the Monastery soon rose to a degree of political and financial power over the other monasteries commensurate with its height when the generous John Uresis, grandson of the Serbian prince Stephen, retired to its summit in 1338. The Monastery is divided into two levels housing a variety of structures, including four churches. Only one of them is open to the public. As you enter the Monastery, you come to the large wooden basket which provided the original means of access to the summit. While they still use it to bring up supplies, the monks themselves wisely make use of the stairs. A stairway to the left leads to the second level and to a kitchen buzzing with flies despite decades of disuse. Adjacent to the kitchen is the Monastery's barrel-vaulted stone dining room, now converted into a museum. Its collection includes illuminated manuscripts dating from the ninth century and carved icons decorated with scenes from the Bible. One of the icons overlaid with tiny sculptured relief reputedly took a monk named Daniel fourteen years to complete. Of particular interest is the beautiful eighteenth-century print displaying a map of the area's original 24 monasteries. The Grand Meteoron stands out in the center of the map, with the monasteries of Varlaam and Roussanou just to the right and the town of Kastraki below. If you step outside onto the terrace of the Monastery you will enjoy this very view. Varlaam stands to the left, Roussanou is framed by the crags in the distance, and Kastraki nestles in the valley.

The central feature of the Grand Meteoron is the sixteenth-century **Church of the Transfiguration,** probably the most beautiful of all the churches at Meteora. The narthex (interior) is decorated with brilliant frescoes depicting the persecution of the Christians by the Romans, an appropriate theme for the secluded refuge of the monks. The main hall is capped by an elegant twelve-sided dome with the characteristic image of Jesus at its center. A friendly old monk who occasionally sings haunting refrains when the church is relatively empty tends the church. If you take the central stairway back down to the first level and face left, you will see a row of small arched cubicles where the monks go for solitary contemplation and prayer. Directly across is a chamber filled with carefully-stacked skulls and bones, the remains of previous residents. (The Grand Meteoron is open daily 9am-1pm and 3-5pm except Tuesday, admission 50dr.)

Just three hundred yards down the road from the Grand Meteoron, the **Varlaam Monastery** is the second largest and next most impressive monastery on Meteora. Built in 1517, its main attractions are the first-rate sixteenth-century frescoes that adorn the chapel. The fresco on the central wall of the church depicting the Apocalypse portrays little devils leading sinners down a long, flaming serpent's tongue to Hell while the faithful rise to Heaven on silky white clouds. In the far right corner of the narthex, a glass case contains venerated relics of bone set in silver. Just above hangs a fresco of Nektarios and Theophanes Asparas, Varlaam's founders, holding the Monastery aloft between their open palms. Also of interest at Varlaam are the museum and chamber containing an enormous wooden wine vat with a capacity of 13,000 liters. The Monastery is easily reached by a metal footbridge connecting it to the neighboring stone pillar. (Open daily 9am-1:30pm and 3:30-6pm, except Fri., admission 50dr.)

A short distance below the main intersection on the road back to Kastraki and visible from most of the valley, **Roussanou** is the most spectacularly situated and frequently photographed of the monasteries. All of its four sides rise continuously from the vertical walls of its rock foundation. Because of steady deterioration, Roussanou was recently abandoned and closed without plans for a future reopening. It is still possible to ascend a trail to the Monastery and walk across the bridge to one of the neighboring boulders for a dizzying view of the valley below. The shade of the mountainside provides good cover for a picnic lunch.

If you continue up the trail all the way to the end, you eventually reach the road leading to the Agios Triados and Agios Stephanos monasteries. A short walk along the road brings you to two lookout areas on the right providing the best view of Meteora. From the second lookout area five of the six monasteries are visible. Hitching along this road to Agios Stephanos and Agios Triados is fairly reliable.

Agios Stephanos, at the road's end, is the monastery visible from Kalambaka. Begun as a hermitage, Agios Stephanos officially became a monastery in the fourteenth century and is now a convent. Cleaner, lighter, more well-kept and spacious. Stephanos has an atmosphere very different from the massive Grand Meteoron and Varlaam. Of its two churches, only the more modern **Agios Charalambos** is open to the public. Built in 1798, Agios Charalambos serves as an interesting contrast to the older churches of the other monasteries. The scholarly young nun who tends the church is well-read in many languages and eager to answer questions. Although relatively small, the museum here is the best in Meteora because of the fine quality and delicate detail of its artifacts. Pay special attention to the abbots's elaborate personal signatures on the ecclesiastical parchment scrolls in the case on the left. (Open Tues.-Sun. 8am-noon and 3-6 pm; admission free.)

The Monastery of **Agios Triados** (Holy Trinity) lies a few kilometers down the road towards the main intersection. Looming directly over Kalambaka, its soaring peak features a striking view of the town's orange-tiled rooftops 1320m below and of the snow-capped Pirdos Mountains in the distance. The monk Dometius built the Monastery in 1476, but the wall paintings weren't added for two hundred years. There are pretty gardens scattered among the wood and stone buildings. (Open 8am-noon and 3-6pm.) A three-kilometer footpath runs from the right side of the entrance to Agios Triados all the way into Kalambaka. Follow the red trail marks into the city and then descend through the narrow streets towards the main drag.

All the way back down the road, past the main intersection and only 2½km from Kastraki, is the Monastery of **St. Nicolas** or Agios Anapafsa (open 8am-1pm and 3-6pm; admission 50dr). Built in 1388 and expanded in 1628, its highlight is the frescoes painted by the sixteenth-century Cretan master Theophanes. His technique of using alternately light and dark bold strokes of the brush make the figures on his icons bristle with life and look as if they were still wet with paint. A particularly delightful mural depicts Adam naming the animals. On a more mundane note, the Monastery also features a traditional Meteora lavatory: a hole in the wooden floor at the edge of the cliff, with a straight drop to the rocks below.

Visitors are only admitted in small groups, so wait in the entrance at the top of the steps and eventually the door will open (open daily 8am-1pm and 4-7pm, admission 50dr). In addition to the usual restrictions regulating clothing, St. Nicolas denies entry to men with long hair, but if you tie your hair back and tuck it underneath your shirt, you'll probably get in.

Epirus

If you came to Greece for striking natural beauty, you should seriously consider coming here (boats from Brindisi stop en route to Patras; and excursion boats from Corfu come here every hour). This hiker's paradise is filled with snow-capped mountains, lush valleys, serpentine rivers, and timeless mountain villages. If you long for the sea, Epirus has plenty of rugged, secluded coastline, and to top it off the ancient oracle here may speak to you in ways Delphi could not.

Igoumenitsa

No one ever goes *to* Igoumenitsa; one goes *through* Igoumenitsa on the way somewhere else. Though a drab port town, Igoumenitsa is an important transportation center for Northern Greece and the Ionian islands. Boats sail to Corfu twelve times a day (two hours, 197dr), and several companies connect the port with four cities in Italy: **Otranto** (Roana Lines, daily at 10am; 1600dr), **Bari** (Stability Lines, even-numbered days at 6am; 2300dr), **Brindisi** (Adriatica Lines and Ionian Glory Lines, daily at 7am; 2400dr), and **Ancona** (Minoan Lines, Tues. at 8am and Fri. at 10am; Ionian Star Lines, Wed. at 8am and Sun. at 7am; 2800dr).

There is almost always a **currency exchange** open at the port; the **National Bank** nearby is open Mon.-Fri. 7:30am-2:30pm. To get to the **bus station** (tel. 22 48 0 or 22 30 9), turn right as you disembark the ferry and then left one block after the little park. There is no train station, and the local people are tired of telling visitors to stay on the boat until Patras if they want to take advantage of railpasses. The bus station can connect you with most major cities nearby.

Merchants in Igoumenitsa clearly realize that most visitors are in a hurry to dash from the bus station to the ferry; most shops and fast food restaurants are located within a four-block radius of the ferry landing. The street along the water has mostly shipping companies and travel agencies; one block in you'll find the shops and restaurants. On the waterfront (towards the bus station) are the **Tourist Police** (tel. 22 30 2), open every day 8am-1pm and 6-7pm. The OTE (open every day 7:30am-10pm) and the **Post Office** (open Mon.-Fri. 7:30am-4pm; overseas parcels and money orders close at 2:30pm) are on Evaggelistrias St., the first left past the bus station. The **hospital** is at 15 Filiates St. (tel. 22 20 5; emergencies tel. 22 11 3). Stores are usually open Mon.-Sat. mornings and Wed. and Sat. afternoons. The **telephone code** for Igoumenitsa is 0665.

If you must stay, there is one cheap pension on Eleftherias Venizelou St. From the port authority, turn right and walk three blocks; past the Hotel Egnatia on the right stands the one-story white building with light blue shutters. The only identification is a sign which says in Greek *Pandoxion E. Osprotia John Diamante*. The second shop on the left (next door to the shipping agency on the corner) sells great souvlaki for 23dr. You can also try the **Rhodos** hotel at 19 Kyprou (tel. 22 24 8) or the **Stavrodromi** at 26 Souliou. Both have clean doubles for 700dr, including shower. The new **Kalami Beach Camping** (tel. 71 24 5) is 10km south of town. A taverna has opened up there, and a mini-market should be in operation by the summer of 1984. 140dr per person, 140dr per tent or car, including showers. **Drepanos Beach,** 6km north of Igoumenitsa, has a fine sand beach and relatively clean water, but no camping. For an inexpensive meal, buy a loaf of bread at the bakery next to the bus station. Across the street, grocery and dairy stores sell yogurt, feta cheese, and salami. But the wisest thing to do in Igoumenitsa is to leave—quickly.

Parga

Parga is settled like an amphitheater around a bay. Flanked by secluded inlets and coves, sandy beaches and offshore islets, its small port looks like a set piece for a landscape painter. The NTOG is trying to build the place up as a major tourist attraction, but luckily hasn't yet succeeded. Thus, the town remains a delightful maze of narrow passageways on steep steps, winding around brilliantly whitewashed buildings and archways.

All buses will deposit you at the bus station disguised as a cafe. Next door is the **Post Office,** open Mon.-Fri. 8am-2pm, and the **police station** (tel. 31 22 2), always open. The **OTE** is located down the street towards the harbor at #3 (open Mon.-Fri. 8am-1pm and 6-10pm). **Parga Tours** (tel. 31 58 0) on the waterfront doubles as a tourist office (open 9am-9pm). Gail and Dinos, the managers, can help you find a room, rent cars, boats, windsurfers, and can also arrange daytrips. Budget Cars rent for 2688dr a day plus 400 free km, 10dr per km thereafter. The **telephone code** for Parga is 0684.

Chances are that as soon as you step off the bus, several people will approach you whispering, "Domatia . . . rooms . . . Zimmer." If they don't find you, find them—better still, get them to bid against each other. Parga has an oversupply of rooms; you should be able to find a place near the water for 400dr for singles and 600dr doubles with bath (20% more in high season). **George Mitsoulis,** Averof 9 (tel. 31 03 8) has immaculate rooms and a good location. He can help you find a room if his are full. Otherwise, walk up the hill towards the ugly and overpriced Hotel Paradisos and turn left to the **Petros House** (tel. 31 38 9), which rents very clean doubles for 800dr (no singles), including the use of a spotless bathroom. Not as nice, but dirt cheap, is the **Acropole** around the corner (tel. 31 23 9). Singles 450dr, doubles 800dr including bath. The **Vasilas House** nearby offers doubles for 900dr. The road on the far left-hand side of the harbor leads to the shaded olive groves of **Parga Camping** (tel. 31 58 6)—like everything else, it's a stone's throw from the beach. In high season the charge is 120dr a person; 100dr a tent or car.

Most of the town's restaurants are on the waterfront. **To Souli** near Parga Tours has a fine view and tangy stuffed tomatoes. Better deals are further away from the water. Or try **To Kantouni** around the corner from the Hotel Acropole. At the top of the hillside next to the fortress, other good restaurants also offer rooms to let. A **supermarket** and a **bakery** are located up the hill from the Hotel Paradisos.

Parga has a number of intriguing sights. On one of the islands outside the harbor lies a remote monastery. Hire a boat to take you over for a few drachmas. The principal beaches include the sandy one right in town next to the harbor, and the long crescent-shaped **Lichos Beach** 3km to the south. Above all, don't miss the **Necromateon Acheron,** a Venetian fortress to the north. Dramatically perched at the top of the hill overlooking the town, the ruins command a spectacular panorama of the surrounding coastline. The fortress is beautifully shaded by pine trees and its gutted ruins are full of empty rooms and cool alcoves. In the heat of the afternoon, it's a perfect spot for a picnic or a snooze. Follow the steps from the harbor up the hill; if the front gate is locked, call out, wait a few minutes, and an old man will saunter out and unlock it for you. Admission 15dr.

Parga's principal attraction is swimming; get a mask and watch the fish down among the rocks. Price masks in the stores before you buy; then bargain. The longest beach is over the hill on the right-hand side of the harbor. The beach at **Lichnos** (5km) is bigger, but crowded. If you're feeling lazy, take a bus for 115dr. Windsurfing on all the beaches is about 150dr per hour off-season, 300dr per hour in July and August. You can take six hours of lessons for 2000dr. At the end you'll be awarded a diploma in Greek and English attesting to your windsurfing proficiency.

Excursions are made daily in summer to Paxos/Andipaxos (400dr) and Ioannina (510dr). The best daytrip, however, is a boat ride up the ancient river **Styx** (the Acheron), the mythological passage to Hades. The trip takes a half hour by boat from Parga to the mouth of the river; another half hour up the river the boat stops, allowing you to walk the mile and a half to the ruins of the **Necromateon Oracle.** On its return, the boat stops at Lichnos Beach for swimming and a late lunch in a taverna. Departure at 9:30am, return at 5pm; 400dr. Buy tickets at Parga Tours.

Nightlife in Parga consists of the Greek *volta,* the idyllic promenade up and down the main street along the bay. The two discos in town are caught in a time-warp, perfectly-preserved 1978 shrines to the Bee Gees and *Saturday Night Fever.* 200dr cover; first drink free. Avoid these overpriced anachronisms and head for **Funny Bar.** At 11pm and 1am Greek music takes over and the men dance traditional dances.

Preveza

The ugly port of Preveza is built on the entrance to Amvrakikos Bay, opposite Aktio, a one-kilometer walk to the harbor from the bus station. If you turn right and walk a few hundred meters, you'll come to the ferry boats. The main drag in town is Eleftheriou Venizelou, on which you'll find the **National Bank** (open Mon.-Fri. 8am-2pm), the **Post Office** (open Mon.-Fri. 7:30am-4pm; 2:30pm for money orders and parcels), and a number of cheap fast food joints. **Hotel Apollo,** 25 P. Tsaldari (tel. 28 71 6), has singles for 562dr, doubles for 815dr, and triples for 1125dr (10% less from Sept. 15-June 1). To get to the **Hotel Actaion,** 1 Colobou (tel. 22 25 8), go to the church tower and cut down the alley. It offers cheaper rooms at 450dr for a single, 800dr for a double, 1100 for a triple (showers 50dr extra). About one mile from the ferry landing is the **Bel Mare Campground** (120dr per person, 120dr per tent). If you have a sleeping bag, you'd be wise to skip staying in town and head to **Monolithi,** a great sandy beach 8-10km outside of Preveza on the road to Igoumenitsa with a campground (120dr per person, 120dr per tent) and taverna on the water.

Preveza is a good base for daytrips and a major transportation center. Buses leave for Igoumenitsa twice a day (280dr), for Parga four times a day (180dr), for Zaloggon twice a day (75dr), and for Athens (990dr) and Patras (510dr) three times a day. Buses also leave about every two hours for Nikopolis (60dr).

If you plan to continue south by bus, car, or thumb, you should take the ferry to **Aktio,** the scene of a great sea battle in 31 B.C. Apparently nothing of the ancient city survived, for it is now nothing more than a ferry landing. Ferries leave every half hour; from Aktio buses leave a few times a day for Lefkas. You can try to hitch a ride to Lefkas with one of the cars disembarking from the ferry.

Near Preveza

Zaloggon (Zalongo), 27km north of Preveza and overlooking the village of Kamarina, makes an interesting morning or afternoon trip. The mountaintop site figures in modern Greek history. On Dec. 18, 1803, sixty women from Souli threw their children off and then leapt from the cliff in order to avoid being taken as slaves by the Turkalbanians. A strange multiform monument honoring the heroines and the magnificent view of the Ionian coast are worth the tiring climb of over 450 steps. At the foot of the mountain is St. Dimitris Monastery.

Ioannina

Although the tourists only stop here to change buses en route to or from Igoumenitsa, Ioannina merits at least a day's stopover. The town is beautifully set on the shores of Lake Pamvotis with a spectacular view of the surrounding mountains. The old town streets are a fine place for a promenade, even during the eerie, deserted hours of a hot afternoon. The parks near **Platia Konstantinou Eleftherotou** and on the island nearby offer an idyllic escape from the summer heat of Northern Greece.

Practical Information and Accommodations

Unless you are coming from Athens, you will arrive at the main Bus Terminal between Zosimadon and Sina Sts. Buses to and from Athens leave from the terminal on Vas. Olgas St. Ioannina is the transportation center for Epirus, with four buses a day to Thessaloniki, ten a day to Athens, and nine a day to Igoumenitsa. If you stay for any length of time, you should get a city map at the bookstore (50dr).

Finding a place to stay is not difficult as there are few tourists. The **Hermes** near the station, is overpriced and noisy, although it's usually rather empty (singles 450dr, doubles 650dr). For more attractive accommodation, walk uphill from the main bus terminal and turn left on Tsinigoti St. Down on the right is the **Paris Hotel** (tel. 20 54 1) which has singles for 300dr, doubles for 400dr (showers 50dr extra). Further down Tsinigoti St. in corridors to the left and right, respectively, are the **Agapi** and **Pogoniou Inns,** where singles are an inexpensive 225dr, doubles 350dr; neither place has a shower. An immediate left after the Pogoniou and then a quick right will lead you to the National Bank of Greece at 10 Venizelou St. (open Mon.-Fri. 8am-2pm).

Uphill several blocks to the right after the Pogoniou you'll find Averoff St., which runs from the main gate of the old city on the waterfront up to Konstantiou Eleftherotou Place. At 10 Neoptlemov St. you'll find the **Hotel Elpis** (tel. 25 32 3) which, although slightly more expensive than the Paris, is closer to the old city. The cheapest inn this side of Mount Olympus, however, is the **Nea Yorki.** Walk past the southernmost parapet on the old wall; it's upstairs from the cafe opposite a small building on the waterfront. It's a very male-oriented establishment, so women might feel uncomfortable; singles 150dr, doubles 275dr.

If you head right and uphill on Averoff St. instead of left, past the white Turkish clock tower in the square, you'll find the **Bretannia** (tel. 26 38 0) and the **Ilion** (tel. 26 51 7) hotels. Each has lofty ceilings, spacious rooms, and beautiful, if noisy balconies, with singles running about 400dr and doubles 625dr. Immediately to the right after the Ilion is the **Post Office** (open Mon.-Fri. 7:30am-8:30pm for most services; *poste restante* until 3:10pm). The **OTE** is open 24 hours, and the English-speaking **Tourist Police** (tel. 25 67 3) are open 8am-10pm. A bookstore nearby has decent maps of Epirus and Ioannina, as

well as English periodicals. One long block behind the Post Office, at 6A
G. Molaimido St, is the local chapter of the **Hellenic Mountaineering Club,**
usually staffed after 5pm on weekdays. This is an excellent place to obtain
information if you are heading into the mountains (see Northern Epirus).

Food and Sights

Ioaninna is an ancient city with many historical riches. Founded by Emperor
Justinian, it was conquered by the Turks in 1430 and remained in their hands
until 1913. Ioannina was made famous, however, by the brutal Turkish tyrant
Ali Pasha, the governor of the province of Epirus just before the Greek Revolution, when he tried to secede from the Sultan and create an independent
kingdom. He is reported to have chained up his wife and harem of sixteen and
thrown them into the lake. He was belatedly assassinated in 1822 by the irate
local populace. The **Aslan Aga Mosque,** a splendid eighteenth-century reminder of the five-hundred year Turkish rule, is even more commonly referred
to in association with the Pasha. Now converted into a public museum, the
Mosque sits at the edge of the old town, overlooking the lake next to
Skilosofou St. (open Mon.-Sat. 8:30am-1:30pm and 5:30-8pm, closed Sun. and
holidays; admission is 22dr). On the southern side of the old town is another
area with deserted Turkish ruins, an old mosque, and isolated poplar trees.
This is an excellent place to spend the lunch hours with a superb view of the
lake and the new sections of the city.

The massive walls of the Castle of Ioannina are probably the oldest structures, having been built near the time of the city's founding in the seventh
century. The castle was further strengthened in the eleventh and fourteenth
centuries, and today its walls mark the dividing line between the old and the
modern parts of the city. Enclosed within the remains of the castle walls are
the narrow streets of the old town, filled with examples of traditional architecture, ancient plane-trees, and stone churches. As you walk through the old
town, listen for the clinking hammers of the silversmiths; you can look through
the windows and see them practicing their trade.

The **archeological museum** in Ioannina has been growing slowly in importance each year. The most interesting pieces in the collection are the detailed
panels on its three sarcophagi and the minute stone tablets etched with political, romantic, and cosmological questions that Roman emperors put to the
oracle at Dodoni (sixth to the third century B.C.). The museum is in a park
back from Averoff St. and below the clock tower. (Open Mon., Wed.-Sat.
8:30am-12:30pm and 4-6pm; Sundays 10am-4pm; closed Tues.; admission
50dr, 30dr for students.)

Ioanina's chief attraction, however, is the idyllic island near the western
shore of Lake Pamvotis. Boats leave every half hour in both directions from
8am-11pm (20dr); in Ioannina they leave from the lakeside northern corner of
the city wall, and are usually piloted by pre-teens under the proud supervision
of their fathers. The tiny village on the island has no cars; chickens wander on
narrow stone paths between immaculate whitewashed houses, many of which
have elaborate gardens. The interior of the island is pine forest with secluded
paths wandering between curious monasteries. Some have restored frescoes.
The most outstanding group can be found in **St. Nikolas.** It was here, in the
cellar of the church of St. Panteleimon, that Ali Pasha took refuge—in vain (he
was also killed here). The island has the best eating in Ioannina; select your
own trout *(pestropha)* from the tanks outside the restaurant (360dr per kilo,
and half a kilo is a *huge* fish). You can also get eel *(xeli)* and crayfish
(karavideo).

The dockside restaurants will suffice, but for even better food and a quieter atmosphere head for **To Sari** along the shoreline to the right or follow the signs to the Museum. You may be able to stay on the island (provided all the rooms aren't booked by Greek tourists). Singles are 450dr, doubles 750dr.

About 5km northwest around the lakes from Ioannina on the Konitsa highway is Perama, with some of the finest stalagmite and stalactite caves in Greece, stretching for about two kilometers and averaging about ten meters in height. The guided tour of the caves (admission 100dr) lasts close to an hour and includes a series of elaborate accounts of the names of different rock formations; if you don't understand Greek, you might wish to browse through one of the brochures sold at the entrance. Take the #8 bus from Konstantin Eleftheroton Place to the end of the line and then follow the signs.

Dodoni

Sheltered in a lush green valley at the foot of some enormous mountains (21km south of Ioannina), ancient Dodoni was the site of the oldest oracle in the Hellenic world. The ruins that remain are possibly the finest in Northern Greece and are surprisingly deserted.

Dodoni became a religious center when the first tribes of the Hellenes occupied the area around 1900 B.C. Worship first centered around an earth-mother goddess, but later shifted to a giant oak tree. Cauldrons were placed around the tree to resonate in the wind and thus drive out the evil spirits. Around Homeric times (800 B.C.) the site became an oracle dedicated to Zeus, who was believed to reside in the roots of the tree. A temple was built there around 500 B.C., then destroyed along with the oak tree by the Romans in 167 B.C. What little was left of the old religion was further subverted by the Christians who built a basilica on the site (the ruins are still visible) in an attempt to destroy the old pagan beliefs.

The main thing to see now at Dodoni is the beautifully-restored third-century **theater.** Second in magnificence only to the theater at Epidavros, it originally seated 18,000 spectators. The stage of the theater was rearranged during Roman times so that it could be used for gladiatorial games and other bloody spectacles that constituted the Romans' idea of entertainment. In the first week of August, the theater hosts a festival of classical drama performed in front of a capacity audience. The remains of the Oracles and the foundations of several buildings, such as a temple to Aphrodite and a hall for pilgrims, are next to the theater. A small oak tree has been replanted thoughtfully in the middle of what is left of the sanctuary of Zeus (open 7:30am-7:30pm; admission 50dr, 30dr for students, free on Sun.)

The peaceful village of Dodoni is adjacent to the ruins. The place is peaceful for a good reason—getting here is so difficult, it wouldn't hurt to have advice from an oracle. Municipal buses leave for Prevaze from the northern side of Pl. Pyrrou near the clock tower, on Bizanou St. in Ioannina (check at the Tourist Office for times as they are apt to change). Unfortunately, the buses turn around and come back almost immediately after they get to Dodoni. Once you're out there, though, it is not too difficult to sweet-talk your way onto one of the tourist buses heading back to Ioannina. If you have a lot of people you can take a taxi (700dr one way, 860dr round trip). The only other alternative is to hitch. Start walking out the Dodoni road from the Pl. Pyrrou to the Preveza road. The turnoff to Dodoni is 8km down the road; the last 13km is almost completely deserted. When hitching the last stretch, a sign may help to attract other tourists.

Northern Epirus

North of Ioannina, the countryside turns rugged and beautiful, a fairy-tale land of mountain hamlets and remote forests. The climate is dry in this region, so the mountains boast less of the vegetation encountered in the Metsovo area; you'll quickly acquire a fascination for this arid landscape.

Metsovo

Nestled on a mountainside just below the 1850m Kakara Pass midway between the Kalambaka and Ioannina, the exquisite village of Metsovo outshines even the surrounding Pindos Mountains in beauty. In the past few years, the main artery of the town has been transformed by the tourists who stop here for half an hour on the way from Thessaloniki to Ioannina. Houses with intricate woodwork line its narrow streets and the material grace and friendliness of its people are entirely undiminished. Here, the traditional Vlahi culture survives as a distinct sub-community in Greece. A group of Romanian shepherds migrated to the area over a century ago, and their descendents remain in the surrounding mountains for most of the year. The old men of the village spend their time in the main square watching the crowds of tourists and posing for photographs.

The buses stop in the heart of the main square, in the lower part of the village. Someone from the **Hotel Acropolis** (tel. 41 67 2) or **Hotel Victoria** will probably offer you a single for 450dr or a double for 600dr. Try to bargain them down since both hotels are a long, hard walk back up the hill to the main highway. If you decide you wish to spend more time wandering through the surrounding mountains, the best combination of price and location is the **Athenai** (tel. 41 21 7), located just off the main square behind the bank. Prices are similar to those at the Acropolis, but again, bargaining them down can bring them to a more reasonable level. If you are in the mood for a splurge, go up the main street from the square to the **Egratia,** which charges 800dr for a single, 1160dr for a double—try to bargain for a lower price.

Metsovo's merchants specialize in handmade clothing and trinkets which are hard to resist. Price attractive items and then bargain them down furiously; start to walk away if necessary. When you get tired of shopping, relax by wandering through the cobble-stoned streets. The church **Agios Paraskevi** near the square contains a beautiful wooden screen dating from 1511 and an elongated pulpit with a winding, wooden staircase. Although the **Tosita Museum** is touristy, it is interesting nonetheless and houses a large collection of utensils, riding equipment, costumes, tools, and weapons from an eighteenth-century Metsovo aristocrat. In the evening, lounge in the park near the square, and watch the old men talking and the children playing.

Metsovo is located half-way between Kalambaka and Ioannina. There are three daily buses to Trikala and Kalambaka and four buses to Ioannina. Both routes offer spectacular views of high peaks covered with unusually luxuriant vegetation. During the winter a very small ski area operates at Mount Pindos just outside of the town. The single lift operates daily 8am-5pm except for Wednesdays.

Zagoria Villages

The remote Zagoria villages, between Ioannina and Konitsa, have a century-old tradition of sending skilled masons abroad. Lately, fewer migrant workers have chosen to return to the ancient life-style, and many of the 43 villages have dwindled in size and lost their former prosperity. The government has declared them "traditional settlements" and has halted the development of tourism in the area. Roosters wander on paths between ancient stone houses erected without mortar, and shepherds usher goats down through the town every evening from the high mountain pastures. If you can, try to get some hot goat's milk with sugar in it—it's soothingly delicious.

For exploring the area, your first task will be to get a good map. Unfortunately, the army has forbidden the making of topographical maps (presumably because of the proximity of Albania). You may be able to get a 1902 ordnance survey map in Athens. The most easily available map is the 1:250,000 survey of Epirus, but this is of little use for trail information. If you are passing through Thessaloniki, the Greek Mountaineering Club there has some old topographical maps that cover the southern end of **Vicos Gorge**. The branch in Ioannina has a couple of rough contour sketches of the area between Papingo and Mt. Astraka; with some friendly persuasion, you will be allowed to photocopy these across the street (see Ioannina).

Getting up here without a car is very difficult since bus service is sparse and hitching is about impossible. During July and August, **Kipi, Tsepelovon,** and points in between—**Kepesouo, Kaukooli, Dilofo,** and **Asprageli** are served twice a day by bus from Ioannina, with **Monodendri** serviced only by the earlier run. A bus leaves Monodendri for Ioannina every afternoon. More distant **Laista, Illohori,** and **Vrisahori** are served by bus only once or twice a week, though a taxi operates out of Tsepelovon. Check all the bus times first in Ioannina, along with the schedule of the five daily buses linking Ioannina and Konitsa; you cannot flag down these buses along the way, but there are stations at all intersections and in all villages along the Konitsa-Ioannina highway.

If you come, bring some food and be prepared to camp (possible if done discreetly). There are no hotels but you might be able to arrange to room with locals. Remember that these villages are not prepared to handle tourists—they generally have only enough food for the village and are on the xenophobic side. Be extremely polite and do not trespass. If you are coming from Ioannina, you might consider leaving any heavy luggage behind and taking more water canteens instead; most trails are quite long and water sources scarce (there is no place to check in luggage, but you may be able to arrange something with the Tourist Police).

Vicos Gorge

For spectacular hiking, head for the Vicos Gorge. In this deep, twisted pathway, the air is always still, the sun seldom intrudes, and trees cling just barely to the cliffs. The trail along the gorge starts from near the **Agia Pakaskeni** monastery half a mile above Monodendron. The trail weaves across the river and along the cliffs all the way to the northern end of the Gorge, in the village of Vicos. It is possible to hike this distance in about eight hours, but one should allow even more time before sundown. It is impossible and dangerous to camp anywhere along the Gorge. Although rare, poisonous snakes and poisonous spitting frogs are found in this region. The trail is seldom used, not marked, and often obscured by undergrowth. Since this is not a national park, rangers do not patrol the trails, and it is not a good idea to walk the trails alone.

The tiny village of **Vicos,** at the bottom of the canyon, is situated on the road between Aristi and Papingo, served by a daily bus that leaves Ioannina at 9am and returns at 4pm (once again, check these bus times). The bus ride to Papingo is a thrilling adventure that seems to excite the otherwise implacable Greek travelers. If you have less confidence in the bus than in your own legs for climbing, you can reach Papingo by trail from Vicos in about four hours (the same trail extends back to Arista, on the other side).

In **Papingo,** life seems to revolve around a Mr. Kristodoulos who will sell you everything from a flashlight to a pork chop. He may also be able to get you the keys for alpine huts in the region, although these are often booked by expeditions. The main trailhead is further up the road at the tiny stone village of **Micro Papingo.** It is a good idea to ask Mr. Kristodoulos about the trail conditions. It is a three-hour climb to the main hut, below Mt. Astraka (2436m). There is a direct approach leading from the hut to the north face of the mountain, but the second half of this climb is quite challenging. The easier way to get to the top is to follow the trail that starts about 200m before the cabin and follow it around to the southern side of the mountain.

From the cabin, another trail leads north to **Mt. Lapatos** (2251m; two hrs.) for a fantastic view of the gorge formed by the **Aoos River.** The village of Konitsa will be in sight, on the other side of the precipice. Unfortunately, it is impossible to descend in this direction without hang-gliding equipment. To the southwest of Mt. Lapatos is the abandoned church **Agia Kiziaki** and a group of mountain shelters. If the main hut is full, the **Bristoureli Cabin,** about a mile along the trail to Mt. Lapatos, on the left side, is less often occupied.

The next two trails heading north off the main trail after the Astraka hut lead to alpine lakes. The **Stanitsoumani Hut** is visible from the main trail after the lake.

For the most spectacular view of the surroundings, it is worth making the three-hour climb to **Mt. Gamila** (2497m). The trail is quite easy and starts on the left of the main trail, about 100m after the lake. The main trail continues all the way to Tsepelovon (eight hours).

Macedonia

Alexander the Great came out of Macedonia and conquered the world. It's hard to know why; Macedonia is world enough with spiritual austerity at Mt. Athos, vibrant natural splendor in the Lake District, modern prospects in Thessaloniki and ancient projects at Vergina and Pella, Alexander's birthplace. Not widely explored by tourists, this largest of Greek provinces has more to offer than many think. Since the most interesting sights, whether landscape, waterfalls, or archeological excavations, are located in the countryside, there is often no need to get stuck in the often bland modern cities.

Kastoria and the Lake District

Jutting out on a peninsula into a beautiful, mountain-ringed lake, Kastoria is by no means a peaceful, picturesque little town. A thriving fur industry has spawned a bustling and filthy metropolis swept by strong mountain winds kicking up clouds of dust from the broken streets. To escape the city's despair, walk down to the water's edge where little wooden dinghies bob on the lake. Kastoria's many churches are well known for their unique and elaborate, serrated masonry. Two churches in particular merit a visit: the Byzantine **Panagia Koubelidiki** and the wooden **Church of the Prophet Elias** overlooking the lake from a beautiful spot just outside of town. About 4km north of Kastoria, along the lakeside is the eleventh-century **Church Malovitsou** with some well-preserved frescoes and a small museum displaying typical Macedonian house furnishings. Father Nicholas will let you camp on the waterfront in exchange for buying some of his postcards in the morning.

Of Kastoria's two inexpensive hotels, the **Kallithea** at 4 Artemidos St. (tel. 22 26 9) is less dingy. With rooms reached by a green spiral staircase winding outdoors through fur workshops, the roof provides a great view of the lake and the town below. The rooms smell slightly musky; singles go for 380dr, doubles 460dr, and triples 590dr. More expensive, the **Palladion** on 40 Mitropoleos St. (tel. 22 79 3) has singles for 580dr, doubles 775dr, and hot water every other day. The **Tourist Police** is on 24 Grammou St. (tel. 22 69 6), around the block from the **Main Bus Terminal,** and the OTE is south of Platia Davaki on Leo. Ay. Athanasiou St. Buses run to and from Neapoli, Edessa, and Thessaloniki four times a day and to and from Athens and Florina. In Athens the Kastoria bus leaves from Kavalas and Kifissou St.

If you really can't stand Kastoria, inexpensive rooms are available in **Maurohori** on the same lake ten kilometers down the road towards Edessa. Better still, head for the peaceful and serene **Lake District.** Since tourists don't usually venture north of Kastoria, this region of unspoiled lakes and rivers remains one of Greece's best-kept secrets. Many large lakes besides Kastoria's dot the mountainous area. **Florina** offers a good home base for exploring the area, easily reached by train or bus from Edessa, Kastoria, and Thessaloniki. There is an afternoon train to Bitola, Yugoslavia that arrives in time to catch a bus to Lake Okrid. Although the town itself has nothing to offer except a fragrant market *(agora)*, the **Tolis** has singles for 450dr and doubles for 625dr. 22km to the west is a mountaineering refuge near the village of **Pissoderi** on Mount Verna.

Northwest of Kastoria and 34km west of Florina, the Great and Small Prespa Lakes straddle the borders of Greece, Albania, and Yugoslavia. These Lakes cannot be visited without a permit (check the U.S. Embassy in Athens for details) but the **Great Prespa Lake,** largest in the Balkans, can be viewed from the hamlet of Agios Germanos. The tiny fishing village of **Psarados** is the nicest spot in the area and accommodations are available here. Easiest to reach from Kastoria is **Lake Vegoritis,** bordering the main highway to Edessa and Thessaloniki. A nice stopping-point here is Arnissa, 2km from the highway, a peaceful and untouristed village overlooking the lake. All of the lakes remain unspoiled by tourism and industrialization.

Edessa

A pleasant, clean little city filled with tiny plazas, fountains, and aromatic rosebud trellises, Edessa's main sight is the waterfall at the edge of town. Edessa ends abruptly on the brink of a deep ravine where the streams flowing under the town's arched stone bridges suddenly shoot into a gaping abyss and plummet over 25m to the floor of the valley below. The largest waterfall, Katarrakton, is in an opulent tree-filled park (walk along Filipou St. from the main bus station and then follow the signs). When you reach the park, be sure to descend the steps for a view of the frothy waters roaring over the edge of the cliff. Real waterfall enthusiasts should continue down the path at the bottom of Katarrakton into the valley to see the three more sizeable falls near the hydro-electric plant.

Aside from the cascades, Edessa offers little to excite the tourist. A small archeological museum exhibits findings from the area in the Tsami Mosque on Stratou St. at the back of town. Despite the town's historical antiquity and importance in the ancient Macedonian empire, little of Edessa's archeological past has yet been unearthed.

The **Hotel Pella** (tel 23 54 1), two blocks from the main Bus Station at 30 Egnatsia St., features high ceilings, a working elevator and clean doubles for 600dr in high season, and 450dr in low season. Diagonally across from the Pella is the large green and white **Hotel Olympion**, 1 Vas. Georgiou St. (tel. 23 48 5) which has a wider selection of rooms with singles for 420dr, doubles 580dr, and triples 820dr. Edessa's only E-class hotel is the **Olympia** at 69, 18th Octovriou St. (tel. 23 54 4) near the Train Station (singles 325dr, doubles 470dr, showers 50dr). A few doors down from the Pella Hotel, the **I. Omonia Restaurant** has an especially wide moderately-priced selection.

From June 1 to October 31 a **Tourist Police** office operates at Fillippou and Iroon Polutehneio Sts. (tel 25 35 5). The Bus Terminal on the corner of Paulou Mela and Filipou Sts. has fifteen daily buses to Thessaloniki. Buses to Kastoria and Florina leave from Egnatia St. next to the Pella. Trains depart three times a day from the end of 18th Octovriou St. for Athens via Plati, three times a day for Florina, and eight times a day for Veria, Naoussa, and Thessaloniki. Buses following a similar route leave the main terminal six times a day for Veria and stop at the modern town of Naoussa, 43km from Edessa, where more superb waterfalls can be found. Eighteen kilometers up the road from Naoussa at the village a small ski area operates in the winter.

Vergina

The discovery of the ancient ruins of Vergina, 11km southeast of Veria, only four years ago marks the greatest archeological event in recent history. Archeologists have determined that the royal tombs and remains of a large palace date from 350-325 B.C., though the identities of the royal deceased remain in dispute. Given the high-quality workmanship of the magnificent treasures found in the tombs, some have concluded that they could only belong to the royal family of Macedonia—that of King Philip II, father of Alexander the Great. Others disagree, but cannot suggest who else could have received such an honorable burial.

The ruins are located near the village of Vergina. Unfortunately, the site has not been excavated fully and does not really deserve a visit unless you are either an archeology buff or simply near the area. As you proceed down the road leading out of the village, you will see a sign pointing to the left for "The Royal Tombs" while "The Archeological Site" is straight ahead. The tombs to the left are still being excavated and are not open to the public. There are, however, plans to reconstruct a full-scale Macedonian Tomb. You should proceed straight ahead, 2km from the village, to the ruins of the third-century **Palace of Palatitsa.** Look for the exquisite mosaic floor, still in excellent condition, on the south ring of what remains of the palace.

Shortly before the site, a short climb up from the site to your left takes you to a beautifully-preserved and partially-excavated royal tomb. Archeologists found a gold chest within that contained the cremated remains of some royal personage (presumably Philip II) along with a great many artworks and pieces of jewelry. All of the findings from the tombs of Vergina are on display at the archeological museum in Thessaloniki. Since the site has not yet worked its way into the itineraries of tour buses, it is usually fairly deserted. It is probably a matter of only a few years before this situation changes for the worse. (Open Mon.-Sat. 9:30am-6pm, Sun. and holidays 10am-3pm; admission 50dr.)

The closest city of any size to Vergina is the noisy, unattractive town of Veria, 74km from Thessaloniki. Buses run every thirty minutes between Veria and Thessaloniki and seven times daily between Veria and the town of Vergina.

Thessaloniki

Like an amphitheater surrounding its graceful circular harbor and long waterfront promenade, Thessaloniki, the capital of Macedonia, wears the modern and uniformly drab architecture of an earthquake-plagued metropolis. Greece's second largest city has an ancient past as well. Though there's nothing here comparable to the Parthenon, Thessaloniki hosts a rich array of fine Byzantine churches, an excellent archeological museum, and some Roman ruins. The castle-like White Tower, the symbol of Thessaloniki, presides over the harbor like an oversized chesspiece. About fifteen blocks up from the waterfront, just to the north of Athinas St., lie the winding streets of the old town—good for afternoon perambulations.

On the crossroads of the important trade routes, the city has flourished ever since it was founded by Cassander, the brother-in-law of Alexander the Great, in 315 B.C. Named for Cassander's wife, Thessaloniki prospered after the Roman conquest of Greece, being the only port on via Egnatia, the ancient east/west highway. Egnatia St., six blocks from the waterfront, still serves as the city's main avenue. During a period of cultural decline in Athens, Thessaloniki became the most important city in the Byzantine Empire after Constantinople. After the tenth century, the missionary followers of the Brothers Cyril and Methodius (hence the Cyrillic alphabet) exerted a considerable influence over the culture of the Balkans.

Orientation and Practical Information

The transportation center of Thessaloniki is located towards the western end of the city around **Monastiriou St.** This central avenue runs parallel to the waterfront and is transformed into **Egnatia St.**, which leads towards the old city. Your first stop should be the helpful **Greek National Tourist Organization** (tel. 27 18 88 or 22 29 35), half a block up from the waterfront at 8 Platia Aristotelous (open daily 8am-8pm.) They can provide you with a good map of the city, hotel listings, train, bus, and boat schedules, and generally answer any questions you may have. Be sure to ask about local cultural events, especially the **Film and Song Festivals** in September and the October **Demetria Festival** in honor of St. Demetrius, patron saint of the city. A celebration of art and drama, the Demetria includes traditional music and folk dance performances. Less helpful are the **Tourist Police** in the hotel district at 10 Egnatia St. and the New Railway Station. Both organizations also have offices at the airport.

Sitting at the juncture of three major domestic rail lines, Thessaloniki is a center for nearly all forms of Greek public transportation. Trains leave from the **Main Railway Terminal** (tel. 51 75 17; Monastiriou St., in the western part of the city) for Athens six times a day via Larissa, Levadia, and Thebes, seven times daily for Edessa and four times daily for Florina in the west, twice daily for Alexandroupolis in the east, and once a day for Istanbul. There are also four train lines which pass through Thessaloniki on the way to numerous destinations in western and eastern Europe. The **State Railway Offices** (OSE) (tel. 27 63 82) are at 18 Aristotelous St. To get to the Train Station itself, take a bus (100dr) headed west down Egnatia St. The Station is the monstrous cement building on the right.

Two bus companies serve Thessaloniki: the State Railway Organization Coaches (OSE) and the private KTEL with stations around the city serving different destinations. Eighteen OSE buses depart for Athens from the Railway Station each day. Immediately adjacent to the station on Monastiriou St., four KTEL buses go to Athens for less money than the OSE buses. Four daily Trikala-bound buses leave from here as well. Buses for Kastoria (ten daily runs; five hours), Florina (five buses daily; two hours), Pella (21 daily; one hour), and Volos (four daily runs) leave from points along Anagenniseos St. a few blocks from the Train Station towards the waterfront. Just around the corner at 26 Octovriou St., ten buses go to Veria a day. Also on the west end of town at 19 Christoupipsou St., behind the Hotel Rei, buses for Kalambaka and Ioannina leave four times daily. Finally, for those going southeast to the Halkids Peninsula, the KTEL Station is at 68 Karakassi St., on the east end of the city (take bus #10 to Leofouion).

Tickets for the Railway Organization Coaches can be purchased at the OSE booking office at 18 Aristotelous St. (tel. 27 63 82 or 51 75 19); tickets for KTEL buses can be purchased at the branch stations before boarding the bus. For schedule information, check the NTOG office or individual stations.

Thessaloniki's **airport** serves London, Paris, Munich, Frankfort, Vienna, Dusseldorf, Amsterdam, Tel Aviv, and Cairo as well as other major cities around the world. Domestic flights are made to Limnos, Lesvos, Kavala, Kozani, Skiathos, Kastoria, and Alexandroupolis. For more information, contact Olympic Airways (tel. 26 01 21) at 7 Vas. Konstantinou St. on the waterfront. Other international airlines have offices nearby. Considering its stature as a port, Thessaloniki has remarkably little passenger ferry service. The *Sappho* leaves from the pier near Platia Elephtheria every Saturday and Sunday for Lesbos, Chios, and Piraeus. For tickets contact Vladimiros Karakharissis at 19 N. Kountouriotou St. (the western extension of Vas. Konstandinou St.) on the second floor (tel. 53 22 89) or Doucas Tours at 8 Venizelou St. (tel. 27 74 56).

Tourist Police: 10 Egnatia St. (tel. 52 25 87) or at the New Railway Station (tel. 51 70 00). Office at the airport.

Central Post Office: Tsimiski St. between Aristotelous and Karoloudil Sts. Open Mon.-Fri. 7:20am-9:30pm. Package-wrapping service in the basement.

OTE Offices: Main office on Vas. Irakliou St. (one block north of the Post Office; entrance from Ermou St.) is open only Mon.-Fri. 7:45am-1pm. Two others in the western part of the city at 26 Octovriou St. and at 26 Agelaki (near Sintrivanion Square). Open Mon.-Fri. 7:30am-11pm, weekends and holidays until 1:30pm.

American Express Travel Office: 10 Venizelou St. Do not confuse with **American Express Bank** around the corner on Tsimiski St. which sells and refunds travelers checks.

Currency Exchange: National Bank of Greece, 11 Tsimiski St., is open for exchange 8am-7pm. Smaller banks charge higher commissions for exchanging checks.

U.S. Consulate: 59 Vas. Konstantinou St. (tel. 27 39 41).

U.K. Consulate and Library: 11 Vas. Konstantinou St.

Magic Bus: 32 Tsimiski St. (tel. 28 32 80). Departures every Wed. and Fri. at midnight for Germany and England and every Tues., Wed., Fri., and Sat. at 8pm for Italy, France, and England.

Hospital: Agios Paoulus, 37 Frangon St. (western extension of Ermidou St.; tel. 53 80 21).

ELPA: Greek Motorists' Association. On Antheou St. in the eastern part of town just off the waterfront.

Travel Agent for the Disabled: Lavinia Tours, 101 Egnatia St. (tel. 23 44 89).

Laundromats: four in town. The best one is the Bianca, 3 Vas. Antoniadou St. next to the Arch of Galerius. Open until 2pm Mon., Wed., and Sat. and until 8pm other days. 100dr per load. Around the corner is Zerowatt at 2 Episkopou St. Also try in the basement of 46 Olibou Cor Olympou St. and the Canadian at Platia Navarino.

Book Stores: Near the National Bank at 10 Tsimiski St. is the excellent Molcho Books, with extensive selections in English, French, and German. Open Mon.-Fri. 7:30am-2:30pm, Sat. until 1:30pm.

Bicycle Rental: great for Thessaloniki's long and flat waterfront. Ask for Ramattis Michalis at Reutra Bicycles and Motorcycles at 66 Filipou St.

Accommodations

The main hotel district is along and on either side of the western end of Egnatia St., roughly between J. Mextaxa Square and Dikasterion Square. This concentration of hotels in one area makes shopping and bargaining for a room simple and convenient. Minimum rates for a D-class hotel, with and without bath, are singles 375 and 450dr, doubles 520 and 575dr, and triples 675 and 760dr. Best along Egnatia St. are **Nea Niki** at #15 (tel. 52 22 32), the **Alexandria** at #18 (tel. 53 61 85), the **Illisia** at #24 (tel. 53 21 00), and the **Avgoustos** at 4 Helenis Svoronou St. (tel. 52 25 50). The nicest D-class hotel by far is the **Hotel Tourist,** 21 Metropoleos St. (tel. 27 05 01), two blocks west of Aristotelous Square and two blocks up from the water.

Minimum rates for E-class hotels, with and without bath, are singles 290 and 380dr, doubles 450 and 525dr, and triples 570 and 660dr. Of the four E-class hotels, the **Atlantis,** 14 Egnatia St. (tel. 53 69 09) with its interesting architecture, and the relatively new **Argo,** 1 Helenis Svoronou St. (tel. 51 97 70) have accommodations of the same caliber as D-class hotels. The other two E-class hotels are the **Patris,** 3 Helenis Svoronou St. (tel. 52 22 50) and the **Nea Orestias,** 20 Selefkidon St. (tel. 51 94 11).

Thessaloniki has one **Youth Hostel** conveniently located near the Arch of Galerius on 44 Nikolaou St. The reception office is open 8:30-11am and 6-11pm, dorm beds are 250dr each, and showers (which can be taken only 6-11pm) are 25dr. All hours are strictly observed: doors close for the night promptly at 11pm and the rooms are locked from 11am-5pm though a small sitting area is kept open during the day. The hostel is clean and comfortable.

The **YWCA** (*XEN* in Greek) at 11 Agias Sophias St. (tel. 27 61 44) has dormitory beds for 240dr per night.

Food

Interesting as well as cheap, the marketplace or *agora* is in the middle of town, bounded on four sides by Irakliou, Egratia, Aristotelous, and Venizelou Streets. This is the place to go for fresh bread, cheese, olives, fruits, vegetables, and dried meats. Several inexpensive restaurants stand nearby, including the **Thomas Restaurant-Taverna** on 39 Irakliou St. They often have fresh fish, and Thomas himself speaks English pretty well and is very friendly. Another inexpensive restaurant is a block behind to the Arch of Galerius on the corner of Antoniadou St. Several small *psistarias* or charcoal-pit grills line the strip of Tsimiski St. between Dragoumi and Dodekanisson Sts. There are a few more inexpensive restaurants near the **Rogoti** at 8 Venizelou St. and the **Shetis,** in the Akropolis area. The **Galaxy Pastry Shop** on 34 Nicolaou St. near the Thessaloniki Youth Hostel offers the best baklava in town.

Sights

If you have time for only one stop in the city, you should definitely head for the **Archeological Museum** (tel. 83 05 38), one of the finest in the country. The high point of the museum's exhibits is the superb collection of Macedonian treasures from all of Northern Greece. Located in a side wing of the building, the collection features the recent findings from the Tombs of Vergina, including radiant gold jewelry and gold *larnakes* (burial caskets), which contained the cremated bones of members of the royal family of Vergina. Some of the findings are currently on a world-wide tour, but the great majority of the artifacts remain in Thessaloniki. The Vergina wing should not be allowed to outshine the rest of the museum's beautiful exhibits. Arranged clockwise in chronological order, the displays consist of extraordinary sculptures and mosaics from Archaic to Byzantine times. (Open Mon.-Sat. 9am-3pm, Sun. 10am-2pm.) Admission is 100dr, 50dr for students. To reach the museum, take bus #10 or 31 east on Egnatia St. Next to the museum is a pleasant park with a small open-air zoo (no admission charge).

On the other side of the park on the waterfront at the start of Vas. Sofias St. looms the **White Tower.** The tower is all that remains of a Venetian seawall. Known as the Bloody Tower because an elite corps of soldiers was massacred in it, the structure was once painted white in the hope that a more cheerful color would dispel the gruesome connotations. Far more extensive ruins, the **Eptapirigion Walls,** erected during the reign of Theodosius the Great, stretch all along the northern edge of the old city. To get to the ancient walls take bus #22 from Eleftherias Square on the waterfront. That is also where buses #5, 7, or 33 leave for the **Ethnological Museum of Popular Art** (Folkloric Museum), at 68 Vas. Olgas St. in the eastern part of the city (tel. 83 05 91), which contains examples of many different forms of traditional dress from all over Northern Greece (open 9:30am-2pm).

Thessaloniki possesses several interesting ancient Greek and Roman ruins, the finest of which is the celebrated **Arch of Galerius.** Erected to commemorate the victories of Emperor Galerius over the Persians in 297 A.D., the arch stands at the end of Egnatia St. at the corner of Gounari St. Next to it is the **Rotunda,** originally constructed as an emperor's mausoleum. Constantine the Great converted the structure into a church dedicated to St. George, hence its present name, Agios Georgios. Constantine also furnished the church with impressive fourth-century mosaics, the oldest and perhaps the greatest in Thessaloniki. The Rotunda served as a Turkish mosque for four hundred years before being restored to Christianity in 1912. The church has been under restoration since the 1978 earthquake, and officials don't know when it will be reopened to the public.

For more ancient ruins, head north of Dikastirion Square to the recently-excavated Roman ruins between Fillipou and Olibon Sts. The ruins, which include a somewhat over-restored theater, are still being excavated. The work should be completed in the near future. Already fully excavated are the remains of the **Palace of Galerius,** featuring a well-preserved octagonal hall (near Navarino Square). No Roman city would be complete without **Roman Baths.** You'll find their ruins next to the church of Agios Dimitrios, at the corner of Agios Dimitrious and Aristotelous Sts. The entrance is in the front left-hand corner of the church (open Mon.-Sat. 9am-1pm and 4-6pm, Sun. 10am-4pm; closed Tues.).

Thessaloniki is one of the best places in Greece to see Byzantine art. Only twenty churches survived the earthquakes, but many of them contain outstanding mosaic work. **Agios Dimitrios** is the largest church in Greece and contains some famous fifth-century Byzantine mosaics similar to those in Ravenna, Italy: look on all three inner sides of the pillars at the end of the central nave for some examples. Most of the old church was destroyed in a fire in 1917, but a chapel in the far right corner retains its original frescoes. In the basement of the church beneath the altar there is an ancient crypt where St.

Dimitrios, Thessaloniki's patron saint, was imprisoned and martyred (open 8am-noon and 4-7pm).

Besides the frescoes in the two churches mentioned above, the most noteworthy example of Byzantine art in Thessaloniki is the splendid ninth-century mosaic of the Ascension in the dome of the **Agia Sophia** (in the park of the same name at the corner of Ermou and Agia Sophias Sts.). Modeled after Sancta Sophia in Istanbul, the church is also famous for the unusual representation of the seated Virgin in the apse. Currently undergoing restoration, the church is still open to the public. For more good mosaics, visit the Panagia Ahiropiitos just two blocks further north on Agia Sophias St. Many of Thessaloniki's other churches contain superb frescoes from the late Byzantine era. The Guild church of Panagia Halkeon in Dikasterion Square, Agia Ekaterini, and Dodeka Apostoli (the church of the twelve Apostles) are particularly impressive. The churches in Thessaloniki all close for a long siesta. (Open approximately 8am-noon and 4-7pm except for Sundays and holidays when services are held in the morning.)

Art in Thessaloniki is not restricted to the ancient. On the northern side of Egnatia St. near the Arch of Galerius there are some interesting little icon studios where artists still use the technique and style of the Byzantine period. The artists prop a long pole against the wall to stabilize their hands for painting the delicate details of the icons, resulting in the rigid yet harmoniously balanced quality of Byzantine painting. The **Thessaloniki Art Gallery** in the building of the Society of Macedonian Studies at 2 Vas. Sofias St. features works by contemporary artists from Greece and abroad.

Jews have lived in Thessaloniki since before the Christian Era. The once flourishing community was largely decimated during the holocaust of World War II, but the beautiful **Old Synagogue,** now no longer in use, can still be seen if you ask for the caretaker at the Jewish Community Center on 24 Tsimiski St. under the covered arcade.

For a good view of Thessaloniki, the Aegean, and the legendary peaks of Olympos and Ossa, climb up to the **Vlatadon Monastery,** on the corner of Eptagiriou and Dimadou Vlatadon Sts. A couple of blocks away on Epimenidou St. is the church of **Ossios David,** which contains a beautiful fifth-century mosaic showing the dream of Ezekiel. For an even better view of the surrounding countryside, take the bus from Dikasterion Square 12km up Mount Hortiatis to the village called, appropriately enough, **Panorama.** Because of its refreshingly cool altitude, the village is a popular destination for summer excursions, and is consequently rather touristy and overpriced.

During the summer, weekend nightlife centers in the suburb of **Nea Krinis.** You'll find plenty of Greek music, dancing, and company. Take bus #5 from Platia Aristotelous east of Mitropoleos St.

Pella

Discovered by a farmer in 1957, the famous ruins of ancient Pella are a rewarding and interesting daytrip 38km west of Thessaloniki. Pella served as a port in ancient times, when the surrounding plain was covered with water and was chosen as the site for his palace by King Archeolonos around 400 B.C. It rapidly grew into a great cultural center and the largest city in Macedonia. Under Philip II, Pella became the first capital of a united Greece. The birthplace of Alexander the Great, Pella served as the starting point for Alexander's lifelong mission to unify the entire world under Macedonian rule. A century and a half later, Hellenic rulers fell on hard times and the city was plundered by the Romans (168 B.C.).

The outstanding attraction on the grounds of the site are the incredible mosaic floors. Although made out of rough natural pebbles of various colors, the mosaics exhibit a remarkable degree of expression and artistic perfection. Particularly striking are the *Deer Hunt* and the *Rape of Helen*. Restoration work is still being conducted on many parts of the site; a very good restoration job has been done on the Ionic Colonnade of the interior court of a mansion. (Open Mon. and Wed.-Sat. 8:30am-6pm, Sun. 9am-3pm, closed Tues. Admission 50dr, students 30dr.)

On the other side of the highway is the **Pella Museum** (tel. 31 27 8), which ranks among the five best museums in the country. Its small but excellent collection is highlighted by the mosaics of *Dionysus Riding a Panther* and *The Lion Hunt*. (Open the same hours as the site.)

The nearest hotels are in the town of **Giannitsa**, 12km west of the ruins. Although there is no official campground in the area, you can camp near the site without difficulty. The cafe/restaurant next to the site offers the necessary amenities: food, restrooms, and an outdoor sink. Buses to or from Thessaloniki pass by the site, which is right on the main highway, two or three times an hour. To go between Pella and Vergina, change buses at Halkidona, only a few kilometers east of Pella.

Mount Olympos

Rising from the coastal plain less than 100km southwest of Thessaloniki, Mt. Olympos so impressed the seafaring ancient Greeks that they deigned it the lofty home of the gods. First climbed in 1913, the mountain's rugged 3000m slopes have since become a popular hiking spot for hardy Greeks and foreigners alike, while remaining largely ignored by the majority of tourists who prefer the less strenous life offered on Greek coasts. While Olympos' prestigious mythological credentials have partially waned with human intrusion, the two-day climb is nevertheless spectacular and perfect for the physically fit but inexperienced hiker.

The best point of entry to Olympos is the rather plain village of **Litochoro**, conveniently situated a mere 6km from the Athens-Thessaloniki highway and accessible by both bus and train. Local buses make the run between Litochoro and Katerini hourly between 6am and 10:30pm and stop at the gas station at the intersection of the Athens-Thessaloniki highway and the road leading to Litochoro. You can hitch from the crossroads to town. Although there is not much to do in Litochoro, the town is big enough to have a **bank** (open Mon.-Fri. 8am-2:30pm), **Post Office** (open Mon.-Fri. 7:30am-2:30pm), and an **OTE** (open Mon.-Fri. 7:30am-9pm), which you'll find in the square where the main road ends. Near the bus station is the **SEO Mountaineering Club,** which provides maps and information about the mountain. (The Youth Hostel also provides a free map.) Above the square there are several bakeries and grocery stores where you can buy provisions for your hike. The **telephone code** for the area is 0352.

In Litochoro, try the small (14 beds) **Litochoro Youth Hostel** (tel. 81 31 1 or 82 17 6 during the day), located on a side street not far from the town park. They generally have beds available costing 180dr with a hostel card, 200dr without; showers 40dr; luggage storage 40dr. (If you want to leave luggage but not sleep in the hostel, you will have to pay for staying one night anyway; try to make an arrangement with someone who is staying there.) There is nobody in the hostel during the day, but you can come in and drop off your stuff. The **Markesia,** above the square 150m and to the left (tel. 81 83 1/2), has singles for 675dr, doubles for 810dr, 20% more for each additional bed, all with private bath. Just below the square, the **Hotel Myrto** (tel. 81 39 8, 81 49 8) offers singles for 887dr (675dr in off-season), doubles 1180dr (990dr in off-season), with private bath. At the lower end of town, the **Park** (tel. 81 25 2) has singles for 630dr, doubles for 830dr, and triples for 960dr, all with private bath, 30% less in off-season.

No special equipment is required to climb Mt. Olympos except a pair of hiking boots or a sturdy pair of shoes and at least a liter and a half of water per person. (The plastic water bottles available throughout Greece are sufficient for this purpose, but bring a plastic bag and a rubber band to keep the cap from flying off.) If you plan to stay up on the mountain, bring long pants, a sweater and a windbreaker; for hiking during the day in summer you will want to wear only a T-shirt and shorts, but keep the windbreaker handy. You can camp on Mt. Olympos, but to be within striking distance of the peaks you must camp above treeline where the groundcover is fragile and the wind ferocious. Plan to stay in one of the SEO Refuges; leave your pack in Litochoro, and climb with just clothes, water and food in a small day pack or shoulder-bag.

Two routes lead to the summit of Mt. Olympos (actually Mt. Olympos has five separate peaks); to reach the beginning of both trails you must take the road which winds upward just before the square in Litochoro. Since there is no bus service between the trails and Litochoro, it's best to hitchhike. This is usually not a problem, but get an early start since most climbers drive up in the morning. Fourteen kilometers from Litochoro, at Diastavrosi, the first trail slopes up to the right of the road. This route offers spectacular views of the Aegean, the Macedonian plain to the north, and (cough!) the smog layer over Thessaloniki, thankfully far below. You can find water in two places along this trail—the turn-off between Barba and Spilia (1½ hours from the trail-head), marked on the trail but not on maps, is easier to find than the spring at Strangos. It's a long (five to six hours) but not too steep haul from the start of the trail to the SEO refuge, **Giosos Apostolidis**. Here you can spend the night (ample blankets provided) for 180dr with a Youth Hostel card, 200dr without. The fare here is no more expensive than at any slightly over-priced taverna in Greece, but the food is plain. The shelter's major assets are the expansive view of the bowl-like "Plain of the Muses," and a convenient and exhilarating approach to the peaks—the furthest is only 1½ hours away.

A more popular trail begins 19km from Litochoro at **Prionia**, where a broad icy stream emerges from the mountain. A sustained three-hour hike winds through deciduous and then evergreen forests in **Maurolongos Gorge** to the comfortable Refuge A (tel. 81 80 0), just at the treeline. This large shelter has spacious dorm rooms and as many services as most C-class hotels, plus food, first aid, and guide facilities. To stay here costs 250dr per person; the food is fairly expensive as well. From Refuge A, the peaks are 2-3 hours away.

The routes to the top of the two lowest peaks, **Toumba** (2785m) and **Profitis Ilias** (2786m) are self-explanatory; they are a mere hop, skip and a jump from the SEO Refuge. **Mitikas** (2917m), the highest and most often climbed peak, is reached by traversing the main trail that runs between refuges, then turning up the steep skree-slope beneath the peak. Look for "Mitikas" painted on the rocks, and follow the orange blazes. It is a steep scramble requiring both hands and feet to the top of the pinnacle ("Mitikas" means "needle".) You should not attempt to bring a large pack up to this peak. The exposed trail connecting Mitikas to Skala, the next ridge to the south, is not as hard as it looks, but it's not recommended for acrophobics. From Skala, it's an easy walk along the ridge to **Skolio**, the second highest peak, and the best vantage point for viewing the whole Olympic massif and its sheer western face. Skolio may also be climbed the long-way-round, from a turn-off a few kilometers from Refuge A; for inexperienced hikers, this route up Skolio is the safest and most rewarding climb on Olympos.

The most challenging peak on Olympos is **Stefani** (Thronos Dhios). The turn-off for the ridge is very close to that for Mitikas and indeed, the first part of the scramble is very similar. Once you have reached the narrow ridge, however, you must work your way along it, with several hundred meters of empty space on either side of you. The final section entails crossing a narrow ledge above the abyss, then climbing a crack in a boulder up to the summit. Only if you've had your Wheaties and are feeling your oats should you try this part.

Because winter storms bury Mt. Olympos in six or more feet of snow, the climbing season lasts only from May to October, when Refuge A is open; Apostolidis is open only from mid-June through August. You may notice the small bronze monument along the trail leading from the SEO Refuge to the peaks. It is dedicated to Giosos Apostolides, founder of the Greek Mountaineering Club (SEO) and avid year-round climber. He died in a fall on the mountain in May, 1964.

Halkidiki

Like the three-pronged trident of Poseidon, the Halkidiki points menacingly downward into the Aegean. Yet the narrow peninsulas of this curious geographical formation are hardly as threatening as the sea-god's weapon; rather, they are among the most benign areas in Greece, and are shared by three extremes of Greek society. On the far eastern prong is the restricted region of **Mt. Athos,** the largest enduring monastic community in Western society. On the other side, geographically and socially, **Kassandra** serves as a playground for sun worshippers from Thessaloniki and Athens. Sandwiched between the lands of Greece's past and present is the peninsula of **Sithonia,** which is content being free of tourist development and religious retreats, and retains much of its wild, pristine state.

Thumbing is good for short lifts around Kassandra and Sithonia, but for longer hauls, you will have to rely on public transportation. Buses bound for all three areas depart frequently from Thessaloniki's KTEL station in the eastern part of the city at 68 Karakassi St. (take bus #10 from Monastiriou or Egnatia St.—tell the ticket-seller you want to get off at Stathmos Halkidikis). Six buses a day go to Ouranopolis on the Oros peninsula (6am-5:30pm); four a day go to Sarti on the Sithonia peninsula, via Nea Marmaras (9am-5pm; 480dr); eleven a day go to Kassandria on the Kassandra peninsula (5:40am-8pm; 240dr).

While most of the beautiful Halkidiki northern interior is better viewed from a bus rather than from a day's visit to a village, you might consider breaking the trip for a few hours in **Poligiros,** where there is an archeological museum, or in **Arnea,** a town known for its wines and handwoven fabrics. Further west, and more difficult to get to, is the much-celebrated cave at **Petralona,** where the skull of a primeval man from 700,000 B.C. was found. The beaches on the west of the Halkidikian mainland and on the bays between the peninsulas are best avoided altogether.

Kassandra

Kassandra attracts Greeks by droves for a reason: its sands are as soft and its waters as blue as any this side of Samos. The entire coast is gorgeous—and over-touristed everywhere but in the southwest. To beat the prices and crowds, you'll need to freelance camp in undesignated campsites or on a secluded stretch of beach (even the official campgrounds sometimes fill up). Although the tourist buildup on the coastline in Kassandra has effectively squeezed out the low-budget traveler, one happy outcome is the plethora of free outdoor, freshwater showers available on most of the popular beaches. This makes sleeping on the beach no hardship at all.

Kassandria is the administrative and transportation center of Kassandra; the **OTE, post office** and **banks** are all there. It's also the place to catch buses running down the west coast. But unless you like being far from the water, you should probably get off the bus in **Kalithea**, the last stop before Kassandria. Once the site of a temple to Zeus Ammon, new high-rise temples to Mammon now open their doors to tourists for several thouand drachmas a night. This is the liveliest spot on Kassandra however, and you might want to stay here. A store in the back of town will change money and handle postal services. Start your room search around the corner from the bus stop, on the main street at the **Kentikon** (tel. 22 35 3)—ask the Greek owner for help, not the Scandinavian travel agents entrenched there. He only has doubles, at 900dr (Oct. 10-May 15), 956dr (May 16-June 30), and 1069dr (July 1-Oct. 10). South on the main road you'll find the **Toroneon** (tel. 22 18 2), with the same prices. If you arrive in late afternoon, you may be out of luck at either place and have to pay for a much more expensive room elsewhere. In a jam, and only then, the hotel above **Nikos Greek Art** (behind the Kentikon) might give you the small double bed in their unofficial roof-top room for 500dr, negotiable. There are some rooms to let on the same street as Nikos, running parallel to the main road. For camping, walk past the Toroneon and turn down the dirt road to the left, which leads to an idyllic pine grove on some bluffs overlooking the water.

The coast from Kriopigi to **Pefkohori** is mostly waterfront homes and apartments, but the more traditional village of **Haniotis**, with its tavernas arranged around the square, is fun at night. **Paliouri** is a long 3km away from the beach-campground complex of the same name, and perhaps not worth the bother, but the town has several lively tavernas, small hotels and rooms to rent.

The western coast has more to offer. Hitching is good; otherwise you can get a bus from Kassandria, or rent a motorbike in Kalithea (for high prices). Just after you pass Siviri, heading south, watch for a dirt road that forks right by a "prevent forest fires" sign. The road switches back down about 1km to a vacant beach of sun-splashed gold, next to a small church. At **Fourkas Beach**, farther south on the main road, a few sullen, dirty buildings scowl over a long thin strip of sand. You can camp at either end of the beach, if you can survive the dullness. The next point, however, is lovely once more: **Posidi** is neither crowded nor developed, except for a campground (160dr per person, tents 140dr). The woods brush the coast out on the deserted point of land. The very Greek fishing village of **Nea Skioni** has lately become the favorite spot of a Scandinavian travel agency, but like Penelope with her many suitors, it has not given in yet. Two small hotels, the **Olympia** (tel. 71 21 0) and the **Skioni** (tel. 71 22 3) rent double rooms for around 600dr; the Skioni is the better of the two. If both are full, rooms to rent are in either direction down the main street, tucked in between stores that sell inflatable toys, suntan lotion and trashy books out front, and fishing supplies in the back. And, as always on Kassandra, Nea Skioni has a considerable stretch of beach for camping.

Sithonia

Sithonia is less developed than Kassandra, but during high season you'll encounter similar difficulties finding cheap rooms in the more popular spots, and you might find no rooms at all. Freelance camping is a wise option. Before arriving at Nea Marmaras, Sithonia's largest town, you'll pass the sparkling beach at **Agios Ioanis**, where you might consider camping. If you go as far as **Nea Marmaras**, you might find a room in the cove north of the bus stop. If the restaurant at the BP station can't give you a room, they can help you find a double nearby for about 700dr. Don't forget that the local tourist police (or regular police, in lieu of tourist police) have a list of rooms to rent, and can usually fix you up in a pinch.

Just below Marmaras is the anomalous, ultraluxury **Porto Carras,** a slick, exclusive development patronized by the likes of Mick Jagger and Jackie Onassis. The bus-trip around the peninsula to **Sarti** (four times per day; 480dr) passes by the most deserted and desirable turf on Sithonia. After climbing the road 5km south of Porto Carras, you'll see an unbelievably beautiful beach wrapped in the ajutment near **Agios Kiriaki,** complete with a small reef and an island to swim to. Be warned that it is a long, hard climb down from here, or a long hike along a road lower on the coast. The beach at **Tristinika** can be reached along a dirt road branching off from the highway near Toroni. Very few bathers use this beach; it is long, sandy, with tall evergreens at one end and the smell of sage pervading the air.

At **Toroni,** the next beach down the coast, an Australian archeological team is conducting a dig each July and August. You can walk to the ruined wall out on the promontory, or up to the remains of the city Kastro atop the 280m hill behind the beach. The beach itself is fairly crowded, but long enough to absorb the hordes gracefully. **Porto Koufos** is a better yacht harbor than beach, and finding rooms to let could be a problem, given the lack of buildings of any sort. The official campground here is unique—the tentsites hang from the hillside on terraces shaded by bamboo canopies—but expensive. **Kalamitsi** is a gorgeous beach, which everyone in southern Sithonia knows. **Sarti,** a lazy seaside resort town, has many tavernas and an exceptionally long beach with free freshwater showers. After a little searching you can find a room to let even in summer. Doubles go for 800dr, considerably less for longer stays. **Zorba**'s bar on the road out of Sarti is home for a curious menagerie of sculptures by the local artist, "Uncle Zifiris." They look rather like a cross between Easter Island monoliths and something you once made out of Play-Doh. Because the bus serving the western and southern coasts of Sithonia goes only as far as Sarti, then turns around, it's best to go to **Vourvourou** direct from Thessaloniki (some of these buses do continue around the peninsula). The **Vourvourou** (tel. 91 26 1) has doubles only for 1000dr. Look for a tan building with a tavern, visible from the bus stop above the water.

Mount Athos

Athos *(Agion Oros)* is a world apart. Halkidiki's easternmost peninsula harbors twenty Eastern Orthodox monasteries comprising an autonomous monastic state where the way of life has remained unchanged since the Byzantine Era. With few exceptions, Athos has no electricity, no roads, no telephones. It uses the Julian rather than our Gregorian calendar and a variable time system based on the rising and setting of the sun. Its monks attempt to transcend the confining material pleasures of the outside world and lead a completely spiritual life. Food, dress, and possessions at Athos are very modest. Visitors wearing shorts will not be admitted; those with long hair should tie it in a bun at the nape of the neck as the monks do. An edict of the emperor Constantine from 1060 A.D., enforced to this day, forbids women or even female domesticated animals from setting foot on the peninsula. The consequent absence of any foraging goats or other livestock has allowed the luxuriant forests that closely blanket the hillside to remain in their natural state. This lush tangle of dark green heightens the mystical aura pervading Athos, intensified by the jagged grayish-white marble peak of Mount Athos itself, soaring 2033m above the encircling waves of the Aegean.

Practical Information

A special **entrance permit** is required in order to visit Mt. Athos. To get this permit, you must first get a letter of recommendation from your embassy or consulate and procede with it to either the **Greek Ministry of Foreign Affairs** (tel. 36 26 894) at 2 Zalokosta St. in Athens or to the **Ministry of Northern Greece** at Platia Dikitirou in Thessaloniki (tel. 27 00 92, rm. 218-219, open Mon.-Fri. 8am-2pm). There, you will receive more forms to complete; you must take them to the **Foreign Police** in Thessaloniki (25A Megalou Alexandrou St.). The police in turn will give you a paper for the Aliens Police in Karyes. Citizens of countries with consulates in Thessaloniki can conduct the entire process while in this city (see Thessaloniki for consulate addresses). U.S. and British consulates can give you the form letter in very little time. However, as only ten foreigners a day are admitted and the wait to get into Athos is currently at least ten days, you'd do better to set the visit well in advance unless you plan a long stay in Thessaloniki. Permit in hand, simply arrive in Halkidiki a day or two before your scheduled entry into Athos. Although the rules are not strictly enforced, keep in mind throughout the whole procedure that officially only persons having specific academic or religious interest in Mount Athos are supposed to receive visitors' permits. If you are a student (21 years or older), a letter from your university stating your academic interest in Mount Athos could also be helpful. If you want to take photographs of any of the art in the monasteries, a separate permit is required. Most visitors' permits allow a total stay of four days. Again, however, extra letters of recommendation might come in handy for obtaining a permit for a longer stay. Alternatively, extensions can be obtained with relative ease once you're already in Mount Athos from the monastic authorities at Karyes. Be sure to have your passport with you for all bureaucratic procedures. The NTOG office in Thessaloniki can give you more information.

It should be kept in mind when visiting Mount Athos that visitors from "the world" inherently conflict with the spiritual goals of the monastic life. The monks, however, have an old tradition requiring hospitality to all guests, so a bit of awareness and sensitivity is essential to keep from disrupting the delicate atmosphere of holiness.

The standard approach to Athos is via **Ouranoupolis,** by boat to **Daphne,** then by bus to the capital city of Karyes where some final bureaucratic procedures take place. Buses leave for Ouranoupolis from Thessaloniki six times a day departing from the KTEL Halkidikis station (see Thessaloniki bus information). Ouranoupolis is a very touristed resort town because of Mount Athos as well as the good beaches nearby. You will probably stay in Ouranoupolis overnight in order to catch the boat to Daphne in the morning. The best deal for accommodations is usually one of the pension owners who may approach you at the bus stop. Otherwise, try the **Hotel Ouranoupoli** (tel. 71 20 5), with doubles for 800dr, singles 500dr, or the **Hotel Galini** (tel. 71 21 7), with doubles for 900dr, triples 1200dr. You'll be doing a lot of long, tiring hiking at Mount Athos so you should arrange to leave all of your belongings behind in Ouranoupolis or elsewhere, except for what can be carried in a small light shoulderbag. Theoretically, you are required to wear long pants even while hiking; bring a light pair. Water is readily available along the Athos' trails, but you might want a small container for carrying it. Also, consider bringing some compact food both for hiking and because sometimes the number of visitors to a monastery exceeds the cooks' expectations and you can't pop out for a souvlaki.

A boat to Daphne leaves from Ouranoupolis every morning but the exact time varies and is best found out in Ouranoupolis the night before. Like all of the small boats servicing Mount Athos, the skiff for Daphne occasionally leaves a few minutes early, and it is best to arrive at the wharf at least a half hour in advance. With few stops en route to Daphne, the trip takes about two hours. Your passport and entrance permit are taken as you board to be returned later in Karyes. Boats return to Ouranoupolis daily from Daphne and from Agia Annis. Another boat leaves Ierissos daily at noon stopping at Nea Roda, Esphigmenou, Vatopediou, Pantokratoros, Stavronikita, Iviron, and Megitsi Lavra and returns along the same route leaving Megitsi Lavra at 6am daily.

From Daphne, an old decrepit bus will take you up Athos's one rocky cliffhanging road, built in 1963 for Athos' milleniary celebration, to the capital city of Karyes. Karyes is a tiny hamlet built around a well-restored, tenth-century church. The town also contains an OTE office and two inexpensive hotels which need not be used since the monastery accommodations are free and much more interesting. Your first stop in Karyes should be the **Aliens Police** located at the top of an alley on the side of the church opposite from where the bus lets you off. The final permit *(Diamonitirion),* obtained from the **Monastic Authorities** in the headquarters of the Athonite Holy Council, costs a hefty 500dr (300dr for students). These funds reimburse the monasteries for the costs of their hospitality.

Remember, walking is an integral part of the Athos experience. Except for the occasional skiff, once you leave Karyes much of your time will be spent hiking along rocky mountainous trails.

Accommodations and food in the monasteries are free regardless of the length of your stay. Two meals are generally served each day, and the gates of the monasteries close promptly at sunset, although if you do arrive a few minutes late you will probably be let in.

History

According to a very old legend, the Christian history of Mount Athos begins when the aging Virgin Mary, on a sea trip to visit her old friend Lazarus in Cyprus, was thrown off course by a storm and led by divine sign to the Athonite coast. The peninsula, known then as *Akte,* was a notorious center of paganism, but the moment Mary's foot touched its soil the false idols all smashed themselves to bits in frenzied proclamation of their own worthlessness. Mary then declared Athos to be her holy garden, forbidden to all other women for eternity, and blessed the land before sailing back to Jaffa.

Following indeterminate centuries of occupation by Christian hermits and ascetics, the oldest monastery (Agia Lavra) was founded in 963 A.D. by Athanasius, a rich man's son turned monk. Under the protection of Byzantine emperors, the building of monasteries flourished until, at its zenith in the fifteenth century, Mount Athos harbored forty monasteries and some twenty thousand monks. When Constantinople fell to Turkish armies in 1453, the monastic community wisely surrendered, thus remaining unplundered and relatively autonomous. Because of gradual attrition and the diminishing supply of young novices (now on the upswing), Mount Athos has slowly declined over the centuries. Now only twenty monasteries and about twelve hundred monks remain.

In 1926 a decree of the Greek government made Mt. Athos officially part of Greece while allowing it to retain autonomous theocratic government. Athos is the oldest existing democracy in the world. The abbot who governs each monastery is elected by the monks, as is the representative of each monastery to the Holy Council at Karyes. The Holy Council serves as the central governing authority of the peninsula.

Throughout its long history, the Holy Mountain *(Agion Oros)* has suffered from repeated incursions at the hands of pirates, looters, and foreign invaders, resulting in the fortress-like appearance of the Monasteries. Typically located in a large central courtyard, the church is surrounded by the monks' cells forming a solid defensive wall equipped with heavy iron doors and a tower. Even today, government police guard the peninsula from treasure-seekers.

Athos contains an unsurpassed wealth of Paleologian and Late Byzantine art, manuscripts, and architecture. **Megitsi Lavra**, for example, is a veritable warehouse of crucifixes inlaid with precious metal and stones. Its antique libraries contain well over 42,000 tomes. The Athonite churches are stylistically unique, having a double narthex with side chapels. Graceful frescoes and painted ikons, including numerous masterpieces by great artists of the Cretan and Macedonian Schools, adorn the church interiors. Any visit to Athos will be greatly enriched by reading about the art, history, and legends of the individual monasteries. *Athos the Holy Mountain* by Sydney Loch and *Mount Athos* by Norwich, Sitwell, and Costa are both highly readable and informative.

Monasteries of the Mountain

Although Athos contains stunning works and breathtaking natural scenery, the most rewarding aspect of a visit there often proves to be the conversations with the people at the monasteries. A certain spirit of camaraderie quickly forms among the guests and the monks. The numerous monasteries at Athos have differences in character based on their remoteness from tourism, degree of commercialism, and the ages, level of education, and nationality of their monks. At one time there were nearly equal numbers of Greek and Slavic monks at Athos. The Russian Revolution cut off the supply of funds and novices at its source and today only two Slavic monasteries remain. The Russian **Panteleimon** and the Serbian **Chilandari** serve as an interesting contrast to the largely Greek monasteries on the rest of the peninsula.

While at Athos, you should definitely try to visit some of the smaller and more remote monasteries which don't have grandiose art attracting swarms of visitors. Although Megitsi Lavra and **Iviron** are beautiful and well worth seeing, these two largest, oldest, and most frequently visited of the cloisters were aptly referred to by one novice at Stravronikita as the "museum monasteries." For a better experience of the monastic way of life and to meet younger, better educated, and more international monks (always addressed with the title Pater) head for the monasteries of **Simonos, Petras, Dionysiou, Philotheou,** or **Stavronikita.** Knowing French helps, understanding Greek is of course best of all, but most monasteries do have a few monks who can manage reasonably well in English. There is one very friendly monk from Illinois who's been at Dionysiou for about twenty years.

For a day or two of invigorating hiking crowned by an awe-inspiring once-in-a-lifetime view, climb Mount Athos. Its soaring pinnacle affords a vantage point from which you can see the rambling dark green hills of the entire peninsula stretching out into the distance, with the enveloping sea shimmering below. The ascent takes about seven or eight hours from Megitsi Lavra and five hours on the return. During the summer if you leave early in the morning, you can make the round trip in time to reach the gates of Lavra before they close for the evening. Alternatively, the climb can be shortened considerably by setting out from the Agias Annis Monastery instead of Lavra, or you can make the climb in two days, spending the night in the cliffside church of

Panagia before continuing on to the top. The monks have constructed a reasonably good trail along the whole route since there is an annual service on August 19 held at the church on the top of the mountain.

Kavala

On the Macedonian coast at the northern edge of the Aegean, Kavala (pronounced Ka-VAH-lah) is an attractive modern port city. Although it is the fifth largest city in Greece, a small-town atmosphere prevails. The town's jewel is its charming old section, known as the **Panagia District.** East of the port, enclosed by ancient walls, the old town sits on its own peninsula and is a delightful place to explore.

Practical Information

Kavala is accessible from Thessaloniki by frequent bus (390dr), with two different routes. The coastal road, the more scenic, passes by **Lake Korona** and **Lake Volvi,** each still unmarred by tourist trappings. The inland route passes through the city of **Serres,** where there is an interesting Byzantine church.

National Tourist Organization of Greece (NTOG): at Eleftheria Sq. (tel. 22 24 25 or 22 87 62), one block from the water. Very well informed. They can provide you with a map of the city, hotel listings, and can arrange cheap, private rooms. Open Mon.-Fri. 8:30am-2:30pm and 3:30-8:30pm, Sat. 8am-1pm.

Tourist Police: 41 Omonias St. (tel. 22 29 05), four blocks up from the port. Less friendly than the NTOG, but, as part of the police station, open 24 hours.

Currency Exchange: Any hour at the Hotel Galaxy, on the port, or the back door at 51 Venizelou St. By 1984 they should be licensed to exchange travelers checks. Otherwise, the only place to cash travelers checks when banks are closed is the NTOG campground (see Near Kavala).

Main Post Office: at the corner of Omonias and Averof Sts. seven blocks directly up from the OTE office. Open Mon.-Fri. 8:30am-8:30pm for most services.

OTE: on the main port at Vassileos Pavlou St., across from where the boat for Thassos leaves. Open 24 hrs.

ELPA: Greek Motorist's Association, on Plateia Eleftherias (tel. 22 97 78).

Bus station: on H. Mitropolitou St., one block from Vass. Pavlou St. and the waterfront. Buses leave here for Thessaloniki, Philippi, Keramoti, and the beaches to the west. Hours for the bus station are 6am-8pm, if you plan to leave your bags there.

Telephone Code: 051.

Boats travel back and forth from Kavala to Thassos twelve times daily (8:30am-9:30pm) during the summer, eight times off-season. Most go only to Prinos; fare of 147dr is paid on the boat. Boats from Keramoti, a town 45km east of Kavala, run the short distance back and forth to Limenas seven times daily (80dr). Two agents have boats connecting Kavala with other Greek islands. **Nikos Miliades** runs four boats a week to Limnos (684dr), two of which continue on to Lesvos (1100dr), and one boat a week to Samothrace (623dr). All run year round. The office is at the east end of the port, 36 Karaoli Dimitriou St. (tel. 22 61 47), and is open daily until the last boat leaves. In July and

August only, and even then unreliably, the F/B *Kyklades* makes one round trip per week passing through Limnos, Lesvos, Chios, Samos, Ikaria, Leros, Kalymnos, Kos, and Rhodes; contact **Alkyon Shipping Agency**, 59 Venizelou St. (tel. 83 28 32).

Accommodations

George Alvanos, 35 Anthemiou St. (tel. 22 84 12 or 22 17 81). The best place to stay in Kavala, and the only place in the Panagia District. Bathrooms are spotless. Access to kitchen and refrigerator. Comfortably furnished singles around 400dr, doubles 600dr, triples 800dr; very bargainable. He'll even give a 10% discount if you show him your *Let's Go*.

Pageon, 12A K. Palama St. (tel. 22 36 89), near the Palatia 28 Octavriou, two blocks from the main port. Not terrific, but the cheapest hotel in town. Singles 500dr, doubles 750dr; showers 75dr extra.

Camping Irini, a minimum half-hour walk east along the coast from the port, (tel. 22 97 85). Closest campground to town. 120dr per person, 120dr per tent.

Sights

A good way to spend an afternoon is to stroll through the narrow stone passageways and delightful houses of the old town. The neighborhood contains several interesting sights, the most conspicuous of which is the sprawling gray, thirteenth-century **Byzantine Fortress.** Kavala is most enchantingly approached from the sea, and it is only from that perspective that you can really appreciate the fortress's immense, turreted walls. A walk along the top of the walls provides a fine panorama of the city. (Open daily sunrise to sunset; admission 20dr).

The two other noteworthy sights in the old town are of Moorish origin, both built during the long Turkish domination of the city. The first, located on Pavlidou St., is the **Imaret,** the largest Muslim building in Greece. The elongated hall with its numerous little domes is best viewed from the water or from the fortress above. Presently used as a warehouse, the building is not open to the public. For an inside view of a Muslim building, you must try the second of Kavala's noteworthy Moorish constructions, the **House of Muhammad Ali,** which stands on the corner of Pavlidou and Mehmet Ali Sts., at the tip of the little peninsula. Not to be confused with the famed boxer of the same name, Muhammad Ali was the self-appointed King of Egypt in the eighteenth century and the founder of a dynasty of Egyptian rulers. He was born in this house in 1769 and lived in Kavala during the early part of his career. The most interesting part of the beautifully-preserved old wooden house is the upstairs, where Ali's harem of seven women lived. The desired one would stay in the handsome bedroom while the others remained in a large dormitory room. Curiously, three bodyguards lived in the room between Muhammad Ali and his wives. Admission to the house is free, but the guide asks for a tip.

At the northern edge of the old town, near Nikotsara Square, the colossal sixteenth-century **aqueduct** is hard not to notice. Suleymein the Magnificent ordered the graceful double-tiered monument built to transport water from the mountain springs above the city. On the other side of town, overlooking the water, the **Archeological Museum,** Erithrou Stavrou St. (tel. 22 23 35) contains finds from Philippi Amphipolis, and other nearby sites. Open Wed.-Mon. 8:30am-2:30pm, closed Tues. For a good view of the town, climb up to the church of the Prophet Elias. On the waterfront, east of the port, is a small and crowded beach.

Near Kavala

Several beautiful sandy beaches lie to the west of Kavala, accessible by bus. The closest is just outside the city of Kalamitsa. As you move further along the coast to Batis, Iraklitsa, and Peramos, they become progressively less crowded. At **Batis,** 3km outside of Kavala, there is also a fancy and expensive NTOG Campground (tel. 22 72 51); 140dr per person, and 145dr per tent, and 30dr to swim. The campground will change money here any day of the week until late in the evening. Direct buses run from Kavala to Batis during July and August. A forty-minute bus ride to the east of Kavala is the small port of Keramoti with ferries to Limenas, the capital of Thassos. Keramoti's two inexpensive hotels, both on Plateia 14th Septemvriou, are the **Exasteron** (tel. 51 23 0) and the nicer but more expensive **Evropi** (tel. 51 27 7). Nearby is **Camping Keramoti** (tel. 51 27 9).

About 15km north of Kavala, the ruins of ancient **Philippi** represent the material remains of one of the more crucial moments in European history. The city was founded by Philip II of Macedonia (father of Alexander the Great), who built a fortified city here to protect Thassian gold-mine workers from occasional Thracian attacks. Philip thought it only appropriate that the city be named after him. In 42 B.C. the soldiers led by Octavius and Marc Antony defeated the Republican army of Brutus and Cassius, winning the crucial battle of the Roman civil war.

Less than a century later, Philippi was the site of Christianity's entrance onto the European stage, when the Apostle Paul came here to preach in 49 A.D. The first European Christian was a woman named Lydia whom he baptized here; the rest of Philippi converted when, after Paul was imprisoned for his preachings, an earthquake struck the town.

Most of the ruins that are seen today date from Roman times. The archeological site is divided in half by the modern highway which follows the same route as the ancient Via Egnatia. The ruins to the west of the road are further divided by a fence that closes off the part of the site which is still under excavation. Here you'll find the remains of the Roman latrines, a well-preserved colonnade, and a Roman basilica with splendid Corinthian capitals; it was so large that it collapsed before it was finished and was never completed. The entrance on the other side of the highway leads up to the Acropolis and a theater which dates from the Hellenistic period. With the upper tiers reconstructed, the theater is now used for performances of classical drama during July and August—worth attending even if you don't know Greek. The performances take place on Saturday and Sunday nights. Tickets and information are available at the NTOG in Kavala or at the theater itself. The site is open every day from sunrise to sunset; admission 25dr, 10dr for students, and free on Sundays.

To get to Philippi, take the bus bound for Drama (30dr); one leaves every twenty minutes. The bus back to Kavala stops down the road, so do not wait at the entrance to the site. If you are driving from Kavala, follow Erithrou Stavrou St. along the waterfront and turn north onto Merarchias Ave. The archeological site is right on the highway.

Thrace

If you plan to go overland from Greece to Turkey, you will pass through Thrace, the easternmost province of Greece. It is a highly agricultural, sparsely populated area of rolling hills, rivers, and swamps. Only officially passed over to Greece in 1912, the land still bears evidence of Turkish influence. Although the majority of the population speaks Greek, small Turkish and Albanian communities can be found throughout the region.

Alexandroupolis

The most likely stop on a route through Thrace will be the modern town of Alexandroupolis. It's a convenient embarkation point for travel into Turkey, as well as the closest port on the Greek mainland to the islands of Samothrace, Limnos and Lesvos. It isn't the worst place in the world, though it's somewhat grey and dusty, and many travelers catch their breath here before setting off for the Northeastern Islands, Turkey or Bulgaria.

Buses and trains from Athens and Thessaloniki stop here en route to Turkey and Bulgaria. Five buses a day head east, and the same number pass through on the way west; seven trains also stop here. The bus is faster, the train more comfortable. Across the street from the railroad station is the **Aktaion Hotel,** where you can get a bed for 300dr per night. The kind owners will get up to let you in at any hour of the day or night; as most of the beds are simply cots in a large living room, there is almost always room for one or two more. Private doubles run 600dr; triples 900dr. Should you arrive by bus, you will find both train station and hotel by the waterfront, downhill from the bus station. One kilometer west of town is a large **campground,** well-situated on a beach far better than the town beach (tel. 28 75 5 or 28 73 5). They charge 100dr per person, 200dr per tent. The **telephone code** for Alexandroupolis is 0551.

If you are in town between July 9 and August 15, the annual **wine festival** will give you a chance to sample a variety of local wines for only 90dr. Cheap food is for sale at the festival as well; the dancing is great. The festival is held just outside of town; the Alexandroupolis **Tourist Police,** on a small street between the waterfront and the main shopping street, can give you further details (open Mon.-Fri. 8am-8pm). Otherwise, you can eat and pass the evening in one of the restaurants and tavernas by the waterfront (cleaner than those in town), or follow the crowd to the fair in the plaza below the lighthouse.

Ferries leave for Samothrace at 7am and 4pm daily (400dr). The *Skopelos,* run by the Nomikos line, leaves once a week for Samothrace, Kavala (623dr), Limni (623dr) and Mytilimi (1238dr). The best way to get to Turkey from Alexandroupolis is by local bus; the train is frustratingly slow, and stops at the border for six hours. Take the bus from the main bus station in town (not the smaller terminal near the railroad station) to **Kipi** on the border. Walk through passport control and customs, telling the Turkish Police that you are going *autostop* (hitch-hiking) and that you don't have a car. On the other side, take a *dolmuş* (shared taxi), if one is available, to **Keşan.** (If not, take a taxi to **Ipsala** nearby, and get the much cheaper dolmuş from there.) Hourly buses connect Keşan and Istanbul (four hours). The whole trip from Alexandroupolis to Istanbul will take around eight hours if bus connections run smoothly (crossing the border and changing money on the otherside will take at least an hour) and will cost less than $5.

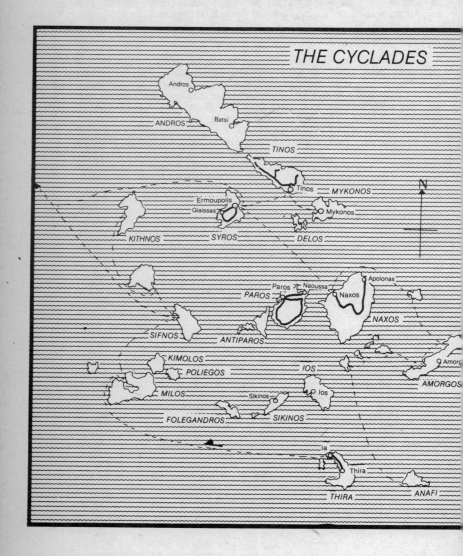

CYCLADES

Once upon a time, the Cyclades were the prototypical remote Greek islands with lovely secluded beaches and sleepy port towns. Then, a few years ago, travel magazines began advertising the islands as ideal getaways, magical paradises far from the hustle and bustle of the city. The advertising has worked a bit too well: now each summer the Cyclades are jammed to the hilt with young and active tourists seeking cosmopolitan nightlife.

Historically, the islands share a complex and bloody past. Archeological excavations suggest that the Cyclades were inhabited as far back as 6000 BC. The Phoenicians, who took control of the archepelago around 3000 BC, developed a culture known as the Early Cyladic, which lasted for over 1000 years. Later, Minos of Crete conquered the islands during a time known as the Middle Cycladic period; the period dating from the fall of Crete to the rise of the Myceneans makes up the Late Cycladic. The Myceneans were in turn defeated by the Dorians, the first Hellenic people in Greece.

In 478 B.C., the Cyclades came under the rule of Athens which had created a league comprising all the different island groups. After Athens' power was broken, the residents of the Cyclades then suffered successive conquests by the Romans (in the second century), the Venetians (in the thirteenth century), and finally the Turks (in the sixteenth century). Foreign rule lasted until the Greek War of Independence, in 1827.

Despite the large number of tourists who flock to its shores every year, the Cyclades are still among the most beautiful islands in Greece, with whitewashed houses, winding narrow streets, abundant flowers and tiny, jewel-like churches. Shutters and doors, painted blue and green, harmonize with the sky and sea. By contrast, the land is brown, rocky and dry, and many islands (especially Ios and Santorini) suffer from a shortage of water.

If you want to share in native Greek life, visit the islands in May or June, or after September when the crowds die down, the prices decrease, and life becomes more equable. But for nightlife, nothing compares with the Cyclades in summer. In July and August, the Cyclades play host to an international assortment of hippies, tourists on package vacations, and yacht-toting sons of shipping tycoons. Peasant homes are turned into discotheques and boutiques, and sleepy villages echo with the sounds of rock, disco, and new wave well into the night. If your vision of the ideal vacation includes images of gathering around a guitar and drinking wine or dancing until dawn, you may find the Cyclades a dream come true.

Transportation in the Cyclades

During July and August, boat connections between the major islands of Syros, Paros, Naxos, and Ios are extremely frequent—at least once a day. The islands are served by huge car ferries, small excursion boats, and the fast but expensive "Flying Dolphin" hydrofoils. In June and September, service decreases, and in the other months it is sporadic at best. For some of the northern Cyclades (Andros, Tinos), boats leave from Rafina, rather than Piraeus. To get there, take the orange-and-white striped bus from the corner of Mavromateon St. just off Leoforos Alexandras in Athens. Buses leave every hour on the hour; fare is 65dr.

Ferry prices are carefully regulated by the government. Passage costs 250-500dr between islands a few hours apart, and 958dr between Piraeus and

Santorini. For long hauls the prices are reasonable, but the cost of transportation can add up quickly if you're planning to do a lot of island-hopping. If you're doing inter-island travel, remember that direct connections will always be less expensive—the more stops, the higher the price. Don't assume that the best way to get between islands is the shortest in nautical miles. For more detailed discussion on the Greek boat system, turn to the Boats section of the General Introduction.

Mykonos

When Narcissus drowned, gazing at his reflection in a pool of water, his spirit is said to have been reincarnated on the island of Mykonos. While archeologists have yet to unearth substantial proof of his existence, one visit will alleviate all doubts—Narcissus and his followers are alive and well on Mykonos.

It is good to know what you are in for when you visit this island, the most popular of all the Cyclades. If you are looking for chic, international social life—gay or straight—you've come to the right place. There is really nothing to compare with Mykonos. The island has a few traditional attractions, which we will bravely name, but it would be ridiculous to pretend that people come to Mykonos to experience cultural enrichment or indigenous Greek life. Connoisseurship is strictly reserved for the *haute couture,* which includes a heavy dose of discos and drugs. At night, Mykonos looks like New York's Upper East Side without the traffic—slick, elegant and expensive. People are dressed to kill, things happen fast, and at $3 or $4 a drink you better have a sizeable wad of bills to keep up with the crowd.

Town of Mykonos

The town of Mykonos is a maze of freshly-painted white buildings with a large number of tourist shops and cafes, all staffed with Greeks who have at their disposal a repertoire of English, French, and Japanese phrases. Depending on how homesick you feel, you will be either delighted or shocked by the availability of such American products as cheeseburgers, milk shakes, fur coats, and the *Wall Street Journal.* All offices of importance are located on the waterfront, including the **OTE** (open Mon.-Fri. 7:30am-midnight, weekends to 3:10pm) and the unusually helpful and competent **Tourist Police** (open every day 8am-8pm). Here you'll also find a doctor's office, the ticket agencies, and the town's two banks. Behind the OTE is a special **currency exchange,** open Mon.-Fri. 9am-1pm. At the edge of the beach you'll find the **Post Office** (open Mon.-Fri. 7:30am-2pm) and an Olympic Airways office. Behind the banks one block from the water, on Kambani St., is a foreign newspaper and periodical store. The **telephone code** for Mykonos is 0289.

The island has a long tourist season, lasting from May to October. During that time you will find, more than on the other Cyclades, that the residents try to divorce themselves from tourist life. Most are indifferent to, or worse, offended by the yearly influx, and keep their distance. Despite this attitude, even in the height of the season, a few words of Greek, however halting, will work wonders in surmounting the barriers of habitual distrust, and may even secure reduced prices.

Accommodations and Food

While the bars and discos are costly, accommodations are not much more than on the other Cyclades. You can thank government regulations for that. Still, during the summer hotel rooms are hard to find. You should start your search for a room early in the day—the hotels are certain to be full by evening. One sensible strategy, of course, is to make a reservation by phone. As you disembark from the boat, you will be greeted by a handful of little kids and elderly women offering you private rooms. During high season bargaining for a room immediately can save you a lot of searching later in the day. The best rates you can get are about 500dr for a single, 800dr for a double, and 1100dr for a triple—and this is if you are very lucky. The Tourist Police in the southwest end of the harbor, have lists of available rooms and are generally well-informed on other matters as well. Some of the most reasonably-priced rooms in town are owned by **Maria Stefano** on Agio Artem St. She charges 400dr per bed, very cheap for couples who don't mind sharing a small bed. The **Megas** store (tel. 22 26 0) on Andronikou St. has rooms both in town and on the beach. The best deal on the island is to be found at **14 Metropolis Street,** in a house that looks like an old Venetian mansion. Most of the suites are triples, and cost 900dr. It's a real find right in the center of town.

In addition to private rooms, there are also a number of D-class hotels in town, unaffordable in high season. Prices for the hotels listed below are at the very least 20% lower in the off-season and decrease 10% if you stay more than two nights; they hover in high season around 1000dr for a single and 1400dr for a double. But in high season you won't have to worry about losing an arm and a leg to the hotel manager—all his rooms will be full. The **Apollon** (tel. 22 22 3) has singles and doubles, both without bath. On Kalogera St., the **Hotel Philippi** (tel. 22 29 4) has clean singles and doubles, and a beautiful flower garden. The **Hotel Maria** (tel. 22 31 7) has doubles only. On Andronikou St., three blocks up from the waterfront, you'll find showerless singles and doubles at the **Hotel Karboni** (tel. 22 47 8). The **Karbonkai,** on the corner of Panairandou and Etairias Sts. (tel. 22 46 1), has the same to offer. The **Delfines** (tel. 22 29 2) has the same and is located just up from Mavroyenous Square (Taxi Square).

Outside of town there are a few more hotels, but even these are booked solid in high season to tourists who pay through the nose. The **Mina Hotel** (tel. 23 02 4) has singles and doubles without private bath and is at St. Stephanos beach, near good sports facilities. If you make it to Megali Ammos beach, you can try the **Markos Beach Hotel** (tel. 22 81 1). The same goes for Ornos beach and the **Hotel Christina** (tel. 23 01 3). If you feel like camping, **Paradise Beach** has an excellent campground with a disco, a self-service cafeteria, and lots of room. They charge 200dr per person.

Though it usually tastes great, the food on Mykonos will cost you an arm and a leg to enjoy. Cheap restaurants are an extinct species here. Good service, too, is fairly high up on the list of endangered animals. But redeeming the culinary establishments of Mykonos is the incredible selection each offers—some restaurants even boast they'll never turn down an order, no matter how exotic it is. **Nikos Taverna** in the center of town serves filling meals, and the nearby **Fisherman's Taverna** offers great seafood. **Sundown,** located in a secluded part of the harbor, also serves aquatic fare.

Entertainment

There are too many bars and discos to name, and the shades of difference will take the *cognoscenti* to sniff out. The following are among the best, whatever your taste or sexual preference.

Pierros, in town, mostly a gay bar and disco, with a floor show as well. Straights are also welcome. About the liveliest place in Mykonos.

Seagull is good for quiet conversations and a peaceful drink. One of the most relaxed bars in town, on the waterfront at the edge of the beach.

Windmill Disco, in the center of town, is one of the most popular discos, made out of an old windmill. Good music and dancing. Open until 2am.

The Yacht Club, right on the pier, is the place to go for night owls. Open after the other bars and discos have closed—until 5am. Dancing and drinking.

Kastro's Bar, in town; relaxed and mellow, it's a welcome change of pace.

If you prefer to try some traditional Greek dancing, go to **Baboulas Tavern** at the corner of Anagirm and Georgouli Sts. There are also two cinemas in town, the **Artemis** and the **Leto.**

Sights

Shopping is the prime daytime activity on the island. While there are beautiful handicrafts in the other parts of Greece, this is the only place where you will find designer clothes of international repute. (**Galatis,** to the left of Maveroyenous Square as you face the town, is the place to shop.) You will find the fine, brightly colored handwoven goods much more affordable. Two of the best stores are a shop opposite Galatis, which sells jackets, shawls, scarves, and hats, and **Panos** on Matogianni St. The latter sells handwoven bedspreads, table mats, sweaters, shawls, and bags, and will do work to order (goods shipped anywhere). Neither store is cheap by Greek standards, but their work is beautiful and considerably less expensive than in the U.S.

The only in-town daytime diversion to compete with shopping is the **Archeological Museum,** located on the waterfront between the ferry dock and the center of town. The collection includes the findings from the tombs of Delos, Attic black figure vases from the sixth century B.C., grave *stelai* from the first and second centuries B.C., and the museum's prized possessions, a seventh-century B.C. *pithos* (large earthenware vessel) with relief scenes from the Trojan War and a bronze *kouros.* Open Mon.-Sat. 8:30am-2pm, Sun. 9am-3pm; admission 50dr, 30dr for students. The other museum in town, with a somewhat kitschy collection of folklore, has wisely decided not to compete with either beach-going or bar-hopping—its strategically chosen hours are Mon.-Sat. 4:30-8:30pm, Sun. 5:30-8:30pm, admission free. The **Folklore Museum** is located on the northern edge of town just behind the OTE office, next to the **Paraportiani,** a glistening hive of several white churches twisted on top of one another which should not be missed.

Around the Island

Without a doubt, the beaches are one of the main attractions of Mykonos. The nearest one to town, dismissing the eminently dismissable town beach, is at **Megali Ammos,** a 1 km walk past the windmills on the southwestern corner of the harbor. For some others, bus schedules are posted in front of the Tourist Police. **St. Stephanos** beach, a ten-minute bus ride from town (departures hourly from the town beach) is not spectacular, but is convenient and has a very good water sports center. **Psarou Beach,** also close to town, has the cheapest wind surfing around. The nudist beaches are reached by taking a bus to **Plati Yialos,** not a bad beach in its own right, with windsurfing for 300dr an hour. The bus leaves every half hour from 8am until midnight from a bus stop about 250m up the hill along the street that runs beside the windmills (look for painted signs pointing to "buses for Plati Yialos"). From the same bus stop, buses also run hourly to the beach at Ornos. From Plati Yialos, small boats go to **Paradise Beach** (30dr, nude and straight) and **Super Paradise Beach** (50dr, nude and gay). Boats also leave from the harbor in town for Paradise and Super Paradise in the morning (60dr). Check the schedule post in chalk near the Tourist Police. Finally, if you are going by car, Paradise Beach is connected to the town by a 7km strip of road.

If you feel like divorcing yourself from the hordes of other tourists, visit **Ano Mera**, the island's only other village. The main item of interest is its **Tourliani** monastery with an ornate sixteenth-century marble steeple. Bus schedules are available from the tourist police, though the bus leaves hourly.

Transportation

Boat service between Mykonos and the other islands and ports has improved quite a bit in recent years. Boats run to Tinos (271dr), Andros (550dr), Syros (271dr), Paros (339dr), Ios (607dr), Santorini (644dr), Rafina (730dr), and Piraeus (814dr). The *Chrissi Ammos* runs Tinos-Andros-Rafina once or twice a day. The *Ios* sails daily at 3:30pm for Paros-Ios-Santorini. For certain destinations, the *Naïas* and the *Panagia Tinou* alternate. They take turns making the daily 3pm run to Syros. The *Panagia Tinou* sails Tinos-Piraeus Tues., Thurs., and Sat. (other days Tinos-Syros-Piraeus), while the *Naïas* sails Mon., Wed., Fri., and Sun. Tinos-Piraeus. Similarly, on other days, the *Naïas* runs Tinos-Syros-Piraeus. On Tues. and Thurs. the *Kamiros* begins its Patmos-Leros-Kalymnos-Ios-Rhodes run. On Wed. and Fri. it runs to Piraeus. The adventurous or the boat-loving can take the *Sol Phryne* Wed. at 11am, arriving in Limassol, Cyprus, Sat. at 10am and Haifa, Israel, Sun. at 7am (cheapest fare is 4300dr).

Olympic Airways flies from Athens to Mykonos ten times daily (1890dr, 75 minutes). A special bus runs between the airport and the Olympic Airways office on the waterfront. There is only one hotel next to the airport, **Le Village** (tel. 22 96 1), with doubles including private bath for 1200dr.

Delos

It seems rather ironic that Mykonos, where tourists worship the flesh, is also the point of departure for most pilgrimages to Delos, where ancient Greeks worshipped the gods. The sacred heart of the Cyclades, Delos is the site of the famous Sanctuary to Apollo built to commemorate the place where legend reports that Apollo and his twin sister Artemis were born. When their mother, Leto, became pregnant, Zeus, fearing Hera's wrath, cast her off. The rest of Greece and the islands followed suit, and Leto, searching desparately for a place to give birth, came upon Delos, a barren island floating moorless in the sea. Here at last she was welcomed, and as she stepped on the island, four pillars rose from the sea to anchor it. On its ground—some say on Mt. Kythnos, others, by the Sacred Lake—Artemis was born, and the next day assisted at her brother Apollo's birth.

The mere mortal history of the island is somewhat less charmed. Colonized from remote prehistoric times, Delos had long been a religious and commercial center for the Cyclades when the Ionians brought to it the cult of Leto in the tenth century B.C. By the seventh century B.C., Delos had become the political and trade center of the Aegean League of Islands, thus beginning three centuries of struggle between the Delians and the Athenians for its control. During these years, the Athenians ordered at least two purifications of the island, the latter in 426 B.C., when they decreed that no one should give birth or die within the sacred island. Delians facing either exigency were removed to the nearby Rheneia. Following the purification, the Athenians instituted the quadrennial Delian Games, dominated by the Athenians themselves.

After the defeat of Athens in the Peloponnesian Wars (fourth century B.C.), Delos enjoyed a brief and prosperous independence until the Roman occupation in the second century B.C. The Romans, who had a knack for this sort of thing, turned the religious festival into one grand trade fair, and earned for the island the dubious distinction of being the slave-market of Greece—on a single day, as many as 10,000 slaves were sold.

By the second century A.D., after successive sackings, the island was left virtually uninhabited, although under Turkish occupation it was a pirates' haunt. Today its only residents are members of the French School of Archeology, which since 1873 has been excavating and watching over the extensive ruins of a millenium of worship of Apollo.

Unfortunately, circumstances conspire to make the pilgrimage to Delos less than the transcendant experience it ought to be. Unless you want to pay 600dr for the private afternoon tours or a charter boat, the only way to see the island is to take the 9am ferry over and to return with it at 12:30pm. These boats depart from the pier in front of the Tourist Police in Mykonos; fare over to the island costs 176dr round trip. It is not possible to stay overnight on Delos legally, so if you want to explore the site in depth, several morning trips on successive days is probably the best strategy. The water, often choppy, can make you seasick, so bring along your dramamine.

Occupying over three quarters of a square mile of this tiny island, the archeological site neatly divides into four parts; the central part of the city, including the Sanctuary of Apollo and the Agora, the outlying parts of the ancient city, Mount Kythnos, and the theater quarter. While it takes several days to see the ruins, the tour suggested below is perhaps the most efficient way to catch a glimpse of the highlights during a three-hour visit.

From the dock head straight to the **Agora of the Competaliasts,** where different Roman guilds built their shrines. To the left are several parallel rows of porticos known as **stoas,** the most impressive of which was built by Phillip of Macedon. This line of altars, pillars and statue bases (you can still see the statues' prints) forms the western border of the **Sacred Way.** Follow this road to the **Sanctuary of Apollo,** once considered one of the most sacred places in Greece. Today its most impressive remain is an immense, partly hollow rectangular pedestal that once supported a 24-foot-high statue of Apollo. The famous **Delian Lions,** a gift of the people of Naxos to the holy island, lie 50m to the north. In the seventh century B.C., nine marble lions were placed in a row on a terrace facing the sacred lake, but today only five remain (a sixth was pirated by the Venetians, and to this day guards the entrance to the arsenal in Venice).

To the left of the lions, proceed up the small crest to the appropriately named **House of the Hill.** Much remains of this edifice because it was dug deep into the earth, and it serves as an excellent example of the layout of a Roman home. Continuing downhill and to the right, you'll reach the **House of the Lake,** with a well-preserved, patterned mosaic decorating its atrium. Turning back south toward the docks, pass along the wall that defines the long, dry **Sacred Lake.** If you head up the path of Mt. Kythnos (where Zeus watched the birth of Apollo), the **Temples of the Egyptian Gods** will appear on your left, demonstrating the international range of those who paid homage on this island. From the top of the 368-foot hill, there is an impressive view of ruins as well as the surrounding Cyclades. As you descend, keep an eye out for the **Grotto of Hercules.** The great size of the blocks that form its entrance halfway down the mountainside seem to date the Grotto's origins to Mycenean times, though some experts suggest it is a Hellenistic imitation of such architecture.

Bear right (north) at the bottom of the hill to reach the **House of the Dolphins** and the **House of the Masks,** which contains the renowned mosaic of **Dionysus Riding a Panther,** considered by many to be the high point of the visit to Delos.

A bit further down the hill is the **Ancient Theater.** Descend its steps to reach the **House of the Trident,** with a mosaic of a dolphin twisted around a trident, and the **House of Dionysus** with its austere white columns. Finish up at the **House of Cleopatra,** where you can drink fresh water from the cistern and admire the white marble statues of Cleopatra and Dioscourides (the house's Athenian owners) until the boat whistle signals the end of your visit.

A map to the sprawling site is highly recommended, whether you want to follow the tour above or improvise. They are sold at the island's tourist pavilion (which also has refreshments) or in the harbor at Mykonos (50dr). Admission is 100dr, 50dr for students. If possible purchase one of the many books on Delos (250dr) in Mykonos before you visit the site. Unless you do some background reading before your visit you may feel overwhelmed by the site, and confused by the multitude of unmarked ruins. The site is open Mon.-Sat. 9:30am-3pm, Sun. 9:30am-1:30pm.

Tinos

Its streets filled with incense, icons and pilgrimage candles, Tinos is an abrupt and refreshing change from the other Cyclades. Considered by many to be the "Lourdes of the Aegean," Tinos was a sacred island as far back as the fourth century B.C., when pilgrims flocked to its shores hoping to be healed by the god Poseidon and to participate in the Poseidonia festivals. Today the island's main attraction is an icon of the Virgin and the Archangel Gabriel. Discovered in 1822 by a nun named Sister Pelagia (now canonized), it is claimed to have miraculous curing powers and is covered with gold, diamonds, and pearls. Even today, the faithful line up to kiss the holy relic currently housed in the **Panayia Evangelistra.** Try to visit on one of the major pilgrimage days (Aug. 15 or March 24), when tens of thousands flock to the church. These festivals are the largest *panayieria* in Greece. The church is open daily 8:30am-8:30pm. Dress properly if you want to enter. Upstairs are two museums exhibiting the distinctive sculpture for which Tinos is famed.

Facing the docks from the water, you'll see Leoforos Megalochares St. to the left, a main road with important services. On the right a few blocks up you'll find the **OTE** (open Mon.-Fri. 7:30am-midnight, weekends 7:30am-3:10pm). The **Post Office** is in the same building (open Mon.-Fri. 7:30am-4pm). Looking from the water, the first road to the right of Leoforos Megalochares takes you to a part of town filled with tourist shops and cheap restaurants, a section unto itself. Turn right onto Gafou St. and you'll come to **Michalis Taverna,** which has all the tasty Greek specials. If you go straight and take your fourth right (rather than turning onto Gafou), you'll find Lazarou Sohou St., on which are located the **police.** In the center of the wharf is a **bank** (open Mon.-Fri. 8am-2pm). Nearby, in front of the Tourist Information Center/ Windmills Travel, are the **bus** schedules to the other parts of the island. To cool off, the beach in town, **Agios Fokas,** is only a short walk to the east.

Singles in a pension shouldn't cost more than 350dr. Fortunately, you won't have to search for one; several eagle-eyed pension owners will approach you and try to rent you a room as you walk along the waterfront. **Kostas Petas,** 12 Leonida Filipidoe St. (tel. 22 05 6), has doubles set in a beautiful garden for 800dr, hot showers included. You can also have an outdoor bed in the garden for 200dr. To get to it, walk up Leoforos Zannaki Alavanou (the road up from the large "coffee shop" sign) and follow it to the top, a five-minute walk. The pension will be on your left, and the last moped rental before it has the cheapest rates in town (500dr a day). Tinos also has one relatively cheap hotel, the **Thalia,** 7 Panatiou St., with singles for 600dr. The **Aegli,** 7 El. Venizelou St.

(tel. 22 24 0), charges 900dr for a single, but it does have a good restaurant with a fine view of the harbor. Also try the **Yaro Taverna** on the waterfront.

The **Archeology Museum** is across the street from the Post Office. Open Mon.-Sat. 8:30am-12:30pm and 4-6pm, Sun. and holidays 10am-2pm, closed Tues.; admission 50dr, 30dr for students. It contains many artifacts from Poseidon's sanctuary and a fascinating first-century B.C. sundial.

Tinos is very well serviced by boat. To find the most convenient schedule you'll have to shop around on the waterfront; all lines charge the same. Fares to the four most common destinations are as follows: Mykonos (271dr, ¾ hour), Andros (394dr, two hours), Syros (244dr, one hour) and Rafina (632dr, 3½ hours). The *Chrissi Ammos* sails once or twice a day for Rafina, with a stop at Andros, Syros, or direct, and sails daily to Mykonos. You can also take a daily excursion to Mykonos and Delos (550dr), which leaves at 9am and returns at 6pm every day except Sunday, when it leaves at 11am. The *Panagia Tinou* sails daily to Mykonos and Syros-Piraeus (802dr). The *Naïas* runs Syros-Piraeus Tues., Thurs., Sat. at 4pm and straight to Piraeus other days at 3:20pm. It also sails to Mykonos daily. The *Kamiros* leaves every Fri. for Rhodes (802dr), with stops at Patmos, Leros, Kalymnos, and Kos.

Andros

Andros Town is one of the most attractive island capitals of the Cyclades. With winding stone streets, impressive views of the surrounding sea, and a soothing "pedestrians only" policy, it's a lovely and relaxing village. Accommodating it's not, however. Andros Town is filled with vacationing Greeks who rent out rooms for extended periods and resent short-term visitors. Lodgings are extremely difficult to find in town; you'll probably have to spend a night in the port town of Gavrion or nearby Batsi before you can locate a room in the solidly-booked capital.

To reach the island from Athens, take the orange-and-white-striped bus to Rafina from the corner of Mavromateon St. just off Leoforos Alexandras. Buses leave every hour on the hour; tickets are 65dr and the trip to the port lasts an hour. From Rafina, at least two boats a day head for Andros, one around 7:30am, the other 2:30pm (410dr, 2½ hours).

All boats land at **Gavrion,** a nondescript port town more than an hour's bus ride from the capital. From there you can get right on one of the buses to Andros Town (95dr), which depart shortly after each boat arrival—usually around 7am, 10am, 11am, and 5pm. If you don't want to take the chance of finding no vacancies, then head for the Gavrion **police** (tel. 71 22 0), located up the street next to the taxi stand and open every day 24 hours. They will tell you that there's plenty of room in Andros Town or that you'll have to see when you get there, but if you pester them relentlessly, they'll call the Andros police or the **Hotel Egli** to confirm space. If you still don't want to take the risk, ask the police to help you find a room in the port town or stop by the **Hotel Galaxias** (tel. 71 22 8). Doubles in Gavrion run about 1000dr. You could also head for Batsi, whose beautiful beach will not (you hope) have attracted too many to the "rooms to let" signs that dot the road.

The *Anna L* runs daily from Gavrion to Rafina at 11:20am and 6pm. The *Chrissi Ammos* runs Mon.-Fri. at 10:50am and 5:30pm, Sat. 5:30pm, and Sun. 5:30pm and 7:50pm. Two boats a day run from Gavrion to Tinos, continuing to Mykonos, at 10am and 6pm. (Andros to Tinos is a two-hour trip costing 386dr.)

Once in Andros Town, you'll need to find your way around. Make sure you get off the bus at the **police station** on the main road, Ebirikou St. Closed to cars, paved with stone, and a pleasant place to stroll, the street is also lined with all the important services. After the police station is a square; take a right at the bottom to reach the **bus station,** one block up. Buses leave for Gavrion six times a day. Continuing down Ebirikou, you'll find the **Post Office** (open Mon.-Fri. 7:30am-2:30pm), the **OTE** (open Mon.-Fri. 7:30am-10pm), and the **bank** (open Mon.-Fri. 8am-2pm). Almost in the next square you'll find the **museum** (open Mon.-Sat. 9am-3pm, Sun. 9am-2pm, closed Tues.). To the right in this square is a clean and modern **restaurant**—it has a great view of the beach you may have to sleep on. Through the breezeway, down several flights of stone steps, stands a colossal statue of an anonymous but friendly-looking fisherman.

Syros

The two churches, one Orthodox and one Catholic, which command the two hills of Syros' largest city once surveyed the premiere port in Greece: Ermoupolis. The growth of Piraeus and the invention of the steamship, however, led to the city's gradual demise. Today the nineteenth-century mansions in Dellagrazia reflect the island's opulent past. Most tourists only visit the island to make ferry connections to the more popular Cycladic islands. Yet perhaps because they see fewer tourists, Syros' inhabitants are friendly and eager to help.

If you decide to spend a day or two on Syros, there are several hotels and places advertising rooms to let in the main port town of **Ermoupolis.** The **Hotel Akteon** (tel. 22 67 5), on a side alley off High Street, around the corner from the **NTOG,** offers singles for 480dr, doubles for 760dr, both including shower. Near the **Post Office,** facing the main square, the **Kykladikon** has singles for 500dr and doubles for 680dr, all atop a flight of solid marble steps. The proprietor speaks no English, so be prepared to gesture. The **Apollon Rooms to Let** is the most delightful place to lay your pack and head in Ermoupolis; at 300dr per person with free showers (unless the local water supply is low), it's a bargain besides. Vines and flowering plants cascade over the sunny front stairway; inside, the walls are papered with posters and postcards from fellow travelers. You may stay on the roof for 130dr and still share use of the refrigerator and kitchen with the other guests. Proprietors Tassos and Nikos are very hip. The Apollon also rents motorbikes for 600dr per day, or 900dr per day for a two-person Vespa.

A night on the town in Ermoupolis might start with dinner at one of the several tavernas up on the two hills. **Tempelis Taverna,** on Anastaseos St. below the church on the right hill, is a favorite of the locals. The garlic sauce (*skorthalia*) and fish are highly recommended. Or, you can skip dinner, sip ouzo and snack on grilled octopus tentacles (succulent in more ways than one) in one of the numerous outdoor cafes on and around the Main Square.

Ermoupolis provides somewhat tame entertainment for the highbrow, lowbrow, and jejune in all of us. The **Apollon Opera House,** newly renovated along the lines of Milan's La Scala, has something on the hill most nights throughout the year. Meanwhile, around the corner, the **Disco Margarita** rocks to a different beat; there's no cover charge unless you sit down. Or you can take in the arcade to the north of the port, but don't ride the ferris wheel too soon after the ouzo and octopus.

Galissas, a fishing village to the west of Ermoupolis, has a fine beach and an inexpensive taverna on the shore. On the hill overlooking the village is a pristine, whitewashed church, which stands in stark contrast to the nude bathing and impromptu camping that occur in the adjacent cove. There are several pensions along the beach road; **Angela's** is among the cheapest and cleanest.

The more sheltered beach at **Vari** is also pleasant, but **Agathopes** is a battleship cover, not a beach, and not worth the trip. All the beaches and larger villages on Syros can be reached by frequent buses from Ermoupolis; a schedule is posted in the NTOG office on High Street.

If you are merely waiting for a ferry, stop in at the free **Archeological Museum** next to the Town Hall, open Mon.-Sat. 9am-3:30pm, Sun. 9am-2pm. The collection is no great shakes, but it displays some unusual proto-Cycladic and Roman artifacts, as well as those retrieved from Chalandriani, the site of the old acropolis of Syros. From Syros, there are daily connections to Piraeus, Tinos, Paros, Mykonos, Ios, Naxos, and Santorini. Boats also run daily from Rafina (on the Greek mainland), stopping at Andros and Tinos.

Paros

Located in the geographical center of the Cyclades, Paros has become one of the most popular islands with tourists. At first, this may seem perplexing; it has neither the serenity of Tinos, the rugged beauty of Naxos, the archeological interest of Santorini, nor the flash and glitter of Mykonos. Nevertheless, Paros does have its own subtle charm: its unpretentious, friendly, and relaxed atmosphere is refreshing, especially for those seeking to escape the tourist hassles inherent in many of the other Cyclades. In addition, Paros offers some excellent beaches as well as a plentiful and easygoing nightlife. Unfortunately, the herd instinct has definitely inundated Paros.

While several of the towns in the interior remain free of tourists, the major coastal villages—Parikia, Naoussa, Pisso Livadi—are packed in summer. Prices are high, and if you don't have prior reservations, hotel rooms are often hard to find. The numerous pensions, starting at 600-700dr, are often full as well. Private rooms, even at around 400dr, get snapped up fast. If you can't find accommodations in any of the main tourist centers, don't panic. Just try one of the small villages, Antiparos, or any of the island's secluded beaches. The **telephone code** for Paros is 0284.

Parikia

The main port of the island is Parikia, also known as the town of Paros. Its architecture is classic Cycladian and its houses and churches are dazzling white with blue and green shutters and doors; its gardens are scented with yellow honeysuckle and lemon trees. Wander through the winding streets near the thirteenth-century Venetian *Kastro* (built on the site of an ancient temple to Demeter and Apollo) and climb to the summit by the Church of Saints Konstantines and Eleni (seventeenth century) for the best view. On a clear day you can see not only the bay and Antiparos, but the island of **Sifnos**, which lies to the west.

Nightlife is Parikia's major attraction. The majority of visitors to Paros are under 30, making the port somewhat of a giant youth center. Discos and music-playing bars abound, and many remain open until after 2am, the "pumpkin hour" set and enforced by the police.

Practical Information

Parikia serves as a convenient base for touring the island. The well-informed **Tourist Information Center** in the windmill by the dock will help you locate a room and supply you with a map of the island. Three main boat agencies in town arrange rental of private rooms and provide general information. The **Paros Travel Agency** (tel. 21 58 2) and the **Cyclades** (tel. 21 44 7) are to the right as you disembark, and the more helpful **Scopas** (tel. 22 30 0) is to the left, across from the church. The Paros is the place for plane reservations from Mykonos or Santorini. If none of these proves satisfactory, you can always try the **Tourist Police** (tel. 21 67 3), sandwiched between the Paros and Cyclades agencies. Parikia is the main business center for the island, with most of the important offices located near the waterfront: behind the Oasis Hotel one block from the harbor is the **Post Office,** open Mon.-Fri. 7:30am-2:30pm; the **OTE,** one block south of the windmill, is open Mon.-Fri. 7:30am-midnight, Sat. and Sun. 7:30am-3:10pm. The best way to see the island is by motorbike. Most of the bike rental shops are north of the main pier, past the hotels, along the waterfront. **Dimitris Kypraios** (tel. 21 38 3) has a particularly good selection. Public restrooms are beside a small church near the main pier.

Accommodations

Most of the hotels are just to your left as you disembark from the ferry, on the road leading directly away from the water and into the old town. All the hotels listed below cut their prices approximately 20% during the off-season, and reduce them by 10% for stays of over three nights.

Oasis Hotel (tel. 21 22 7), near the dock. Doubles 1401dr, 1055dr in the off-season, triples 1681dr, 1265dr off-season, both with private bath.

Hotel Parko (tel. 22 21 3), a few doors down from the Oasis. Singles 700dr, 500dr in the off-season, doubles 800dr, 600dr off-season, triples 1000dr, 800dr off-season; hot showers 70dr extra.

The Kypreous (tel. 21 38 3), on the same street as the previous two. Singles 400dr, 300dr off-season, doubles 700dr, 600dr off-season, triples 1000dr, 900dr off-season; showers 70dr extra.

The Akropolis (tel. 21 52 1). Follow the signs around from the end of the street where Kypreous is located. Doubles 900dr, 800dr off-season, triples 1200dr, 1000dr off-season, including showers.

Gallinos (tel. 21 48 0) and **Luiza** (tel. 22 12 2), situated next to the Akropolis, have singles for 1000dr, 800dr off-season, doubles for 1400dr, 1050 off-season, and triples for 1600dr, 1300dr off-season.

The Dina (tel. 21 32 5), on the main shopping street. The best place to stay in Parikia. Quietly immaculate and with a beautiful garden, it has singles for 700dr, 650dr off-season, doubles for 800dr, 750dr off-season.

Kato-Yalos (tel. 21 40 3), south of the dock near the park. Doubles 100dr, 850dr off-season.

Livadia (tel. 21 59 7), on the beach north of town. Singles 675dr, 560dr off-season, doubles with bath 1125dr, 900dr off-season.

Rooms Mimikos, around the corner from the main shopping avenue on Agorakntou St., has singles for 500dr, 420dr off-season, doubles for 800dr, 600dr off-season.

For cheaper rooms, try the pensions east of town (take a right by the Akropolis Hotel). Most places charge 400-500dr per person. The other alternative for finding private rooms is to bargain with the people who meet the boats as they dock, although the Tourist Police are trying to eliminate this practice on Paros.

There are two camping sites in Paros: **Paros** (tel. 21 67 0), north of town, and **Loula** (tel. 22 08 2). Both charge 90dr a night. There is also camping at Antiparos, and at **Kolybithras Beach** near Naoussa.

Food

Most of the restaurants in Paros are located along the harbor. Almost all of these establishments display their menus in a glass window box, so wander around until you find something that catches your eye. **John's Take Away,** down at the end of the street, is one of the friendliest and cheapest in town. **Taverna Effkaloptos** (follow the signs in town) also has good food and reasonable prices. If you are feeling homesick for America, try **Nick's Hamburgers,** which is run by a former employee of McDonalds from Ohio. For a splurge, break away from the main drag of sea front eateries and dine at **To Tamarisko** (open from 7pm every day except Monday). To get there, walk past the National Bank onto the side street, take your first left, and look for the signs (or ask). The Greek food, rumored to be the best on Paros, is served on tables set under trellises in a garden filled with the fragrances of flowers and good cooking.

Nightlife

Both the harbor and the old town are filled with discos, but you'll find the best ones along the waterfront. The most popular is **Sirocos,** which attracts an international crowd. **Hesperides,** at the end of the street, is also popular but has a small cover charge (200dr). **Magic Disco** (follow the signs) is also recommended. For its part, the new wave set displays its frightening finery in the **Kiaola Bar,** which also faces the water.

Sights

Anyone with a taste for Byzantine architecture will not be disappointed by the **Panagia Ekatontapiliani** (the Church of Our Lady of One Hundred Gates), an imposing sixth-century edifice that houses three separate adjacent churches. The main structure is the huge **Church of the Assumption,** flanked to the north by the **Church of St. Nicholas** (the oldest of the three) and to the south by the **baptistery,** which contains what is reputed to be the oldest baptismal font in Greece. Dress properly when visiting the church; entrance is denied to men and women wearing shorts. Open 7am-noon and 4-8pm daily. If you happen to be in Paros on Aug. 15, come to the church to watch the island's biggest festival—the Assumption of the Virgin.

Behind the church and next to the schoolyard is Paros' **Archeological Museum,** which houses Archaic, Hellenistic, and Geometric period artifacts, including a fifth-century B.C. statue of the Wingless Victory and a piece of the Parian Chronicle. Open Mon., Wed.-Fri. 8am-2pm, Sun. 8am-1pm.

You don't have to be an entomologist to enjoy the **Valley of the Butterflies.** Just 10km south of town, this lush little valley filled with countless brightly-colored moths that dot every bush and tree is a visual feast. Sporting handsome black and white tiger stripes, these moths reveal bright red underwings when provoked to fly. A private tour bus leaves at 5:15pm from in front of the Paros Travel Agency for the Valley of the Butterflies; fare is 250dr. Unfortunately, the valley cannot be reached by public transportation, but for 300dr you can hire a donkey (round trip takes 2½ hours) to take you there and back. If you don't take the tour bus, the other alternative is the taxi, which costs about 500dr. The valley has a 25dr admission fee. One warning: make sure it's butterfly season when you visit (spring, especially May); if not, the excursion is a waste of time and money.

Around the Island

Daily tours of Paros depart from in front of the travel agencies in Parikia around 10am every morning. Unless you are very pressed for time, they are unnecessary; hourly bus service connects Parikia to Naoussa and to the route cutting across the island down the east coast. Schedules for public buses are posted at the bus depot inside the information windmill in Parikia.

Five kilometers east of Parikia, near **Marathi,** are the quarries where the marble which made Paros famous in ancient times was mined. Parian marble is still held by many to be among the finest in the world, translucent up to three millimeters in depth, three times that of most other marble. After being abandoned for centuries, the quarries were again mined by the French in the nineteenth century, to get the marble for the tomb of Napoleon. The quarries are no longer in use, but you can climb down into them a little ways. The interconnecting shafts are over one hundred meters deep. To the left of the entrance is a relief carving dating from the fourth century B.C.

Lefkes, 7km from Marathi, was the largest village on the island in the nineteenth century when Parians moved inland to avoid the pirates menacing the coastal towns. It is now a quiet village of four hundred inhabitants, with a lovely post-Byzantine church and several excellent studios where ceramics are produced. Continuing east, you come to the even smaller town of **Prodromos.** Few tourists ever stop off at this village. If you do, the two churches at the entrance to the town are worth visiting. The one on the right dates from the year 1687, and houses some unusual icons.

The little town of **Pisso Livadi** on the east coast of Paros provides a quiet place to spend time while on the island. Once a bustling harbor, the long cove now serves as an anchorage for a few fishing boats and a haven for windsurfers. There's a windsurfing school on Logaras Beach where boards can be rented at 400dr per hour or 1200dr per day. Behind Pisso Livadi, the untouristed town of **Marpissa** lies at the foot of a large hill. The **Monastery of Agio Antonios** shines a brilliant white from the top of the hill. Unfortunately the monastery is not open to visitors, but an expansive view from the summit rewards the climber.

There are scores of available doubles in Pisso Livadi; solo travelers, however, must rent a double at a slightly reduced rate, or take their chances with mosquitoes and Tourist Police on the beach. If you're traveling alone, try to befriend a fellow individualist and go in on a double together. Don't worry—twin beds are the rule. The **Marpissa Hotel** is one place to try: it enjoys a fine view of the harbor, and does have singles at 600dr and doubles at 800dr, showers extra. The **Coralli Hotel** (tel. 41 28 9), near the Marpissa, is itself expensive, but the manager rents out doubles (with a shared bath) in the building below the hotel for 700dr, 600dr in the off-season. **Captain Kafkis Camping** has singles at 350dr and camping at 80dr per person, including hot showers. Follow the signs a half mile back along the road towards Parikia.

The destination for most tourists is the beaches on the east coast, of which the justly named **Chryssi Akti** (Golden Beach) is the most beautiful. There are rooms to rent on the beach (500dr for doubles), but most people camp in the coves a short walk down from the beach. From Chryssi Akti, the public bus continues south along the coast to **Dryos,** where there is also a good beach. Another public bus runs twice a day to Pounda and Aliki on the west coast, where you will find still more good beaches. From Pounda, it is only a fifteen minute hop by boat over to Antiparos.

There are also a number of good beaches on the west coast, accessible by boat from Parikia (50dr). **Krios Beach,** the first stop, is a family beach, and **Kamines,** the next beach, is known for its excellent swimming and snorkling. **Agios Fokas,** the last stop, is the most secluded of the western beaches, and for this reason alone considered by many to be the best.

Like Pisso Livadi, **Naoussa** is an alternative to Parikia as your home-base on Paros. A quiet fishing village only recently discovered by tourists, Naoussa now has a tourist office of its own and is serviced by hourly buses from Parikia, twenty minutes to the south (30dr). These buses stop at the popular Kolybithras Beach on the way to Naoussa. Bring your windsurfer. The snack bars and cafes which flank Naoussa's main square advertise "pizza, hamburgers, toast" (yes, toast), but for fine Greek fare, go to one of the seafood tavernas by the harbor. **Delphini Ouzeri** serves up fresh fish at 150dr per portion, and the manager boasts that his ouzo is so cheap by the bottle that if you only want to drink one glass he'll give it to you for free. If you happen to be in town on August 23rd, you may feast your eyes and ears as well when local Naoussans turn out in traditional costume to commemorate a victorious naval battle over the Turks with music and dance.

Pension accommodations in Naoussa are expensive, averaging about 1400dr for a double, 1150dr in the off-season. But the **Naoussa Hotel** (tel. 51 20 7) offers rooms with balconies overlooking the sea and breakfast for the same prices, and has singles for 670dr. Furthermore, the Tourist Offices can help you find private rooms at around 600dr per person, 450dr in the off-season. Look for a sign proclaiming "Tourist Office, Katerina Simitzi;" she is particularly helpful.

Transportation

Paros is rapidly overtaking Syros as the transportation hub of the Cyclades. During the summer months, boats depart several times a day to all of the major islands nearby. The most complete ferry schedule is posted in front of the main pier. In addition, individual boat agencies post the schedules of boats for which they sell tickets. When buying tickets at the boat agencies, make sure the agency you go to sells tickets for the boat you want. During the summer, boats leave at least twice a day for Naxos, Ios, and Thira; at least once a day to Syros, Tinos, Mykonos, and Piraeus; and about five times a week to Crete. There are also excursion boats to Delos/Mykonos, and to Sifnos.

Antiparos

The hour-long boat ride from Parikia makes it hard to believe that Antiparos is almost within spitting distance. In fact, the two were one island until about a thousand years ago. But the small channel that now runs between them has been sufficient, at least so far, in keeping Antiparos tranquil and set in its own ways. One side effect of the recent tourist boom is Paros has been increased traffic to Antiparos of people unable to find accommodations on the larger island.

Little of this small island is developed—virtually all of its 540 inhabitants live in the town where the ferry docks, and there is no bus service to any other points on the island. There is a modest beach alongside the dock, with delightful waterfront restaurants (delightful atmosphere, at any rate) and several hotels and pensions. The center of town, up the road about three hundred meters, has a wide-open plaza, with cafe bars under its large shade trees, and flowers and trellised plants bedecking most of its sparkling houses.

The street leading from the dock to town and then bearing left is lined with cheerful pensions with rooms to let. The cheapest hotels are the **Anargyros** (tel. 61 20 4) and the **Mantalena** (tel. 61 20 6), with singles for 500dr (400dr in the off-season) and doubles for 700dr (600dr in the off-season). There's also an organized campground northwest of town, and many people take to the more remote beaches. One of them is reached by following the sign for Bonos on the far side of the town plaza—a pleasant beach backed by the barren fields characteristic of this windy island. The best restaurants on the island (located in the main town) are the **Taverna Yorgas** and the **Taverna Kalmatarie**.

Since there's no bus service on the island, all excursions are by foot or by boat. Although it's nothing spectacular, the most popular one is to the stalactite caves at the southern end of the island; privately-owned excursion boats leave from the dock at Antiparos three times a morning, at 9:30, 10:30, and 11:30am, and return starting at noon. It is also possible to make the trip on foot—allow a few hours round trip—which has the added advantage of allowing you a closer inspection of the island. Once you're at the foot of the path leading to the cave, it is an arduous climb, or 200dr donkey ride, up to the entrance. Recently tourists have taken to writing graffiti into the stalactite formations, greatly depreciating their aesthetic appeal.

In high season, there are three excursion boats daily that stop at Antiparos and the caves. Also, a passenger ferry makes frequent trips between Antiparos and Pounda (on the west coast of Paros) during July and August. In the off-season, try opening the door of the small church by the shore in Pounda. Apparently, this will signal the ferryman to come over from Antiparos.

Naxos

Tradition has identified Naxos as the land of Ariadne, the daughter of King Minos of Crete. After Ariadne saved Theseus from her father's labyrinth, he fled toward Athens, taking her with him. But en route, he landed at Naxos, and after abandoning the sleeping Ariadne on the islet off the Chora, made his way back to Athens alone. There Dionysus (in some accounts himself a son of Naxos) found her, married her, and when she died, put her bridal wreath among the stars, where it still shines as the Corona Borealis.

It is not hard to understand how Naxos came to be the site of such a legend. With its lushly cultivated, terraced mountainsides, remote mountain villages, and the magnificent Tragea, Naxos is a land for true connoisseurs of sensoral delights. Its rich soil supplies the neighboring Cyclades with produce; for the visitor's pleasures there are tomatoes, peaches, and fresh fish in abundance; and when the grapes are in season, they are about the best you will find in Greece. Locally produced wines and a variety of graviera (called "Naxos" cheese) both deserve their high reputations.

All of this bounty has made Naxos one of the richest of the Cyclades, a fact which is apparent on a short walk through the town of Naxos (called the Chora). Rather than the usual depressing coexistence of poor native homes and luxury hotels and services catering to tourists, the best of this beautiful town belong to the people of Naxos. Glimpses into homes—invited by open windows and doors, but unavoidable in any event in these narrow streets—show a degree of comfort and expendable income not to be found on the islands dependent on tourist trade. Jasmine trees crowd tiny front yards, plants and artwork fill many of the houses, and patios with trellised arbors open out onto the sea. Most of the private homes in town do *not* rent rooms, another sure sign of material comfort; and if you have difficulty locating a room and find the natives preoccupied with matters other than serving tourists' needs, just bear in mind that the compensations of an independent, thriving culture are too obvious to need enumeration.

Until now, most of the tourists in Naxos have been Greek, although the influx of Europeans increases each year. Another sign of the relative unimportance of tourist trade is that there is still no Tourist Police or National Tourist Office for the island. As on all other Cycladean islands, the agencies selling boat tickets and running bus tours are an invaluable source of information. You'll find them along with most of the town services right on the Paralia, the long promenade running along the water.

Getting to Naxos

Because of Naxos' climb in popularity, boat connections to the other Cyclades and to the Greek mainland have improved steadily in the past few years. During the summer, often as many as four boats go from Paros and two from Mykonos a day, making Naxos one of the easiest Cyclades to reach. Boats run from Naxos to Santorini and Ios six days a week. Naxos is the best access point for Amorgos—in summer there are up to four sailings a week, two of which stop at **Iraklia, Shinoussa, Koufonissia,** and **Donoussa.** At least two boats sail every day of the summer from Piraeus to Naxos, the first departing at 8am.

The Town of Naxos

A short foray into the town of Naxos (or Chora) will leave you wondering whether King Minos perhaps built his labyrinth here, and not on Crete. The maze of narrow alleys and streets makes it difficult to find where you want to go, but you'll hardly mind, for, along with the handsome villas and beautiful flowers, they make Naxos one of the most enchanting cities in the Cyclades.

Maps of the city's layout are available on the back of the Naxos Island maps and in the one Naxos guidebook sold throughout the town, but the city cartographers neglected to mark street names, nor would the names help much even if they were included. Some of the hotels and restaurants have painted arrows all over the old town to direct the confused visitor. The best strategy for locating a place is to remember which of these establishments it is close to; then you can safely find your way by following the brightly colored arrows.

Practical Information

Currency Exchange: The several banks on the Paralia are open Mon.-Fri. 8am-2pm. In summer, the bank in the center of town is also open 6-8pm. Shops and the boat agencies will also change money.

Post Office: Walk down the Paralia, turn left after Hotel Hermes, then take your first right. Open Mon.-Fri. 7:30am-2pm; closed Sat. and Sun.

OTE: beneath the Hotel Coronis at the other end of the Paralia. Open Mon.-Fri. 7:30am-midnight, Sat. and Sun. 7:30am-3:10pm from mid-June through mid-September; open Mon.-Fri. 7:30am-10pm, Sat. and Sun. 7:30am-3pm in the off-season.

Bookstore: The Naxos Popular Art Shop on the waterfront buys and sells used books, as do several other shops.

Clinic: Papavasileiou Street (tel. 22 34 6, afternoons and evenings, 23 19 7), just after the big bend, on the left. The doctor speaks some English, and is in the clinic from approximately 8:30am-1pm each day. He also makes housecalls.

Public W.C. and Showers: on the street parallel to Paralia St. Mount the stepped alley to the left of Cafe-Bar Nikos and turn left.

Telephone Code: 0285.

Accommodations

Naxos offers a number of cheap hotels and pensions, some with spectacular ocean views. Most of the hotels are clustered either in the center of town or next to the beach south of the main town. Try any one of the following:

The Dionysus (tel. 23 33 1), in the old market section near the Venetian Kastro (follow the red arrows). Run by friendly **Katarina Villa,** who keeps the old house impressively clean. A good buy—400dr for doubles, 600dr with private bath.

Youth Hostel, run by the same woman, in the basement of the Dionysus. A non-licensed hostel, but who cares? The beds cost an unbelievable 150dr. The dormitory is a little cramped, but the bathrooms are clean.

The Anixix (tel. 22 11 2 or 22 78 2), in the old town, next to the Dionysus. Clean, with a superb ocean view. Doubles are 700dr, 500dr in the off-season. 1000dr with private bath.

Evripiotis Pension, near Mavlis Garden Taverna. Go to the old town and ask someone for Betty and Tassos Evripiotis. Simple, tasteful, with a bonafide hot shower. Singles 400dr, 350dr off-season, doubles 700dr, 600dr off-season.

Hotel Apollon, on Neofitou St., past Jasons (tel. 22 46 8). A real hotel with lounge and reception desk, but cheaper than you'd expect with singles for 600dr, 400dr in the off-season, doubles 877dr, 600dr in the off-season, showers included. Breakfast is available for 120dr.

Hotel Anna, next to the Hotel Apollon (tel. 22 47 5). Anna has a variety of rooms to let with various features (with and without bath, a five-bed suite with bath and kitchen, etc.), and might accept a (polite) offer below her list price of doubles for 1125dr, 900dr in the off-season, triples for 1350dr, 1125dr in the off-season.

Hotel Proto (tel. 22 39 4), on the side of the harbor near the Palatia. The crusty manager, who is author of a guide to Naxos, speaks fluent French (but not English). Singles 700dr, 560dr off-season, doubles 1000dr, 800dr off-season, triples 120dr, 1080dr off-season.

Hotel Ariadne (tel. 22 45 2), on the ocean at the southern end of town, with some spectacular views. The hotel is run by a charming Greek woman, who charges 800dr for singles, 500dr off-season, 1000dr for doubles, 600dr off-season, shower included. Breakfast on the terrace costs 130dr.

Sanoudos (tel. 22 36 9), at the end of the road just before you come to the beach. Doubles 950dr, 697dr off-season, and triples 1102dr, 837dr off-season. Prices include private bath.

Camping: a small community of freelance campers usually unrolls sleeping bags on the town beach. Watch out for late-night motorcycle traffic to and from the waterfront discos. Others congregate in the inlets just beyond Agia Anna beach.

Food

There are a number of good, relatively inexpensive restaurants in Naxos. The best are located on **Nikodemos Street. Vassilis Taverna** is particularly inexpensive. **Flora,** in the old town, has the island's best seafood. For a good view of the harbor, try **Nikos Cafe-Bar** (it looks pricey, but it isn't), or the **Meltimi,** right on the beach south of town. Dinner hours in Naxos start earlier and end later than elsewhere in Greece. If you show up past 7pm, you may have to wait for a table. For truly late eaters, **Thomas' Grill** ("the best grill in Naxos") stays open to satisfy the inner man with souvlaki, fried kalamari (squid) and similar fare. Look for the signs near the OTE.

Nightlife

After a cursory stroll through the town, the tourist with itchy feet might worry that discos had not found fertile ground on Naxos; they have, but not along the Paralia, where diners linger over their meals, coffee, or local citron liqueur to pass the cool evening. A crop of semi open-air discotheques has taken root along the town beach, Agios Giorgios, instead. **Asteria** is the only club with live music: rock until midnight, bouzouki after that. Back in town, at

Joe's Pub and **Mike's Pub,** you'll hear (slightly slurred) English spoken in a wide variety of accents.

Sights

Although you could spend weeks exploring the streets of Naxos, you should make a point of visiting the old **Venetian Kastro,** a set of mansions still inhabited by the descendants of the original Frankish and Venetian nobility. One of these buildings, originally a French school, now serves as the town's excellent museum. It contains a large collection of vases, sculpture, jewels, and implements found in Mycenaean chamber tombs from the twelfth century B.C., and Geometric tombs from the eighth century B.C., as well as Cycladic artifacts over four thousand years old. The museum is open Mon.-Sat. 8:30am-12:30pm and 4-6pm, Sun. 9am-3pm, closed Tues.; admission 50dr, 30dr with student ID.

Some say the marble archway atop the **Palatia,** an islet connected to the town by a causeway, was part of a palace Dionysus built for Ariadne on the spot where he found her. But facts, which always seem to intrude on more delightful fictions, suggest that the archway, along with the platform and some columns, are all that remain of an Ionic temple to Apollo, begun by the tyrant Lygdamis in the sixth century B.C., and left uncompleted at his death.

If the sun proves too hot for sightseeing, you can always cool off at one of Naxos' many beaches. There is a small town beach on the causeway to the Palatia, and a far more substantial one at the other end of the Paralia; it's a bit crowded during summer, but undeniably beautiful. But the best beach in the area is at **Agia Anna,** a series of beautiful coves to the south. Buses run to Agia Anna approximately every hour during the summer, starting at 10:30am (36dr). You can also take an excursion boat every hour between 8:30am and 7:30pm during the high season, or spend a pleasant 45 minutes and walk. For an incredible view, climb to **Aplomata** just north of town. There are ancient Cycladic tombs here (4500 years old), and excavations from this site are displayed in the town's museum.

Around the Island

Islands tend to be judged by their harbor town and beaches. This is a mistake with Naxos, because the splendor of the island is hidden in its wildly undulating interior. Anyone who leaves having seen only Naxos town and its environs will be disappointed—and rightly so, as he will have missed the heart of Naxos entirely.

If you had unlimited time on Naxos, the ideal way to see the island would be on foot. Villages are so spaced that food and shelter are available at propitious intervals; many, at least in the interior, are connected by footpaths through the countryside, and there are few places in Greece that would more richly reward the time and attention thus spent. For those with only a couple of days, some difficult choices will have to be made. You can rent a moped (from 400dr per day without gas) or a small motorcycle (from 700dr per day without gas) to cover more ground, but it's not recommended for inexperienced riders—the machines are poorly maintained, as are Naxos' mountain roads, and help can be a long time in coming. Moreover, it is impossible to insure bikes on Naxos, and you will be held responsible for any damage. Since you must leave your passport as a deposit, this has lead to a practice by at least one motorcycle rental shop in Naxos of renting at a cheap rate, then charging exorbitantly for tiny or imagined damages, while holding passports for ransom. If this happens to you, go straight to the police.

Nevertheless, a moped or motorcycle can be a terrific way to see the island, taking you places where feet or public transportation can't. One of the best rental shops in Naxos is **Jasons** on Neofitou St. at the northern end of town. Their bikes are new and in good shape. The mechanics at Jasons are good at teaching beginners to ride mopeds and can recommend safe, interesting places to go. One of the workers, Theoharis, speaks fluent English and is a fountain of information on Naxos island in general.

What most people do is take the bus to Apollon, a small fishing village on the northern tip of the island. The two and a half hour trip (155dr), heading east to Filoti and then north to Apollon, takes you through the most beautiful part of the island. Several of the villages along the way deserve closer attention than they can get from a bus window; if you're so inclined, you can stop en route, and catch the next bus (there are five a day) or continue on foot along your way. This trip may also be taken by moped or motorcycle, though the second leg, from Filoti to Apollon, requires more experience.

The first hour of the ride, from Chora to Chalki, takes you through rich cultivated mountainsides, with olive trees, whitewashed churches, and wild flowers that erupt on schedule each spring and summer. Before you reach Chalki there's a turn-off for Ano Sangri, one kilometer west of the road. You can take the Chora-Chalki bus to the turn-off and then walk, or walk the entire way from Chora if you have time (about an hour and a half). An isolated town of winding flagstone streets, it is worth a visit anytime, but particularly during its folk-arts festival (the second and third weeks of August). An old house, originally a monastery, has been fitted out with the traditional furnishings, farming, and housekeeping implements, and clothing of Naxos. Admission is 35dr, and the friendly young men and women of the village act as guides.

At Chalki, one of Naxos' prettiest villages, the magnificent **Tragea** begins—a huge arcadian olive grove of absolute stillness. Stop in at the **Panagia Protothonis,** the parish church of Chalki, right across from the bus stop: restoration work on the church has uncovered beautiful wall paintings from the eleventh through thirteenth centuries. The well-marked turn for **Moni** branches off from the main road in the middle of Chalki. Three kilometers from the turn-off, a short path on the right leads to the eighth-century stone church of **Panagia Drossiani.** As you stand in front of this solid building, the whole Tragea lies spread along the terraced valley before you.

Soon after Chalki you reach Filoti, where the Tragea ends as the road climbs the flanks of Mt. Zas. These slopes offer superb views extending all the way to Poros and the sea beyond, and in another fifteen minutes you are in **Apiranthos,** another delightful small village with a traditional arts museum. From there to Komiaki, an hour's drive away, the road snakes among the interior mountain ranges. The landscape, its terraced slopes carefully planted with fruit and olive trees, descends dramatically into valleys far below—it has been compared to a Japanese brush painting. The only tip-off that you're in the Mediterranean and not the Orient is the occasional stark white church perched on an isolated plateau over the valley, with a lone foot path leading up to it.

From Komiaki, the road descends slowly around mountain ridges, reaching the sea at last at the village of **Apollon.** Considered remote only a few years ago, Apollon now has a sizable tourist trade with several pensions and restaurants, and a fairly crowded rocky beach. But the town is still quite lovely, and many people choose to pass their whole time on Naxos there. Rooms run from 550-650dr for a double. People do sleep on the beach, but the local police come around in the middle of the night and ask you to move.

A short walk from the harbor is one of the two famous **Kouroi** found in Naxos. The other, smaller but more developed, is in the town of Flerio, unfortunately not en route to anywhere, but worth a trip out of your way. The kouros, a larger than life idealized sculpture of a male figure usually found at tombs or local shrines, was first made in Greece in the seventh century B.C. under Egyptian influence that is apparent in the finished product. The Kouros at Apollon, ten and a half meters long and cut into the marble hillside, was never completed, probably because the marble broke while being sculpted. To reach it from the village, head back up the main road away from the beach, and turn right at the small sign for "kouros." From there, it is about a twenty-minute hike up the path to the sculpture.

On your return trip from Apollon to Chalki, you might consider getting off the bus at **Filoti** (about two kilometers away) and walking through the Tragea, which begins shortly after Filoti on the left. There is a footpath that starts on the main road just outside of Filoti directly across from the sign for Kerami. It leads to **Agia Apostoloi,** a beautiful Byzantine church dating to the tenth century with wall paintings from the thirteenth century. If the door is locked (it usually is), you can climb through the window, but make sure you have the means to boost yourself out again. Following the footpath southwest from Agia Apostoloi, you'll come to a lovely post-Byzantine church, the **Panagia Metochiotissa,** dating from the seventeenth century. It is delightfully easy to get lost wandering through the Tragea, and those with time to spare might well do it voluntarily. For the rest, keep heading west and you'll soon return to the main road.

Besides the popular ones near Naxos, the best beaches serviced by bus are **Kastraki, Aliko,** and **Pyrgaki,** along the southeast shore of Naxos. Here the desert meets the sea: on the dunes behind you grow scrub pines, prickly pear and century plants; in front of you the blue ocean is cool and refreshing. And despite four buses per day from the Chora, this piece of shoreline remains secluded. A German company has recently purchased part of the area around Pyrgaki and Aliko, and rents out attractive three-person bungalows with kitchen and bath for 1220dr per night or 8540dr per week in the off-season. The bungalows fill up in high season, so for July and August rentals write to Adolphe Maes, Manager, Pyrgaki Bungalows, Nakopro E.P.E., Athens. Follow the dirt road that veers off from the bus route by the sign "Pros Kastraki" and you will come to Kastraki beach. **Zorba's Taverna** offers food, dancing, and dirty but serviceable rooms (200dr per person with shower) in a beach house atmosphere that is at once bucolic, with cattle grazing nearby, and alcoholic, thanks to manager and lay philosopher Michael's well-stocked bar. An anachronism in the middle of nowhere, this place may seem to be a mirage, brought on by too much mopeding in the sun. But the taverna is worth a visit even if you decide to sleep on the beach. Naxos' best secluded beaches are on the eastern coast and accessible only by car—or motorbike, if you are very confident astride one. Try **Moutsouna, Psili Ammos,** and **Kildo.**

There is a complete bus schedule for all routes on the island posted in the town of Naxos at the bus stop by the dock. It's a good place from which to begin trips around the island, but be forewarned—it isn't entirely reliable. Sometimes the earliest buses don't leave, sometimes extra buses are put on short hauls (i.e., to Agia Anna), and most times, especially on the Apollon route, the buses are so crowded you may not get on from any intermediate stops en route. (It is also advisable to get to the first stop early if you don't want to stand for two and a half hours). As ever in Greece, the most reliable information on buses is gotten from the drivers themselves. The easiest of the villages to visit from the town of Naxos is Chalki. Five buses a day run between the two towns. To visit any place else, you will have to plan on a full-day excursion, since the bus schedule is organized primarily to meet the needs of the local people.

Amorgos

When people tell their friends about Amorgos, it is usually on the condition that they don't tell anyone else. So far these gentlemen's agreements seem to be working, as this island remains among the most peaceful in the Cyclades. The only reason visitors become noticeable during the summer months is that a single boatload of tourists can fill Amorgo's few pensions and only bus to overflowing. To date, several delightful beaches have provided safety valves, as much to the relief of locals as to that of roomless visitors.

Most ferries disembark on the west side of the island at **Katapola,** the main port, which has the post and boat offices along its harborside. The only public telephone is in a private home on the other side of the harbor, but may be used if you ask. **Pension Amorgos** (tel. 71 21 4) offers pleasant, tidy doubles without bath for 751dr, 600dr off-season. If it is full, ask for a spot on the roof, where for 200dr you have access to the showers. Up the hill, **Nikitas Koveos** (tel. 71 21 8) runs a pension surrounded by his beautiful garden, but call early, for savvy Greek vacationers tend to book his doubles well in advance. Doubles are 900dr, 700dr off-season, showers included. Impromptu camping takes place on the town beach when the boats arrive late, but for long-term stays, head up to Panteleimon Beach in the cove on the left side of town.

Katapola, which literally means "below the town," is best left as soon as you have your bearings. In this case, "the town above" is **Chora,** sometimes known as Amorgos. Six kilometers from the harbor by the island's only bus, it makes for a far more restful if slightly less convenient headquarters. Chora's landmarks are a fourteenth-century Venetian fortress and a row of defunct windmills that dominate its hills, but the town's real attraction is its streets, so unspoiled and uncluttered they initially seem desolate. Keep an eye out for **Agios Fanurios,** the smallest church in the Cyclades, which can only hold three people. Appropriately named after the patron saint of lost objects, this church can be found by the number 240 painted on its facade, but even that is disappearing under layers of whitewash. In the main square, **Kostas Getabis** cuts traditional Greek silhouette puppets in his shop. There are no hotels, but many of the locals offer rooms which can be had for as little as 200dr per bed. There are a couple of friendly tavernas along the main street that winds through the center of Chora. **D. Kastanis** serves hearty fare at startlingly low prices, and occasionally hosts live Greek music in his taverna. At the last taverna, on the far edge of town, you can drink real retsina—resinated in the barrel, not the bottle.

A twenty-minute walk or five-minute bus ride from Chora down the east slope of the island brings you to the path to the remarkable **Chozoviotissa,** or Monastery of the Presentation of the Virgin. Pressed against a slight hollow on the sheer rock face, the edifice looks like an American Indian cliff dwelling painted white. Not only is it visually one of the most spectacular monasteries in Greece, but it is also one of the most delightful to visit as long as you observe the dress code: long pants for men, dresses or skirts for women, and no bare shoulders. If you arrive between sunrise and 2pm (additional hours in summer, 5-7pm), the monks will greet you with coffee or their homemade liqueur and sweets. After you've signed the register, the tour begins in the chapel, where to the right of the altar is the famous icon of the Virgin which arrived miraculously about the same time that Byzantine Emperor Alexis Comnenus granted the monastery its charter. The ornate charter can be seen in a small alcove one flight below. Next to it is a room with ecclesiastical silverware, accessories for liturgical vestments, and eleventh-century illuminated manuscripts.

A twenty-minute scramble further down the hill to the right, cutting across a switchback in the road, takes you to Agia Anna, a spectacular white pebble beach. Don't be seduced by temptations of the first cove. Further to the right is a much bigger beach with plenty of room for the nude bathers and freelance campers based there. A spring running down the cliff provides water, but for food you must catch the bus back to Chora and Katapola (four a day—two in the morning, two in the afternoon) or hoof it.

If sand beaches are your fancy, head to the inlet of **Egiali** on the northern tip of Amorgos. Although no daily means of transportation exists linking Egiali to Katapola, some inter-island ferries stop at the small harbor town of **Ormos,** so you can wait for the next ferry to stop en route. Rooms can be had at **Pension Lakki** (tel. 71 25 2), halfway down a long beach where informal camping takes place. Singles go for 350dr, doubles for 500dr, showers included. Egiali occasionally has water shortages, but evidently Lakki has water even when other places have run out. A short hike along the cliffs opposite Ormos brings you to isolated coves with unblemished sand. Should you feel like exploring, the towns of **Potamos** and **Langada** on the hills above Ormos offer an abundance of whitewashed churches and locals who still consider visitors a novelty. The windswept town of **Tholarea,** inhabited by farmers and their donkeys, all of whom return the favor to gawking tourists, commands a ridge from which both sides of Amorgos can be seen. To get there from Ormos, walk to the end of the beach and follow the stone path leading up the valley to the town (half hour). You can slake your thirst at an old, sweetwater well along the way.

Transportation

One factor which keeps tourists away from Amorgos is the difficulty inherent in getting there, and, having arrived, in leaving again. Amorgos is linked to Naxos, Paros, Syros, and a handful of the smaller Cyclades, but only by infrequent boats. Do not expect to reach Amorgos from Ios or Santorini (or vice versa) without changing ships in Naxos. In fact, except for weekly boats from Piraeus and the Dodecanese, you almost have to be in Naxos in order to make connections to Amorgos (four sailings weekly). Moreover, Amorgos-bound ships are "locals," not expresses—they invariably stop at one or all of the smaller islands near it, adding between three and six hours to what should be a three-hour hop from Naxos. As if that weren't enough, Amorgos lies in some of the roughest waters of the Aegean, and when the wind blows, more than one traveler has found himself leaning over the rail of one of the smaller ships which ply the Amorgos route (beware the good ship *Marianna!*).

Ios

In the past few years, few islands in Greece have changed as much as Ios. Once a hippie hangout known for its 1960's Woodstock atmosphere, Ios has moved into the 1980's. Mellowness is out; new wave is in. Still, although styles may have changed considerably, the main preoccupation of the island's tourists hasn't. Ios is for partiers. The summertime visitors come to Ios as much for each other as for the natural splendor of the island and it once had more counter-culture types per square foot than any other place in the world. Nowadays, it's more middle-class, meat-market, nude and lewd than counter-culture. There are few drugs (none visible or discussed), no politics, just hedonism. Unfortunately, as in any place where a high concentration of people exists in a small area, there have been problems of noise, theft, fights, litter, and poor health conditions. The United Nations High Commission on Refugees has not been called in yet, but in an attempt to ease the strain on Ios' natural and social environment the local police have started to crack down on illegal camping and to urge tourists with little money to stay in one of the three established campgrounds. Another result of increased tourism in recent years has been a cooling of the once amicable relationship between the island's residents and tourists. Still, most islanders remain friendly and if you respect local customs, you won't get any dirty looks or resentful grunts.

Life is not completely free on Ios—it takes a little money (though less than on other islands)—but it comes close. If you go in for sunbathing, music, and general revelry, you can't ask for a more perfect setting: a beautiful beach, a charming town, and all the *simpatico* company you could want. The good life for tourists centers on three locations—the port, with several restaurants, cheap hotels, and shops; the village of Ios, a half-mile up the hill, where most people stay; and the beach at Milopatos, a short bus ride away.

Getting to Ios

On the main run from Piraeus and the northern Cyclades to Santorini and Crete, Ios is serviced by several boats a day. Boats run from Iraklion three times a week, from the Dodecanese once a week, and from Paros (527dr), Naxos (446dr), Syros (682dr), and Santorini (250dr) at least twice a day during the summer. At least one boat leaves every morning from Piraeus, bound for Ios, at 8am. Third-class passage from Piraeus costs 1004dr.

The Port

Though it may take you a few minutes to realize it, the port, where the boat lets you off, is not where you want to be. The port has been unable to capture any of the atmosphere and charm that characterizes the community on the hill directly above it. Perhaps this is because it has become the hang-out for most of the tourists over 40 who came here because they knew Ios was famous for something, but weren't quite sure what. The contrast with the village is striking—people in the port are more aloof and cold, the water stinks of sewage, and everything is considerably more expensive. Simply join the rest of the visitors who pile on the bus that runs from the ferry landing to the village (12dr).

The Village

Cut into the hillside, the village of Ios is a tumble of houses connected by a labyrinth of winding whitewashed alleys lined with restaurants, high quality leather shops, a few expensive clothing and jewelry stores, two wonderful bakeries, and above all, the many discos and bars that come alive at dusk. Prices here reflect what most young people can afford to pay, making the village by far one of the cheapest towns in which to stay in the Cyclades. Restaurants and rooms are reasonably priced, and in the cafes you won't find yourself under the usual pressure to order something or leave. Cocktails in bars will set you back a bit, but if you think how cheap 150dr is by American or Northern European standards, your drink will go down smoothly.

Practical Information and Accommodations

Most of the important offices—**OTE, bank, boat agencies**—are located on the main street of the village. A large hall by the bus stop houses the **police** and also the **Post Office** (open Mon.-Fri. 7:30am-2:30pm, closed weekends).

The many rooms to rent in town start at about 500dr (600dr in July and August) for a double; beds in pleasant hostel-like pensions (e.g. **Papa Antonio's** at the western end of town) can be had for as little as 200dr per night, including a shower. Other accommodations include the following:

Poditi Strati, up the steps behind Hotel Philipou (tel. 93 49 4). Doubles for 500dr, showers 50dr extra.

Anna S. Mettou (tel. 91 44 5) has some nice rooms to let above the Deja Vu Cafe, directly behind the post office. During the summer, doubles with private bath run 600dr, triples 900dr, shower included.

Georgios and **Michalis Stavraki,** two houses two doors apart, behind the Deja Vu (tel. 91 48 6). Clean doubles for 500-600dr, depending on the time of year; triples 750dr. Michalis (to the right) also has some singles.

Afroditi Hotel, further along the road towards Milopatos Beach (tel. 91 52 6). A bit expensive, but pleasant. Doubles with a double bed, 796-910dr; with twin beds 910-1137dr.

Dimitrios and Angeliki Amoussi (tel. 91 45 4). Diagonally up the hill from the Afroditi, going toward the harbor. The best deal around. A large new pension with doubles for 550dr, 650dr with private bath; triples for 750dr, hot showers included.

Hotel Philipou, in the village. Expensive. Doubles for 900dr with private bath.

Food and Entertainment

Ios has a number of excellent restaurants. For the best value, try **The Nest,** a little taverna in the middle of the village, or **The Mill,** at the top of the hill next to an old windmill. **Agiris,** a neighboring taverna adjacent to The Mill, serves excellent seafood at a reasonable price. Or snack, as you barhop, in the numerous souvlaki stands along the main street.

Half the reason to come to Ios is to share in the nightlife. By late afternoon, the chairs and tables in "the square" (on the main street) begin to fill up with people eager for the fun to begin, but the bars and discos usually don't come alive until midnight. The following list of recommended nightspots is by no means exhaustive.

Scorpio's and **Fanaris,** on the main road going toward the beach, are the most popular discos. Definitely for the "in" crowd.

The Friend, on the main street in the village. Good rock, good dancing, and crowded.

The Orange, one block up from the Friend. Quieter lounge with low tables. Good for conversation and getting away from the mob scene.

Kalimera Pub, on the main road. Specializes in low-key jazz, but occasionally features orgies of Renaissance and Baroque music.

Boby's Club, next to the bus stop and down the hill from the post office. Plenty of room and plenty of rock music for dancing outdoors.

Ios Club. Very popular spot along the footpath to the harbor, next to Boby's. Around 7pm they feature two hours of classical music for those wishing to watch the sunset, and then at 9pm switch on the latest tunes so disco enthusiasts can pound the floorboards. Delightful amphitheater provides an escape from the noise, crowds, and heat of the discos in town. Program is posted next to the bar.

Why Not. Video has come to the Cyclades. Free movies in the evenings, live music at night. They also serve a variety of non-Greek meals and cocktails.

Traditional tavernas, such as **Zorba's** (down the street from the Orange), feature live bouzouki music and fiddling.

Milopatos Beach

During the day most people head for Milopatos Beach on foot (about 25 minutes from the town) or by regular bus service from 8am-10:30pm (12dr from the village, 17dr from the port). The beach is magnificent, and while it tends to be crowded, it is large enough to offer relative seclusion to those willing to hike to its outer parts; the farther down the beach you go, the fewer clothes you see. There are some rooms to rent, starting at 500dr for doubles, but they are usually full. Try **Draco's Place,** down the beach. The **Delfini Hotel** (tel. 91 34 0) has fancier doubles at 900dr, including shower, but you may have no luck with it either. **Camping Stars** (tel. 91 30 2) near the bus stop charges only 100dr per person, but has no water and looks more like a parking lot. There is a more pleasant campsite on the beach, the **Soulis Campground,** which charges 100dr per person and rents tents for 50dr (hot showers, cooking and washing facilities as well as safekeeping of valuables are provided), but as the row of backpacks perched on the back edge of the beach demonstrates, many people simply take to the beach at night. This practice, however, is subject to periodic police action.

Around the Island

With the exception of a solitary monastery and a modest pile of ancient rubble reputed to be Homer's tomb, the only other places of interest on the island are the beaches. Since roads leading to them have not been completed as yet, they can only be reached by excursion boats from the harbor or by jeep. Most of them have been colonized to varying degrees by nudists, particularly **Kalamos Beach,** on the opposite coast. The most popular of the secluded beaches is **Manganari** (a boat leaves every morning from the port at 10am and returns at 6pm; 200dr). Inquire at any of the travel agencies in town or at the harbor about boats to **Koumbaka** beach. A jeep trip to **St. Theodoti** beach sets out at 10am every day and returns in the afternoon (sign up 1-2 days in advance; 200dr), but you will have to walk to far-away **Psathi** beach. There is also a weekly boat that circles the island, stopping at various sights on the way (every Wed. at 10am, 400dr), as well as excursions to the islands of **Sikinos** (400dr) and **Folegandros** (500dr), some of the less populous Cyclades.

Santorini

Santorini, with its whitewashed houses perched atop sheer vertical cliffs, is pure magic. From about 2000 B.C. to 1600 B.C., one of the most advanced societies in ancient Greece flourished on the soil of this volcanic island, also called Thira; the society was influenced strongly in its later years by Minoan Crete, only 56 miles to the south. But around 1500 B.C. a massive volcanic eruption blew out the center of the island, burying every sign of civilization beneath the millions of tons of lava and pumice spewed up onto the rim. In the centuries since the catastrophe, fact and legend have mingled, leading some to identify Santorini as Plato's lost continent of Atlantis, while others have found in it the source for the biblical parting of the Red Sea. More serious historical speculation has convinced some that the eruption of Santorini triggered a tidal wave large enough to account for the contemporaneous destruction of several Minoan sites in Crete.

Professor Spyridos Marinatos, one of the strongest proponents of the last theory, began excavations on the island in 1967 in an effort to prove it. He resumed work begun at the Akrotiri site by the French School a century before, and worked steadily until his death in 1974. Excavations, still continuing under the Greek School, have so far shed no additional light on the Crete connection; they have, however, unearthed one of the most impressive archeological finds in the past several decades—a complete town, preserved virtually intact, like Pompeii, beneath layers of volcanic rock. Its paved streets are lined with one-, two-, and three-story houses, with wooden-framed doors and windows.

But even those with no interest in the island's illustrious past will find ample delights in its present—good beaches, small towns precariously pitched on cliffsides, and most of all, spectacular land formations left by centuries of eruptions from its smoldering volcano. The modern Santorini is really only the eastern crescent of the originally circular island; the explosion in 1500 B.C. left the center of the island hollow under a crust of volcanic ash, and when it caved in, water broke through the rim to fill the basin that now makes up Santorini's harbor. The two seemingly separate islands to the west, Thirasia and Apronisi, are in fact a continuation of the rim of the original island; their connection to Santorini is now submerged in the water.

Orientation

Santorini is a stopover for all boats on their way to or from Crete; during the summer months, three boats arrive every day from Piraeus, two boats a day from Paros and Naxos, one a day from Ios and Crete, and two a week from Mykonos. Buses only leave for the new port of **Athinios** from Thira 1½ hours before the scheduled departure time of ferries, which causes problems: you have to wait in Athinios, where there is nothing to do. Before you board the bus, you might ask the travel agency whether your boat is on schedule. Make sure to buy your ticket in Thira; it costs 20% more on the boat, and the ticket agency at Athinios is often closed. If one of the agencies tells you they can't sell you the ticket, go to a different one.

Olympic Airways has daily flights between Santorini and Athens (1850dr) and, during July and August, also has direct flights between Santorini, Mykonos, and Rhodes. The airport is next to Monolithos, and is connected by bus to the Olympic Airways office on the main road in Thira.

The approach to Santorini is most impressive at dawn, when the sun throws shadows over the dark waters from behind the red-black volcanic cliffs that line the west coast of the island. Boats land at three different ports on the island, a fact explained inadequately if at all over the ferries' loudspeakers to bewildered first-time visitors. Ferries may stop at Athinios, or at one of the two old ports, **Ia** (at the northern tip of the island) or **Thira** (in the center). Smaller boats stop at one or the other of the old ports; larger boats generally call at Athinios. From the old port in Thira, the only way up the cliffs is along a 587-step path. As you disembark from the ferry, you will encounter a small band of entrepreneurs eager to rent you a mule for the ride up. Don't pay more than 150dr per mule (a little more if you are wearing a pack) and fix the price before you get on the mule. Or you can take the path by foot (about 25 minutes), but remember that the mules can be stubborn about right of way and they're bigger than you. There is also a newly installed cable car that will take you to Thira for 180dr.

Thira

The center of activity on the island is the capital city of Thira (Fira). The west edge of town, perched on a rocky precipice, commands spectacular views of the harbor, Santorini's west coastline, and the neighboring islands. On the east side, the island's characteristic barrel-vaulted houses spread out on more secure footing, their quiet tree-arched streets trailing off into the surrounding countryside. In the summer, the town is overrun with tourists, mostly Americans and Europeans, who come on mammoth cruises that dock in the harbor. But it almost doesn't matter—nothing can destroy the pleasure of wandering among the narrow cobbled streets, inspecting the fine craft shops, and arriving at the western edge of town in time to watch the sun bathe the harbor in a deep magenta glow.

Practical Information

Thira has no Tourist Police, but the regular **police** are located on 25th of March St., north of Theotokopoulou Square and next to the Olympic Airways office. All of the travel agencies are also clustered around Theotokopoulou Sq., where both private excursion and public buses leave. The most helpful of the agencies are **Pelikon Tours, Damigos Tours,** and **Kamari Tours** (where you should ask for George or Gisella Nomiko). They also cash travelers checks at a rate slightly less than at the bank. Damigos offers a free left-luggage service.

Exchange: The **National Bank of Greece** (ATE) is off the square on Joseph Dekigala St. Open Mon.-Thurs. 8am-2pm, Fri. 7:45am-2pm; additional summer hours for exchange only 6-8pm. Closed Sat. and Sun.

Post Office: on 25th of March St., south of the square. Open Mon.-Fri. 7:30am-2:30pm.

OTE: behind the bank, atop the cliff on Ipapantis St. Open Mon.-Fri. 7:30am-midnight, Sat. 7:30am-3:10pm. Collect calls may be made up until two hours before closing.

Hospital: along the highway to Messaria, at the southeastern edge of town. Across from the Olympic Airways office.

Public bathrooms: on 25th of March St., down from the post office and taxi stand. They probably haven't been cleaned since they were built.

Telephone Code: 0286.

Accommodations

Most visitors to Santorini stay in Thira; a central location and good bus service make it the logical base for exploring the island. As a result, hotel rooms are often impossible to find in the summer if you arrive without reservations. But if you look among the numerous pensions in the northeastern part of town, you will probably find something. The other alternative is to accept one of the offers made to you as you arrive at the top of the steps from the ferry landing. If you arrive before the crowds, you can bargain with the children and the middle-aged women and get a good rate.

IYHF Youth Hostel: 400m north of town (tel. 22 72 2). Good facility with 80 beds. No IYHF card required. Open Apr.-Oct. 185dr per person per bed; roof space 125dr per person. Both include a hot shower.

Hotel Loukas (tel. 22 48 0). If you take the path, turn right on step #567. The main entrance is in town, down from Ipantis St. Singles 650dr, 550dr in the off-season, doubles without private bath 800-1000dr, with private bath 1000-1300dr. Hot showers included in all prices.

Hotel Tataki, 354 Danezi St. (tel. 22 38 9). In the middle of the shopping district. Brand new. Doubles 1080-1350dr, including private bath.

Hotel Lygnos, on main north-south highway (tel. 22 04 5). Go past the main square to the eastern edge of town. Singles 618-736dr, doubles 900-1012dr, triples 1012-1125dr. Showers included.

Hotel Roussou, across the street from Lygnos (tel. 22 87 9). Clean and comfortable. Singles 618-736dr, doubles 900-1012dr, triples 1012-1125dr, all including private bath.

Pension Thirasia (tel. 22 54 6), down from Hotel Lygnos on the same street. Singles 500dr, doubles 900dr, both with private bath. Doubles without bath 700dr.

The Santorini (tel. 22 59 3), in the southeast corner of the city. Doubles with private bath 1125-1350dr.

There are also pensions in the private homes lining the north-south highway at the eastern edge of town. They generally charge 600dr for modest rooms. The farther from town you walk, the cheaper they get. There are also a few cheap ones to the left of step #551 as you ascend from the ferry. Most comfortable and best bargains are the pensions to be found on the cliff walk, heading northwest beyond the museum and the cable car. The **Panoramic View Pension** (tel. 22 98 9) is quite far from town, but its clean, airy doubles (702dr, 850dr with bath) command a view of Thira and the surrounding cliffs. Inquire at Mendrinos Travel, around the corner northeast of the museum.

Rooms to let are much cheaper and easier to come by in **Karterados** (2km from Thira) and **Messaria** (4km from Thira) than in Thira, and with the frequent bus service, it is easy to reach the towns. Moreover, all of the excursions organized by the travel agencies will pick up passengers in Karterados and Messaria on their way to points south.

Food

If you look hard enough, you can find the right combination: excellent food, reasonable prices, and a spectacular ocean view. **Nicholas** and **Leonidas Tavernas,** facing each other at the top of the steps, both serve tasty moderately-priced meals (try the octopus at Finari's). **Leschi** restaurant, a little farther up, is more intimate and offers a spectacular view. For relaxed outdoor cafes, try **Canava** on the water, which along with playing Brahms and Bach serves the best cappuccino in Santorini. **Aresana,** on a side street between the water and the town square, is an art gallery-cafe. The interior is decorated with sculpture, paintings, and plants—a quiet place for rest or conversation. Wherever you go, be sure to sample some of the island's wine. Grapes thrive in Santorini's volcanic soil, and the island produces some of Greece's best vino. Although the reds are quite sweet and often taste like cough syrup, the whites are good (try Nikteri white). For a small price, you may taste a variety of Thiran wines at **Canava Roussos,** just off the road to Kamari.

Sights

If you're interested in buying handicrafts while in Greece, Santorini is one of the better places to shop for them. Numerous shops sell handmade sweaters starting at 1100dr; handmade leather sandals start at around 400dr; and the island has a large cottage industry of handwoven rugs and wall-hangings. The women of the island, working on looms at home, sell their goods through several outlets in town—the two best are **Step 566,** on the cliffside step of that number, and a store located at the south end of the waterfront right past the OTE office. Both stores will ship goods anywhere in the world. Since their prices and selection vary, check both.

The town's **Archeological Museum** has an impressive collection of prehistoric, early Cycladic, and Geometric vases, mostly from the site of ancient Thira (see below). There are also a few black figure vases from the sixth-century B.C. gravesites on Santorini. A new museum is being built which will house a magnificent collection of finds from Akrotiri. Open Mon.-Sat. 9am-3pm, Sun. 9am-1pm, closed Tues.; admission 50dr, 30dr for students.

If you take a walk up the hill behind the museum, you will have a fine view of Thira, the harbor, and the donkey path you narrowly avoided by landing at Athinios. In the evening, join the ritual of watching the sunset at one of the waterfront cafes. **Franco's,** with comfortable lounge chairs, is pricey, but worth the splurge. Drink a *frullati* and listen to Handel's *Messiah* while the sun sinks behind the craters. **Canava** is a less expensive, but equally fine choice. For nightlife, try **Victor's Disco,** or the **Tropical Bar,** both by the water. Back in town, the **Town Pub** and **Paradise Cocktails** are popular bars playing rowdy rock music. The jazz bar, **Kira Thira,** serves its own special sangria.

Around the Island

If you have only a day or two to spend, you might consider taking one of the several organized tours to various points on the island. For 600dr (500dr for students), you can take a whirlwind tour of all the major sights—buses leave at 10:45am from in front of the travel agencies around the main square in Thira. Alternatively, you can rent a moped (500dr with gas) or a Vespa motorscooter (1000dr) for the day. But with two or more days to spend, it's quite possible to cover the island by bus, supplemented by foot and donkey. Schedules are posted in the main square. Tourist maps on sale for about 50dr will tell you all you need to know to decide where to go and how to get there.

Ia

Ia (pronounced "eeya"), with its pumice caves, ancient churches, and winding streets, is one of the most beautiful and architecturally pure of the Cycladic villages. A small town clinging to the rocky northern point of the Island, Ia was devastated by the earthquake that hit Santorini in 1956. Its present inhabitants, three hundred strong (strong at least in faith, since there is every indication that the island will be hit again), have done a wonderful job of rebuilding the town. Their new houses, almost as if carved out of rock, are interspersed among the blown-out ruins of the old. A walk to the promontory at the tip will give you a splendid view, and a long climb (twenty minutes) down the stone stairs brings you to the rocky beach at Amoudi, with a few boats moored in its surprisingly deep swimming lagoon. Buses run from Thira to Ia nine times a day 9:30am-10:30pm (51dr).

Accommodations and Food

Tourism has yet to become "big business" in Ia, making accommodations and restaurants both cheap and plentiful. Hotels are mostly in the new part of town, below the crest of the hill. The **Anemones** (tel. 71 22 0) has doubles for 1058dr, 872dr in the off-season, triples for 1154-1403dr. Right down the street, the **Fregata** (tel. 71 22 1) includes breakfast in its prices of 1250-1477dr a double, 1337-1622dr with private bath. The **Delfini** rents doubles with private bath for 700dr. The unofficial **youth hostel** on the road 300m before Ia charges 200dr per person, and 50dr for showers. Some people simply sleep on the roofs of deserted houses.

For breakfast, pick up some freshly baked bread at **Nikolas Passare's bakery.** **Cafe Loutza** is an excellent place to have a leisurely lunch or just sip iced coffee. For dinner, try the **Kyblos Restaurant** on the tip of the island, built beautifully into the nearby caves and grottos.

Southern Santorini

The rest of the places most worth a visit are in the southern end of Santorini. There is, first of all, the excavation site at **Akrotiri**. This is one of the archeological sites in Greece where you may most appreciate a guided tour—the extent of the excavations, still underway, and the superficial similarity of many of the buildings, can bewilder the undirected eye. If you're interested, inquire at one of the four travel agencies located in the central square of the town of Thira. If you possibly can, join a Kamari tour led by Kathy, who is unusually thorough and well-informed. Tour buses leave from each of the travel agencies at around 10:45am, and the tours include visits to the **Profitias Elias Monastery, Perissa,** and a winery, as well as to Akrotiri (600dr, students 500dr). There are also half-day tours to the monastery and Akrotiri which leave at around 8:45am (350dr). Public buses run eight times a day to Akrotiri from Thira; the fare is 60dr.

Professor Marinatos found the paved streets of Akrotiri lined with multistory houses all connected by a sophisticated central drainage system. Most of the ground-floor apartments were used for storerooms, and hundreds of pithoi jars and other utensils have been found within them. The upper floors were the living quarters for what appear to have been wealthy families; each house had at least one room lined with frescoes, some among the most magnificent yet found in Greece. These, along with the best of the pottery and stone vases unearthed at Akrotiri, are on temporary exhibit in a special room in the Athens archeological museum, pending completion of the new museum at Santorini, due to open in 1984.

The original inhabitants of the town, used to the hazards of life on a volcano, had enough warning from earth tremors to clear out before the eruption; the only remnant of a living thing found during excavations was the skeleton of a pig. What happened to the people once they left remains a mystery: they may have made it to safety, although no traces have been found, or they may all have died while escaping in the tidal waves that followed the eruption.

Marinatos and his successors have added cement support to walls already leaning before the earthquake, and have replaced the wooden beams and frames that were carbonized by the heat of the volcanic eruption. Otherwise, no changes have been made in the site, except to cover it with a protective roof. The site is open Mon.-Sat. 9am-7pm, Sun 9am-2pm; admission 100dr, 50dr for students. A hundred yards down the road from the site is a small beach where one can cool off.

Santorini's two most popular beaches are also on the southern end, at Kamari and Perissa. Both beaches, with black volcanic sand, look like something out of Poe's *A. Gordon Pym*. Bring along a straw mat and sandals; the sun bakes sand to scorching temperatures. The water here, as elsewhere on the island, is brisk and clear, and the rock and seaweed bottom offers some tame snorkeling if you've brought along equipment. **Perissa** is the more distant and less crowded of the two. It offers many rooms to rent for 200-300dr per person, depending on the season and the proximity to the water. The **Perissa Youth Hostel,** 600m along the road leading out of town, has beds for 120-150dr, beds with sheets 180-200dr. But most people take to the small, crowded, and expensive campground by the beach, or improvise one wherever they find a private niche.

Kamari beach, more developed than Perissa, has several posh hotels and rooms to rent starting at 1050dr in high season for doubles along the water, 750dr away from the water. The **Hotel Asteria,** on the right hand side of the road as you come into town, provides breakfast and a double with private bath for 709dr. People also camp on the beach at a discreet distance from the hotels.

In high season, two or three buses leave Thira for Kamari every hour, and one leaves approximately every hour for Perissa, starting at 7am; the last bus is at 10pm. One word of warning: buses leave when they are full, regardless of the time, so it's a good idea to get to them early.

The highest and most charming of Santorini's villages, **Pyrgos** is surrounded by medieval walls and dotted with the towers and blue and green domes of its many churches. About an hour's hike up the mountain from the little town of Pyrgos is the **Profitias Elias Monastery,** now sadly sharing its magnificent site with a radar station. In addition to the beautiful view of Santorini (especially at sunset), the monastery's museum contains an interesting assortment of seventeenth- through nineteenth-century paintings, saints' relics, and old manuscripts. The museum is open Mon.-Sat. 8am-1pm and 3-6pm; admission is 40dr, and robes are supplied for those insufficiently clad. A different path leads to the **Monastery of Episcopi Gonias,** another worthwhile sight to visit.

If you are interested in viewing traditional Greek ceremony, on July 20 there is a **Festival of St. Elias** beginnning with an all-night vigil at the monastery's main church the night before and culminating in a procession of worshippers to the chapel before the gate at 11am or so. All in attendance are then served a meal of *fava* (specially prepared chick peas).

From Profitias Elias, it is about an hour's hike to the **ancient city of Thira.** Leaving from the northeast side of the mountain top, the footpath follows the stony cliffside, with breathtaking views of northern Santorini (not recommended for acrophobics). From the plateau at the end of the path, the site of the ancient city is a short climb up the hill directly to the southeast. Much of the original layout of this Ptolemaic city is still recognizable, and with a guidebook (for sale in Thira) and some imagination one can piece together certain aspects of life on Thira in the second and third centuries B.C. under Alexander's successors. Look for the stone in the middle of the ruin which bears a carved phallus with the inscription *Tois Philois* ("for friends"). The ancient city is open to visitors Mon.-Sat. 9am-3pm, Sun. 9am-1pm. From the base of the hill, Kamari beach is another thirty minutes on foot down the snaking dirt road, and Perissa is equidistant on the other side via a footpath.

If you plan to follow the route from Pyrgos to Kamari on foot, be sure to plan your time carefully to avoid the 3pm closing at the Monastery and Ancient Thira. You can also do the hike in reverse, beginning at Kamari or Perissa and ending at Pyrgos, but allow more time for the mostly uphill climb, and bring some water—it can get very hot climbing on the exposed mountain faces.

The southern end of the island also has a few nice villages where you can spend the night. The cheerful whitewashed village of **Eborio,** some 3 km inland from Perissa, has frequent bus connections to the beach and to Thira. Rooms go for as little as 200dr here. If you are looking for something a little more plush, the very comfortable **Hotel Archaia Elefsina** (tel. 22 64 3) has luxurious singles for 600dr, doubles for 800dr.

Santorini now hosts a music festival and concert series each summer, featuring classical and Greek traditional music. Inquire at the travel agencies for details.

At some time during your stay, you'll want to visit the volcano which was, in a way, responsible for making Santorini famous. The crater of the volcano is located on a small island, between the larger islands of Santorini and Thirasia. Boats leave from Thira at 11am and 3pm for Nea Kameni, the small port at the foot of the volcano. The boats return two hours later; the fare is 250dr round trip. A slightly longer trip takes in the hot springs on Palea Kameni near the volcano, as well as the volcano itself. These boats leave at 4pm from Thira, return at 7pm, and cost 350dr.

Thirasia

Santorini's unspoiled junior partner Thirasia is worth an excursion. The island's two villages, **Potamos** and **Manolas,** built along its upper ridge, feature excellent views of Santorini's dramatic western coast. Visitors seldom spend the night on Thirasia, since neither of the villages has running water or electricity. Excursion boats leave the harbor of Thira at 10am for a round-trip tour of the volcano, Thirasia, and Ia. They return at 4pm (fare is 450dr). Boats also leave from Amoudia in Ia for **St. Irene,** the tiny port of Thirasia, at 11am, returning at 5:30pm; round-trip tickets cost 100dr.

Western Cyclades

Although these islands are not widely advertised, that doesn't mean they should be avoided. The Western Cyclades offer the same fine beaches and quaint villages as the other Cycladic islands, and chances are that here you'll find the seclusion you originally came for. Of course, the word about these islands has been spreading quickly.

Milos and Kimolos

Most people know **Milos** as the place where the Venus de Milo lay buried before she was spirited off to the Louvre. To others, the island is the subject of Thucydides' moving *Melian Dialogues,* in which the Melians argue the injustice of the Athenian invasion of their independent island during the Persian Wars. In a prime example of "might makes right," the Athenians attacked anyway, massacring the men and enslaving the women and children. But few people, even the yearly hordes of pilgrims to the larger Cyclades, know of Milos' sun-drenched beaches, tucked away amidst startling geological formations. Ferry connections to Milos are not forbiddingly indirect or infrequent; the island lies along a main route between Santorini and Piraeus and receives three ships weekly from Piraeus and four weekly from Ios and Santorini. From Milos, there are departures for Ios and Santorini (three days a week), Serifos (four days a week), Sifnos (five days a week), and Piraeus (six days a week). Two flights daily to Athens take off from the small airport on Milos.

Ships dock in **Adamas,** a port which comfortably accommodated the Allied fleet during World War I, but which tourists find less satisfying today. Milos has always been preoccupied with mining—obsidian in the Early Bronze Age, salt and a variety of minerals today—and Adamas wears the dreary countenance of a busy export harbor with its cement jetty and freighters anchored on the grey water, waiting to be loaded with tons of rock. Unfortunately, 90% of Milos' tourist industry is centered in Adamas, so you probably cannot avoid spending at least one night in the town.

The **OTE, Post Office, Bank, International Bookstore** and **travel agencies** (good for general information as well as boat tickets) are all situated along the main street facing the harbor. The **police** have their headquarters in the nearby town of Plaka. Most of the hotels are either on the beach to the west, or facing the square to the east of the pier. Doubles cost around 1000dr per night at most places during the high season. **Georgantas,** above a taverna in the square (tel. 41 63 6), has slightly dingy doubles for 832dr, 697dr in the off-season, triples

1012-1181dr. **Semiramis,** on a side street running diagonally to the left of the road to Plaka (tel. 41 61 7), has clean, new rooms with private bath and Norwegian wood furniture, all for the price of 400-500dr a single, 600-800dr a double, and 700-800dr a triple. Guests are invited to pick grapes (when they're ripe) from the arbor. Several houses in town offer rooms to rent. **Nikos Mallis Kanaris** (tel. 41 74 6), around the corner to the right of the Coralli Hotel, offers doubles for 600dr in high season, and has an attic with a double bed for 300dr; hot showers included. Campers may pitch their tents on the beach in **Bombarda,** a few hundred meters west of Adamas. The stony path leading over the hill to Bombarda may even be negotiated after dark, by the light of a harborside disco.

There are few restaurants in Adamas, and fewer still open at mid-day. For lunch, you can buy bread or cheese-pies at the local bakery (on the hill in town, to the east of the main church), or snack at one of the harborside cafes that stay open through the afternoon siesta. For dinner, you can try **Barbarossa,** which serves reasonably priced standard Greek fare in a pleasant garden. **Aphrodite's Arms** *(Ta Cheria tis Aphroditis),* on the waterfront, offers a good selection of fish, and is a favorite of sleek local alleycats who may beg at your feet.

Milos' main attractions are all away from the port, at the ends of the island's four main roads. **Pollonia,** to the northeast, is a quiet fishing village with rooms to rent (doubles 400-500dr per night), two tavernas, and camping on the town beach with a free outdoor shower. From Pollonia there are frequent but irregular launches to **Kimolos.** Ask at the tavernas when the next boat disembarks, if you wish to visit that chalky, deserted isle. Kimolos is graced with fine beaches and two spotless Cycladic towns, but little else of interest.

British archeologists discovered 5000-year-old frescoes of lilies and flying fish in the rubble of **Filakopi,** 3km from Pollonia back along the road from Adamas. Today the ruins still merit a quick ramble, but you may find your time more pleasantly spent swimming nearby. Just below the ruin, the ocean has carved a series of caves in the soft volcanic tufa, one of which is accessible by means of steps cut into the rock; a small beach of black sand and clear water waits at the bottom. The diminutive **Archeological Museum** in **Plaka** houses the Cycladic Minoan and Mycenean artifacts unearthed at Filakopi, including a few amusing *rhyta* (zoomorphic drinking vessels). The town of Plaka itself is bathed in the stillness and light that Adamas lacks; walk to the terrace of the **Church of Panagia i Korfiatissa** for the best view on Milos. South of Plaka, outside the small town of **Trypiti,** are several more sights of archeological interest. The **catacombs,** tombs cut into a cliff-face where two thousand people were buried, comprise the oldest site of Christian worship in Greece. Archeological finds in the **Ancient City** on the hillside above the catacombs represent three periods of Greek history: a wall of hewn stone hexagonal blocks built by the Dorians between 1100 and 800 B.C., a plaque marking the spot where the Venus de Milo was buried around 320 B.C., and an ancient theater dating from the Roman occupation. The town of Trypiti itself is exceptionally quiet, so the ancient magic can operate.

The finest beach on the island is in **Paliochora.** Wade through the hole in the rock south of the taverna to the less populous cove beyond. **Hivadolimni Beach,** on the harbor south of Adamas, is long and clean, its black edge shaded by pines.

All of the sights can be reached by buses, which run several times a day from Adamas (the schedule is posted in the town square). Also, mopeds and motorscooters (Vespas) are for rent: mopeds cost 450dr per day, Vespas 700dr; both prices include third party insurance and a helmet, but no gasoline.

Sifnos

Sifnos is one of the most resplendent of the Cyclades; its verdant hillsides are covered with groves of olive and tamarisk trees, its valleys ablaze with oleander, its village streets cascading with bougainvillea. In ancient times the island was famous for its gold. Legend has it that each year the islanders, in an effort to appease the god Apollo, would send a solid gold egg to Delphi. One year, however, the locals decided to keep the gold for themselves. As a result of this insult, Apollo cursed the land, and the island became empty, or in Greek "sifnos." While it might have been empty centuries ago, Sifnos' beauty is no longer going unnoticed, and the island is rapidly becoming more widely touristed.

Sifnos is serviced by several boats a week that stop at all the Western Cyclades along the north-south arc between Piraeus and Ios/Santorini (including Kithnos, Serifos, Kimolos, and Milos). There are also five boats a week to Paros, and one a week to Syros. All boats dock at **Kamares,** the port, and from there buses make the twenty-minute trip to the capital, **Apollonia,** every hour or whenever boats arrive. The buses then continue on to one of the other towns of Sifnos: **Artemon, Kastro, Faros,** and **Platis Gialos** (look for the signs on the front of the buses). There are two bus stops in Apollonia, one for Kamares-bound buses (in the square), and another for buses bound for all of the other towns (around the corner). **Boat agencies** are in both Kamares and Apollonia. The **Post Office** (open Mon.-Fri. 7:30am-2:30pm), **bank** (Mon.-Sat. 9am-1pm and 6-8pm) and **police** are all located in Apollonia, close to the square. The **OTE** (open Mon.-Fri. 8am-1pm and 4-10pm) faces the second bus stop.

Accommodations are difficult to find in Sifnos during the high season, when Greek tourists book up the island's hotels, pensions, and private rooms. But if you start looking early in the day and remember that the outlying towns fill up more slowly than Kamares and Apollonia, you should be able to find somewhere to sleep. Camping is a legal and popular option. Kamares' accommodations are slightly more expensive than elsewhere on the island; clean doubles with hot water and private bath at the **Kamari** and **Stauro Hotels** cost 1350dr, and rooms to let run only slightly less than that during the high season. There are shower facilities on the Kamares beach (20dr) and trees to camp under. In Apollonia, rooms to let go for as little as 200dr per person in the off-season, but in July and August they average 600dr a double. Inquire in the "Tourist Shop" on the street with steps directly to the north of the square. The **Guest House-Auberge** down the street from the second bus stop in the direction of Platis Gialos offers singles for 620dr and doubles for 800dr, both with an ocean view. The **Hotel Sophia,** back in town (tel. 31 23 8), has doubles for 900dr, 872dr in the off-season. Many people camp in Platis Gialos and Faros, where there are also a few rooms to rent. In Kastro, as well, you will see signs advertising "domatia."

Sifnos is famous for the high quality of its olive oil, and the food on the island is generally quite good. The seaside tavernas in Faros have a fine selection of fish, along with the usual Greek fare. The **Alexis-Zorba Taverna** in Kastro enjoys a view from its shaded patio that will make you feel like you are eating on the ramparts of a castle—in fact, you are. Sifnians are known to be fond of pastries; if you've developed a sweet tooth after weeks of souvlaki and Greek salads, the cafeteria by the second bus stop has a wide selection of delectables which should satisfy you.

If you enjoy excursions to churches, the **Taxiarchis** in **Vathi** is the island's most famous Byzantine edifice. For the afficionado of ruins, there is a crumbling Venetian fortification in Kastro, its grounds overgrown with weeds and cluttered with rubble and donkey spoor.

Tired of sightseeing? The beaches on Sifnos are superb. Besides the service-able beach at Kamares, there are several choices. **Platis Gialos,** easily accessible by bus, is reputedly the longest beach in the Cyclades; **Faros'** shoreline is shorter but sweeter—the first cove is full of boats, so walk through the village to reach the second. Follow the path over the headland to the south to reach the third, still quieter beach. An excursion boat leaves Kamares harbor three times a day for **Vathi** beach (73dr each way).

Serifos

Medusa smiled on Serifos, and the island has never been the same since. As the story goes, when Danae bore Perseus, Acrisius, her husband, put the mother and child to sea in a chest. They landed on Serifos, where King Poly-dectes took a liking to Danae, and, hoping to rid himself of Perseus, sent the young hero to kill Medusa. Much to the king's chagrin, Perseus returned just in time to interrupt his plans for Danae, and used Medusa's head to petrify Polydectes and the other islanders; hence Serifos' "drear reaches of wreck" which spoke to Lawrence Durrell "of poverty and silence."

Like its partners in the Western Cyclades, however, Serifos has lately been speaking of drachmas and disco, as tourism has begun to play an increasingly important role in the island's economy. Serifos caters to a somewhat older crowd than Ios or Mykonos, but there is plenty of room for younger tourists on the island's undeveloped beaches and in the tavernas along the waterfront in the port, **Livadia.**

Serifos is difficult to reach, since few of the boats that sail the western route between Piraeus and Ios or Thira stop here. But in high season there is gener-ally at least one boat per day stopping at Serifos en route to Piraeus (often late at night), and one per day from Piraeus bound for Sifnos and other points south. The direct trip from Serifos to Piraeus take approximately four hours. In addition, boats headed for Syros leave Serifos several times a week.

The **police** and the main **OTE** office are located in **Pano Chora,** the island's capital, a twenty-minute bus ride from Livadia; you can also make phone calls and buy stamps from the cigarette and candy kiosk in Livadia. The **Mini-Market** acts as the local bank agent and currency exchange. Two other grocery stores serve as boat ticket offices: the first faces the harbor on the main square, and the second is one block back from the water, next to the small church.

If you arrive in Serifos at night during the high season (and many of the boats will drop you there after 10pm), you may be hard put to find a room for the night, even at one of the more expensive hotels that line the beach. Make reservations in advance, or be prepared to camp. Although there are signs prohibiting it, long and short term campers set up tents and unroll their bags in the coves that make up **Karavi** beach. To reach it, walk up the steps at the south end of the harbor (don't try to skirt around the jetty). If you don't want to rough it, try the **Galanos Hotel,** above the bakery in the center of town (tel. 51 27 7), where tidy rooms cost 300dr, 60dr extra for a shower. The manager, Anna, has a heart of gold and a smile to match. The **Cavo d'Oro** is more posh: doubles with a private bath cost 1000dr, 700dr in the off-season. There are many places with rooms to rent in town, where doubles go for 500-900dr; you can also try along the town beach past the Hotel Haistrali.

The fine **Karavi beach** is less than a fifteen-minute walk from town; since the only structures along it are the bamboo huts built by dedicated campers, it feels almost uninhabited. But the best beach on the island is **Psili Amos,** which may be reached by a fifty-minute walk along the shoreline to the north, or from the town of Pano Chora. Tumbling down the hillside like a cubist's attempt at city-planning, the town is worth a visit in itself. Hourly buses run from the square in Livadia, but the walk up the stone steps that wind curiously past gardens and chicken coops is worth a spell of heavy breathing. The **Church of St. Konstantine,** crowning the town, commands a heady view of Pano Chora, Livadia, and the stony interior of Serifos.

Kithnos and Kea

Kithnos and Kea could be termed the semi-precious gems of the Cycladic treasury. Although closer to the Greek mainland, irregular ferry schedules make them, paradoxically, more remote than the other Cyclades. Ships go to **Kithnos** from Piraeus, Serifos, Kea, and Lavrion, and stop at the port of Kithnos, **Merichas.** Kithnos is known for its caves and thermal spa. There are beaches at **Loutra, Lefkes,** and in the port town.

Kea, the birthplace of fifth-century B.C. poets Simonides and Bacchylides, is also famous for two pieces of sculpture: the **Kea Kouros,** now in the Athens Archeological Museum, and the **Lion of Kea,** which may still be found near the island capital of **Ioulis** (Kea), a short bus ride from the port, **Korissa.** Kea can only be reached from Kithnos, or from the mainland port of **Lavrion** (one hour by bus from Athens). It is a favorite retreat of Athenian tourists.

SPORADES

Breathtakingly beautiful, with lush, thickly-wooded interiors and steep, jagged coasts interrupted by tiny coves and sea caves, the Sporades have long been a well-kept secret among the Greeks. These are the Aegean islands as Homer described them, their forested slopes abounding with goats and other game. Ancient seafarers found the island ports to be sporadically situated—scarce in some places and plentiful in others—indeed, that is why they gave the island chain its name. Today, however, the four major islands—**Skiathos, Skopelos, Alonissos, and Skyros**—are all easily accessible.

The Cretans first colonized the islands in the sixteenth century B.C., and started the cultivation of olives and grapes. The Athenians later liberated the islands in the fifth century B.C., and of all the island groups, the Sporades retained the most amiable ties with Athens. Athena, in fact, was the most popular goddess in the islands' pantheon. The Sporades were later occupied by the Romans in the second century B.C., and by the Venetians in the thirteenth century; both left ruins on many of the islands. The Venetians were later forced out by the Turks, who controlled the islands until the revolution of 1821, when the Sporades came under Greek rule once again.

The only thing sporadic about the archipelago today is its tourist traffic. In comparison to the Cyclades or Saronic Gulf islands, the sheer number of visitors is modest, and so is the beach dress. Moreover, tourists tend to arrive almost exclusively in July and August. Yet in the past few years word has gotten out about the Sporades, and tourist facilities have been rapidly developed to meet the demands of the increasing number of European tourists. Skiathos, the most popular of the islands, has fallen victim to the disfiguring scars that accompany tourist traffic. Skopelos, its sister, shows signs that it may soon follow. Alonissos and Skyros, however, are relatively unspoiled and far enough off the beaten track to provide you with a peaceful vacation and some of the best beaches in Greece.

On most of the Sporades, the population tends to cluster in harbor towns, which are connected by bus if there is more than one on a given island. Otherwise, there are few roads, for obvious topographical reasons. These islands are the exposed summits of the submerged tail end of the Pelion Mountains, a geological heritage that has given them little flat ground. It has, however, produced some spectacular coves embracing pristine beaches. Such gems, decorating the plunging coastlines of these islands like strings of pearls, are often so isolated that they can only be reached by motorboat. But these excursions are well worth 200-300dr, if only to get you well away from the roads.

Transportation

The major islands are serviced by the gigantic Nomikos line, which has a virtual monopoly over the Sporades. Two or more boats a day run between Volos, Skiathos, Skopelos, Alonissos and Kimi in July and August, and several boats daily pass between Kimi and Skyros (fewer during off-season). Excursion boats go from Skiathos to Skopelos and Alonissos, and caïques make frequent trips between the latter two islands. You can reach the islands from the mainland part of Agios Konstantinos as well, or fly from Athens to Skiathos (1890dr one-way).

Skiathos

Skiathos is the most sophisticated and expensive of the Sporades. It beats with a steady, though not overly-pronounced cosmopolitan pulse: clothing boutiques and stylish jewelry shops (many managed by foreigners) line its main shopping street, hotels sprout more readily and grow higher here than on Skiathos' eastern cousins, and sun-worship and nightlife have eclipsed the native expressions of culture still visible on the other Sporades. For these reasons, many people think of Skiathos as "the straight Mykonos." And it is easy to see why the tourists keep coming, with over sixty beaches scattered across the coastline and plenty of rolling green countryside waiting to be explored. Yet Skiathos attracts a slightly different type of tourist than do other islands. Besides being home for a sizeable year-round community of British expatriates in high season, Skiathos welcomes many package tours, as well as numerous Greek families on vacation. As a result, Skiathos presents some problems for the traveler on a tight budget. Restaurants and accommodations are pricey, discos have a cover charge, the official camping facilities are inconvenient, and you cannot unroll your bag and sack out just anywhere. Nevertheless, many young tourists choose to give Skiathos a whirl, so you'll be in good company here.

Town of Skiathos

The picturesque town of Skiathos has weathered the impact of the tourist industry far better than much of the coastline. The town divides roughly into two sections: the residential sector, which contains private homes and a few pensions; and the commercial sector, which blatantly caters to tourists. Yet, even the latter has managed to retain some of its charm. Its cobbled streets and red-roofed buildings are both cheerful and inviting. It is, however, the residential quarter which is really the special part of town. Everywhere, balconies overflow with magenta bougainvillea and white gardenia blossoms, and the omnipresent grape vines provide each terrace with a path of shade. And here, at least, is one corner of Skiathos where you won't find tourists at every bend.

Practical Information

As you disembark from the ferry in the town of Skiathos, to your immediate right you will see the maritime agency that sells tickets for the ferry. Continuing to the right along the waterfront, you will pass Miltos Travel Agency, Budget Rent-A-Car, and a bicycle/moped shop that leases mopeds for 400dr a day, and motorbikes for 800dr a day, not including gas. Buses leave every thirty minutes from the bus stop next to the taxi stand on the wharf and travel the one road on the island, which ends at the pine grove of Koukounares (38dr). The **Post Office** and the **OTE** are in the same building on Papadimadi St. (the main shopping street); the OTE is open Mon.-Sat. 7:30am-10pm, Sun. 7:30am-3:10pm, and the Post Office closes after 2:30pm and on weekends. Several banks in town will exchange money Mon.-Fri. 8am-2pm, and 6:30-8:30pm; during the summer, the Central Bank of Greece opens Sat. mornings as well. The **police** are at (tel. 42 00 5), the hospital is at (tel. 42 04 0), and the Emergency Medical number is (tel. 42 34 7). The Skiathos telephone code is 0424.

Skiathos is easily reached from the mainland and the other Sporades. Boats leave three times a day to Skopelos (250dr) and Loutraki (230dr); twice daily to Alonissos (290dr); and at least once a day for Kimi (1140dr) and Skyros (820dr). Ferries head to the mainland ports of Agios Konstantinos (660dr, 1113dr price includes the bus to Athens) and Volos (490dr). There are also

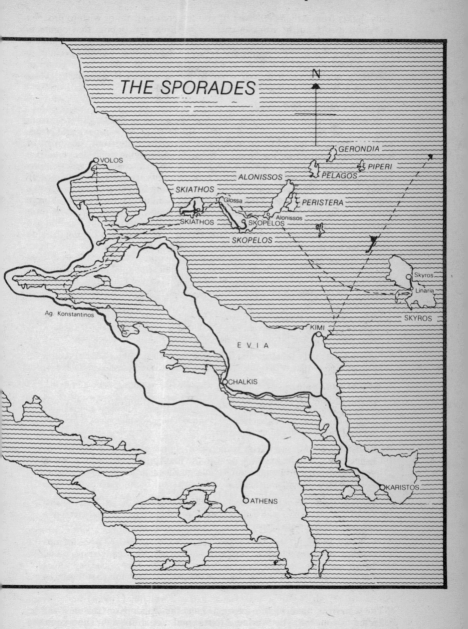

daily flights from Athens (1890dr). If you are coming from or wish to proceed to Pelion to the north, you can catch a small excursion boat that connects Koukounares beach with the mainland town of Platania. Boats leave Platania three times a day in the morning and return in the evening, weather permitting (200dr round trip). If you have to get to Platania and have a large group of people, it might be worth your while to hire a boat in Koukounares. Most captains will agree to make the trip for around 500dr.

Accommodations and Food

In July and August, tourism in Skiathos takes on a character different from that of most other Greek islands. The telltale signs of footloose travel are missing: there is no array of backpacks along the waterfront, no crush of women and children crying "rooms, rooms!" and tugging your sleeve as you get off the boat. Instead, new arrivals in town bear suitcases and reservations for hotels and fancy villas. Most of the private rooms are booked in advance by Greek tourists. Wandering around town and asking for rooms may land you a good deal, but it may not. Your best strategy will be to make a reservation in advance (though many proprietors are reluctant to rent to short-term transients) or go to one of the travel agencies in town early in the day and ask them for help. Nassos Prapas at **Skiathos Tourist Organization** (facing the side of the harbor where small boats dock) manages many pensions and cheap hotels in Skiathos; he may also give student discounts of up to 30% (tell them you read about it here). **Skiathos Tours** (on a small street just off of Papadimadi St.), managed by a kind Scottish woman, is also very helpful. In general, inexpensive doubles and triples are much easier to find than singles.

Hotel Akti, 26 F. Giorgiadou St. (tel. 42 02 4). Go to the right as you get off the ferry. Most rooms have ocean views. Doubles in high season 1300dr (without private baths); 850dr off-season; triples 20% more. Hot showers included.

Rooms-to-let, 33 F. Giorgiadou St. (tel. 42 20 6). Near the Akti (the road takes a hairpin curve to the left). Doubles 700dr; 550dr off-season. Hot showers included.

Hotel Avra, 3 Antipl. Laskou St. Somewhat gloomy and dirty, but with fun balconies over the street. Very close to the ferry landing, 20m down a side street perpendicular to the water. Doubles 750dr, triples 1200dr. All rooms considerably cheaper in off-season. Hot showers 50dr extra. If no one is in, inquire at Skiathos Tourist Organization around the corner.

Pension Kostis, 5 Evangelistrias St. (tel. 42 97 9). Go down Papadimadi St. (the main shopping street) away from the harbor. Turn right on Evangelistrias, which is right before the Post Office. Bright, clean doubles. In season 1125dr without bath (1600dr with); 900dr off-season.

Australia House (tel. 42 48 8). Down an alley which is to the left after Pension Kostis. Doubles 1100dr with bath; 900dr without. If this is full, the manager runs a pension next door with similar prices.

Aselinos Camping, at Megalos Aselinos beach. Good facilities and a fine location near one of Skiathos' best and least crowded beaches. No public transportation, though, and it's a long haul across the island. The other campground on Platinos Bay was recently shut down for sanitation reasons, though people do still camp on the site.

The waterfront tavernas are expensive and the grandness of the view will be reflected in your bill. The **Marimari Restaurant**, set off from the others (on the far left end of the harbor), has the best food and the lowest prices. **Taverna**

Stavra on Evangelistrias St. is also a good choice for seafood. One good dish to try while in Skiathos is *pikália,* a selection of spreads such as *tzadziki* and *taramousalata.* Eaten as an appetizer or with bread as a light lunch, these dips provide a piquant break from the olive oil routine.

Nightlife

Skiathos nightlife runs the gamut from sitting in waterfront tavernas to getting down in discos. But Skiathos is a step ahead of many islands since the discos are not so jerry-rigged, and don't resemble converted cinderblock garages. You pay a price for the more sophisticated decor, however: 150-250dr at the door (redeemable upon purchase of your first drink).

Disco Retro, roomy, with one of the best dance floors and light shows in the islands. A good place to go if you want to dance.

The BBC Disco, the main scene to make while in Skiathos, though it has its on and off nights.

The Kelari Bar, this bright, airy bar has a distinctive chi-chi feel with music to match.

The Bortzoi, a large bar with room for dancing and tables in the garden outside. Curiously decorated with two huge millstones, a gazebo and palms, all glistening wetly under lush green lighting.

Disco Bonaparte, couldn't be cosier without being cramped; even the dance floor is intimate. But the people who fill the place are chic and interested in others.

Captain Nemo Disco, a veritable coliseum of a disco, but it seems as if it's 20,000 leagues out of town, on the road to the airport. Nevertheless, it's large and popular among foreign and Greek tourists.

Adagio Bar, as the name suggests, this place features classical music and is generally slow-paced. It's quiet, lit by candles, and attracts mostly couples.

Around the Island

The bus that runs along the 12km coastline (38dr; departures every thirty minutes) will let you off within walking distance of some of the island's best beaches. Unfortunately, many are now dominated by hotels and villas. Despite these eyesores, the bus ride offers excellent views of the coast and several reasonably-priced pensions are along the route.

Mitikas beach, near Ftelia, is the closest to town, and a convenient place for a quiet dip. In the bay formed by the eastern corner of the Kalamaki peninsula, **Nostes Beach** is quiet, and has sail boats to rent (600dr per hour). Just around the point, a small beach with a comfortable taverna is at **Kanapitsa.** Further down the road are the beaches **Vromolimnos, Platanias,** and **Troulos.** Try the small taverna, up the path from Platanias, close to the church of Agia Paraskevi, or **Taverna Troulos** on the beach by that name, which is picturesque and reasonably-priced for dinner. In the next cove is **Maratha Beach,** and where the road ends abruptly amidst the pine trees and "no camping" signs is **Koukounares.** This beach is the most famous, most photographed, and most jampacked of all the beaches in Sporades. It was once considered one of the best beaches in Greece. Today, however, its crystal-clear blue-green water and the soft white sands are covered in July and August with lobster-red European sunbathers, and the scent of the nearby pines is eclipsed by the smell of suntan lotion. **Christo's Boatline** and **Astir Windsurf School** on the beach rent sailboats, pedal-boats, and windsurfers, starting at 500dr an hour. A short walk from Koukounares is the famous nude **"Banana Beach"** (called Krassa on maps).

From Troulos, a road turns off for **Aselinos.** Two kilometers further, this road forks, the right fork leading up the hill to **Panagia Kounistra,** a small monastery with a grape arbor and a taverna within its walls. If you follow this fork past the monastery, you will enjoy a fine view where the road bends: to the north is the beach of Megalos (Big) Aselinos; to the south, Micros (Small) Aselinos. The latter is the more secluded of the two (though neither is crowded); it can be reached by a short scramble from the end of the right fork. Megalos Aselinos, the end of the road on the left, is a large sandy beach, with rocks at either end that make for good snorkeling. Because of Aselinos' northern exposure, the water here is choppier than on Skiathos' southern shore. Megalos Aselinos also has a campground and a taverna (see above); it can only be reached by car, moped, or a long walk from Troulos.

The northern coast of the island is only accessible by boat. If you have only a short time on Skiathos, spend at least part of it on one of the many excursion boats that leave the town of Skiathos for this part of the island every morning. The most popular destination is **Lalaria Beach,** a giant pebble beach set in its own secluded cove visible through a natural stone arch on one end. Nearby are the ruins of the medieval walled city of **Kastro** (about a two-hour walk on a path from Skiathos Town). The Greeks built Kastro on top of this huge, impregnable headland during the sixteenth century to hide from marauding pirates. After the Greeks won their independence in the beginning of the last century, Kastro was abandoned and work was begun on what has since blossomed into the present-day town of Skiathos. Kastro was originally connected with the rest of the island by a drawbridge, but now it can be reached by steps. All that remains intact of the ancient community are two churches, of which the **Church of the Nativity** is the better, containing a number of fine icons and some frescoes.

Also on the northern coast, near Lalaria Beach, is **Skotini Spilia** (the "Dark Grotto"), a striking sea cave, **Glazia Spilia** (the "Blue Grotto"), and **Chalkini Spilia** (the "Copper Cave"). The caves are near the **Panagia Evangelistria,** the most beautiful of the island's monasteries. Lalaria Beach, Kastro, and the caves can be reached by excursion boats which leave from the harbor in front of the main town in the morning, stop over at Lalaria before visiting the other spots, and return in the evening (400dr). For history buffs, there are also boats that go only to Kastro and only to the Evangelistria Monastery (600dr per person), and mule trips to the Monastery only (700dr). For those who want a full day of swimming, there are small boats which leave the Skiathos harbor every hour for the nearby island of **Tsougria,** which has some good beaches (150dr). Other excursions include a circumnavigation of the island (400dr), and fishing trips (700dr; includes a meal). Finally, boats leave the harbor in the town of Skiathos for a full-day excursion to Skopelos and Alonissos for a very reasonable round-trip fare of 700dr.

A road was recently built from just north of Ftelia to the northwestern coast of the island. Although intended as a fire-break and a way to allow islanders to reach the olive groves in Bostrani more easily, the road affords grand views and a chance to escape the crowds on Skiathos' beaches. The road ascends the ridge dominating the interior of Skiathos. On the way up, you can see over the red-roofed town of Skiathos and its harbor, past the small islands at the harbor's mouth to Skopelos beyond. If the haze is not heavy, the hills of Alonissos are visible above Skopelos. The main road continues over the ridge (a few smaller tracks branching off) and finally disappears in the underbrush of the untended olive grove on a rise above the northwest coast. From here, you can view the mountains of Pelion rising smokily on the distant mainland. This vantage point on Skiathos thus provides a strong sense of the continuity of Pelion and the northern Sporades, of the long chain of wooded summits hanging down into the Aegean. Although you can most easily travel this cross-island road by car or motor bike, it would also make a challenging but worthwhile hike. Allow 3-4 hours one way, and bring water and the best map you can find in town (if possible, get a local to trace the course of the new road onto your map). About 2km before the road ends, there is a footpath marked with a sign for Kastro. From here, you can walk to Kastro and Lalaria Beach, and catch the excursion boat back to Skiathos in the afternoon (200dr). Make sure to get to Lalaria by 3:45pm, as the boat is scheduled to swing past Lalaria on its return route at 4pm.

Skopelos

Skopelos (which means "cliff") is a rugged island covered with forests, fruit orchards, and over three hundred small chapels. In ancient times, Skopelos was a Cretan colony ruled by King Staphilos, whose grave lies near one of the island's best beaches. While Skopelos is the only island in the Sporades that boasts two major towns, it manages to remain less touristed than Skiathos and relatively untouched by modern oversized hotels. A tasteful job has been done of incorporating accommodations, restaurants, and tourist offices into the white-washed houses and narrow passageways of the main port, somehow still maintaining the town's serene character.

The town itself is an eclectic architectural mix; besides the ruined walls of the Venetian Kastro and dozens of Byzantine churches, Skopelos' houses contain elements of Turkish, Macedonian and Neo-Classical building styles, reflecting the island's turbulent history. The roofs of overlapping, irregular slate tiles are a common feature of the houses on Skopelos and on its neighbor, Alonissos. Such roofs are extremely heavy, weighing up to ten tons for an average-sized house, and require special expertise in their construction—otherwise they not only leak, but absorb water and drip for days after a rainstorm. Thus they are expensive to build, replace or maintain, and are gradually giving way to red ceramic tiles. The best way to see the town is to climb the steps on the north side of town, past a series of small churches to the top of the castle walls. From here you can look over Skopelos' rooftops and then descend into the town itself. Skopelos enjoys an airy quality because of its Turkish wooden balconies, wide streets, and many gardens and plazas. Moreover, the islanders have an exquisite though apparently effortless taste for color, as seen in the flowers and paint with which they decorate their town, making Skopelos an ideal place for sketching, photography, or simply looking around.

Practical Information

Skopelos Town is usually the first stop for the ferry from Kimi; boats from Volos and Skiathos often stop at another port, Loutraki, as well as at Skopelos Town, but you probably won't want to get off here as all the action is at Skopelos. A third, more sheltered port at Agnondas is used by small boats when the seas are high. The public bus runs four times a day to Loutraki and ten times a day to Agnondas; times are posted on a tree near the bus stop in Skopelos. Taxis cost 1200dr to Loutraki. It's a good idea to rent a moped or motorbike on Skopelos since bus service is infrequent and good paved roads exist. Mopeds are 500dr a day, motorbikes (capable of seating two) are 700dr; neither price includes gasoline. If you specifically want a moped, rent it early in the day, before supplies run out.

As you disembark from the ferry in Skopelos, you will see three tourist offices to your right. They can book private rooms, supply maps, and show you pictures of the island's beaches. Helen at **Skopelos Tours** is extremely helpful. These agencies also sell ferry tickets to the other islands and the mainland. In high season, car-ferries run five times a week to Alonissos, Kimi and Skyros, three times daily to Volos, and four times daily to Skiathos. In addition, several smaller boats make the trip to Alonissos every day. Once a day, a ship sails for the mainland port of Agios Konstantinos, from which Athens may be reached by bus.

The **Post Office,** on a street sloping up from the waterfront, is open weekdays 7:30am-2:30pm. The **banks** are also facing the harbor, and the **OTE** is one block up in town, on Skoufa St.

One thoroughly practical aspect of pre-tourism Skopelos remains today: S.I. Lemoni runs a knife shop near the tourist agencies where he forges and hones blades by hand. If you happen to be waiting for a ferry by the harbor, take a peek into the dark interior of his shop to see a real craftsman at work.

Accommodations and Food

A number of rooms to let are along the waterfront, as well as in the old town. Try the street behind the Commercial Bank, or the main road where it heads away from the water past the big hotels. If you can't locate a room by scouting around yourself (often the case late in the day during high season), the tourist agencies will help you find a room in a hotel or pension; for private rooms, go to the wooden shed next door to Skopelos Tours. The going rate in high season at most hotels is 1000dr for a double; in pensions and private rooms it is 650-800dr. Don't expect to pay less than 500dr for a single, unless you arrange to sleep on a roof, in which case you could get away with paying only 300dr. The town beach is free, but exposed. For longer stays, try **Velanio Beach.**

Some of the best rooms in town are in a pension run by Maria Abelakia (tel. 22 66 2) to the left of the tourist agencies. Doubles 650dr, triples 900dr (off-season 500dr and 700dr respectively), but try bargaining. In a house advertising rooms to rent up the steps on the north side of the harbor, Nikko has a few double rooms for 600dr a night. They are not the cleanest, but the location on top of the cliff which gives Skopelos its name is quite dramatic. The **Hotel Amerika** (tel. 22 33 1) further along the waterfront to the left, just up the narrow street from the Post Office, is the only cheap hotel in town. Singles 675dr, doubles 956dr, triples 1125dr; less in off-season.

The restaurants in town are expensive, but **Ta Kymata** at the northern end of the harbor and **Ioannis Taverna** with green leatherette chairs in the middle of the paralia are the best tavernas. **Platanos,** between the two, serves a "natural breakfast": sip *nescafe,* and eat corn flakes, yogurt and fruit salad while listening to Little Feat or John Coltrane. (This shady spot is popular among young Europeans and Americans.) After dinner, most of the Greek and foreign tourists sit by the water drinking frappes (whipped iced coffee) and eating *loukoumades* (deep-fried honey pastries). If you feel more energetic or a little guilty about consuming so many calories, try dancing at the **Livadia** or **VIP's** (pronounced "veeps") discos, the most popular nightspots on the island. Or do the *volta* on the waterfront. For the truly sedentary, the **Jazz Farm Bar** is a good place to relax and listen to music after a hard day on the beach.

Around the Island

For those who are only planning on spending a day or two on Skopelos, a good strategy for seeing the island is to enter by one of the ports, work your way along the road, and then leave from the other port. Beaches are all along the coast from Skopelos to Loutraki. **Staphylos** is long and sandy, but it is also the primary family beach on the island, and very crowded as a result. Archeologists discovered the tomb of an ancient Cretan general, Staphylos, on a hillside near here, as well as a gold-plated sword dating back to the fifteenth century B.C. (now in Athens). If you walk the length of Staphylos beach and climb over the ridge at its eastern end, you'll come to the sandy **Velanio** beach. Because this is advertised as the one legal nude beach on Skopelos, it is considerably less crowded, less noisy, and less strewn with toys, or children's toys, at any rate. But it is, if anything, more beautiful than Staphylos. Continuing along the paved road, the next place of interest is the harbor of **Agnardas**. The beach at Agnardas is small, crowded, and too close to the boats, but from here you can catch the caïque every half-hour to **Limonari** beach, a long, uncrowded crescent of golden sand (80dr round-trip). **Panormos beach** is crowded, but has several lively tavernas. Around the point to the north lies **Milia**, the most beautiful beach on Skopelos. It is accessible from the main road by means of a dirt track, where the bus-driver will stop if you ask. You may reach two other beaches from Skopelos town by boat: **Sares** and **Agios Konstantinos** (don't confuse this with the mainland port of the same name).

If you follow the road all the way to **Loutraki,** you will notice plastic bags mounted under the incisions on the area's many pine trees. They are collecting pine sap, one of Skopelos' major exports (besides olives and plums) used primarily to flavor and preserve retsina. The peaceful—one might even say boring—town of **Glossa** hangs from a large hill on the northern end of Skopelos. Probably because of its distance from the shore, Glossa does not cater to tourists. It is better to look for accommodations and a sandy beach in the town of Loutraki. If you are facing the harbor, at the right end of the small port is the **Hotel Flisvos** (tel. 33 77 6), which has doubles for 800dr. Almost next door, towards the center of town, the pension above the cafe-grill offers doubles with balconies, flowers and a view of the harbor for 700dr, showers 50dr extra. An agency on the harbor sells ferry tickets. The ride to Skiathos only takes forty-five minutes from Loutraki, as opposed to one-and-a-half hours from Skopelos, but the fare is about the same.

Three monasteries are situated in lofty seclusion on Mt. Palouki, which faces the town across the water. The town's main road splits just after the **Amalia Hotel,** the left fork circles the harbor, and ascends the mountain. **Evangelismos,** perched among the rocks across from Skopelos, dates from the eighteenth century; the gold-plated altar-screen, produced in Constantinople, is four hundred years older. The Monastery of **Metamorphosis** stands amid pines on a breezy knoll. The little chapel, set in a courtyard bedecked with flowers, dates from the sixteenth century. From Metamorphosis, **Propromou** is visible on the next ridge. Although it was a monastery at the time of its reconstruction in 1721, this cloister, dedicated to St. John the Baptist, is now inhabited by nuns. The sister who shows visitors around speaks fluent French, and is a stickler for proper apparel—"one cannot walk naked into the house of God!" All three monasteries are open from 8am-1pm and 4-8pm, and can be reached from Skopelos by taxi, moped or a pleasant walk (3 hours round trip). The travel agencies in town also run bus excursions which take in the three monasteries for 350dr.

For a superb hike to a lovely, spectacular spot, take the bus to Glossa, and walk the dirt track across the island to where the monastery of **Agios Ioannis** clings to a massive boulder above the ocean. A map and directions from a native are essential in getting you on the right dirt track; after that it's clear sailing. The road traverses several ridges through olive groves which in summer shimmer with locusts and heat. At the road's end, a steep path drops down to the sea, and stone steps cut in the escarpment lead up to the monastery. According to legend, the builders had originally intended to establish the monastery at the base of the rock, but each day after they finished work, St. John moved all their tools and supplies to the boulder's summit. In the end, therefore, they built the monastery, to the greater glory of God and St. John, on top of the rock. Another miracle, more interesting to hikers, is the cistern of potable water in the rock. To cool you off further, there is a small sandy cove below the steps. Allow at least four hours round trip to visit Agios Ioannis, and bring at least a liter of water per person. The road is also passable part of the way on motorbike, although the inappropriate noise will ruin your chances of glimpsing the nymphs and satyrs who dart here and there through the olive grove along the way.

Alonissos

With only fifteen hundred inhabitants, Alonissos is the least populated and most isolated of the Sporades. Its story is also one of the saddest in the tumultuous post-war history of Greece. In 1950, the island's vineyards were wiped out to the last grape by a fast-spreading plant disease. This destroyed the island's once-lucrative wine industry, and left the local economy in such dire straits that much of Alonissos' male population was forced to take on construction work in Athens. By 1965, when the island had recovered some measure of prosperity through other forms of farming and fishing, an earthquake struck, damaging both the harbor of Patitiri and the town of Alonissos on the hill above. In ensuing years, through bureaucratic bungling and inflexible economic policy, the Greek junta government decided to erect cheap new houses in Patitiri, rather than rebuild the old island capital. With a government-supported housing development going up in the port town, die-hard residents of Alonissos found it impossible to secure loans to repair their damaged homes, although many buildings had suffered only minor structural damage; indeed, many of the houses, including some which dated to the eighth century, were torn down after erroneously being judged unsafe. Eventually, all but nine Alonissians moved to Patitiri. Speculators bought up their deserted village at bargain rates, and turned it into a colony where wealthy Europeans—mostly Germans—spend the summer. The islanders are understandably resentful about the way their town was expropriated, but foreigners and Athenian Greeks have restored Alonissos with obvious respect for its original architecture, and native resentment has not turned into hostility towards tourists. Vacationers have, moreover, made the most of Patitiri, cloaking its drab architecture behind a riot of exuberant flowerboxes, thereby creating a rarity—a cheerful modern island town.

Alonissos is one of those places where, once you arrive, you don't want to leave. It is small enough so that most shop and restaurant owners recognize you after one or two days and begin to treat you like an old friend. You also get to know the local characters—the playboy priest who frequents the disco, the local fishermen who make excursions to the nearby beaches. Despite a slight air of sleepy melancholy which pervades Alonissos, it is without doubt one of the friendliest islands in Greece—as well as one of the least touristed.

Practical Information

Ferry service to Alonissos is not as frequent as to Skiathos and Skopelos, but in the summer boats run almost daily and there are excursion trips as well from Skiathos and Skopelos. In addition, there are small local boats zipping back and forth between Alonissos and Skopelos (the trip takes less than an hour) three times a day, making Skopelos the easiest place to reach directly from Alonissos. Skyros is one of the hardest, with only four boats sailing a week.

All boats stop in the small semi-circular port of **Patitiri**. Fifty yards from the dock is **Ikos Travel**, the most helpful travel agency in the Sporades. It is run by Panos Athanassiou, a native of Alonissos, who speaks highly articulate English. He is as willing to discuss economics or English literature as he is to talk about the island's history. He also changes money, finds rooms, and gives 10% student discounts on rooms and on his excursions.

The **OTE** is on Ikion Dolopon St., to the right as you disembark from the ferry. To get to the **Post Office**, walk past the OTE and turn left at the sign for the Post Office; it's just beyond the chickens. (Open weekdays 7:20am-3pm.) The official **exchange** is on the corner of Ikion Dolopon and the main street by the harbor.

Accommodations and Food

There are many rooms to rent on the island, and even in high season, islanders mob the incoming boats trying to get you to stay with them. Most are willing to bargain with you, especially for longer stays. If you'd rather hunt around on your own, try **Babis** on 15 Ikion Dolopon St. (upstairs from the OTE). Singles 400dr, doubles without bath 600dr in high season, 300dr and 500dr in off-season. There are also rooms to let on the other side of town, along Pelasgon Ave. The **Pimakis Pension** has doubles for 750dr, with bath for 1050dr, 600dr and 900dr in off-season. There is an official campground, **Ikoros Camping** on Steni Vala beach (tel. 65 25 8) that charges 100dr per person. The town beach by the port is unsuitable for sleeping, as it consists of stones the size of baseballs. (Since some ferries leave around 6am, however, people nap there before departure time.)

At the waterfront tavernas you have the choice of dining under canvas, or under a canopy of leaves; the tavernas are similar in all other respects. The **Mouria**, under the trees, is one of the cheapest, and serves large portions. **Metoikos**, in front of the town beach, has good pizza, special ice cream, and friendly service. Alonissos opened its first disco, **Disco for You**, in 1982 and the locals are very proud of it, although it may remind you of a cross between a bowling alley and a Mexican restaurant. The even newer **Disco Rocks** lies on a peaceful if somewhat distant knoll south of town.

Around the Island

After abandoning Alonissos, most islanders moved to the towns of Patiri and Votsi in the south. Only the southern end of the island is inhabited, leaving the mountainous central and northern sections to dense pine forests. Alonissans say the best way to see the island is by foot—they have a point, given that Alonissos' roads are not paved, and there's no public transportation. But several places can be reached by excursions from Patitiri. One of the best is the trip to **Old Alonissos**, a forty-five minute walk or 100dr round trip by excursion bus. The town is quiet, breezy and cool, with two small plazas that afford wide views of the island. The twelfth-century **Christ Church** in Old Alonissos is one of the few churches in the Greek islands where men and women were separated during services; a small narthex was constructed above the entrance to the basilica to seat the women and children. While in Old Alonissos, try the **Paraport Taverna** (at the end of the stream) for excellent food and views.

Another interesting jaunt will take you to **Gioura**, a near-nemesis of Odysseus. Several islands claim the honor, but this little island to the northeast of

Alonissos best fits Homer's description of the island of the Cyclops: its large cavern, replete with thousands of splendid stalagmites and stalactites, could easily house an owner of monstrous proportions. Its steep cliffs are ideal for hurling boulders seaward, and Gioura is home for herds of goats—not as wooly as those that saved Odysseus and his crew, but unique in their coloration. The beasts are brown, with black crosses across their spines and shoulderblades. Because of the goats, the island was designated a national park in 1930. Excursions from Patitiri to Gioura run three times a week, and stop also on the island of Kyra-Panagia to visit its monastery.

One of Alonissos' greatest attractions is its isolated beaches. For 150dr round trip you can take a boat to **Marapounda** and **Vithisma** beaches, sheltered beneath steep pine-clad slopes on the southern tip of the island. Or you can walk to these beaches along a dirt road in an hour. Further around the southern coast, in the Bay of **Tsoukalia,** you may search for ancient pot-shards, dating from the fourth century B.C. (Remember, you can't take them home.) At that time, the island was known as "Ikos," and Isoukalia was the site of the island's pottery workshops. Thus, many of the shards discovered at Tsoukalia are marked *Ikion:* "product of Ikos."

In the other direction, also for 150dr, caïques will bring you up the coast to **Milia, Chrisimilia** (considered the most beautiful beach on Alonissos), and **Kokkinokastro,** where the ancient acropolis of Ikos has been inundated by the sea. For an additional 100dr you can continue to **Steni Vala** or **Kalamakia,** or further still to **Agios Dimitrios,** an unusually lovely beach stuck out on a point. All of the main beaches except Agios Dimitrios have tavernas or cafe-snack bars. Should you want to shop around before deciding, there is a boat for 850dr which circles the island, stopping at several beaches.

If you are willing to go to the expense of chartering a boat, Alonissos is the best place from which to visit some of the smaller members of the Sporades. Shepherds are the only inhabitants of the lovely **Skantzoura** to the east besides the one monk who cares for a small cloister affiliated with the Lavra monastery in Athos. The islands and ocean around **Piperi** to the north of Alonissos are a protected National Sea Park, unique for its species of sea birds and large populations of seals. (When sailing anywhere in these waters, keep your eyes open for the seals, as well as for dolphins, which occasionally escort ships.) Check with Ikos Travel about arranging an excursion to these islands; in summer, with enough people, it is neither difficult nor prohibitively expensive.

Skyros

The largest and southernmost of the Sporades, Skyros is arguably the most beautiful and enchanting, and definitely the least spoiled. Tourists mostly avoid the island, perhaps because it's isolated from its northern cousins, or maybe because of the scarcity of amenities. No matter what the reason for this phenomenon, the consequence is that Skyros, unblemished by a high-powered tourist industry, retains much of its natural charm. Moreover, Skyrians are proud of their island's uniqueness, proud of its legendary importance as the place where Achilles was raised, and proud of its traditional way of life.

Skyrian traditions remain vigorous today. Much of the native population of 2700 still produces the same local crafts that their grandparents did. Throughout the labyrinth of step-streets you will see old women weaving rugs and old men making sandals. The main products of the island come from the woodworking shops—handsome handcarved chairs, tables, and chests. Another distinctive feature of Skyros is the traditional dress: the men are often clothed in black caps, puffy blue bloomers over black leggings, and the island's sandals (which resemble foot binding devices); the women wear embroidered skirts, and tie their hair with long, colorful, printed scarves.

Orientation

The island's only paved road connects the port of **Linaria** with the capital, Skyros; a spur splits off near Skyros for the beach. When you get off the boat in Linaria there will be two buses waiting: one destined for Skyros town and the other for the Xenia Hotel and **Molos,** on the beach (both buses 35dr). Be sure to ask the drivers where they are headed, as the buses may be marked somewhat counter-intuitively (e.g. *To Pikon*—"the place"—for the town, and "Skyros" for the beach). A taxi to Skyros runs 350dr.

The only boats to Linaria are from Kimi, and the trip takes two hours (435dr). There are two lines: the giant Nomikos line, with a virtual monopoly on the Sporades, runs daily boats from Kimi to Skyros, and five boats a week for the return trip. Their competitor, the *Anemossa,* is owned collectively by Skyrians, who have been able to put their "underdog" status to good advantage by billing the ship as "the boat of the Skyrian people." The *Anemossa* now handles most of the Kimi-Skyros traffic, making two round trips daily during the summer, in the early morning and afternoon. Both companies have offices in Kimi and Skyros; neither will tell you about the other's boats or honor the other's tickets.

Only the Nomikos line serves the other Sporades, and only one boat a week sails direct from Skyros to Alonissos, Skopelos and Skiathos. The other four runs originate in Skyros and transfer to Kimi before turning north towards the other islands, adding two and a half hours and at least 150dr onto the trip. If you can, catch the direct boat; if not, have a good book ready, for the Skyros-Kimi-Alonissos leg alone takes 6½ hours.

Town of Skyros

The town of Skyros, shaped like a bulky question mark, winds around the side of an enormous cliff that rises up dramatically from the water. By far the most unspoiled town in the Sporades, Skyros owes its preservation to its steep passages that are virtually impregnable to the assault of the automobile. The side streets of the central part of the sprawling town climb the steep backside of a huge rock wall, finally ending in the **Monastery of St. George** and the remains of a medieval fortress, both of which afford spectacular views of the eastern coast of the island. Legend has it that the Athenian hero Theseus met his end falling off this cliff, having been double-crossed by Skyros' King Lykomedes, with whom he had sought asylum. Skyros was also the home of Atalanta, the princess who refused to marry anyone who could not beat her in a footrace. Her suitor Melanios, however, eventually slowed her down by throwing golden apples from the Garden of the Hesperides in her path and finally won her hand in marriage.

A bit further down the crest, on the tip of the town, is a plaza containing a most unlyrical statue of English poet Rupert Brooke, another victim of Skyros hazards. He died of fever here en route to Gallipoli during the disastrous Dardanelles campaign of the First World War. The poet's tomb was constructed near a bay in southern Skyros.

Practical Information

The **OTE** (open weekdays from 7:30am-1pm, 4-9pm) and **Post Office** (weekdays 7:30am-2:30pm) are just below the square where buses stop. A hardware store managed by A. Fragkoulis and Stamati Sarri's foreign newspaper and book shop, across from each other on the main street (Agoras St.), both change money and cash travelers checks. The police (tel. 91 27 4) are around the corner from Skyros Pizza, off the main street.

Accommodations and Food

You can stay in Skyros Town or on the beach 1 km away; buses run to both places (get off at Xenia Hotel to be near both beach and town). Within Skyros Town itself, private rooms are the best way to go. The rooms are decorated with family heirlooms: crockery, copperware, dolls, icons, portraits, hand-carved furniture—you are a paying guest in a part of the house where the family lives during the rest of the year. (One hazard of this is that you may feel like a bull in a china closet when you stagger in hot and dusty, lugging a monstrous backpack—remember how careful you used to be at your grand-parents' house?) One such place to stay is with **Elefteria Phtoules** (walk up the main street to the kiosk and ask children). If she has no room, her many neighbors will be glad to help you out. All are willing to bargain; they charge more for stays of only one or two nights. The high season rate for longer stays is around 300dr per person per night. **Nic Mantzourakis** has a pension near the square in town (600dr for doubles) but the spartan rooms pale in comparison with most Skyrian homes.

If you decide to stay on the beach, **Manolis Balotis** just at the end of the steps leading to town (tel. 91 38 6) rents doubles for 700dr. The campground next door charges 110dr per person plus 60dr per tent for stays in a pleasant, though buggy, grass field. Camping on the beach itself is free and not frowned upon. In **Molos**, 500m down the road, **Diethnes** and **Venetsanos Pension** (tel. 91 38 6) both offer doubles with private bath for 900dr; these places are often full, so inquire early in the morning, or after a boat has left the island. About 1.5km in the other direction, **Petroula Restaurant**, near **Bassale** on the shore, has singles for 300dr, doubles for 600dr, slightly less in April and May. They are closed from September until March.

A number of good tavernas in town cater more to the locals than to the tourists. Try **Kabanera** or the nearby **Aquarius** (follow the signs) for the best and cheapest fare. If you want a view, try the roof garden across from the square, or the one overlooking it. Both serve good basic Greek food. The **Restaurant Moraiti** on the main street is always lively and provides a good perspective for people-watching. While on Skyros, taste the island's fine ret-sina. Most of the tavernas have rosé in the keg—much preferable to bottled retsina—and will bring you a freshly drawn carafe if you request it *apo bareli*.

While most of Skyros goes to bed by 11pm, some of the locals keep surpris-ingly late hours. The main street cafes, along with the **Sisyphus Pub** (which serves mixed drinks and plays rock music) are open until midnight. The real night-owls can be found in the town's two discos, **On the Rocks** and **Sky-ropouk**. After 1am, pop gives way to Greek music, and the Greek youths hit the floor to show their stuff. No tame, Sunday night folk-dancing this; the dances show a strong Middle Eastern influence, with moves hotter than any Saturday night fever.

Sights

The **Archeological Museum** (down the marble stairs to the right before the statue of Brooke) has a lovely 1200 B.C. Mycenean jar decorated with octopus and ship motifs, showing the extent of Minoan influence on Mycenean art. The museum also houses a collection of tenth century B.C. *fibulae* (safety pins), and some Classical and Roman treasures. A pamphlet is available to lead you through the exhibits in chronological order, and explain the significance of the more important pieces. The museum open Mon.-Sat. 9am-3:15pm, Sun. 10am-2:30pm, closed Tues.

Equally fascinating is the **Faltaits Museum,** one of the best folk-art exhibits in all of Greece. The building and its contents were left to the island by Manos Faltaits, a descendant of one of Skyros' 20 *archon* families, who led the island from the thirteenth century up to the 1820s. The display includes a superb collection of the island's embroideries, carved wooden furniture, pottery, costumes and copperware, as well as rare books (such as a 1795 edition of poems by the pseudo-Celtic poet "Ossian"). Relics from the island's yearly carnival (April 23) include a goat mask and a goatskin costume. The museum also has a gallery set up as a traditional Skyrian home, with walls decked with hammered copper plates, shelves laden with hand-painted ceramics, and all other available surfaces coated with colorful woven and embroidered textiles. While viewing this gallery is a pleasure, even greater delight is in store when you wander down the streets and discover that the locals actually live this way. At night, their living rooms are brightly lit so as to invite inspection from passersby. If you feel at all a Peeping Tom, stick your head in the door, point, and crack an appreciative grin—you may be treated to a guided tour. Even the exteriors of some of the modest, weather-beaten stucco houses, such as the finely varnished window panels and the carefully arranged mosaics of pebbles and polished stones that adorn the entrances, offer some clues as to the splendor of their interiors.

While in Skyros, be sure to climb up to the **castle** which crowns the town. It's generally believed to be of Venetian vintage, but evidence indicates that the Venetians merely repaired and added to an earlier Byzantine fortification. The reclining marble lion set in the stone wall above the entrance to the castle dates from the fourth century B.C., when the Athenians used it as a symbol of their dominion over Skyros. On the southeastern side of the castle peak lie the well-preserved remains of an aqueduct. From the roof of this structure one may peer down into the aqueduct's main shaft, used as a prison.

If you are on Skyros on April 23, you will witness the **Skyrian Carnival,** a festival which is part religious, part folk satire. Groups of three to five men dressed in elaborate, ponderous costumes consisting of capes, goatskin masks, shepherd's pants, and 50-80 copper bells dance wildly through town on their way to the Monastery of St. George. The ritual is a commemoration of a legendary land-use dispute between shepherds and farmers, and is unique to Skyros.

Around the Island

The dark sand beach below the town is one of the longest in the Sporades, stretching along the coast through the villages of Magazia and Molos and continuing around the point. In July and August it can be crowded, when it crawls with ill-behaved Greek children. But it's undeniably convenient: a fifteen-minute walk down stone steps will get you there from the center of Skyros; and in the summer, buses run to the beach approximately every hour during the day, departing from the main square or the Post Office.

Kalamitsa is the only other beach on Skyros that may be reached cheaply. Take the bus to Linaria and walk 45 minutes along the dirt road south of the port. The walk itself affords breathtaking views, and the crescent of sandy beach with a shaded taverna are well worth the effort. Summertime excursions by bus and boat, organized by Skyros Travel (in town), will drop you off at Kalamitsa, as well as at **Pefkos beach**, north of Linaria (100dr); the boats leave in the morning and return to pick you up in the evening. Longer trips go to beaches at **Atsitsa**, fringed with pine trees, and **Tris Boukes**, the site of Rupert Brooke's tomb. If you can afford to rent a moped (800dr per day, including gas) or a motorboat (180dr per day for 3-4 people), you can make the entire island your playground, with two restrictions: some of the roads are extremely dusty, rough, and remote, and getting to certain corners of the island could be difficult for both bike and rider. The beach at the northernmost tip of Skyros is off-limits, even if you can get there; it is reserved for personnel of the nearby air force base.

If you don't have the cash to rent transportation, try walking around Skyros. Much of the island is clad with pines, and where it is not, you will have a chance to see how the island's rural inhabitants—farmers, shepherds, sheep and goats—scratch out a living from the dry soil. Besides the beaches, two small chapels are near the town of Skyros, both about an hour's walk along the road that forks to the right of the main street by the OTE office. Inquire at Skyros Travel a day in advance to arrange to have the walled **Monastery of Agios Dimitrios** opened for you. Sections of this Byzantine edifice date back to pre-Christian times, evidence of the Christian policy of destroying pagan monuments, and reusing the same materials to build churches, often on the same site. The chapel of **Agios Antonios**, or *Ta Kria Nera* (cold water), is set in a magical garden with a spring and many varieties of trees. Bring water yourself anyway, especially during the summer, for this or any hike around the island. Do not be afraid to get off the roads and head across country. You can always find a path—it's merely a question of finding one that leads where you want to go. With a good map, a sense of direction, and a facility for crossing physical and cultural barriers, you can go anywhere you want in the wild interior of the island.

During your rambles on Skyros, you might see one of the island's unique and indigenous ponies, descendants of a breed believed to have inhabited the island 17 million years ago. In recent centuries, the population of Skyrian ponies grew very large, until over-grazing and subsequent starvation decimated the herds. Today there are only about one hundred of the animals left. Because of their paleontological importance as well as their interest to equiphiles, an effort has been made to care for the animals and protect the purity of the stock by preventing cross-breeding with other types of horse. Each summer around July 15 the Skyrian ponies, now domesticated, are assembled in a field near Magazia Beach, where village children ride them in a makeshift rodeo. It's reminiscent of the "Caucus" race in *Alice in Wonderland*—they have a square track, and neither horse nor rider knows quite what to do at the corners.

SARONIC GULF ISLANDS

In ancient times, no matter how many people crowded the shores of the Saronic Gulf Islands, the higher rocky interior of each remained serenely vacant. That's why you'll find temples and sanctuaries on these islands built at such impressive heights: sanctuaries were no place for the hubbub of the ancient masses. In modern times, oddly enough, the same holds true. For all the cultural earthquakes of the millennia, Athenians, tourists, and other weekend warriors still inundate the coastal villages of **Aegina, Poros, Hydra,** and **Spetsai**—the four main Saronic Gulf Islands—while those who venture to the dry upland areas can still gaze at the molten silver sea in windswept solitary silence. Some of the holy buildings, the divine residences at these lofty retreats, have crumbled under the joint onslaught of years and elements and are now no more than pitted rubble. But don't let that stop you from paying them a visit. Whether or not you'll find any gods at those altitudes, you will certainly find arresting views, and you won't marvel at these islands unless you leave the tourists at the shore and journey inward and upward.

Unfortunately, the Saronic Gulf Islands are among the most expensive places in Greece. At 300-500dr a night for a single, the cheapest lodgings are pensions and private rooms. The best strategy is to look for the "rooms to let" signs which dot all of the major towns. Compare prices and try bargaining, especially if you plan on staying for a couple of nights. Camping is illegal on all of the Saronic Gulf Islands (except on the islet of Moni), though during the off-season the Tourist Police tend to look the other way if you pitch your tent in a secluded spot for a night. Finally, a word of advice: because the islands (especially Aegina and Poros) are such a short hop from Athens, many Greeks go for the weekend, making an already crowded situation unbearable. Try to stay on the islands during the week and never arrive on a weekend.

There are basically three ways of traveling between Piraeus and the Saronic Gulf Islands. In descending order of cost, they are: the package tour, the hydrofoil, and the ferry. Definitely not advised are the one-day, three-island (Aegina, Poros, Hydra) cruises sponsored by all of the Athens agencies. You're better off arranging your own transportation. Although this makes long-range planning difficult, the money you save and the leisure you gain will make the effort more than worthwhile. The fare for ferries between any two adjacent islands is roughly 180dr; the hydrofoil costs about 120dr extra but cuts travel time in half, runs more frequently, and reaches places much farther away, such as Nafplion, Tolo, Leonidio, Kyparissi, Monemvassia, Kythira, and Neapolis. Remember that we list high season prices for ferries and hydrofoils; these drop by 15% in the low season. Ferry and hydrofoil schedules are posted in the port of each island and even though departure and arrival times fluctuate greatly from week to week, boats are careful to adhere to the posted timetable. But keep in mind that recent accidents have encouraged the authorities to stop service in bad weather or even when the water is slightly choppy. Many travelers who depend on that last hydrofoil to catch a connecting boat find themselves "lost in Spetsai" because of this official caution. If you have any questions, the main passenger service is provided by the **Argosaronikos Line** (tel. 45 11 311), while the **Flying Dolphins Line** (the **Delphini**

Iptamena) provides the hydrofoil service (all Saronics except Aegina tel. 45 27 107; Aegina only tel. 45 31 716/17).

The **telephone code** for the Saronic Gulf Islands is 0298.

Aegina

Aegina, about an hour by ferry from Piraeus and an easy daytrip from Athens, has had little trouble attracting visitors. The verdant, sun-dappled island is blessed with sumptuous mountain scenery and endowed with many small, rocky coves that are perfect for swimming. Long the favorite Athenian retreat, Aegina bears some of the scars caused by an expanding tourist industry, but the island is large enough to allow refuge from the crowds.

In ancient times, though, Athens and Aegina weren't so friendly. Aegina led the other Greek states in such areas as shipping and coinage—it minted silver "tortoises," the first Greek coins ever—from as early as 1000 B.C., and had angered its growing neighbor on the mainland. In the Persian War, for example, Aegina eventually submitted to the invading Persians (491 B.C.), a move which Athens could not forget, and over the next thirty years, when Athens ruled many of the Greek states, Aegina sided with Sparta. Though the island's inhabitants flourished and even built the magnificent **Temple of Aphaea** during these thirty years, Athens defeated Aegina in 459, forcing it to join the Athens league. Some thirteen years later the poet Pindar was inspired to close his eighth Pythian ode with an appeal to the patron heroes of Aegina:

> *Man's life is a day. What is he?*
> *What is he not? A shadow in a dream*
> *Is man: but when God sheds a brightness,*
> *Shining life is on earth*
> *And life is sweet as honey.*
>   *Aigina, dear mother,*
> *Keep this city in her voyage of freedom:*
> *You with Zeus and lord Aiakos,*
> *Peleus, and noble Telamon, and Achilles.*

(from *Pindar: The Odes*, translated by C. M. Bowra. Penguin Edition, 1969)

But the heroes couldn't help, and by 431 B.C. Athens had expelled the entire Aeginetan population, replacing it with Athenian colonists, until Sparta restored it in 405 B.C. Thenceforth, great historical events bypassed Aegina until the 1820s, when it briefly became the capital of the new Greek state. Today few clues—scars or otherwise—remain of Aegina's trials and tribulations.

To get to Aegina from Athens, take green bus #40 from Filellinon St. and get off at the Public Theater *(Demotikon Theatron)* in Piraeus. From there you can see water and the pier where the ferries leave for Aegina. Alternatively, take the subway to the stop at Piraeus and walk to the left for a few blocks along the water until you reach the pier. The fare is 222dr one-way, 324dr by hydrofoil; both types of vessel make the run several times daily. Unless you know exactly when you plan to return, buy your return ticket on Aegina.

Town of Aegina

You will most likely disembark in the port town of Aegina, which happens to be one of the better places to stay and is the central point of departure for buses around the island. The town has managed to preserve its original charm surprisingly well, probably because it lacks a good beach (although there are nice swimming spots close by). Archeologically, the town is a bust—half a column remains of a temple of Apollo. The **archeological museum,** however, is reputed to have a good collection and is located right near the column, a few hundred meters to the left of the ferry landing as you look from the water to land. The museum's hours are 9am-3:30pm daily and 10am-7:30pm on holidays. The ruins are open 9am-7pm, though the hours may change.

The town's **Tourist Police** (tel. 22 39 1), located on Aiakou St. off the waterfront, provide an accommodations service and information. (Open 8am-2pm and 4:30-9pm.) For excursions to other parts of the island, go to the **bus station** on the waterfront to the left of the ferry landing. Buses leave hourly for Souvala, Perdika, and Agia Marina, and run 5am-10pm from the terminal and 5:30am-10:30pm from other points. Just behind the bus station is the **Post Office;** the OTE is located up Aiakou St. and is open 7:30am-10pm. The **bank** is on the waterfront, open Mon.-Thurs. 8am-2pm, Fri. 7:45am-2pm. If you wish you can rent a two-wheeled vehicle at the shop a few steps before the bus terminal. Bikes go for 80dr an hour/250dr for the day, motorbikes 250dr an hour/800dr for the day, and Vespas 250dr an hour/1200dr for the day. The last two come with a full tank of gas and all must be returned by 6pm.

Accommodations and Food

As always, the most reasonable places are the pensions and rooms to let. Since the island has to ship in its entire water supply from Poros and Piraeus, expect to pay up to 100dr for a short shower. There are cheap places in town, but they fill up fast in the high season. The cheapest hotels in town are D-class and their rates fluctuate 20-40% between the high and low seasons. Bargaining is particularly helpful if there are only a few tourists in town, but it will get you nowhere on a full weekend. Try the **Hotel Artemis** behind the bus station (tel. 25 19 5), which has singles for 972dr, doubles for 1350dr, and triples for 1575dr, all with shower; singles for 900dr and doubles for 1125dr without shower. **Hotel Marmarinos,** up Leonardo Lada St. from the harbor (tel. 22 47 4), has slightly cheaper rooms. Singles with shower go for 956dr and triples with shower go for 1350dr. Singles without shower cost 675dr and doubles without shower cost 1012dr. **Hotel Miranda** (tel. 24 55 5), on the waterfront past the playing field, has singles for 765dr and doubles for 1069dr, both without shower. Located just past the large, domed church, set back from the waterfront, **Xenon Paulou,** 21 Paulou Aeginitou St. (tel. 22 79 5), has doubles with shower for 1575dr, singles without for 675dr and doubles without for 1350dr, and they'll throw in breakfast for 100dr. Bargaining may bring these prices down. If after bargaining and discussion you can't make suitable hotel arrangements, try sleeping on the beach, under the trees near the museum. It's supposed to be illegal but can often be done without hassles from the police.

For a good, reasonably-priced meal, try the **House of the Fisherman (To Spiti Tou Psara)** at #41 on the waterfront, or **To Maridaki,** a few doors farther down. In the morning, take a walk through the covered fish market. Behind the market, fresh fruit is sold and there are also several inexpensive *souvlaki* stands. Be sure to sample the pistachio nuts, an important product of the island; they're sold everywhere. A disco at the end of the pier, and music and dancing at the "Retro" next to the post office are two of Aegina's more long-lived but rather dull nightspots. Check the signs on the fence near the museum for more information about nocturnal events.

Near Aegina

The little island of Angistri is a half-hour boat trip from Aegina. Boats leave three times a day in summer, and because there is no ferry from the mainland itself, Angistri is pleasantly undertouristed. Try it for a relaxing week on the beach. Skala is the best place for swimming, though you might want to explore

Milo and Limenario. The **Aktaeon** (tel. 91 22 2) has singles for 540dr, doubles for 756dr, and triples for 864dr, all without shower, and doubles for 864dr and triples for 1080dr with shower. On the beach, the **Anagennissis** (no phone) has doubles for 1080dr and triples for 1276dr with shower. The **Angistri** (tel. 91 24 2) offers singles for 675dr, doubles for 900dr, and triples for 1125dr, all with shower.

On the road between Aegina and Agia Marina in the middle of the island is the village of **Paliohora.** The inhabitants of the island used to take refuge here from the attacks of invaders. At one time the village had 365 churches; indeed, it is more commonly referred to as "the town of three hundred churches." Only 28 of these remain, and some of them have wonderful frescoes. Of particular interest is the monastery **Agios Nektarios.**

Buses run from the town of Aegina along the northern coast to the small resort town of **Souvala.** The cheapest place to stay is the **Saronikos** (tel. 52 22 4), which has doubles with shower for 1125dr, doubles without shower for 675dr, and triples without shower for 900dr. Buses also travel along the west coast to the fishing port of **Perdika;** from here you can catch a boat to the tiny island of **Moni,** the only place on the Saronic Gulf Islands where camping is permitted. For more information on sights, pick up the map and guide to Aegina at the Tourist Police.

Even if Greek ruins don't tickle your fancy, the well-preserved **Temple of Aphaea** is worth a visit. Unless your trip happens to coincide with one of the infrequent bus tours of Aegina, you will be able to enjoy the fifth-century B.C. building in eery solitude, as winds whisper in the pines and the sun smiles down on you. It's almost like an ancient ghost town—you half expect to see tumbleweeds blow by. The structure is the only surviving Hellenic temple with a second row of small superimposed columns in the interior of the sanctuary. The view of the island from the site is also spectacular—worth the trip itself. But watch out for the cactus and briars, which can poke right through the sole of any shoe. To get to the ruins, take the Agia Marina bus from Aegina town (48dr one-way), sit back, and watch the pistachio and fig groves. Admission to the site is 50dr, 30dr for students.

Try to avoid the town of Agia Marina, since it is a textbook example of how tourism can ruin a beautiful island village. Its **beach,** though, is broad, sandy, and on the whole not too crowded.

To continue your journeys from Aegina, you don't have to hop from island to island. Hydrofoils leave twice daily for Methana (284dr), Poros (411dr), Hydra (495dr), Ermione (626dr), Spetsai (647dr), and Porto Heli (750dr). They also leave less frequently (two to six times a week) for Tolo and Nafplion (1018dr each), Leonidio (916dr), Kyparissi (1226dr), Monemvassia (1374dr), and Kythira and Neapolis (2668dr each).

Poros

Nobody knows who thought of it, but Poros' name, which means "passage," certainly is apt. The name refers to the narrow channel that separates the island from the Peloponnese. It's such an easy swim to the mainland you'll have trouble believing large ships actually go through—but they did, and so the name stuck. Historically, Poros' claim to fame is the great orator Demosthenes—or rather, his suicide before the **Temple of Poseidon** in 322 B.C. Demosthenes spoke with marbles in his mouth to improve his enunciation, and if you make it up to the mountain crest to enjoy the spectacular view from the temple ruins, you may never stop talking about it—whether you've got your marbles or not.

Poros is small, lush, and rich in beaches and beautiful scenery. Although less crowded than Aegina, it's filled to the gills on weekends, mostly with Greeks making the short hop over from the mainland but also with very white English tourists on package vacations. Your first glimpse of the island, if you come by ferry, will be of the white houses and bright orange rooftops of the cheerful town of Poros. The town, built on a large hill with its highest point in the center, is actually shaped like an inverted amphitheater. But don't spend all your time on the touristy and overpriced waterfront; escape the crowds by climbing up the narrow passageways that lead to the top of the city, where you can enjoy an excellent view of the area.

Accommodations and Food

To the left of the ferry landing a sign will direct you to an agency, **Family Tours,** at 14 Iroon Square (tel. 22 54 9 or 23 74 3), that locates inexpensive accommodations and sells a comprehensive map of and guide to Poros for 40dr. Open Mon.-Sat. 8am-9:10pm, Sun. 8am-5pm. An accommodations service is also provided by the **Takis Travel Bureau** (tel. 22 04 8), to the right of the ferry landing; climb the steps up and around the back of the building to enter. Open 8am-9pm every day, though hours are sporadic on Sunday. The cheapest pensions and private rooms cost about 800dr for a double. The **Tourist Police** (tel. 22 46 2) will sometimes help you find a room, but for the most part, they're useless; rely on Takis. Turn right as you get off the boat to find the Tourist Police; they're on the other side of the harbor, about one hundred meters away, in the same building as the regular police. They're open Mon.-Fri. 8am-2:30pm, mid-June to September, but you may get help at other times if it's an emergency.

During the summer months, smaller and cheaper boarding houses are officially allowed to operate, and they are often located without the aid of an agency. If you're lugging a backpack around, sharp-eyed men and women will spot you and lure you to their homes where, with a little bargaining, you can stay quite inexpensively. Three reputable pensions are located near the Hotel Lahtsi, several hundred meters to the left after you leave the boat along the waterfront. If they don't find you first, call **Nikos Douras** (tel. 22 63 3), **George Douras** (tel. 22 53 2), or **Dimitras Alexopoulou** (tel. 22 69 7). The first two are extremely helpful, speak a few words of English, and are expanding their businesses. The third is reputedly more expensive. Expect to pay about 400dr per person including hot showers. There are also some lovely rooms to let located up the hill near the clock tower where the view is superb. Prices vary, but you should be able to find a double for about 800dr. Avoid all of the Poros hotels since the cheapest onces are class C.

The town also has quite a few good restaurants. For great seafood and grilled meats at a reasonable price, try either **Caravella** or its next-door neighbor, both a good walk to the right along the wharf as you face inland, and both with covered tables right at the water's edge. In the square to the right of Takis, **K. Bissias** and, opposite it, **7 Brothers,** have wonderful atmosphere and full portions of well-cooked food, as do **3 Brothers,** opposite the museum, and **Dionysus,** near the Hotel Lahtsi. There are also a few tavernas near the monastery and even a restaurant, **Paradissos,** close to the Temple of Poseidon, whose only real advantage is location. **Zorba's** serves up tasty dishes and offers traditional Greek dancing about half a kilometer up the road to the left of the wharf facing inland, across the canal. You can also find fairly inexpensive *souvlaki* and chicken at the restaurant next to the **Diana** movie theater (#50 on the left hand side of the port facing inland). The theater itself often plays American and British films. For a more exciting evening, try the discos **Kavos** and **Corali,** which are popular watering holes for the younger crowd. The latter features Greek dancing at about 1am each night. Both are located at the extreme right end of the wharf. Another good new disco is the **Siroco.**

The **OTE** can be found to the left on the wharf (open 7:30am-10pm), the **bank** to the right past the church (open 8am-2pm), and the **Post Office** in the first square to the right along the water. The **archeological museum** is also to the right along the water. Open daily 9am-3pm, holidays 9am-2pm, and closed Tuesdays, it is small but has some interesting inscriptions and photographs of the ruins at Troizen (so you can decide if you want to visit in person).

Near Poros

Small boats travel back and forth constantly to sandy **Neorion beach** (15dr), about two kilometers from town. The main sight on Poros, the **Monastery of Zoodochos Pigis** (Virgin of the Life-Giving Spring), is a scenic twenty-minute bus ride (25dr) from the bus stop next to the main port in town. Buses leave every half hour and run 7am-9:30pm. Open daily, 6am-1pm and 3pm-sunset, the monastery has an excellent view and is situated in an overgrown glade. If it's the life-giving spring, there must be more than water in it—even the bees are big as helicopters. The site was used as early as 200 A.D. and inside you'll find a twenty-foot high, three-tiered series of panels illustrating scenes of Jesus' and the Apostles' lives, inlaid with gold. Notice the striking skull and crossbones at the foot of the cross that crowns the front board. It is cool and silent inside and empty except for a busy Greek Orthodox priest whose industry somehow harmonizes with the serenity. Dress properly to visit; men wearing shorts and women wearing pants are forbidden to enter, and though a few skirt-like coverings are available at the door, you'll have to wait for them on a busy day. Along the route to the monastery is the little, uncrowded beach of **Askeli,** a 25dr bus ride.

Unless you're a Greek history buff, the main reason to visit the ruins of the **Temple of Poseidon** atop the mountain is the stunning view of the Saronic Gulf. If you walk, watch out for sunstroke and heat exhaustion: it's a long way uphill, and after an hour of climbing you'll agree that either old Demosthenes was a trooper or he landed at an extraordinarily high tide. The best way to reach the top is on one of the motorbikes you can rent by the shore in Poros. From the monastery, backtrack half a kilometer along the road until you get to the turn-off leading to higher ground. Little remains of the temple but knee-deep rubble. The structure dates to the sixth century B.C. and was traditionally used as a sanctuary for all refugees, especially victims of shipwrecks who needed shelter. It was here that Demosthenes, a powerful Athenian thanks to his titanic tongue, took refuge from his Macedonian pursuers, and, you could say, outwitted them by killing himself. From the steps of the sanctuary, he called out to his enemies that he would surrender but first needed time to write his family a farewell letter. Chewing on his pen for a while, he crouched down, shaking. His pursuers taunted him, mistaking his movements for tremors of fear, and before they knew it their prize had died. He had put poison on the end of his pen.

Dominating the harbor is the **Battleship Averof** (tel. 22 25 4). It's hard to miss—it's the monstrous one hundred-year-old grey warship on the left side of the harbor. Open Sat. 5-7pm, Sun. and holidays 10am-12:30pm and 5-7pm; admission free. Right behind it is the naval school.

Boats of all different sizes, including car ferries, run back and forth between the Peloponnese coast and the harbor of Poros. They usually cost 6 to 12dr, but beware—ferry operators will occasionally try to milk unsuspecting tourists for as much as 60dr for the short ride. Take the short caique ride across the channel to **Galatas** on the Peloponnese mainland for the sunny beaches of **Aliki** (the nicer of the two) and **Plaka,** both quite a distance to the left as you walk along the shore. A ten-minute walk from Plaka Beach is the enormous lemon grove of **Lemonodassos.** Try the fresh-squeezed lemon juice at **Cardassi Taverna.** Donkey rides, at 100dr each way, are definitely a rip-off. Although camping is officially forbidden in the area, tents do crop up behind Plaka and Aliki beaches. Be discreet, however, since the Tourist Police are getting progressively more strict. There is camping in a lemon grove nearby but the owner of the site has threatened to close it for lack of business.

For a pleasant excursion, take a caique ride to Galatas (the mainland) and catch one of the buses to **Trizinia.** Bus schedules are available at Takis; the telephone number of the Galatas bus station is 22 48 0. (There are no Tourist Police at Galatas.) Walk up through the carnation fields to Devil's Gorge and the site of ancient **Troizen.** The archeological sites are only moderately interesting, but the walk is quite beautiful.

Poros makes a good daytrip from Athens or from cities in the Argolid area of the Peloponnese, although (as with the other Saronic Gulf Islands) you will have more fun if you come for several days. Try to avoid the island on the weekends when it is filled with day-tripping Athenians. Buses leave for Galatas from Nafplion four times daily (210dr). Hydrofoils (674dr) and boats (336dr) leave Piraeus for Poros several times daily. From Poros hydrofoils also run to Aegina (411dr), Methana (264dr), Hydra (219dr), Ermione (238dr), Spetsai (364dr), Porto Heli (411dr), Tolo and Nafplion (787dr each), Leonidio (672dr), Kyparissi (1086dr), Monemvassia (1085dr), and Kythira and Neapolis (2327dr each). En route between Poros and Aegina, the boats stop at the up-and-coming resort town of **Methana** on the peninsula of Methana, which offers some nice rock beach. Avoid the bland tourist village and its extremely modest strip of sandy beach. All in all, Poros is nicer, so there's no reason to stop off.

Hydra

The entrance into the Port of Hydra (or Idra as the Greeks call it) is one of the highlights of a stay in Greece: the white and gray orange-roofed buildings rise up out of the water on all three sides, with cannons jutting out of the barricaded walls and windmills perched high above on either side. The harbor, lined with jewelry stores, gift shops, and expensive restaurants and cafes, is an enormous tourist trap. The town, however, with alley-like streets winding their way up and down narrow staircases, possesses a certain nobility and impregnable grace that the herds of tourists are somehow unable to corrupt. Hydra has recently become an artists' colony, and so far the effort has not succeeded. Though the jewelry stores feature "original pieces" and Americans, palette in hand, appear occasionally, the town is by and large unpretentious once you get away from the harbor. And it's quiet. No private cars, bicycles, or other moving vehicles are allowed—only feet or donkeys.

Accommodations and Food

The **Tourist Police** (opposite the OTE, tel. 52 20 5) are open 24 hours; walk along the wharf and turn left at the church with the clock tower. There you can find travel information and a small supply of maps of the island, and arrange rental of private rooms, the cheapest way to lodge. Though singles are practically impossible to find, doubles cost about 600dr. The cheapest hotel in town is the **Sophia,** 2 A. Miaouli St. (tel. 52 31 3), right at the center of the wharf, with singles for 560dr, doubles for 850dr, triples for 1000dr, beds in the hall for 280dr per person, and showers for 80dr extra. The other two D-class hotels,

Argo (tel. 52 45 2) and **Dina** (tel. 52 24 8), are significantly more expensive, and often fully booked during the high season. A popular island for European jet-setters and wealthy Greek vacationers, Hydra can be an almost impossible place to find a room without prior reservations. When there are no rooms, the Tourist Police allow people to sleep on the beaches, which are rocky—a very uncomfortable proposition. But even when rooms are available, Hydra is far and away the highest-priced of the Saronic Gulf Islands.

Food can be expensive as well. The only cheap place in town is **The Three Brothers,** just off the harbor behind the marble clock tower. This is a really excellent, inexpensive restaurant, so all is not lost. For even cheaper food, try the market one block from the water, behind the **National Bank of Greece.** If you're dying for a bite to eat with a view of the port, try **Cafe Laikon** to the left of where the boats disembark—it's cheaper and friendlier than the other tour-ist-hustling cafes. **Antonio's** is probably the best of these because its waiters can say, "How are you? Peach Melba?" in languages you never dreamed could be slaughtered like that. Up Ikonomou St. is a movie theater and, next door, a charming taverna called the **Garden.** But for Hydra's soft ice cream, which may be the best in Greece and is well worth the 35dr, stick to the harbor. Too much ice cream? Dance it off at either **Disco Cavos** or **Lagoudera** (where drinks are half-price with a student ID). Lagoudera is located on the right corner of the harbor as you look from the water, and is embedded in the stone fortress. Cavos is in the same direction but further down the stone path and around the bend. To write home about your experience you'll find the **Post Office** in the alley to the right of Ikonomou St., up a few steps.

Sights

Since there are no cars and virtually no roads on the island of Hydra, you'll have to walk to see anything. The large **clock tower** that dominates the wharf belongs to the Ecclesiastical Church with a fine courtyard accessible by the side gate on N. Votsi St. Also of interest are the frescoes of the **Church of St. John** in the Place Kamina. On the right of the harbor as you look from the water one flight up from the Quinta night club is the **House of Koundourioti,** a great leader in the Greek War of Independence and a descendant of one of the shipping families that put Hydra on the map. Since the house is maintained for viewing by certain family members, opening hours are extremely unpredict-able; it's best to check with the Tourist Police first. On the left side of the harbor, just past the Cafe Laikon, the **Pilot School** sits on top of a flight of white stairs. Look for the very serious Greek captains in the class pictures from the 30s: Greeks don't take their sailing lightly. Open 8am-10pm.

But don't spend all of your time on the waterfront with the rest of the tourists. Explore the port of Hydra and the rest of the island. Any of the following three hikes from town are strongly recommended. The first and shortest, featuring a beautiful view of the town, continues down A. Miaouli St. from the waterfront (the road takes you out of the town) and up a hill to the twin monasteries of **Elias** (for monks) and **Efpraxia** (for nuns), both open 9am-5pm. To return to the harbor, climb down the monastery steps and follow the steps and passageways down through the town. The second hike is to **Epis-kopi,** a deserted monastery an hour or more's walk west from Elias along goat paths (you'll need to ask directions; the Greek word for footpath is *monopati*) that take you through beautiful uninhabited country side. You can return to town by cutting down to the north coast via the tiny village of **Vlihos.** There is a small pebble beach here, deserted even in high season, where you can dis-creetly pitch a tent. The third and most challenging walk follows goat paths east to the convents of **Agia Triada** and **Zourvas:** the former is located on a hill one and a half hour's walk east of town, and the latter is at the eastern tip of the island. For the less adventurous, skiffs can be taken to Palamadas beach on the west coast, about an hour's walk. Avoid the once nice beach at Miramare. It has been ruined by the construction of a "Water Sports Center."

Hydra makes a challenging daytrip from either Poros or Spetsai. Hydrofoils (833dr) and boats (370dr) run several trips between Piraeus and Hydra, often stopping at the other Saronic Gulf Islands first. From Hydra hydrofoils run to Aegina (495dr), Methana (401dr), Poros (219dr), Ermione (284dr), Spetsai (296dr), Porto Heli (331dr), Tolo and Nafplion (549dr each), Leonidio (447dr), Kyparissi (617dr), Monemvassia (982dr), and Kythira and Neapolis (2073dr each). On the way between Hydra and Spetsai, the boat and hydrofoil stop at the resort town of **Ermione** on the Peloponnese; get off here to go to Epidavros or Nafplion. Stay on the boat if you're continuing on to Spetsai. Locals joke about the tourists who disembark at Ermione, walk around, and, not realizing they're on the mainland, unwittingly remark about what a big island it is.

Spetsai

At the southern end of the Saronic Gulf, Spetsai (also called Spetses) offers the most picturesque stony beaches and the most luxuriant vegetation of all the nearby islands. Jasmine, lemons, and honeysuckle perfume the air, giving the town of Spetsai scents more often found at the French Riviera than on a Greek island. Once the least touristed of the group, Spetsai is now crawling with English sunworshippers.

The town of Spetsai is small and compact. The **Tourist Police** (tel. 73 10 0) are located on Botassi St., around the corner from the **Post Office,** and are open 24 hours to help you find accommodations and obtain information. From the harbor you will see the two tourist bureaus and the two cheapest hotels, both of which have signs which require the aid of a telescope to be seen. The **Saronicos** (tel. 72 64 6), to the right of the Flying Dolphins hydrofoil office, has singles for 675dr, doubles for 878dr, and triples for 1215dr. The **Acropole** (tel. 72 21 9) has doubles for 1100dr and triples for 1700dr. (In season, they are booked months in advance.) One of the tourist bureaus, **Takis Travel Office,** to your left as you disembark (tel. 72 21 5 or 73 02 1), has 90% of the rooms in town at their disposal; that's 3,500 beds. Singles are virtually non-existent, and doubles go for about 800dr. Make sure you avoid the Takis tours of Spetsai, which cater to bibulous Brits. For a laugh you can peruse the pamphlet. Takis (the owner) is a wily shyster, but then he, not you, has masterminded a monopoly of beds on one of the Saronic Gulf Islands. His office is open 9am-1:30pm and 4:30-9pm. The **bank** and **OTE** are on Santou St., overlooking the water on the right side of the harbor. The bank's hours are Mon.-Fri. 8am-2pm; in summer they will also change money 6:30-8:30pm.

You'll find some good pensions along Botassi St. Doubles usually go for 600-750dr, although bargaining will substantially lower the rates in the off-season or if you're staying for more than one night. Sleeping on the beach, technically illegal, is common on Spetsai. There are two beaches near the port: **Agios Mamos** (the small town beach) and, twenty minutes further away, a larger beach near a pine forest. Across from the beach is the **Anargyrius and Korgialenios College** (we would call it a high school). John Fowles taught here and memorialized both the institution and the island in his novel *The Magus*. For a beautiful walk, especially at dusk, go left past Takis and continue along the stone path between the water and the high, whitewashed stone walls that could withstand any tidal wave. The old harbor, where your walk will lead you, is quieter and has fewer tourist shops than the new port—the higher prices show it.

On the rise above the town is a naval museum housed in the mansion of Hadjiyanni Mexi, the first Governor of Spetsai. It contains coins, ship's models, weapons and other memorabilia from Spetsai's past. It was closed for repairs in 1983 but may reopen by 1984. To find it, follow Hadjiyanni Mexi St. through several twists and turns until you see the signs pointing to the museum. The most heroic Spetsiot, however, was a woman named Lascarina Bouboulina, a captain in the Greek War of Independence. Says the historian Filimonas, she "put cowards to shame and brave men made way for her." Under Bouboulina's leadership, Spetsai was the first island to rebel against the Turks (April 3, 1821). **Bouboulina's house** is located near the **Dapia,** or pebble square.

Food and Nightlife

The cheapest (and one of the best) restaurants is **Stelios,** along the wharf past Takis. A large English-speaking population livens up the evenings in Spetsai; the best place to dance is at the **Delfinia,** a very popular disco near the Rendezvous to the left along the wharf. **El Paginos** is a much quieter place for pizza, but the largest English-speaking contingent seems to migrate to the roof garden at the **Hotel Myrtoon.** Ask the bartender for a Metaxa and coke—that'll prove you know the secret ways of the islanders. If you wake up very hungry, the **Palm Tree Cafe** serves a full English breakfast for 180dr. For a worthwhile splurge, eat at the **Trechantiri** restaurant in the old harbor. Dinner will cost about 500dr but the dining area is on a rooftop overlooking the water. In Agia Marina, **Fever** is, according to natives, "a very special disco" and is next door to **Tzourtze's (George's) Bouzoukia.**

The best way to see Spetsai is by motorbike (or bicycle, if you're hardy enough), and there are bike shops to the left of the harbor, past Takis. With your wheels you can ride to Spetsai's four excellent beaches: **Agia Paraskevi** (the best), **Agia Marina** (the most crowded), **Zoghena** (somewhat rocky and reputed to have sea-urchins), and **Anargyri** (also great). A bus (35dr) usually leaves twice a day for Anargyri from the bus stop to the left of the harbor. A boat, the *Nautilus,* leaves the harbor once daily for Paraskevi and Anargyri (round trip 140dr). Since only registered cars are allowed on the island, the only other means of transportation are motorboats and horse-drawn carriages, which are expensive except for large groups.

A ferry runs back and forth between Spetsai and the town of **Kosta** on the Peloponnese (33dr), as do small boats (about 30dr); avoid the sea taxis, which cost 500dr. Kosta has the broadest sandy beach in the area and from there you can catch the bus to **Porto Heli,** which features a cemetery from the Classical period, or to **Kranidi** (30dr), where you may have to change buses for Epidavros and Nafplion (200dr). To find out when buses leave Kosta, call the bus station in Kranidi (tel. 21 21 8) or ask the tourist bureaus on Spetsai. Whether or not you know when the right bus leaves Kosta, do your waiting at Kosta: sometimes the boats won't leave Spetsai until they have enough people. The bus stop at Kosta is to the left of the boat landing, on the road between the hotel and the restaurant. Hydrofoils (931dr) run between Piraeus and Spetsai several times daily; one boat per day also makes the trek. Hydrofoils can also be taken to Nafplion, where buses can be caught to Athens. Other hydrofoil trips from Spetsai include Aegina (647dr), Methana (594dr), Poros (364dr), Hydra (296dr), Ermione (284dr), Porto Heli (167dr), Tolo and Nafplion (498dr each), Leonidio (326dr), Kyparissi (449dr), Monemvassia (795dr), and Kythira and Neapolis (1915dr each).

IONIAN ISLANDS

While other Greek islands have succumbed to the ravages of the rapidly expanding tourist industry, the Ionian Islands have retained a refreshingly untouched quality. This diverse group of islands has some of the finest beaches in Greece, and unmatched natural vistas. From the lush countryside of Corfu to the barren, rocky cliffs of Ithaca, each island has a different geography and a distinctive personality—each reacted in its own way to the invasions of Venetians, Turks, French, and English. Greener and less commercial than the Aegean islands, this archipelago possesses a unique blend of Byzantine tradition and Renaissance culture. From north to south the islands are: Corfu, Paxi, Lefkas, Ithaca, Cephalonia, and Zakinthos. The seventh island, Kythira, is located south of the Peloponnese, and is not related to the others geographically or historically.

As a rule, stay away from the main towns; they are normally packed with tourists. You need only take a bus or, better still, a moped to a village along the coast where you'll find paradisal stretches of sand, with much cheaper restaurants and accommodations all to yourself. Watch where the crowds are going and head in the opposite direction.

Most travelers come to the Ionians by ferry from Brindisi or other cities in southeastern Italy; regular boats sail between Corfu and Brindisi, Bari, Ancona, and Otranto. Several ferry lines link Corfu with the other Ionian islands. Boats leave daily for Paxos (274dr, two hours) and every other day for Ithaca and Cephalonia (620dr, six hours). Lefkas and Zakinthos, by contrast, are best reached from the mainland (Patras). Boats leave Corfu daily for Igoumenitsa and Patras. Finally, boats leave three times a week for Dubrovnik (2619dr, twelve hours). The New Port is thronged with agencies selling international tickets; the Old Port tends to sell tickets to the other Ionians. There are also airports on Corfu, Cephalonia, and Zakinthos.

Corfu (Kerkyra)

> There was an old man of Corfu,
> Who never knew what he should do,
> So he rushed up and down
> Till the sun made him brown,
> That bewildered old man of Corfu.
> —Edward Lear, *Views in the Seven Ionian Islands*

Corfu was once the Homeric isle of the Phaeacians, where King Alcinous reigned and Odysseus, shipwrecked, met the lovely Princess Nausicaa. Some locals claim it was also the magical isle conjured up by Shakespeare in *The Tempest*. Since ancient times Corfu has had a long history of being plundered, conquered, and occupied by foreign invaders. After its liberation from Venice in 1797, the island was ruled by the French under Napoleon, the Russians, the French again, and the English before becoming a part of Greece in 1863. In sharp contrast to the jagged landscape of mainland Greece, parts of the luxuriant countryside are more like an English country club than anything else, and the food exhibits a healthy Italian influence.

Sound wonderful? It certainly does to almost everyone who consults NTOG brochures. Unfortunately, to enjoy Corfu now is an exercise in tourist-dodging, for the island in innundated with visitors, some en route from Brindisi to the mainland, some in search of an idyllic retreat. Jampacked with British, German, and especially Scandinavian aliens, Corfu must be one of the few areas in Greece where nearly everyone you see is blond. More than that, prices are high, beaches are overcrowded, and pidgin English is its native tongue. The sad thing about Corfu is not only that it's being destroyed, but that it gives such willing assent to the act. The only place to escape this disaster is to head to the inland regions where (if you look hard enough) you'll still find traditional Greek culture. Elsewhere, Corfu may strike you as a prosaic island filled with gift shops, discos, fast food, and people wishing they were at Club Med.

Getting Around

Buses run frequently between Corfu Town and major points on the island (though fewer run in the afternoon and on Sundays), and no trip will cost you more than 100dr. Schedules for the main KTEL line are chalked up on a billboard outside the office in New Fortress Square in Corfu Town, from which the green and cream colored KTEL buses leave. Other (blue) buses, including buses to Kontokali (Youth Hostel) leave from around San Rocco Sq.— schedules are printed on the signs. To enjoy the view, get a seat on the right when traveling north, on the left when going south. The best and most popular way to see the island is on a moped: not only can you stop at any secluded beach you find, but driving the twisted mountain roads can be fun and the surrounding countryside is a feast for the eyes. If you've never ridden a moped before, be careful when making your selection: make sure the brakes work. Rental places are everywhere; you shouldn't pay more than 500dr a day for a moped, 800dr for a two-seater Vespa, or 1200dr for a small motorcycle. Gas costs about 1dr per kilometer. You are responsible for any damage incurred. If you want to rent a car, the going rate for a Ford Fiesta is 2100dr plus 13dr per kilometer (the first 100km free). In the off-season, the same car goes for 1750dr plus 11dr per kilometer. A van (nine person mini-bus) costs 3450dr a day, plus 33dr per kilometer (off-season 2850dr a day plus 30dr per kilometer). Prices exclude gas, the 18% tax, and full collision insurance. Many places automatically add a minimum kilometer charge, but you can avoid this and get unlimited mileage if you rent for two or three days. Hitching is another option, although be warned that there is no traffic off the main roads. Confine thumbing to early morning or late afternoon; roads are deserted from 2-5pm (closing hours for most stores).

Corfu Town

The main town is the natural base for touring the island; all ferries and most bus services originate here. Parts of the town are simply a jungle of rooms to let, boats to catch, scooters to hire, and pizzas to go—everyone in town seems to be an entrepreneur. But the *Spianada* (Esplanade) and the old town, especially the streets behind Arseniou St. (an area called Platia Kremasti), can provide an uncrowded respite. Visit the town's churches and palaces; notice how the improbable melange of Byzantine, Venetian, and Greek architecture is matched by the incongruities of the streets, where shirtless kids and bearded Orthodox priests freely mingle.

Orientation

Face it: you're going to keep getting lost for at least the first few days. Before long, you'll be cursing the Theotokis: four of Corfu's main streets are

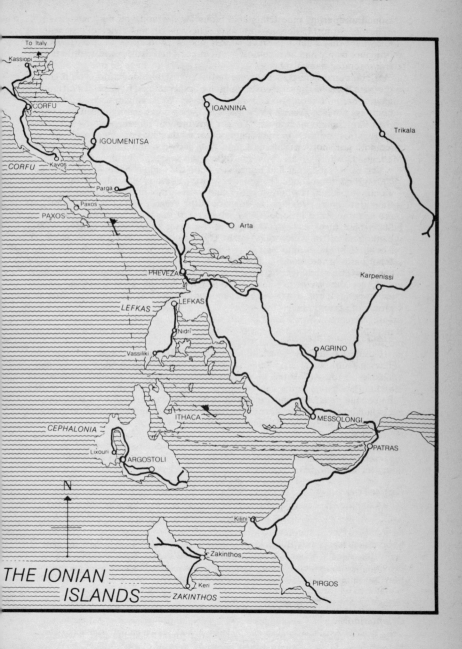

THE IONIAN
ISLANDS

named after members of this ubiquitous family, and you may pass from N. Theotoki St. to M. Theotoki St. to G. Theotoki St. to I. Theotoki St. without knowing what's hit you. The wisest policy is to bring a map (the Corfu brochure is free and available all over Greece); luckily, most main streets have transliterated names.

If you come here by ferry from Italy, Yugoslavia, or Patras, you'll land at the **New Port,** next to the customs house and crammed with places offering to let rooms, rent scooters, and store baggage. Walking along the quay, you'll first pass the **Neo Frourio** (New Fortress), then come upon the **Old Port** with a park-like Square next door. To get downtown, slip through **New Fortress Square** (just off the top right-hand corner of the Old Port Square as you face inland), turn left on Solomou, and then right on the small main street **N. Theotoki.** Alternatively, you can follow the sea, walking down **Arseniou St.,** which rounds a corner and brings you upon the famous **Spianade** (Esplanade). This grand promenade, ringed by smart cafes and graced with occasional games of cricket, is where scantily clad tourists and imperturbable locals strut their stuff every evening. On one side is the **Palace,** on the other, jutting into the sea, the **Paleo Frourio** (Old Fortress). Off the Esplanade runs **Voulgareos St.,** which turns into **G. Theotoki St.**—a main street which houses several banks and off of which the **Tourist Office** and **Post Office** can be found. G. Theotoki St. leads into **San Rocco Square,** from which blue buses leave for other parts of the island, and from here, I. Theotoki St. will take you back to the New Port. Practice the circuit once and you'll have the town mastered.

If you come by plane, you'll have to hope that the Olympic Airways buses are running. If not, a taxi will cost 400dr and a walk will take thirty minutes and plenty of perseverance.

Practical Information

Business hours on the island are normally Mon., Wed., and Sat. 8am-2pm; Tues., Thurs., and Fri. 8:30-1:30pm and 5-8pm (5:30-8:30pm in summer). Thanks to tourists, some shops and banks are open on Sundays and late at night. Public restrooms can be found on the harbor at the Old Port, on the Esplanade near the bandstand, and in San Rocco Sq. Pick up a free copy of *Corfu News:* apart from chronicling the doings (and undoings) of British expatriates, it has lots of good information in English.

National Tourist Organization of Greece (NTOG): Diekitiriou St. (tel. 39 73 0). To get there, turn off G. Theotoki St. into Dessila St.; it's just a block and a half from San Rocco Sq. Friendly, crowded, and filled with brochures, maps of Greece, and schedules of special events, this place is a treasure house of information. Ask for the free pamphlet, *The Mythos Guide to Corfu 1984.* The board outside has a complete list of accommodations, a boat timetable, and a map. Open May 15-Oct. 15 Mon.-Fri. 7am-2:30pm and 6-8pm, Sat. 9am-noon. Off-season open Mon.-Fri. only 7:30am-3pm.

Tourist Police: 31 Arseniou St. (tel. 30 26 5). Open every day 7am-10pm and until midnight in high season. Complete lists of hotels and bus schedules. They'll give you names of private houses with rooms, but may be reluctant to call on your behalf. A good place for leaving messages for friends.

Currency Exchange: The four main banks are on G. Theotoki St. near where it narrows and becomes Voulgareos. They are open Mon.-Fri. 8am-2pm; the National Banks may also be open 5:30-7:30pm during high season, and the Ionian Bank at Akadimias Square may be open in high season on Sat. 9am-noon. The lines are enormous in most of these places; in mid-morning, it may take 45 minutes to change money. The change window at the Port Customs house is also open weekends 9-11am. You can usually change money at the airport every day until 3 or 4pm. If you end up desperate for funds, any of the tourist agencies near the Old Port will bargain, and many hotels are authorized to change money. Their rates are about 10% lower than the official rate.

Post Office: In the same building as the Tourist Office. Open Mon.-Fri. at 7:30am; stamp windows and Poste Restante close at 8:30pm, parcels abroad window at 2:30pm.

OTE: The main office is around the corner from the post office at 9 Matzarou St. Open Mon.-Fri. 24 hours and Sat.-Sun. 8am-10pm. A smaller office at 78 Kapodistriou St. is open 8am-10pm. No collect calls on weekends. Also at the OTE office are the blue pages, and English telephone directory.

Olympic Airways Office: 20 Kapodistriou St. (tel. 38 69 4; airport 30 18 0). Office open Mon.-Fri. 7:30am-10pm, terminal usually 24 hours.

Bus stations: KTEL office in New Fortress Square; other buses leave from San Rocco Sq. Tickets for island destinations can be bought on the bus; all others must be purchased in the office. (Buses leave three times a day for Athens and three times a week for Thessaloniki.) English spoken at the KTEL office. A good place to leave luggage—no lockers, but safe. Open 5:30am-8pm.

Boat Agencies: Any agency should be able to direct you to the place which carries the ticket you want. **Hellenic Mediterranean Lines** are at 74 Xen. Stratigou St. (tel. 39 74 7 or 31 56 9), opposite the New Port; **Ionian Lines** are at #76, **Epirus** at #50, and **Mancan Travel** (for trips to Yugoslavia) at #38. **Tourinvest**, at 12 Kapodistriou St., runs one-day excursions to Paxos (leaving at 9am, returning 7pm; 1400dr) three times a week. **Vikentios Manessis Travel** (tel. 32 66 4 or 36 93 5), also opposite the New Port, is the agent for **Jadrolinija-Rijeka Lines** and offers a 10% reduction and a free ticket to the leader of a group of twenty. A real go-getter could earn a free trip to Italy or Yugoslavia. **Adriatica Lines** has regular trips to Brindisi. Always check the taxes that are (or are not) included, and remember that you must buy a ticket for a specific time and place.

Emergency: tel. 100.

Hospital: Polihroni Kostanda (tel. 30 06 2).

Car Rental: International at Greek Skies, 20 Kapodistriou St. (tel. 33 41) offers the best prices. **Just Rent-a-Car** at 34 Xen. Stratigou (tel. 32 20 4) is reliable and also rents scooters. Replacement service for breakdowns with no extra charge. Minimum age 23 (25 for vans), but they'll sometimes drop it to 21. Full payment in advance or major credit card required.

Boat Rental: Zodia Water Club, New Port (tel. 39 94 8). 3000dr a day (2400 off-season) for a 10-horsepower Evinrude (4000dr for a 20-horsepower). Gas not included. Minimum age 27; 6000dr deposit or credit card required.

Luggage Deposit: Upstairs at 130 Anrami St. opposite the New Port charges 40dr a day (open 6:30am-9pm). Lots of places are nearby on I. Theotoki St. Otherwise, just use the KTEL bus station in New Fortress Square.

English books: Most souvenir stands carry English best-sellers, as well as foreign magazines and newspapers. **Lycoudis** at 63 Voulgareos St. has the most comprehensive selection.

Telephone Code: 0663.

Accommodations

Prepare yourself for daylight—and nighttime—robbery. Although hotel prices are strictly regulated by the Tourist Office, proprietors in Corfu can find all kinds of cunning loopholes: obligatory breakfasts, freely interpreted high season rates, etc. Believing that two beds are better (or more lucrative) than one, hotel managers tend to fill their rooms with camp beds, which they then offer as dorm accommodations at the same price as singles cost elsewhere in Greece. Solo travelers may well be grateful for the system, since singles are impossible to find (the alternative is accepting a double and trying to bargain). Also be advised that hotels near the water fill up most quickly and the morning hordes from Brindisi arrive at 7am. Bargaining power diminishes as the night wears on, and if you carry a backpack. If arriving late from elsewhere in Greece, try reserving by phone; a two-minute phone call from Athens is less than 100dr. The only good news is that prices decline by perhaps 100dr per person off season, and if you're planning a prolonged stay, it's not hard to negotiate lower long-term rates in the small pensions.

As you disembark the ferries you will undoubtedly find yourself beleaguered by throngs of hotel grapplers and women offering you rooms in their homes. You can often find a clean, conveniently located room at a rate considerably cheaper than a hotel, but agree on a price before you leave the dock area. Otherwise, you may end up paying exorbitant sums in some remote part of the island.

Hotel Europe, 10 Gitsiali St. (tel. 39 30 4). Small rooms in a central location. Crafty management, however, so establish a firm price for showers and breakfast. Doubles 630dr, triples 760dr.

Hotel Akropole, 3 Zavitsianou St. (tel. 39 56 9), on Old Port Sq. Friendly and slightly crazy proprietor speaks a little English. Clientele can be noisy, and beds uncomfortably hard. Some doubles on the top floor with a fantastic view for 900dr. Other doubles 840dr, shared rooms 450dr per bed. Less than lukewarm, handheld shower included.

Hotel Konstantinoupolis, 11 Zavitsianou St. (tel. 39 82 6), on Old Port Square. Rooms are smaller than in Akropole, but cleaner and better furnished. Ask for a room with a view—same price. Manager speaks English. Singles 550dr, doubles 900dr, shared rooms 400-450dr per bed. All prices include real live hot showers down the corridor.

Hotel Zorbas, Alykes Potamou St. (tel. 37 65 4). Not easy to find, and no prize, but quiet and clean with hot showers. A bargain, except in the middle of high season. Doubles 600dr, some triples 720dr.

Hotel Mitropolis, 14 Konstantinou St. (tel. 31 15 6). Konstantinou runs off the far left-hand corner of Old Port Sq.; the hotel is at the end of the street next to the church. Rooms are clean, well-furnished, and quiet, the beds are soft, and the proprietor is friendly. Singles 550dr, doubles 900dr; showers 70dr extra.

Hotel New York, 21 Ipapantes St. (tel. 39 92 2). On the left-hand side of Old Port Sq. as you face away from the water. Often full. More comfortable than the bleak exterior and grumpy proprietor (who speaks English) would suggest. Pleasant rooms with balconies. Singles 600dr, doubles 900dr, triples 1100dr.

Hotel Spilia, 2 Solomou St. (tel. 37 61 8). Solomou is the street opposite 121 N. Theotoki St., near the bus station. Cheap and dilapidated, you get only what you pay for. Doubles with shower 700dr, dorm beds 310dr. Showers included, but hot water extra.

Hotel Elpis, 4, 5H Parados N. Theotoki St. (tel. 37 65 4), in an alleyway opposite 128 N. Theotoki St., near St. Anthony's Church. Clean, quiet, and well-kept rooms. English spoken. Double beds only 615dr, but if pressed, they'll let you share for 280dr per person.

Hotel Kriti, 43 N. Theotoki (tel. 38 69 1). Very centrally located, but dingy and sometimes noisy. Doubles and triples (one big and one little bed) 700-900dr.

Hotel San Rocco, 10 I. Theotoki St. (tel. 36 64 0 or 30 15 0), off San Rocco Sq. The kitschy kittens on posters at the entrance are highly unpleasant. Comfortable TV lounge. English spoken. Rooms with twin beds 1000dr, including breakfast and shower. Longer stays or singles may be able to bargain.

Hotel Cyprus, 13 Agion Pateron (tel. 30 03 2). Turn right just after the National Bank on Voulgareos St. and follow the signs. A quiet location and very helpful proprietor help make up for the drab rooms and poor shower facilities. No singles; doubles 615dr, but prices come down for longer stays. Dorm rooms are 300dr per person with shower.

Room-finding Service: Agios Spuridon, 43 Arseniou St. (tel. 22 10 1). On the road following the sea between the Old Port and the old fortress. Double or twin rooms in nearby private houses are 600dr with bath (solos can talk this down to 400dr). Ask for a room with an ocean view. English spoken. Open every day 9am-noon and 4:30-7:30pm. The Tourist Police down the street also find rooms for similar prices, but not necessarily nearby and they probably won't phone for you.

IYHF Youth Hostel, 4½km north on the main road from the port (tel. 91 20 2). Take the #7 Dassia-Kontokali bus from the long side of San Rocco Sq. nearest the center of town. Ask the driver for the hostel; the bus goes by the gates (just after the turn-off for Paleokastritsa by the BP gas station). A taxi to the hostel is 175dr per carload plus 40dr per bag. Inconvenient location, crowded, rowdy, with cold showers and no toilet paper, this is the rock-bottom cheapest place to stay on the island. Crabby manager, but good, inexpensive restaurant on the grounds with dancing until midnight. Mini-market and scooter rental. Reception open 7am-noon and 6-9pm. IYHF card required. No curfew. 190dr per person. The office also serves the adjacent **Camping Kontokali** with tents under shady olive groves for 120dr per tent and 120dr per person. Ask at the NTOG office for a complete list of campgrounds.

The **Nikos Pension** (tel. 94 28 7) operates an unofficial youth hostel in Pelekas on a hill above the beach. Take bus #11 to Pelekas Beach from San Rocco Sq. 350dr per person, including breakfast.

Food and Nightlife

The best area to find restaurants is around N. Theotoki St. near Old Fort Square; lunch is served at outdoor tables until 3pm, dinner until 11pm. The **Dionysus** at 17 D. Dona, in an alleyway opposite 150 N. Theotoki, is perhaps the best, although the *moussaka* (145dr) and stuffed tomatoes (110dr) tend to be oily. Their Greek salad at 100dr is very tasty. The service and the food at **Korakinites,** 1, 5H Parodos N. Theotoki, the next alleyway down, are both less appealing but still good. At **To Nautikon,** 150 N. Theotoki, the waiters are surly, but the food is delicious and the prices are reasonable. A new restaurant called **Edem** (around the corner from the bus station on Solomou) lacks atmosphere with its artless Burger King decor, but don't let the plastic façade fool you: it offers bona fide Greek specialties at cut-rate prices. Try the rice and tomato-cheese casserole (60dr). The owners are amiable, keep late hours, and will change money if you eat there. Your other option is to pay for the romance and coolness by the sea: **Pizza Mouragia** at 21 Arseniou St. has overpriced pizza for 200-330dr and is open until 1am; **Pizza Pete** next door is virtually identical, but claims that it has the only fresh and homemade pizza around. You may be better off eating cheaply and then having an after dinner drink at one of the places next to the Old Fortress (like the **Acteon**), which also over-look the sea and are full of locals.

In the evenings, it seems as if almost everyone on the island parades up and down the Esplanade and the adjacent park. As you approach the bandstand and Rotunda, you'll come across more and more Greeks and fewer bronzed Swedes. Buy a bag of popcorn here, then install yourself at one of the cafes by the park and watch the show. Look but don't eat: the food on this street is incredibly overpriced.

It's best to avoid discos like **Studio 54** (every sign in town seems to point you there). These joints charge 300-400dr entrance fee, which only includes the first drink. The **Mermaid Bar,** 9 Ag. Pontou St. (starting behind the Esplanade, just before Voulgareos) is cozier, and also open until 2am. There are two **bouzouki** clubs, both on the road leading north out of town. They're expensive, but they provide a traditional Greek evening with *syrtaki* dancing. Plate smash-ing is encouraged (of course, you have to pay for them).

Every morning you'll find a large open-air **market** on Dessila St., near the base of the New Fortress. Some stalls stay open all afternoon, but it's best to arrive early in the morning, around 7:30am. The **Supermarket Avenes** on Sol-omou St., near the bus station, has everything you could ask for, including huge sugar doughnuts for 15dr. Open Mon., Wed., Sat. 8am-1:30pm, Tues., Thurs. and Fri. 5:30-8:30pm as well.

Sights

The most imposing site in town is the **Old Fortress** (Paleo Frourio), a huge relic of Venetian rule, located west of the Esplanade, that commands regal views of coastline and town. The fortress is open daily 8am-7pm, but every night from June 15-Sept. 15 it hosts a **Folk Dancing** and **Sound and Light Show.** The dancing begins at 9pm, followed by the 45-minute Sound and Light Show at 9:30pm. Admission to the shows is 200dr (100dr for students); Sound and Light only is 150dr (70dr for students). The spectacle is in English every night except Sunday, when it is in French. The dancing, accompanied by guitarists crooning "Never on Sunday," is similar to the shows arranged by enterprising cafe owners; alas, the dancers seem more amused than the audience. The Sound and Light Show is also a joke, except for the heavily breathing woman moaning "Kerkyra, Kerkyra." You'd be wiser spending your time swimming off the rocks near the fortress.

At the northern end of the Esplanade is the **Palace of St. Michael and St. George.** Unmistakably English, the palace was originally built as the residence for the British Lord High Commissioner and was later used for the Ionian Parliament. Now part of it is a **museum of Asiatic Art,** which includes snuff bottles, tobacco pouches, hideous Noh masks, and Samurai trappings, as well as more familiar Japanese screens, Indian and Nepalese sculptures, and ceramics. Another wing displays mosaics from the early Christian basilica in Paleopolis and some fifteenth-century paintings. It's open daily except Tues. 9am-3pm, Sun. 10am-2pm; admission 45dr, 15dr for students.

At the waterfront south of the Esplanade (at 5 Vraila St.) is an **Archeological Museum** which contains some impressive ancient sculptures found on the island. Of all Corfu's churches, the most beautiful is **St. Spiridon,** built be-tween 1589 and 1596 and named after the island's patron saint. To get to the church, turn off Kapodistriou St. onto Spiridonos St. or follow its bell tower and cherry red roof. The rococo church is so cluttered with silver chandeliers and medieval paintings that it looks as if it will sink under the weight of its holdings. It houses a spectacular icon screen and St. Spirodon himself—his embalmed body stands upright in a glass-topped reliquary (coffin) through which you can see his raisin face. He doesn't look too bad, considering he's been dead over fifteen hundred years. His body is paraded around the town four times a year during festival celebrations: Palm Sunday, the Saturday before Orthodox Easter, August 11, and the first Sunday in November. More than half the men on the island are called Spyros in his honor. The **Greek Orthodox Cathedral of Corfu,** dedicated to St. Theodora Augusta, contains the remains of her headless body. It is a block up from the Old Port off Filelinon St.

About 2km out of the center of Corfu's port, **Mon Repos** overlooks the blue waters of the Ionian Sea. The **Royal Villa** is the summmer residence of Greece's former imperial rulers and the site of a public beach. Four kilometers south of Mon Repos, at the tip of the short peninsula jutting southward from the port, is **Kanoni,** where there is a French gun emplacement. From Kanoni you can take a ferry (40dr) to the small islands of **Vlakerena** and **Pondikonissi** (Mouse Isle). Vlakerena is barely big enough for the one church and solitary cypress tree it holds; Pondikonissi isn't even big enough for a church—there is only a small chapel and a few trees. According to Homer, Pondikonissi is the fabled ship which took Odysseus back to Ithaca and was turned to stone by Poseidon when it returned to the Phaeacians. Poseidon was pissed because Odysseus had blinded the Cyclops Polyphemus, Poseidon's son. You can walk to Kanoni, or take bus #2 from the Esplanade (one leaves every half hour).

Southern Corfu

The trip down the southern coast covers some of Corfu's most striking scenery. The renowned **Achilleion Palace** stands 9km south of the port of Corfu in the village of Gastouri. Overbearing and ostentatious, it was commissioned by Empress Elizabeth of Austria for a summer residence and later bought by Kaiser Wilhelm II of Germany. He was responsible for the inscription on the statue of Achilles that reads "to the greatest of Greeks from the greatest of Germans." The gardens are especially wonderful—you may recognize the entire scene from the James Bond flick *For Your Eyes Only,* filmed here. To get there, take bus #10 from San Rocco Sq. (one leaves every three hours and takes thirty minutes). The mansion is open Mon.-Sat. 8am-7pm, Sun. 9am-5pm; admission 50dr. The Palace was a casino at night, but the new German company which owns Achilleion is currently renovating the gambling salons. While at the Palace, do what most tourists don't—visit the intriguing little village of **Gastouri**.

Further south is the crowded, nouveau-chic former fishing village of **Benitses** (take bus #6 from San Rocco Square). Still further south is **Messonghi** (45 mins., 60dr; twelve buses daily from New Fortress Square). The beach here isn't bad—there aren't pebbles at least—but it's best to steal through the spacious lawns of the Messonghi Beach Hotel and recline under a straw parasol. **Kavos** is at the southern tip of the island, 47km from Corfu Town (twelve buses daily leave from New Fortress Square). The beach is pleasant enough, but the water's very shallow.

Without a doubt, the most deserted spots on the island are along the shores of the southwestern tip, in part because few roads go there. You can go to **Spartera, Perivoli,** or **Kritika** by bus, leaving Corfu at 5pm and returning to Corfu at 6am the following morning.

Northern Corfu

The first 20km of the coastline north of Corfu have been ruined by the tourist industry. The resort towns of **Dassia, Ipsos,** and **Pyrgi** (twelve buses daily from New Fortress Square, 30dr) consist of a long string of hotels, nightclubs, and boutiques. Dassia is perhaps best seen as a daytrip. The scenic beach offers the best views for parakiting (900dr, 1500dr for two). With a parachute strapped to your back, you zoom two hundred feet in the air for a glide over the ocean as the boat takes off. Ipsos has the best campground, right across the street from the main stretch of beach. **Wooden Pier Camping** charges 120dr each per person, per tent, and per car, plus 5% tax. 50dr for a scooter. If you're looking for nightlife and a chance to practice European languages, head to any of these cities. For less spoiled and more aesthetically appealing country, go further north.

You can take buses all the way to **Kassiopi** and **Sidari** (eight times daily from New Fortress Square, trip takes one hour and costs 80dr). Stopping at towns along the way is complicated and inconvenient; rent a moped instead. The views on the coast road after Pyrgi are breathtaking: on one side of the road, massive mountains rise three thousand feet; on the other, steep cliffs shoot down to the rocky coast. Be extremely careful of buses or trucks coming around the blind curves. The highway winds its way past a pleasant beach at **Nissaki** and the most secluded sandy beach on the northeastern part of the island at **Koulora,** which is described in Lawrence Durrell's book, *Prospero's Cell*. This part of the highway also features the best view of the Albanian coast available anywhere, only two miles away from Corfu at the closest point.

Although more and more tourists (especially British) have found it out, **Kassiopi** remains one of Corfu's most idyllic spots—visitors come here for a quick look and end up staying a month. It's not hard to understand why. The people are friendly, accommodations are all clean, and, especially during the off-season, the rates are reasonable. If you plan to spend a lot of time on Corfu, spend it here.

Kassiopi was founded in 300 B.C. by Pyrrhus of Epirus. Its main attraction is the incredible rock beach that stretches along the coast for several kilometers to the east of the little town; follow the dirt path that starts on the left-hand side of the harbor as you face the water all the way to the Kassiopi Peninsula. For a cheap thrill, try parakiting here. It costs 900dr; both Leo's Ski School and Spiros Boats leave right from the beach. More sedentary attractions include the ruins of a ninth-century fortress overlooking the rock beach, destroyed by the Venetians in 1836, and the **Panagia Kassiotropi** church, which contains stark seventeenth-century frescoes.

You will see many "rooms to let" places as you come into town. Prices are reasonable everywhere, so you might as well stay near the water (for all practical purposes, however, singles do not exist). In high season, the pension most likely to have space is the **Ta Dixtya,** on the left-hand side of the harbor as you face the water. Doubles are 800dr—large, well-furnished, they come with their own bathroom and shower. The telephone here (81 20 9) is the only one in town. Maria Sarakinou, the proprietor, can also find you a room if hers are all filled. For July and August phone ahead. The food at Ta Dixtya, while not full meals—mostly salads and pizza—is ample and cheap.

If you continue from the Ta Dixtya down the dirt path to the end of the road, you will come to the **Villa Irini,** where doubles with balconies overlooking the water are only 600dr. On the right-hand end of the harbor, the **Vraicha Taverna** is also very nice; if you stay for several nights, doubles go down to 400dr (but it's almost always full in high season). As for food, remember that although prices are regulated, quantity is not. Most places near the harbor are exorbitant; instead, try near the bus stop. The best food and the most generous portions are served at Restaurant **Da Franco** (Italian cuisine). The supermarket on the harbor stays open until 10pm in the summer.

For nightlife try **Kassiopi by Night,** a disco-bar built around the oldest olive-press in the region. It's a ten-minute walk south on the left-hand side of the road. (Open Mon.-Fri. 9:30pm-2am, Sat. until 3am.) The **Kan-Kan Bouzouki Club** is just down the road.

To get farther off the beaten track, explore some of the mountain villages in the northern part of the island. A bus from Kassiopi occasionally runs to the village of Loutses. On the way, the bus passes the little hamlet of Perithia, near **Mt. Pantokrator,** Corfu's highest peak at almost three thousand feet. If you have a moped, the trip from Kassiopi to Paleokastritsa on the western coast is a very good way to see the rugged, spectacular interior. Above all, have a good map; not even the local police seem able to give accurate directions. Gas stations in this area are few and far between (dangerous, since most mopeds have no gas gauges). The station nearest Paleokastritsa is 15km back towards Corfu Town on the main road.

Following the main road north from Kassiopi (winding up and down mountain roads), you begn to head west to the beach resorts of **Roda** and **Sidari.** These two beaches are the best sand beaches on the islands, with sparkling clean water. From the two towns it is possible to hire a motorboat for a daytrip to the tiny islands of **Othoni, Erikoussa,** and **Mathraki.** These three islands are the northernmost points in Greece in the Ionian Sea and are completely untouristed; they're inhabited only by farmers and fishermen.

Western Corfu

For beautiful beaches, lots of young people, and a dazzling jagged coastline, come to the western coast of Corfu. **Paleokastritsa** ("Old Castle" in Greek) is carved into a bay amidst some of the loveliest scenery in Greece. The main road into town winds past several spectacular bays, with small coves and sea caves that jut into the headlands. Swimming here is surreal; the crystal water dazzles you with infinite gradations of turquoise and blue. As you come into the main beach in town, walk up the winding road to the thirteenth-century fort of **Angelokastro** (there is a natural balcony called **Bella Vista** half way up). Jutting out over the sea is the chaste white **Panagia Theotokos Monastery.** The place radiates serenity (even the chapel is restrained and free of the gilded chaos of most Greek churches) and gazes majestically over the sea in every direction. Be sure to come as early as possible; in the daytime it is one jangled mess of cameras and tour buses. Also be warned that you cannot enter in your bathing suit.

Beauty has its price, however. Paleokastritsa is easily the most chic spot on Corfu and charges outrageously. The best way to see this haunt of the rich is by daytrip. Buses leave from Corfu Town six times a day from New Fortress Square (60dr) and take about 45 minutes. The only place to stay within budget range is **Paleokastritsa Camping** (tel. 41 20 4), about 3km from town on the main road from Corfu Town. Tents 120dr, 120dr per person, open mid-May-Oct.

The food situation is not much better. **Le Pirate** offers good food for a little less than its neighbors. Appropriately named, it's only slightly cheaper than the others; they're all pirates. Although the supermarket (as you come into town, on the right a few hundred yards before you hit the main beach) has rip-off prices on tourist items, it sells basics like bread, cheese, and salami. There are numerous other beaches and resort towns along the western coast. To the north of Paleokastritsa, you will find the somewhat overrated resort town of Sidari, featuring striking beaches and rock formations.

South of Paleokastritsa is **Pelekas**, a popular hilltop village with the best panorama of the island. Eight buses a day leave from San Rocco Sq. (40dr, twenty minutes). From Pelekas, it's less than a half-hour walk to **Glyfada Beach**, especially beautiful at sunset (six buses a day travel directly from New Fortress Sq.). Glyfada has become the main haunt of the young and is certainly one of Corfu's best beaches; you can stay here, but unless you're successful at bargaining, you'll have to pay 2500dr for a single.

At night those with terpsichorean tendencies should go to the **Top Sail Night Club** (in the Glyfada Grand Hotel) for good tunes and Greek music. This is a good place to learn the *syrtaki*. (Open Mon., Wed., Fri. 9pm-1am; no cover, but proper dress required.)

A little north of Glyfada and accessible by a dirt path off the main road are the isolated beaches of **Moni Myrtidon** and **Myrtiotissa**, which Lawrence Durrell called the most beautiful in the world. A section of the beach at Myrtiotissa is the island's nudist beach and often has volleyball and other group activities. If the net is not up, ask the taverna owner and organize a group.

Everything here is very casual, although once in a while the local monks complain to the Police, who reluctantly bring offenders to court. Clear-sighted judges usually let them off scot-free. Perhaps the most beautiful, and probably the most crowded, of the sandy beaches is **Agios Gordis**. Buses leave three times a day for Agios Gordis from New Fortress Square. Not to be confused with Agios Gordis is the long remote sandy beach of **Agios Georgios** at the southwestern edge of the island (two buses daily come here from New Fortress Square).

Paxos (Paxi)

Just five miles long, the tiny island of Paxos can be reached by boat from Corfu (900dr, three hours) and Parga (400dr, 1½ hours). During the off-season boats are cheaper, but run less frequently—only once or twice a week. This is an island on which there is absolutely no sign of visitor exploitation. Choose your own strip of beach and swim in solitude or go to one of the sea caves and swim with the seals. Be careful: the seals sometimes play rough.

Upon reaching Paxos, all boats sail through a narrow channel to the picturesque little harbor of **Gaios**, the island's main village. There are no hotels, but you can find rooms to rent. (Singles be warned: on Paxos the charge is always per room, not per person.) Clean rooms go for 800-1000dr including shower. The islanders are tolerant of freelance campers. Ask permission first if you're near someone's house, otherwise head for the beach.

You can walk over the whole island in just a few hours, winding along dirt paths that go to and from the beach through olive groves. One road leads to the even smaller port of **Lakka**, where you'll find a deserted sandy beach. The **Byzantine Church** in Lakka has some unusual Russian bells that the locals are quite proud of. Ask them to ring the bells and watch them beam. On the south side of the island is the islet of **Mogonissi**, connected to Paxos by a private caique run by the restaurant owner. Every night he ferries visitors and locals over to dinner. Prices are pretty much the same in all tavernas on Paxos, but you'll get ample servings here instead of the Lilliputian portions elsewhere.

On the west coast are the **Mousmouli Cliffs** and the **Seven Sea Caves**. According to Homer one of the caves, Ipapando, was Poseidon's Cave, with walls of glittering gold. **Panayia**, an islet on the east coast, features a religious shrine honoring the Virgin Mary, and, on the Feast of the Assumption (August 15), visitors from other islands and the mainland crowd together to make a pilgrimage. Drinking, dancing, and general merry-making go on all night in the square at Gaios. Just off the south coast of Paxos is the satellite island **Andipaxos** (Andipaxi), whose population consists of only 56 families. Here you'll find a few small vineyards and sand beaches, and no tourists.

Trips and daytrips to Paxos can be made from Corfu at **Corfu Sun Club**, 45-49 Arseniou St. (tel. 33 85 5), near the Tourist Police, and from Parga at **Parga Tours** on the waterfront (tel. 31 58 0).

Lefkas (Lefkada)

Only a narrow canal (75ft) separates Lefkas from the mainland, leaving the island peculiarly vulnerable to those tourist invasions that become the welfare, and the downfall, of many Greek islands. Sure enough, once you've crossed the channel (via a bizarre ferry that never seems to move) and taken the causeway into Lefkas Town, you're greeted by a familiar pastiche of movie posters, unclad women, and signs in English. But, unlike its northern Ionian neighbor, commercialism only affects the main town; walk a few steps off the beaten track and you can have peaceful beauty all to yourself.

Thucydides wrote that Lefkas was a part of the mainland in 427 B.C. and that the island's inhabitants had separated themselves by digging a canal. Octavian (Caesar Augustus) built a new canal when the old one had filled up—the same one is reputedly used today, having been maintained by the Venetians, the French, and the English.

Thanks to an unusual raft that is pulled back and forth across the canal with chains and pulleys, Lefkas is quickly and easily reached by bus. The crossing itself takes only three minutes, but in the height of the season you're likely to wait thirty minutes or more for your turn to cross. From Patras (leaving the small Favierou St. "station") the trip takes four and a half hours and leaves at 6:15am daily, for 420dr. There are also three buses daily from Athens (six hours, 910dr). Buses leave Athens at 7am, 1pm, and 9pm. Buses leave Lefkas for Athens and Patras (same bus 420dr to Patras, 910dr to Athens) at 8:30am, 9:30am, and 12:30pm. Last year, in July and August, Ionian Lines ran boats from Vathi in Ithaca to Nidri three days a week for 600dr. This year the times and dates will almost certainly be different, so check with the Ionian Lines agent for the new schedule. From Vassiliki the town Fiscardo on Cephalonia is agonizingly close (26km), but we've never seen a ferry. You might try asking, since rumor has it that they run sporadically in high season. You can always hire a fishing boat to make the crossing for 2800dr. Since the alternative route to Cephalonia means taking the bus to Patras and the ferry from there (four and a half hours, 420dr to Patras, and another four hours and 510dr on the ferry), even a group of three people will save money and enormous amounts of time on a fishing boat. You can bargain with the fishermen as there are no set prices. There are also excursion boats to Ithaca and Fiscardo from Nidri, leaving daily at 8:30am and returning at 8:30pm.

Lefkas Town is an amalgamation of poor dusty houses and plush gleaming tourist facilities. As you come off the causeway onto the street that runs along the waterfront, the first little alleyway going inland (Dairpfeld St.) will take you to the main drag. Going past the little cafe on the corner, at 4 Dairpfeld St. you'll find the immaculate and centrally located **Hotel Byzantion** (tel. 22 62 9). The proprietor's son John speaks some English and will let a single room for 550dr and a double for 750dr, with showers for 70dr. Much cheaper is the seedy and dilapidated **Hotel Averof**, at #40 (a block past the Byzantion, also on the right). There is no sign outside, but just push open the door and go upstairs to the second floor office. Singles 300dr, doubles 450dr, and triples 560dr. Across the street in the plain white building is a great restaurant run by George Logothetis, boasting the cheapest beer in town.

If you continue down Dairpfeld, you'll soon reach the town's main square on your left, where you'll find the **Banque Nationale de Grece,** open Mon.-Thurs. 8am-2pm, Fri. 7:45am-2pm. Continue straight, and the street becomes Siratigou loan Mela St. At #183 is the **Post Office** open Mon.-Fri. 7:30am-4pm (parcels till 2:30pm). Also off Siratigou St. is the **Police Station** (upstairs on the side street Mitopoulos, but you can see the emblem from Siratigou), tel. 22 34 6. Siratigou St. eventually brings you to a church with a clock in an unusual metal tower; make a sharp left at the next street and you'll arrive at the bus station. Buses to Athens run three times daily (910dr), to Patras three times daily (420dr), to Preveza four times daily (50dr), to Nidri seven times daily with returns a half hour later (40dr), and to Vassiliki three times daily (90dr).

For really cheap food try **MacDonut's** in the square. Appropriately named, the decor is an eclectic blend with all the charm of MacDonald's and Dunkin Donuts, but they serve low-priced hot dogs and hamburgers. For more Greek fare, **El Greco's** (near the Hotel Byzantion) has *pita souvlaki* for 31dr.

The **telephone code** for Lefkas is 0645.

While Lefkas Town has no beach, the northern half of the west coast offers miles of deserted white pebbles and clean water (rent a moped to get there—the going rate is 1000dr per day). The best stretch is north of **Agios Nikitas.** Buses leave from Lefkas Town to Agios Nikitas three times a day; unfortunately they turn around upon arrival (but there are rooms to rent in the town).

Much of the interior of Lefkas is austere and barren, but the eastern coast is dotted with orange and olive groves. Seventeen kilometers south of Lefkas Town is the beautifully situated town of **Nidri** (seven buses daily to and from Lefkas Town, 40dr). Many "rooms to let" are scattered along the main street running parallel to the water. Moreover, the view of the mainland from Nidri is wonderful. Numerous little islands, accessible by local ferry, punctuate the strait separating the two. From here you can glimpse **Scorpios,** the private island of shipping magnate Christina Onassis. You can hire a small boat (1200dr) to take you around the manicured terrain of this standoffish retreat. Although the private guards will not allow boats to come too close, you can see the spectacular dock, the tennis courts, Christina Beach, and the elaborate burial vault of Aristotle Onassis.

Three kilometers south of Nidri on the main road is **Vliho,** a quaint village in the midst of wild flowers and cypress trees. As you get off the bus, you'll see "rooms to let" signs. Further on, at the top of the hill, is a small, secluded, sandy beach. Continuing south, the tranquil town of **Vassiliki** (three buses daily, 90dr), at the southern tip of the island, is certainly far from the maddening crowd. Set on a cove with a pebble (though somewhat littered) beach and turquoise water, the pace of life here is very easygoing; many people sit for days watching the fishermen fix their nets, or reading in the town cafes. There are no hotels, but you'll see rooms to let in nearly every house. Ask the owner of the cafe at #6 on the extreme left-hand side of the harbor as you face the water; she has some very nice doubles with balconies for 800dr. The cafe right in the center of town, where the bus stops, has cheaper (though less amenable) rooms.

The **Pisitaria** restaurant serves excellent, inexpensive food (except for the seafood, which is characteristically outrageous)—*souvlaki* costs only 31dr on a stick. The tiny **Post Office** branch is open Mon.-Fri. 8am-2pm; there is no money exchange, so be sure to bring enough from Lefkas Town.

At the southernmost tip of the island there is a lighthouse built on the site of the Temple of Lefkadas Apollo. It was here from the two hundred foot high cliffs that the ancient poetess Sappho leapt to her death when Phaon rejected her love. The cliff is called "Sappho's Leap," and is known in Lefkas as *"Kavos tis Kiras."* In the worship connected with Apollo, evil was driven out with an annual sacrifice. An evil person (usually a criminal or a retarded person thought to be possessed) was thrown into the sea from the cliffs. Live birds were tied to his arms and legs with the intention that their wings would lighten this fall. There were boats below that would take survivors (or what was left of them) away to where they and their evil could do no harm.

Cephalonia (Kefallinia)

The largest of the Ionian Islands, Cephalonia is not exactly on everybody's itinerary. All the better—in the height of the season you'll see almost no tourists. The island's west and east coasts are for the most part steep and rocky; most of the sandy beaches are on the south coast. The interior is very mountainous, some parts are relatively lush and almost completely deserted. The island is sometimes referred to as the "Ireland of Greece," both for its location and for the temperament of its inhabitants. Famous as feisty adventurers, they trace their lineage back to Odysseus.

According to scholars, the name of the island is derived from the Cephallenes, who were a people from Western Greece who settled here. According to mythology the name comes from the hero Cephalus who came to the island from Attica. Arkesius, son of Cephalus, married Halkomedussa who gave birth to Laertes, who married Antiklea and fathered Odysseus. According to the *Iliad,* Odysseus was accompanied by "huge Cephallenes" in twelve ships.

In summer, **Ionian Lines** boats link Sami and Patras daily with no stopovers, leaving at 9am (four hours, 510dr), and leaving Sami each afternoon for Ithaca at 5:30pm (one and a half hours, 206dr). Boats leave Ithaca for Sami daily at 7am (also one and a half hours, 206dr). Boats from Brindisi also stop here every other day in summer on their way from Corfu to Patras (Brindisi to Sami takes about sixteen hours and costs 2900dr, 2700dr off-season, for deck space—less with Eurail or InterRail cards). Ask at the Ionian Lines office for specific information to make connections from Sami to Fiscardo (at the northern tip of the island), Ithaca, Lefkas, Paxos, and Corfu. If you've got more money than time, you should ask about the three-hour hydrofoil from Patras to Cephalonia's main city of Argostoli (about 1500dr). In Patras, buy tickets for the regular boats at Tsimaras Agency, 12/14 Iroon Polytechniou St. (also called Othonas Amalias St.), tel. 27 77 83. The boats leave from the wharf right across the street.

Almost all boats deposit you in **Sami,** a town which is basically dull and dusty. As you leave the ferry, there is often a bus waiting to transport you instantly to Argostoli (these leave at 7:30am, 8:15am, 2:30pm, and 5:30pm daily; the trip takes an hour and costs 65dr). If not, you can either wait for the next connection—buses leave from the Ionion Cafe about fifty yards away from the port—or else try to relish the delights of Sami.

Two blocks from the ferry landing is the main square dominated by the Hotel Kyma. Just off the square, around the corner from the hotel, are **OTE** telephones (open Mon.-Fri. 7:30am-10pm, closed Saturday and Sunday). The street bearing right as you face Hotel Kyma, I. Metaxa, will take you to the

Post Office (open Mon.-Fri. 7:30am-2:30pm, closed Sat. and Sun.) and the **Police Station** (tel. 22 00 8); they speak no English and are open 7am-1:30pm, so try to arrange your crisis accordingly. The **bank** next to the cafe is open 8am-2pm, but Ionian Lines and the Balatta Travel Agency (at the opposite end of the quay) will also change a travelers check.

It's not hard to find rooms in Sami: the **Hotel Kyma** (tel. 22 06 4) in the main square is decent with singles for 495dr, doubles 630dr, triples 821dr, and showers for 60dr. If this is full, walk down I. Metaxa, take the first right, then the first left, walk past the old church ruins, and on your right will be the **Hotel Ionion** (tel. 22 03 5). This is an absolutely spotless hotel with singles for 650dr and doubles for 900dr. Showers are 70dr extra. If you're traveling off-season you may be able to get away with a little bargaining.

You can also let a room in a private home during July, August, and the first two weeks of September. Ekaterina Flamiatu (tel. 22 32 1) has rooms in her house for 300dr a single, 500dr a double, and 750dr a triple (50dr for a shower). To get there, turn left up the quay (as you face the water) and walk a quarter of a mile. Her house is 700 feet past the campground. It's the third house (looks like the second) and is white with green shutters. If you don't mind the goats, ask her about camping in the side lot.

Caravomilos Beach Camping (the aforementioned campground) is a rather smooth operation with the KOA motif: 300 organized sites with electrical current (for trailers), a 24-hour snack bar, a restaurant, a disco, and a self-service market. 120dr per person and 120dr per tent (100dr off-season) is the fee with showers included, no charge for the dishwashing and laundry facilities. Valetas is building a beach across from the entrance near the huge sand and gravel piles, but it's not likely to be finished before the summer of 1984, although you can swim here. Scooters, canoes, windsurfing, and water-skiing are all available through the campground (tel. 22 48 0).

Two places near Sami which are easy to reach are the spectacular stalactite and stalagmite cave-lakes of **Melissani** and **Drograti**. The first is the better of the two, and can be reached by foot in half an hour from Sami. Follow I. Metaxa, and turn right at the sign for Ag. Efimia. Follow the signs and, soon after the village of Caravomilos, you're there. A nicer shortcut is to walk along the sea past the campsites, crawling over the sand and rock piles for the new beach, till you come to a cafe situated five feet from the surf. Turn left here to the main road, and a left soon thereafter will get you to Melissani (open all day; 50dr). If you're lazy, take the Fiscardo bus at 1:30pm and ask to be let off at Melissani. At the lake a guide will take you in a rowboat to glide around two large caverns pockmarked with lichen-covered stalactites. Drograti is 4km from Sami and can be reached by walking inland along the Argostoli Road (also open all day; admission 40dr).

While staying in Sami, you could also travel 10km north to the other end of the bay here you'll find the pretty little harbor **Ag. Ephimia.** The only difficulty about visiting this town is transportation: the Fiscardo bus will drop you off here for 65dr (leaving Sami at 1:30pm), but the bus back to Sami is at 7am. Either stay in Ag. Ephimia overnight, take a taxi (400dr for a carload), or attempt the long walk. In Sami, you can hire bicycles or scooters.

Sami's greatest drawback is that it is linked with virtually nowhere by bus; even getting to the nearby villages on the east coast, such as Poros, is almost impossible. A preferable base for exploring the island's smaller, more remote villages is the modern capital of **Argostoli.** Buses leave the Ionian Cafe in Sami for the 24km ride over the mountains at 7am, 8am, and 5:30pm. (Buses to Sami from Argostoli leave the bus station in Argostoli at 7:45am, noon, 1pm, and 3pm. One-way fare is 65dr.) In Argostoli you can leave your luggage free at the bus station 7am-8pm; no lockers, but safe. As you leave the bus station go right (as you face the water), and past the fruit market you'll find a great restaurant called **Estiatorion E. Kalaphate.** For 180dr you can try one of the regional specialties, *stephado,* made of stewed rabbid (or sometimes veal), onions, and tomatoes. Inhabitants of Sami sometimes journey to Argostoli just to eat here.

Cutting inland from the restaurant and turning right on the second street will put you on D. Konstantinou, the city's main drag. You'll soon pass the **Post Office** on your right (open Mon.-Fri. 7:30am-4pm, parcels till 2:30pm); two blocks later, on the corner of Ithakes St., across the street from the Orthodox church, you'll find **Petratos,** an excellent shop for foreign newspapers and magazines. One more block will take you to a square. The plain white building in front of you is the Archaeological Museum; bear left down R. Vergote, and two blocks down, where it meets Zerbou, is the splendid **Cargialenios Library,** housing the Historical and Cultural Museum. If you continue down the main street which becomes Vallianou, you'll soon reach the Platia I. Metaxa, Argostoli's central square, and on your left, the very helpful **Greek Tourist Office** (open Mon.-Fri. 8am-3pm, tel. 22 84 7). Ask for the large pink pamphlet containing invaluable information about the town and the island, including a ferry schedule. They can also help you find a room in a private home. The **Tourist Police** along the waterfront (tel. 22 20 0) is open every day 7am-1:30pm.

For accommodations the small **Dido** (22 31 7) near the main square has singles for 770dr and doubles for 1000dr. It's a bit sleazy, as could be guessed from its obvious nickname. At the same prices for more spacious rooms is the **Allegro** (tel. 22 26 8) on Vergote St. near the bus station. In the off-season, some hard bargaining could halve these prices.

The two local museums could not be more different: the modern, well-organized **Archeological Museum** is elegant but lacks any outstanding artifacts. By contrast, the **Historical and Cultural Museum,** housed in the Cargialenios Library, is chock full of knick-knacks, personal effects, and other household belongings from the nineteenth century. Argostoli's French coffee cups, English top hats, antique dolls, and written accounts of the town by visiting Englishmen all fashion a picture of confident and careful luxury. Best of all are the photographs which give a visual record of Argostoli during the last century, including the huge earthquake of 1953 and the ensuing reconstruction. Both the Archeological Museum and the Historical and Cultural Museum were closed for repairs in 1983 following a slight earth tremor which upset many of the delicate displays. They may reopen by June 1984.

The Venetian **Castle of St. George** is 9km southeast of Argostoli on a hill overlooking the village of Travliata. It's ten minutes away by scooter taking the road to Skala and going right (uphill) when the road splits. Open Mon.-Fri. 8:30am-2:45pm (closed Tuesday), and occasional Sundays 9am-2pm. From the battlements you can view the same panorama that inspired Lord Byron in the 1820s.

There are several options for exploring the other towns on the island. Boats leave eight times daily for **Lixouri,** a pretty town in the center of the western peninsula (half an hour, 55dr). Lixouri was the home of the satiric poet Lascaratos. Here you'll find miles of beautiful coastline practically untouched by tourists. You can rent a moped near the bus station at M. Pephonis, 32 Siteborn St. in Lixouri. Most places are accessible by bus, however—just be sure to check the return times. For more information on the sporadic bus service call KTEL at tel. 22 27 6 or 22 28 1, or pick up a schedule from them.

If the bus schedule does not appeal to you, consider renting a car with a group. **Express Rent-a-Car** at 4 P. Valianou St. near the main square in Argostoli (tel. 22 38 8/ 23 01 4) rents Ford Escorts for 3000dr a day (2500dr in the off-season) with all taxes, insurance, and unlimited mileage, which is reasonable if the cost is split between three or four people. You can also rent a scooter here for 800dr a day.

There are several beaches on the coast south of Argostoli. One of the best is at **Ormos Lourda** (accessible by bus). Buses also go regularly to Platos Gialos. You can visit one of Lord Byron's hometowns—though his house no longer exists—at Metaxata, or see Kourkoumelata, a village completely restored after the earthquake by a Greek tycoon. Poros, on the east coast, is a town much like Argostoli but with a beach, and there are many rooms available in private houses. Buses run four times daily from Argostoli, taking one and a half hours and costing 80dr.

The northern coast of Cephalonia is quite barren, but blessed with spectacular views. There is a beautiful but empty beach at **Myrtos**—you won't believe the white sand and the color of the water. To get here, take the bus just past Deivarata and walk down about 4km from the main road. Continuing up the coast, you'll pass the little and still unspoiled port of Assos, joined by a narrow isthmus to an island with a Venetian fortress (one unhelpful bus daily from Argostoli, leaving around noon and returning the next morning). Continuing to the northern tip of the peninsula brings you to Fiscardo, the only town on the island not damaged by the 1953 earthquake. This tiny fishing village, with its eighteenth- and nineteenth-century two-story houses, has been declared an historical site and is ready to be devoured by tourists. There is an old ruined church here that many believe is eleventh-century Norman. Fiscardo is named after the Norman Robert Guiscard, who conquered the town, as well as Sicily, and died here in 1085. It's already acquired a certain worldly chic. If you come here, you must eat at the **Erodotos restaurant,** which many believe serves some of the finest Greek food in the world. Try the aubergines, chicken, or fish salad; it's all quite inexpensive. Next door is an unusually fine ceramics shop. Buses leave Argostoli for Fiscardo several times a day (120dr).

If you're on Cephalonia in August there is an unusual festival in the village of **Markopoulo** to celebrate the Assumption of the Blessed Virgin Mary (August 15). During the celebration hundreds of small harmless snakes with black crosses on their heads appear and mysteriously vanish again until the next year's celebration. Also that night is the Eve of Agios Gerassimos' Day, and you can climb up to Omala and attend a village festival and all-night vigil in the saint's church.

Ithaca (Ithaki)

It's hard to believe that this small, steep, and rocky island was the legendary home of perhaps the greatest hero of classical antiquity. Indeed, inhabitants of other Ionian islands are constantly advancing claims that Odysseus was from their island, and there is no solid evidence for any alternative theory; out of respect for tradition we must suppose this is the place. Still, classicists on a pilgrimage will not be the only ones attracted to Ithaca's unspoiled and untouristed scenery. Although there is little to do on Ithaca, it's a wonderful place for doing little—and you'll notice that most of the visitors here, regardless of nationality and age, are unorthodox, informed, adventuresome, and drawn to the place for compelling and sophisticated reasons. Getting here is easier than it was for Odysseus, although not by much. (See the Lefkas and Cephalonia section above for complete ferry information).

Vathi (the name means "deep") is the main port and the largest city on the island (pop. 2500). This is not the location of Odysseus' palace (the site is further to the north), but the setting is beautiful: the town forms a horseshoe around the edge of a long, natural harbor and is almost completely surrounded by mountains. The **Ionian Lines** office (opposite the ferry landing) is open whenever boats come in and during high season keeps somewhat regular hours (Mon.-Sat. 6:30am-11pm with a long, irregular siesta in the afternoon, Sun. 10am-1pm; tel. 32 14 5). The owner, Mr. Dellaportas, bills the office as a Tourist Information Center—a euphemism for a center of information where you can spend your money, so that he will pull in a hefty commission. If you don't like his prices, go around the corner, on the waterfront, to the more reliable **Polyctor Tours** (tel. 33 12 0 and 33 13 0). These agencies will help you find acommodations, but you can ask around town on your own for a *domatio ftino* (cheap room in a private home). Unfortunately, the official hotels are expensive. **Hotel Odysseus** (tel. 32 38 1) is considered cheap wiuth singles for 720dr, doubles for 1152dr and showers 100dr extra, so a domatio hunt is a good idea. There is a **pension** at 158 Nostou St. (from the ferry cut inland and turn left onto Odysseus St.; Nostou St. will be on your right) which charges 650dr for a double but is usually full. If you're traveling off-season or phone ahead for a reservation (tel. 32 32 8) you'll probably get a spot.

Almost every shop in town is along the waterfront. The major spots of importance are at the far right-hand corner of the horseshoe as you face the town: one block in is the **National Bank,** open Mon.-Thurs. 8am-2pm, and Fri. 7:45am-2pm. The **Post Office** is upstairs in the building behind the bank and open 8am-3pm (closed Saturday and Sunday). On the other side of the street are the OTE telephones and a bookstore selling English language magazines and paperbacks. You'll see a dozen "Scooter for Rent" signs with mopeds going for around 1000dr a day including a full tank of gas. You can also rent a sailboat for 1000dr a day, or a small motorboat for 1000-1200dr a day without gas. Bargain furiously, especially off-season, as no prices are fixed and modern Ithacans are just as wily as their most illustrious native son.

All of the cafes and restaurants near the ferry are expensive—you pay for the convenient location and the atmosphere. If you walk about a mile, however, to the deserted side of the harbor (opposite the ferry landing), you'll find **To Paliokaravo,** which serves pleasant food in a very quiet location beside the sea. There are two slightly cheaper taverns a little further along the road.

Though the town's spectacular setting forms its main attraction, there are some interesting sites, such as the Byzantine icons in the **Cathedral.** Those with poetic imaginations and sturdy walking shoes will want to climb up to the "Cave of the Naiads" where, so it is said, Odysseus hid the treasure he had been given by the Phaeacians as soon as he returned to Ithaca. To reach the cave, walk southwest down the road on the left-hand side of the harbor as you face the water, then turn left up the hill to *Marmarospilia* (Marble Cave). The climb takes about half an hour. Be sure to bring a flaslight or you'll only see the entrance. If you're in Vathi during late August or early September, ask about the Greek Music and Theater Festival that takes place here.

Amazingly, the loveliness of Vathi's location is matched by the breathtaking beauty of Ithaca's other towns. The usual "around-the-island" circuit is from Vathi to Stravos, Frikes, Kioni, and back again. If you don't have a moped, in the high season you can take a boat from Vathi to Kioni, leaving twice daily in each direction and costing 150dr. Your best alternative, however, is to use the buses. They leave Platsia Drakoule, along Vathi's waterfront, at 7am, 8am, 9am, and 2:30pm, and return from Kioni at 10am and 3:30pm. As you crawl towards Stavros—through the neck of the island—you can see stunning turquoise bays on one side and wide expanses of sea, with the shores of Cephalonia in the misty distance, on the other. At Stavros itself (45 minutes, 80dr) Homeric enthusiasts should ask for the village's schoolteacher: he has the key to a small museum at the alleged site of Odysseus' Palace, reached by walking for about ten minutes out of town, along the left-hand fork. Walking back into Stavros, a pleasant thirty-minute stroll through deserted olive groves will take you to the tiny tranquil village of **Frikes.** If you wish to stay here, there are several houses with rooms to let for around 400dr. Whether you got out of the bus at Stavros or not, you should definitely get out at Frikes; the forty-five minute walk from here to **Kioni** takes you along the sea past a dizzying succession of bays, little coves, and small pebble beaches, all of them empty and washed by a beautifully clean turquoise sea. Kioni itself is charming, but larger and more touristed than Frikes. While you're here ask around for a bakery or taverna that has *ravani,* a dessert specialty found in Ithaca, made of honey, sugar and rice.

Zakinthos (Zante)

Zakinthos is a tidy, tame, and well-behaved island full of respectable, middle-aged (and middle-class) tourists. Although the northeastern half of the island is mountainous and inhospitable, the rest of Zakinthos is gentle, fertile, and overwhelmingly green.

To get to Zakinthos by boat, most people take the ferry from Killini (in the Peloponnese), which leaves seven times a day in summer. Deck fare is 250dr, and boats run only three times a day in winter. (See Killini section).

All boats arrive in **Zante,** the island's main town. As you leave the dock, you will see a large, stately plaza, lined with palm trees and large buildings. If you walk along Dimokratias St., you will soon come to the **OTE** (open daily 6am-midnight). Walking toward the center of the waterfront from the plaza you'll find the **Tourist Police** (tel. 22 55 0), open daily 8am-2pm and 4:30-9pm. Although the employees are gruff, they'll grudgingly help you find a room. On the street just before the Police are the **Post Office** (open Mon.-Fri. 7:30am-4pm, parcels till 2:30pm) and several banks (open Mon.-Fri. 8am-2pm). If you walk a few blocks further down the waterfront and turn right just before the Fina Station, you'll find the **bus station** on Philita St. (three buses to Athens each day). Safari, on Ethnikis Anistaseos St. just off Dimokratias St., makes renting a moped here completely worthwhile by charging only 300dr for a full 24 hours of use. The **hospital** can be reached by calling 22 51 4. If you want your clothes washed, go to **To Magikon laundry** on Foskolou St., to the left off Ioan Filioti St., up from the water. The **telephone code** for Zakinthos is 0695.

If you want to stay in Zante, try the **Hotel Rezenta** 36 Alex. Roma St. (tel. 22 37 5), the third street parallel to the waterfront. Singles 500dr, doubles 675dr; showers 50dr extra. Off-season prices are 50dr lower per person. The friendly proprietor speaks no English, but the facilities are clean. Down the street at 18 Alex. Roma, the **Ionion Hotel** (tel. 22 51 1) charges similar prices, but make sure you ask to see a few rooms before you commit yourself; the manager sometimes tries to stick unsuspecting customers in windowless rooms. The **Hotel Kentrikon,** 25 L. Zoi St. (one street closer to the water than Alex. Roma; tel. 22 37 4) offers unprepossessing accommodations for similar prices. The **Hotel Alfa,** 1 Tertseti St. (tel. 22 41 1), one road farther from the water than Alex. Roma, again has similar rates but slightly more comfortable rooms.

Most people tend to stay outside Zante Town and nearer to the beaches. Every road on the island is plastered with signs advertising rooms to let and free camping. Your best strategy is either to take a room in town for a night while shopping around on a moped, or to ask informally at the bus station or at the Tourist Police. Even if you find a place a few kilometers from the center of Zante Town, buses are frequent and taxis inexpensive. A **Mr. Fotis Giatris** has doubles for 500dr a few kilometers from town and will come and collect you if you call (tel. 23 39 2). If you've brought a sleeping bag, head directly to the **Turtle Bay Club: Camp Dafni.** A sort of unofficial youth hostel with many friendly young people, this place offers sleeping under trees on a secluded bay for 70dr per person, and there is a tavern run by the owners that serves cheap Greek specialties (wine 60dr per liter). Since the spot is inaccessible by public road, look for the owners' blue jeep at the ferry land or go to the Snoopy Cafe on the waterfront. The owners are in town several times each day, usually to meet the ferries. At the camp you can rent windsurfers (250dr per hour) and scuba diving equipment. For 450dr, they will take you by motorboat to see some magnificent sea caves. Closer to Zante Town, yet still in a secluded area close to what may be called the best beach on the island, **Tsilivi Camping** (tel. 24 75 4) charges 120dr per tent and 130dr per person, and has a cafeteria and mini-market. It's probably too far to walk but you can be the judge of that if you buy the map of Zakinthos across from the Hotel Ionion for 50dr. In any case you should look for Tsilvi beach, which you can reach by taking a left onto the asphalt road skirting the shore (left as you face the water). Evening entertainment is available at the **Saturn Club,** a great outdoor discotheque with '60s music. It's about a mile out of Zante on the road to Vasilikos, but the Turtle Bay owners make frequent runs from the camp.

There's not a lot to see in Zante once you've exhausted the endless rows of souvenir shops lining the waterfront and the pleasant arcaded streets. At the church of **Agios Dionysus** (St. Denis) is a beautiful silver chest containing the saint's relics. In **Solomov Place** (near the ferry dock) is the town **museum,** housing icons from the "Ionian School" (referring to the distinctive local mixture of Byzantine and Renaissance styles). Open Mon.-Sat. 8:30am-2:45pm, Sun. 8am-1pm, closed Tues.; admission 50dr, 30dr for students. On the hill behind Zante Town are the ruins of the **Old Venetian Fortress** (follow the signs for Vohali). If you're lucky enough to be here during Easter, you can't miss a **Carnival** in which the locals express their religious joy by smashing plates. Even agnostics are tempted to join in.

The beaches in Zante Town suffered an oil spill some years ago; though the water is once again clean, the beach is scattered with annoying oil pellets. Most tourists flock to the beaches at **Laganas** but steer clear—they have been ruined by the large hotels, souvenir stands, and mobs of tourists. Instead if you can't make it to Tsilivi for some reason, head for the peninsula near the **Vasilikos,** which has relatively uncrowded beaches around **Porto Roma.** Buses leave from Zante Town daily at 8am and 1pm and return immediately. Take the early bus (or your moped) and go straight to the beach; the hordes don't begin to assemble until around 10am (buses take 30 minutes and cost 40dr).

The town of **Keri,** on the southwest tip of the island, is particularly worth a visit. There are two buses daily from Zante. The trip takes forty minutes and costs 45dr. The village itself is uncannily quiet and remarkably unvisited. Half the population sits in a tiny main square just waiting to chat with visitors. There's nothing else to do in Keri, except visit the Lighthouse which is twenty minutes away by boat (ask for the *pharo* and locals will point out the dirt road to you). The lighthouse itself is surprisingly modest, but allows you to peer 600 feet down to the waves below. You can stay in Keri for 300dr a night if you find the right person, or en route in **Limni Keriou** near the beach (doubles 450dr). In the far northern part of the island, the village of **Volimes** offers fine, handmade tapestries. Mopedallists should be warned that the road up the western coast is not nearly as good as it looks on the map. At the extreme northern tip are the **blue caves,** an interesting natural site. From Zante Town, buses leave at 5am and 1pm only two days a week (Wednesday and Saturday; buses return immediately) and deposit you in Korithi (100dr), where you can hire a boat to the caves, known as the "Spillia."

NORTHEASTERN ISLANDS

It is hard to generalize about the islands in the northeast Aegean, for no two are alike. From thickly wooded **Thassos** in the far north to rocky barren **Limnos** in the south, the geography of these islands varies tremendously. But they do have some things in common besides their location: by and large, each is breathtakingly beautiful, relatively inexpensive, and surprisingly untouristed.

For a number of reasons, the islands of **Lesvos, Chios,** and **Samos** could be grouped under a separate heading. They are all extremely close to Turkey (the ferry ride between them affords some beautiful views of the Turkish coast), which raises some sensitive political problems. Especially since the Turkish invasion of Cyprus, a great many Greek soldiers have been stationed on these three islands. The presence of the soldiers can make the situation somewhat uncomfortable for women traveling alone on the ferries and in the main towns.

Thassos

Some of the finest beaches in Greece gird the popular resort island of Thassos, just off the Macedonian coast. Quite a few tourists are here; most are Greek or German. But the number of beaches divided by the number of vacationers leaves plenty of lovely, uncrowded space. After you lounge on the beach, spend some time in the interior, with its lush pine-covered hills, mountainous terrain, and sparkling streams. Although the island lacks quaint seaside towns, it has some elegant and picturesque mountain villages.

Numerous ferries connect Thassos daily with both Kavala (year round) and Keramoti (summer only) on the mainland; see section on Kavala, above. It is not possible to continue from Thassos to the other islands of the northeastern Aegean, so ignore the boat route marked on most maps. You have to return to Kavala for other ferry connections.

Limenas

Limenas, also known as the town of Thassos, is the island's capital and serves as its tourist center. This lively port is crowded, and more expensive than the rest of the island. Stick around here for the nightlife, but not for scenery or quiet.

Practical Information and Accommodations

On the waterfront opposite the ferry are the **bus station** (also a cafe, next to the gas pumps) and, in a marble building, the very friendly **Tourist Police** (tel. 22 50 0), open 7:30am-2pm and 5-9pm, who can give you a map of the island, a list of hotels, and can arrange rental of private rooms from mid-May to mid-September anywhere on the island. Going rates are around 420dr for singles (which are rare), 600dr for doubles, plus 60-70dr for a shower. This is almost always a better bet than a hotel; during the off-season when rental of private rooms is illegal, you can usually get a good deal on one if you look discreetly on your own. Besides being the best place in town to eat cheaply, the **Asteria Restaurant,** run by Ioannou Skoudi on the main avenue, also lets out pleasant doubles for around 600dr.

The only inexpensive hotel is the **Astir,** on the waterfront between Hotel Angelika and Pizzeria Verona. Bare but clean; singles 600dr, doubles 850dr. You can lay out your sleeping bag on the town beach just south of the small-boat harbor; a tent might be too conspicuous.

Although you'll never see a street sign, the main street does have a name: 19th of October, in honor of Thassos's independence from Turkey in 1913. It's parallel to the waterfront street, one block in. Toward the small-boat harbor (usually called the Old Port) is the **OTE,** open Mon.-Fri. 7:30am-11pm, weekends 8:30am-3:10pm. Turn inland at Gregory's Gift Shop to find the **Post Office,** three blocks up; open Mon.-Fri. 7:30am-2:30pm. Gregory is very friendly, speaks English, and is a good source for all kinds of information. He also cashes traveler's checks until 10-11pm. Boats can be hired for fishing or excursions from **Georgios Salonikis** (tel. 23 73 4); look for his *Aristea* docked in the old port. The **telephone code** for Thassos is 0593.

Sights

No Greek island would be complete without some archeological find, and Thassos is no exception. The island's major attraction is the ancient theater built on the remains of the acropolis of ancient Thassos. The ruins are easy to find: turn right at the eastern end of the waterfront behind the old port and continue to a three-pronged fork in the road beyond a recessed ruin. The middle path quickly leads to a long stone staircase that ascends to a grove of aromatic pine trees shading the well-preserved theater. Four to eight performances of classical drama are shown here each year in July and August. (Cheap tickets are available at the NTOG in Kavala or on the waterfront in Limenas.) Admission to all of the archeological sites is free. The museum close to the Old Port contains a fine collection of mosaic floors and sculptures found on the site, including the *Kouros*—a colossal sixth-century B.C. marble statue of Apollo carrying a ram on his shoulder. The museum is open daily 8:30am-2pm, closed Tues.; admission 25dr, free on Sundays.

Near Limenas

Your first glimpse of the island may be the handful of drab, modern buildings at the port-town of **Skala Prinos.** This is really the least attractive spot on the island; there's no reason to stay here. Halfway between Prinos and Limenas is the beachfront campground at **Ioannidis Rahoni** (tel. 71 37 7). The charge is 140dr and 140dr more per tent, with showers and food stores nearby.

Eight and ten kilometers out of Limenas in the other direction are two charming villages, **Panagia** and **Potamia.** Prettier and more peaceful than either of the larger towns, these villages have better beaches and are choice locations in which to base yourself. In Panagia, a crystal-clear stream winds its way through the narrow stone streets and numerous old wooden mansions with their silver-gray slate rooftops down to the small square. Potamia's white-washed houses and brightly painted doorways are set in the green of pine trees and mulberry bushes. Both towns have rooms to let; Panagia also has an inexpensive hotel, the **Helvetia** (tel. 61 23 1), at the entrance into town. Double with bath 800dr, negotiable.

Three kilometers from Panagia, down by the water, runs the seemingly endless golden sand beach **Chrisi Ammoudia;** there is plenty of room for camping here, but little real privacy. The official camping area (140dr per person; 140dr per tent) has a decent food store, and unguarded showers. Potamia's beach is not as nice, but does have plenty of rooms to let right on the water. Either of these beaches surpasses Limenas's own **Glyfada** or **Makriammos,** the most popular, most expensive, and least recommended of all the beaches on the island.

Limenaria

Limenaria is prettier and quieter than its sound-alike cousin to the north, but it has its share of tourists. Twelve daily buses connect the two towns. Finding a private room here should be no problem—there are "Domatio" signs all over town. The least expensive hotel is the towering **Papangiorgiou** (tel. 51 20 5); singles with bath from 700dr, doubles from 850dr. On a cliff at the east end of town is an enormous, abandoned mansion with a commanding view of the waterfront. The small, pine-covered meadows around it are an inviting place to camp out; there's a fresh-water tap on the road leading down the hill to the main highway.

Near Limenaria

The pebble beach right in Limenari is nothing special, but there are good beaches all along the southwest coast. **Pefkari** and **Potos** are only 3km and 4km out of Limenaria. Maybe the best beach on the island is **Aliki,** with a wooded peninsula all its own. You won't lack company if you decide to camp in this idyllic setting, although it never seems to get over-crowded. The only restaurant here is a bit expensive, though there is drinking water nearby. Between here and Potos are four beach-strips generally neglected because of the height of the road above them and the hike necessary to reach them. The beach below the monastery 6km west of Aliki has the most dramatic setting in a slender valley with steep walls on either side.

While the beaches northwest of Limenaria are not very good, several towns have roads reaching inwards to the interior. With infrequent bus service, the mountain towns of **Maries** and **Theologos** are completely free of tourists, and in their lush setting well worth a half-day excursion.

Samothrace (Samothraki)

Although first settled in the seventh century B.C. by colonists from Samos, from whom it derives its name, Samothrace bears little resemblance to the lush, beautiful island to the south. In ancient times, this small, mountainous island was a popular destination for religious pilgrimages as tens of thouands came to the celebrated Mysteries, a secretive sacred ritual initiation rite similar to the one practiced at Eleusis. Today, a mere three thousand people make their home in Samothrace, and it is seldom visited by any type of tourist, religious or not. While excavations have uncovered the famous sanctuary where the ceremonies were held, they are hardly extensive enough to warrant a visit. It is rather the island's untouched natural beauty and its unspoiled village life which make Samothrace an increasingly unique and attractive place to visit, especially in a country so tarnished by tourists.

When you arrive at the island's only port, **Kamariotissa,** you should probably board one of the two buses which will be waiting at the dock. One bus heads southeast to the town of **Lakoma;** the other heads around the north coast of the island as far as Loutra but first climbs inland to the town of Samothrace (also known as Chora). Cradled in mountainside, **Chora** is a charming village, untouched by any outside influences. In fact, its original settlers chose this inaccessible spot five hundred years ago because of the protection it offered against the pirates who repeatedly ravaged the island. Up on the left from where the bus stops you'll see a **pension** (tel. 41 27 0) where singles cost 400dr and doubles, 600dr. Other "domatia" are available as the road curls up to the left, passing the island's only **bank, OTE** (open Mon.-Fri. 7:30am-2:30pm) and **Post Office** (open Mon.-Fri. 7:30am-2:30pm). At the top of the road near the ruins of a small Byzantine fort are the island's only **Tourist Police,** almost always available but not too helpful. From the bottom of the village, a scenic road leads over the pass and a pleasant twenty-minute walk to the tiny town of **Alonia.**

Another road on the far side of the fort leads about 6km down to **Paleopolis,** which is on the bus-route to Loutra. The site of the cult of the Great Gods, or the *Megaloi Theoi,* the ruins here are accompanied by an interesting museum that houses, among the relics, a replica of the *Victory of Samothrace,* which the French took long ago to display at the Louvre in Paris. The museum and the sites are open Tues.-Sat. 8am-7pm, Sun. 10am-6:30pm; admission for the museum is 50dr, the sites are free.

The steep pebble beach at **Kamariotissa** extends past Paleopolis, with several unattractive "domatio" in the port and the **Kaviro** (singles 400dr, doubles 600dr) standing by itself at the base of the road to the museum. The island's best beach, **Pahia Ammos** (literally "large sound"), is a 5km walk southeast of **Lakoma.** Those who feel the urge may want to head inland to tackle the highest peak in the Aegean, **Mt. Ferrangi** (1600m). You should be warned, however, that the five-hour hike from Therma is quite difficult.

The ferryboat *Saos* provides year-round daily service between the mainland port Alexandropouli and Samothrace (one-way fare is 343dr). **Nikos Miliades** runs one boat a week to Samothrace from Kavala (4hrs., 623dr).

Limnos

With a small number of good beaches, the large, rocky island of Limnos is an excellent place for a quiet and scenic vacation. Since few tourists make it here you'll have no problem immersing yourself in the indigenous Greek culture.

The main port of **Mirina** is a charming collection of weather-beaten, white-washed cubical houses completely free of any oversized hotels or resort complexes. A peaceful strip of sandy beach extends along the waterfront; turreted towers of a Venetian fortress peek out from behind the convoluted volcanic rock formations that overlook the town. To complete the scene, old wooden fishing boats huddle together in the cozy inner harbor, protected from the open sea by a white stone breakwater.

As you walk down the pier from the point of disembarkation, on the left side you'll see one of the cheapest hotels in Mirina, the **Aktarion,** 2 Arvanitaki St. (tel. 22 25 8). Singles go for about 600dr, doubles 800dr, and triples 900dr, depending upon the season (high season is July 1-Sept. 15). The **Thraki,** at 23 28th Oktovriou St. (tel. 22 61 7), has similar prices. Both hotels tack on a 10% surcharge if you stay less than three nights. If these places are full, there is a **Tourist Police** in Mirina, but they're not much help and are located quite a distance from the port area. It's best to bargain furiously with the locals who will meet you at the pier. Prices will initially be exorbitant but the lack of tourists and the good humor of Mirina's inhabitants should bring rates down to about 400dr for a single and 600dr for a double.

To get to the center of Mirina, walk to the far side of the pier and head diagonally left up the winding street. 150m down, in the Square, you'll see the **National Bank of Greece** (open Mon.-Fri. 8am-2pm) and the OTE. (The **Post Office** is on the waterfront, open Mon.-Fri. 7:20am-2:30pm). Mirina's cathedral and its archeological museum are both nearby and, although not spectacular, are worth seeing.

There is no public transportation on Limnos, and hitching is difficult due to the lack of automobiles. Fortunately, this is not a problem since everything of interest is close to Mirina. For a great beach, try walking southeast of Mirina

2.5km to **Plati.** Another 4km farther south will bring you to a more spacious beach at **Thanous,** with a taverna where you can satisfy your thirst.

If you make a day's excursion from Mirina, though, you'll find Limnos quite beautiful. The island's livelihood comes from its interior rather than from the sea. Besides Mirina and a couple of other towns, its villages tend to be oases of trees with fields of hay, tobacco, and other crops checkerboarded around them. You'll be the only traveler to pass through in a while wherever you go, so take advantage of the opportunity to explore. Further from the Mirina, toward the eastern end of the island are the beautiful villages of **Atsiki, Kotsinas, Kondopouli,** and **Repanidi. Moudros,** Limnos' other large town, is only moderately attractive, and has a large military compound.

Transportation

Nikos Miliades runs four boats a week to Limnos from Kavala (5 hrs., 684dr), two of which continue on to Lesvos (Mitilini). The same boat also makes infrequent trips between Limnos and Kimi on Evia. The *Alkeos* travels all year between Piraeus-Chios-Lesvos-Limnos and returns along the same route except for a brief stop in Kavala. A third ship connects Limnos with Thessaloniki and Lesvos once a week, in July and August.

Lesvos (Lesbos)

Lesvos, Greece's fourth largest island, is doubly blessed: not only are the natives friendly and solicitous, but the countryside is as beautiful as it is diverse, from rugged mountain terrain to thick groves of olive trees and lush agricultural fields. An increasing number of tourists now come here, but as yet, no crowds; Lesvos still feels much less touristy than many of its neighbors to the south and west.

Legend has it that the population of Lesvos was once entirely female, but there is little evidence to support the claim. Perhaps the notion owes its origin to the decision of the Athenian Assembly in 428 B.C. to punish the Lesbians for attempting rebellion by executing all adult males on the island. After some debate, however, the decision was reversed and the order was never carried out. Another reason for the legend might be that Lesbos was the home of several great female poets, including the celebrated Sappho (seventh century B.C.). In its time, Mitilini flourished as an important center of Greek culture; its inhabitants would have been astonished to know that later millennia would consider fifth-century Athens to be the summit of Greek civilization. Sappho's poems influenced generations of the greatest Greek lyricists.

Later the island was again a great center, this time of Hellenistic culture. It was especially famed for its Philosophical Academy where Aristotle and Epicurus taught. Turks ruled the island for almost five hundred years until, in 1923, it became part of modern Greece.

Transportation

Lesvos is serviced all year long from the three major mainland ports: six times per week to and from Piraeus (13 hrs.); two or three times per week to and from Kavala (12 hrs.); and once a week to and from Thessaloniki (13 hrs.). During the summer, six boats per week connect Lesvos with Chios (5 hrs.). You can also get to Turkey from Lesvos (or Lesvos from Turkey; 2½ hrs.): boats leave three or four times a week May-Oct.; schedule varies. The Turkish port town is Ayvalik; fare is 1500dr one-way, 2500dr round-trip. Should you want to fly, Olympic has daily connections to Thessaloniki (with the exception of Sunday) for 3200dr and to Athens for 1950dr.

Getting Around

The **bus station** in Mitilini is at the corner of Smyrnis and Leoforos Sts., one block up from Konstantinoupoleos Square at the southern edge of the harbor. Buses leave frequently for points all over the island, but on Sundays there is only minimal bus service. Travelers to the northern and western parts of the island must head first for Kalloni, 40km from Mitilini, where the road splits three ways. Drivers or hitchers should follow Zoodochos Pigis St., an extension of the street with the Post Office, out of town until it turns into the highway to Kalloni. The hitching is excellent on Lesvos as long as you stick to well-traveled roads.

Since you always have to return to Kalloni and wait for another bus, it's difficult to see a lot of the island in a short time. Every three doors along the harbor is a travel agency offering a solution—one-day round-trip excursions to different parts of the island. All begin at 9am; fares vary from 300 to 600dr depending on the route but not, in general, on the agency.

Mitilini

Your first glimpse of Lesvos will be the bustling main port city of Mitilini (pop. 16,000), in particular the massive grey walls of the fourteenth-century Genoese Fortress. A block up to your right as you disembark are the **Tourist Police** (no exact hours; generally Mon.-Fri. 8am-2pm and 6-8pm, weekends 8am-noon) who can direct you to one of the many pensions, the best alternative for accommodations. Prices average 400dr per single, 600dr per double, including bath. As a last resort, the least expensive hotel is the **Megali Vrentannia**, in the same building as the Ionian and Popular Bank of Greece, with doubles for 750dr.

The main shopping street, **Ermou Street,** runs parallel to the waterfront one block in. If you follow it south and turn right on Vournazon St. you'll find the **Post Office** open for most services from 7:30am-3pm. A little further on, make a left at the end of the park and you'll run into the **Bus Station.** There are a couple of banks on the waterfront for changing money; all close at 2pm. The **telephone code** for Lesvos is 0251.

Behind the enormous Baroque Church of **St. Therapon** on Ermou St. is a lovely **museum of Byzantine church art,** including a spellbinding portrait of Christ from the fourteenth century and an almost angry Virgin Mary from the seventeenth. (Such stern-faced representations of Christ as *Pantocrator*—ruler of all—are found in every Orthodox church.) Open daily 9am-12:30pm and 4:30-8pm, closed Tues.; admission 25dr. The Church itself is grand if not extraordinary. The **Archeological Museum** near the main pier contains findings from around the island; open daily 8:30am-2:30pm, closed Tues. Otherwise there is little worth seeing in Mitilini; the town is perhaps at its most pleasant in the evening, when the modern buildings don't look so drab and you can sit in one of the waterfront cafes watching the evening promenade *(volta)* and the lights shimmering on the harbor waters.

Near Mitilini

Several excursions are possible from Mitilini; none is particularly exciting. Six kilometers to the north you will find a well-preserved Roman aqueduct at **Moria.** If you continue north another kilometer you'll come to the spa resort of **Thermi** which features thermal springs and one E-class hotel. The village of **Varia,** 3km to the south, has the **Theophilos Museum,** with its collection of works by the famous folk painter. (In the Byzantine museum, you can see a few of his works to decide if you're enticed.) Varia also offers the remains of a

Turkish aqueduct. Finally, a deserted, sandy beach can be found 13km south of Mitilini at **Agios Ermogenis.**

Molyvos (Mithimna)

On the northern coast of Lesvos the town of Molyvos has followed Sappho's dictum:

> *She who wears flowers*
> *attracts the happy*
> *Graces: they turn*
> *back from a bare head.*
> (Sappho, No. 19, translated by Mary Barnard; Berkeley, 1965.)

Leafy vines and fragrant flowers peek out of every corner of the stone passageways, and the main shopping street, **17th of November St.,** is a tunnel of grapevines and flowers. Although many tourists wisely choose to base themselves here rather than in Mitilini, there are no large hotels, and the number of souvenir shops has been kept under control.

In the summer, there are four buses daily between Molyvos and Mitilini; on Sundays and in the winter, two a day. The two-hour ride costs 120dr. You can rent a moped for 600dr per day, 300dr after 1pm, at the base of 17th of November St. This is the best way to explore the island, especially the western half.

The two hotels in town are both overpriced. Fortunately, the **Tourist Office** (on the left as you come into town) can direct you to lots of rooms to let; going rates are 450dr per single, 650dr per double, including bath. If the office is closed, ask anyone for suggestions; if you are here in the height of high season, late July through mid-August, try to look early in the morning.

Molyvos is best suited for strolling and swimming. You could enjoy a full day just exploring the town and its magnificent Genoese Fortress presiding over the straits between Lesvos and the startlingly close Turkish coast. The fortress and the higher sections of Molyvos give a gorgeous view of the area. As for swimming: the crowded pebble beach just in front of the town is less attractive than either the pebble beach to the south or the sand beach to the north.

Near Molyvos

Seven kilometers south of Molyvos, **Petra** has all the elements of the prototypical, remote coastal village: a large church, the eighteenth-century **Church of the Holy Virgin,** which dominates the village from a large rock in its center; and a delightful waterfront covered with bright flowers, small cafes, and topped off by a wide, pebble beach over a mile long. So if Molyvos doesn't fit the bill, Petra will.

There are two roads that lead from Mitilini to Molyvos and Petra. By far the more scenic is the coastal route. There are no noteworthy beaches along this strip of coast, but the scenery is spectacular. This road also goes through the pleasant village of **Madamados,** 38km north of Mitilini, where an eighteenth-century church houses a famous icon of the Archangel Michael. If you don't have a car and still want to enjoy the scenery, buses leave from Mitilini for Madamados three times a day, but there is often no public transportation from there to Molyvos. The quickest route to Petra and Molyvos is the island road via Kalloni. Don't be confused by the poorly marked intersection past Kalloni—the righthand fork leads to Molyvos.

Plomari

Plomari, 42km from Mitilini on the southeastern coast of the island, is an earthier, more modest, and less polished version of Molyvos, with the same quaint old houses and infectiously cheerful atmosphere. The town is best suited for strolling along its narrow alleys and steep street-stairways full of delightful scenes: you'll find cats sunning themselves, chickens pecking the dirt in search of food, and children playing. Unfortunately, Plomari is full of package tour groups in the summer and many of the more attractive areas—particularly on the beach to the west—are full. Try to find a place in the town itself. Cross the second bridge to the left off the main shopping street, veer right around the restaurant, then follow signs two blocks to "Furnished Rooms in Traditional House." This pension is attractive and clean; doubles 800dr. including bath. Plomari has no major sites but the **Church of St. Nicholas** (first bridge to the left off the main shopping street) is worth a visit. Beautifully decorated, the church contains icons from the sixteenth century to the present. Walk up by the altar—some of the best icons are on the back of the podium wall.

Plomari has beaches, though they're hard to find. The breakwater wall along the town's waterfront conceals spurts of pebble beach. The best one around is **Agios Isodoros,** a few kilometers to your left if you're facing the water. It's suitable for camping if you're inconspicuous.

Buses leave for Plomari five times a day from Mitilini; the fare is 120dr. The road hugs the **Bay of Geras,** offering some beautiful views of both the coast and the interior, and passes through the charming villages of **Paleokipos** and **Pappados.** If you are hitching or bicycling from Mitilini, you can take the shortcut across the mouth of the Bay. Head down Konstantinou Kavetsou St. and continue to the village of **Kountourdia** at the end of the road. From there you can take the small passenger boat to Perama, which connects to the road to Plomari. Fifteen kilometers to the north of Plomari, the village of **Agiassos** remains a lively center for ceramic crafts. It also hosts the island's largest name-day celebration for the patron of its church—in this case *Panayia,* the Virgin Mary—every year on August 15. This is worth changing your schedule to attend, especially since traditional name-day celebrations are becoming increasingly rare in Greece.

Western Lesvos

The best beach on Lesvos is, as usual, the farthest away from the main town. **Skala Eressos** is a long, sandy beach that's almost empty and worth the 270dr bus fare; hitching is also a viable option. Not only is camping a breeze here, but "domatios" or private rooms are also readily available. If you ever get tired of the beach, you can go to the village of **Eressos** and visit the medieval fortress and the **Archeological Museum.** For a place to stay, try the **Minavra** (tel. 53 20 20). On the way to Eressos from Mitilini, the road passes by **Adissa,** 5km from which is the twelfth-century **Monastery of St. John Theologos Ipsilos.** Avoid the misnamed **Petrified Forest** nearby; it consists of one petrified tree that gets a little smaller each year as tourists keep breaking off pieces of it. Past Adissa, the road branches off to **Sigri,** an isolated coastal village dominated by an eighteenth-century Turkish fortress. Buses leave for Eressos and Sigri two times a day from Mitilini.

Chios

Chios, allegedly the birthplace of Homer, is a small, untouristed island sandwiched between Lesvos and Samos and equally close to the Turkish coast. The waterfront in Chios Town, the main port, looks like one long souvenir shop, but don't let it fool you—there are relatively few tourists here and almost none anywhere else on the island. In recent years a number of rich Greek shipbuilders have chosen Chios as their exclusive retreat and do what they can to prevent the island from either developing tourist facilities or attracting tourists. The result is that Chios is all the more fascinating for the few travelers who make it to this beautifully desolate island.

The golden age of Chios in commerce and art was the sixth century B.C. Since that time, the island's tenuous geographical location has made it the scene of numerous occupations. The Genoese dominated Chios for two hundred years before the Turks took control in 1566. A failed rebellion in the 1820s resulted in the slaughter of 25,000-30,000 Greeks. A major earthquake brought its own kind of destruction in 1881. Oppressive foreign rule continued until 1912, when the Balkan Wars reunited Chios with the rest of Greece. This long-suffering island suffered again in 1981 when a huge fire destroyed one of its two forest regions, in the north around Volissos.

Transportation

Five boats a week travel between Chios and Piraeus; these ferries also stop at Lesvos. Chios is also on the route of the *Kyklades,* which does an unreliable round-trip once a week between Kavala and Rhodes, stopping at all of the larger islands in between. Excursion boats connect Chios to Samos about three times a week April-Nov. From July 15 to Sept. 15, a ferry runs three times a week to nearby Çesme, Turkey; from June 1 two times weekly, and once a week in May and the last half of September. Fare 1500dr one way, 2200dr round trip with open return; you must leave your passport with the travel agent one day in advance.

The **airport,** a seven-minute drive south of the main town, has daily flights to and from Athens for 1710dr each way. You can purchase tickets in Chios at the Olympic Airways office located on the west side of the harbor. Buses leave from in front of the office for the airport 1½ hrs. before each flight.

The Town of Chios

As you disembark, head for the **Tourism Office/Acceuil** at the northern corner of the harbor (tel. 26 55 5). The couple that runs this office is exceptionally friendly and helpful. They will find you a room, give you boat and bus schedules, and make good suggestions about island explorations. Walk down the waterfront from this office, take the third right, and you'll find two inexpensive hotels, the **Filoxenia** and the **Palladion,** on the left; doubles with bath around 750dr in each, but the Filoxenia is a little nicer. Across the street are two restaurants serving good, inexpensive breakfasts. Both are called **Kalamatis,** because they are run by two brothers who used to own one restaurant but then had a falling out. They fight furiously over each potential customer. Two **banks** and the **OTE** (open 24 hrs.) are around the central square, one block back to the north. Down the waterfront street to the south, past Olympic Airways, is the **Post Office** (open Mon.-Fri. 7:30am-2:30pm). The **telephone code** for Chios is 0271.

The town of Chios is somewhat touristy and not very attractive. Its most impressive sights are the Byzantine **Kastro** to the north and the nineteenth-century **mosque** on the square, which now houses an archeological museum. The southern quarter, **Kambos,** is dominated by the Italian-style mansions of centuries of Greek landowners. In one of them you can visit the **Philip Argenti Museum** (open Mon.-Fri. 7am-1:30pm, Sat. 7am-noon), which elegantly houses numerous paintings, period costumes, and portraits of prominent families, all from the island's illustrious past.

The green buses on the far side of **Vounakio Square** provide adequate service around the island. Routes are all east-west, so to move north-south, you have to return to Chios Town. Try to get schedule information beforehand at the Tourist Office. Hitching is also viable; it's better in the south than in the north.

Nea Moni

The Nea Moni, or "New Monastery," is a world-class monument of Byzantine art that is too rarely seen by visitors. It was founded in the eleventh century by three hermits, at the spot where they found a miraculous icon, depicting the Virgin Mary, hanging from a myrtle tree. The icon remains, hanging to the right of the main altar. Over the centuries, the monastery complex was rebuilt and enlarged, but the thousands of monks living here were slaughtered in the Turkish massacre. The 1881 earthquake was the final blow, destroying much of the complex. The church has been restored, apparently quite accurately, but the interior is still chaotic.

Inside, the eleventh-century mosaics in the dome are especially noteworthy, and their superb artistry shines through their state of partial destruction. The refectory is still intact; if you sit at the solid marble table and put your feet in the foot-holes, you can tell how short most people were nine centuries ago. One other chapel is open; its state of disrepair is somehow appropriate for its content: the skulls (look for sword slashes) and limb bones of many of the massacred monks line the walls.

Located on a secluded mountain slope 16km from the town of Chios, Nea Moni is nearly inaccessible. There is sometimes a bus from Chios on Sunday morning; ask about the time. Otherwise, take the bus to Karies, then walk, share a taxi, or hitch the remaining 9km. Not much traffic, but you'll get a ride eventually. Open dawn-1pm and 4-8pm daily.

About halfway from Karies to Nea Moni, a gravel path to the left leads to the **Monastery of Agios Markos,** worth visiting just for the view. The caretaker will let you into the chapel for a few minutes, then, if you're lucky, invite you to the courtyard for a glass of ouzo.

The South

The southern half of the island, called *Mastikokhoria* in honor of its unique crop, is the lowland area where the famous resin of Chios is produced. Mastica, tapped like syrup from the squat, curvey-branched trees, is used to make chewing gum and strengthen paint. About half of the annual crop is sold to Iraq to be made into a very non-Muslim beverage.

The main "mastic village" is **Pirgi**, 25km from Chios and serviced by eight buses a day. Walk into town past the first seven or eight houses and you'll hit your head against the only hotel. There are also a few rooms to let; ask anyone for suggestions. The curiously beautiful gray and white decoration, called *xysta,* is Pirgi's trademark. Try to get into the **Agioi Apostoloi** church, northeast out of the square. The fourteenth-century building was a copy of Nea Moni, but is now the older of the two since it was never heavily damaged.

Ten kilometers farther west, **Mesta** is a hermetically medieval village, beautiful and deathly quiet. The whole town seems like a single continuous building; the streets are tunnels arched over in a heavy stone. The stonework is no longer necessary for defense, but it works remarkably well in keeping the town cool. Behind and to the right of the bus stop, the tiny church of **Palios Taxiarchis** has the remnants of some eighteenth-century frescoes. It makes an odd contrast in both size and condition with the huge **Megas Taxiarchis** in the square—well-kept but much less beautiful. The town's very sweet specialty,

Mesta wine, is available only at its one cafe. The NTOG has recently restored some of the old houses into lovely guest-houses; a small apartment with kitchen and bath costs 1100dr per night—affordable if shared. A week's vacation in this cool, peaceful setting could work wonders.

Five or six kilometers south of Pirgi is the volcanic black-pebble beach at **Emborio.** Chians claim that this is the best beach in Greece, and they may be right. The water is crystal clear and the surrounding volcano is gorgeous. You'll probably be the only foreigner in this untouristed, enticing spot. The last cove to your right (facing the water), past three short rock climbs, is an unofficial nude beach.

The North

Always the poorer region, the north half of Chios was left particularly destitute after the 1981 fire. As long as you're just visiting, its desolation can be strangely intriguing. One bus route follows the coast; a few kilometers past Marmaron is the beautiful, empty beach at **Nagos.** Another route winds through uninhabited hills toward **Volissos** which legend calls the birthplace of Homer. A few kilometers south, the tiny (four houses) village of **Limnia** hosts another long, empty stretch of sand beach, **Skala Valis.** It would be lunacy to endure Chios-town's two dirty, crowded beaches when such extraordinary beaches as Valis, Nagos, and especially Emborio are available.

Samos

Of the major northeastern islands, Samos has the lushest, most varied landscape. For this reason, and perhaps because of the acumen of some of its travel agents, Samos has built up a brisker tourist trade than any other island in the area. Not that Samos's heavy tourism is undeserved. One of Greece's major archeological sites is here, superb beaches abound, and parts of the island are stunningly beautiful. But to enjoy Samos you'll probably want to stay clear of crowded Samos Town and Pythagorion, and instead find some secluded place on the coast or in the mountains, away from the hordes.

Samos claims a rich history. It was once the wealthiest of the Aegean islands, and one of the great intellectual centers of the world. The island was home to many great ancient Greeks, including Aristarchus, the talented astronomer who argued that the sun was the center of the universe before anyone had even heard the name Copernicus; Epicurus, the famous moral philosopher; and Aesop, the fabulous author of fables. The most famous and beloved of the island's native sons is the ancient philosopher Pythagoras, whose portrait has been adopted as the symbol of Samos.

Transportation

Ferries run between Samos and Piraeus (1090dr) and Samos and Ikaria (375dr) six days a week during the summer. Four times a week the route also includes Paros in the Cyclades (790dr). The only ferries that provide connections with the other Northeastern Islands or with the Dodecanese are the *Kyklades* (north and south) and the *Panormitis* (south; no cars), both with varied schedules. Smaller boats shuttle to Chios and Patmos almost daily, but if your schedule permits you to take the ferry, you'll find it more comfortable and much cheaper. *Panormitis* and other smaller boats heading south leave from Pythagorion rather than Samos. Olympic has daily flights to and from Athens for 1990dr one way.

Getting Around Samos

Bus service on the major routes is good during the summer, but it stops around 6pm. On Sundays and in winter (Sept.-May) service falls off considerably. Fares range up to 75dr for Samos-Karlovassi. The main bus terminal (tel. 27 26 2) in the town of Samos, is located one block up from the waterfront, past Pythagoras Square and the BP gas station. The best way to see the island, and the only way to get around the more mountainous and remote western end, is by motorbike. Standard rental fee for a motorbike is 500dr a day; 150dr a day for a bicycle. Rentals are available in Samos, Pythagorion, and Karlovassi.

Hitchhiking is very good here on the main roads. To hitch out of Samos, walk all the way around the waterfront (to your left facing the water), then head uphill past two or three hairpin turns. If you need a taxi (they're expensive), the main **taxi stand** is at Protagoras Square in the town of Samos, or call 28 40 4.

The Town of Samos

Samos is a large, bustling port town, a little overrun with tourist facilities but still fairly attractive. It is vindicated by its older section, called Vathi or Anavathi. On a hill overlooking the south end of town, this neighborhood is full of handsome, old mansions—a good place to stroll and to escape the crowds.

Accommodations and Practical Information

In July and August, even if you arrive on a weekday morning, you may very well find that no rooms are available. When you get off the boat, go to the new, friendly, and English-speaking **Tourist Police.** From the dock, walk along the waterfront past the main square to the far end of the Hotel Xenia (open April-Oct. 8am-2pm and 5-10pm). The staff is quite willing to call hotels and pensions for you at no charge, not only in Samos Town but all over the island. The **Post Office** is behind the park-zoo nearby.

Equally helpful (and much closer) is **Samos Tours,** located right across the ferry dock and open daily until the last boat comes in. Posted inside is a gold mine of information—a bus schedule, museum and bank hours, a list of hotels all over the island, and a schedule of ferries other than the *Panormitis*. It is important that you check boat schedules here before inquiring in the many ferry company offices on the waterfront, since they often withhold information about their rivals' excursions. Like the Tourist Police, this office will call around the town and island to help you find accommodations.

Pension Ionia, with a friendly owner and two houses full of rooms, is a first-choice bargain accommodation. Turn away from the waterfront at the Aeolus Hotel, then take the second left at the wall; the green building will be on your left. Doubles 700-750dr, one bed in a five-bed room 250dr, both including shower. **Pension Bells** has three- and four-bed rooms for 250dr per person including shower; cramped and not too clean. Follow the signs by the bell tower, a block north of Pythagoras (the main) Square.

Past Samos Tours to the north is a bit of beach where you can spread your sleeping bag; you'll also find people sleeping on the concrete plaza right off the quay.

Sights

The most interesting sight in town is the **Archeological Museum** (tel. 27 46 9), which houses finds from all over the island. Open Mon.-Sat. 8:30am-2:45pm,

Sun. 9am-2pm, closed Tues. Next to it, the small but beautiful **Municipal Gardens** contain a variety of beautiful flowers along with a small zoo. The museum and the gardens are reached from Pythagoras Square by walking down Kapetan Katavani St.

Plaz Gagou, a fifteen-minute walk to the north, is a good beach to cool off at on hot days, but it gets quite crowded during the summer. There's a fresh-water shower here that works during the day, in case you need to rinse your-self off.

The Trip to Ephesus

Many people come to Samos simply to make the short hop over to the ruins of Ephesus on the Turkish coast. The archeological site is the most extensive and perhaps the most interesting remnant of ancient Hellenic civilization. Founded around 1100 B.C., Ephesus rapidly blossomed into the largest me-tropolis of Asia Minor. Most of what remains today dates from the first four or five centuries after Christ, and cannot possibly be seen in a single day.

Ferries leave most days at 8am and 5pm to Kuşadasi from Samos, and about four times a week from Pythagorion; the trip takes 1½ hours. Weather permit-ting, there are five ferries a week through the winter, i.e. end of Oct.-April. If you take the morning boat, you'll need to leave your passport at the ticket agency the night before; drop your passport off at least a few hours before for the afternoon boat. You're going to weep when you hear the fares: 1600dr round trip, 1200dr one way, plus a Turkish port tax of 700dr if you don't stay overnight, 1400dr if you do. There's a 10% student discount on the boat fare (but not on the port tax). The one-day guided tours that various travel agencies will encourage you to buy are completely worthless; see sections on Kuşadasi and Ephesus in Turkish coast chapter.

Pythagorion

The ancient capital of Samos, on the southern coast, is a very lovely city; its setting, with the town's old mansions arranged in a crescent along the harbor, is beautiful. Unfortunately, it has taken on a few too many tourist trappings for its size, especially near the waterfront. Still, smaller and quieter, Pythagorion can be a pleasant alternative to Samos Town; it's also in the center of the island's archeological sites. Buses frequently make the half-hour trip between Samos and Pythagorion (30dr); the last bus back to Samos Town leaves at 6:45pm from a cafe next to the crossroads.

Practical Information and Accommodations

The main street runs perpendicular to the waterfront. Here you'll find a **Bank** (open Mon.-Fri. 8:30am-12:30pm) and the **Post Office** (open Mon.-Fri. 7:30am-2:30pm). The **Tourist Police** (tel. 61 10 0) are combined with the regular police; open daily 6:30am-9pm in the summer. Communication may be difficult, but they're very helpful about finding rooms. Unfortunately, it's un-likely that any will be available.

If you turn left from the main street onto the waterfront, then left again past the Customs House, you'll find a gray and white building on the right, where the street becomes stairs. This unnamed **pension** has clean doubles for 700dr. Follow the main street away from the water, take the second left, and **Pension Arocaria** (tel. 61 28 7) will be on your right just before the road ends at the church. Clean and well-furnished doubles with baths go for 800dr. Pythagorion is relatively expensive, so you'll have a hard time finding anything much cheaper. There are beaches at both the east and west ends of town for camp-ing; the one to the west is better and less crowded.

Sights

The ancient city of Pythagorion, known for a while as Samos, enjoyed its heyday during the second half of the sixth century B.C., under the reign of Polycrates the Tyrant. By Herodotus' standards, Polycrates undertook the three greatest engineering feats in the Hellenic world, all in and around Pythagorion. The most impressive is the **Tunnel of Euphalinos,** a mile up the hill to the north of town, which was built to carry water from a natural spring straight around the mountain to the city below. It is about 1.3km long, and in remarkably good condition. The entrance is in a small building constructed to protect the mouth of the tunnel. The tunnel has been closed since 1981 so that electricity can be installed. But there have been difficulties, so check with the Tourist Police to find out whether the tunnel has reopened. Should you be able to enter, be sure to move along the left side, because there are often deep drops on the right half of the tunnel. Electricity should make the visit safer, if less of an adventure. Round trip takes a bare minimum of ninety minutes but most people survey only the first few hundred meters.

Polycrates' second great feat was constructing the 120-foot deep **harbor mole** (rock pier) on which the modern pier now rests. Actually, this was the feat of certain Lesbian slaves, prizes from one of the tyrant's earlier conquests.

Not everything in Pythagorion was built by Polycrates. On the south side of town is the **Castle of Lycurgus,** built during the beginning of the last century, by Lycurgus, a native of Samos and a leader in the Greek War of Independence. The entrance to the fortress is at the Church of the Transfiguration, just to the east.

Polycrates' third great feat was performed 4 or 5km west of Pythagorion at Ireon. The Goddess Hera had already been an object of worship on Samos for seven centuries when Polycrates decided to enlarge her temple, in 530 B.C. He did so with a vengeance. The result was **Ireon**—the largest temple ever built by this race of temple-builders: 354 feet long, 175 feet wide, supported by 134 columns. The Temple was damaged by a fire in 525 and the rebuilding project was never completed, presumably because in 522 Polycrates came into the hands of some of his many enemies, who dealt with him and his remains without mercy.

These ruins really are ruins, but they're definitely worth seeing. A little way past the entrance on your left is a tablet showing the lay-out of the site. Some German archeologists live and work here; a few speak English, and you may be able to persuade one to show you around. The site is open Mon.-Sat. 9am-3:15pm, Sun. 9am-2pm. There are three buses a day from Samos and Pythagorion. A better alternative is to take the 45-minute stroll along the beach from Pythagorion; the Ireon is a waterfront property with a back gate leading right on to the beach. If you can't go in the back gate, continue along the beach past two houses where a path will bring you inland to the main road and main entrance. This way runs close to the route of the ancient Iera Odos (sacred road) from Pythagorion to the Temple.

Near Pythagorion

For some positively prehistoric sites, head north of Pythagorion (only 12km from the town of Samos) to the village of **Mitilini** where there is the famous **Paleontological Museum,** which contains an interesting collection of animal fossils, some of them fifteen million years old. Mitilini is easily reached by bus from both Pythagorion and Samos, though the last bus returning to Pythagorion leaves at 2pm. The Paleontological Museum is in the Mitilini Town Hall, open Mon.-Fri. 9am-2pm.

More beautiful and less crowded than the beach near Samos Town are the beaches of **Psili Ammos** and **Poseidonion,** on the southern coast of the island. Directly across from the Turkish coast, these beaches afford perhaps the most beautiful view of the Straits of Mykale. You can reach either of these sandy beaches by bus from Samos Town (9:30am and 12:45pm), or by excursion boat from Pythagorion, or by rented motorbike.

Kokkari

If you go to Samos, Kokkari is an essential visit. On a small peninsula, the village is completely encompassed by smooth pebble beaches. Many of the town's picturesque houses almost seem built on the surface of the turquoise water.

Practical Information and Accommodations

Kokkari is only 10km from Samos; six buses a day make the trip. The last bus goes back to Samos Town at 6:15pm. There is no bank here, but several places in town change travelers checks, including the food store just up the hill from the Vicky Hotel. In and around the square are a number of restaurants that are cheaper than those in Samos. Since Kokkari has become a haven for young northern-Europeans, the town is well-supplied with inexpensive, young-European foods like yogurt.

Unlike Samos and Pythagorion, Kokkari has an adequate supply of reason-ably-priced rooms. The best place to look is on the little peninsula that juts out beyond and west of the square. Many houses on the peninsula have rooms to let; ask any one for suggestions. You should be able to get a double for 650-700dr. Slightly more expensive (750dr) but very attractive is the **Pension An-thoula,** on the left side of the peninsula as you face the sea.

Kokkari's police seem to take the many Camping Prohibited signs relatively seriously, but you can sleep on any of the more remote beaches along the coast west of town.

The North Coast

The northern coastline of Samos, particularly the stretch between Kokkari and Karlovassi, boasts a number of beautiful, deserted pebble beaches tucked away in little coves and plagued occasionally by strong winds. Most of the coast is easily accessible from the road that goes to Karlovassi, and the drive or the bus ride is well worth the trip just for the scenery. Two kilometers west of Kokkari is **Tsamadou Beach.** With a cafe and fresh water tap, this is a good place to camp, though it gets more crowded by the day. Soon, the unnamed beach-cove just east of **Avlakia** may become overpopulated as well. The only outstanding sight in the area is the sixteenth-century monastery near the village of **Vourliotes,** 5km inland from Avlakia.

The second major port of Samos is **Karlovassi,** on the western end of the island. Although most boats to Samos stop here, continue on to the town of Samos which offers a far better orientation to the island. Karlovassi is an unattractive, overpriced city full of huge hotels and modern, empty buildings.

Should you use the town as a base for excursions to western Samos, the bus stops in Neo Karlovassi (New Karlovassi). The best place to stay is the unofficial **youth hostel** (tel. 32 87 2) behind the huge Panayia Church; 150dr per person.

You'll find the **OTE** and the **Post Office** down Agios Nilolos St. on the way to the old quarter of Karlovassi Port. While this area is interesting to explore on foot, the beach is much better at Potamia, a twenty-minute walk beyond the harbor.

Western Samos

That Western Samos remains unexplored by most tourists is fortunate for those willing to venture into the region. Speckled with tiny villages and manicured agricultural fields, this area is best covered by moped, though bus service from Karlovassi is adequate. Perched 500m above the Aegean, the charming village of **Platanos** has an exquisite view of both sides of the island. Mr. Menegas runs a new **hotel** (tel. 33 22 9) with doubles for 700dr. Eighty meters to the right down the last dirt road before town you'll find a **pension** which has doubles for 600-700dr; singles 450dr. Two buses a day connect Platanos with Karlovassi, but the last return is an early 2:15pm.

A couple of kilometers west of the peaceful coastal hamlet of **Ormos Marathokambou** is the spacious beach of Votsalakia and another mile farther an even better beach at Hrissi Ammoudia. The fresh-water stream makes this place ideal for camping. Two buses a day service these beaches from Karlovassi. From Hrissi Ammoudia, the unpaved road continues clockwise beneath Mount Kerkis (1440 meters) around the island's western end in a brutal passage rewarded by dramatic mountain views.

Towards the center of the island, near the town of Pyrgos, is the quiet and remote village of **Koutsi,** another good place to escape the crowds. The **Hotel Koutsi** (tel. 61 38 9) has doubles for 700dr.

Ikaria

Legend has it that Ikaria, 42 nautical miles west of Samos, is named after Icarus, the famous mythological character who escaped from Crete by taking flight with wings fashioned by his father Daedalus. Unfortunately, his newly found powers made Icarus giddy and in his confusion he imprudently soared too close to the sun. The wax on his wings melted and he plummeted into the waters just off the coast of this then deserted island. Getting here has become considerably easier since Icarus' time; the island is on the main ferry line from Piraeus to Paros and Samos. From Ikaria's main port, boats leave for Patmos on Wednesdays, Fridays and Sundays. From Evdilos, a little town on Ikaria's northern coast, there are boats twice a week during the summer to Samos (for complete boat information, see the Samos section).

One of Ikaria's advantages is that, until now, it has been largely neglected by tourists. When you first see the western coast, you may be disappointed, for the rugged mountains are quite barren. Much of the island's interior, however, is green and lush, providing splendid mountain vistas.

Unlike many similar towns in the Greek isles, **Agios Kirikos** has remained an authentic Greek fishing village, not a stage set for tourists. As you walk from the dock on the waterfront you'll see Isabella's House and Adam's House right on the main square. On the ground floor of Isabella's is the **National Bank,** which changes money Monday through Friday, 8am-2pm. If you're going to other towns on the island, be warned that there are no banks outside of Agios Kirikos. On the cliff on the far side of the harbor, you'll see the **Hotel Akti,** a whitewashed building with green shutters and an orange sign on the roof (tel. 22 06 4). One single (usually booked) costs 280dr; otherwise doubles are 450dr, and the 50dr shower can be bargained off. There are also numerous places with private rooms for similar prices, but almost none of them are marked. Ask at the Akti if it's full, or at one of the kiosks.

If you take the street that leads up the hill and to the right from the National Bank, after about one hundred meters you'll pass the **Post Office** (open Mon.-Fri. 7am-2:30pm) and the **OTE** (open Mon.-Fri. 7:30am-11pm, Sat.-Sun. til

1:30pm). Just up the hill from here on the left are several houses with beautiful gardens; the third and last (with the biggest garden) surreptitiously lets out doubles at 400dr with shower (cold) and dorm rooms at 200dr per bed.

There are no beaches near the town, but if you take the steps that go up from the far left-hand side of the harbor and continue along the coast for about ten minutes, you'll be able to climb down to some lovely secluded caves. If you continue on this road a bit more, you'll come to the waterfront village of **Therma,** appropriately named for its hot springs, where many elderly people come to alleviate various ailments. You don't have to have rheumatism to enjoy a twenty-minute dunk (40dr) at the Apollo Bath, the only public bath among the six functioning springs. (A seventh spring was closed due to dangerously high radioactivity.) In the same complex, modern **Apollo Inn** has doubles costing 400dr, 550dr for a room facing the sunny harbor. In the gift shop up the main street and across the dry creek bed, and on the left, **Apostolos Manolaros** runs boat tours around the island and to Patmos (tel. 22 43 33).

When you get off the ferry in Agios Kirikos, you'll notice that a large fraction of the backpackers make a beeline for the old bus at the end of the dock without so much as a sidelong glance. If you're looking for sandy beaches, follow them. Most of the riders have not the slightest idea of where they're going, acting on blind faith (based on rumor) that at the end of the ride lurk the best beaches on the island. This happens to be true; the bus goes all the way to Armenistis (58km) on the northern coast, where the sand is fine and white and the water crystal-clear. The tiny road to **Armenistis** offers amazing views of the coast as it traverses verdant hill country and snakes along sheer cliffs—the bus passes so close to the edge that the driver won't let you stand up in the bus.

It has been a couple of years since the beaches at Armenistis were anyone's best-kept secret; although quite isolated, this is where you'll find 90% of the young tourists on the island. Most of them are European kids on shoestring vacations. Most people sleep on the beach, but rooms to let are plentiful and cheap, around 400dr for a double. Be warned that you cannot count on a bus back from Armenistis to Agios Kirikos on any particular day; if you're in a hurry, get several people together and take a taxi (1200-1500dr, but definitely bargain). To really get away from it all, take one of the small boats that run every morning from the dock underneath the Hotel Akti to the Faro Peninsula on the eastern tip of the island. Boats allegedly leave at 7:30am (9:30am on Sundays); in reality they leave whenever the driver is in the mood. Pay equal attention to the pilot's mood for return trip or you may be stranded. The boat takes you to the little village of Panarion, with a long, sandy beach. From Agios Kirikos, there are also boats to Evdilos on the northern coast and occasional boats to the tiny island of Fourni. If you go to the latter, inquire about the availability of drinking water—you may have to bring your own. A boat, leaving periodically throughout the day, also connects Agio Kirikos with Therma (12dr).

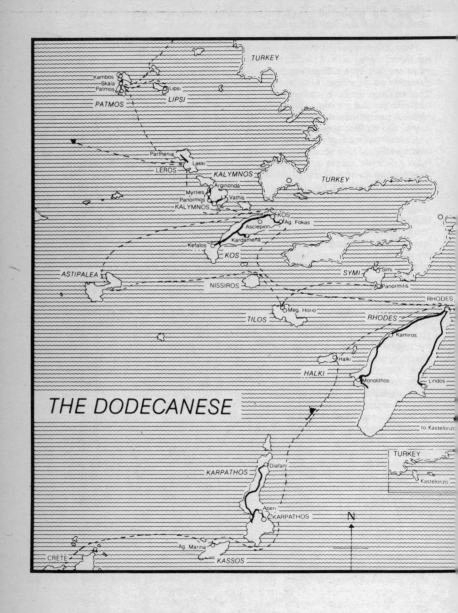

THE DODECANESE

DODECANESE

In the sunny southeastern corner of the Aegean is a glittering cluster of islands known as the Dodecanese. Although relatively remote from the mainland of Greece, these well-endowed islands contain all the elements that make the country the supreme vacationer's paradise—magnificent beaches, superb scenery, handsome villages, impressive medieval fortresses, imposing mountains, and outstanding archeological sites.

Slowly but surely, the Dodecanese are exchanging their unspoiled beauty and individual characters for a more cosmopolitan glitter. The Dodecanese have begun to acquire a tourist trade on the level of the Cyclades, but for now the development is uneven. Rhodes and Kos are solidly packed due to the successful efforts of package-tour companies from northern Europe, but the other islands are still relatively serene.

The Dodecanese were the site of a prominent and flourishing ancient culture, as indicated by the splendid ancient Greek ruins uncovered in recent excavations. For most of the last seven hundred years, however, the history of the islands has been one of successive foreign occupations. In early Roman times, the region continued to prosper, but as the Byzantine Empire slowly waned, the islands became vulnerable to the hit-and-run raids of pirates from many nations. During the final years of the Empire and after its demise, various admirals and merchants from Italy, especially Genoa and Venice, were able to exert control over some of the islands. But the essential force here during this period was the Crusader Knights of the Order of St. John of Jerusalem. They came to the Dodecanese when they were forced out of Jerusalem and settled here through the fourteenth and fifteenth centuries, defending God and the islands together by building tremendous fortresses. The Knights succeeded in holding off the Turks until 1522 when Suleymein the Magnificent invaded. For four hundred years the Ottomans ruled the islands; they converted Byzantine churches into mosques but otherwise kept their distance from the Greeks and changed little. Italian forces ousted the Turks in 1912, and the most pervasive legacy of their occupation is probably the public buildings they erected in the major towns. They also improved trade and conducted archeological excavations and restorations (the value of which has been hotly debated), but their overall record is tarnished because of their reputation for cruelty and oppression. When the Italians surrendered during World War II in 1943, the Germans replaced them in Dodecanese. Three years after their surrender in 1945 to Greek and British forces, the Dodecanese were incorporated into the Greek State.

To and From the Dodecanese

Most of the Dodecanese islands are arranged in a rough, curved line that follows the coast of Turkey, making it easy to hop from one to the next without backtracking or changing boats. The main island row, extending northwest from **Rhodes** to **Kos, Kalymnos, Leros,** and **Patmos,** is serviced during the summer by boats traveling between Crete and Rhodes twice a week in either direction. Two smaller ferries stop three times a week at **Kasterlorizo** and **Astipalea,** the islands at the eastern and western extremes of the Dodecanese chain. Hydrofoils also service most of the islands, all originating in Rhodes.

Ferries run to the Dodecanese from Piraeus (at least one boat a day Mon.-Sat., no boats on Sun.); Kavala (Tues. mornings, but unreliably); and Agios

Nikolaos and Sitia on Crete (Wed. at midnight). Boats to and from Samos and Armorgos call at several of the Dodecanese ports twice a week. Weekly boats connect Rhodes to Limassol (Cyprus), Lattakia (Syria), Alexandria (Egypt), Beirut (Lebanon), and Haifa (Israel). Rhodes has daily (except Sunday) boat connections with Marmaris, Turkey. You can also fly to Rhodes from Athens, Iraklion or Larnaca (Cyprus) and, during the summer, from Kos, Mykonos, Karpathos, and Santorini. Kos has international flights, but they are all chartered.

Rhodes

According to legend, Rhodes rose out of the sea in order to provide Helios with a terrestrial possession after Zeus had divided the earth among his fellow gods. Helios subsequently married the nymph Rhodon who lived there and named the island after her. Less dramatic but similarly inspired is the possibility that the name Rhodes comes from the word *rodon,* meaning rose.

In either case, Rhodes has retained much of its legendary beauty, even though it is the undisputed tourist capital of the Dodecanese. The major resort towns of Rhodes are among the most heavily touristed parts of Greece and suffer from all the accompanying difficulties, but most of the island is uncrowded and beautiful; endless expanses of sandy beaches stretch along the west coast, dramatic rocky cliffs rise from the water along the east coast, and green mountainous landscape dotted with tiny, secluded villages fills the interior. Moreover, Rhodes has three good archeological sites in Kamiros, Ialyssos, and Lindos, and fabulous examples of medieval architecture, especially in the island's largest city and principal port. If the number of tourists grows at all, Rhodes may reach a breaking point, but for now it continues to seduce.

Transportation

Rhodes is without doubt the easiest island to reach in the Dodecanese. Regular ferry service connects the island to Piraeus, Crete, the Cyclades, the Northeastern Islands, Kavala, and the other Dodecanese islands. Many tourists come to Rhodes from Piraeus or Athens. Boats leave at least six days a week from Piraeus bound for Rhodes passing through many of the major Cycladic Islands—the trip takes about twenty hours and costs 1413dr. You can also fly to Rhodes from Athens (3300dr; special night fare 2480dr), and from a few islands: Kos and Karpathos (daily in summer; 1530dr), Mykonos (four days a week, 2740dr) and Santorini (three days a week, 2520dr).

Boats travel four times a week to Limassol, Cyprus (3300dr plus 1000dr tax), and once a week to Beirut, to Lattakia (Syria), to Alexandria and to Haifa. The NTOG or Tourist Police will be able to direct you to the relevant agency for each of these boats. In addition, a small boat leaves for Marmaris, Turkey every day except Sunday at an unpredictable time. From October through April the boat leaves once or twice weekly. Tickets are sold by Bastiyali Agency, 15 Plastira St. (1500dr). To board any of these boats, have your passport stamped with an exit visa by the immigration authorities. You must leave it overnight with the travel agent for this purpose.

The City of Rhodes

During the seventh century B.C., the island of Rhodes began to flourish as a major trading center, with three prosperous cities in **Ialyssos, Lindos,** and **Kamiros.** In the final years of the Peloponnesian Wars, the three jointly undertook to found a fourth city on the northern tip of the island. Determined to create both the most beautiful city in the world and a commercial port capable of handling large-volume trade, in 408 B.C. they enlisted the services of the renowned architect Ippodamus from Miletus on the coast of Asia Minor. The city of Rhodes was born.

Always prudent, ever letting politics follow commercial interests, Rhodes flourished during the next centuries as a center of Classical and Hellenistic culture. Rhodes' history is typically Greek and paradigmatically Dodecanese. Byzantine masters replaced Roman ones, and barbarians and Arabs raided incessantly. Italians, Crusaders, and Ottoman Turks ruled in succession. In recent times Rhodes has struggled for independence and reunited with Greece. Throughout, the city has gained in importance relative to the other cities on the island, only one of which (Lindos) has been continuously populated. Rhodes today shows traces of each period and reminders of each occupying power. But its contours are dominated by the legacy of the Knights of St. John, who transformed the city into a vast, impregnable bastion during their 213-year reign.

As you'll soon discover, Rhodes is more than an archetypal medieval city: it must also provide for the tourists who make it one of the premier holiday meccas of the Mediterranean. Consequently, the new, western part of the city (the famous **Sandy Port** in particular) is so full of luxury hotels it looks like Waikiki Beach. The main beach to the west of the city is probably the most crowded in Greece, and during the summer the tourists are packed thigh to thigh on its surface. So if you are coming to Rhodes to view its rich array of historical sights, your visit to the city will be amply rewarded, but, if you have come to Rhodes to enjoy its natural splendors and to lie on the beach, you would do far better elsewhere on the island. The best guide to Rhodes' history and archeology is *Rhodos,* written by Christos Karousos, the late director of the National Museum. The book costs 250dr at any of the city's sidewalk stands or bookstores.

Practical Information

Most of the services for travelers are located outside the walls of the old city, a five- or ten-minute walk away in the new town.

NTOG: at the corner of Papagou and Makariou Sts. about four blocks from Mandraki Harbor (tel. 23 25 5). Very helpful. This extraordinarily efficient office has complete bus and boat schedules along with a list of boat agencies and their addresses. They also have maps, flight schedules, and information on cultural events in the city. And they'll find a room for you, an invaluable service in July and August. Open in summer Mon.-Sat. 7:30am-8pm, Sun. 9am-noon; in winter (Oct.-March) weekdays 8am-2pm.

Tourist Police: next door to the NTOG office (tel. 27 42 3). They speak English well here and will help you find a room when the NTOG office is closed. Open 7:30am-midnight in summer, reduced hours in winter.

American Express, c/o Georgiadis Ltd. Tourism & Shipping, 41 Vas. Sophias St. (tel. 27 30 0 or 27 49 3). Will hold client mail. Open Mon.-Fri.

Post Office: main branch on the waterfront of Mandraki includes Post Restante. Open Mon.-Fri. 7:30am-8:30pm; closed weekends.

OTE: 91 Amerikis St., at the corner of the 25th of March St. Open daily 6am-midnight.

Currency Exchange: In the old city, the Ionian and Popular Bank of Greece in Symi Square is open Mon.-Sat. 8am-2pm and 2:30-7:30pm, Sun. 9am-noon. In the new town, the National Bank of Greece at Vas. Sofias and Makariou Sts. has the best hours during the summer: Mon.-Fri. 8am-2pm and 2:30-8:30pm, Sat. 8am-2pm, Sun. 9am-noon.

Hospital: Helvetas Street (tel. 25 55 5).

Flight Information: The Olympic Airways office is on Ierou Lhou St., next to the Hotel Plaza and just off Amerikis St. (tel. 24 75 1); open 8am-9pm. The British Airways office is two doors down at 11 Ierou Lhou St. (tel. 26 71 0). Rhodes is connected by daily flights from Iraklion, Athens, Kos, and London. The airport is on the west coast, 17km from town, near the city of Paradisi. The public bus runs frequently; 40dr one way. Be sure to arrive at the airport one hour before your flight is scheduled to leave.

Consulates: The Voice of America (tel. 24 73 1) at the turn-off for Koskinou from the main east-coast highway is equipped to handle certain consular matters, especially if it's an emergency. Open weekdays 8am-4:30pm. A British Vice-Consul is available weekdays 8am-2pm; contact him through the travel bureau at 25 Martiou St. #23 (tel. 27 30 6).

Getting Around the Island

Bus service is adequate for getting around Rhodes. Inter-urban buses leave from two different locations in the city. Buses for Lindos, Faliraki, Kallithea, and Afandou leave from Papagou St. by Sound and Light Square. Buses for other destinations, including Paradisi, Monolithos, Kamiros and Koskinou, leave from Averof St., around the corner and alongside the market. Bus stops along both streets display the destination of each bus that stops there, so make sure you are waiting in the right spot. All tickets are purchased on the bus and bus schedules for all buses are posted at the respective bus stops or in the NTOG office.

Mopeds and motorcycles can be rented at any number of shops in the Old and New Towns. Expect to pay around 500dr for a moped and 700-1000dr for a motorbike depending on the size. You should beware of paying much more than this, but also of paying much less. If you think you're getting an extraordinarily good deal, ask to see proof that the bike is covered by third-party insurance since less-than-scrupulous bike dealers are a perennial problem in Greece. Insurance for the bike you're riding is non-existent. Bicycles can be rented for 150dr a day at 12 Evdimou St. in the Old Town.

One of the less expensive places to rent a car is Nobel Rent-a-Car (tel. 24 00 8), behind the Cairo Palace Hotel at 26 Ethelenton Dodekanision St. The cheaper Fiats and Volkswagens cost a minimum of 2000dr a day to rent, and a car with unlimited mileage costs 8000dr for three days. Remember that the price you're quoted never includes optional insurance on the car itself, which may run 300dr a day extra, or a 20% government tax on the total bill. You must be at least 23 years old and have a valid driver's license at least one year old. Some of the rental companies lease cars to younger drivers, but you must prove you've been driving for at least four years—and even then it's up to them.

Accommodations

The best part of Rhodes is also the cheapest to stay in. Almost all of the town's inexpensive pensions are in the quiet and infinitely interesting Old Town. During high season, you're much more likely to find a place within the ancient city walls, even if it's only a cot on a roof. If you don't like the choice the NTOG has given you, this is the place to begin looking.

Steve Kefalas' Pension, 60 Omirou St. (tel 24 35 7). Just down an alley off Omirou St., within earshot of the folk dancing. Has a pleasant, peaceful garden, and Steve is a delightful host. Doubles for 700dr, 250dr for a cot on the roof or in the garden.

Pension Apollon, 28c Omirou St. Another friendly place, but with plainer rooms. Doubles for 600dr, 150dr to sleep in the garden.

Pension Nikos, 45 E. Aristotelous St. (tel. 23 42 3), hides behind a flower garden facing the Square of the Jewish Martyrs; doubles 800dr, triples with bath in room 1030dr.

Pension Athinea (tel. 23 22 1) in the tunnel at 45 Pythagora St. (just off #29); singles 427dr, doubles 619dr, triples 872dr plus 60dr per shower.

Pension Massari, 42e Irodotou St (tel. 22 46 9). Clean doubles for 800dr, triples 1200dr (probably bargainable), or 200dr for a roof or garden spot.

Pension Dora (tel. 24 52 3), 37 Aristofanous St. At the northern end of the street where it curves around and is hard to track; zany decor and less than spotless bathrooms. Singles 480dr, doubles 670dr.

Artemis Pissa, 12 Dimosthenous St. Fragrant garden but they really pack them in here. A bed in a five- or six-bed room is 250dr.

The hotel district to the northwest of the Old Town features a handful of D- and E-class hotels, but most of them are booked solid through July and August. Cancellations do occur, however. Try the **Efrosini Hotel** (tel. 24 62 9). Located on a little side alley in front of the Ariette Hotel off Apolloniou Rodiou St., it has friendly management and singles for 585dr, doubles for 810dr.

Food

Rhodes seems to have benefited gastronomically from the Italian occupation of the island. Many of the town's restaurants specialize in pasta dishes, and the food is almost always of better quality than that offered in other parts of Greece. Unfortunately, only a small fraction of the fish served every day in Rhodes' restaurants is fresh, and this only in establishments that serve seafood exclusively. A good one in the Old Town is **Coralli,** Ippodamou 13; not much more expensive than many less classy places, and the food is excellent. There are also a number of family-owned restaurants in the Old Town—standard Greek fare, but better prepared and a lot cheaper. Try the ones at 47 Agia Fanourion St. and next door on Omirou St, or around the base of Pythagora St. Although no longer frequented by locals, the **New Market** has restaurants, meatpie stalls, cafeneions, and vegetable stands which certainly give you a wide range of eating options in a colorful atmosphere. The market is housed in a large white Moorish structure with a large open courtyard and stands in the rectangle bounded by Gallis, Averof, and Papagou Sts. and the waterfront. For a splurge, indulge in homemade Italian ice cream in Greece at **Tivoli Garden,** on the corner of Ion. Dragoumi and 28th of October Streets. Prices range from 30dr for a scoop to 200dr for the "Tivoli Special," a shamelessly large mound of hazelnut and vanilla ice cream on a meringue, topped with whipped cream, nuts, chocolate syrup, and biscuits.

Sights

The capital city of Rhodes contains almost no Hellenistic remains, so the twentieth century tourist receives no assistance in imagining Rhodes in its time of greatest glory. The Knights of St. John were voracious builders, and they replaced the Hellenistic structures, most of which had survived the fourteen or fifteen intervening centuries with works of their own. The Knights' hold over the Old Town was complete, and the ancient remains that still can be seen are, with one exception, outside it. Several blocks due west of the southern end of the Old Town, a **stadium,** a small **theater** and a **Temple of Apollo** have all been found and partially reconstructed. The stadium and especially the theater look rather modern, but the Temple still looks like an ancient ruin. You can see the few standing columns from the boat as you arrive or depart from Rhodes. They're just before the last long stretch of modern hotels. The only other pre-Roman ruin is just inside the Old Town near Symi Square: a third-century B.C. Temple of Aphrodite, strikingly out of place amidst the traffic and medieval surroundings.

The Castello

For the most part, the city belongs to the Knights. The Italians imitated them consciously, and even the numerous Turkish mosques bear an odd stylistic resemblance to the Knights' medieval architecture. The Order reserved the northwest section of the Old Town to itself, and its grandest buildings are here. The best place to begin exploring this quarter is at **Symi Square,** inside Liberty and Arsenal Gates, the main passages between the Old and the New City and the Waterfront. Behind Aphrodite's Temple is the **Inn of Auvergne** (1507), with staircase attached to the facade in Aegean style. A jewelry store now uses the main entrance on the south side of the building; the carved doorway is very impressive.

To the west of Symi Square lies **Argykastron Square,** with a relocated Byzantine fountain in the center. Set back on the right (west) of the square is the **Palace of Armeria,** now the **Archeological Institute,** built in the fourteenth century. The door and stairs leading down to the street on the left side of the building indicate where the old chapel used to be. The whole structure looks more like a fortress than anything else, with small windows, embattlements, and heavy Gothic architecture. Connected to the palace is the **Museum of Traditional Decorative Arts** (open Mon., Wed., and Fri. 9am-1pm). By passing through a low archway, you reach Museum Square. On the left is the Church of St. Mary (now closed) which the Turks transformed into the Enderoum Mosque, and beyond it the **Inn of the Tongue of England,** built in 1919—an exact copy of the original 1493 structure. Across the square and dominating it is the former **Hospital of the Knights,** another fortress-like building with an imposing entrance that now houses the **Archeological Museum.** A visit here is an important complement to touring the island, since many of the sculpture and pottery finds from every site are now here. Don't miss the celebrated **Aphrodite of Rhodes,** one of the best-preserved examples of sculpture in the sensual rococo style that flourished around 100 B.C. in the wealthy cities of the Hellenic world. The Museum also contains statues, bas-reliefs, pottery, and cannonballs, dating from Archaic, Hellenistic, and Crusader times. Open Mon.-Sat. 9am-3:15pm, Sun. 9am-2pm, closed Tues. Admission 100dr, 50dr with student ID.

The small cobblestone street next to the Museum sloping uphill is easy to pass—from this end it looks much like some of the other, quieter streets in the Old City—but don't be deceived. This is the historic **Avenue of the Knights,** the main street of the inner city five hundred years ago, which contains most of the houses of the Knights. The Order of the Knights of St. John of Jerusalem consisted of seven different religious orders called "languages" because each came from a different part of Europe. Each group except the Tongue of England and Auvergne had its own building, or "Inn," along this avenue: Provence, France, Italy, Germany, and Spain (later subdivided into Arragon and Castile). Each national section was responsible for guarding one segment of the city wall; this is why parts of the wall are labelled "England" or "France" on the map. Though their Order was officially dedicated to healing, the Knights were warriors first of all, and even these elegant residences feel like fortresses. The Italians tastefully restored the street by removing the makeshift balconies and lattice windows of the last century, and now there are no signs of modern living here aside from an occasional car parked in the street.

If you walk up the Avenue of the Knights from Museum Square, you pass the Inn of Italy, the Palace of Villiers De L'Isle Adam, and the Inn of France on your right. The Inn of France has the most interesting facade, with an off-center main doorway, half-framed second-story windows, and four gargoyles protruding from above between four turrets. Almost directly opposite the Inn of France is an iron gate leading to an old Turkish garden and fountain. Uphill from the Inn after you pass Lahetos Street on the left is the French Chapel, with its Gothic sculpture of the Virgin and Child at one corner underneath a stone canopy. Next to it stands the house of the Chaplain of the Tongue of France. Passing under an arch, on the right is the Inn of Provence, and to the left the Inn of Spain. At the top of the street is a second archway, with ribbed vaulting leading to Kleovoulou Square and, on the right, the prize possession of the city, the **Palace of the Knights of St. John.**

In times of war, this 300-room castle, which dominates the entire city of Rhodes from the northwest corner of the old town, served as an almost impregnable medieval fortress, complete with moats, drawbridges, huge watchtowers, and colossal battlements. The structure survived the long Turkish siege of 1522 reasonably well, only to be decimated in 1856 by an explosion in an ammunition depot across the street. The Italians undertook the task of rebuilding it in the beginning of this century. Determined to outdo even the industrious Knights of St. John, and erect an edifice the likes of which the world had never seen, they completely restored the citadel and embellished many of the floors with famous Hellenistic mosaics taken from the island of Kos. The Italians had big plans for the palace: in the early part of this century, it was used as a seat of Italian government, where such notables as Victor Immanuel III and Mussolini were entertained during their visits to Rhodes. The interior decoration was only completed a few months before the start of WWII, so the Italians had little chance to enjoy the full fruits of their megalomaniacal effort.

The monumental castle is as much an archeological museum as a fortress, since it contains one of the finest collections of Hellenistic and early Byzantine mosaics (mostly dating from the sixth to second centuries B.C.) in Europe. When you first enter the palace, you will find yourself irresistibly drawn towards the impressive main courtyard. But to reach the chambers with the mosaics from Kos, you will have to backtrack and take the grand staircase to the left of the entrance. Particularly noteworthy is the second century B.C. mosaic of Medusa in a small room of its own. A copy of the statue Laocoon, a Rhodian masterpiece of the first century B.C. which is now in the Vatican museum, graces another room. At the bottom of the staircase and to the left is the Chapel to the Virgin Mary. The palace is open Mon.-Sat. 9am-3:15pm, Sun. 10am-2pm, closed Tues. Admission is 100dr, 50dr with student ID. Tours of the walls are given every Monday and Saturday at 3pm, leaving from in front of the Palace of the Knights. Be sure to arrive about fifteen minutes early; the tour costs an additional 50-100dr, but is the only way you can have access to the ramparts.

The Chora

To get a sense of a different era in the city's history, turn right into Kleovoulou Square as you leave the palace. After passing under some arches, turn left onto Orfeos Street, better known as **The Plane Tree Walk.** The large clock tower on the left marked the outer limits of the wall which separated the knights' quarters from the rest of the city. The idea was the same during the Ottoman era, but the boundaries changed: the Old City as a whole was reserved for Turks and Jews, and Greeks had to live outside of its walls.

Just one block from the clock tower stands the **Mosque of Suleymein,** the biggest mosque in Rhodes. The original mosque on this site was built immediately after Suleymein the Magnificent captured Rhodes in 1522. The present one, an early nineteenth-century construction, has red-painted plaster walls, a garden, and a stone minaret that make it a good landmark in the old city and the best-kept symbol of a time Rhodians would like to forget. You can enter from 10am-12:30pm and 6-7:30pm (these hours are unpredictable) if you dress appropriately. The interior, with white ceilings and several light-colored carpets, is surprisingly bright and airy. Across the street from the mosque is the **Turkish library,** built in 1794 and full of Persian and Arabic manuscripts, including a chronicle of the three-month-long siege of Rhodes in 1522, and Qur'ans with extraordinarily beautiful calligraphy. It is open (again unpredictably) Mon.-Sat. 9am-1pm and 5-7pm. The other Turkish buildings and monuments in the Old Town are in various states of decay. The **Mosque of Retjep Pasha,** near Ornirou Street in the southeast part of the city, is only a ghost of what was once Rhodes' most splendid mosque. The old Turkish baths are at Platia Arionos.

Leading downhill from the Mosque of Suleymein is Sokratous Street, Rhodes's main shopping street, lined with yellowed, two-story structures and empty of traffic except for an occasional motorbike. Here you'll find crowded storefronts selling ceramics, clothes, jewelry, and other gift items. The **Mosque of the Agha** about halfway down prevents a clear view down Sokratous St. If you continue eastward along Aristoteleous St., you'll reach the **Square of the Jewish Martyrs** in the heart of the old Jewish Quarter. Two thousand Jews were taken from this square in 1943 to Nazi concentration camps; only fifty survived. Both the **Archbishop's Palace** (or Admiralty Palace) facing the square and the **Church of Ste. Marie du Bourg,** a little further on Pindarou St., to the east, deserve a visit.

For a sample of the Byzantine art which seems overwhelmed by all the other monuments in the city, visit the **Church of St. Fanourios** across from the Paris Hotel on Aghios Fanourios Street. Used as a stable and as a mosque during the Turkish period, it was restored in this century.

The New Town and Mandraki

Mandraki Harbor's most treasured possessions are the bronze Deer, a stag and a doe, flanking the entrance to the harbor. Some say that the two pillars that support the statues occupy the original site of the "Colossus of Rhodes," a 32m statue that stood over the mouth of the harbor: boats passed between the statue's legs to enter. Maybe not. In any case, the statue was commissioned to celebrate a forgotten bit of Rhodian history: one of Alexander's heirs besieged Rhodes in order to force it to join in an alliance against Egypt, a move contrary to Rhodes' commercial interests. After a full year (305-304 B.C.) the island's resistance succeeded and the siege ended. The enormous statue of the sun-god Helios took twelve years to build and was declared by the ancients to be one of the seven wonders of the world, but the famous Colossus stood for only sixty years before it was toppled by a devastating earthquake in 226 B.C.

Set back from the deer are several examples of Italian architecture along the Mandraki waterfront. Massive Mussolini-inspired buildings of large, multi-colored stone preside over wide Elefterias Street and small parks with statues. The Bank of Greece, the Town Hall, the Post Office, and the National Theater are the more notable structures on the far side of the street. Directly opposite, along the waterfront, is the majestic **Governor's Palace** (reminiscent of the Doge's Palace in Venice) and a church to St. John. The church, built by the Italians in 1925, is supposed to be a replica of the original St. John's Church near the Grand Palace, which was leveled in the explosion of 1856. Some Greeks resent these grandiose buildings, others appreciate them. An attempt was made in the last few years to claim the theater as the Greeks' own by completely re-building the inside; unfortunately, in the process, its acoustics were ruined.

The Turkish presence can only be seen a little to the north in the **Mosque of Mourad Reis,** named after Suleymein's admiral, who succeeded in capturing Rhodes from the Knights in 1522 but died in the process. The small domed building to the right as you enter is his mausoleum; the eerie cemetery is full of broken stone turbans and hungry-eyed cats.

Much older and more famous than the Italian and Turkish structures are the three **Windmills of Rhodes,** halfway along the harbor's long pier, which used to mill grain for medieval cargo ships, and the **Fortress of St. Nicholas** at the end of the pier which was built in 1464 and guarded the harbor until the end of World War II. If you walk along the pier at Mandraki toward the windmills, you'll see many private yachts heading to Cyprus, Turkey, etc. looking for crew members. It's one cheap, if unpredictable, way to travel.

The **Aquarium,** situated on the northernmost tip of the city overlooking Sandy Point, offers a pleasant diversion from the seemingly endless series of ancient buildings and sights. Open from 8am-8pm, the price is 50dr, 25dr for students.

Nightlife

The **Folk Dance Theater** on Andronikou (tel. 29 08 5) has performances every night during the summer except Saturday. Shows begin at 9:15, cost 400dr (200dr with student ID), and feature dances and songs from Northern and Central Greece, and, of course, the Dodecanese Islands. The dancing is splendid, definitely worth the admission price. Some of the dancers give instruction (in English) in the late afternoon.

The evening **Sound and Light Shows** given at the Palace are extremely popular with tourists. Performances are conducted in four languages and give an account of the Turkish siege of the city during the Crusader occupation. The entrance to the show is on Papagou Street, across from the New Market, in the fortress gardens. From April 1-May 15 and Aug. 1-Oct. 31, English shows are on Mon., Tues., and Thu. at 9:15pm; Wed., Fri., Sat., and Sun. at 10:15pm. From May 16-July 31, the shows are one hour later. The price is 150dr, 80dr for students. St. Francis Church has organ recitals every Wednesday night at 9pm, and is located at the intersection of Dimokratias and Filelinon Sts. The ancient theater near Monte Smith is only used once or twice a month; check the NTOG office for details.

Rhodes has enough night-spots to satiate even the most restless bar-hopper. A healthy dose of variety is wanting, however; almost all of the bars, clubs, and discos play the same music and attract the same crowd. The **Babylon,** on Voriou Ipirou St. near Kennedy St., offers all you can drink for a 350dr cover charge (which is what one drink costs at many places here), and gets packed on hot summer nights. If it's just too crowded, there's an identical club next door and another across the street. Near Diakou and Venizelou Sts. is another cluster of bars and clubs; the **1960s Bar** on Diakou is, in spite of its tacky sobriquet, a fun place to hang out. As its name suggests, it does not play disco.

Finally, many people make an evening of just walking in the Old Town, as the souvenir shop and clothing stores on Sokratous St. stay open until 10 or 11pm.

Near Rhodes

Several places of interest make ideal half-day trips from the city of Rhodes: Ancient Ialyssos (now known as Filerimos), Petaloudes, and Rodini Park.

The coastline to the west of Rhodes for a stretch of about 8km is a long string of high-rise hotels along the equally long strip of sandy beach. The western end of this luxury hotel district is the town of **Trianda,** or Modern Ialyssos, not to be confused with the archeological site of Ancient Ialyssos, or Filerimos (5km inland on a hill), which, with Lindos and Kamiros, was one of the three great cities on the island in ancient times.

The ruins themselves are rather meager: the most impressive find is the fourth-century B.C. **Doric fountain** decorated with four lion heads. Much more interesting are the **Monastery** and the **Church of Our Lady of Filerimos,** which is actually four connected chapels. Both the church and the monastery are built on the site of a third century B.C. temple to Athena and Zeus Polieus and a Byzantine Church (converted to stables by the Turks), which was rebuilt once by the Italians and then again in the 1950s. Also see the underground **Chapel of St. George** nearby, covered with restored fourteenth, and fifteenth-century frescoes. An interesting historical footnote is that first the Knights, and later the Turks, used the commanding vantage point from this hill to organize their respective attacks on the City of Rhodes. The site is open Mon.-Sat. 9am-3:15pm, Sun. 10am-2pm, admission 50dr, 25dr with student ID. Unfortunately, there is no easy way to get to Filerimos. Taxis from Sound and Light Square will make the round trip for 500dr. Aside from motorbike, the only other alternative is the buses from Rhodes to modern Ialyssos which leave every hour, but you'll have to take a taxi from Trianda, try to hitch (which can be difficult), or walk the five kilometers.

Two other popular excursions from Rhodes are those to Rodini Park and Petaloudes. **Rodini Park,** just 3km from the city and serviced by any bus heading east from Rhodes, is a forested area with streams and little trails and a restaurant. **Petaloudes,** about 25km away, is also known as the **Valley of the Butterflies** because it becomes filled with brightly-colored moths from June to September. Though often crowded with tourists, the valley overcomes their effect with little lakes, wooden bridges, and eighteenth-century monastery. Buses leave at 9am and at noon for Petaloudes from Averof St. and start the return trip at 10:50am and 1:50pm; the trip costs 85dr each way and takes about forty minutes.

Eastern Rhodes

As you drive out of Rhodes, the landscape changes in double-time from city to country. Fifteen kilometers south of Rhodes towards Lindos you pass the popular **Faliraki Beach,** a good place to swim, but only a little less crowded than the beaches around Rhodes during the day. Down to the right side of the beach you can rent windsurfers from **Maryanna** for 300dr per hour, or 2500dr for ten hours. There are plenty of rooms to let near the beach which the Rhodes NTOG can call up for you; expect to pay at least 800dr for a double. Buses to and from Rhodes run at least hourly until 11pm; 40dr one way.

Further south, just before Kolimbia, a road to the right will take you to a dirt road 3km away, which brings you to **Epta Piges** or Seven Springs. This area is ideal for nature walks, but most people come to eat at the restaurant next to the main stream. All the tables are in the shade next to the rushing water, and the waiters hop from rock to rock to serve their customers. If you like Byzantine churches, it's worth continuing another 10km or so inland past Epta Piges to the **Church of Agios Nikolaos Fountoucli,** 3km past Eleousa. Built on a rare four-apse design, it has some excellent thirteenth- and fifteenth-century frescoes.

Back on the road to Lindos, the next place of note is the **Tsampikas Monastery,** a little Byzantine cloister sitting high on Mt. Tsampikas. A cement road on the left near the top of a hill (just before the Tsampikas Beach turnoff) will take you three-quarters of the way there, if your motorbike has very good low gears, but you'll have to walk the rest of the way. At the top, white stone walls surround five small rooms and a chapel, and the views are great. If you have trouble deciding whether to go to Kolimbia or Tsampikas Beach, the new perspective ought to help you choose. Ten kilometers further down the road (15km shy of Lindos), if you take the turnoff to **Charaki,** you can swim next to the hill with the crumbling **Castle of Feraclos** at its top, built by the Knights of St. John. This is a beautiful spot, almost undiscovered, although there are already hints of impending tour-group colonization. Among the circle of houses along the beach are a few rooms to let and a few restaurants. The beach is ordinary, but the setting is unbeatable. At the end of the beach, a path leads up to the castle. When the tourist wave hits Charaki, you can try **Lardos Bay** a few kilometers southwest of Lindos; as beautiful as Charaki but without the castle.

Lindos

Lindos should be the showpiece of Rhodes. The town has it all—a fabulous Crusader fortress, a splendid ancient acropolis situated on a precipitous clifftop, a well-protected cove with a large sandy beach, and enchanting little streets. Unfortunately, Lindos' magnetic qualities have drawn crowds of tourists to its streets, making the town the most expensive in Rhodes. To make matters worse, many of the Greeks in Lindos have lost all patience with the excessive numbers of foreigners, and, having become accustomed to wealthy, middle-aged tourists, are often hostile and rude to younger, more budget-conscious travelers. If you visit Lindos in the summer, you will find yourself torn by a love for the enchanting and idyllic setting, and a disgust for the crass commercialism that pervades the town.

You might want to consider just making a daytrip to Lindos, to avoid the tourist trappings as much as possible. If you come in the summer, arrive later in the afternoon when most of the tour buses have cleared out and you can explore the town in relative solitude. The town itself is like an outdoor picture gallery—streets, doorsteps, and inner courtyards are all covered with delicate black and white pebble mosaics arranged in striking and intricate patterns, and many of the village's alleys are paved with wall-to-wall mosaics. In addition, the doorways of Lindos are an artform in themselves—carved into intricate patterns and freshly painted in the same rich shade of brown. Each one of them is different, and yet they share a common style that is one of the fundamental features of the village's beauty.

Six buses a day go between Rhodes and Lindos; the ride takes an hour and costs 140dr.

Accommodations and Practical Information

Lindos has one main avenue, Acropolis Street, leading from the Main Square through the eastern part of town and up to the Acropolis. The second main street, Apostolous Paulou, runs perpendicular to Acropolis St., westward from the Church of the Assumption Madonna (whose stone bell tower rises up in the middle of town). Houses are indicated only by a number and not a street address. House numbers increase as you ascend Acropolis Street and as you move west away from it, whether you take Apostolou Paulou St. or any of the smaller alleyways. Although initially frustrating, after a while locating any house number in town by watching the numbers progress becomes relatively easy.

If you come in summer, the only cheap, and sometimes the only possible place to stay in Lindos is the beach. There are no hotels in Lindos, one reason why it is such an attractive place. Unfortunately, this means all tourists stay in pensions and private homes. There are only a handful of pensions which are not filled by vacationers on tour with Olympic Holidays, Inc., for the entire summer. In the few independent pensions that still exist (and there seem to be fewer every summer) doubles run 800-900dr per night, and singles are nonexistent. Some of these are **Pension Lindos** at #70, the **Pension Elektra** at #63, **Pension 416** (which hasn't changed its name though it has changed its address—#511) and houses #58, #412, and #506. You can also visit **Pallas Travel Agency** (tel. 31 27 5) at #178, open Mon.-Sat. 9am-1pm and 5-8pm. Most of the tour groups have representatives here, and if any of their houses has a vacancy, you can get it; it's a slim chance but worth a try. They rarely arrange stays of less than three days. On summer nights the beach is lined with sleeping bodies, and no one complains. It appears to be safe to leave a pack here during the day, behind the umbrellas.

Most of the town's services are on or just off Acropolis St. The **OTE** at #156, up the stairs on the left behind Alexis Bar, is open Mon.-Fri. 8am-2:30pm. The **police** are at #521 and a **laundromat** is at #456, where you can use the machines yourself for a steep 300dr. **Panayotis Motorbike Rental**, #336 (tel. 31 32 8) will rent motorcycles for 700-900dr. The **Post Office** and **pharmacy** are up the hill to the right from the donkey stand; follow the signs. Beyond them at #381 is a small lending library which rents books for 15dr a day with a 250dr deposit.

Daily boat trips leave Lindos at 10:30am for the more secluded beaches of **Agathy Heraki** and **Vleha** to the north and to **Pefkos Beach** in the south, returning at 5pm. The two operators, Captain Tassos and Captain Stergos, take reservations at Pericles Taverna and Yannis' Bar, respectively. Round trip price is 500dr. If you want to go to Pefkos Beach and skip the boat ride, you can walk the 4km south and maybe get a lift from another beachgoer if you set out at around 9am. Just out of town you'll see some spectacular, rocky scenery and **St. Paul's Bay,** the protected little cove where the Apostle Paul supposedly landed in a storm, bringing the teachings of Jesus to this corner of the world. Paul's name-day, June 28-29, is the occasion for a festival here. The cliffs here also served a more secular crew filming *The Guns of Navarone*.

Food and Nightlife

Eating cheaply in Lindos poses a real challenge: restaurants range from moderately expensive (like the Pericles) to out of this world. The only alternative is the souvlaki-pita bars or grocery stores on the two main streets.

Lindos has a lively, loud nightlife. Most people visit the town's bars until the music is turned off at 11pm and then saunter down to the discotheques along the road on the other side of the main square leading to the beach. You may want to avoid the busier bars in town if you're not interested in drinking very much—the waiters keep asking you to order and occasionally ask you to leave. Most proprietors in Lindos are accustomed to watching foreigners unload money at a prodigious rate; if you fail to keep pace with your neighbors at other tables, it is quite possible you will encounter a lack of hospitality that would be considered disgraceful in most other parts of Greece. The **Cafe-Bar Poseidon,** just past the Church at #173, is a small place with a less-pressured atmosphere.

Sights

Lindos' main attraction, the ancient **acropolis,** stands at the top of the sheer cliff walls that rise 375 feet up from the town, and is enclosed in the impenetrable walls of a Crusader **fortress.** On the left as you enter the site are three cisterns with remarkable acoustical qualities—throw the tiniest pebble down, then listen. Across the courtyard, the relief of a second century B.C. ship serves as an elegant frontispiece to the fortress. Up the stairs and through a little storehouse of ancient rubble are the ruins of castle chambers and of the Knights' basilica, built in the thirteenth century and dedicated to their patron saint. The nave and side aisles are still discernable. Thirteen restored columns of the imposing **Doric Stoa** (arcade) dominate this whole level. The arcade, built around 200 B.C. at the height of Rhodes' glory, consisted originally of 42 columns laid out in the shape of the Greek letter pi. Notice how the side wings, by limiting perpendicular movement, help to focus the whole structure on the apex at the top of the steps. The design serves to heighten the anticipation for what comes into view at the top of the steps: the **Temple of the Lindian Athena.**

According to myth, a house of worship had been on this spot since 1510 B.C., probably dedicated to some matriarchal goddess who demanded the sacrifice of fruit and vegetables rather than of live animals. This custom persisted in Lindos long past the Dorian invasion. The remains you see are of a temple built originally by the tyrant Cleoboulos in the sixth century B.C., and rebuilt and expanded two centuries later to its present dimensions. Surprisingly small, the temple was one of the most important religious sites in the Mediterranean. Now it is one of the few ancient Greek temples with inner walls intact and colonnades on both sides. A glance down over the medieval walls next to the temple will reveal St. Paul's Bay which looks like a small lake of crystal blue sea water.

If nothing else, enjoy the acropolis of Lindos for its natural setting; it affords a breathtaking view of the town and beach of Lindos, the large quiet harbor with its long natural stone breakwater, and the dramatic coastline that extends in either direction. The acropolis is open Mon.-Sat. 9am-3:15pm, Sun. 10am-2pm; admission 100dr, 50dr with student ID. Don't hire a donkey to take you up to the acropolis; it's too expensive at 150dr up to the acropolis and 100dr down. (If someone tells you that it's a long haul up to the acropolis, they are talking about the circuitous route taken by the donkeys.)

Between the town and the acropolis are a few sights worth seeing. The graceful stone bell tower that rises up from the middle of the town belongs to the **Church of the Assumption Madonna,** rebuilt by the Knights of St. John around 1489. The interior of the church is adorned with brightly-colored eighteenth-century frescoes which were retouched by the Italians in 1927. If you can get someone to let you in, the burial chamber at the far end has some lovely icons. As usual, dress properly. At the southwest foot of the acropolis is the intact **ancient theater.** It is across an asphalt lot from #422; follow Pavlou from the Church to the Agricultural Co-op foodstore, then take the left of the pair of almost-parallel streets. On the way up to the acropolis, you can look west and see a **Hellenistic cave-tomb** from 200 B.C. on Mount Krana. At #202 by a leftward turn of the steps is an odd house with a five-hundred-year-old wood ceiling where you can see the self-proclaimed "famous Lindian plates," antiques noted for their beauty and passed down for generations. On the northern side of the rock face of the acropolis is the **Voukopion,** a natural cave which the Dorians transformed into a sanctuary dedicated to Athena. It is believed to date back to about the ninth century B.C. and to have been used for special sacrifices that could only be performed outside the premises of the acropolis proper.

Outside of the city of Rhodes, Lindos has the most crowded beach on the island. During the summer it's packed with British vacationers either sunbathing or pausing from the heat in the shade of one of the numerous beach umbrellas. Windsurfers can be rented for 300dr per hour or 2500dr for ten hours worth of tickets with all the instruction you want or need. If you're willing to have an audience, you can take water-skiing lessons: 500dr for some instruction and about ten minutes in the water.

Western Rhodes

South of Filerimos along the eastern coast, the two historical spots worthy of attention are the ruins of Ancient Kamiros and Castle of Monolithos. There are also several interesting towns along the way. Two of the island's biggest religious festivals take place on the road to Kamiros. At Kremasti, 12km outside of Rhodes, the name-day of the Virgin Mary (Panayia) is celebrated for nine days beginning on August 14. Off the inland road at Kalavarda, the Monastery of Aghois Soulas puts on an especially grand name-day festival for its patron saint on July 28 and 29.

Ancient Kamiros, 35km from modern-day Rhodes, was a prosperous city surrounded by good farmland in the sixth and fifth centuries B.C. What survives are the stone walls of the houses, a cobblestoned main street, the reservoir cisterns, and the fallen pillars of temples and public places. Individually, the ruins are not all that interesting, but taken together the site becomes a lifesize blueprint of a small ancient city. Down a small flight of steps and past the entrance to the site are the remains of an ancient Doric temple on the right. Just to the left stands a larger sanctuary with seven pillars remaining, though in various stages of ruin. From the main street, you can get a good sense of how big the place is. Most of the ruins of private houses are on the left. Up the street before the hill, there are seven standing, restored pillars which belong to a **Hellenistic House.** A long porch (over 200m) sits on the top of the hill, where the market used to be. Behind this third century B.C. structure, which originally bore two rows of columns, stands a temple to Athena. Two rows of stones, those farthest up on the hill, are all that remain. In front of the market are two large reservoirs which provided water for the town: enough, say archeologists, for 300-odd families for half a year. The Kamiros site is open Mon.-Sat. 9am-3:15pm. and Sun. 10am-2pm; admission is 50dr, 25dr for students.

Some 15km beyond Ancient Kamiros, the village of Kamiros Skala has a few houses, tavernas, and a boat launch. Boats leave here for Halki once a day at 3pm, returning at the same time the next morning (700dr round trip). Beyond Kamiros Skala at Kritinia there is a turn for **Embona,** a village famous for its dancing and traditional costume. Not very striking from a distance, Embona is a large group of low-lying houses above farmland and forests and below the barren, rocky slopes of Mt. Ataryros—at 1215m, the tallest mountain on the island. The town itself is busy and conducts a thriving tourist trade on summer evenings. Two restaurants offer traditional Greek dancing for tour groups which come from Rhodes. You don't need to join a group if you don't want to, however, and **Bake's Cafe** (near the large Church of the Holy Trinity in the southeast part of town) will give you dinner and the show for 500dr. Rooms to let above the dancing square are 500dr for two people, but an empty one is hard to come by.

From Embona, the road south traverses a mountain ridge, and from these heights you can get beautiful views of Alimnia and Tragousa and the other small islands off the coast before continuing to Monolithos. On the way you may want to stop in **Siana** and purchase its local specialty, honey. If you stop here, be sure to visit the **Cafeneion** on Main Street with the "English Spoken Here" sign and the old-timer who spent his boyhood days in Sacramento, California, as he says, during "the years of Roosevelt, Taft, and Wilson."

There isn't much to see in the town of Monolithos, so proceed southwest (2km) to the **Castello of Monolithos,** which some say is one of the most beautifully-situated castles in the world. The fortress is now in ruins, but it still looks majestic on the top of a single rock rising five hundred feet into the air (monolithos means "single rock"). You can walk around inside the castle and the small chapel of St. Panteleimon, but be careful of the steep drop while you are enjoying the views.

Southern Rhodes

The area south of Lindos in the east and Monolithos in the west could almost be considered a different island. This is a farming and goatherding countryside, whose yellow, grassy flatlands gradually slope into green hills covered with low-lying bushes. There isn't much of specifically historical interest to see in these parts, but there are numerous secluded beaches and coves, especially on the east coast. You'll find plenty of Greeks here, and (with few exceptions) prices unaffected by the tourist invasion. If isolation is what you are looking for, you can take the dirt road to the **lighthouse** at Akro Prassonisi at the southern tip of the island. The couple who lives there rarely gets any visitors in the summer. During the winter they get none at all, as the sea covers the narrow stretch of land connecting the lighthouse to the island. Doubtlessly the most picturesque place to stay at this end of the island, however, is the rustic **Skiadhi Monastery,** situated halfway up a hill on a steep, alternate road between Apollakia and Messanagros. The views of the western coastline below stretch for miles, which is ideal for sunsets. No monks live here, but an elderly couple will almost always put you up for the night. Be sure to bring your own food—there is nothing around you but forest and hills. Occasionally a group of villagers will come here by car (sometimes even a bus) with a hired priest and hold services at midnight and in the early morning. Accommodations may then be something of a problem. To get there from Messanagros, take the posted turnoff 2km to the southwest and follow the winding road downhill for about 4km. From Apollakia, go south about 7km before taking a left for 4km.

Symi

The island of Symi, two hours away from Rhodes by ferry, is a small yet dramatic showpiece of the Dodecanese islands. As your boat makes its final turn into the harbor of **Ghialos,** the island's main village, you'll quickly see why. White and stone houses with red-shingled roofs climb up the sides of the surrounding hills, and beautiful churches proudly stand all around. The whole setting is reminiscent of another time. Many houses of neoclassical style, in fact, date from the island's nineteenth-century glory. During this period, shipbuilding, sponge diving, fishing, and commercial trade all flourished while the Symians received concessions from the Sultans. Ships made in Symi have a reputation for being yare (a reputation which has lasted, though to a much lesser degree, until today).

Most of the shipbuilding, sponge diving, and fishing industry is gone now, along with a large segment of the population. The villages, however, manage to retain their romantic, elegant beauty. In 1983, a project to enlarge the harbor brought a lot of noise and ugly machinery into Ghialos, but everyone says, or prays, that it will be completed by 1984. The Greek government has actively joined the preservation effort: in 1971, it declared the town of Ghialos a historic site. Many of the islanders now seem to work in the tourist trade, catering to the daily excursion boats filled with visitors who come from Rhodes for the afternoon. What happens on many Greek islands certainly applies to Symi: the restaurants fill, the stores hike their prices, and the locals, at the point of irritation, become that much harder to meet. You can avoid the crush of people by going to the beach for a few hours, but if you're coming from Rhodes, it won't seem crowded anyway.

If possible, stay after the excursion boats from Rhodes leave the island in the afternoon. The whole atmosphere becomes much more peaceful. In the evening, it is mostly Greeks who will sit in the taverns drinking ouzo and retsina. Symi (Ghialos) is connected by ferry three times a week to and from Rhodes (250dr) and two times a week to and from Piraeus (1200dr). Excursion boats also travel between Rhodes and Symi (see Panormitis monastery).

All important offices are found in Ghialos: a **Post Office, OTE,** and a number of banks. During the summer a one-man tourist information office is open Mon.-Sat. 11am-1pm in the clock tower, and the regular police are located on the second floor of the next building. The **Glafkos Hotel** (tel 71 35 8), on the village square just back from the waterfront, has small singles and doubles for 500dr and 700dr a night, respectively. There are outdoor tables for eating and reading, and the top four rooms have an excellent view of the harbor. The **Haskas Hotel** (tel. 71 34 0), almost exactly opposite on the same square and up the stairs, has the same under somewhat cramped conditions. Rooms to let throughout the village cost 450dr for a single and 650dr for a double. There are few enough of them that during the high season you may have trouble finding a place, so look early in the day.

Eating can be expensive in the waterfront restaurants, since the daytime tourists keep prices high. Even if you don't eat there, be sure to notice the plaque above **Les Caterinettes Restaurant** one hundred yards from the clock tower: this is the house where the Italians signed the agreement surrendering the Dodecanese to the Allied Powers on May 8, 1945. A good place for dinner is **George's Restaurant** near the castle, where you sit on a veranda looking down on the harbor.

Although Symi has weathered several historical epochs, there is relatively little of historical interest. The best thing to do is to walk through the village's back streets up to the houses in and around the castle ruins at the top of the hill. Chorio, as this neighborhood is called, was built when locals sought protection from pirate raids. Even today many of the houses make use of the castle walls as part of their structure. To get to Chorio, you must walk along the waterfront to Okonomou Square in front of the Symian Holidays Agencies, take a right, and start walking up the 500-odd stairs, also known as Kali Strata, the main road in Ghialos and Chorio.

Nos Beach, ten minutes by foot from Ghialos (head north along the waterfront, past the shipyard), is very small, but it is also the closest beach to the port. It has a small taverna-discotheque next to it. The hamlet of **Pedi** (pronounced Pethi) is behind the hill of Chorio and takes about thirty minutes to reach. The beach there is not especially good, but at least it's quieter. If you're especially ambitious, you might continue on past Nos Beach about 45 minutes to Emborio. The beach that runs all along this hamlet is not great but the views along the way and the remnants of a Byzantine mosaic in a church courtyard 200m from the water make it worth the walk.

Panormitis Monastery

At the center of a remarkable horseshoe-shaped harbor in the southern part of the island is the grand Monastery of the Archangel Michael the Panormitis. The monastery was founded at the spot where a local woman chanced upon a miraculous icon of Michael. Although taken to Ghialos, the icon kept finding its way back to Panormitis, and the hint was taken. The palatial white buildings of the monastery, dominated by an elegant bell tower (built in 1905) in the center, have been a popular stopping place for Dodecanese sailors in years past. Within the monastery complex are several restaurants, a small museum, a library, and rooms to let. The monastery church is small with an exceptionally crafted wooden altar screen. The guest rooms in the complex, which are actually old monk's cells, are inexpensive at 500dr a night for a three- or four-bed room—a great place for rest and contemplation. Most of the other overnight visitors are vacationing Greek families, and it remains quiet here except between 3 and 4pm when the excursion boat arrives. Inside the church, don't forget to dress conservatively.

A road is being built from Ghialos through Panormitis, but until it's completed the only plausible way to get to the Monastery is by boat. Various excursion boats from Rhodes come to Symi in the morning and then stop at Panormitis for an hour and a half before the return trip. The full excursion costs 700dr.

Halki

If life on Rhodes seems a little too fast-paced or impersonal, or you think there are just too many people around invading your peace and quiet, a few days on Halki may prove the answer. The visitor who steps off the boat in Halki's harbor, **Niborio,** will be immediately struck by the relaxed, easygoing pace of life on the island. Even during the summer season, there is a good chance that aside from a handful of Europeans renting houses on the island for a month, you will be the only tourist there.

Niborio is a peaceful village, a group of box-shaped stone houses arranged in a semi-circle around the still, clear waters of the harbor. In its heyday it was an active fishing and sponge-diving community with several thousand inhabitants. Most of the year-round villagers still fish for a living, although the population is far smaller than it once was. Many of the locals have moved to Tarpon Springs, Florida, to start an expatriate community there. Evidence of their exodus can be seen in a number of uninhabited, run-down buildings still standing side by side with the freshly painted white houses with orange roofs.

Niborio has only a few small tavernas and restaurants, a grocery store, a bakery, and a post office (open Mon.-Fri. 7:30-9am, 10am-2pm). There are no hotels or pensions, but some private homes rent rooms (300dr per person) along the waterfront, so you should have no problem finding accommodations. The beach nearest to the village, **Pandemos Beach,** is a modest stretch of sand on the other side of the small hill which rises above the town. Follow the cobblestone street which starts behind the post office and snakes its way up through the village (the walk takes about ten minutes).

If you take the road up the hill towards the middle of the island, you will eventually reach **Chora** (4km from Niborio), a largely deserted village that thrived in the eighteenth and nineteenth centuries when the islanders were trying to avoid the frequent pirate raids. Those willing to climb some more can go to the Medieval Castle for a magnificent view of the entire southern coast. The ruins of a church lie behind the fortress walls, and you can just make out a few wall paintings which have faded in the sun.

Halki can be reached by ferries traveling between Rhodes and Karpathos three times a week. A small boat also leaves Kamiros on the island of Rhodes at 5:30am for Halki, returning at 6pm (332dr one way).

Kos

Kos has all the ingredients for a superb island vacation—and every travel agent in Northern Europe knows it. With some of the finest archeological sites in the Aegean, superb beaches, and an active nightlife, Kos is an attractive target for hundreds of German and Scandinavian charter tours. As a result, this one-time island paradise is packed in July and August and the once friendly islanders have become sullen and indifferent to the continuous influx of foreigners. At the same time, the island handles its heavy load of tourists with grace. If you are really allergic to the tourist scene, go elsewhere for the summer and leave Kos for the off-season.

Kos is best known as the home of Hippocrates, father of medicine and composer of the 2400-year-old oath still taken by doctors today. In ancient times the island prospered as a major trading power and as the sacred site of Asclepion, the healing god. Several hundreds of years later, Kos served as an episcopal seat under Byzantine rule. Before and after the fall of the Byzantine empire, pirates and naval forces from various nations repeatedly invaded the island. The Knights of St. John finally took the island in hand in 1315, and promptly transformed it into one of their invincible outposts. From then on its history followed that of the other Dodecanese islands.

Transportation

Six ferries a week travel between Kos and Rhodes (591dr), and six a week go to and from Piraeus (1256dr) via Kalymnos, Leros, and Patmos. Olympic has daily flights to and from Athens (2520dr) and Rhodes (1530dr). A number of hydrofoils travel to and from Samos, Rhodes, and Patmos several times a week, fast but considerably more expensive than the ferry. Ferries travel twice a week to Astipalea, Amorgos, Samos, Lipsi, Arki, and Agathonisi, and three times a week to Symi, Nissyros, and Tilos. In addition, excursion boats make daytrips to Kalymnos (one-way 250dr), Patmos (500dr), and Nissyros (400dr); these generally leave from the harbor between 8 and 9am, and you can buy your ticket right there. Ask at the NTOG or Tourist Police for details.

It is possible to get to the Turkish port of Bodrum, near the ancient site of Halicarnassus, from Kos. The boat is Turkish and the schedule irregular; during the summer it sails about three times a week. There is no agency in Kos, only an elderly man named Mr. Politis who often spends his mornings at Sifi's Restaurant on the waterfront. He doesn't speak English, but will write down the current schedule and fare—in 1983, 1400dr one way.

Getting Around the Island

It is especially true in Kos that the mode of transportation you choose will depend on your destination and the amount of time and energy you are willing to spend. Bicycles are the best way to see the island, but you are probably going to walk up no small number of steep hills if you're headed for the southern end of the island or one of the little villages in the mountains. Otherwise, they're fine for getting around. The landscape is often beautiful, so a slower form of transportation is preferable. The popular alternative, especially for those traveling longer distances, is the motorbike. Both can be rented for reasonable rates around the town of Kos. Bicycles usually cost 150dr a day, motorbikes from 300 to 600dr depending on the size. **Pantelides'** Shop on Mitropoleos Street (tel. 28 69 8) might be more willing than others to give you a discount for two days or more.

Many of the island's roads are unpaved. For those going to only one or two places in one day, bus service is reliable but infrequent, and in summer the public buses are usually crowded. Hitching is perfectly viable as long as you're not in too much of a hurry.

The Town of Kos

No other place in the Dodecanese bears the marks of as many different historical traditions as Kos's largest city and principal port. In the town of Kos towers of Turkish mosques stand side by side with grand Italian mansions and the massive walls of a Crusader fortress. Masses of brilliantly-colored flowers and date palms embellish the streets, squares, and ancient monuments, framed by the exotic backdrop of immense architectural diversity. But above all, the town of Kos is one great archeological park with ruins—ancient, Hellenistic, Roman—around every corner. These diverse and somewhat incongruous architectural styles form a strange but colorful whole, leading many to declare Kos one of the Aegean's most beautiful cities.

As in Rhodes, the great mass of bronzed tourists remains in or near the main town. Even the most gregarious will not be pleased with the hustle and bustle of the city during the height of the tourist season. Germans and Scandinavians have spent all day frying in the sun and occupy their evening hours by parading through the streets of Kos in white clothing to show off their tans. Despite the crowds, the town is especially clean, and most of the junky souvenir and clothing stores are confined to the side streets.

Practical Information

NTOG: On the waterfront at the corner of Pavlou St. (tel. 28 72 4). Open Mon.-Sat. 8am-1pm and 6-8pm. Very helpful; boat and bus schedules and a complete list of hotels with prices. For private room bookings, though, you'll have to turn to the **Tourist Police** next door, open every day 7:30am-1pm and 2-9:30pm.

Boat Agency: On the waterfront, next to the NTOG. If this is the wrong agency for your particular boat, they can get you to the right one.

Currency Exchange: After bank hours you can change cash and travelers checks at V-Tours Travel Agency on the first block of Pavlou St. Open Mon.-Sat. 9am-1pm and 6-8pm.

Post Office: Venizelou St. near Vironos; open Mon.-Fri. 7:30am-8:30pm; for packages only until 2:30pm.

OTE: Corner of Vironos and Xanthou Sts. Open Mon.-Fri. 7:30am-midnight, Sat. and Sun. 7:30am-3:10pm.

Bus Station: Kleopatras St. a block west of Pavlou St.

Olympic Airways: Pavlou St. south of the market (tel. 28 33 1); open daily 7:30am-7:30pm. Shuttle buses run from here to the airport 30km away.

Public Restrooms: Along the Avenue of Palms (also called Finikou St.) behind the fortress walls. Filthy.

Police: (tel. 22 22 2). Only some English spoken here. In the Town Hall, next to the Plane Tree of Hippocrates. Open 24 hours.

Hospital: On Hippocrates (Ippokratous) St. (tel. 22 30 0). There are also several pharmacies down the street.

Accommodations

During July and August, hotel and private room vacancies are non-existent, so start your room search early. The NTOG or Tourist Police is the best place to start. If your boat lands around 3am, which it often will, you probably won't have a chance of finding a room—camp out on the beach or in the little park along the Avenue of Palms at the western side of the city (turn left away from the town as you disembark). Be prepared to waken with the early morning traffic, however.

Kalymnos Hotel, 9 Riga Ferrou St. (tel. 22 33 6). Just off the center of the waterfront. A little run down, but the rooms are clean and the price is right. Singles 400dr, doubles 600dr including shower.

Hotel-Pension Australia, 39 Averof (tel. 22 10 4). On the western section of beach. Singles 600dr, doubles 870dr, baths in rooms. Rita, the friendly Greek-Australian woman who runs the place, will do her best to find you a room with one of her neighbors if her place is full.

Hotel Dodecanessos, 2 Alex Ipsilantou St. (tel. 28 46 0). Just up the road from the Hotel Kalymnos. Singles 560dr, doubles 790dr. Shower is 100dr extra, but you might be able to bargain this down.

Kos Camping (tel. 23 27 5), 2.5 km out of town. Follow the road along the water going east of Agia Fokas. Not only is it far from town, but it's also on the wrong side of the road, away from the beach. 120dr a night per person, tents up to 100dr, depending on size.

Food

Most of the town's tavernas and cafes are along the old horseshoe-shaped harbor of Mandraki, or at one of the two adjacent main squares of Kazouli and Eleftherias. Near the ruins on Nafklirou St., **Drossia** has generous portions and a few out-of-the-ordinary dishes; try the eggplant. If you really want to get away from the hustle and bustle, take Kouroukli St. out of town (about a ten-minute walk) to **Troumoukhi's Restaurant;** good food served on a vine-covered terrace.

The big yellow building in Eleftherias Square houses the municipal **market,** or "agora"; it has the best selection of fruits and vegetables.

Sights

If today Kos seems to live very much for the present, it does so under the watchful eye of the past. You can hardly walk a block here without coming upon some structure of historical interest, living or in ruins. Most sites are readily accessible, either in or near town.

Your first sight from the boat will be of the colossal walls of the **Castle of the Knights of St. John.** This Crusader castle was built in the fifteenth century and expanded during the sixteenth in response to Turkish raids; the elaborate double walls and inner moats are remarkable architectural achievements for their time. The Order of St. John on Kos was originally dedicated to nursing and healing. Their actions fell short of their ideals, however; the Knights spent most of their time engaged in warfare rather than medicine. Both building materials and design elements were borrowed from the ruins of the ancient acropolis on the same site. The top of the ramparts afford a breathtaking view of the harbor of Kos, and, across the deep blue waters of the Aegean, the

Turkish coast. (The rows of columns in the distance on the Turkish coast are the remains of the ancient sanctuary of Halicarnassus.) Enter the castle by means of the splendid stone bridge that traverses the Avenue of Palms, originally the site of the outer moat of the castle. Summer hours are Mon.-Sat. 9am-3:15pm, Sun. till 2pm, closed Tues; admission 50dr, students 25dr, free on Sundays.

Before you cross the stone bridge, between the Avenue of the Palms and the ruins of the agora, you'll see the **Plane Tree of Hippocrates,** allegedly the oldest tree in Europe, named after the great physician of antiquity who is said to have taught his pupils and written many of his books under its shade. (A highly unlikely claim, by the way, since plane trees live several hundred years at most, and Hippocrates lived over 2500 years ago.) The area around the plane tree contains a bewildering array of different architectural styles. In front of the tree, the Platanos Restaurant occupies one of the many fanciful mansions built during the Italian occupation of the island. (The most splendid example of Italian architecture is the monumental **Town Hall,** originally the Italian Governor's Palace, with a turreted white clock tower and mosaic entrance.) Flanking the tree is a Turkish structure built of multicolored stones, the rectangular **Loggia Mosque** (1786). Another Turkish structure is the **Mausoleum of Hadji Pasha,** at the corner of Hippocrates and Metreopolis Sts.

The town **archeological museum** (continue down Nafklirou St. alongside the ruins of the ancient Agora to Kazouli Square) exhibits the celebrated statues of Hippocrates and a first-rate collection of other Hellenistic sculpture. In the central courtyard is a magnificently preserved second-century A.D. Roman mosaic, depicting Hippocrates and a colleague welcoming the god Asclepius. Same hours of admission as the castle. For a sample of Byzantine architecture, visit the city's **Greek Orthodox Cathedral,** located on the corner of Korai and Agios Nikolaou Sts.

The ruins of Kos Town are grouped into two large sites: one near the harbor and castle, and the other several blocks southwest. If your archeological patience is limited, the southwest site, with ruins dating from the third century A.D., is more interesting and the better place to begin. Two short stairways lead down into the site from Grigoriou St. Across the stretch of original paved road are the remains of houses; each has bits of interior decoration intact. Toward the center of the site, the **House of Europa** contains a striking mosaic floor depicting the abduction of the nude Europa by the god Zeus. As the story goes, Zeus disguised himself in the form of a white bull and with the aid of Eros managed to seduce the Phoenician princess. Nearby are the ruins of an early Christian basilica, built over the ruins of a Roman bath; you can see both the church and the earlier structure. A large mosaic of the Judgment of Paris covers the floor of the domed bathhouse; it's protected by a blanket of sand. An elaborate building with a colonnaded *loggia* (inner balcony) was probably the latrine. Ask the curator of the museum if you would like to see it from the inside. Walk back along Grigoriou St. and you'll find a **Temple of Dionysus** on the left, just past Pavlou St.

Across Grigoriou near Pavlou, an Italian archeologist uncovered a Roman house in 1933. It turned out, however, that the third-century A.D. Roman structure concealed the ruins of an even more impressive Hellenistic mansion, two centuries older. The mosaic floors and frescoes that are now in the **Casa Romana** are Roman. Only one piece of mosaic survives from the earlier house, but it is a gem. See it in the town museum—its intricate composition manages to capture the sheen on the scales of the fish it depicts. The Casa is open the same hours as the museum and castle; admission is free. The second vast field of ruins, near the waterfront, is usually referred to as the "agora." The remains of a **Temple of Aphrodite** are here, as well as a second-century **Temple of**

Hercules that contains a fragment of a mosaic floor (third century B.C.) depicting Orpheus in the company of animals. In the corner of the site, near the Loggia Mosque, are the remains of a fourth-century A.D. Roman **basilica**. A small Christian chapel, which is still used by the local people for private prayer, has been incorporated into the ruins. The ancient agora is open 24 hours a day and admission is free. All of these ruins are particularly enjoyable in the evening when the air is cooler and the grounds less crowded.

Beaches

The town of Kos has a very modest and narrow strip of beach running southeast of town and a much wider and better strip running north of town, but both are crowded during the day and flanked by large hotels. If you follow the beach far enough to the west, you'll avoid most of the tourists and all of the hotels and restaurants. Eventually, you will reach the beach of **Lambi**, a sandy point at the northernmost tip of the island 3-4km from Kos.

Two other good beaches are located a little farther away from the port. **Agios Fokas**, 8km southeast of Kos, is accessible by a good road, but is unfortunately not serviced by a public bus. **Tigaki**, perhaps the better of the two, is 10km away from Kos on the western coast of the island. This beach, which can get crowded in summer, has a handful of restaurants and pensions (rooms 400-700dr). Camping is technically illegal, but no one seems to mind the tents that are invariably set up under the trees. Buses run to and from Tingaki three times a day on weekdays, and twice a day on weekends, arranged to allow full- and half-day excursions to the beach. It's also easy to hitch.

Asclepion

Most visitors make a pilgrimage of sorts to the workplace of Hippocrates. The Asclepion is an ancient sanctuary dedicated to the god of healing and site of the world's first medical school (applications no longer accepted). In ancient Greece there were three hundred or so Asclepions, the ancient equivalent of a hospital or medical center, and the most famous and influential were those at Epidavros and Kos. It all really began in the fifth century B.C., when Hippocrates opened up his school and encouraged the institution of a precise and systematic science of medicine. Hippocrates combined early priestly techniques with his new ones, and made Kos the foremost medical center in ancient Greece.

Most of the ruins at Asclepion actually date from the fourth century B.C. The complex was built on five different levels on a 35m hill which commands a spectacular view of the town of Kos and the Aegean. Adjoining the site is a forest of cypress and pine trees, held to be sacred in ancient times. No one was allowed to be born or to die in this area, which may explain why the inhabitants of the district had a reputation for good health. Hippocrates himself is reputed to have lived until the age of 105. The three central terraced planes, called andirons, contain the most interesting remains. They are connected by a series of superbly-crafted marble staircases.

The first andiron is most notable for the large complex of buildings that comprised the **School of Medicine.** A massive stone wall decorated with a row of niches that originally housed statues stands along the southern side of the andiron. The statues depicted various deities from which curative waters poured forth. A figure of the god Pan (half goat, half human) is still in place, and water from a natural spring flows beneath his feet. Scattered about the perimeter at this level are the ruins of Roman baths and two underground rooms that housed patients suffering from venereal disease.

Walk up the thirty steps leading to the second andiron and you'll come to the best-preserved and most interesting remains of the Asclepion: the elegant, slender, white columns of the **Temple of Apollo** from the Hellenistic Period to the left, and the two propped-up columns belonging to the third-century B.C. **Minor Temple of Asclepius** to the right. An altar stood in the center of the Temple of Asclepius for offerings to the god; his spirit was called on by nobility and laborers alike in the belief that it would free them of illness.

After sixty more steps you reach the third andiron, and the remains of the sanctuary which supported the second-century B.C. Doric-style **Main Temple of Asclepius.** The structure was reputed to be of monumental dimensions, possessing 104 columns and measuring 34m by 18m wide. Traces can be seen of a Hellenistic portico that surrounded the temple on three sides.

The site is open Mon.-Sat. 9am-3:30pm, Sun. 9am-2pm; admission 50dr, 25dr for students. Asclepion is not serviced by public bus, so if you choose not to rent a bicycle or motorscooter you must walk, hitch, or take a taxi, which will cost about 50dr. Ask for an estimate beforehand, and make sure the cabbie turns the meter on. If you want to walk one way: the return trip is downhill; from Kos, follow Grigoriou St. west out of town.

The road to Asclepion has its own rewards. Halfway there, Platani is a small Muslim village with a pleasant mosque; services are Fridays at noon. Near Platani is a Muslim cemetery, and not far off a Jewish one, with graves in Hebrew and Italian.

Central Kos

Much of the traditional Kos lifestyle can be found in the inland towns along the main road. The modern village of **Zipari** adjoins the ruins of the early **Christian Basilica of St. Paul,** 11km southeast of the main port. From there, a winding road slowly makes its way through the green foothills of the Dikeos Mountains to **Afsendiou** consisting of five small settlements with a total population of around 1600. The first one, **Evangelistia,** is disappointing. The Greek army has posted some soldiers there and the main square resembles a big asphalt parking lot. A kilometer or two farther is **Zia,** which advertises a "Greek Wine Festival"—actually a newly-created package deal for tour groups that come from Kos by bus. Everyone sits at long picnic tables and is dancing to Greek music by the end of the evening. There's a good chance your fellow merrymakers won't speak English or Greek. If you're interested, you can buy a ticket for the evening—transportation, dinner, lots of wine—for around 1100dr at a number of travel agencies in Kos Town. **Hatzivasili's Restaurant** next door has more food and better company for less money. The owner, who speaks a smattering of almost any language, makes a wonderful cinnamon juice.

For examples of the traditional way of life in these hills—goatherding, farming, weaving—try the other settlements. **Lagoudi** is the most beautiful village of the group. A project is underway to restore some of the older houses throughout Afsendiou and open them to the public; you'll have to check on the current status with the NTOG in Kos. The best part of Afsendiou may be the spaces between the settlements; you could hike for hours in the beautiful hilly woodlands and not meet anyone. Two buses a day travel to Afsendiou and one back, Mon. through Sat. If you hitch up the hill from Zipari, you'll eventually get a ride on a tractor or a farm truck.

Further south on the island, on the way to the airport, is a rotary with turnoffs for Mastihari (North) and Kardamena (South), the two resorts of central Kos. Both offer good beaches, streets with few cars, and places to eat with good, fresh food, but the similarities end there. **Kardamena** is a popular resort for tour groups from Europe, a fair-sized town with a small, active main street and a walkway behind the beach lined with cafes. Finding a room here will undoubtedly prove difficult, given all the German, English, and Scandinavian tour groups. Try the **Hotel Alma** (tel. 91 36 5) with singles for 520dr and doubles 670dr. Or ask around for a private room. Four buses a day run to Kardamena, with the last one at 8pm; four back to Kos, the last one at 5:15pm.

Mastihari, to the north, is a much quieter, smaller village with less action but more natural beauty. It's also windy most of the time. The **Fenareti Hotel,** a typical D-class hotel, has singles for 383dr and doubles for 554dr, plus 50dr for a shower. Two buses a day run to Mastihari (last one 5pm) and two run back to Kos (last one 1pm); none on Sunday.

Halfway between Kardamena and Mastihari lies the **Castle of Antimachia.** About 1km short of Antimachia from Mastihari on the main road, near a windmill, a path leads north 3km to the castle. This is another enterprise of the Knights of St. John, but its isolation enhances the grandeur.

Kefalos

Taken as a whole, the southern part of the island is something of a disappointment. The general rule that an island gets better the farther you get from the main port doesn't hold here. The landscape has the rolling hills and ravines patched with green, but the town of Kefalos, on the hill at the end of the island, is mediocre at best, with the huge Club Mediterranee spoiling an otherwise good beach and picturesque coastline. *Kefalos* is Greek for head (as in encephalitis), which is why towns on rounded peninsulas all over Greece are named Kefalos. There are no bargain hotels here; least expensive are the **Maria** (tel. 71 30 8) in Kamari, with singles 675dr, doubles 956dr, and the better-situated **Sydney Beach** (tel. 71 28 6), on Kamari Beach just before the hill to Kefalos, singles 745dr, doubles 853dr. A room-to-let will almost certainly be a better deal; ask around, or at the Tourist Police in Kos beforehand.

The beach to the east of Kamari is beautiful and unspoiled. The best beach on the island is called **Paradise Beach,** 5km east of town, accessible by a turnoff from the main road. To the north, the ruins of the eleventh-century **Christian Basilica of St. Stephen** are the most interesting Byzantine sight on this section of the island. Even though the basilica is surrounded by the bungalows connected to the huge hotel, it retains much of its simple beauty. Three buses a day travel from Kos to Kefalos; last bus out at 8pm, last return 2:45pm.

Kalymnos

The people of Kalymnos are fiercely proud of their island—and not without reason. The island's history is closely tied to that of the rest of the Dodecanese archipelago, but the independent spirit of its inhabitants has long been felt. Kalymnos was the first island to revolt against Ottoman Turkey in the 1820 Greek War of Independence. In the past Kalymnos' claim to fame was its sponge-fishing tradition. Most of its menfolk would depart for five or six months to fish for sponges in the southern waters of the Libyan Sea, off the coast of North Africa. Theirs was a unique solution to the problem of feeding themselves while living on a large, barren rock. Now the industry has declined, but because sponge fishing is very dangerous, the islanders are letting it go with a sigh of relief. One or two family members will usually work in Sydney or Ontario and send money home. There's even a town of emigrant Kalymnians in Tarpon Springs, Florida.

Transportation

Kalymnos is reached by ferries six days a week en route between Rhodes-Kos and Leros-Patmos-Piraeus. The fare from Rhodes is 755dr; from Piraeus, it's 1065dr. The *Panormitis* makes weekly stops in both directions, on its way to every island from Samos to Rhodes. A small fishing boat shuttles daily between Xerocampos, on the island of Leros (7:30am) and Myrties (1pm) on the western coast of Kalymnos; fare is 250dr. Three different agencies on the waterfront in Pothea run round-trip excursions to Kefalas Cave (400dr), Pserimos (350dr) and Masticheri (350dr). Kefalas Cave is large, with stalagmites, stalagtites, and now, colored electric lights. Zeus reputedly hid from his father here before killing him. The excursion goes here for a few hours, then stops at a beach on the southern coast for a few hours before returning to Pothea. The excursion to Pserimos is purely for the beach, but you'd do better on the beaches of Kalymnos or Telendos.

Getting Around the Island

Almost everyone seems to ride motorbikes. Many of the roads are extremely hilly and several interesting things to see are on different parts of the island. A bus from Kyprou Square goes six times daily along the western coast of the island, stopping at Panormos (35dr), Myrties (40dr), and Massouri (45dr). Two of these continue to Arginontas (70dr), and four buses a day run along the eastern coast to Vathis. Both rides are very scenic. A slightly more expensive alternative is the taxi-bus, i.e., a regular taxi with at least four or five passengers which charges a set rate per person, 5 or 10dr more than the bus. There are taxi-bus stands in each town, but you can flag one anywhere; they run until 10pm. If you're the only person in the car, it's not a taxi-bus.

Pothea

In the early morning hours, Pothea, the largest port in Kalymnos, presents a cheerful patchwork of colors. Arranged in a half-circle around the large harbor, the town's white, green, yellow, and light blue houses radiate from the waterfront promenade. As morning turns into afternoon, however, the area around the waterfront becomes a noisy and congested mass of pedestrians, motorbikes, and cars trying to make their way on overly narrow sidewalks and streets. After you perform any necessary errands—changing money, renting a motorbike—get out of Pothea to the quieter, more scenic spots on the island.

The main pier of Pothea runs parallel to Elefterias Street, the waterfront promenade. The second most important avenue, Venizelou Street, intersects Elefterias at the northern part of the harbor, next to the Agois Christos Church. This narrow street, filled with appliance, cosmetic, and gift shops, leads to Kyprou Square and eventually to the western part of the island.

Practical Information

Surprisingly, Pothea has no Tourist Police. The regular police, located on Elefterias Street, between Christos Church and the water, don't speak English, although they can be helpful anyway (tel. 29 30 1).

The Blue Islands Travel: in Pl. Elefterias at the southwest corner of the harbor, has complete bus and boat information posted. The staff is very friendly, speaks English, and can answer almost any question about the island.

Post Office: (tel. 28 34 0). Just west of Kyprou Square. Open Mon.-Fri. 7:30am-4pm.

Currency Exchange: After bank hours, you can change money in a hotel or in Blue Islands Travel.

OTE: Near the taxi stand. Open Mon.-Fri. 7:30am-10pm, Sat. 7:30am-3:30pm, Sun. 7:30am-1:30pm.

International Bookstore: Newspapers from Europe and the *International Herald Tribune* are sold in Kyprou Square.

Motorbikes: Several places on the waterfront on Pothea rent mopeds (400dr a day) and 50cc motorbikes (600-700dr a day). If they ask you to buy your own gas, remember, you don't have to fill it all the way.

Taxi Station: Kyprou Square (tel. 29 55 5).

Accommodations

The easiest way to find a room is to deal with one of the pension owners who greet your boat. Otherwise, just ask around; Pothea is large for the size of the island, but it's still a small town. You can also try the **Hotel Alma** (tel 28 96 9), just off the center of the waterfront. Singles 405dr, doubles 580dr, triples 800dr, plus 70dr shower; clean sheets, not so clean bathrooms. **Hotel Krystal** (tel. 28 89 3) is right on the waterfront at 25th of March Square; singles 450dr, doubles 650dr, shower 80dr. It's a little more spacious.

Sights

Pothea is a busy town, but the lives of its inhabitants don't revolve around tourism. As you stroll around you might stop into the **Restaurant N.O.K.,** on the waterfront behind the Port Police, and see their collection of ancient amphoras and odd-shaped sponges that divers have brought up. On the wall is a goofy but informative painting of a sponge diver; the equipment is very different from a James Bond scuba diving set-up.

On a hill overlooking the south end of town, the **Monastery of Agios Pantes** is worth a visit. A Father Savvas, a church official at the monastery (a convent, really) died in 1948. At the traditional reburial nine years later, his body hadn't decomposed at all. Such an unequivocal call for sainthood couldn't be ignored, so Father Savvas was promptly canonized. The monastery was re-dedicated in his honor, and new chapels were added. The gate on the right side is generally open; if you enter here (dress appropriately), the first chapel on your left contains Father Savvas' bones in an elaborate sarcophagus. After he became a saint, his body did evidently decompose, which says something about the corrosive power of high office. Saints aside, the view from up here is splendid; you can see all the way to Telendos Island and beyond.

Western Coast

Kalymnos has two main roads: one running northwest out of Pothea, the other northeast. The fortress of the Knights of St. John, here called the **Kastro Chrissocherias,** is the first point of interest on the northwest road. A few kilometers out of Pothea, a side road to the left leads up to the castle, whose walls seem to grow organically out of the rock it's built on. Hidden away in the remains are a number of little chapels, all open to view. You might notice sections of wall or floor that look newly painted. These are places where modern-day privateers dug holes to search for buried treasure.

The view from the fortress takes in much of the island; northward across the valley the **Pera Kastro** is in plain view. This even larger structure was originally Byzantine but was enlarged and fortified by the Knights. Nine tiny churches—this time not hidden since they're bright white—are scattered throughout the ruins, maintained by some elderly women from Chorio. You can climb to the summit from Chorio by passing through some backyards and scaling a fence or two; about a half hour walk.

Back across the valley is the site of ancient Argiens. Hardly any remains are to be seen, and Argos is merely a tiny suburb, but again, the view from these heights is spectacular.

Both the Pero Kastro and Argos overlook the town of **Chorio,** once Kalymnos' capital but now a small quiet village. Pothea has expanded so far now that it's impossible to say where it ends and Chorio begins. A kilometer or so beyond Chorio, a few white steps leading up from the road on the left are the only marker of one of the island's most important historical remains, the **Church of Christ of Jerusalem.** This Byzantine church was built by the Emperor Arcadius to thank God for sparing him in a storm at sea. Only a shell is left of the church, but it is still grand. The stone blocks with carved inscriptions are from a fourth-century B.C. Temple of Apollo that stood on the same site. This church was seen as a symbol of Christianity's victory over paganism. The inscription on the stone at shoulder-level just to the right of center is said to be of the document that joined Kalymnos to the fifth-century B.C. Athenian Alliance; if you can translate it, let us know.

The western road finds the sea again near **Kantouni,** 6km from Pothea. Unlike Myrties and Massouri to the north, Kantouni hasn't been discovered yet; it has a few pensions and sits at the southern end of 3-4km of very good beach called Platis Yalos. **Myrties** and **Massouri** aren't exactly crowded either (by Greek standards), but they have their share of Scandinavian package-tour groups and it may be difficult to find a room. **Hotel Myrties,** on the main road, has singles with bath for 400dr, doubles 800dr. Myrties' finest attraction is a short boat ride out of town: the tiny, rocky islet of **Telendos,** severed from Kalymnos by an earthquake in 554 A.D. A city occupied the site where the island cracked; traces of it have been found on the ocean floor, but you cannot see anything from the surface.

The ruins on Telendos are at best modest, but on the far side of the island, you'll find two sandy, secluded beaches. Since almost all of Telendos' visitors return to the main island in the evening, finding accommodations is not a problem. You can either pitch a tent on the beach or stay in one of Telendos' two pensions. If you have the time, a walk around the southern part of the island rewards the adventurous with some startling scenery. Telendos is connected to Kalymnos by a number of tiny ferries that frequently cross the channel for 25dr (last ferry at 8pm). Before leaving Myrties, take a look at Telendos and notice the woman's face in profile along the left-hand side of the mountain; the picture is best at sunrise or sundown. According to the islanders, she is looking forlornly out to sea, weeping for her estranged husband. If you have a motorbike, ride along the coast toward **Argynontas** just for the spectacular view.

Vathis

Six kilometers northeast of Pothea, Vathis presents a totally different landscape. Most of the island can support only grass and a few masochistic wildflowers, but the valley at Vathis is a lush garden of tangerines, limes, and grapevines. The valley starts at the smallish village of Rina, where the sea comes in to create a kind of fjord. There is no beach here (you can swim off the pier), but the exquisite scenery and complete absence of tourists make sand a negligible sacrifice. On the north side of the inlet is a stalagmite cave, **Daskaleios,** that you can swim to; you'll probably need to persuade a local kid to swim out with you to point it out. There are no official pensions in Rina, but if you ask around, you'll likely find someone willing to rent you a room.

Inland of Rina, the pretty stone farmhouses become sparse and the roads more rutted. This is a good area for hiking: it's not too hilly, and if they're in season, you can pick grapes or tangerines to eat as you go. You'll find genuine Greek hospitality as you forge your way inward—friendly folk may invite you to come in out of the sun to share a slice of watermelon.

Leros

Locals describe Leros as an island of lakes. The six bays plunging deep into the island's coastline create pristine waters and natural harbors that often appear entirely landlocked. Halfway between Patmos and Kalymnos, Leros has thus far had much less tourist traffic than its Dodecanese counterparts. Lacking the nightlife and antiquities of Kos or Rhodes, Leros's charm lies in its quiet, friendliness, and relative seclusion. On daytrips and walks around the island, you will sometimes feel that all the striking vistas exist for your benefit alone.

To and From Leros

Boats stop seven days a week at the main dock in Lakki, headed to Patmos and Piraeus and leaving around 7pm. Six days a week (not Sunday), boats head south for other ports in the Dodecanese. A weekly boat goes to Mykonos. Schedules are subject to change: a windy day can delay a boat for as long as two hours. Tickets are sold at the cafe across the street from the dock by a ticket agent who appears around two hours before the boat's scheduled departure.

A small boat also leaves from Xerocampos in the southeastern part of the island for Myrties, on the western side of Kalymnos, at 7:30am (returning, if you like, at 1pm). The one-way fare is 250dr. On Tuesdays, a small boat also arrives from Patmos. If the sea is too choppy, these smaller boats will not make the trip.

Getting Around the Island

Leros is best explored on bicycle. You can rent one for 100dr a day in Lakki at **Kosta's** shop on the waterfront (he also has mopeds for 500dr and scooters for 650dr). There is one bus that runs from Platanos to Lakki and Xerocampos and back, leaving Platanos six times a day (35-50dr). The same bus goes from Platanos to Partheni via Alinda three times a day. Taxis also tend to be a reasonable means of transport—four people in a taxi from Lakki to Platanos is easily affordable.

Lakki

You will probably disembark in Lakki, the main port which has an island **Police Station** (at the southern end of the waterfront) as well as a **Post Office** (7 Martiou St.) and an **OTE** (open Mon.-Fri. 7:30am-3pm). The least expensive hotels on the island are in Lakki—try the **Acropolis** (tel. 23 38 5) on Lord Vironos St. with beds for 350dr per person. Pensions are also available in and near the town with doubles for 600dr and quads for 850dr. A ten minute walk from the beach is Leros' only official campsite (tel. 23 37 2), a nice one situated in an olive grove, where you can stay for 180dr per person, less if it's uncrowded. The numerous pizza joints near the OTE are the cheapest places to eat (except for the *souvlaki* stand next to the port cafe). Lakki also has an open-air cinema, which often shows movies in English.

Around the Island

Instead of staying in Lakki, try exploring one of the three adjoining towns located just to the east. **Platanos** is the capital of the island, and has both an OTE and **Post Office** in the same building on Karami St. off the main square. Rooms to rent are available at 600dr for a double, but try bargaining. For a treat, stay at **Madame Doukissa Deligeorgi's** pension (tel. 22 34 0) in Pantheli; her 120-year-old home has painted ceilings, and this French teacher from

Athens is a delightful hostess. Singles are 450dr, doubles 650dr. The best restaurants in these three villages are beachside in **Pantheli**. In the evening, if it's not too windy, dinner is served at tables on the beach. The atmosphere is delightful. **Zorba's** has the widest selection and the best food, though portions tend to be small. Next door, to the left if you are facing the beach, there is another restaurant with no name that has only one or two main dishes on the menu. Most of the other diners are Greeks, and the prices can't be beat. The nearby town of **Alinda** has a fantastic beach, and the **Byzantine castle** overlooking the island (now used by the Greek military to scout the Turkish coastline) is worth a visit for its spectacular view of the island.

Patmos

> . . . I greatly desired
> There to be lodged, and there
> To approach the dark grotto.
> For not like Cyprus,
> The rich in wellsprings,
> Nor any of the others
> Magnificently does Patmos dwell . . .
> —Friedrich Hölderlin

If Delos was the sacred heart of the Aegean for the ancients, then for Christians, the spiritual center of this great sea will always be the beautiful, rocky little island of **Patmos.** One of the first outposts of the Christian faith was established on Patmos, and St. John is believed to have written the Book of Revelations in a grotto overlooking the main town. Something of the spirit of this place must have gripped Hölderlin, who wrote "Patmos" without ever actually seeing the island. When the teachings of the Gospel flourished under Byzantine rule, Patmos became a popular destination for religious pilgrims. Until recent centuries only monks inhabited the island, but its spectacular coastline, strikingly beautiful scenery, and enchanting hilltop village of Chora could not remain secret for long. Today the island bears a thriving tourist trade that seems to increase year after year. But whether by divine intervention or shrewd management, many of the island's more hallowed spots have retained a refreshing uncommercial character.

Transportation

Six ferries a week run during the summer to and from Piraeus (1051dr) and six a week along the Leros-Kalymnos-Kos-Rhodes route (968dr to Rhodes). During the off-season, three or four ferries run each week in either direction, weather permitting. Four ferries a week run to Samos. The two ferry agencies are near the square: one in a grocery store and the other in a candy/newspaper store. Excursion boats shuttle to Samos, Ikaria, Lipsi, Kalymnos, and Kos; they're generally more expensive than the ferry, but occasionally offer special deals—in 1983 the Stefamar had a student fare of 250dr to Kos.

Patmos is covered with scores of monasteries for the historically inclined, and numerous secluded coves for those who want to enjoy the island's unspoiled coastline. The best way to get around Patmos is by motorbike; you can rent them on the waterfront in Skala for 400-700dr, depending on the size of the bike. Bicycles can be rented for 150dr a day at a few shops near the waterfront. Test-drive any bicycle or motorbike before you set out. Nine buses a day go to Chora and back (7:40am-10:30pm), four to Kampos (8:15am-9:30pm), and five to Grikou (9:15am-10:30pm). Fares run 30-40dr. The current schedule is posted outside the police station, where the buses stop.

Skala

The pleasant, modern port of Skala is the main touring base for Patmos. Nearly all the tourist facilities and accommodations are located in the town. You may want to stay in the quiet town of Chora, however, since Skala can be a bit too touristy.

Practical Information

The island has no tourist police. The regular police (open Mon.-Sat. 8am-1pm and 4-7:30pm, Sun. 8am-1pm, tel. 31 30 3) speak a little English and do not consider it their duty to find lodgings for tourists, but if you are having difficulties finding rooms or getting around and are able to communicate it, you will probably find them most helpful. They're located just to your right as you get off the boat, before the main square and facing the water.

Post Office: on the main square. The large building with the following inscribed greeting: "Welcome to Patmos. Enjoy its beauties. Respect our traditions." Open Mon.-Fri. 7:30am-2:30pm.

Currency Exchange: Main Square. The Ionian and Credit Banks are housed in a gift shop, while the National Bank has its own storefront in a corner of the square. After closing hours, try a hotel.

OTE: located to the north, along the waterfront. Open Mon.-Fri. 7:30am-10pm, Sat.-Sun. until 3:10pm.

Hospital: (tel. 31 30 3). Take the bus to Chora and get off at the clearly marked turn-off. One hundred yards downhill from St. John's cave.

Accommodations

During the summer, Skala's few hotels are almost always full, but finding a room in one of the numerous pensions and private homes is usually a simple matter. Even the boats that arrive at 1am are greeted by an array of people offering singles for 450dr and doubles for 650dr. Since most of the boats from Piraeus and the other Dodecanese do arrive very late in the day, it is strongly recommended that you come to terms with someone in the harbor as you get off the boat. Otherwise, you may find yourself sleeping on the sidewalk. Another reason for opting for private rooms is that most of Skala's hotels are quite expensive. The affordable ones are:

Hotel Rex, turn left as you disembark and take the first right (tel. 31 24 2). Singles with bath are 625dr, doubles 825dr.

Hotel Rodon, turn right as you disembark, walk past the main square, then take the first left: three blocks down on the right (tel. 31 37 1). Singles are 650dr, doubles 1000dr.

An excellent **campsite** is at **Meloi,** a twenty minute walk north of Skala. Run by Stefanos Grillis (tel. 31 28 7), it is only two minutes from the beach and has its own cafe. Across the street is a restaurant with Greek music and dancing some nights. Camping costs 150dr per person per night, only 30dr if you camp on the beach and shower at the campsite.

Beaches

The town beach is crowded and small. The nearest good beach is at **Meloi,** a twenty-minute walk north along the waterfront and over a small hill. Ask any Patmian to recommend his or her favorite beach—the answer will vary, but will always be prefaced by "After 4pm . . .," since the excursion boats haul their loads daily to the main beaches, leaving Skala at 10am and returning at 4pm. Round trip to **Agriolivado** or **Kampos** costs 100dr; 300dr to **Lampi** or **Psili Ammos.** Try staying past 4pm at any of these; you'll probably have to camp out at Lampi or Psili Ammos. Otherwise try **Sapsila,** off the road to Grikou about two-thirds of the way there from Skala.

Chora

From any part of Patmos, you can see the white rectangular houses of Chora and the nearby majestic gray walls of the Monastery of St. John the Theologian. Chora needs no advertising; this enchanting village sells itself. It's enjoyable just to roam its labyrinthine streets, peek into doorways, and view the Patmos shoreline with the archipelago of tiny islands on all sides.

Practical Information

Due to the intricate, maze-like character of the town's layout and the almost total absence of street names, it is next to impossible to give precise directions for places in Chora. Furthermore, most services and offices of importance on the island are not located in Chora, but in the main port of Skala. It is advisable to take care of all important details—like money—before coming to Chora.

The bus lets you off at the top of the hill, outside the town; this is the point of departure for buses to other places on the island. Once you climb up to the town, if you continue to the left (west), you will pass the public restrooms and will eventually come to the **police station.** If you go to the right you will come to Xanthos Square, and beyond it the village's **clinic/pharmacy.** The **OTE** office is next to the Church of Agias Levias and the square of the same name, in the northwest part of town. In the little village of Chora alone, there are 22 monasteries and churches, and many of them are only open a few hours a day. Many of the old churches are quite beautiful; if you decide to explore them, both men and women should have shoulders and legs covered.

As if by natural selection, most of the tourists stay in Skala and most of the natives of Patmos are to be found in Chora. There is a conspicuous lack of restaurants, nightlife, hotels, and other tourist facilities, but if you are willing to dig around a little for a room, you will find that Chora is a peaceful and refreshing place to stay. Chora's few pension owners do not hang around the dock at 1am to meet the boats, so you'll probably have to spend the first night elsewhere and start looking early the next morning. **Marouso Theologos** (tel. 31 02 6) has clean doubles for 700dr, bath and use of kitchen included. Facing Vacelis' Restaurant (you'll see signs), go right out of the square, take the first left, and go about four blocks. Again because of natural selection, Chora's restaurants are generally better and cheaper than those in Skala. Even if you're staying in Skala, the late bus (or a pleasant walk) allows you to come to Chora for dinner. A block before Vacelis' (following signs from the bus stop), you'll see a small restaurant on the right with long tables which serves a great combination plate for 120dr. For a splurge, try the classy **Patmion Restaurant,** in the back of Xanthos Square.

Sights

Strolling about Chora's winding streets is a popular activity, and you'll quickly understand why. Somehow these tiny streets never seem to get crowded. In your wanderings, you will notice above most of the doorways the sign of the Byzantine cross, and often the date the house was built. Both testify to the considerable age of many of the houses in the older quarters of Chora.

Most tourists come to Chora for its monasteries, and few of them are disappointed by the monumental **Monastery of St. John the Theologian.** From the outside, its massive turretted walls and well-fortified gateway bear much more resemblance to a fortress than a place of worship, but then this is no ordinary house of God. The monastery was founded in 1088 by St. Christodoulos, nearly one thousand years after St. John's celebrated stay on the island. Christodoulos had been granted the island by Byzantine Emperor Alexios Comninos the First, and was provided with financial assistance to build the structure. But pragmatics proved more important than aesthetics—the proximity of Islamic Turkey made the monastery a constant target of pirate raids, so it was only a matter of time before the memorial to St. John was transformed into an impregnable citadel with formidable battlements and watch towers.

In the church itself, perhaps the finest works are the frescoes in the **Chapel of the Virgin,** to the right of the main sanctuary. Be sure to look at the ones behind the screen, to your left as you enter.

In 1983, the **Treasury** and **Library** were being remodeled; the best pieces from each were on display in the refectory. By 1984, they may be open again in their entirety. The treasury contains an outstanding collection of Byzantine and medieval artworks, featuring ornate liturgical garments, thirteenth-century icons, hand-painted gospels, hand-carved wooden crosses, and an unusual twelfth-century mosaic icon of St. Nicholas. Also interesting is the parchment Imperial Order of 1088 from the Byzantine emperor, ceding the island to St. Christodoulos. Admission to the treasury is 50dr, no student discount.

The brightly-colored mosaic of St. John over the entrance to the monastery is quite striking. The main church, next to the splendid inner courtyard, is embellished with beautiful Byzantine-style frescoes dating from the seventeenth century (which, unfortunately, are in desparate need of restoration), and the famous icon of St. John. The library has a wonderful collection of manuscripts, some illustrated. One page of a fifth or sixth-century New Testament hardly looks weathered.

The monastery is open Fri.-Tues. 8am-noon and 3-6pm, Wed-Thurs. 8am-noon. Try to visit early or late in the day during the summer—toward midday, the monastery become uncomfortably crammed with tourists and hollering tour guides. If you come during the off-season, one of the monastery's 25 monks (there were once a hundred times as many) may volunteer to show you around the closed-off sections. The admission to the inner courtyard and the chapels is free. The monks are particularly insistent that visitors enter the treasury only if "properly" dressed (women, for example, may not wear pants). Informal dress is not appreciated in any part of the monastery.

Halfway up the hill on the winding road that connects Chora and Skala is a turn-off for the **Apokalypsis Monastery,** a large, white complex of interconnected buildings. The tiny **Church of St. Anne,** carved into the cliffside underneath the monastery proper, deserves a look, but most people come for the **Sacred Grotto of the Apocalypse,** adjacent to the church. *Apocalypsos* means uncovering or revelation; the English word takes its meaning from the great vision St. John is said to have had in the cave. Here also he dictated the entire Book of Revelations (the last book of the Bible) to his companion and pupil Prochoros. St. John had originally come to the then uninhabited island from Asia Minor in 96 A.D. when he was exiled by the Roman Emperor Domitian for preaching the teachings of Christ. As he wrote in the prologue to Revelations: "I dwelled in an island of which the name is Patmos, so as to preach the word of God and have faith in the martyrdom suffered by Jesus Christ." According to his writings, while St. John was resting in a cave staring up at a recess in the rock, he suddenly heard the voice of God explaining to him "the things which are and the things which shall be hereafter" (Rev. 1:19). The present cave, of course, has the legendary crack through which St. John received the ominous news. Silver plating also marked the spot where St. John presumably rested. St. John's cave is open the same hours as the Monastery of St. John.

While most of St. John's activity was up on the hill, he did leave one mark in the port below. It is said that he was engaged in a duel of miracle-making with a local priest of Apollo named Kynops. Since Greece is a Christian country, the winner was, of course, John. The Saint, a graceful champion, threw the loser into the water at Skala where Kynops turned into a rock. Ask any native to point out which rock was Kynops.

Grikos and Kambos

Most visitors to Patmos spend only a day or two on the island, visiting the historical attractions, taking in the breathtaking views, and perhaps catching a quick swim. Those with more time can visit the two other villages on the island. Grikos, more popular with tourists, has a comparatively empty sandy beach, one luxury hotel, and a couple of restaurants. The **Vamvakos Hotel** (tel. 31 38 0), which overlooks the southern end of the beach, has doubles for 750dr (20% less during the off-season) and exceptional views. Tents are often pitched on the beach beyond the hotel. Some visitors to the island have been known to live in the big rock called the Kalikatsou, jutting into the bay.

To the north is the smaller community of **Kambos,** with a modest beach and a handful of pensions with doubles for 600dr. Both villages can be reached by bus, car, taxi, moped, thumb, or fishing boat from Skala, along the coastal road running in either direction from the port; hitching is a little slow.

Lipsi

Some say the tiny island of Lipsi is where Homer's Odysseus met the beautiful Kalypso; some say it's not. Even a small island wants to have some claim to fame. At any rate, Lipsi is a rocky, scenic, one-village island where the word "tourist" has not yet become common usage. Excursion boats visit from Patmos six days a week (300dr one-way, 400dr round-trip). Almost everyone returns to Patmos the same day, so if you choose to stay over for a few days, you'll find Lipsi peacefully secluded.

The stepped street by the school leads up to the central square, with a **Post Office** and OTE. Rooms are no problem to find and cheaper than almost anywhere else. Next to Pension Flisvos on the waterfront is a no-name pension with doubles for 600dr, including shower. If you ask Lipsians about special sights on their island, they shrug. One item of interest is a government rug-making school on the waterfront where you can watch artisans weaving Oriental rugs and see the splendid results.

You can camp on and swim off the fine town beach, but it becomes congested in the afternoon, when Lipsian children are let out of school. A narrower, less crowded stretch of beach can be found ten minutes north on the path to the right just before the last pair of restaurants. But the best beach on the island is **Katzadia**, a half-hour walk out of town to the south on the road that runs behind Pension Flisvos and parallel to the waterfront.

Astipalea

Shaped like a butterfly, Astipalea is the westernmost of the Dodecanese archipelago, and its location (150km from Rhodes) has assured that fewer visitors come to its shores than to most other Greek islands. Unfortunately, isolation is the only reason to visit Astipalea. It has neither spectacular natural scenery nor interesting ancient ruins. And, surprisingly, despite the lack of any tourist trade, its inhabitants are not especially receptive to visitors.

Getting to Astipalea is relatively easy. Four boats a week stop at Astipalea on the way between Piraeus and Rhodes. The fare to Rhodes is 804dr. Traveling in Astipalea is a very difficult task unless you can find a friendly islander to take you around. For most tourists, the best way to see the island is by foot or by boat. Caïques run fairly frequently to many points around the island, but more than a little inquiry is needed to find out their exact schedules. One boat goes daily at 9:30am from Astipalea to Livadia, Agios Konstantinos, and Maltezana. Far cheaper is the sea-taxi run by Peter the Welshman; look for a boat flying both Greek and Welsh flags.

There are only three D-class hotels in the town of Astipalea: the **Astynea** (no phone) on the wharf, with bed for 300dr per person, the **Paradissos** (tel. 61 22 4) with singles for 450dr, doubles for 650dr, and triples for 850dr, and the **Aegeon** (tel. 61 23 6) with singles for 440dr, doubles for 700dr, and triples for 850dr. In the last two, bargaining may help lower the price if they're not full—which is most of the time. The **OTE** (open Mon.-Fri. 7:30am-3:10pm) is next to the Paradissos, and the **Marine Agency** (for boat tickets) is across the street. The **Port Police** can be found to the right of the Astynea cafe. The **Post Office** (open Mon.-Fri. 7:30am-3pm) is located at the top of the hill by the seven windmills. Food is inexpensive in Astipalea; all of the outdoor cafes overlooking the wharf offer standard Greek fare at reasonable prices.

From the town of Astipalea, a 20-minute walk to the west (over the hill) will bring you to **Livadia,** where Nicholas Kontaratos (tel. 61 26 9) rents doubles and triples for 600dr. The pleasant beach is crowded with tents and Greek children during July and August, but on the nearby beach of **Senaki,** further along the coast to the southwest, nude bathing proceeds in near-solitude.

Maltezana, also known as Analipsi, is a peaceful fishing village to the east of Astipalea town; Helios Kalis' pension offers doubles for 600dr. In the winter when the winds are too strong for boats to dock at Astipalea, the ferries use the port of **Vathi,** which has a well-protected harbor. A caïque goes back and forth twice a week between Vathi and **Agios Andreas**—a great place for swimming off the rocks.

Kastelorizo (Megisti)

Geography has been a blessing for Kastelorizo, a quiet and beautiful island sixty-five miles from Rhodes. As the easternmost island in the Aegean, it is so small and distant that it has long been ignored by tourists. And for good reason: it almost never appears on a map of Greece, and was not even counted when the Dodecanese (12 islands) were named. Although it is less than two miles from the Turkish coast, Kastelorizo has distinctly Greek character and its traditional fishing and farming economy remains largely unadulterated.

Finding cheap accommodations on Kastelorizo is not a problem, and one or more pension owners will probably greet you as you disembark from the ferry. **Despina Mavros'** pension (tel. 29 07 3) is on a side street a few blocks from the water; she offers rather untidy singles for 250dr, and doubles for 400dr. Despina has an extra bonus though; swallows fly through the windows to their nests in the rafters of some of the rooms, leaving their droppings on the floor, bed, and you, if you don't move quickly enough. **Esodia's** pension (no phone) is slightly more luxurious, with singles for 300dr and doubles for 500dr.

Kastelorizo is *the* place to eat seafood; if you're lucky, you'll see piles of immense swordfish stacked on the harbor, or boys pounding squid or octopus on the cement to make them tender. All of the restaurants along the wharf are inexpensive, but as the fare differs each night, it's best to ask what is available before you sit down. **Karpouzis,** at the south end of the harbor near the mosque and just past the **Tomb of the Unknown Soldier,** is a friendly watering hole frequented by the island's youth during the summer (it's closed in winter).

The town's other services, the **OTE, Post Office,** and **Police,** can be found in the same building at the northern end of the harbor next to the steel tower. Hours vary, depending upon when the employees choose to open or close, but someone will usually be working Mon.-Fri. 7:30am-2:30pm.

In the evening, try climbing the stone steps leading to the mountains overlooking the town for an unforgettable view of the harbor. The fourteenth century castle also merits a visit for its splendid view of the entire town and, to the north and east, the mountainous coastline of Turkey. Kastelorizo's one-room **museum** houses a few modest archeological finds and folk art objects. It's supposed to be open 9am-1pm and 3-5pm, but its curator, Diakakias, is rarely at the museum. He can be found drinking coffee in the mornings at Mavros' cafe on the wharf.

Two pleasant excursions can be made if you band together a group of four or five tourists and ask one of the local fishermen for a lift. **Parasta's Cavern,** on the eastern coast of the island, can be entered through its nearly invisible opening at low tide in a small boat; the aqua blues of the water inside the immense cave are stunning. The other excursion is to the small fishing village of **Kaş** on the Turkish coast. (See Turkish Mediterranean Coast for information). There is thriving black market trade between the islanders and this coastal town; Turkish carpets and other goods can be purchased and brought back to Greece as long as it's kept quiet. Greek currency cannot be used in Kaş so bring some US dollars and your passport. The round trip to Turkey should cost about 500dr per person.

Four boats a week stop at Kastelorizo, leaving Rhodes' Mandraki Harbor and arriving in Kastelorizo six hours later, starting on the return voyage after about one hour. The one-way fare is 554dr.

Karpathos

In relative isolation halfway between Rhodes and Crete, southwest of the main line of Dodecanese islands, sits the large, elongated island of Karpathos. Because of its location, Karpathos has fewer ferry connections and fewer tourists than other Dodecanese islands. But those who come here swear by it, and pray that the secrets of Karpathos will be kept from the masses on Rhodes and Kos. Geographic seclusion is the one feature of the island responsible for its serenity; it's also what keeps many aspects of a centuries-old lifestyle alive here, especially in the northern town of Olymbos. If you take the time to explore Karpathos, you may find it an unusual alternative to the usual island round of beaches and ruins.

Karpathos' history is unusual for the Dodecanese since the Knights of St. John ruled here for only two years. During the 200-odd years the rest of area was under their control, Karpathos was under Venetian rule, so there's no Knight's castle on Karpathos. The recent history of Karpathos, like that of other dry, rocky islands, has been dominated by the flux of emigration. Even more than by tourism, the island's traditional patterns of life are threatened by the influence of Karpathians who return after several years in the U.S. If you will spend any time on the island, the guidebook *Karpathos,* written and published privately by Yvonne and Klaus von Bolzano, is worth the 300dr—it's very thorough.

Four boats a week go from Rhodes to Karpathos (690dr) and two a week from Piraeus (2100dr) via Crete or Rhodes. The *Kamiros* stops only at Pigadia; other ferries call at both ports. Olympic Airways has flights between Rhodes and Karpathos three times a day (twice on Thursdays) during the summer; fare is 1530dr one-way.

Getting Around the Island

Back toward the center of the waterfront, the road leading up to the Karpathos hotel has a car rental, and, right before the hotel, the main bus stop. Bus service around the island is minimal: four buses a day on the Aperi-Volada-Othos-Piles route, one a day to Menetes and Arkasa (returning only the next morning), and two to the beach at Amopi. Even this sparse schedule is unreliable, subject to the vagaries of old buses and idiosyncratic drivers. Hitching is slow, but with so little other transportation, it becomes a viable option. On the same street as the Post Office and OTE, you can rent mopeds for 600dr per day, larger bikes from 1000-1200dr. Don't even think about trying to drive through to the north—Olymbos or Diafani—except on the largest cycle (i.e. 90cc), and even then not unless you're an experienced driver.

Southern Karpathos

The island's main port, **Pigadia** (also called Karpathos Town), is the administrative and transportation center of the island. Pigadia's **Police** are just across from the complex of Italian buildings at the far end of the waterfront (to the left if you're facing the water). They don't speak much English, but are happy to fulfill whatever Tourist Police functions they can, including calling around for rooms to let. Around the corner from the police is the **OTE,** open Mon.-Sat. 7:30am-10pm, Sun. until 3pm. Two blocks inland from the OTE is the **Post Office,** open Mon.-Fri. 7:30am-2:30pm.

Accommodations in Pigadia include the **Karpathos** (tel. 22 34 7) at 25 Vas. Konstantinou St. (two blocks up from the center of the waterfront), which has clean singles including shower for 550dr, doubles for 900dr; and the **Anessis** (tel. 22 25 6), in the block beyond the OTE, with singles for 560dr, doubles 620dr, shower included.

Pigadia is mostly modern and not especially attractive. The remains of **Agia Fotini,** a fifth-century basilica, can be found on the road north to Aperi on the right just past the island's one gas station. Near the basilica is Pigadia's beach, pretty and uncrowded.

The rest of southern Karpathos features green, gentle beautiful landscapes. This is a place to visit for the land: all you'll see are empty stone farmhouses, tiny isolated chapels, and views over terraced hillsides to the sea. Some of the towns, too, are charming, but you shouldn't go from town to town and miss the real treasures between.

On a branch of the road south out of Pigadia are **Menetes** and, on the west coast, **Arkasa.** The huge church of Menetes seems to flow upward out of the terraced houses below; its marble pillars are from the ruins of an early Christian basilica. A few kilometers beyond Menetes, 600-700m along a dirt side-road to the north, the tiny chapel of **Agios Mammas** is one of the island's choice gems, rarely visited. Through the minature doorway you'll find the remains of some superb fourteenth-century frescoes. Lie on your back to look at the Christ Pantocrator in the dome. Absurdly vulnerable, the icon of Mary with the infant Jesus is lovely; don't take it, but do move it to see its subtle, rich colors in the sunlight. The most interesting part of Arkasa is the peninsula southwest of town with the remains of not one but five parallel cyclopean walls. They are said to be 3000 years old and suggests that a massive Mycenean fortress must have stood here.

The island's only other paved road leads north and then west out of Pigadia. This is the lushest part of the island, and definitely the place to hike. **Aperi** is the most important town historically; it became the capital in medieval times when Arab raids forced the Karpathians to abandon the coastal town, and is still the island's bishopric, although Pigadia is now the capital. **Mertonas** and **Katodio,** in the foothills of Mt. Kalolimni, both have lush gardens fed by the mountain's streams. You can hike to either from Aperi, and in the summer, pick grapes as you go. **Piles** is perhaps the prettiest town accessible by bus.

Farther north on the coast, **Lefkos** is difficult to reach, but worth the trek. This tiny fishing hamlet has a handful of rooms to let (doubles for 600dr), two tavernas, and a very good beach. A ten-minute walk up the hill to the north is a large cave with pillars supporting its ceilings. An occasional bus is reputed to go to Lefkos and Mesochori, so ask.

The nearest approximation to a crowded beach on Karpathos is **Amopi,** on the southern road just past the turn-off to Menetes. If you've been in Rhodes, you'll feel isolated by comparison. For the ultimate in seclusion, stalk the several miles of sand beach that stretch southward from below Amopi, interrupted only occasionally by a hotel or taverna.

Northern Karpathos

The fact that no adequate roads connect the north and south parts of Karpathos in one sense shows how much of a physical obstacle Mt. Kalolimni is, and also demonstrates how slowly modernization has come to Karpathos. A track was completed in 1979, but it could hardly be called a road. Whatever development might have occurred in this beautiful, arid region will probably be slowed even further due to the huge fire in the summer of 1983, which devastated most of the pine forests between Spoa and Olymbos. As villagers telegraphed for help to Athens and even the U.S. Seventh Fleet, the fire continued out of control for three days and came within a few hundred meters of Diafani.

The best way to get between the south and north is the excursion boat that makes a round-trip three or four times weekly. Fare is 350dr one way; details at Possi Travel in the center of the waterfront in Pigadia. You might be able to use one of the larger Rhodes-bound ferries; most stop at Pigadia and then Diafani. A small fishing boat will pick you up (50dr), since Diafani's harbor is too small to handle large ships. The daily shared taxi organized through Possi Travel costs 5000dr total round-trip; reserve a place one day ahead. You can probably get a better price if you get a group together and ask a taxi driver yourself. The overland route is scenic enough, with distinctive and gorgeous vistas around each hairpin turn; you might even want to hitch. Start off early in the morning where the road begins to degenerate past Aperi, and you'll probably get a ride within a few hours.

Don't stay in Diafani longer than you need to make travel arrangements. The cafe of the **Golden Beach Hotel,** front and center on the waterfront, serves as the town's travel agency, with schedules and ferry tickets. Diafani's four hotels have doubles for 600-700dr.

From Diafani, most people go to **Vananda,** a pleasant beach and campground a half-hour walk to the north, or to Olymbos, an amazing clifftop village 8km away overlooking the west coast. If there is one village to see on Karpathos, if only for a day, it is **Olymbos.** Ethnologists and linguists have known it for years as a place which has preserved centuries-old customs and a dialect with several phrases and words that date from three thousand years ago. You won't find western-style action and nightlife if you come here, but if you want to see a community following a traditional lifestyle, you've come to the right place. The women all wear long-sleeved white shirts and flowered aprons every day, and it's not for show. Any day you can find women baking bread in huge stone ovens built into the hillside. On weekend nights, the men usually gather in the *cafeneions* to play their traditional musical instruments, entertaining themselves and whatever tourists may be staying in the village. If you visit in the months of July, August, and September, you may be able to watch one of the elaborate wedding ceremonies or religious feasts, the largest of which is the name-day of the Virgin Mary (Panayia) on August 15.

If you're willing to scramble over a few stone walls you can visit the oldest chapel on Karpathos, **Agia Anna.** It's one of two stone chapels right next door to each other, easily visible from the town above. The frescoes inside are purely geometric, dating them to the time of the eighth- and ninth-century iconoclastic controversy. Watch out for mules on the way back up. Unfortunately, it is not clear how much longer this city with its rich traditions will last—emigration, recently-installed electricity, the north-south road, and tourism cannot help but take their toll.

The **Artemis Pension,** run by hard-working Marina, costs 400dr a night for a double. She'll probably want you to eat in her kitchen, which might not be a bad idea since she's a good cook and there's only one other place to eat in town. **Pension Olymbos,** run by the equally industrious Anna (you'll quickly notice that the women seem to do all the work around here) costs 200dr per person. Anna hopes to open her restaurant by 1984. To get between Olymbos and Diafani, you can take a taxi (400dr total one way) or the small "bus" (80dr per person), but the ninety-minute hike along a valley floor, through streambeds and over rocky hillsides graced with wildflowers, is easily the best alternative.

The truly adventurous can hike to **Vrugunda** on the northwest coast, two or three hours from Diafani. The landscape is dramatic, and in Vrugunda, the site of a pre-Dorian-invasion settlement, ancient burial chambers are cut out of the rock face overlooking the water. St. John's name-day is celebrated here August 27-29.

Just north of Karpathos, within swimming distance if it weren't for the very strong tides, is another small island called **Saria.** You might be able to persuade a fishing boat to bring you here to visit **Ta Palatia,** a deserted village halfway up the eastern coast with odd, cone-roofed houses built by Syrian pirates in the seventh to ninth centuries A.D. Don't get stranded here—the island is still deserted and there is no fresh water available.

CRETE

There is a saying in Greece that the people of Crete are Cretans first, then Greeks. As it happens, the dictum reflects historical truth: Crete won union with Greece only in 1913, eighty years after the formation of the Greek state and following a century of bitter uprisings against the Turks. But, even more, it reflects the cultural differences that still keep Crete apart from the rest of Greece. Crete has its own folk dances—infinitely delicate and intricate affairs performed to the accompaniment of a lyra (a bowed, three-stringed instrument), bouzouki, and singer—its own handicrafts—brightly painted pottery, leather footwear, woodworking, featherwork, and weavings—and its own traditional dress of thorn-proof high black boots, pantaloons, sash, and embroidered jacket. Gardens are carefully tended, flowers erupt everywhere, and each foot of arable land is cultivated with the rich produce that abounds in every town. Cretan wines are among the best in Greece—smooth, slightly sweet, and you can drink all you want and never rue it in the morning.

The rugged terrain of this, the fifth largest island in the Mediterranean, has kept most Cretans relatively isolated. Other Greeks will invariably tell you that Cretans are a hard lot to get along with—chauvinistic, stubborn, volatile, and very proud. But they will say it with unmistakable admiration and affection. The popular novel *Zorba the Greek,* by the Cretan author Kazantzakis, is an excellent portrayal of the reckless and rugged individualism that characterizes the natives of this island. The protagonist of the story is a potter who one day takes a knife and lops off his index finger because he feels it has been interfering with his work. So it is with these wonderful, if somewhat mad, people—they are never dull, and often fascinating, but be careful: sooner or later, their explosive tempers are bound to catch you by surprise.

The Cretans have much to be proud of in their long history. The Minoans, coming over from Asia Minor in around 2600 B.C., were the first to settle Crete and established a flourishing civilization—the first in Europe. Bringing with them knowledge of the use of bronze, they erected palaces as early as 1950-1900 B.C. A major catastrophe, thought to be an earthquake, laid waste to these buildings in about 1650 B.C. After their destruction, the palaces were rebuilt in a different style, known to archeologists as Middle Minoan II or the Neo-Palatial Period. Most of what has been unearthed at Phaestos, Malia, Kato Zakros, and what is simulated at Knossos dates from this period. During this era, Minoan seafarers, according to Thucydides, dominated the Mediterranean from Syria to Sicily. In roughly 1450 B.C., all the palaces were suddenly destroyed by a disaster of proportions major enough to affect the entire island. Some scholars believe that an invading tribe was responsible, but the current prevalent theory (also the romantic one pushed by tour guides) is that these cities perished from the tidal waves and volcanic fallout that followed the contemporaneous explosion of the island of Santorini, some 60km to the north.

Following the downfall of Minoan cities in the fifteenth century B.C., Crete had to reconcile itself to a more modest role in world affairs. Although the island was colonized by the Dorians in the eighth century B.C., it never became a center of either Classical or Hellenistic Greek civilization. In 69 B.C., the Roman conquest marked the beginning of Crete's long history of occupation by foreign powers. When the Roman Empire was divided in 395 A.D., Crete became part of the Byzantine Empire, under whose authority it remained until the thirteenth century. In 1204, Venetians took control, and proceeded to build numerous fortresses, many of which still stand today, at strategic points along the northern coast of the island. In 1669, after 25 years of battle with the Venetians, the Turks seized Crete and began a long and bloody domination which provoked a number of uprisings by the Cretan people. Their tyranny was finally brought to an end in 1898 when the island became an English protectorate. Fifteen years later, Crete succeeded in joining the Greek state after the Balkan War of 1913.

But these episodes pale in the minds of the Cretans before their magnificent display of courage and tenacity in World War II. Having suffered costly defeats in mainland Greece, British and Commonwealth troops fled to Crete in the spring of 1941, and, on May 20, the Germans came in pursuit. For ten days, Cretan civilians fought side by side with the British with whatever weapons they could muster, and against insuperable odds inflicted severe losses on the enemy. Finally, on May 30, Crete fell. Cretans, justifiably proud of their record, still remind visitors today that while France with its many millions of people fell in three days, Crete with its 400,000 inhabitants held off the Germans for two weeks.

Today, in more peaceful times, hundreds of thousands of foreigners still make their way to Crete for the more affable but sometimes devastating pursuit of holiday-making. Somehow, miraculously, Crete has survived this onslaught as well. A system of felicitous cooperation has taken care of those sincerely interested in sharing Cretan life—the Cretans have opened their arms to visitors who have, in turn, learned to love the island as their own. As for the rest of the tourists who transport their own life, complete with discos and high fashion, to warmer Cretan shores, the inevitable herding instinct has kept them clustered in a few coastal and resort towns, mostly on the north coast. In the rest of Crete—the western end, most of the southern coast, and virtually the whole interior—the indigenous culture has remained intact. The land awaits innumerable explorations—for speliologists, there are hundreds of limestone caves riddling the mountainsides and coasts; for hikers, the mountains themselves, with peaks over eight thousand feet; and for amateur and serious students of history, many of Greece's more significant archeological sites. The interior of Crete offers some of the most beautiful landscape in Southern Europe, and no visit to the island is complete without a drive through its remarkably lush countryside.

For the beach bum lurking in all of us, there is good news and bad. First the bad news: Greeks, tourists, and developers, in concert, have managed to muck up most of the "official" beaches on Crete. Developers have generally taken flat, uninteresting coastline, stripped it of what few trees it had, and then slapped up hideous concrete hotels, many standing half-completed for years. The Greeks, inexplicably, do not believe in garbage cans: any beach frequented by them looks like a free-form town dump. And tourists, inevitably, all converge on the same handful of remaining "deserted" beaches. A few of the better-known beaches, particularly those at Matala, Vai, and Paleochora, are still worth the trip, although even these are likely to disappoint the most exacting beach connoisseurs. Town beaches tend to be narrow, perfunctory affairs at best, with highways running alongside, but on a hot summer afternoon you'll note with pleasure that at least the water is still wet.

Now the good news. Most of Crete's magnificent coastline is still untouched by developers—Greek or foreign. If you are willing to forego refreshment stands and bus stops and do a little walking, you will find all the truly deserted beaches you could possibly need. The best areas are the south and west coasts, but even the built-up north coast has long stretches where cliffs have so

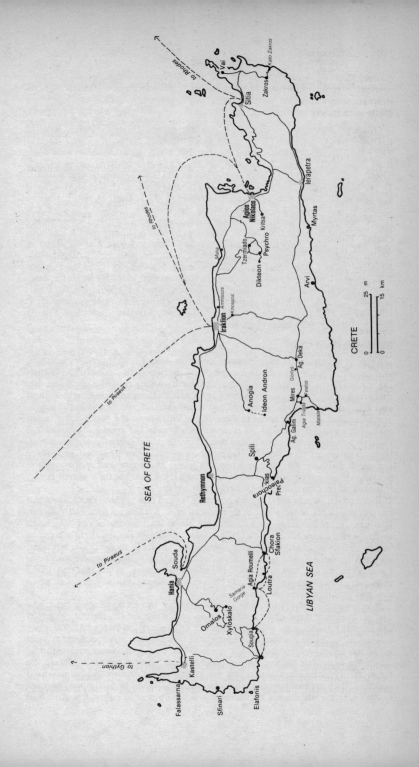

far discouraged the many; for the price of a short hike, they will delight the few.

Getting to Crete

Olympic Airways has flights to Iraklion from Athens (2500dr), Rhodes (2430dr), and Santorini (1730dr), but most travelers arrive in Crete by ferry. The island is well-serviced during the summer: boats depart at least twice daily from Piraeus to Iraklion. Deck class fare for the twelve-hour voyage is 1059dr. There are also daily departures from Piraeus to Hania (eleven hours, 1014dr). Every Monday and Thursday a boat sails from Gythion on the Peloponnese to Kastelli at the western tip of Crete (six hours, 879dr). There is also extensive sailing to and from the Cyclades. During the summer, boats run at least ten times weekly from Santorini, Ios, Naxos, Paros, and Syros. Twice-weekly service connects Mykonos, Milos, Kimolos, Sifnos, and Serifos with Iraklion. A boat sails from Piraeus to Agios Nikolaos once a week, making stops in Anafi, Santorini, Folegandros, and Milos. You can also get to Crete from Rhodes (fifteen hours, 1180dr). Boats leave Rhodes for Sitia and Agios Nikolaos on Tuesdays and Thursdays in the summer, stopping at Halki, Karpathos, and Kassos. Every Monday the *Vergina* leaves Haifa, Israel, for Iraklion and Piraeus, with a stop in Limassol, Cyprus. The boat returns from Iraklion to Haifa on Friday mornings. One-way student deck-class fare is 4000dr, Iraklion port taxes included.

Getting Around Crete

Crete is divided into four separate counties—Hania, Rethymnon, Iraklion, and Lassithi—each with its own capital city on the north coast. In the following chapter, the counties of Hania and Rethymnon, roughly speaking, are discussed in the section on Western Crete, and Iraklion and Lassithi in Central and Eastern Crete respectively. Major transportation routes cover the northern areas, but no roads connect most of the villages on the south coast, so to visit them you must zigzag back and forth across the island. Tourism is a relative newcomer to the southern part of Crete. Until recently, the inaccessibility of many of its coastal villages by any means but boat had kept them remote from other Cretans and tourists alike. But more and more visitors, seeking a haven from the crowded north coast, are making their way there by ferries, and by cars and buses where roads exist.

Bus service is very good to all frequently visited parts of the island. Between each of the major north coast cities (west to east: Kastelli, Hania, Rethymnon, Iraklion, Agios Nikolaos, and Sitia) there are at least ten buses per day. Each intercity trip along this stretch costs roughly 200dr and takes slightly over an hour. Just about every village of consequence has daily bus service, but often on "market buses" which load up early in the morning with people who have business in the city and bring them home in the evening. While this may make rural day-trips unworkable, staying the night in these small villages is an obvious and usually delightful solution.

If you want to see as much of Crete as possible, have a bit of spare cash, and can get together three or four companions, a car can be the ideal way to tour the island. Rentals with unlimited mileage and insurance start at 13,000dr per week, and gasoline is about $2.50 a gallon (40dr per liter). Nevertheless, a car gives you an unparalleled chance to explore the island, spontaneously heading down the unbeaten tracks, for less than $60 per person per week. While the open jeep-type vehicles are terrific for getting down crude roads to deserted beaches, they are insufferable when August winds and the accompanying dust storms kick up and cannot be used for locking up gear in cities. It's not a bad idea to stick to the bottom-of-the-line Fiat 127s, which can be serviced anywhere in an emergency. Another possibility is to rent a Suzuki van, which sleeps two (16,000-18,000dr per week), thus saving on accommodations.

Motor scooters and small motorcycles are excellent for daytrips out of the cities, but are uncomfortable on long rides along windy major highways, and dangerous on rocky, dusty dirt roads. The 50cc models (less powerful mopeds may not get you up those steep Cretan hills) run 700-800dr per day, including tax and insurance, or 3500-4500dr per week. The 150cc and 200cc models cost about 20% and 30% more, respectively. "Insurance" only provides third-party liability coverage, and does not cover damage to your machine or your person. The best policy available on Crete (or in Greece for that matter) insures your bike with a 16,000dr deductible. Bargaining over rental rates often proves fruitful: 10-20% discounts are not uncommon. If you do intend to rent long-term, plan to do so in Agios Nikolaos, Malia, or Hania, where the supply of bikes is greatest and the prices are lowest. Try not to rent long-term in Iraklion. A tacit price-fixing agreement keeps prices there extremely high.

As elsewhere in Greece, hitching isn't great, but the patient seem to succeed at it. Often you have better luck on the tiny dirty roads leading to monasteries and desolate beaches than on highways, since people driving up these dead end tracks have a fair idea of what you want. As always, a wholesome appearance and minimal luggage are your best tickets. While there probably isn't much that can be done about the former, stashing your luggage in a city is a great idea. Whether you tour by crowded car, bus, motorbike, or thumb, you'll be thankful for the items you didn't bring.

A good map of the island is a worthwhile investment no matter how you plan to travel. Most have a complete road map of the island on one side and a modest street map of each of the four major cities (Iraklion, Hania, Rethymnon, Agios Nikolaos) on the other. They are sold everywhere for about 60dr.

Central Crete

Iraklion

There are two compelling reasons to end up in Iraklion: your boat just landed there, or you want to see the archeological museum. With both of these things accomplished, the casual visitor will find that, by and large, what remains are most of the vices and few of the virtues of urban life. Iraklion, the major city of Crete and the fifth largest in Greece, has grown uncontrollably in recent years, sprawling up and down the coast in a most unappealing way. Modern, drab concrete hotels have been plunked down even in the old city's imposing Venetian walls; it appears that one innovation for which civilization is not indebted to Greece is the zoning law. To make matters worse, Iraklion is one of the most expensive cities in Greece. But, as in any city in Crete not yet totally ceded to the tourists, a longer stay, spent getting to know its people and their way of life, will prove very rewarding. Even here, beneath the superficial anonymity of big city life, is a spirit unmistakably Cretan.

Orientation

Should you arrive by ferry, you'll probably want to head directly downtown. Turn right as you disembark and then proceed down the 25th of August St., which begins just under the sign for Hotel Florida. While Iraklion spreads for miles, most of what you'll need is located in the circle formed by **Diokesinis Ave., Handakos St., Duke Beaufort Ave.,** and the waterfront. The twin hubs on this wheel are **Venizelou Square** where Handakos St. meets Diokesinis and 25th of August Avenues and **Eleftherias (Liberty) Square,** at the intersection of Diokesinis and Duke Beaufort Avenues.

Catching or changing buses in Iraklion can be a complicated affair. There are five separate bus stations, each serving a different part of the island. The **main bus terminal** (or Bus Terminal A) only services points east of Iraklion (Agios Nikolaos, Lassithi, Ierapetra, among others); it is located to the east of the harbor on the waterfront (turn left as you disembark, or take bus #2, 3, or 5 from Eleftherias Square). If you turn right as you disembark and continue west along the waterfront, you will come to the **Hania/Rethymnon terminal** which services the northwest coast; it is next door to the Historical Museum. A third terminal of importance to tourists is the **Hania Gate Bus Station** (or Bus Terminal C), named after the Venetian gate in the city walls next to it, just off of Politechniou Square. It connects all the towns along the major route that stretches south from Iraklion, including Phaestos, Matala, and Agia Galini. **Bus Terminal D,** just to the north along the city walls, services towns to the southwest of Iraklion, such as Tilissos, Anogia, and Fodele. To get to Terminals C and D, take bus #1 from in front of the Astoria Hotel in Eleftherias Square. Finally, there is the **Oasis Bus Station** (or Bus Terminal B) which services the area to the southeast of Iraklion, in particular the village of Arvi. The terminal is at the end of Evans St., just outside of the city walls past Kainouria Gate. Buses for destinations in the immediate vicinity of the city leave from different parts of Iraklion, usually Eleftherias Square or Venizelou Square.

Practical Information

National Tourist Organization of Greece (NTOG): 1, Xanthoudidou St., opposite the archeological museum in Eleftherias Square (tel. 22 24 87). They provide maps of the city, lists of hotels, and bus schedules for the entire island. They can also supply you with the most up-to-date, comprehensive boat schedules for departures from Crete; as always, however, all times should be verified directly with the company when you purchase your ticket. Open Mon.-Sat. 8am-7pm, closed Sun. Reduced hours in winter.

Tourist Police: on Diokesinis Ave., just off Venizelou Square (tel. 28 31 90). Less knowledgeable than the NTOG office, but sometimes more helpful. Open every day 7am-11pm.

Student Travel: Summerland Travel, 2 Vironos St., just off 25th of August St. (tel. 28 46 28). Sells budget air tickets for flights out of Athens. Does not handle mainland trains or buses. Open every day 9am-2pm and 5-8pm.

American Express: in the same office as the Creta Travel Bureau at 20-22 Epiminidou St. (tel. 24 38 11). Handles client mail and arranges check-cashing privileges with local banks for card-holders. Does not cash or sell American Express travelers checks. Open for mail collection Mon.-Fri. 9am-7pm. For check-cashing services, open Mon.-Fri. 9am-1:30pm.

Banks: on 25th of August St. Open Mon.-Fri. 8am-2pm. The National Bank of Greece at #35 keeps additional hours in summer; Mon.-Fri. 5:30-7:15pm. Gift shops in Venizelou Square do after-hours exchange at slightly lower rates.

Post Office/Poste Restante: off Gianari St. near Eleftherias Square. Open Mon.-Fri. 7:30am-8:30pm, closed Sat. and Sun.

OTE, Telephone/Telegraph: El Greco Park, just off Venizelou Square. Open every day 7am-midnight.

Olympic Airways: at Athonos St. in Eleftherias Square (tel. 22 51 71). Buses (30dr) leave from here to the airport one hour before each departure and return 20 minutes later. Otherwise, city bus #1 (20dr) goes to within 500m of the airport. Open 6am-11pm.

Boat Offices: on 25th of August St.

Emergencies: tel. 100.

Medical Services: The **Public Hospital** is on Venizelou St. (tel. 23 19 32), on the road to Knossos. Each day a different pharmacy stays open 24 hours; its name is posted on each pharmacy door every morning.

Foreign Bookstores: all over, but the one at 6 Dedalou St. has the widest variety.

Laundry: 25 Meramvellou St., near the museum. Open 8am-8pm.

Telephone Code: 081.

Handakos St., El Greco Park, and 25th of August St. are all lined with discount motorbike rental places. Prices fluctuate significantly; the price quoted one week may be higher the following week. The quality of the bikes, service in case of breakdown, and the honesty of the proprietor are all as important as price. Don't believe anyone who boasts that insurance covers damage to your bike—this does not exist in Greece. Prices usually range from 700-800dr a day and from 4000-5000dr a week for a 50cc bike, tax and third-party liability insurance included. **Caravel,** at 3 Mintavrou in El Greco Park, **Nikos Rent-a-Vespa,** at 14 Duke Beaufort Ave., **Hercules Rent-a-Scooter,** at 36 Handakos St., and **Mike's Rent-a-Scooter,** at 28 Handakos St., regularly offer low prices. Because of the enormous amount of competition, many of these rental places will arrange 10-20% discounts, especially if you show them your *Let's Go.* Remember, however, that Iraklion is probably the most expensive town on Crete in which to rent a motorbike. **Ritz Rent-a-Car** (tel. 22 36 38 or 24 21 89), which operates out of the Hotel Rea (see below), offers the Fiat 127 at a rock-bottom 13,000dr per week, with unlimited mileage, tax, and insurance included. **Itanos Rent-a-Car** (tel. 22 41 14 or 22 42 04), at 2 Kandanoleon St. in El Greco Park, has cars for the same price as well as mini-buses with double beds for 18,000dr per week. Ritz and Itanos are relatively honest agents in a less than entirely scrupulous business. Both require either an international driver's license or a national license held for at least twelve months.

Accommodations

Iraklion is a pretty good city for cheap accommodations. Most of the inexpensive hotels, as well as the Youth Hostel, are located on or near Handakos St., conveniently close to the center of town. A few more are located on Evans St., right near the market. If you arrive on one of those ferries scheduled to get in at 11pm, which invariably arrive at 2:30am, the best, and the only inexpensive, course of action is to sack out in the grassy park around Kountouriotou Square, next to the port. The police know that most of the sleeping bodies that appear in the park every night belong to innocent victims of the boat company, and you don't have to worry that they'll interrupt your sleep.

IYHF Youth Hostel, 24 Handakos St. (tel. 28 62 81). Has 180 beds and a restaurant on the top floor, but is a bit of a sardine can in terms of both spaciousness and scent. Showers in the afternoon only. Closed 10am-1:30pm, ostensibly for cleaning. 200dr per person. Midnight curfew. No card necessary.

Hotel Rea, Kalimeraki St. (tel. 22 36 38 or 24 21 89), one block off Handakos St. The owner, Michalis Hronakis, could get a lot more than the 700dr he charges for doubles and 900dr for triples, hot showers included. Quiet location.

Hotel Ideon Andron, at 1 Perdikari St. (tel. 28 36 24), has the cheapest rooms in town. Walk down Dedalou St. from Venizelou Sq. and take the first left. Doubles 500dr, triples 700dr.

Kretan Sun, 10 1866 St. (tel. 28 32 17 or 23 18 67), just off Venizelou Sq. Not especially clean and very noisy in the morning, but cheap. Doubles 600dr, triples 770dr. Showers 80dr extra.

Hotel Ionia, on Evans St. (tel. 28 17 95), just off Diokesinis. Dirty and noisy, but large enough to accommodate late arrivals. Very eager management. Most rooms have balconies. Doubles 600dr, triples 900dr.

Hotel Hania, 19 Kidonias St. (tel. 28 42 82 or 28 28 32), off Handakos. A sign outside the door proclaims "For hospitality, Hotel Hania," but the owner, George Thiakakis, is about as unfriendly and inhospitable as they come. An alternative to the Youth Hostel, which is around the corner. Beds run 200-250dr per person, depending on your sex and the proprietor's whims.

Camping: Camping Iraklion (tel. 28 63 80), 5km west of town, is brand-new and very well run. Take bus #1 or 6 from Eleftherias Sq. 120dr per person, 120dr per tent.

Iraklion has a number of cheap pensions, the most reasonable of which is **Pension Karpathos,** at 8 Gazi St. (tel. 24 11 61 or 28 64 26), near the Hania/Rethymnon bus station and the historical museum. Run by Anna Kourti. Even during the high season you can manage to get a clean double here for 600dr, a triple for 750dr (showers 50dr extra). **Rent Rooms Mary,** at 48 Handakos St. (tel. 28 11 35), has doubles for 550dr and triples for 800dr; showers 50dr extra. The following charge about 750dr for doubles and 950dr for triples: **Pension Gortys** (tel. 28 06 13), two blocks from the Phaestos bus station at 4 Akrotiriou St.; **Pension Vains** (tel. 28 57 51), run by Marika Katsirdaki, at Korytsas St. (take bus #1 or 5); **Pension Kalimera,** 6 Gramvoussis St. (tel. 24 21 76); **Pension Achilleas,** 1 Giamalaki St. (tel. 22 42 60); and **Pension Vergina,** 32 Chortatson St. (tel. 24 27 39), near the historical museum.

Food

During the day, the best show in town is the open-air market on 1866 St., which starts just off of Venizelou Square. Both sides of the narrow street are lined with stalls piled high with spices, fresh fruits, vegetables, cheese, meat, and delicacies. Two dairy shops, one at #53 and the other just opposite, compete at selling fresh yogurt to the morning shoppers. Carved in slabs out of huge ceramic bowls in which it has set overnight, this yogurt far excels the usually filtered, often pasteurized brands sold elsewhere.

Running between Evans and 1866 Sts. is tiny Theodosaki St., also called "Dirty Alley." If not the most elegant place in town to dine, it is certainly the most colorful, with its ten taverns jammed side by side, and territorial rights hopelessly undecipherable to the untrained eye. The cheapest dishes go for about 100dr here, and the helpings tend to be generous. It is wise to get the price straight before you sit to eat.

For more appealing fare at only slightly higher prices, try **Antigonis,** 40 Knossou St., about 1km from downtown Iraklion. At the base of 25th of August St. is **Ta Psaria** (the Fish Tavern), where excellent seafood dishes are served at moderate prices. For the best Greek pizza in town, try the **Pizzeria Napoli** in Eleftherias Square. Most pies are less than 300dr.

Sights

Even if you've managed to make all the boat connections outside of Iraklion, the **Archeological Museum** is still worth a special trip into the city. Outside of the National Museum in Athens, it is the finest in Greece. It houses the numerous Minoan vases discovered at the caves of Kamares, and the major finds from the excavations at Knossos, Agia Triada, Phaestos, Zakros, and Amnissos, as well as lesser archeological sites on Crete. The collection covers all of the Cretan history until Roman times, but what most of the people come for is the world's finest collection of Minoan art. The collection is huge, but well enough planned to make even a quick visit worthwhile. The thirteen rooms on the ground floor are laid out chronologically and geographically; their walls are covered with photographs of the sites and artist's renditions of what they might have looked like in their prime. Gallery III contains the puzzling "Phaestos Disc," whose hieroglyphics have yet to be decoded. In IV is a libation vase shaped like a bull's head, complete with gilt horns. Room VII has a series of double-headed axes *(labrys)* which were apparently intimately linked to the matriarchical religion. Room XIII is filled with *larnakes*, elaborately decorated Minoan sarcophagi that are so short that the bodies have to be doubled over in order to fit. Room XIX features eighth-century B.C. bronze shields decorated in relief found in the Ideon Cave near Anogia. Room XX is filled with Classical Greek, Hellenistic, and Greco-Roman sculpture.

You have to go up to the second floor, however, to see the main reason for visiting the museum: The Hall of the Minoan Frescoes! The frescoes are composites of bits of the originals, with the missing details filled in by imaginative restorers. The most renowned are the Bull-Leapers (from Knossos), an action portrait of the lost art of bull-dancing that is so rhythmical and graceful that danger seems absent; the Red and White Lilies (from Amnissos); and the Blue Monkey and Prince of the Lilies, which, along with the priestess called La Parisienne in the next room, are also from Knossos. In the center of the main room is one of the museum's prize possessions: a sarcophagus from Agia Triada, dating from about 1400 B.C., carved from limestone and painted on all four sides with a beautifully preserved representation of the sacred rites for the dead. The upper floor was closed in the summer of 1983, but should be open by 1984. Museum open every day 8am-7pm in summer; admission 100dr, 50dr for students. If you are starting and finishing your visit to Crete in Iraklion, you might consider two visits to the museum—one before you go to the archeological sites and one after.

Iraklion also has an **Historical Museum,** located near the waterfront off Grevenon St., two blocks from the Xenia Hotel. It contains a very interesting and varied collection, including frescoes, sculpture, and liturgical objects from the early Christian and Byzantine periods, a fine collection of Byzantine coins, Turkish gravestones, finely woven tapestries from Chora Sfakion, and photographs connected with the invasion of the Germans in World War II. In addition, on the second floor is a room reconstructed as the study of Nikos Kazantzakis, Crete's most famous native son. Open Mon.-Sat. 9am-1pm and 3-5:30pm; admission 70dr. Since the museum is privately owned, there is no discount for students.

Iraklion contains three interesting churches—the **Cathedral of Agios Minas,** built in 1735 and featuring six icons by the Cretan master Damaskinos; **St. Catherine's Church,** which served as the first Greek university after the fall of Constantinople in 1453 and now houses an icon exhibition (open Mon.-Sat. 9:30am-1pm, Tues., Thurs., Fri. 5:30-7:30pm; admission 30dr); and **St. Titus Church,** originally a Turkish mosque until it was converted into a Christian church several years ago. The first two are located on Agia Ekaterinis Square, the third next to 25th of August St. But perhaps the most interesting of Iraklion's sights are the various monuments built during the long Venetian occupation of the city. The most popular of them is the seventeenth-century circular **Morosini Fountain,** a fountain decorated by handsome marble lions on Venizelou Square. Several of the other monuments also deserve a visit: the **Venetian Loggia,** also at Venizelou Square; the thirteenth-century **Basilica of St. Mark** (on the 25th of August St.) now used as an exhibition hall; the **Venetian Arsenal,** off of Kountouriotou Square, near the waterfront; **Koules Fortress,** which guards the old harbor; and last but not least, the impressive fifteenth-century **Venetian walls** that encircle the city. If you walk around the top of the walls, at the southern corner of the city at Martinengo Bastion, you will come to a small zoo, and just to the west of it, the **Tomb of Kazantzakis.** The austere grave of the celebrated novelist is a popular place for evening pilgrimages for locals, since the spot offers a nice view of the town, the water, and the mountain of Zeus to the east. Due to his heterodox beliefs, Kazantzakis was denied a place in a Christian cemetery and was buried up here on the wall without full rites of the Orthodox Church; his simple gravestone bears the bold inscription from one of his own novels: "I hope for nothing. I fear nothing. I am free."

Nightlife

Iraklion has quite a few good discos, but most adhere to the dubious policy of admitting men only if they are accompanied by an equal number of women. The **Piper,** behind and below the Astoria Hotel on Eleftherias Square, is one of the most popular dance clubs. A number of bars and discos, some of which have video machines, electronic games, and other paraphernalia from the '80s, are located along Dimokratias St. A popular hangout for both Greeks and tourists is **Venizelou Square,** a plaza surrounded by cafés and featuring the Morosini Fountain.

Near Iraklion

Iraklion's location makes it an obvious base for exploring central Crete. Some sites, including the great Minoan palace complex at Knossos and lesser Minoan finds at Malia, Tilissos, and Arhanes, are within a half-day's excursion from Iraklion. Others a bit further away, including the Lassithi Plain to the east and the twin Minoan sites at Phaestos and Agia Triada, the Roman ruins at Gortys, and Matala Beach all to the south, can be visited on the way to other points in Crete, and are described later.

Knossos

Knossos, a mere 5km from Iraklion, is undoubtedly the most famous archeological site on Crete, and few visitors to the island have left without at least a quick trip to view this impressively reconstructed palace. The palace of Knossos is richly shrouded in mytho-historical associations. Here King Minos, the son of Zeus and Europa, ruled; and within the palace walls, Daedalus, at Minos' command, constructed an intricate labyrinth to hide the Minotaur, an enormous bull conceived by Minos' wife. The Minotaur was eventually slain by Theseus, an Athenian prince who was sent to Knossos with a party of young men and women as a gift to King Minos. Theseus succeeded in escaping from the labyrinth with the aid of a skein of golden thread given to him by Ariadne, the daughter of King Minos, whom he promised to rescue from her treacherous father.

And the myths go on and on. During the first millennium before Christ, Cretans were renowned throughout the Hellenic world for their overdeveloped sense of fantasy, and ridiculed for imagining that they could possess such impressive forefathers. In time, the Cretans were shown to be more right than wrong. In the first years of this century, excavations at Knossos showed that from 1700 to 1400 B.C. Knossos was indeed a great city, and had stood at the center of Minoan civilization. The modern saga of Knossos began in the 1880s when Heinrich Schliemann, the discoverer of Troy, Mycenae, and Tiryns, used his uncanny intuition to select a then-undistinguished hill near Iraklion. Arthur Evans, one of his British friends, purchased the hill and proceeded to spend the next 43 years and his entire fortune excavating it.

Evans' work at Knossos has provoked a great deal of controversy, the source of which will be obvious the moment you set foot on the site. He took the liberty of restoring large portions of the palace to what he believed to be their original configurations, based on all the internal evidence unearthed during excavations. Walls, window casements, stairways, and columns were reconstructed in reinforced concrete, and copies of the magnificent frescoes found on the palace walls (originals in the Iraklion museum) were mounted in their original places. While purists feel that the complex at Knossos is an outrage and an obstacle to science, there is no question that the whole is impressive. Indeed, when you visit the other, less adulterated Minoan sites on Crete, you'll probably be thankful for the running start your imagination was given at Knossos.

The palace of Knossos was built around a great central court similar to those found at Malia and Phaestos. All three palaces, or at least most of what can be seen today, were built after the 1650 B.C. earthquake in the so-called Neo-Palatial period (see Crete Introduction). Sprawling around this court, several stories high, is a series of rooms connected by one grand staircase and a secondary private one. The rooms were illuminated by shafts of light from strategically placed minor courtyards, and the whole complex shared a sophisticated water and drainage system, still evident in the gutters woven throughout the site, which can twist an unwary ankle. The functions of various areas have been more or less deduced: the official state rooms, most notably the throne room with its original gypsum throne still in place, the queen's bedroom with its toilet and quarters for attendants, and the granaries with their rows of *pithoi*, the huge, round pottery containers for oil and grain as tall as a man.

There is no point in suggesting a route by which to tour the various areas because you are bound to get lost in the maze-like site—the word "labyrinth" doesn't come from here for nothing. As classical etymologists have pointed out, however, the word derives literally from two separate words, "labrys" and "nthos," meaning "house of the double axe," a fitting name for a palace filled with that ancient Minoan symbol.

A guidebook to this extensive site is a great help; the best and most comprehensive is *Pendlebury's Handbook to the Palace of Minos, Knossos, and its Dependencies*, on sale at the site and in most foreign bookstores on Crete. The ruins at Knossos are open Mon.-Sat. 8:30am-3pm, Sun. 9am-2pm; admission 100dr, 50dr for students. Rooms can be rented in the small community of tourist shops adjoining the site for 1000dr a double, but the expense is hardly necessary. Take bus #2, departing every twenty minutes from in front of the Astoria Hotel in Eleftherias Square (20dr for the fifteen-minute trip).

Lindo and Amnissos

Iraklion's harbor is unswimmable, but there are two public beaches nearby, at **Lindo,** 4km west, and at **Amnissos** (the better of the two), 8km east. Amnissos is also the site of the ancient port of Knossos; among the remains is a villa in which the frescoes of Amnissos, now in the Iraklion museum, were found. For Lindo, take bus #1, which leaves from in front of the Astoria Hotel in

Eleftherias Square and stops at several free hotel beaches, including **Creta Beach, Agapi Beach, Apollonia, Akti Zeus,** and **Dolphin Bay.** Bus #6, which leaves from a stop across the street from the Astoria, takes you to Amnissos.

Tilissos, Anogia, and Fodele

Although Knossos ranks as the most popular site on Crete, it cannot lay claim to being the oldest. The archeological site at **Tilissos** wins that title; just 14km southwest of Iraklion archeologists have unearthed the oldest Minoan city to date. Unlike the ruins of Knossos, those at Tilissos remain relatively unblemished by modern modifications. Open Mon.-Sat. 10am-4:15pm, Sun. 9am-2pm; admission 30dr, 20dr for students. Tilissos has one pension, which charges 600dr for a double.

Another 22km along the same road brings you to **Anogia,** a center for weaving and folkcraft and a popular destination for excursion buses. The reason for Anogia's high level of craft is a bitter one. During World War II, the villagers hid the British kidnappers of German General Kreipe, and in reprisal, the Germans shot all of the village's menfolk, thus leaving the widows with no other recourse for their livelihood. Today Anogia celebrates its renewed vigor with a traditional music festival at the end of July. From the village it is a four-hour hike to the **Cave of Ideon Andron,** an ancient sanctuary dedicated to Zeus in which a number of archeological discoveries were made. The hike itself is spectacular, taking you through the beautiful **Nidha Plain,** one of the most scenic spots in all of Crete. Anogia has two cheap hotels: the **Imarmeni** (tel. 31 36 5) and the **Psiloritis** (tel. 32 23 1). Both charge 500dr for a double. Halfway between Tilissos and Anogia are the remains of the Minoan villas at **Sklavokambos.** The roadside ruins are unattended and always open, but warrant only a brief stop. Buses for Tilissos and Anogia depart five times a day from Bus Terminal D (100dr one-way).

Also accessible from Iraklion is **Fodele,** a pleasant village full of orange trees. Fodele is famous as the home of El Greco, the celebrated Cretan painter whose real name was Domenikos Theotokopoulos. El Greco left Fodele at the age of 20 to study under Titian in Venice, and from there he moved on to Toledo, Spain, where he lived most of his life and did his finest work. Buses depart twice a day from Bus Terminal D for those who wish to make a pilgrimage to the master's hometown.

From Iraklion to Matala

If you immediately flee Iraklion by taking the north coastal route east or west, you'll miss the best part of Central Crete—the south, with its remarkable archeology and beaches. Even if you want to head west eventually, you can travel to Rethymnon via Agia Galini and see far more than you would on the north coast freeway. From Iraklion, buses head south from Bus Terminal C, first climbing and then descending into the fertile Messara Plain, whose agricultural wealth supported the Minoan centers at **Phaestos** and **Agia Triada,** and the Roman capital of Crete, **Gortys.** While these sites can be seen in a full daytrip from Iraklion, if you have the time it is far more pleasant to continue south and spend the night in the coastal resorts of **Matala** or **Agia Galini.** From the latter, you can continue up to Rethymnon, a route described in the Western Crete section.

Gortys

The first stop of historical interest on the road south, Gortys contains the ruins of a Greco-Roman city, whose chief prize is a series of stone tablets containing the Law Code of Gortys. The code uses over 17,000 characters, and is inscribed in the ox-plow manner: one line is written left to right, the next right to left. The characters are written in a Dorian dialect of Greek, and date to about 500 B.C., when Gortys was flourishing under Greek control. Although it mandates that slaves be punished with more severity than citizens, the content of the code is, on the whole, surprisingly liberal for its time. The code grants slaves the right to sue free men, whether masters or other citizens, and grants the children of slaves the status of free citizens if at least one of the parents is also free.

Gortys fell to the Romans in 67 B.C. along with the rest of Crete, and was designated the capital of the island. Most of the remaining ruins to be seen are from the Roman occupation, including the **Roman Odeon,** or music hall. One of the few remains from the Hellenistic city, the Law Code tablets survived because they were so handsomely and evenly cut that the Romans used them as building materials for the Odeon, without realizing their significance. The part of the structure which covers the Law Code now was tastefully restored by the Italian archeologist Halbherr, who excavated the site at the turn of the century.

The large ruined stone church which you pass on your way to the Law Code is the seventh-century **Basilica of Saint Titus.** It was built to house the tomb of Titus, Crete's first bishop, who died in 105 A.D. Titus was installed by St. Paul himself, who was obviously less than enthusiastic about the job, writing in Titus 1:12-16 that the Cretans were lazy, gluttonous liars. Several sketchier remains of a Roman city (a sanctuary, theater, and amphitheater) are located across the road from the site of the Basilica and Odeon.

The site of Gortys is next to the road to Phaestos, 1 km beyond the town of **Agii Deka.** Though the site technically closes at 7pm, you can always let yourself in. Admission is free, and the attendants are often helpful, providing unofficial guided tours. Beds can be rented for 250dr per person at either of the two tavernas in Agii Deka. The seven daily buses from Iraklion to Phaestos all stop in the town and at the site.

Phaestos and Agia Triada

Situated on a plateau with a magnificent view of the surrounding mountains and Messara Plain, the palace at **Phaestos** once housed a Minoan royal family whose power, if not equal to that of Knossos, certainly approximated it. Phaestos was originally excavated at the turn of the century by the Italian archeologist, Halbherr, who also discovered Gortys. He originally unearthed two palaces dating from successive periods, but in 1952, another excavation effort uncovered signs of two earlier palaces still further beneath the site. Like Knossos, the palace built in Phaestos in the Middle Minoan Period was largely destroyed along with all the other major Minoan cities in about 1450 B.C. Since the excavations, minor reconstruction has been done on the walls, chambers, and cisterns, but nothing approximating Evans' work at Knossos—the impressive site at Phaestos remains pretty much the way it was found.

Built on the typical Minoan plan, and resembling Knossos in practically all architectural details, the palace contained a great central court, off of which radiated the private royal quarters, rooms for attendants, store rooms, and rooms for state occasions. The palace was constructed on several levels, with a grand staircase (still in place) and several lesser ones connecting them. Close inspection has also revealed identical masons' marks at both Knossos and Phaestos, suggesting that the same workmen labored at both palaces. The similarities in design between the two sites allow the visitor a rare opportunity to compare a reconstructed and an untouched version of a Minoan palace. The rich finds from Phaestos, including vases, jewelry, altars, and the famed Phaestos Disc imprinted with as yet undeciphered signs, are all on display in the Iraklion museum.

The tourist pavilion right at the site has doubles for 700dr; reservations are advisable in summer (write to Xenia Hotel in Phaestos or call 22 83 6). The guards at the box office can direct you to local, cheaper (but more inconvenient) pensions if the hotel is full. The site is nestled in a valley surrounded by mountains and is usually blessed with a cool breeze, making it one of the few archeological sites in Greece that can be enjoyed on a hot summer day. Open Mon.-Sat. 8am-7pm and Sun. 8am-6pm (Mon.-Sat. 10am-4pm and Sun. 10am-2pm in the off-season); admission 50dr, 30dr for students, free on Sundays. Unfortunately, much of the palace is poorly labeled. The glossy 200dr Gortys-Phaestos-Agia Triada guidebook available at Phaestos provides little help in deciphering the ruins. Bus service from Phaestos is excellent: seven buses a day run to Gortys and Iraklion (the last one is at 5:15pm), six a day to Agia Galini (last one at 6:50pm), and six a day to Matala (last one at 4:20pm).

Three kilometers from Phaestos is the smaller Minoan site of **Agia Triada.** A kind of miniature version of the great Minoan palaces, Agia Triada is believed to have had some close tie to Phaestos, perhaps as a private retreat for the royal family. Although the site itself is not nearly as impressive as Phaestos, important finds unearthed during excavations—including frescoes, Linear A tablets, and the painted sarcophagus considered among the greatest treasures of the Iraklion museum—have contributed to its fame. Oddly enough, its name comes from the small Byzantine church at the southeast corner of the site, now so overshadowed by the once-buried pagan site to which it has lent its name that it almost escapes notice. The site is open Mon.-Sat. 10am-4:15pm, Sun. 9am-2pm; admission 30dr, 20dr for students. To get to Agia Triada from Phaestos, follow the road to Matala, and take the right fork (uphill) 200m beyond the parking lot. Agia Triada is 3km past the fork.

Matala

From Agia Triada or Phaestos you can make the journey 12km south to Matala, a small coastal community surrounded by marvelous beaches and terrific scenery that looks like a Hollywood set left over from a filming of Beach Blanket Bingo Meets Frankenstein. The deep-set swimming cove in front of the village is backed with high cliffs, in which, over the centuries, elaborate caves were carved out as tombs. The caves were further widened and outfitted by the Germans during World War II, when they were guarding the south coast of Crete from English submarines.

Years ago, Matala gained fame as a retreat for hippies who took up long-term residence in the caves. Its prestige was further enhanced by an article printed in *Life Magazine* on the "Hippie Caves of Matala." The police have taken to clearing out some of the caves, at least intermittently, but the reputation as a gathering ground for youth has stuck. Large numbers of young people of all nationalities still flock to Matala every summer; however, only a minority of them still take to the caves at night, especially now that the ones nearest the village have been fenced off by barbed wire. Today, most sleep at the campsite near the beach. Although many of the present-day pilgrims to Matala are considerably more clean-cut and better financially endowed than the original generation of hippies that made its beaches and caves famous, it has not yet entirely lost its romantic flavor. Matala retains a cheerfully informal atmosphere, and most of the night spots still play '60s rock tunes as if they were trying to keep the old tradition alive.

Accommodations and Practical Information

Matala has over a dozen hotels and pensions, but there are few bargains. It helps to start your search early in the day, since rooms fill quickly in this popular hideaway. Solo travelers are advised to find a temporary roommate, since singles often cost as much as doubles; consider yourself lucky if you find a single for 500dr during the summer.

The **Zafiria Beach Hotel** (tel. 42 36 6), just before the town square on the main road, and the **Kimata Hotel** (tel. 42 36 1), just past the square on the street closest to the ocean, have clean doubles for 800dr. The best of three new pensions in Matala is run by **Nikos Kefalakis** (tel. 42 37 5), and costs 565dr for a double (take a left down the dirt road just before the square; Kefalakis' pension is the second on the right). Room prices drop slightly as you move inland from the village. **Hotel Tsiterakis** and **Hotel Acropol** both charge 600dr for dingy but sufficient doubles. **Pensione Jannis** (tel. 42 35 8), farthest inland from the town, charges 700dr for a double—inquire at the Hotel Chez Xenophon. The **Matala Beach Hotel** has doubles for 600dr, but the owner, Stefano Kotsifakis, is an excitable, ill-tempered fellow who can be extremely unpleasant. **Matala Camping** (take a right just before the Bamboo Sands Hotel) is probably the best deal in town, at only 50dr per person, 50dr per tent, 50dr for a car or motorcycle, and 100dr to rent a tent. The site is spacious and right behind the beach, and the perpetually cold showers will wake you up no matter how much you had to drink the night before.

It is not recommended that you spend the night either on the main beach or in one of the impressive caves on the north side of the cove (if you can get through the fence), since both are subject to sporadic police raids. If you decide to ignore this piece of advice, then leave your passport elsewhere, for the police punish freelance campers by confiscating their passports and selling them back for about 5000dr. At both of the above locations there have also been repeated instances of theft.

The village consists of essentially two main streets: one on the waterfront, and one behind it. On the former, you will find cafés, restaurants, and music, and on the latter gift shops, motorbike rental agencies, and stores. The **Mermaid Gift Shop** and **Sport Rent-a-Car** both change cash and travelers checks at rates a few drachmas below the official standard. Buses run back and forth between Matala and Iraklion four times a day during the summer (195dr one-way). The last bus leaves from Iraklion at 3pm, and from Matala at 5pm. To get to and from Agia Galini, you need to change buses in Phaestos. The **telephone code** for Matala is 0892.

Sights

The main beach at Matala is beautiful but crowded. For an equally good beach and more secluded caves, head for **Red Beach**, known for its long and cheerful tradition of nudism. Follow the path which starts where Matala's two streets converge and veer right; it's a twenty-minute hike over the hill to the south. On the way, you will pass numerous caves within easy climbing distance. Here the veteran cave-dwellers now reside, for the police never bother to hike up here, nor do most of the tourists—they both seem to be sufficiently amused by the caves to the north of the village. The cliffs between Matala and Red Beach all offer spectacular views of the Mediterranean, and most paths take you back down to the beach.

Another secluded beach with its own small community of freelance summer residents is **Kommos Beach**, a 5km walk from Matala (walk towards the village of Pitsidia, and take the second dirt road on your left). The beach is quite long, and leads you to the makeshift beach-town of **Kalamaki** (a half-hour walk), where beds can be rented for 150dr in one of the two pensions. If you keep walking towards Pitsidia on the main road (3km from Matala), you'll find rooms for 250dr per person, and sometimes even less.

Nightlife in Matala centers around its two discos, **Zorbas,** a few hundred meters inland, and **Aquarius,** in the town itself. Wine and beer flow freely and cheaply at any of the restaurants which line the harbor and the main square.

Agia Galini

Agia Galini, west of Matala on the southern coast, was once a pristine and peaceful fishing village, but is now a casualty of the tourist trade. The main shortcoming of the town is that it is about as Greek as Frankfurt. The area has become very popular among Northern European charter operators, and the mass influx of package tour patrons has driven up hotel and restaurant prices. Though clever bargaining can land you a double for as little as 400dr in the off-season, by midsummer even the dirtiest dives fill quickly for 800dr a double.

Escaping the tourists who flock to the small, rocky beach is difficult; a fifty-foot-wide river blocks access to the rest of the coast after only five hundred meters. At the moment, there is little to see here during the summer but your fellow tourists kicking up their heels at the **Soroco,** the only disco in Agia Galini (on the beach).

Accommodations and Practical Information

In the summer, it is very difficult to find a cheap room in Agia Galini. The **Pantheon Hotel** (tel. 91 29 3), at the top of the stairs leading up from the main square on Vass. Ioannis St., is probably the best deal in town, with relatively clean doubles for 700dr and delightful management to boot. **Hotel Selena** (tel. 91 25 0) charges 800dr for doubles with a beautiful view of the ocean, 600dr for rooms less well-situated. Take the first right off Vass. Ioannis at the Pantheon Hotel. The adjacent **Hotel Akteon** (tel. 91 20 8) has reasonably clean rooms with a good view of the sea for 700dr a double. Farther along the same street is **Hotel Acropol**—less than aromatic, but cheap at 600dr a double. **Kydon,** just before the square on the main road into town, has rock-bottom rates starting at 450dr a double. **Camping Agia Galini** (tel. 91 23 9) is probably the most pleasant place to stay in Agia Galini. Nikos and his family are wonderful hosts, and charge only 150dr per tent, 100dr per person (100dr for tent rental). The site is located down a dirt road 2km east of town on the road to Matala, 200m from the beach.

On Vassili Ioannis St., which leads from the water and is lined with tables, relatively cheap restaurants abound. A drop-off laundry is located on the main road out of town (about 500m from the main square) charging 120dr per kilo. If the National Bank agent is closed, the Candia Travel Agency on Vass. Ioannis St. can change your money.

Eight buses a day connect Iraklion and Agia Galini (210dr one-way). Four buses a day travel between Rethymnon and Agia Galini (180dr one-way). The **telephone code** for Agia Galini is 0832.

Near Agia Galini

Fifty-five kilometers from Iraklion, along the isolated northern route to Agia Galini, is the mountain village of **Kamares,** a good place to view the twin peaks of Mount Ida (8000 feet high). Kamares is also a good base from which to make the excursion to **Kamares Cave,** the grotto sanctuary where the famous collection of nineteenth-century B.C. polychrome pottery, known as Kamares Ware, was found (now exhibited in the Iraklion museum).

During the summer, the village of **Kokinos Pirgos** celebrates "Cretan Night" every evening, a lively affair featuring traditional food and entertainment, but entirely for the benefit of tourists. Tickets for the festivities run a steep 900dr, and can be purchased at the **Candia Travel Agency** on Vass. Ioannis St. in Agia Galini.

If you want to continue west to Rethymnon (there are four buses a day), then see descriptions of the various sights along the way—the **Preveli Monasteries, Plakias,** and **Spili**—in the Western Crete section.

Western Crete

Rethymnon

The pleasant harbor town of Rethymnon, 81km west of Iraklion, is an intriguing slice of Crete's past. The Venetian and Turkish influence to be seen all over Northern Crete is nowhere as obvious as in this charming town, with its Turkish minarets, narrow arched winding streets dating from the 1500s, and the imposing Venetian Fortezza crowning the west end of its long harbor. The much-celebrated wine festival during July and August is an enjoyable affair, but Rethymnon deserves a visit at any time of the year.

Practical Information

The well-informed **Tourist Police** (tel. 28 15 6) are next door to the museum at 216 Arkadiou St. (disregard the maps which say otherwise), and can provide you with a map of the city and a list of hotels in Rethymnon. The office is open Mon.-Fri. 8am-2pm, closed weekends. The same services are also provided by the **National Tourist Organization of Greece** office at 100 Kountouriotou St. (tel. 29 14 8), open every day 8am-1:30pm and 5-7:30pm. The office is literally a one-man show, with Kostas Palierakis, who has received honorable mention in just about every guidebook, as the star. The accolades are well deserved: Palierakis runs one of the best tourist offices in Greece. In addition to regular duties—providing maps to the towns, bus and boat schedules, museum hours, and a list of all-night pharmacies—he can suggest day trips in the area, tell you what is scheduled in Rethymnon's tavernas, help you find a room, and negotiate car payments with the car rental companies for you. Since he manages to get as much as 50% off, this makes Rethymnon an appealing place to rent cars.

Rethymnon's two bus stations face each other on opposite corners of the intersection of Dimokratias and Moatsou Streets, one block inland from the Venizelou monument on Kountouriotou St. Buses leave every hour or two for Iraklion and Hania, four times a day for Spili and Agia Galini, twice a day for Plakias, and once a day for Chora Sfakion. Buses also leave three times a day for the Arkadi monastery from Kountouriotou St.

You'll find almost everything you need, including most of the town's craft shops, in the rough triangle formed by Gerakari, Antistasseos, and Arkadiou Streets. To get to Arkadiou St. and the waterfront from the bus station, walk down Dimokratias St. to the Venizelou monument, cross Kountouriotou St. (the NTOG office will be to your right), and walk straight on Varda Kellergi St.

Post Office: 104 Kountouriotou St., next to the Tourist Office. Open Mon.-Fri. 7:30am-4pm.

OTE: two blocks west at 28 Kountouriotou St. Open 6am-midnight.

Motorbike Rental: Daskalakis, at 44 Palelogou St. near the museum (tel. 24 50 7), quotes the lowest prices (500dr per day for a 50cc bike). **Stavros Papadakis,** two doors down at 14 Palelogou St. (tel. 22 85 8 or 23 70 7), has 50cc bikes for 600dr a day.

Hospital: on Iliakaki St. (tel. 22 26 1). Or try the **Ippokration Clinic** at 74 Kountouriotou St. (tel. 29 15 5).

Supermarket: The biggest is at 2-8 Hatzidaka St., between Kountouriotou and Moatsou Streets.

Telephone Code: 0831.

Accommodations

IYHF Youth Hostel, 7 Pavlou Vlastou St. (tel. 22 84 8). One block inland from the Tassos restaurant on the waterfront. The owners, Barbara and George Kalogeraki, do everything they can to create a cheerful, informal atmosphere. The place is small and usually crowded in the summer. If you check in late, the best you can hope for is a bed on the floor. Mercifully for wine festival goers, there is no curfew. 180dr per person, no card necessary, free showers (put your towel in line for the only hot shower).

Hotel Paradissos, 35 Ag. Gavril St. (tel. 22 41 9). From the bus station, walk down to the Venizelou monument and go left on Kountouriotou, which becomes Ag. Gavril. Clean and friendly, with a cheerful management. Singles 450dr, doubles 620dr, triples 870dr. Showers 70dr extra. Midnight curfew.

Hotel Minoa, 60 Arkadiou St. (tel. 22 50 8). Just to the right of the intersection of Arkadiou and Varda Kallergi. Large and likely to have space. Doubles 900dr, triples 1000dr; 200dr cheaper in the off-season.

Hotel Akropol, 2 Makariou St. (tel. 23 47 7), just off Iroon (Agnostou) Square. From the Venizelou monument, go right on Kountouriotou for two blocks. Attractive decor, but otherwise unremarkable. Doubles 600dr, triples 800dr.

Hotel Achillion, 151 Arkadiou St. (tel. 22 58 1). Go left from the corner of Arkadiou and Varda Kallergi Streets. A once-fancy place on the waterfront, now fallen on hard times. Conditions are pretty grim for Rethymnon. Doubles 700dr, triples 900dr; 200dr cheaper in the off-season. Showers 60dr extra.

Pensions: Arkadiou St. and the harbor between the Fortezza and the Venetian port are lined with inexpensive rooms-to-let. Two of the best and cheapest places are run by **Barbara Dokimaki** (behind 9 Plastira St., tel. 22 31 9) and **Mr. Kokonas** (303 Arkadiou St., tel. 29 12 9). Both have doubles for less than 650dr and triples for less than 900dr.

Camping: For some reason, Rethymnon has the lion's share of Crete's few organized campgrounds: **Elizabeth Camping** (tel. 28 69 4) is 3km east of town, at the beginning of the old road to Iraklion. **Arkadia Camping** (tel. 28 82 5), the best of the lot, is 500m beyond Elizabeth. Both charge 120dr per person and 80dr per tent, and are accessible via the buses to Loutra, Platanes, or Kiriana. **George Camping** (tel. 61 36 3), 16km west of town (all Hania-Rethymnon buses pass it), charges the same rates, but has a smaller, rockier beach.

Food

Unlike most other Cretan cities, Rethymnon is well-endowed with small stands and tavernas offering *souvlaki-pita* and other inexpensive fare. There is also an open-air market on weekdays next to the park, between Moatsou and Kountouriotou Streets.

Restaurants are uniformly expensive in Rethymnon, with the cheapest dishes available (*moussaka,* spaghetti, etc.) costing at least 120dr. In the winter, most of the town's tavernas are to be found near the center of the city, but in the summer, serious eating shifts to the harbor. If you've been holding out for one good fish meal, this may be the place to get it. All of the many restaurants that line the old harbor specialize in fresh seafood and you will find a variety not easily come by elsewhere (although the one local catch of the day may be just as good, and cheaper than at Rethymnon). Fish here, as everywhere in Greece, is sold by the kilo (except shrimp, squid, and small fish like chopa). Kilo prices fluctuate from day to day with the local catch, ranging 500-800dr; an average one-person meal of fish weighs ⅓ to ⅔ kilo. You'll find that the prices are standard at most restaurants (probably set by a daily price-fixing colloquy over ouzo and backgammon). Quality varies mostly for the accoutrements—vegetables, bread, and salad. The harbor is definitely the most entertaining place to eat, but for a non-fish meal you will do well also at **Tassos,** at the east end of the waterfront (at the corner of Therissou St.). If you have access to a car or feel like taking a walk, try **Zizi's Taverna,** 4km east of town on the old road to Iraklion. It's only open at night (closed Wednesdays) but is the most popular place to eat among the locals.

Sights

Rethymnon has a one-room **Archeological Museum** (on Arkadiou St. at the corner of Palelogou St.) which occupies an old Venetian Loggia dating from about 1600. Its motley collection includes Minoan and early Hellenistic pottery and ornaments, Roman coins, a number of Minoan sarcophagi, and, curiously enough, Egyptian figurines not found on Crete. Open Mon.-Sat. 8am-5pm, Sun. 9am-4pm; admission 50dr, 30dr for students. One block to the west of the museum you will find the **Arimondi Fountain,** one of the city's numerous Venetian monuments.

At some point during your residence in Rethymnon, you should make a pilgrimage to the colossal **Venetian Fortezza.** The fortifications date from around 1580, and the walls of the enormous citadel are still in excellent condition. Most of the buildings in the interior of the fortress were destroyed by the Turks in the seventeenth century, with some help three centuries later from German bombing during World War II. During the summer, the Fortezza is open Mon.-Sat. 9am-7:30pm, Sun. 9am-4pm; admission 40dr.

Rethymnon is filled with reminders of the long Turkish presence in the city. To name a few: the **Neratzes Minaret** on Antistasseos St.; **Nerdjes Mosque,** one block further, which was formerly a Franciscan church; the **Kara Pasha Mosque** on Arkadiou St. near Iroon Square; and the **Valides Minaret,** which presides over **Porta Megali** gate at the beginning of Antistasseos St. in 3 Martiou Square. The Neratzes Minaret is open every day 10:30am-1:30pm and 5:30-8:30pm. Kara Pasha can also be seen from 11am-1pm. Admission to both sites is free.

Entertainment

If you've heard that there's a wine festival in Rethymnon the last week in July and the first week in August and arranged your itinerary to make it, don't bother. Although good fun, it's a bit of Walt Disney, complete with papier-mache rocks, a miniature windmill, and an electric band playing Hello Dolly. (It's not, as one might imagine, that the festival is mounted for the benefit of tourists; the Greeks themselves go in for this sort of stuff in a big way.) The drinking part of the festival works as follows. You can pay 100dr to enter the park, which entitles you to as much wine as you can drink from the barrels at several strategic spots on the grounds. Each station has a barrel of white, rosé, and red, but you need a glass, or, better yet, a carafe, to be served (unless you are very good at cupping your hands). Both are sold on the grounds for 20dr and 70dr respectively, but unless you want them as souvenirs, bring your own. As the evening gets going, the Hello Dolly contingent is booted off the stage to make way for a traditional Cretan trio of lute, viol, and singer, and a local dance troupe performs in traditional costumes. If this is your only opportunity to see Cretan dances performed, then it is worth a special trip—papier-mache rocks and all. Nothing captures the gentle exuberance of this island and its people's sheer joy at the gift of life better than their dances and festivals.

An exhibition of Cretan handicrafts is also scheduled in Rethymnon to coincide roughly with the Wine Festival. The work is worth a look, but you won't pick up any bargains—better prices can usually be gotten at local artisans' shops in each major town.

Near Rethymnon

One popular excursion from Rethymnon is to the **Arkadi Monastery** in the mountains 22km southeast of the city. This monastery, like many on the island, has a long history of resistance to foreign incursions against Crete. But it is chiefly owing to the events of November 9, 1866 that Arkadi is held sacred by the Cretans. The monastery had been storing gunpowder for the war against the Turks, and over one thousand Cretans had taken refuge there. When thousands of Turks besieged the monastery and defeat was imminent, the abbot ignited the gunpowder, blowing up the building to prevent its capture. Hundreds, and perhaps thousands, of Cretans and Turks died in the explosion, bringing worldwide attention to the Greeks' struggle for independence. Throughout Greece the Arkadi Monastery is today regarded as a symbol of freedom and independence. The anniversary of the holocaust is observed annually (November 7-9) with solemn celebrations at Arkadi and in Rethymnon. The monastery is open every day 7am-8pm.

Although the excursion to Arkadi is charged with more significance for the Greek than for the foreign visitor, the trip is well worth taking for the handsome stone buildings of the monastery, including the sixteenth-century church erected during the Venetian occupation, which combines classical and rococo architectural idioms. The roofless gunpowder room is in the far left corner of the courtyard, near the unused eastern entrance to the monastery. The historical museum on the right (southern) side of the courtyard contains various mementos connected with the war. (Closed 1-2pm; admission 30dr, no student discount.) To the left as the bus enters the site is the octagonal **Sanctuary of the Heroes,** a memorial to the victims of the blast. Inside are displayed the skulls of thirteen Cretans who perished in front-line combat. Several tour companies offer expensive one-day excursions to the monastery, but you can easily do it on your own; public buses to Arkadi leave three times a day from Iroon Square in Rethymnon.

The east end of Rethymnon opens onto a long beach, extending for about 10km. It is wide and spacious for a town beach, but somewhat dirty; on a typical Cretan summer afternoon you probably won't be too picky, and will find it more than adequate. The beach gets a little better as you continue east, but not enough to justify the trouble of getting there without private transportation. Many of the local Greeks prefer to swim off the rocks at the foot of the Fortezza's walls. If you take any bus about 10km west along the new coastal highway, you'll soon be passing one of the longest stretches of sand beach in Crete, which extends all the way around the **Gulf of Georgiopolis.** The road is a mixed blessing. While it has taken some of the beach's splendid solitude away, it has also preserved the remainder by running so close to the water that almost no hotels could be built (there are also some oleander hedges which protect the privacy of bathers). Although cars and motorbikes can pull over along the road, the nearest inexpensive accommodations are in the quiet coastal village of **Giorgiopolis.** The **Amfimalla** hotel offers doubles for 600dr, triples for 800dr, and quads for 1000dr. The nearby **Hotel Penelope** has doubles for 650dr, triples for 800dr, showers 50dr extra. Similar prices are quoted by the many "rent-rooms" establishments, but a little bargaining will bring the prices down.

From Rethymnon to Agia Galini

This route can be seen as two directions, either as a trip southeast from Rethymnon (the way it is described here), or in the reverse direction, heading northwest from Agia Galini. Either way, it should ideally be combined with the itinerary "From Iraklion to Matala" in the Central Crete section, as the two together form a delightful southern circle between these two major cities on the north coast.

You can head south from Rethymnon on either the bus to Agia Galini (four a day) or the bus to Plakias (two a day). After 23km, a right turn toward Koxare leads south toward Preveli and Plakias. After passing through the spectacular gorge of Kourtaliatiko, you reach the town of Asomatos. At the first intersection in the village, bear right to stay on the road to Plakias. A left turn and another left onto a dirt road puts you on the path to Preveli.

There are actually two monasteries at **Preveli.** The older one, dedicated to St. John the Baptist, is on the left, below you on a hillside about 2km after the turn-off for Preveli. Until World War II, it was used as a granary, but after the Germans vandalized it, only the curious peaked corner watchtowers were left to preside over the crumbling ruin. Goats now have the run of the monastery; a goatherd inhabits one of the buildings, and his charges leave their marks on every corner of the grounds.

The newer **Monastery of St. John the Theologian,** about 4km further along the scenic but rough dirt road, perches magnificently on a hill overlooking the sea. This monastery did its part during the German occupation of Crete in World War II by hiding Allied soldiers within its walls until they could be safely smuggled out in submarines. The monastery still operates, but just barely. In recent years, it has fallen into disrepair due to lack of support and reduced staffing. The monastery and its small museum can be visited 8am-1pm and 5-8pm (admission to museum 20dr). Proper dress is required, but this dictum is not likely to be enforced unless one of the three monks is around.

There is no public transportation to Preveli. The morning bus from Myrthios and Plakias to Rethymnon goes through Asomatos. From there, it's a 7km (two-hour) uphill trek to the latter monastery. Alternatively, scooters can be rented in Plakias.

There are two good beaches in Preveli, although both are difficult to find. **Limni Beach** is closest to the monastery—walk on the dirt road which begins about 1km below the upper sanctuary. **Preveli Beach** is about 6km from the road to Preveli, and does have a small taverna—cross the bridge about 2km after the dirt road to Preveli begins and follow the intermittent signs. Camping is tolerated on this dirty but secluded beach.

In contrast to Preveli, the simplicity of getting to **Plakias** guarantees that you will not be alone, although it is unlikely that you will regret the trip. A beautiful beach served by buses from Rethymnon twice a day, Plakias is increasingly popular with travelers seeking a quiet place to stay for a week or two—you can live quite happily here for about $6 a day. The newly-opened **Youth Hostel** at Plakias is clean, friendly, and charges only 160dr per night (no card necessary, no curfew). Phillipus, the warden, has an extensive tape collection with music for all tastes. He also rents windsurfers for 300dr an hour, including a quick lesson. His parents run an equally superb **Youth Hostel** in **Myrthios** (tel. 31 20 2), a twenty-minute walk uphill from Plakias. Although somewhat primitive, it offers a spectacular view and its host, Giorgio, is terrific. If the hostels are full, they'll usually make room for you on the roof. If you prefer privacy, the **Hotel Livicon** (tel. 31 21 6) offers doubles for 800dr during the summer (600dr in the off-season). There are also rooms-to-let for comparable prices. A makeshift (read: free) campground can be found at the far eastern end of the beach. The official camp site, **Camping Marcel,** charges 100dr per person.

Although the beach at Plakias is nothing to complain about, several swimming coves to the east are even better. The closest is **Damnoni** (walk 1km on the road to Lefkogia and take a right on the dirt road), which has an informal campsite, two tavernas, an expensive pension (doubles 900dr) and cold public showers. The lone cove to the west also deserves a visit. Miraculously, it has escaped the onslaught of tourist buildings that has scarred Plakias and Damnoni.

The rest of the main route from the Koxare turn-off to Agia Galini winds through wide-open mountainous terrain, much of it covered with lush vegetation that makes it an unusual sight on this arid island. **Spili,** 8km southeast of the turn-off, is a beautiful village with cascading waters, cobblestone streets, and shady trees. The **Green Hotel** (tel. 22 22 5) on the western edge of town is a delightful, though expensive, place to stay the night. True to its name, the interior is a veritable orangery, with ferns winding up the stairs and sparkling rooms (singles without bath 450dr, doubles without bath 900dr; 100dr more per person for private bath). **Pension Pandocheion,** at the opposite end of the village, is far less pleasant but much cheaper: 200dr per person, showers 50dr extra.

If you have a jeep, or a vehicle which can take a pounding, some of the most beautiful scenery in all of Crete is along the mountain roads in the area of Spili and **Gerakari.** Very few maps show these routes, but if you follow the mountain ranges, you won't get lost. Just 2km southeast of Gerakari is a lovely shaded spot with running water—perfect for camping. Across the road is a tiny, ruined eleventh-century Byzantine monastery, **Agios Ioannis Theologos,** containing some well-preseved frescoes. You'll find no tourists here.

Hania

Sit down at a restaurant in Hania and order a beer, and the waiter will gently urge you to try a Hania wine instead—it is, he tells you, nothing like the foul stuff they force on you in less richly endowed parts of Greece. Can I have some feta to go with it, you say—would you perhaps like to try some Hania cheese instead, he suggests, I think you'll like it. And so it goes. The Haniots may have more pride in their city than you will encounter anywhere else in Greece, and it is richly deserved.

At first glance, the city may seem unremarkable—its Venetian harbor and the narrow, winding streets in the old town are a busier version of Rethymnon's, its market a covered version of Iraklion's market street. The town beaches, like those in most of Crete's northern cities, are unimpressive, and like everywhere else in Greece, people drive madly.

But something about Crete's second largest city is different. Partly it is the combination of big town activity and small town hospitality which have joined in a remarkably harmonious marriage here; partly it is the richness of the region—rich in produce, local arts and handicrafts, and in history to those interested in Greece's long struggle for independence. But most of all, it is simply that Hania has so far survived tourism. Fewer tourists make it to Western Crete than to other parts of the island. The city won't appeal to everyone—it's definitely not a resort town, although there are good beaches not far to the west. But many of those smitten with its charms have stayed for years, some even for lifetimes, making up a small but significant community of foreign artists, writers, and retirees in residence.

When you first drive into Hania, you won't be overwhelmed by its beauty. It's a large city by Greek standards (pop. 41,000), and the outlying districts are quite unattractive. But soon you will pass all the modern concrete apartment houses and enter Hania's charismatic core: the picturesque harbor with its faded old mansions and wooden fishing boats. When evening rolls around almost the entire town saunters out for a promenade underneath the brightly-colored lanterns that illuminate the wharf, with their reflections glimmering soundlessly in the water. Unlike Agios Nikolaos or Ierapetra, Hania has chosen to retain its traditional garb rather than take on a glossier, more polished look.

Practical Information

The layout of the town is confusing, and when you arrive, a judicious first stop would be at the **Tourist Police** at 44 Karaiskaki St. (tel. 24 47 7, open every day 7am-9pm), or the **National Tourist Office** (open Mon.-Fri. 7:30am-7pm), in the converted Turkish mosque at the east end of the harbor, to pick up a map of the town. The latter office can also provide you with a bus schedule for Hania, a ferry schedule, a sheet of information on visiting the Samaria Gorge, and a list of festivals and ceremonies in the area. Both offices have a complete list of the cheap hotels and rooms to rent, car rental agencies, and all-night pharmacies. To get to the tourist office and the harbor from the **Central Bus Station** at the corner of Kidonias and Kelaidi Streets (tel. 23 05 2 or 23 30 6), walk right on Kidonias St. for two blocks to Zimvrakakidon St. and go left. Zimvrakakidon St. becomes Halidon St., which leads to the harbor. From the market, where the bus from the port of Souda arrives, walk on Gianari St. to Halidon and turn right.

Even armed with a map, it is no cinch to find your way around Hania, for street names change with alarming frequency—sometimes block by block. But once you locate the covered market on Tzanakaki St. and the harbor, you're on your way.

Post Office: 3 Tzanakaki St. Open Mon.-Fri. 7:30am-8pm.

OTE: 5 Tzanakaki St. (next door to the post office). Open every day 6am-midnight (closes at 11pm in the off-season).

Banks: The **Credit Bank,** at 2 Kanevaro St. on the east side of the harbor, is open Mon.-Sat. 8am-2pm during the summer. The **National Bank of Greece,** on

Kidonias St. next to the bus station or across from the market at Tzanakaki St., is open Mon.-Fri. 8am-2pm.

Boat Office: A.N.E.K., 28 Sofoklis Venizelou St. (tel. 23 63 6 or 25 65 6). For tickets to Piraeus.

Olympic Airways: 88 Tzanakaki St. (tel. 27 70 1). Buses for the airport leave from here. Open every day 6:30am-11pm.

Laundry: Oskar Laundry, at 1 Kanevaro St. on the east side of the harbor, charges 60dr per kilo to wash and dry.

English Bookstore: 98 Halidon St.

Telephone Code: 0821.

If you are thinking of renting a motor scooter or bicycle to tour the island, Hania is a good place for it—prices run as much as 100dr cheaper for a week's rental than in Iraklion. **Steve's** motorbike rental (tel. 29 09 4) on Sfaka St. near the harbor and across from the Pension Kidonia offers a Vespa 50cc at 550dr per day or 3400dr for the week, with helmet and insurance included, but shop around and try bargaining. Avoid the clip joints right on the harbor.

Accommodations

It is fairly easy to find cheap rooms in Hania, but not so easy to find cheap and pleasant ones. Most of the inexpensive hotels are located by the harbor—noisy, but scenic and convenient. The Tourist Police can supply you with additional names and locations of hotels and pensions in your price range.

IYHF Youth Hostel, 33 Drakonianou St. (tel. 53 56 5). On the southeastern outskirts of the town. Quiet but very inconvenient. Take the Agios Ioannis bus from Kotsabasi Square (opposite the market hall) and get off at the fifth stop. 180dr per person, 30dr extra for a hot shower. Cold showers are free. Midnight curfew; no card necessary.

Hotel Fidias, 6 Sarpaki St. (tel. 52 49 4). From Halidon St., go right at the cathedral on Athinagora St., which becomes Sarpaki. Very helpful management. Friendly atmosphere. Singles 400dr, doubles 550dr, triples 750dr.

Hotel Manos, 17 Kountouriotou St. (tel. 29 49 3 or 52 15 2). Enter on Zabeliou St. From Halidon St., go west on Zabeliou St. Just above the Dionisos Taverna on the waterfront. Airy, old building which has been gracefully restored and converted into a good, inexpensive hotel. Doubles 750dr, triples 1000dr.

Hotel Ariadne, (tel. 50 98 7). On Aphentoulief St. at the east end of the harbor, past the tourist office. Spanking new establishment with trim Scandinavian wood furnishings, carpeted floors, clean bathrooms, and polite management. Doubles 850dr, triples 972dr, showers 75dr extra.

Pensione Kasteli, 39 Kanevaro St. Walk on Kanevaro from the east side of the harbor. Small, but spacious and as clean as you'll find in Hania. Tastefully and authentically decorated. Singles 500dr, doubles 700dr, triples 900dr.

Hotel Averof, 11 Plateia 1866 (tel. 23 09 0). From the bus station, walk right on Kidonias to the second street of the square. In an elegant building, convenient to the bus station. Doubles 688dr, triples 828dr, showers 50dr extra.

Pensione Kydonia, 15 Isodion St. (tel. 57 17 9). From Halidon St., walk east on Athinagora St. for one short block to Isodion. One of the few places in Hania which regularly rents by the bed. 300dr in a double or a triple, 250dr in a quad.

Meltemi at 2 Angelou St. and **Theresa** at 8 Angelou St. (tel. 26 12 2), both near the Naval Museum at the west end of the harbor, have drab doubles with mediocre bathrooms for 700dr.

Camping: Camping Hania (tel. 51 09 0), 4km west of town, charges 110dr per person, 80dr per tent. **Camping Agia Marina** (tel. 48 55 5), 4km further along the road to Kastelli, charges 110dr per person and 70dr per tent.

Food and Entertainment

The harbor is the best place to eat in Hania, offering both the best food and the best view. Cheap dishes (*moussaka,* spaghetti) usually go for about 140dr, but shopping around is recommended to avoid overpriced establishments. **Dionisos,** at the corner of Kondilaki St., usually offers the widest variety at the standard prices. If you happen to be in Hania in the cooler months of the off-season, visit **Aposperida,** at 37-39 Kondilaki St. A three-story palace, this eatery closes down for the sweltering summer months (usually early June to mid-September).

For really cheap sustenance, try the souvlaki stands on Halidon St., or visit the excellent market between Gianari and Tsouderon Streets.

Hania's romantic harbor is a relaxing place to pass a lazy Cretan evening. Nearly all of the countless restaurants and cafés offer a good selection of Greek and not-so-Greek refreshments. If you're anxious for a more serious alcoholic experience, head for the **Taverna Annitsaki** at 27 Gianari St. The twenty enormous wine barrels lining the walls of this cavernous hall give you an indication of its purpose: the owner calls his taverna "the parliament," because it is for serious drinking. He jokes that music isn't allowed in this alcohol sanctuary, and insists that water is strictly forbidden. **Faka,** behind the Customs House on Plateia Katehaki (follow the harbor around to the east), is much less crowded than the harborside places, very pleasant, and popular among the locals. Hania's handful of loud, tasteless discos is situated at both ends of the harbor.

Sights

One corner of Hania that is responsible for seducing many a visitor into a longer stay is **Topanas,** the enchanting Venetian quarter of the city, with its handsome stone villas and narrow alleys. If you find yourself in need of indoor diversion, Hania's **Archeological Museum,** in a restored Venetian church at 25 Halidon St., has a small but growing collection of Neolithic and Minoan pottery, jewelry, and implements found during excavations in Western Crete. Open Mon.-Sat. 8am-2:45pm, Sun. 9am-2pm, closed Tues.; admission 50dr, 30dr for students.

The main harbor also has a **Naval Museum** (open Tues.-Fri. 9am-noon, Sat. and Sun. 9am-2pm and 4-7pm; admission 25dr) and a graceful Venetian light-house. To the west of the main harbor is the earlier Venetian harbor with its original stone breakwater and arsenal still in place. If you're a true scholar of Turkish and Venetian history, then head to the **Historical Archives Building** on Sfakianaki St. in the southeastern part of town, which contains an impressive collection of Turkish and Venetian manuscripts (open daily 9am-1pm, closed weekends).

For a taste of Cretan exuberance at its most endearing, try the large, bustling indoor produce **market,** laid out in the shape of a cross in the style of Italian covered markets. The market is located on Gianari St. at the base of Tzanakaki St. Following Tzanakaki St. south you will come to the small town zoo.

Above all, Hania is a city to stroll around in, and merits a slow walking tour through the lovely public gardens, along the long walkway west by the waterfront, through the old quarters of Evraiki and Kasteli around the harbor, and by the numerous craft shops (pottery, leather goods, furniture-making, and weaving) in both the old and new sections of town. Hania is one of the best cities in Crete for purchasing handmade items and souvenirs of Crete.

While Hania itself does not have any usable beaches, **Galatas,** a short bus ride to the west, has a decent beach; buses leave every half hour from Plateia 1866.

Near Hania

The entire region around Hania is rich in places to explore but, with the exception of the Samaria Gorge, few of these are visited. **Akrotiri** makes a good sidetrip from Hania. This large peninsula northeast of Hania forms the boundary of the magnificent Souda Bay and features three monasteries, as well as several good beaches. The well-preserved pink buildings of **Agia Triada** (not to be confused with the Minoan site of the same name) house a small but interesting collection of icons. **Gouvernetou,** also called **Agios Ioannis,** 4km to the north, is even more intriguing. The church, featuring a fascinating Venetian carving, contains several 500-year-old icons and a fresco on the building's copper dome. (The church was knocked down so many times that an unbreakable dome was finally installed, to avoid the trouble of repainting.) Because the monastery is much less popular with tour buses than its southern neighbor, the monks are much more hospitable, and will explain the history of the buildings and of Agios Ioannis in German, or if you're lucky, in English. A half-hour walk from Gouvernetou brings you to the ruins and cave of Katholiko, the first monastic settlement on Crete (circa 700 A.D.). The monks at Gouvernetou will show you the well-marked path. If you do decide to visit the monasteries, dress conservatively, and try to get an early start, since the two inhabited sites are closed from 2-5pm.

But the reason most Greeks venture out to Akrotiri is to visit the **Hill of the Prophet Elias.** In addition to its fine view of Hania and of the bay, the hill contains the grave of Eleftherios Venizelou (1864-1936), the great Cretan revolutionary and statesman who served as Premier of Greece for several administrations in the early part of this century. Venizelou is fondly remembered by all Greeks, but especially by Cretans who are fiercely proud of their native son. In a sense, Venizelou is the George Washington of Crete. In every town on Crete, you will find a street or a plaza named after him, as well as numerous memorials. The hill also has an older significance for Cretans, for here, in 1897, Cretan fighters raised the Greek flag in defiance of Turkish forces.

There are also two fine, sandy beaches on the peninsula, at **Choraphakia** and **Stavros.** The latter is the setting for the film "Zorba the Greek." Akrotiri is ideal for touring by motorscooter: distances are short, traffic is light, roads aren't bad, and you'll feel good about the investment once you see how rarely buses pass. To get to the monasteries, follow signs for the airport. From the airport, there'll be signs for Agia Triada (most maps don't show a road).

One short trip to make by car, hitching, bus (about three daily), or taxi (80dr one way) is to the little village of **Mournies,** 4km south of Hania. Famous as the birthplace of Venizelou, it offers a fine botanical tour of Greece. Mournies trees, from which the village gets its name, line the streets. In the summer, ripening grapes hang from the trellises on the patios, and the air is rich with the mingled scents of jasmine, rosemary, dahlias, roses, and eucalyptus. Walking south from town for about 1 km, you'll pass carefully cultivated orange and mandarin orange trees, fig trees, walnut trees, and of course the ubiquitous olives. Herds of goats graze on the mountainside to the west; to the south loom the Lefka Ori, or White Mountains, and if you come in winter or early spring you'll know why—the peaks are snow-covered, even on this southernmost island of Greece.

Boats to Hania usually dock at the port of Souda, 5km to the east. Once the site of one of the most impressive Venetian fortresses along the north coast, Souda is now a major NATO naval base, as evidenced by the numerous crew-cut American sailors strolling through Hania. When Hania celebrates "Naval Week" in early July, the port comes alive with festivities, but otherwise it is rather drab and does not merit special attention. If you are arriving or leaving by boat at an inconvenient hour, the **Parthenon** (tel. 89 24 5), on the main square by the port, has clean doubles for 800dr. The **Knossos** (tel. 89 28 2), also on the main square, offers doubles for 900dr. Buses run every fifteen minutes to and from Hania, departing for Souda from in front of the market.

Samaria Gorge

The most famous excursion from Hania, and perhaps the only real "must" in any trip to Crete, is the splendid hike down the Samaria Gorge—an 18km pass worn in the White Mountains by thousands of years of run-off from the mountains. The longest gorge in Europe, Samaria has managed to retain its beauty despite the vast number of tourists, both foreign and Greek, who come to the area every year (as many as six hundred to a thousand people trek through the gorge some days). One visit here and you'll know why it's considered one of the most beautiful parts of Crete. Wild flowers and low shrubs adorn the otherwise sheer-rock walls, and—although few people catch a glimpse of the nimble creature—the *agrimi,* or Cretan wild mountain goat, still thrives here, one of its few remaining natural habitats.

The twelve-mile hike begins at the Omalos Plain, in Xyloskalo, 42km south of Hania and reached by bus or car. Passing between cliff walls of up to one thousand feet, and at the narrowest point only three meters across, the path winds its way slowly downward along a dry (in summer) river bed, ending in the small town of **Agia Roumeli** on the southern coast. From there, a boat takes you to **Chora Sfakion,** whence buses take you back to Hania. The hike down-hill (Omalos Plain to Agia Roumeli) favored by most people takes anywhere from four to seven hours, depending on the pace you set. You should wear good walking shoes and bring some trail snacks. Because of its altitude, the top of the gorge can be cold and rainy, so you might also consider bringing appropriate clothing. Although 2km will not go by without a natural spring, a canteen is still useful, as it allows you to picnic away from these crowded watering holes. Finally, be careful—though less tiring than uphill climbing, downhill hiking is tricky, and twisted ankles are not at all uncommon.

The gorge is only open from May 1 to October 31 because during the winter and spring, the river goes back to work cutting its trail through the rock. Passage is officially allowed through the gorge between 6am and 3pm. From 3pm to sunset you can visit any part of the trail within 2km of either entrance. The Hania Forest Service forbids the following activities in the gorge: camping, staying overnight, making fires, smoking, hunting, cutting and uprooting plants, and, believe it or not, singing.

The 42km drive from Hania to Omalos and Xyloskalo offers some of the most spectacular scenery on Crete. Try to catch the early bus to see the incredible sunrise. The road climbs increasingly higher, passing by the enchanting village of Laki and through the Omalos mountains at an altitude of 1500 meters. In Omalos, two tavernas rent doubles. Call 93 26 9 for reservations. The first as the bus enters town charges 500dr, and the second charges 770dr, cold showers included. Both tavernas are often filled with tour groups. Five kilometers past Omalos is **Xyloskalo,** where the Samaria Gorge trail begins. Just above the trail head is the tiny **Xenia** guest house (tel. 93 23 7), where one of the two double rooms costs 1728dr, and the sole triple costs 1944dr, cold showers and Turkish toilets included. Last summer, the management allowed desperate travelers to sleep on the floor or the roof for 150dr, but this cannot be relied upon. The hotel has only a half dozen blankets and a few foam pads. Camping at the top of the gorge is a reasonable, feasible alternative, since the local goatherds seldom trouble with the occasional backpacker. Buses for Omalos and Xyloskalo leave Hania at 6am, 9:30am, and 4:30pm—check with the bus station for possible schedule changes. The ride takes 1½ hours; one-way fare is 120dr.

At the other end of the gorge, the small village of Agia Roumeli is connected by boat to Chora Sfakion. It is therefore possible to make the complete round trip from Hania in one day, leaving by either the 6am or the 9:30am bus. The 9:30am bus will allow you plenty of time if you don't dawdle excessively. The 6am bus, besides giving you more time, will insure cooler weather and less company. Alternatively, you can plan a leisurely hike and spend the night at either of the two quiet coastal villages of Agia Roumeli or Chora Sfakion. If you only want to catch the dramatic tail of the gorge, you can start from Agia Roumeli and hike a few kilometers, but it is not recommended that you walk the entire twelve miles in the reverse direction unless you are prepared to do some hefty uphill hiking along the last half of the trail. It is also possible to go on an organized excursion, which essentially consists of your paying for someone to hike along with you and a lot of other people.

The attractive little community of **Agia Roumeli** at the bottom of the Samaria Gorge serves as a kind of oasis for numerous hikers who, having completed the twelve-mile trek, collapse in this secluded coastal village every summer afternoon thirsty, hungry, and exhausted. The village's one hotel, the **Roumeli,** charges an outrageous 1060dr for doubles and 1300dr for triples, but you can easily find a room in one of the town's pensions for 400-600dr a double. Be prepared to bargain furiously, however. Many young people camp out around the wide river mouth, which is mostly dry in summer. Agia Roumeli is surrounded by good pebble beaches (a 7km-long beach stretches around to the east), a small strip of dark sand, and several large sea caves which more than make up for the colorless resort town, but you might consider moving on to some of the less-crowded resorts along the Southwest Coast. Boats leave every day in hiking season from Agia Roumeli for Loutro and Chora Sfakion, at 9am, 2pm, and 5pm. The fare for the hour-long journey is an outrageous 320dr. You can save 71dr by taking the 2pm boat to Loutro (160dr), spending several hours in this pleasant and relatively empty village, and then catching the boat to Chora Sfakion (89dr). All buses to Hania and Rethymnon from Chora Sfakion are scheduled to depart after the arrival of the ferry from Agia Roumeli. Don't delay, since the drivers are in the habit of leaving very soon after the boat docks (220dr, the trip takes just over two hours). There is also a boat from Agia Roumeli to Sougia (180dr) and Paleochora (360dr) at noon on Mondays, Thursdays, and Saturdays (after July 1, every day).

The bus to Hania from Chora Sfakion passes through the lovely village of **Vrises,** where there are rooms to let for about 600dr a double. You may be lucky enough to catch a glimpse (or a whiff) of the charcoal burning which is frequent in this area. Huge olive trunks are burned and broken into bits of charcoal before they are bagged and sold as heating fuel.

Southwest Coast

A recent investigation conducted by a German company revealed that the most unpolluted waters in the Mediterranean are those off the southern coast of Crete. The stretch between Frangokastello and Elafonisi remains virtually untouched by the commercialism that pervades Crete's northern coast. The few small communities scattered along its length are still unspoiled and strikingly beautiful.

Chora Sfakion and Frangokastello

The crowded but pleasant resort town of **Chora Sfakion** (or Sfakia) has a small beach backed by an unattractive concrete wall. The town is connected by bus to Hania and by boat to the entire southwest coast, and thus serves as a good starting point from which to explore the region. The **post office** and **OTE** office stand on the street behind the waterfront. On the same street is the coast's only **supermarket**—this is the place to stock up on food if you're planning an extensive tour of more remote beaches. The **Hotel Stavris** on the port can change money. Although your time is best spent elsewhere on the coast, inexpensive accommodations are common here. **Rooms Sfakia** on the waterfront has doubles for 400-600dr. **Livicon,** nearby, charges 500dr for a double and 600dr for a triple. **Pension Sofia,** next to the supermarket, has dormitory-style accommodations for 200dr per person. For reservations, call 91 29 9 (the village switchboard). The **telephone code** for Chora Sfakion is 0825.

Frangokastello, 12km east of Chora Sfakion, features an excellent sandy beach and an impressive fortress at the water's edge. Though facilities are somewhat limited and primitive, one of the two tavernas rents doubles for only 500dr. Discreet camping along the broad, clean stretch of sand is accepted, as is nude bathing. One bus a day from Hania (2pm) and Chora Sfakion (4pm) serves Frangokastello.

Loutro, Finix, and Agia Roumeli

Loutro, halfway between Chora Sfakion and Agia Roumeli, is accessible by regularly-scheduled boats from either town. Few tourists make it to this charming old fishing village, with its handful of whitewashed houses, its ruined castle, and its lone palm trees. There are five pensions in Loutro, located side by side at the western end of the cove. All quote prices of 600-700dr a double, 700-800dr a triple, except for the middle one, which has doubles for 450dr. The easternmost pension can change money for you. There is one small, inadequate supermarket in the town, and a kiosk that is open only in summer.

The coastline between Chora Sfakion and Agia Roumeli boasts some of the finest beaches on Crete. A path runs between Chora Sfakion and Loutro (2½ hours), and on to Agia Roumeli (5-6 hours more). Both walks are highly recommended. The trails are relatively easy, but seldom-traveled, so you can contemplate the beautiful turquoise-and-emerald waters of the Libyan Sea in undisturbed isolation.

Halfway between Chora Sfakion and Loutro is **Sweetwater Beach,** so named because several natural springs just below the surface of the pebble beach provide fresh drinking-water for the campers who frequent this all-nude beach. (Sweetwater is the first cove if you're coming from Chora Sfakion, the third from Loutro).

Just over the hill from Loutro (head towards the castle and then down the other side) is the gloriously remote settlement of **Finix.** Sifis Antithakis, his wife, mother-in-law, and five children are the only permanent residents of this former archeological site. His taverna serves the freshest fish and dairy products on the coast at remarkably low prices, and beds in his spotless, spanking new pension only cost 250dr per person. Or you can sleep on the roof for free.

A 30-45 minute walk west of Finix leads past several excellent caves to **Marble Beach,** a magnificent black-pebble lagoon framed by elegant formations of stunning white marble. Here again, "clothing" is a four-letter word. The rest of the footpath from Marble Beach to Agia Roumeli is not especially well-marked, but you're sure to be alone for four hours, and the ever-present ocean makes navigational errors almost impossible.

(See the Samaria Gorge section for information on **Agia Roumeli.**)

Boats to Loutro and Agia Roumeli leave Chora Sfakion in the morning (10:30 and 11:30am), and retrace the route from Agia Roumeli at 9am, 2pm, and 4pm. They arrive in Loutro 30-45 minutes after departure, but don't dawdle—the captains won't hesitate to leave you behind. Buses (200dr) from Hania to Chora Sfakion depart at 9am, 11am, and 2:30pm, and return as soon as the boats from Agia Roumeli arrive.

If you plan to walk from Agia Roumeli to Marble Beach, Finix, and Loutro, ask Yanni at the Cafe Kri-Kri in Agia Roumeli for directions (make sure you ask about the path which follows the coastline). From Chora Sfakion, take the path which begins about twenty minutes from town where the paved road to Anopolis doubles back. To go east from Loutro, go left after building #23 and climb up to the top of the ridge (about 20m), where the well-marked path begins. To go west, climb over the hill (there are many paths; the "official" one begins at the western end of town) and ask for directions at Finix. Avoid walking in the sweltering midday heat, and be sure to bring a water bottle. Boats and buses along the southern coast don't begin running until mid-May, so you will need to do a little hiking if you visit this region in the off-season.

Paleochora and Sougia

Just as the British retreated behind the impassable walls of southwestern Crete to hide from the Germans in World War II, so has the embattled rear guard of 1960's youth culture chosen to make its last stand in the corner of this island. Base camp is the isolated village of **Paleochora,** 77km from Hania. The hamlet has all the elements for a get-away-from-it-all vacation—a wide, sandy beach with a pine grove that offers excellent impromptu tent sites and one main street (named Venizelou, of course) with a few delightful tavernas and other necessities.

The town's one inexpensive hotel, the **Livikon,** is at 1 Venizelou St. (tel. 41 25 0) and offers light, airy doubles for 600dr, triples for 800dr, and single beds for 500dr. Paleochora also has a few inexpensive pensions. On the main beach, they are usually more primitive but less expensive (400-700dr for a double), while pensions on the main road to Hania offer more sumptuous accommodations at 900-1000dr a double. Try the nameless pension next to the post office; its sparkling rooms, with bathrooms, are approximately 800dr for a double. Most young visitors, however, camp either on the main beach, which is popular but technically illegal and slightly unsafe, or at the official campsite 1 km east of town on a dirt road starting from the wharf side of town (100dr per person, no charge for a tent). **Zorbas, Glavos,** and the **Rock and Roll Café,** all on the beach, offer basic Greek dishes at standard prices. Several small supermarkets and a bank are in the center of town on the road from Hania. Buses for Hania arrive and depart from the same square. The post office (open Mon.-Fri. 7:30am-2:30pm) is on the beach near the Studio Music Club.

An even more isolated outpost than Paleochora is **Sougia,** 10km to the east, with a pleasant, pebbly beach. Rooms are available for as little as 400dr for a double, and the cafes are attractive and inexpensive. The boat that sails from Paleochora daily (in July and August only) at 2pm to Agia Roumeli, Loutro, and Chora Sfakion usually stops at Sougia. Buses to Sougia leave Hania Mon.-Sat. at 9am and 2pm and on Sunday at 8am. There is a footpath from Paleochora to Sougia and Agia Roumeli, but it's an arduous trek and should only be attempted by those proficient at orienteering.

A very difficult journey, but one that will prove extremely satisfying, is to **Elafonisi,** a small island at the southwest corner of Crete. No boats make the passage, but at low tide the ocean is so shallow that you can wade out to the island. Food is available at Kefali and Vathis, and the residents of **Moni Chrisoskalitissis** can provide water. Stock up on provisions ahead of time, since there is no food or water on this beautiful deserted island. No buses run past the island from either Paleochora or Sfinari, so you must hitchhike from either town to Kefali, and walk or hitch from there.

Kastelli and West Coast

It is quite possible that the whitewashed houses of Kastelli (or Kisamos) will be your first glimpse of Crete, since that is where the bi-weekly ferry from the Peloponnese and Piraeus docks (ferries leave for Gythion on Tuesdays and Fridays at 8am). The advantage of starting or ending your tour of Crete in Kastelli is that it will allow you to see a lot of the island without having to backtrack.

For practical purposes, **Tzanakaki Square** is the center of Kastelli. The bus station and the boat office are both located here, and buses from the wharf (1½km west of town) stop here. East of the square along the town's main street is its one cheap hotel. The **Morfefs** (tel. 22 47 5) has singles for 350dr and doubles for 550dr, but you'll do better, in terms of both cleanliness and price, at one of the many pensions along the beach. **Papadakis Restaurant,** by the sea in Teloniou Sq., serves the best squid in town. The **Fish Restaurant,** in a lovely little harbor just beyond the town line to the west, is cheaper, and a favorite among the locals. The **telephone code** for Kastelli is 0822.

A highly recommended walk from Kastelli takes you to **Polirinia,** a tiny village with a mediocre archeological site (not worth visiting) and a splendid café. You can rest after the 7km, 1½ hour walk at the **Restaurant Polirinia.** The veranda of the restaurant, canopied by grape vines, offers a commanding view of the gloriously unspoiled countryside, and the village itself has remained untouched by tourists. To get to Polirinia, take the road that begins across from the Mamadakis gas station on the road to Hania.

The area west of Kastelli, around **Kaliviani,** is well worth exploring. Interesting footpaths and enchanting unmapped villages await the curious in this region.

The area around Kastelli is mostly farmland, marked by small villages and filled with fruit stands selling local produce. A few stray hotels have sprung up along the coastal road to Hania, but not enough to alter the tenor of the region. The residents of the area have built their homes along the sandy shoreline, and chickens and tethered donkeys meander by the water's edge. Here, more than any other place in Crete, you can simply stop at your fancy and go for a swim—the patches of beach are usually visible from the road. Don't be afraid to leave the bus because they run hourly between Hania and Kastelli, and there is no danger of being stranded. If possible, visit the **German War Cemetery** just inland from Malleme. The site, with 4465 German graves in a field of flowers, is as much a tribute to the Cretan spirit of forgiveness as it is a monument to the waste of war. It is kept blooming exquisitely by its caretaker,

George Psychoundakis, a member of the Cretan resistance forces in the second World War, who accepted the job because he was a "firm believer in the movement for reconciliation among nations."

Seventeen kilometers west of Kastelli is the beautiful and deserted beach at **Falassarna.** This vast expanse of sand is hardly unspoiled, however. Falassarna has fallen victim to industrialization, apparently. Local fishermen regularly clean their boat engines in the waters off the west coast, and much of this black mess has reappeared in solid, thick clumps on the sand. There are two new tavernas at Falassarna, both of which will rent you a room, if one is available, for 200-400dr.

To get to Falassarna, catch the bus to Platanos (three times daily). From there, walk or hitch another 5km along a dirt road to the long, flat beach. Hitching is fairly good—there aren't many cars, but they'll usually stop if they're not already full. You may find yourself hitching back from Platanos to Kastelli—the buses scheduled for the morning only run if one of Platanos' handful of residents needs to get to Kastelli. The last bus back to Platanos leaves at 5:30pm, but only when school is in session. Some people solve the problem of insufficient transportation by pitching a tent and staying put. Freelance camping on the beach is tolerated here.

Sfinari, a secluded fishing and farming village 15km south of Falassarna, has suffered a similar fate. The rocky beach here is not as dirty as its northern neighbor, but deposits of oil are still frustratingly present. The two seaside restaurants in this windy coastal town, **Diolinis** and **Antigonis,** have made a wonderful symbiotic arrangement with foreign visitors; you can camp for free behind their tavernas, and use their toilets and showers, as long as you eat there. Otherwise, they charge 200dr per person. Since there is no hint of a market in Sfinari, this is a good deal after all. If it's a bed you're after, try **Nikos and Athina** (on the short dirt road which begins across from building #20) or the **Psaro,** above the restaurant of the same name. Both are within fifteen minutes of the beach and charge only 400dr for a double.

If you plan to spend much time at Falassarna and Sfinari, change your money before you come, since there are no facilities outside Kastelli. Buses for Sfinari leave on Mon., Wed., and Fri. at 1pm from Hania (about one hour later from Kastelli).

Eastern Crete

From Iraklion to Agios Nikolaos

Most of the coast from Iraklion to Agios Nikolaos has fallen victim to the tourist boom in Crete. High-priced, unattractive hotels and holiday villas litter the flat, uninteresting shoreline. One of the largest of the resorts along this overdeveloped strip is **Chersonissos,** a once-peaceful fishing village now crammed with dozens of overpriced luxury hotels. The only inexpensive alternatives are the **Pension Selena** at 13 Maragaki St. (tel. 22 41 2) and the **Hotel Samantha** at 9 Vitzenzou Kornarou St. (tel. 22 49 8). Both charge 900dr for clean doubles. There are two good campsites along the coast. **Camping Kreta** (tel. 41 40 0), 14km east of Iraklion (and then another 2½km on a seaside dirt track), is brand new, clean, and charges 120dr per person and 110dr per tent. **Caravan Camping** (tel. 22 02 5) is 1½km east of Chersonissos just off the main road, and charges 100dr per tent and 100dr per person. They also have the cheapest rooms near Chersonissos—a bungalow for two is 800dr. Buses to Malia and Agios Nikolaos pass by the Camping Kreta turn-off, and stop in Chersonissos and at the nearby campsite.

Malia

Malia, 34km east of Iraklion, is a prime example of the overcommercialization that plagues the northern coast of Crete. This resort town boasts one of Crete's finest archeological sites, streets lined with pensions, restaurants, hotels, shops selling local crafts, a nearby golden sand beach, and a handful of endearing windmills. Unfortunately most of the hotels are full, the shops sell mostly junk, the beach is packed with multitudes of deep-fried sunworshippers, and the beautiful windmills are overshadowed by the advertisements for rooms and tourist shops. Although Malia's natural charm has not entirely disappeared, it has been squelched by the devastating effects of the tourist trade.

The palace at Malia, one of the three great cities of Minoan Crete, lacked the elaborate architecture and magnificent interior decoration of Knossos and Phaestos, but was, nonetheless, an imposing structure. First built around 1900 B.C., the palace was destroyed along with the other two around 1650 B.C. Rebuilt on an even more impressive scale, it was destroyed again around 1450 B.C. The city presumably prospered as a major port, and the bricks used in the construction of its buildings were made from an unusual mixture of clay and seaweed. Most of what is of primary interest to someone who has only time or patience for a quick visit to the site is to be found around the large central courtyard, notably the **Hall of Columns** on the north side, named after the six columns supporting the roof, and the famous **Loggia** on the west side, a raised chamber which was used for ceremonial purposes.

To the west of the Loggia lie the main living quarters and the archives. To the northwest of the Loggia and main site is the **Hypostyle Crypt,** believed to have been a social center for the intelligentsia of Malia. As in Phaestos, only minor reconstruction has been attempted; the ruins remain, for the most part, exactly as they were found. Since most of what is left of the palace presently stands at about knee-level, a preliminary visit to Knossos can greatly aid the visitor's appreciation of Malia's original splendor. (To get to the ruins proceed by bus, car, or foot 3km east of the village and then left towards the sea.)

The main beach at Malia (follow the road which begins across from the Avis office) is sandy but small and extremely crowded. For more private sunbathing and swimming, walk east until you find a suitable spot.

Fortunately, you don't have to ransom your wallet to stay in Malia. The town has a small 35-bed **IYHF Youth Hostel** (tel. 31 33 8) with a large, pleasant garden (180dr per night, hot showers 30dr extra, cold showers free; no curfew). To get to the hostel from the bus stop, head east along the main road to Agios Nikolaos, take the second right, follow the small signs around to the left, and the building will come into view after 500m. The town's cheapest hotels and pensions are to be found along the backstreets on the inland side of the main road. Both the **Pension Menios** (tel. 31 36 1) and the **Hotel Apostolos** (tel. 31 48 4) charge 600dr for a double. To get to the Menios, take the second left off the road to the youth hostel, and then the second right—the pension is on the first corner on the right. To reach the Apostolos, go right on Eisodion St., which begins at the Avis office. On the main road, the **Hotel Rousakis** (tel. 31 25 1) charges only 550dr for a double if you have your own sheets or sleeping bag, and 750dr for a triple.

Malia Camping (tel. 31 46 1) lies 800m down a side road off the main road to Agios Nikolaos. It comes complete with a bar/disco, restaurant, and grocery store. It is so urbanized that the campsites are in blocks with curb-stones, and the "campers" sweep the dirt away from their tents. It charges 100dr per person, 90dr per tent, 60dr per car, and 100dr for a sleeping bag, plus 10% extra during July and August and a 6% tax. Reception is open from 7:30am-10:30pm. **Camping Sissi** (tel. 32 08 6) is 5½km east of town (4km on the main road and then 1½km on a dirt road). Fees are 100dr per person and 100dr per tent. There is no beach, but a swimming pool has been installed.

Food in Malia is distinctly uninspiring; the restaurants offer strikingly similar fare—only the prices vary. The **Sirtaki Restaurant,** on the road to the beach, is one of the cheapest, and features a spicy pork dish. There are over a dozen supermarkets throughout the town (don't be fooled by the fact that most of them stock more liquor than foodstuffs).

The **telephone code** for Malia is 0897.

Buses leave Iraklion for Malia every half hour from 6:30am to 9pm (100dr). Malia can also be reached from points on the Lassithi Plain. A bus leaves Psychro for Malia every day at 1:30pm. Halfway between Malia and Agios Nikolaos is the inland town of **Neapolis,** whose one hotel, the **Neapolis** (tel. 33 26 8), has doubles for 850dr and triples for 1150dr.

Lassithi Plain

You can avoid much of the messy coastline and at the same time see some of the most interesting and breathtaking parts of Crete by taking an inland route to Agios Nikolaos through the Lassithi Plain. A fertile plateau irrigated by hundreds of sail-rigged windmills, the plain also features the Dikteon Cave at Psychro, the legendary birthplace of Zeus. The plain is alive with the rural Cretan culture so often lacking in the more touristed parts of the island. Here you'll find the whitewashed buildings, overburdened donkeys, and mustachioed Greek men sipping coffee that you expect to find on Crete. Even if you have no desire to continue on to Agios Nikolaos and eastern Crete, the trip to Lassithi and Psychro is worthwhile just for the view of the plateau and the dramatic mountain scenery on the way, and can easily be made as a daytrip from Iraklion.

By car or scooter, the most direct route is to take the coastal road from Iraklion until five miles past Gournes, and then turn right on the road to Kasteli (not the one on the West coast). This is also the route the bus follows. After about three miles, the road forks right to Kasteli; you stay left, heading towards **Potamies.** Just above the town is the Byzantine church **Panagia Gouverniotissa,** noted for its fourteenth-century frescoes. Ask Vassilos Vavachis, the owner of Potamies's only cafe, for the key. The road soon starts to climb. If you have the time and the means, take a 1 km detour at the sign for **Krassi** to see the giant plane tree in the village center. Bypassing Krassi, the main road winds around mountain ridges, with beautiful views on all sides. In the tiny town of **Kera,** you will see the turn-off for the monastery which contains a twelfth-century icon of the Virgin. The road continues to climb to the Seli Ambelou pass, with its abandoned stone windmills, and then finally descends into the Plain of Lassithi.

The residents of the region, long ago anticipating our current energy problems, have harnessed the plain's persistent winds with thousands of wind-powered water pumps. When the sails are unfurled—usually mid-morning—the whole plain is filled with their spinning, a magnificent if anomalous vision after twenty kilometers of mountain vistas. Even the houses have small windmills sitting on the back fence to supply water for household needs.

Because of its prime location, which enables it to collect the run-off soil and waters from the surrounding mountains, the plain is one of the most fertile areas in Greece. In harvesting season (July and August) wheat is everywhere—leaning on church porches, stacked in the fields, and piled so high on donkeys that all you can see of them are the ears and tail.

The first and only "major" town you pass through is **Tzermiado,** capital of the subprovince of Lassithi, with a few gift shops and two hotel-restaurants catering to day tourists. But at night, Tzermiado returns to its own peaceful ways, with the entire male population divided among its ten or so cafes, drinking, arguing, playing backgammon, and watching subtitled spaghetti westerns on television. Not many tourists stop over in Tzermiado; if you do, you will be welcomed with warmth and curiosity. At the **Kronias Restaurant** in town you get a good meal and a glimpse of rural Cretan life. The town also has two hotels. The **Kourites** (tel. 22 19 4), surprisingly plush for this out-of-the-way place, has singles for 663dr, doubles for 870dr, and triples for 1080dr, all with private bath. More affordable is the **Hotel Kri-Kri** (tel. 22 17 0), where singles run 250dr, doubles 450dr, and triples 550dr; showers 50dr extra.

Though only a scratch in the hill compared to the Dikteon Cave, the **Kronion Cave,** the mythical home of Cronus and Rhea, parents of Zeus, merits a quick side trip. There'll be clear signs in Tzermiado directing you to the famous grotto 2km outside of town. (The last kilometer is only traversible on foot.) Be sure to bring a flashlight.

Leaving Tzermiado, a right fork at the church 2km southeast of town will take you to **Agios Konstantinos,** a quiet rural village where **Maria Vlassy** (tel. 37 22 9) rents doubles for 500dr. **Agios Georgios,** 2km further down the same road, boasts a tiny **folklore museum.** The children who are the caretakers proudly claim it is "an alive monument to the rural life," and will gladly point out the bed on which the entire family slept, the loom, the stable, and the tool shed. Its comic models and stuffed fowl provide more amusement than edification. Open 10am-4pm in summer, closed winters; admission 25dr. Agios Georgios is perhaps the best place to stay in the Lassithi Plain, since food is cheap and the town's two hotels, the **Dias** (tel. 31 20 7) and the **Rea** (tel. 31 20 9) both offer clean doubles for 475dr (showers 50dr extra).

The next village, **Psychro,** is the only town in the Lassithi Plain where the full impact of tourism can be felt. The cheapest of the town's three hotels is the **Dikteon Andron,** with singles for 200dr, doubles for 400dr, and triples for 600dr; showers 50dr extra. From the small sign on the main road, walk up one block and go right; the Dikteon Andron is the building just before #93. The **Hotel Helen** (tel. 31 41 6) is less primitive than its nearby competitor. Singles are 300dr, doubles 450dr, triples 550dr; showers free. To reach it, go right at the Platanos Restaurant.

One kilometer past Psychro is the **Dikteon Cave,** designated at least by the tourist officials as the mythological birthplace of Zeus. Legend suggests that Zeus spent his infancy in a secluded grotto on Crete. The story goes that Cronus, Zeus's father, after hearing a prophecy that a child of his would dethrone him, took to eating his newborn children as a precautionary measure. When Cronus's wife Rhea gave birth to Zeus she gave Cronus a stone to eat instead, wooing him with harp music and song to divert his attention, and kept the baby hidden in the cave near Psychro. Almost everything else you will hear has been amended to the original myth by local tour guides. The cave, a dramatic cleft in the side of the Dikteon mountain with several chambers and impressive stalactite formations, is worth a trip, whether or not you subscribe to its mythological associations. Tour groups start arriving around 10:30am; if you stay in one of the nearby villages the night before and arrive at the cave by 9:30am, you should have a chance to explore it in relative solitude. Admission to the cave is 50dr, 30dr with student ID, but if you come at an odd time, the attendant may not be around to take your money. If at all possible, bring a flashlight. The cave is quite dark, and the candles sold in the restaurants at the base of the path are fast-burning and provide little light. Donkeys take visitors to the entrance of the cave (240dr round trip), but it's better to walk; the view of the Lassithi Plain below is so spectacular that you'll want to enjoy it at your own pace. Avoid any guided tours of the cave—the guides seldom speak more than a few words of English, and have been known to demand sums even more exorbitant than the rates posted at the bottom of the path (240dr plus 25dr per person).

Buses leave from both Iraklion and Agios Nikolaos for Psychro and Lassithi twice daily. One bus passes between Malia and Lassithi daily. If you decide to visit the region by scooter, consider bringing a windbreaker; even in summer, the mountain wind is quite cool.

Agios Nikolaos

The very picture postcard of a port town, Agios Nikolaos is now largely the property of tourists. You won't find many signs of indigenous culture along its sparkling tree-lined streets, at least not during the high season. But with convenient town beaches, an energetic nightlife, and two waterfronts on which to sit and people-watch, Agios Nikolaos is a popular spot for one-stop vacations. American, English, and Scandinavian tourists on their whirlwind tours of Greece jam the outdoor tables that line the "lake" and the harbor, reloading their cameras, guzzling soft drinks, and gazing out over the turquoise waters of Mirabello Bay. The cute if somewhat glossy waterfront merits a look; a longer stay is not recommended.

Practical Information

Agio Nikolaos is one of the easier towns on Crete to find your way around in—the center of town is actually a small peninsula, with beaches on three sides and most services, hotels, restaurants, and discos located in the middle. The bus terminal is at Atlandithos Square, on the opposite side of town from the harbor. If you've just gotten off the bus, follow Venizelou St. north to get to the port and the center of town.

Tourist Police: at the foot of the stairs on the southern corner of the bottomless lake (tel. 22 32 1). They have maps of the town, a bus schedule, and a list (with prices) of all the hotels and pensions. In summer, open 7am-2pm and 5:30-8pm (sometimes later).

Post Office: 28th of October St, #9. Open Mon.-Fri. 7:30am-4pm.

OTE: on 25 Martiou St., three blocks east of the lake. Open 6am-midnight.

Boat Office: Massaros Travel, at 29 Roussou Koundourou St. (tel. 22 26 7 or 23 07 7), sells tickets for departures from Agios Nikolaos and most of Crete.

Hospital: (tel. 22 36 9).

English Bookstore: 5 Roussou Koundourou St. An excellent collection of books on Crete. There is another good bookstore across the street at #8.

Motorcycle Rentals: Cheaper than in Iraklion. There are loads of agencies, so shop around and try bargaining.

Car Rentals: Try **Ilias Rent-a-Car** at 1 Sfakianaki St. (tel. 22 64 7), across from the Akratos Hotel.

Telephone Code: 0841.

Buses make the trip along the north coast from Agio Nikolaos to Malia and Iraklion every hour on the half-hour. Buses leave from Iraklion on the reverse trip at roughly the same time interval. Nine buses a day connect Ierapetra and seven a day connect Sitia to Agios Nikolaos. Agios Nikolaos is also a major port with several ferries a week arriving from Piraeus and the Cyclades. The ferry to Rhodes and the Dodecanese leaves at 10am on Sun. and 3:30am on Wed. in the summer.

Accommodations

As a result of Agios Nikolaos' excessive popularity, many of the better hotels are booked months in advance by European tour groups, and the few cheap places in town have a slow turnover rate. Fortunately, there is a Youth Hostel, but even it is often full. The town has almost as many pensions as it does hotels, but these are often booked 6-12 months ahead of time as well. Those we list are quite small, but not likely to be the exclusive territory of charter operators. If you plan to stay in town, arrive early in the day or make reservations. You can also head for the town of Kritsa (only 9km away) for the night (see below).

IYHF Youth Hostel, 3 Stratigou Koraka St. (tel. 22 82 3). From the bus station, walk on Venizelou to the waterfront, go left, and take the second right (there are signs). Crowded and dirty, but quite friendly. 180dr per bed in a dormitory room or on the sociable roof. More rooms should be built by 1984. No curfew.

The Aigeion, 28th of October St. (tel. 22 77 3). Large and reasonably clean rooms. Conveniently located. Doubles 625dr, triples 880dr; showers 50dr extra.

The Green House, 15 Moudatsou St. (tel. 22 02 5). From the station, go left on Kapetan Tavla St., which becomes Moudatsou. This multilingual couple has packed beds into the rooms of their cavernous home. Pleasant garden. 300dr per person or 400-500dr for a double.

Pension Achilles, 8 Moudatsou St., up from the Green House. Quite clean and inexpensive at 500dr a double. They sometimes let overflow sack out on the roof for 200dr per person.

Pension Argiro, 1 Solonos St. (tel. 28 70 7). Take the first right after the Green House and then go left after one block. Friendly management, and clean, too. Sizeable and likely to have space. Doubles 700dr.

Pension Marilena, 14 Stavrou St. (tel. 22 68 1 or 28 92 5), six blocks north of the Youth Hostel. Clean but distant. Doubles 700dr.

Pension Kri-Kri, on the ocean road to Elounda, above K Tours (tel. 23 72 0). Quite small, but has a kitchen available for guests' use.

Food and Entertainment

Food is quite expensive in Agios Nikolaos. Most restaurants can be found around the town's attractive harbor or immediately west along the waterfront. The **Haris** is one of the cheapest on the harbor, with fresh fish usually available. The numerous "Tost" places around town (the Greek equivalent of a hamburger joint) cook decent omelettes for low prices, and most sell souvlaki-pita sandwiches. Far cheaper and less touristed cafes can be found at **Venizelou Square,** although they don't offer the same harborside views.

The cafe-bars along the "bottomless lake" are the best places for watching the sunset and the early evening fashion show. Bars and discos can be found all over the town—most are located on Akti Koundourou and 25 Martiou Sts. They're quite expensive—100dr for a beer, 250dr for a mixed drink. Some of these watering holes jack up their prices after 11pm.

Sights

The town's three beaches are all within easy walking distance of the main harbor, and of course there is always the possibility of swimming off the rocks. At the southeast end of town by the bus station there's a long, narrow stone beach. A smaller and more crowded beach by the Sgouros Hotel at the eastern tip of town has several reasonably-priced tavernas. At the northwest corner of town at the Dolphin Restaurant there is a tiny sand beach—most sun-worshippers are forced to lie on the surrounding concrete. For a beach somewhat better than the town offerings, catch one of the frequent buses headed to Ierapetra or Sitia and get off at **Almiros Beach,** 2km east of town. The beach at **Kalo Horio,** 10km further along the same road, is less crowded, but also less clean (get off at the Kavos Taverna).

The **Archeological Museum** has a modest collection of Minoan artifacts from the Lassithi area. It's located just outside the center of town, a few blocks down the road to Iraklion (which begins at the lake). Open Mon.-Sat. 8:30am-2:30pm, Sun. 9am-2pm, closed Tues.; admission 50dr, 30dr with student ID.

Near Agios Nikolaos

A popular daytrip from Agios Nikolaos is to the fishing village of **Elounda,** 11km to the north. The attractive port town now swells with hotels, restaurants, and holiday villas, and serves as a point of departure for the islet of **Spinalonga** and its sixteenth-century fortress. The walls of the fortress were so impregnable that the Venetians were able to maintain control over the complex for half a century after the Turkish conquest of Crete in 1669. Later, the island became a leper colony, and the fear and bad associations of this era have prevented the island from being resettled. Small fishing boats leave roughly every half hour from Elounda (300dr round trip). Tickets can be purchased at **Alma Tours** (tel. 22 80 0) in Elounda's main square, or on the boats if they're not full. Taverna owners in **Plaka,** a few kilometers beyond Elounda, will usually ferry the curious across for less. Only Agios Nikolaos-based operators give guided tours of the island, however. The six-hour, 600dr excursion also includes a stopover at **Makriki Island,** a sanctuary for the *agrimi,* or wild Cretan mountain goat, and a swimming break at **Kalikitha Island.** To avoid paying a 50-100dr agent's commission, buy your tickets in Agios Nikolaos at **K Tours** (tel. 28 98 4 or 22 71 8), on the waterfront next to the Hermes Hotel.

Nineteen kilometers east of Agios Nikolaos are the remarkably well-preserved ruins of the ancient Minoan town of **Gournia,** just 50m from the highway. Just 3km farther is the less overrun seaside retreat of **Pahia Ammos.** Unfortunately, the beach has more garbage than sand. You can find several pensions offering doubles starting at 500dr.

Kritsa

Although only a 9km strip of road separates Kritsa from the touristy port of Agios Nikolaos, the towns seem worlds apart. Perched on a hillside high above Agios Nikolaos, the village of Kritsa has maintained a peaceful, endearing, and traditional character. Every balcony and rooftop is trimmed with trellised grapevines, heavily laden with ripening fruit. In the shade of these fruitful bowers, the women of the village sit and nimbly weave delicate garments. The main streets are lined with crafts shops selling embroidered shirts and handwoven blankets, sweaters, and sacks.

Unfortunately, these traditions could not continue to thrive without the sponsorship of the tourist industry. Come midday, tour companies deposit herds of cackling old ladies in Kritsa, who fly into action like bargain hunters at a discount store. Many of the crafts are embarrassingly cheap, considering the hours of work required to create them. Be cautious, however. The quality of the goods is uneven, since the women don't actually make all the items themselves. If you come to Kritsa during the off-season you'll avoid the bargain basement scene, for the town's artisans will be hard at work creating the next summer's merchandise.

But it is not the craft shops alone that put Kritsa on the itinerary of tour buses. One kilometer before the town is Crete's greatest Byzantine treasure: the **Panagia Kera.** The interior of the church is adorned with biblical scenes from the darkly-colored archaic wall paintings in the central nave (dating from the twelfth century) to the fine Byzantine frescoes (dating from the thirteenth century) in the two adjoining wings. The church is open Mon.-Sat. 9am-3:15pm, Sun. 10am-2pm; admission 30dr, 20dr for students. The church of **Agios Georgios,** in the town itself (look for the small signs pointing the way), also contains several attractive Byzantine frescoes; it's worth a quick visit while you're there.

At night, Kritsa returns to a more serene, tranquil atmosphere, mostly because tourists seldom stay overnight. As a result, the village provides an inexpensive solution to the problem of finding affordable accommodations in Agios Nikolaos. The best and cleanest place to stay in Kritsa is the **Pension Kritsotopoula** (tel. 51 44 9), the first on the road from Agios Nikolaos (doubles 650dr, including showers). For more spartan conditions, inquire at one of the two tourist shops advertising rooms on Plateia Thedoraki, just up from the bus station. **Mrs. Despina** (tel. 51 29 8) runs the first on the left, and offers doubles for 600dr with shower. **Maria Zachariadi** (tel. 51 71 7) has a pension straight ahead as you come from the bus stop; she charges 700dr, and her facilities are cleaner than those of her nearby rival. Beds are cheapest at the home of **Eleftherios Koutantos,** at house #165 on 28th of October St. (tel. 51 57 6). Rustic doubles go for 500dr. To find it, go left from the bus station towards the small church, turn left and walk on Papadothou St. until 28th of October St. appears on your right (follow the road around when it bends).

The village's handful of restaurants and cafes are very reasonably priced: souvlaki and potatoes go for 85dr. Buses leave every hour on the hour (with a few exceptions) for Kritsa from the bus station in Agios Nikolaos 6:15am-7:30pm (30dr one way). During the summer, afternoon buses from Kritsa fill up surprisingly quickly and you may find yourself waiting for the next bus if you don't arrive early.

Ierapetra

Crete's southern coast offers beautiful, uncrowded beaches, a slower pace of life than the tourist-infested north, spectacular scenery—and Ierapetra. The whole area would be far better off without this eyesore. Urban and oppressive, Ierapetra is one of the least attractive places to spend your holiday; it has little to offer except the dark sand beach that stretches for several kilometers to the east of town.

Most of the town's services are located on the streets running parallel to the waterfront. At Kothri Square, one block up, you'll find the **Post Office** (open Mon.-Fri. 7:30am-4pm), and at 25 Koraka St., three blocks up from the water, the **OTE** office (open Mon.-Sat. 7:30am-midnight). If you're thinking of renting motor transportation long-term, don't do it here. For daytrips, try **Rena Motor-bike Rental** at 18 Stratigou St. (tel. 28 41 8), near Neapoli Square. The bus station is on Giannakou St., a half block from the waterfront, just off Venizelou Square. Buses leave Ierapetra for Agios Nikolaos, Malia, and Iraklion ten times a day, for Myrtos seven times a day, for Sitia, via Lithines, five times a day, for Iraklion via Vianos twice a day, and for Makrigiolas five times a day. The **telephone code** for Ierapetra is 0842.

Ierapetra's cheapest, and smelliest, hotel is the **Venizelos** at 11 Koraka St. (tel. 28 67 5; walk west on Koraka, which begins at Venizelou Square, behind the bus station). It's 200dr per person plus 50dr for a disappointing shower. The **Livikon,** just around the corner from the bus station (tel. 22 37 0 or 28 79 2), is just as grim; 250dr per person, showers included. Though slightly more expensive, the **Cretan Villa,** 16 Lakerda St. (tel. 28 52 2), offers more attractive surroundings in a quieter neighborhood. Lakerda is the middle road heading inland from Venizelou Sq. The price is 600dr per double, 750dr per triple (more for single night stays), including use of a well-equipped kitchen until 8pm. The **Coral Hotel,** 10 Ioannidou St. (tel. 22 74 3 or 22 84 6; follow the waterfront west for about five blocks—you'll see signs), has doubles for 600dr, showers included. Across the street from the Coral is one of the best of Ierapetra's many pensions, run by **Chris Ichlakas** (tel. 23 46 3). Doubles 700dr, triples 1000dr, including use of the kitchen. One block west on the same street is the **Ierapytna** (tel. 28 53 0), with clean doubles for 600dr, including shower.

Nearly all of Ierapetra's restaurants are strung along the waterfront, and they all offer more or less the same fare at the same prices. Spaghetti dishes, sold everywhere, usually cost 120-140dr. Most of the town's shops and grocery stores are located one block up from the waterfront on Kountourioti St. At 3 Theotokopolou St. you'll find a good foreign bookstore.

Near Ierapetra

Perhaps Ierapetra's only positive characteristic is that it provides a base for exploring the southeast coast of Crete and the blissfully clear waters of the Libyan Sea. Several small towns dot the coastline to the east of Ierapetra, with numerous swimming coves and occasionally a small pension or two. Many are overpriced, however; food and lodging prices tend to increase as you move east, but at least the region is relatively untouristed. The closest and cheapest of these hideaways is **Agia Fotia,** where you can easily camp on the sandy beach or rent a double room in the town's only pension for 500dr (ask in the restaurant). Nearby **Gallini** has a restaurant and a pension, but the latter charges 700dr for a double. **Koutsouras,** about 5km further east, has two pensions—the one on the main road is slightly cleaner and less expensive at 400dr per person. Just beyond Koutsouras is the fast-growing resort town of **Makrigiolas,** where a half-dozen or so pensions rent rooms for 600-800dr per double, depending on the length of your stay and the current demand. Freelance camping is only feasible at Agia Fotia. Where the main road to Sitia turns away from the sea, a rough dirt road continues along the ocean for 13km to **Goudouras,** where the town's one taverna can fill campers' dietary needs.

One of the loveliest villages on the south coast lies 15km west of Ierapetra. **Myrtos** is quiet, relatively secluded, and has a gorgeous black-sand beach. Myrtos has cheap food and accommodations; rooms in pensions in Myrtos go for as little as 500dr for doubles. The one hotel, the **Myrtos** (tel. 51 21 5), has doubles with bath for 600dr, 500dr without. Buses stop at Myrtos seven times daily from Ierapetra and twice daily from Iraklion (via Viannos).

The beach stretching 5km west to the town of **Tertsa** is popular with campers

(Ierapetra's only tourist policeman seldom makes it out here). It's accessible by a good dirt road which straddles the shore.

The coast to the west of Myrtos leads eventually to the not-so-secluded village of **Arvi,** which, despite its inaccessibility, balloons with German and Greek tourists during the summer. It offers a pleasant beach and a monastery. Here, as almost anywhere along this unspoiled coast, you can easily get away with camping out on the beach. Pension **Gorgona** (tel. 31 21 1) is a bit expensive with singles for 400dr, doubles for 600dr, and triples for 700dr (more with private bath), but the view of the Libyan Sea from the hotel is superb, and there is a pleasant shaded restaurant below. There are two buses a day from Ierapetra to Iraklion via the town of **Viannos,** 10 km from Arvi. From there you can walk or hitch. There are also three buses a day on the Viannos-Iraklion leg of the route. One bus a day runs from the village of **Amiras** to Arvi, usually making the trip down the dusty dirt road in the evening.

Sitia

A lovely 74km drive from Agios Nikolaos by coastal and mountain roads brings you to Sitia, a pleasant port town only recently discovered by tourists. Situated only 27km from Vai beach and 46km from the Minoan ruins and beach at Kato Zakros, Sitia is an excellent—and popular—base for exploring the eastern coast of Crete. Add to this the good town beach, the friendly youth hostel, and the boat connections to the Dodecanese, and Sitia becomes an extremely compelling place to stay.

Sitia's major export is raisins *(sultanas),* and every year in mid-August a **Sultana Festival** (really a wine festival) is held in the town. The 150dr admission buys you an assigned seat at a table to watch Cretan dances, and all the locally-produced wine you can drink. Tickets are on sale during the week of the festival at a booth right by the harbor. A **cultural festival** featuring concerts, theater, ballet, and other artistic events is held throughout the summer (most events are in early July). The rest of the year, life in Sitia centers around the cheerful waterfront. Most of the old quarter of the town is terraced along the hillside on the western part of the city just above the harbor. The fortress at the top of the hill affords a fine view of the town and the entire Bay of Sitia. Sitia's long, lean sandy beach extends for about 3km east of the town. It's right next to the road, and the more distant half of it is usually quite free of people. The strand is apparently a hard-luck spot for ship captains—two semi-sunken boats beckon adventurous bathers.

Practical Information

You are effectively on your own in Sitia, since there is no Tourist Police or town map to guide visitors. The bus station is at 4 Papanastasiou St., a five-minute walk from the harbor. To get to the waterfront from the station, head for the sign for Vai and Kato Zakros, and bear left. Buses run from Sitia to Agios Nikolaos (200dr) and Iraklion (390dr) seven times daily, and to Ierapetra (165dr) four times daily. The bus to Ierapetra runs via Lithines and the southern coastal road.

Post Office: 2 Papanastasiou St., next to the bus station. Open Mon.-Fri. 7:30am-4pm.

OTE: 22 Sifis St. Open Mon.-Fri. 7:30am-10pm.

Boat Office: the **Tzortzakis Agency** (tel. 22 63 1 or 22 73 1) at the west end of the waterfront sells tickets for the *Elli* to Karpathos, Rhodes, and northern Greece

(Sun.) and Agios Nikolaos, Santorini, Ios, Naxos, Paros, and Piraeus (Thurs.). They are also likely to be helpful in providing practical information about Sitia.

Police: 24 Mysonos St. (tel. 22 25 24).

Motorbike Rentals: Motor Tours, 4th of September St. #7, by the harbor. Has 50cc scooters for 700dr.

Telephone Code: 0843.

Accommodations and Food

By all means, try to stay at the hospitable, informal **IYHF Youth Hostel** (tel. 22 69 3), 400m up the road from the bus station at 4 Therissou St. (walk back towards Iraklion). The friendly management has supplied a kitchen, an outdoor garden with music, and tables for writing and eating. They also bravely offer rooms for couples in addition to men's and women's dormitory rooms. The hostel has only 50 beds, but you are always welcome to sleep on the veranda or the floor. All beds go for 180dr. No curfew. Reception open 9am-1:30pm and 4:30-9pm (if no one's around, just find a bed and register later).

Sitia also has five inexpensive hotels. The **Myson,** at 82 Mysonos St. (tel. 22 30 4), is a dive, and priced accordingly at 500dr per double.The nearby **Pressos,** 9 Mavrikaki St. (tel. 22 32 5 or 28 55 5), is a sizeable step up in quality. Doubles 600dr, triples 900dr. Both of these hotels fill fast because of their convenient location west of the bus station. To reach them, follow the street behind the bus station two blocks for Myson, four for Pressos. The **Hotel Archontiko,** 16 Kondylaki St. (tel. 28 17 2), in the old quarter two blocks up from the boat office, has clean, attractive doubles for 600dr (triples for 900dr) and a pleasant patio. The manager, Apostolis Kimalis, also has private rooms at about the same rates at 27 Kazanzaki St. (tel. 22 12 2 or 22 99 3). Rooms are easier to get at the **Hotel Star,** 37 Kolyvaki St. (tel. 22 91 7), one block in from the waterfront at the western end of the harbor, and at the **Hotel Minos,** 31 Therissou St. (tel. 28 33 1), halfway to the youth hostel. Both have doubles for 700dr; the Star provides a kitchen for guests' use.

Private rooms can be hard to find in Sitia during the summer, and a search of the streets around the waterfront will usually prove fruitless. But the pensions farther up the hill usually have vacancies. **Victoria's** (tel. 28 08 0), a three-minute walk on the road to Ierapetra, has interesting doubles for 650dr and a lovely garden. The availability of rooms in hotels and pensions fluctuates greatly. The worst times are just before the weekly departures of boats for Rhodes on Sun. mornings and during the Sultana festival.

Many of the restaurants specialize in fresh fish and lobster, and most of their selection is mounted on stands in front to help you decide. **Zorbas Restaurant** on the west side of the harbor has a large selection of inexpensive dishes, starting at 130dr. **Russo's,** at 4th of September St. #9, just off the harbor, is a colorful taverna where you can sample Cretan "escargot," and sometimes enjoy bouzouki music that is distinctly not a put-on for tourists. But perhaps the cheapest and one of the finest places to eat is **Yuras Restaurant,** at 4 Dimokritou St., one block inland from the harbor and Plateia Iroon Polytechniou, the city's main square (take the street heading towards the bus station). A few doors down is the cheery **Peacock Pub,** a favorite hangout for local youths and a good alternative to the tacky waterfront discos.

Near Sitia

The region around Sitia begs to be explored. For those with an archeological bent and a means of transportation, the half-excavated ruins of **Praisos,** which have yielded many fine small bronzes, lie to the south of Sitia. **Mochlos,** a popular and pleasant fishing village, lies halfway between Agios Nikolaos and

Sitia. The **Hotel Mochlos** (tel. 28 24 0) has doubles for 600dr. Rooms to let in pensions are about 500dr during the high season. Since public buses don't stop in Mochlos, you have to disembark in the village of Sfaka and walk or hitch the last 6km north to the town.

Toplou Monastery

Although you'll first think the Monastery of Toplou looks much more like a fortress, don't be fooled. You've come to the right place. The original church dates back to the tenth century, but after the destruction of the monastery by the Turks in 1471, the entire complex was rebuilt and fortified. The impressive three-story structure now contains a number of interesting treasures, the most famous of which are the second-century B.C. Hellenistic inscription of a treaty between the ancient Cretan cities of Itanos and Ierapytna and the province of Magnesia in Asia Minor (to the left of the entrance of the church of Panagia Akrotiriani), and the elaborate icon by the eighteenth-century master Ioannis Kournaros, a frenetic composition that looks a bit like a Hieronymus Bosch without the grotesquerie.

Public buses do not go directly to the monastery; you must get off the Vai bus at the Moni Toplou turn-off 12km outside Sitia and walk the last 3km. If you are driving, follow the road east out of Sitia along the coast and turn left at the same junction. Farther north on the same road (past Vai) is the archeological site of **Itanos,** where the treaty displayed at Toplou was found.

Vai

Not so long ago, tourists headed east to the palm tree-covered beach at Vai for a secluded and idyllic refuge from the relatively crowded beach at Sitia. The construction of a paved road and tourist facilities has changed that—despite its isolated location, Vai is no longer secluded. Several buses roll into this outpost every day, depositing tourists eager to gawk at Europe's only natural palm forest. Still, it remains a strangely anomalous stretch of the Caribbean transplanted to the shores of Crete.

There is a restaurant and a cafe on the beach, and a new (and, amazingly enough, clean) bathhouse (toilets 10dr, showers 20dr), but there are no accommodations. This, however, has not deterred a great many young Europeans from sleeping either on the beach or in the palm grove behind it. Tent-pitching in the grove itself is not always tolerated, but a sleeping bag is both sufficient and acceptable. If the number of people occupying the palm grove disturbs you, walk five or ten minutes in either direction from the main beach to one of the nearby coves where nude bathing proceeds undisturbed.

If sleeping on the beach doesn't appeal to you, rent a room in the quiet town of **Paleokastro,** 8km back toward Sitia. The town has two cheap hotels—the **Itanos** (tel. 22 50 8) and the **Paleokastro** (tel. 22 06 3). Both charge 500dr for doubles. The town's pensions average 400-600dr for doubles.

Most travelers visit Vai by public bus from Sitia. Since many summertime vacationers go back and forth from Sitia to Vai every day, the bus tends to be uncomfortably crowded. Buses leave Sitia for Paleokastro and Vai and return again four times a day, the last one leaving Vai at 5pm. One-way fare is 80dr.

Kato Zakros

Historians are convinced that the remains of the **Palace of Zakros,** 46km from Sitia, mark the site of the fourth great center of Minoan civilization. Excavations at the site were first begun in the early 1900s, but it was not until

1962 that an additional late Minoan palace and a township of surrounding dependencies were uncovered. Built on a similar plan to those at Knossos, Phaestos, and Malia, with domestic, state, and religious rooms all radiating off a central court, the palace was mostly destroyed by the catastrophe of 1450 B.C. Fortunately, the city of Zakros seems to have escaped the plunder that devastated other major Minoan sites. As a result, archeologists were able to recover the rich contents of the palace (now on display in the Iraklion museum).

Besides boasting one of Crete's most expansive and interesting archeological sites, Kato Zakros also has a gorgeous sand beach suitable for camping, and a number of interesting caves and niches, most of which are inhabitable. For less hardy souls, doubles in one of the town's two pensions go for 700dr, showers included. The village has three tavernas and a cafe-bar. The **Kato Zakros Bay Restaurant** and the **Anexis Taverna** both change money and offer their toilets and showers to camping customers.

The public bus from Sitia goes only as far as the village of Zakros, so to get to Kato Zakros you have to walk, hitch, or take a taxi (400dr) for the last 8km on a dirt road that stretches along the rim of a beautiful, steep canyon known as the "Valley of the Dead" (don't fear—the name has nothing to do with autos or motorcycles). Buses from Sitia leave for Zakros twice a day. If you have your own transportation, travel via Paleokastro, since the well-paved road is faster and infinitely more comfortable than the direct dirt road over the mountains.

CYPRUS

$1 = .54 Cyprus Pounds (C£)   **$1.85 = 1C£ = 1000mils**

Set far off in the eastern Mediterranean on the popular passenger routes between Greece and the Middle East, the island nation of Cyprus sparkles with remote mountain monasteries, crusader castles, ancient Greek mosaics and temples, and fine sandy beaches. Mysteriously overlooked by most tourists, Cyprus is perfect for a vacation spent slightly off the beaten track. Though long influenced by the Greeks, Cyprus is surprisingly unlike its Hellenic neighbor. The food, architecture, and character traits of its people all reflect an intriguing combination of the island's proximity to Greece and its century-long history of British occupation. Because many Cypriots are educated abroad, more people understand English here than in Greece, and more signs are in both the Greek and Roman alphabet. The major cities of Cyprus—Nicosia, Limassol, and Larnaca—are noisy, charmless industrial eyesores, so try to strike out for the smaller, inland towns, where you will experience the disarmingly genuine hospitality of the islanders.

Only independent since 1960, Cyprus is at present a divided nation. Turkish forces invaded the island in 1974, and have since occupied the northern half of the island. Though the Turkish government seems content with the current stand-off, the southern Cypriots and even many Turkish residents in the north are anxious to reunify the young nation. Currently, the battle of political rhetoric continues, while soldiers on both sides stand ready. Tourists are only allowed to make daytrips to the Turkish quarter unless they land in Turkish-occupied Cyprus, in which case it is impossible to cross into Greek Cyprus.

To and From Cyprus

The third largest island in the Mediterranean (after Sicily and Sardinia), Cyprus lies forty miles from Turkey, 100 miles from Israel and Lebanon, 250 miles from Egypt, and 300 miles from the nearest Greek islands. It can be reached by boat or airplane. Five boats connect Greece to Limassol; three of them also travel to Haifa, Israel; a fourth sails to Beirut, Lebanon, and Latakia, Syria; a fifth goes on to Alexandria, Egypt. The *Vergina,* owned by **Stability Line** (in Greece: 18 Voulis 126, Athens (tel. 32 22 119); in Israel: Jacob Caspi Ltd., 76 Ha'Atzmaut St., Haifa (tel. 67 44 44); in Cyprus: Louis Tourist Agency, 636 Gladstone St., Limassol (tel. 63 16 1)), originates in Piraeus on Thursday evenings, stops in Iraklion on Friday mornings, in Limassol on Saturday mornings, and arrives in Haifa on Sunday mornings before making the return trip. **Sol Maritime Ltd.** (in Greece: 4 Filellinon St., Athens (tel. 32 33 176); in Cyprus: Takis Solominides Ltd., 1 Irene St., Limassol (tel. 57 00 0); in Israel: Jacop Caspi Ltd. (see address above)) has two boats stopping in Limassol. The *Sol Phryni* leaves Piraeus at noon on Thursdays and stops in Rhodes and Limassol before proceeding to Haifa. The *Sol Olympia* originates in Venice (Spersenior Shipping Agency, Ltd., 5 Crose 276, 30125 Venice (tel. 70 36 88)), stopping at Piraeus, Rhodes, Limassol, and Haifa. From late June to mid-September, the boats run every eight days; otherwise every ten days. The *Sun Boat* (in Greece: Manos Travel System, 39 Panepistimiou St., Athens (tel. 32 50 711); in Cyprus: Dafnis Travel Ltd., 101 Spyro Araouzas St., Limassol (tel. 60 00 0)) leaves Piraeus every Wednesday at noon for Rhodes, Limassol, Beirut, and Latakia. The *Odysseus Elitis*, run by the **Louis Tourist Agency, Ltd.** (in Greece: 3 Kar. Servias 126, Athens (tel. 32 27 852); in Cyprus: 54-58 Evagoras Ave., Nicosia (tel. 42 11 4); in Egypt: Mr. Gavalas, 63 Nebi Daniel St., Alexandria (tel. 30 05 0)), leaves Piraeus on Wednesdays at 10pm for Rhodes, Limassol, and Alexandria. **The Black Sea Shipping Company** (in Greece: Transmed Shipping S.A., Akti Miaouli St. 85, Piraeus (tel. 41 31 402/3); in Egypt: Amon Shipping Agency, Adib St. 7, P.O. Box 60764, Alexandria; in Cyprus: Francoudi and Stephanou Ltd., New Port Rd., Limassol, (tel. 55 33 1)) operates ferries approximately twice a month originating in Odessa, USSR and stopping in Varna, Bulgaria, Istanbul, and Piraeus on the way to Larnaca. It then continues to Latakia and finally Alexandria. Stopovers are allowed on all boats, but be prepared to pay about $10 in port taxes. If you are coming from Turkey, the **Turkish Maritime Lines** (in Turkey: Istanbul Ac. Rihtim Caddesi, Karakoy, Istanbul (tel. 44 02 07); in Cyprus: Turk Bankasi Ltd., Famagusta, (tel. 03/66 54 94)) operates three times weekly between Mersin, Turkey, and Famagusta. The *Ertürk* also runs three times a week in summer from Taşucu to Kyrenia. Remember, you cannot go from Turkish to Greek Cyprus if you enter the island on the Turkish side. By air, Cyprus is accessible from Greece or Egypt as well as other European and Middle Eastern countries on **Olympic Airlines, Egypt Air, Cyprus Airways,** and other commercial lines.

Orientation and Practical Information

Travel in Cyprus is very easy along the main highways between the bigger cities, but can be somewhat more difficult on the smaller roads and in the mountain areas. Buses and service (shared) taxis run regularly on weekdays (until 7pm) between Limassol, Paphos, Larnaca, and Nicosia. There are also connections between Ayia Napa and Larnaca, Polis and Paphos, from either Nicosia or Limassol. Service taxis generally cost C£1-C£1.5 between the four major cities, while the buses, although slower and less frequent, cost about half as much. The advantage of using service taxis is that they will pick you up at your hotel or hostel and drive you to your final destination rather than to a remote bus station. There is no direct taxi or bus service between Nicosia and Paphos, so expect to pay twice as much since you will have to travel via Limassol.

Direct buses to the Troodos Mountains travel once a day from both Nicosia and Limassol. From Paphos, it's a little more difficult to get to the mountain resorts; you must choose between hitching the hundred or so miles or taking several buses, preferably via Limassol. Hitching in Cyprus is very common, especially on secondary roads not serviced by public transportation. You should have little problem securing a lift since Cypriots are extremely hospitable.

Regular taxis in Cyprus are fairly cheap and can be found everywhere. With the meter, the charge is about 150mils per mile. Drivers almost never use them, though, so have a rough idea of the distance you're traveling and the corresponding price; that way, you'll know where you stand when bargaining. Cypriots drive on the left side of the road. Distances are always measured in miles.

The tourist information bureaus in the four major cities and the branch offices at Pano Platres, Ayia Napa, and the Larnaca airport are all extremely helpful and efficient; each office has stacks of tourist literature and maps of the island and each of the four major cities. Make use of them and be sure to get a copy of the *Cyprus Hotels and Tourist Services Guide*. While this booklet does not list all of the country's cheap hotels (since many are unofficial), it does

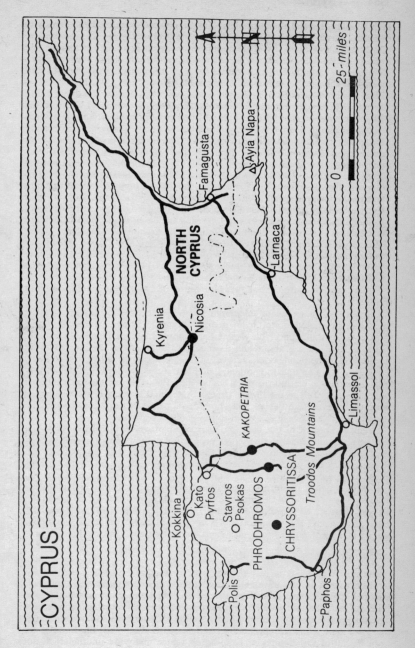

CYPRUS

CYPRUS

NORTH CYPRUS

Kokkina
Polis
Kato Pyrfos
Stavros Psokas
PHRODHROMOS
CHRYSSORITISSA
Troodos Mountains
Paphos
Limassol
KAKOPETRIA
Kyrenia
Nicosia
Larnaca
Famagusta
Ayia Napa

N

0   25 miles

include all hotels and pensions which are government-regulated and gives you the latest approved prices, the facilities, and different types of accommodations available in each. If you are quoted or charged a price higher than the one listed in the booklet, you can register a complaint with the nearest tourist office and, unless the hotel has managed to have its price increase approved (very rare), you will get the appropriate reduction.

The legal tender of Cyprus is the Cyprus pound (C£), which is divided into 1000 mils. Prices are sometimes quoted in shillings, a term left over from the British occupation that refers to fifty-mil pieces. Official banking hours are 8:30am-noon, but nearly all banks in the four major cities provide an afternoon tourist service in summer (usually 4-7pm). Stores are open Mon.-Sat. 8am-1pm, and on Monday, Tuesday, Thursday and Friday 4-7pm as well. Government offices are usually open 7:30am-1:30pm, with occasional afternoon hours, most often on Monday and Thursday. Museums and archeological sites are a notable exception, open Mon.-Sat. in the afternoons. Restaurants are open in the early evening, and public transportation services stop at 7pm. Nearly all establishments, notably museums, are closed or have reduced hours on Sundays. Cyprus observes the following holidays, when most places are closed: New Year's Day, Epiphany (January 6), Archbishop Makarios III Day (January 19), Green Monday, Good Friday, Orthodox Easter (Saturday through Monday), Cypriot National Holiday (April 1), Labor Day (May 1), the anniversary of the death of Archbishop Makarios III (August 3), Independence Day (October 1), Christmas Eve, Christmas, and Boxing Day (December 24-26). Two Greek national holidays, on March 25 and October 28, are also honored.

Cyprus has an excellent telecommunications network (**CYTA**). Overseas calls can be dialed direct from nearly all public phones; rates to North America, Australia, and New Zealand are approximately C£1.300 per minute. Calls to England are about half as much. Country codes are posted in all booths and in the phone books (copies in English are surprisingly easy to find). For information on unlisted numbers, dial 191; if the number is listed, call 192. For information on international calls, dial 194, and for the international operator, 198. Telegrams to the United States and Canada cost 180mils per word (delivery within twelve hours) or 55mils per word (within 24 hours). To Australia or New Zealand, expect to pay 100mils per word.

Greek is spoken in the southern part of Cyprus, Turkish in most of the northern section. A surprisingly high proportion of the population speaks or at least understands English—another leftover from the British occupation. The Popular Bank of Cyprus distributes a free booklet listing useful Greek phrases as well as helpful practical information.

Cyprus is rich in folklore and tradition, and hosts a number of festivals every month. A general list of the major activities can be obtained by writing to the **Cyprus Tourism Organization** (in the U.S.: 13 East 40th St., New York, NY 10016; in Cyprus: 18 Theodotou St., Nicosia). Once in Cyprus, you can obtain a copy of *This Month's Principal Events* from any tourist information office.

Accommodations and Food

Because Cyprus is so often bypassed by budget travelers, inexpensive hotels are few and far between. Except in the larger cities (Nicosia, Limassol, Paphos), the cheapest places tend to be unofficial and thus not listed in the CTO guide. There are **IYHF Youth Hostels** at Nicosia, Limassol, Paphos, and Troodos, and a loosely-affiliated forest station at Stavros tis Psokas. Although there are only a few campgrounds in Cyprus, it's often possible to sleep on beaches and in wooded regions, as long as you choose your site discreetly; try to find a deserted area outside of town and away from the tourist hotels.

Cypriot food is closely related to both the Greek and the English cuisine. Meats are often grilled over charcoal as in Greece, and English-style lamb and meat cutlets and beef steaks are sold everywhere. Try *meze,* a platter of twenty or so appetizers, for two to four people, and *kleftiko,* lamb roasted in spherical charcoal ovens. *Souglakia* is similar to Greek souvlaki-pita, but the sandwiches are larger, more expensive (500-600mils), and served without a sauce. Pita pockets are sometimes filled with *sheftalia,* a homemade sausage.

History

Cyprus first achieved historical importance at the onset of the Bronze Age because of its wealth of copper ore—it is not clear to linguists whether *kypros* first referred to the island or the metal. At the end of the Trojan War, many homeward-bound heroes visited the island and founded the great city-states of **Salamis, Limassol,** and **Paphos** that would last until the fourth century B.C. During this time the Achaean Greeks introduced their language and culture, proclaimed Cyprus the birthplace of Aphrodite—goddess of Love and Beauty—and erected an important temple in her name.

After the conquest by Alexander the Great in 310 B.C., annexation by Rome in 58 B.C., and a visit by the Apostles Paul and Barnabas (actually a local boy), Cyprus became a Byzantine province in 395 A.D. As Islam became a powerful force in the Middle East, Cypriots fortified their towns and built several castles, including those at **Limassol, St. Hilarion,** and **Buffavento.**

In 1191, Richard the Lion-Hearted set sail for Jerusalem with his English fleet as part of the Third Crusade. A storm forced several of his ships to stop at Limassol, including the one with his fiancée, Berengaria of Navarre, and his sister. The rude treatment they received in Cyprus precipitated a vengeful attack and conquest by King Richard. In the midst of his military successes, he married his fiancée in Limassol Castle, and she was crowned Queen of England. Richard then sold the island to the Knights Templar to finance his crusade, and one year later it passed into the hands of Guy de Lusignan, who had helped Richard to take the island.

Under the Lusignan dynasty (1192-1489), Cyprus became an island dependent on the West. For three hundred years, the Greek Orthodox Church was suppressed by the Latin Church. The great cathedrals of Nicosia and Famagusta were built, as well as Bellapais Abbey. After 1291 and the fall of Acre to the Egyptian Mamelukes, Famagusta expanded its commercial interest and Cyprus became the wealthiest island in the eastern Mediterranean. The Venetians, who forcibly annexed Cyprus in 1489 without contributing to its commerce and cultural life, remodeled and strengthened the military defenses, most notably the walls of Nicosia, in fear of Turkish invasion. These proved little difficulty for the Turks, who in 1570 took Nicosia after a two-month siege and Famagusta a year later. Turkish rule, characterized by continued economic decline and heavy taxation on the locals, also relaxed restrictions on the Greek Orthodox Church.

When the Turks sided with the Germans in 1914, the British, who already had defensive installations on the island, promptly occupied Cyprus and offered it to Greece the following year in exchange for military alliance, but the Greeks turned it down. In 1925, Cyprus became a Crown Colony, and the first violent uprisings in the name of *enosis* (union with Greece) occurred six years later. The Government House in Nicosia was burned down, but the movement was quickly suppressed and the leaders deported. The Orthodox Church held a plebiscite in mid-January, 1950, in which 96% of the Greek Cypriots favored *enosis*. That same year, the Archbishop died, and the Bishop of Kitium was elected Archbishop by an Assembly on October 18, 1950, at age 37. Over the next 27 years, Archbishop Makarios III would rise to become the central and most popular figure in Cypriot politics, pursuing the occasionally contradictory politics of *enosis*, nonalignment with the superpowers, and a firm line with the Turkish Cypriots at the negotiating table. In 1954, when the United Nations turned down an appeal by the Greeks to grant Cyprus self-determination, riots broke out and soon guerrilla warfare began, initiated by General Grivas and the EOKA, or National Organization of Cypriot Fighters. Archbishop Makarios was exiled because it was well known that the Church was actively supporting the EOKA movements. Cyprus officially achieved independence on August 16, 1960, entered the U.N., and joined the British Commonwealth shortly thereafter.

Independent Cyprus was rocked by internecine conflicts almost from the start. The Turkish-speaking minority felt they were being treated as second-class citizens—oppressed both politically and economically by the more numerous Greek-Cypriots. The intermittent violence suddenly exploded into an international affair in 1974, when, five days after the Greek Cypriot National Guard staged a coup to oust Archbishop Makarios in hopes of forging unity between Greece and Cyprus, the Turkish army invaded the northern part of the island in an apparent attempt to forestall National Guard hegemony and prevent what they believed would be the wholesale slaughter of Turkish Cypriots. Since that summer of fighting in 1974, there has been relative calm, with both sides working towards a political rather than a military solution. While Greek Cypriots are pushing for reunification and a return to the status quo, Turkey seems to be content with controlling approximately 40% of the island and has, in fact, sought to strengthen its grip, with the apparent hope of creating an independent Turkish-Cypriot state. Negotiations between the two governments have gone through seven rounds and are temporarily stalled with no solution in sight.

Limassol

Limassol (pop. 100,000), the port of entry for most of the passenger boats which stop in Greek Cyprus, does not offer the best inroduction to an otherwise beautiful island. Rapid growth and lack of foresight in urban planning have led to the construction of an endless row of hotels extending east along the coast, and a sprawl of residential and commercial structures lining the major city arteries. Today Limassol is the industrial center of the island, with narrow rocky beaches, a rapidly decaying city center, and on any given day dozens of ugly merchant ships anchored offshore. Its location makes it a good base for daytrips in the area, but aside from the castle and the museum, there isn't much to see in the town itself.

Practical Information

The new port where the passenger boats arrive is actually about 5km southwest of the center of town. Although there is no bus servicing the port terminal itself, if you walk out of the port and north on Omonias St. (the main street after the traffic circle) for about 500m you will see the Bank of Cyprus building and next to it, a blue bus marked 20A parked on the side street to your right. The bus makes seven runs a day from this point to downtown Limassol (150mils) with the last bus leaving at 5:35pm. Insist that the driver give you some sort of ticket or receipt, since he sometimes overcharges new arrivals. If you decide not to take a bus or arrive in Limassol too late, you can share a taxi to or from the town. This should cost C£1-C£1.500, depending on the number of passengers and amount of luggage. With the meter the fare should be just under C£1, so insist on it if you're quoted an unreasonable price.

Cyprus Tourism Organization Office: on the waterfront, one block east of the castle at 15 Spyro Araouzas St. (tel. 62 75 6). Th extremely capable and helpful staff here will tell you just about anything you want to know, suggest daytrips, and provide maps, bus schedules, and general information for the entire island. A wise first stop. Open Mon.-Sat. 8am-1:15pm and Mon. and Thurs. 4-6:15pm. (Afternoon hours in winter are 2:30-5:30pm.)

American Express: 130 Spyro Araouzas St. (tel. 62 04 5), in the offices of A. L. Mantovani and Sons. Holds mail and arranges check-cashing for cardholders. (Expect a $15 charge from the bank.) Open Mon.-Fri. 9am-noon and 3-5pm, Sat. 9am-noon for mail only.

Central Post Office: on Archbishop Kyprianou St., one block inland from St. Andrew St. Open Mon.-Sat. 7:30am-1pm and Mon., Tues., Thurs., Fri. 4-6pm.

CYTA (Telecommunications): on Markos Botsaris St. Open 24 hours.

Bus Stations: Public buses on Andrea Themistoklis St., near Anexartisia St. Catch #6, 25, or 26 to go east along the coast as far as Amathus (10km). The #30 bus will take you as far as the Miramare Hotel. **KEMEK** intercity buses to Nicosia, Platres, and Paphos leave from the station on the corner of Enosis and Irene Sts. **Lefkaritis** buses to Larnaca leave every hour from the waterfront terminal at 107 Spyro Araouzas St., just east of the Limassol Palace Hotel. **Platres** buses to the Troodos Mountains depart from Eleftherias St.

Service Taxis: Kyriakos on Pasteur St. east of Anexartisia St. (tel. 64 11 4). **Makris** on Gladstone St. opposite the Rio Cinema. **Kypros-Akropolis** on Spyro Araouzas St. two blocks east of the tourist office (tel. 53 32 2 or 63 97 9). **Karydas,** 119 Spyro Araouzas St. (tel. 62 06 1). All go to Paphos and Nicosia. Makris and Kypros-Akropolis go to Larnaca. Karydas sends two minibuses daily (one in winter) to Platres.

Police: The headquarters are located at the intersection of Gladstone and Leonides Sts. (tel. 63 11 1), next to the hospital.

Hospital: on Leonides St., next to the police station (tel. 63 17 1).

Bicycle and Motorbike Rentals: All shops are located near the luxury hotels at the eastern edge of town, on the shore road. A motorcycle license is required to rent anything, but most agents will take you to the police station, where if you've "forgotten" your license, you can be issued a temporary Cypriot license. If you plan to rent long term, you'll do better for quality and price in Paphos.

English Bookstore: the Ioannides shop at 30 Athens St.

Telephone Code: 051.

Accommodations

The good news on Limassol accommodations is that they are the cheapest on the island. The bad news is that they are also the dirtiest and most primitive.

IYHF Youth Hostel, 120 Ankara St. (tel. 63 74 9), a few blocks west of the castle. C£1.600 includes bed and breakfast, but laundry, showers, and coffee are 150mils extra. Closed 9am-5pm. 11pm curfew.

Guest House Icaros, 61 Eleftherias St. (tel. 54 34 8). Cleaner and greener than the rest of the town's offerings. Try to ignore the Turkish toilets. Singles C£2.500. Otherwise, C£2 per person.

Guest House Stalis, 59 Eleftherias St. (tel. 68 19 7), next to the Icaros. The rooms aren't bad, but the toilets certainly are. C£3 for a single or double. Otherwise C£1 per bed.

Hotel Troodos, on Eleftherias St. at the Irene St. intersection (tel. 55 74 9). Dirtier than the Stalis, but the beds are as cheap—all are C£1 each. Some rooms are walk-throughs.

Guest House Excelsior, 35 Anexartisia St. (tel. 53 35 1). Rooms follow an unusual, interesting color scheme, and most have electric fans, a welcome luxury on hot summer nights. Pricey for Limassol, with singles C£4, doubles C£8, triples C£10.

Guest House Luxor, 101 Ayios Andreas St. (tel. 62 26 5). The floors and sheets are a bit cleaner, and the rooms more spacious than in most other Limassol dives. Singles C£3, doubles C£5.

Hotel Hellas, 9 Zig Zag St. (tel. 63 84 1). The hotel faces Ayios Andreas St. Only for the really desperate. The monoglot owner asks C£4 for disgusting doubles, but don't pay more than C£3.

Food

Food in Limassol is remarkably mediocre. Most restaurants are located near the big hotels at the eastern end of town, several kilometers from the center. For more conveniently-located eateries, try the following:

Mimosa, on the waterfront at 83 Christogoulou Hagipavlou St. A pseudo-chic eating gallery left over from the British occupation. Steak, vegetables, and chips for C£1.500.

Lefteris, at the intersection of Gladstone and Anexartisia Sts. The best kebab in town. Souglakia for 500mils is the only food they serve.

There are loads of kebab shops along the waterfront, and in the evening sidewalk vendors along the road sell *sytorai* (roasted corn-on-the-cob) for 250mils.

Sights

In the town itself, the labyrinthian **Limassol Castle** is the only building of historical importance. The actual building in which Richard married his queen was destroyed by earthquakes and Genoese assaults, so the only traces of the old Byzantine fort are in the west wall of the compact building which stands today. The Lusignans first leased the castle to the Knights Templar, who thickened the walls and covered the Gothic windows in the early fourteenth century. Later the Knights of St. John converted the great Western Hall into a Gothic church and made the chapel into a series of prison cells. The Turks claimed the castle in 1570, and the large West Hall was used as a prison until 1940 under the British regime. The castle is open Monday through Saturday from 7:30am to 1:30pm, admission 200mils. The **Archeological Museum** on Byron St. across from the Curium Palace Hotel houses a small collection of pottery, terracotta figurines, jewelry, statues, funerary steles. Most notable is the head of Aphrodite in the north room. Closer to the ocean on Byron St. you'll find a town **zoo** and **public gardens**.

If you want to see what today's Limassol is all about, or if you just want free samples of Cypriot wine, visit the **KEO factory** on Franklin Roosevelt Street, a short walk from the castle. Free tours here Mon.-Fri. at 10am close with complimentary bottles of wine and beer. You can also visit the **Haggipavlu Brandy Distillery** Mon.-Fri. 8am-3pm.

The city's long stone beach is nothing to write home about. **Dassoudi Beach,** 3km east of town, is far better. Take bus #6, 13, 25, or 26 from the market (on Kanaris St.).

Limassol plays host to a number of annual celebrations, including a Shakespearean Festival at the end of June, a two-week International Art Festival in the first half of July, a Wine-Fest in mid-September, and a Carnival fifty days before Orthodox Easter (usually in Feb.). For details about these and other special events, contact the Tourist Office.

Near Limassol

Several historical sights near Limassol warrant a visit: Curium, the ruins of an ancient Greek city-state with a Sanctuary to Apollo, the Kolossi Castle, and the Stavrovouni Monastery.

Curium, 12km west of Limassol, is actually within the British Sovereign Base Area which includes all of the Akrotiri Peninsula. First settled during the Neolithic Period, Curium became famous for its sanctuary to Apollo (eighth century B.C.) and its stadium (second century A.D.), both located west of the main settlement. The ruins of the town itself lie just to the south of the highway. The **House of Achilles,** which faces the highway at the entrance to the site, has a splendid mosaic depicting a transvestite Achilles revealing himself to Odysseus as he reaches for a spear. Unfortunately, the house is fenced off from the public and can only be viewed from a bad angle. If you scramble a bit, you can see it by climbing along the inside of the fence that runs along the access road. The ruins of the fifth-century **Christian Basilica** are imposing and contain several fine mosaics; more impressive are the theater and the Baths of Eustolios, two hundred yards down the road. The reconstructed **theater** commands an expansive view of the Mediterranean and is occasionally used for a handful of concerts in June, July, and August and weekend theater in September. The adjacent **Baths of Eustolios,** built by the Romans in the fifth century A.D., contain several superb, well-preserved mosaic floors. The ruins at Curium are open every day 7:30am-7:30pm or sunset, whichever comes first; admission 250mils.

Less than a half-mile west up the hill you can see the low walls of the **stadium** on the right side of the highway. Originally, the seven-row deep stands could hold six thousand people, but today only a small section of the original seating remains (in the southwest corner). Another half mile further lies the **Sanctuary of Apollo,** at one time second only to the Temple of Aphrodite (in old Paphos) as a center of religious worship on the island. Apollo was worshipped here as God of the Woodland. Virtually none of the original temple—in use from the eighth to the fourth century B.C.—still exists, and most of the present ruins date from 100 A.D. At the southern end of the site, which contains the reconstructed five-columned portico, there were five rooms intended for visitors. The temple and altar were located in the north, and only seem small because most of the religous rites were performed out-of-doors. The unattended stadium is always open. The Sanctuary of Apollo is open every day 7:30am-7:30pm (sunset in winter); admission 200mils. To get to either site take a KEMEK bus bound for Paphos and let the driver know where you want to get off. You might consider disembarking at the more distant Temple of

Apollo, since the road back to Curium is all downhill. To get back, hail a
KEMEK bus or book a seat on a Paphos-Limassol service taxi (you'll still
have to pay the whole fare).

The **Kolossi Castle,** its square-shaped, three-story structure visible from the
road about five miles west of Limassol, was one of the more important castles
in Cyprus during the Crusades. Both the Knights Templar and the Knights of
the Order of St. John made the castle their headquarters for a short while.
When the Knights of the Order of St. John moved to Rhodes in 1310, Kolossi
remained their richest overseas possession, garnering wealth from the surrounding vineyards. The castle is open every day 7:30am-7:30pm (sunset in
winter); admission 200mils.

Halfway between Limassol and Nicosia (six miles from the main highway) is
the **Stavrovouni Monastery.** It is believed that the monastery was founded in
327 A.D. to house a fragment of the "True Cross" donated by Helena, the
mother of Roman Emperor Constantine. The monastery is open for men only
on Monday, Wednesday, and Friday, and for both sexes on Sunday. Seven
miles closer to Limassol is the turn-off for **Pano Lefkara,** the center of the
Cypriot lace-making industry. Both locations are only accessible by thumb or
foot from the main highway. Be sure to tell the bus or service taxi driver where
to drop you off.

Nicosia (Lefkosia)

Situated on the site of the ancient city of Ledra, Nicosia was, during the
Roman occupation, just another city state, loosely protected from invasion by
its distance from the sea. It prospered up until the fifteenth century without
any substantial fortifications, until the Egyptian Mamelukes pillaged the town
in 1426. As Egyptian strength waned, the Venetians took over and, in 1567,
built massive walls around Nicosia with the intention of withstanding Ottoman
Turkish cannonball salvoes. Only three years later the Turks attacked—it took
them seven weeks to capture the city. Only when the British took over three
centuries later did the city begin to prosper again. When independence was
finally achieved in 1960, Nicosia became the capital of Cyprus.

Today, Nicosia (Lefkosia, in Greek) consists of two parts. The new city,
with its government buildings, luxury hotels, wide shopping avenues, and
modern residential housing, has become the center of life for most Nicosians.
But the old city, situated within the circular Venetian walls, contains most of
the interesting sights and is much more exciting for the 1980s explorer.

The most obvious and disturbing fact about Nicosia, however, is that, like
Berlin, Beirut, and Belfast, it is a divided city. The presence of Greek Cypriot
and Turkish border patrols as well as a significant number of U.N. troops serve
as constant reminders that violence and bitterness lie just below the surface.
While the life of modern Greek-speaking Nicosia, with all its bustle and modern buildings, will impress you, you need only walk towards the Green Line,
with its emptier streets, boarded up storefronts, and sandbag barricades to
realize just how serious the situation is.

Practical Information

You'll find most places of interest within the old city walls of the southern
half of Nicosia; banks, travel agencies, embassies, and other official buildings
are usually located on the major avenues just outside the walls.

Cyprus Tourism Organization Office: 5 Princess de Tyras St. (tel. 44 26 4), two
blocks down Evagoras Ave. from Eleftheria Sq. Extremely helpful and well-

informed. Open Mon.-Sat. 8am-1:15pm, Mon. and Thurs. 4-6:15pm. The national headquarters of the C.T.O. (tel. 43 37 4) is in the same building, at 18 Theodotou St., 2nd floor Open Mon.-Sat. 7:30am-2pm.

American Express: 35-37 Evagoras Ave. (tel. 43 77 7), in the offices of A. L. Mantovani and Sons, Ltd. Will hold mail. To buy travelers checks with your card and personal check, obtain a letter from AMEX and go to the Popular Bank on Archbishop Makarios III Ave. The bank charges $15 plus a 1% commission for this service. Open in summer Mon.-Fri. 8am-1pm and 3:30-6:30pm, Sat. 8am-12:30pm. In winter, afternoon hours are 2:30-5:30pm.

Post Office: on Constantinos Paleologos Ave., just east of Eleftheria Sq. Open Mon.-Sat. 7:30am-1pm, and Mon., Tues., Thurs., Fri. afternoons 4-6pm.

CYTA: On Egypt Ave., around the corner from the museum. Open every day 24 hours.

Bus Stations: KEMEK (tel. 63 15 7) buses to Limassol, Paphos, and Platres leave from 34 Leonidos St. **Lefkaritis** (tel. 42 56 6) buses to Larnaca leave from Stassinos Ave., just east of Eleftheria Sq. outside the walls. The tourist office has a complete list of village buses. City buses leave from Dionysos Solomes Sq., the next one west from Eleftheria Sq. Route maps are available at the KEMEK station and at the tourist office.

Service Taxis: Makris (tel. 66 20 1), **Akropolis** (tel. 63 84 1), **Kypros** (tel. 64 81 1) and **Kyriakos** (tel. 44 14 1) are all located on Stassinos Ave. **Karydas** (tel. 62 26 9) is nearby at 8 Homer Ave. All travel to Limassol and on to Paphos; Makris, Akropolis, and Kyriakos go to Larnaca; only Karydas goes to Platres and the mountains.

Police: on Archbishop Makarios III Ave. (tel. 40 35 35). In an emergency, dial 199.

Hospital: between Hilon and Homer Sts., near the Municipal Gardens (tel. 51 11 1).

U.S. Embassy: at the corner of Dositheos and Therissos Sts. (tel. 65 15 1; general information tel. 73 14 3), near the Hilton Hotel, just off Archbishop Makarios III Ave. Take bus #16, 50, 55, or 58. Open Mon.-Fri. 7am-3pm.

British High Commission: on Alexander Pallis St. (tel. 73 13 1), west of the old city (take bus #23). Open Mon.-Fri. 8am-noon.

Australian High Commission: 4 Annis Comninis St. (tel. 73 00 1), just south of the city walls. Open in summer Mon., Tues., Thurs., Fri. 7:30am-2:30pm; open Wed. 7:30am-1pm and 2-4:45pm.

Egyptian Embassy: 3 Egypt Ave. (tel. 65 14 4). Visa section open Mon.-Fri. 9-11am (but it's best to arrive before 10am). Wait for visas is one day.

Lebanese Embassy: 1 Queen Olga St. (tel. 42 21 6). Visa section open 9am-noon. The wait can be up to a few weeks.

Syrian Embassy: at the corner of Androcleous and Thoukidides Sts. (tel. 74 48 1). Visa section open Mon.-Fri. 9am-1pm. No wait.

The American Center: 33B Homer Ave. (tel. 73 14 3), around the corner from the museum. No books on Cyprus here, but you can read current issues of the New York *Times* and other periodicals in air-conditioned surroundings. Open Mon.-Fri. 9am-1pm and 4-6:30pm. In winter, open 10am-1pm and 3-5pm. Closed Thurs. afternoons.

British Council: 3 Museum Ave. (tel. 42 15 2). Two doors down from the museum. In summer, open Mon.-Fri. 8am-1pm and Mon., Tues., Thurs., Fri. 4-6:30pm. Afternoon hours in winter are 3-5:30pm. Open all year Sat. 9am-noon.

English Bookstores: Phillipides Charalambos and Son, at 10 Constantinos Paleologos Ave., across from the central post office. Also try the **Bridge House Bookshop,** at 13-14 Byron Ave. Both open Mon.-Sat. 8am-1pm and Mon., Tues., Thurs., Fri. 4-7pm.

Self-service Laundry: located in the parking lot behind the Exagonon Cafe, at the junction of Prodromos St. and Grivas Dhigenis Ave. Open Mon.-Sat. 8am-1pm, and Mon., Tues., Thurs., Fri. 3:30-6:30pm. Wash C£1, spin 100mils, service 250mils, soap 325mils, drying 250mils for ten minutes (use the sun instead).

Telephone code: 021.

Accommodations

Nicosia is not known for the cleanliness of its budget accommodations. Moreover, the staffs of Nicosia's many "cabarets" tend to frequent a number of the cheapest places, so a seedy atmosphere pervades. Nearly all of the inexpensive places are conveniently located within the walls of the old city.

IYHF Youth Hostel, 13 Prince Charles St. (tel. 44 80 8), opposite the Asty Hotel. About a 25-minute walk from the center of town; if you haven't arrived in a service taxi, take bus #27. C£1.750 for members, C£1.900 for non-members, cold showers, sheets, and breakfast included. 350mils cheaper on the second and subsequent nights. Closed 10am-4pm. 11pm curfew.

Tony's Bed and Breakfast, 13 Solon St. (tel. 66 75 2 or 63 79 4). Tony lived in England for two decades and keeps the small rooms of his respectable place quite clean. The English breakfast included in the price is good and filling. Pleasant roof garden. Singles C£4-5, doubles C£8-10, triples C£12, all with fans.

Kypros Hotel, 16A Vass. Voulgaroktonou St. (tel. 63 46 5). The cheapest place in Nicosia, but you get only what you pay for. Very, very noisy. A stone's throw from the Green Line. Singles C£2, doubles and triples C£3.

Guest House Femina, 114 Ledra St. (tel. 65 72 9). Legions of "cabaret" performers hang out here. Really racy, but kept fairly clean. Singles C£4, doubles C£5, triples C£7, quads C£9.

Peter's, 5 Solon St. (tel. 63 52 6). If you can stomach it, apartment-style accommodations go for C£2.500 per person. Avoid the restaurant.

City Hotel, 209 Ledra St. (tel. 63 11 3). Tacky and not especially clean. Very friendly management, however, and in a good location. Singles C£6, doubles C£10, triples C£12, all with breakfast.

Food

Nicosia has many restaurants, but few good ones. You're better off buying your own food at the **municipal market** at the junction of Dhigenis Akritas and Kalipolis Sts. Every Wednesday, a colorful streetside **produce market** sets up shop along Constantinos Paleologos Ave., east of Eleftheria Sq. A great place to go is the **Food Bazaar** on Byron Ave., at the Homer Ave. intersection. It's obscure and uncrowded, and the sizeable portions are always served hot. All dishes go for under C£1.500. Although it doesn't always have a large selection, the **Leventis Tavern** at 4 Tagmatarchis D. Poulios St. (a twenty-minute walk from the old city) is very popular among U.N. staffers. It has good, authentic food at very reasonable prices (*sheftalia* for C£1.250).

Sights

All of the important sights, with the notable exception of the Cyprus Museum, are within the walls of the old city. Four of them are next to each other and next to the palatial Archbishopric of Cyprus (not open to the public). The interior of **St. John's Church,** a small cathedral built in 1662, is adorned with eighteenth-century frescoes depicting biblical scenes, including, to the left of the Archbishop's throne, the discovery of the tomb of St. Barnabas at Salamis. Behind the church is the newly-opened **Byzantine Museum,** containing icons from the eighth to the eighteenth centuries. The museum boasts one of the finest icon collections in Europe and, thankfully, every painting is labeled in English. On the second and third floors of the same building you'll find an excellent collection of unsigned Northern European paintings from the sixteenth through the nineteenth centuries.

In the same courtyard is the **Folk Art Museum,** housed in the old Archbishopric, a former Gothic monastery of the fifteenth-century. The museum displays examples of traditional arts and crafts, including pottery, costumes, jewelry, weaving looms, and carved wooden furniture. Open Mon.-Fri. 8am-4:30pm, Sat. 8am-1pm. In winter, open Mon.-Sat. 8am-1pm and Mon.-Fri. 3-5pm; admission 150mils. For a more exciting interpretation of Cypriot culture, drop in at the **Museum of National Struggle** next door. Founded in 1961 by the Greek Communal Chamber of Cyprus, the museum contains photographs, documents, and other relics from the struggle for *enosis* and independence, including thirty volumes containing signatures of Greek Cypriots who favored *enosis* in a 1950 plebiscite. The room opposite the entrance is called the Hall of Heroes, and includes the pictures of those who died in both the 1931 uprising and others who have died in the EOKA struggle. The museum is open June-Aug. Mon.-Sat. 7:30am-1:30pm. The rest of the year, open Mon.-Fri. 7:30am-2pm, Sat. 7:30am-1pm; admission 100mils.

Down Koreas St. from the Archbishopric you'll find the unusual monument to the Cypriot struggle for freedom. The monument depicts fourteen Cypriots, each representing a period of the island's history, as they are released from jail by soldiers and overseen by a religious figure. The life-like figures and the white marble jail, designed by the Greek artist Falireas, are as yet unchristened, and await the day when Cyprus will once again be unified.

The other interesting site in this area is the **Konak Mansion,** also known as the **House of Hadjigeorgakis Kornessios,** at 18 Patriarch Gregory Street, the luxurious eighteenth-century residence of a famous Turkish dragoman.

A visit to the **Cyprus Museum** is an absolute necessity when you're in Nicosia. Well-preserved artifacts from archeological excavations conducted at Khirokitia, Lapithos, Sanskiou, and other sites in Cyprus have bequeathed to the museum a small but well-deserved international reputation. Clay models, terracotta figurines, pottery of different periods, and monumental sculpture form the bulk of the exhibits. Be sure not to miss the large display of hundreds of seventh-century B.C. terracotta figurines at the sanctuary at Ayia Irini, where pilgrims practiced the Minoan cult of the bull (Room IV). Open in summer Mon.-Sat. 8am-1:30pm and 4-6pm and Sun. 10am-1pm. In winter, Mon.-Sat. 7:30am-2pm and 3-5pm, Sun. 10am-1pm; admission 250mils.

Nicosia is blessed with two central **parks** where one can escape the midday heat. The larger and dirtier one is in the "moat" (which was never actually filled with water) at the base of the old city walls from Eleftheria Sq. to the beginning of Egypt Ave. A short walk west brings you to a cleaner and more colorful enclave behind the Garden Cafe (enter on Homer Ave.). Here you'll find aviaries containing most of the bird species indigenous to Cyprus.

Paphos

Paphos, the westernmost province of the island, with its capital city of the same name, is of great historical and cultural significance for Cyprus. Rich in sights, the city of Paphos is an ideal base for exploring some of the least traveled and most beautiful parts of the island.

Practical Information

The city of Paphos is divided into two sections: the upper, called Ktimapaphos, and the lower, about a mile to the south, known as Katopaphos or Nea Paphos. Most services, shops, and budget hotels are located in Ktimapaphos. Katopaphos is full of luxury hotels, holiday villas, and other supertourist facilities. The following places are in Ktimapaphos, unless otherwise indicated:

Cyprus Tourism Organization Office: 3 Gladstone St. (tel. 32 84 1), next to the Cyprus Airways office. The staff is helpful, and you'll find all the practical information about the region that you'll ever need here. Open Mon.-Sat. 8am-1:15pm and Mon. and Thurs. 4-6:15pm (afternoon hours in winter 2-4pm).

Post Office: on Nikodhimou Mylona St. in the District Administration building. Open in summer Mon.-Sat. 7:30am-noon, and Mon., Tues., Thurs., Fri. 4-6pm. (Afternoon hours in winter are 3-5pm.)

CYTA: on Grivas Digenes Ave. in the southeastern part of Ktimapaphos. Open every day 8am-8pm.

Bus Stations: Bus #11 between Ktimapaphos and Katopaphos leaves every half hour until 7pm from the *stasis* across the street from the post office in Ktimapaphos, and from in front of the Municipal Baths in Katopaphos (150mils one way). Intercity buses leave from the Pervola Station on Fallahegou St.: **KEMEK** goes to Limassol and **Alepa** goes to local villages.

Service taxis: Kyriakos, 19 Pallikaridi St. (tel. 33 18 1), **Karydas,** 29 Pallikaridi St. (tel. 32 42 4 or 32 45 9), **Akropolis** and **Kypros,** Archbishop Makarios III Ave. in Kennedy Sq. (both tel. 32 53 3), **Makris,** Athens St. in the northern part of town (tel. 32 53 8).

Police: on Grivas Digenes Ave. in Kennedy Sq. (tel. 32 35 2). For emergencies, dial 199.

Hospital: on Neophytos Nicolaides St. (tel. 32 36 4).

Bicycle and Motorbike Rental: Most shops are located in Katopaphos. **Psomas Rentals** (tel. 35 56 1) and **3-Star Hire** (tel. 35 83 4), are both on Poseidnos St. across from the Paphos Beach Hotel. Expect to pay C£1 per day for bikes and C£3-4 per day for small motorbikes.

English Bookstore: Axel Bookshop at 62-64 Archbishop Makarios III Ave. (tel. 32 40 4). Open Mon.-Sat. 8am-1pm and 4-6pm.

Telephone code: 061.

Accommodations and Food

Paphos' handful of cheap hotels are both reasonably priced and relatively clean. All but one of the following are in Ktimapaphos:

IYHF Youth Hostel, Eleftherias Venizelou Ave. (tel. 32 58 8). On a quiet residential street northeast of the town center (signs point the way). The location is inconvenient, and the hostel is not particularly clean, but the easygoing warden doesn't charge extra for laundry, showers, etc. C£1.500 includes a continental breakfast. The hostel is crowded in summer, partly because a hostel card is not required. 11pm curfew, but you can come in after hours.

Paphos Palace Hotel, 10 Grivas Digenes St. (tel. 32 34 6), on Kennedy Sq. Don't be fooled by the name or the appearance. Bed and breakfast for C£3 per person, C£2.500 for bed only. Spacious and clean.

Hotel Trianon, 99 Archbishop Makarios III Ave. (tel. 32 19 3). Very dreary. Don't expect much. Singles C£3, doubles C£5, triples C£7.

Hotel Kinyras, 89 Archbishop Makarios III Ave. (te. 32 52 2). Significantly cleaner than its nearby competitor, but more expensive. Singles C£4, doubles C£7, triples C£9, all including breakfast.

Pelican Inn, 102 Apostolos Pavlos Ave. in Katopaphos (tel. 32 82 7), almost directly opposite the pier (don't confuse it with the expensive holiday flats further inland). The only cheap place to stay in Katopaphos. Doubles are C£7.500 (including breakfast), but the inn only has six rooms, so it's often full. Call before you hike all the way down there with your luggage. The pet pelicans walking around are rapidly becoming a city symbol, and you can get pelican T-shirts and postcards if you want.

Most restaurants are located in Katopaphos, within easy range of the big-money tourists. Those on the harbor are more expensive (C£2-3 for meat or fish dishes) than those on the road between Ktimapaphos and Katopaphos, but the view of the setting sun can be quite spectacular. If you prefer to stay in Ktimapaphos, you'll find a good assortment of grill houses and shops selling souglakia. Try the **Nicandros** restaurant at 139 Archbishop Makarios III Ave. in Ktimapaphos for a simple but superb meal.

Sights

Paphos boasts two excellent museums and a number of interesting archeological sites. The sights are relatively close together and can be visited in one day if you get an early start.

The mosaic floors of the **House of Dionysus** are unquestionably the most dazzling and worthwhile of Paphos' many ancient treasures. Discovered accidentally in 1962 by a farmer ploughing his fields, the superbly-preserved mosaics subsequently proved to extend over fourteen different rooms of a large Roman villa, built in the second century A.D. and destroyed in a fourth-century earthquake. One of the mosaics of Dionysus portrays the god of wine being driven in a chariot pulled by panthers while a satyr, Pan, and other figures dance nearby (the *Triumph of Dionysus*). You'll find it on the east side of the great hall. The other internationally acclaimed mosaic shows Dionysus and Acme drinking wine with true Dionysian spirit. It's the second panel between the west side of the atrium and the *Triumph of Dionysus*. All of the other mosaics are equally beautiful in this unparalleled collection. The mosaics are open 7:30am-7:30pm (sunset in winter); admission 250mils.

One hundred yards to the south (toward the water) is the **House of Theseus,** overshadowed by its impressive neighbor but still worth a look. Whereas the House of Dionysus was the private residence of a rich merchant, this building was probably the place where the Roman governor of Cyprus lived around the fourth century A.D. The two mosaics accessible by walkways here are of *Theseus killing the Minotaur* and the *Birth of Achilles,* the latter looking re-

markably similar to later Byzantine mosaics and paintings showing the birth of
Christ. The House of Theseus is still under excavation, so there are no closing
times or admission fees.

On the road to the mosaics, you'll find the remains of a **Roman theater** and
agora, both also built in the second century A.D.

The **Archeological Museum** on Grivas Digenes Ave. in Ktimapaphos houses
a fine array of Bronze Age pottery and tools, Classical sculpture, and statues
unearthed at Paleopaphos and Nea Paphos, and artifacts discovered at the
nearby House of Dionysus and House of Theseus. There are several archeological digs in process throughout the region, so the museum's superb collection is always growing. You're likely to see the museum's curator
reassembling an ancient vessel or arranging a new exhibit when he's not selling
tickets. The museum is open in summer Mon.-Sat. 8am-1:30pm and 4-6pm. In
winter, open Mon.-Sat. 8am-2pm and 3-5pm. Sunday hours are always 10am-
1pm. Admission 250mils.

Just south of the town center at 1 Exo Vrysi St. is the private **Ethnographical
Museum.** The 500mils admission charge includes a guided tour in English
conducted by Mrs. Eliades, the museum's effervescent curator. Fiercely
proud of her well-traveled ancestors, she'll eagerly explain the origins of the
objets d'art they've collected from all over the world. You'll also receive an
excellent cultural tour of Cyprus. Pottery, tools, costumes and other utensils
made and used by the rural Cypriots are distributed among five rooms and the
courtyard. The museum is open every day 8am-1pm and 4-7pm (3-5pm in
winter). Unless you have a particularly keen interest in the House of Dionysus, be prepared to fend off a push to buy Mr. Eliades' book at the end of the
visit.

Several other sights in Paphos warrant exploration. The **Catacombs of Ayia
Solomoni,** a refuge for Christians in Byzantine times, include a chapel with
badly damaged frescoes. The opening is on the side of A. Paulos Ave. At **St.
Paul's Pillar,**near the Chryssopolitissa Church, St. Paul was allegedly tied and
whipped for preaching Christianity. Two castles near the ocean are worth a
trip. The **Byzantine Castle,** on a hill overlooking the harbor, was built in the late
seventeenth century to protect its inhabitants from Arab pirates. The Lusig-
nan-built **Medieval Castle,** on the harbor, was used by both Venetians and
Turks.

To the west of Ktimapaphos, a road runs half a mile to the Paleokastra, or
Tombs of the Kings—a curious appellation, since those interred in these striking hewn stone tombs were not royalty, but merely the local aristocracy. The
larger tombs consist of an open court surrounded by burial chambers, with
Doric columns carved out of the rock below ground level and stairways leading
down to the interiors. Used as a burial ground during the Hellenistic and
Roman periods, the necropolis contains almost one hundred tombs, many of
which remain unexcavated. The tombs are open every day 7:30am-7:30pm
(sunset in winter); admission 200mils.

There are two good stretches of beach in the town of Katopaphos: in front of
the Paphos Beach Hotel (east of the Municipal Baths), and a public beach
further south along the main road.

Near Paphos

On the coast some fifteen miles southeast of Paphos along the main Limas-
sol-Paphos road is **Petra ton Romiou,** the mythical birthplace of Aphrodite.
According to Homer, "The moist breeze of Zephyr brought her there on the
waves of the sea with a noise of thunder amid the soft foam." There are no
ancient ruins here, just a good, although rocky, beach surrounded by stunning

boulders and rock formations which the signposts tell you are the "Rocks of Venus."

Five miles closer to Paphos, adjacent to the modern village of **Kouklia,** lie the ruins of the great **Temple of Aphrodite,** and the remains of **Paleopaphos,** once the capital of a kingdom encompassing nearly half of Cyprus. The temple itself was the religious center of the island and a pilgrimage for worshippers from throughout the Roman world. Its origins can be traced back to the twelfth century B.C.; it thrived until the fourth century A.D., when a combination of the anti-pagan edicts of Emperor Theodosius and a series of earthquakes reduced it to relative unimportance. The remains are not very notable in themselves and are difficult to understand without a guide. Highly recommended to help you around is the booklet published by the Cyprus Department of Antiquities entitled *A Brief History and Description of Old Paphos,* available at most of the museums for 350mils.

The modest **Archeological Museum** at the site houses a small collection of pieces uncovered by excavations during the last century. The **Epigraphical Museum** next door contains a variety of carved stones representing aspects of life in the once-grand capital. The 200mils entrance fee includes admission to the ruins of the temple and the city as well as to both museums. The sites and museums are open every day 7:30am-sunset. ALEPA buses to Kouklia leave from the Pervola station in Paphos three times a day.

Just north of the modern town of Paphos are the painted caves and buildings of the **Monastery of Ayios Neophytos** and the often crowded beach at **Coral Bay.** There are no buses to the monastery. ALEPA buses for Coral Bay depart from the Pervola Station in Ktimapaphos four times a day. Two of the buses stop at the Tombs of the Kings. One-way fare is 200mils.

In the mountains about 25 miles northeast of Paphos, Archbishop Makarios III was born in the village of **Pano Panayia,** and lived there before going to the Kykko Monastery. A monument to Cyprus' most revered figure has recently been erected in the town square, and the small house in which Makarios was born has been converted into a museum (open every day 9am-noon and 1-5pm; admission free). About a mile from Pano Panayia is the **Chryssorroyatissa Monastery**—perhaps the most picturesquely situated monastery in Cyprus. According to legend, the church was built in the twelfth century by Ignatius to house the icon of the Virgin Mary, one of three such icons painted by St. Luke. Though a fire destroyed much of the monastery's property in 1967, the church's fine collection of eighteenth-century icons and frescoes is still very much intact. The monastery will provide free accommodations to guests upon request—ask the staff of the restaurant at the monastery to translate for you. About two miles south is the abandoned **Monastery of Ayia Moni,** whose reconstructed buildings date from the seventeenth and nineteenth centuries. ALEPA buses make the trip past the two monasteries twice a day to Pano Panayia, leaving the Pervola station in Paphos in the afternoon and returning the following morning. Hitching is fairly reliable in this area, so you might consider thumbing to the monasteries and the town.

About 25 miles north of Paphos is the small seaside village of **Polis.** Many regard this area and the coastline to the west as having the best beaches in Cyprus. Freelance camping is practiced quite openly on a number of bluffs above the shore, and there are several restaurants along this stretch which provide free or almost-free camping and the use of facilities to customers. Six miles west of Polis, where the paved road ends, are the exotic **Baths of Aphrodite,** where today mortals can bathe in the thigh-deep waters of the small, shaded pool. Another lush spot is the pool called **Fontana Amorosa,** situated five miles further west, at the end of a very rough dirt road. It can be reached on foot or with a sturdy off-road vehicle.

Service taxis connect Paphos to Polis three times a day (750mils one way), and there is a minibus service to Polis which also runs three times day (400mils). Buses leave from the Pervola station in Ktimapaphos. Once there, you can easily hitch to the Baths. The one inexpensive hotel in Polis, the **Akamas** (tel. 063/21 33 0), charges C£2.500 per person in rooms with 2-5 beds. A better alternative is the seaside **campground,** which charges 750mils per tent, 150mils per person. The well-marked campground is 1 km from the town center (tel. 063/16 52 6). The **Kamares Restaurant** in town serves meat dishes for under C£1.500 on a spacious veranda overlooking the nearby hills.

Larnaca

Unless you're flying in or out of Cyprus, try to avoid Larnaca. This dingy, dirty city is loaded with tacky restaurants, discos, and tourist shops catering to fast-spending vacationers. Larnaca's harbor has fewer supertankers and its beach fewer stones than Limassol, but the city is at least as ugly as its metropolitan neighbor to the southwest.

Practical Information

You'll find most services on or near **Dimokratias (King Paul) Square.** Unfortunately, no public or airline buses serve the airport. Taxis run C£1 regardless of the number of passengers. Drivers will not allow you to round up companions on the spot, so try to arrange a group on the plane or at your hotel.

Cyprus Tourism Organization Office: Dimokratias Sq. (tel. 54 32 2). Be sure to stop here to get maps and information for the entire island. Open Mon.-Sat. 8am-1:15pm and Mon. and Thurs. 4-6:15pm. In winter, afternoon hours are Mon. and Thurs. 2:30-5:45pm. Another office is in the airport.

American Express: Dimokratias Sq. (tel. 52 02 4 or 52 02 9), in the offices of A. L. Mantovani and Sons, Ltd., across from the tourist office. Holds mail and approves personal checks (expect a $15 bank charge). Open Mon.-Fri. 8am-1pm and 3:30-6:30pm. In winter, open Mon.-Fri. 8am-12:45pm and 2:30-5:30pm. Sat. 9am-noon, year-round.

Post Office: Dimokratias Sq., next to the tourist office. In summer open Mon.-Fri. 7:30am-1pm and Mon., Tues., Thurs., Fri. 4-6pm, Sat. 7:30am-12:30pm. In winter, open Mon.-Fri. 7:30am-1:30pm and Mon., Tues., Thurs., Fri. 3:30-5:30pm, Sat. 7:30am-12:30pm.

CYTA: on Lord Byron St., the second right south of the tourist office. Open every day 24 hours.

Bus stations: Lefkaritis buses to Nicosia depart from the waterfront terminal on Athens Ave., south of the pier (tel. 52 14 2). Buses to Ayia Napa leave from behind the Marina Pub.

Service taxis: Makris, 13 King Paul St. (tel. 52 92 9), across from the tourist office. **Akropolis,** corner of Archbishop Makarios III Ave. and Grigoris Avxentiou Ave. (tel. 55 55 5), just north of the tourist office.

Police: Archbishop Makarios III Ave. (tel. 52 00 1) two doors down from the tourist office.

Hospital: off Grigoris Avxentiou St. (tel. 52 00 7).

Telephone Code: 041.

Accommodations

Since Larnaca attracts so few budget travelers, its two cheap places are often empty; you might be able to bargain them down a bit.

The Rainbow Inn, 140 Zenon Kiteus St. (tel. 55 87 4). The dirtiest, emptiest, and believe it or not, the cheapest at C£5.500 a single or C£9 a double, both with breakfast.

Harry's Inn, 75 Athens Ave. (tel. 54 45 3). As unappealing as the Rainbow, but on the ocean. Singles C£5.700, doubles C£9.600, triples C£14. A popular hangout for Arab sailors.

La Maison Belge, 103 Stadium St. (tel. 54 65 5). New, and quite clean. Singles C£7.500, doubles C£12, breakfast included.

Pavion Hotel, 11 St. Lazarus Sq. (tel. 56 68 8). Aging and drab, but more convenient than La Maison Belge. Doubles C£11.650, triples C£15.955. Private bath, air conditioning, and breakfast included.

Camping: Forest Beach Camping (tel. 22 41 4), 5 miles northeast of Larnaca on the road to Famagusta. Accessible only by taxi (C£1 from Larnaca). C£1.500 per tent.

Food and Entertainment

Most of Larnaca's restaurants, discos, and pinball arcades are on the beach between the pier and the fort. Try the following, both right next to the castle:

Dionyssos Restaurant. Generally expensive, but a good fish *meze* dish for C£2.500.

Megalos Pefkos. Cheaper than the Dionyssos for anything but *meze*. Meat dishes C£1.250-1.750.

Sights

Larnaca's biggest tourist attraction is its sandy central beach, which, though somewhat dirty, manages to satisfy the hordes of holiday-makers who bake on it every day. Larnaca's historical sights can easily be seen in a day. The **Medieval Fortress** at oceanside is the most imposing and noticeable of the lot. Built by the Turks during the seventeenth century, the castle contains a very small museum housing a tiny collection of artifacts and photographs from recent archeological digs in the district. The fortress is open Mon.-Sat. 7:30am-7:30pm or dusk, whichever comes first; admission 200mils. The first left north of the fortress will bring you to the **Cathedral of St. Lazarus.** The outside gates to the courtyard are always open; the church itself is open April-August every day 7:30am-1pm and 3-7pm. From September to March hours are 7:30am-1pm and 2:30-5pm. Larnaca has a two-room **archeological museum** between Kimon and Kilkis Sts., containing pottery found in the region, a beautiful assortment of Roman glass, and stone statuary. The museum is open Mon.-Sat. 7:30am-1:30pm; admission 200mils.

Undoubtedly Larnaca's most significant historical sight is the ruined city of **Kition.** It was long believed that the city was first settled by Phoenicians in the ninth century B.C., but excavations over the last twenty years have proven that the city dates to the early part of the thirteenth century B.C. To get to the ruins, follow Kimon St. away from the water to the Chryssopolitissa Church, cross in front of the church and go straight on Sakellariou St. This route will take you past the almost unrecognizable **Acropolis of Kition.** The ruins are open Mon.-Sat. 7:30am-7:30pm (sunset in winter); admission 200mils.

Near Larnaca

Twenty-six miles east of Larnaca are the small resort town of **Ayia Napa** and the beautiful—if crowded—white sands of **Nissi Beach.** Unfortunately, there are no inexpensive accommodations in Ayia Napa. Beach-lovers should take to the town **campground** (tel. 21 79 6), which charges C£1.500 for a site. If you prefer to stay in Larnaca, there is frequent bus service from the Marina Pub in Larnaca to the Nissi Beach Hotel (500mils one way). The last bus back to Larnaca leaves at 4:30pm, but arrive early if you want a seat.

Troodos Mountains

If you can tear yourself away from the beaches, the Troodos Mountains, with their forests of flat-topped pine trees, provide a welcome escape from the summer heat and are the perfect place for hikes or visits to the oldest monasteries on the island. On summer weekends and in August, nature-loving Cypriots flock to the mountains, so you can't be assured of solitude. Unfortunately, there is a shortage of blazed hiking trails through the woods; those that exist are either crowded or difficult to find. Since there are many well-traveled roads through the mountains, however, bushwhacking should be fairly safe. From mid-January to mid-March, Troodos itself becomes a ski retreat with three short ski lifts.

The village of **Troodos,** the hub of the region, has only a few restaurants and hotels, a bank, a post office, a CYTA office, a youth hostel (open July-September), and a campground. Beds at the **IYHF Youth Hostel** (tel. 15 24 9) are C£1.600 per night, breakfast included. Curfew at 10pm. A much more expensive alternative is the green-roofed **Jubilee Hotel** (tel. 21 64 7), 500 yards up the road from the hostel, with singles for C£7.400 and doubles for C£12, all with private bath and breakfast. The **Troodos Hotel** in the village center is cheaper (singles C£5.250, doubles C£10.500), but the obnoxious manager dislikes backpackers and has been known to overcharge young travelers. The cheapest place to stay in town is the **campground** half a mile down the hill on the road to Nicosia, which charges 750mils per tent. The toilets are disgusting and the showers are the iciest imaginable. The **Louis Restaurant** in town serves fine and inexpensive fare. The **telephone code** for Troodos is 054.

To reach Troodos from Limassol, take a KEMEK bus running daily (except Sunday) via Pano Platres, Prodhromos, and Pedhoulas, leaving from the corner of Enosis and Irene Sts. at 1pm. A village bus also runs daily to the same destinations and leaves from Eleftheria St. in Limassol at 2pm. In the summer, there are two minibuses a day to Troodos departing from the Karydas taxi station. One bus a day goes to Troodos from Nicosia (Mon.-Fri. only) from the KEMEK station on Leonidos St.; or you can take a village bus from the Constuza Bastion, next to the Bayraktar Mosque.

The villages in the area, all of which are kept fairly busy with tourists during the summer, somehow manage to retain their charm and relaxed pace of life. Most have hotels and guest houses in the C£3-4 range for singles, but if you prefer to camp it isn't difficult to find a satisfactory location outside of town. There are occasional local buses connecting the main villages, but hitching is very good. In the northern part of the Troodos mountain range, **Kakopetria** and its smaller neighbor **Galata** have five interesting Byzantine churches between them. Ten miles to the northeast of Kakopetria is the tiny **Assinou Church,** which houses some excellent twelfth-century frescoes. To visit the church, find the priest in the nearby village of Nikitare, and take him with you in a taxi (C£1 round trip). Ten miles southeast of Kakopetria is the church of **Panayia ton Arakou,** which also has some beautiful twelfth-century frescoes.

Kakopetria is serviced by frequent **Solea** buses from Nicosia; catch them at the Constuza Bastion.

Between the villages of Pano Platres and Prodhromos is the modern **Troodhitissa Monastery** (open June 15-Sept. 15 6am-noon and 2-8pm; no overnight guests). Between Troodos and Prodhromos is **Mt. Olympos** (elev. 6401 feet), the highest peak on the island—on a clear day you can see to the ocean. Just north of Prodhromos is the small village of **Pedhoulas,** with its **Church of Archangel Michael** and mural paintings from 1474. Just north of Pedhoulas are the villages of **Kalopanayiotis** and **Moutoullas,** with the nearby **Church and Monastery of St. John Lampadhistes.** If you're visiting one of the churches and it's closed, just ask the village priest to let you in; usually he'll be happy to oblige and give you an impromptu tour in the process.

A little more difficult to reach, but definitely worth the effort, are several places in the northwestern part of the mountain range. The palatial **Kykkos Monastery,** located about ten miles northwest of Pedhoulas, was first constructed in the eleventh century, but most of the structures you see are from the early nineteenth century (a fire destroyed much of the original complex). It is the wealthiest monastery on the island and possesses one of the three icons of the Virgin Mary attributed to St. Luke. You'll find it half-covered by a curtain, gilded in silver, and in a mother-of-pearl shrine just to the left of the church altar. Kykkos has gained new fame in this century as the monastery where Archbishop Makarios III lived. The grave of Cyprus' patriarchal figure is just a few miles away—ask at the monastery for directions. Because of the Archbishop's lifelong association with the monastery, the place is very popular with Cypriot pilgrims—you'll find a supermarket, an outrageously-priced tourist pavilion, and several sweet shops on the hilltop. If you are interested in spending the night, you must speak with Father Sofraniyos.

About ten miles northwest of Kykkos is the forest station at **Stavros tis Psokas.** It's often crowded with schoolchildren and city-dwellers by day, but the **guest house** provides a wonderful opportunity to enjoy near solitude in a natural setting. The guest house has only seven double rooms (C£3 each), so it's very wise to book in advance, especially in August (tel. 067/16 33 8 or 074/17 45 4). If the place is full, you can camp (500mils per tent, no reservation necessary). On the road between Kykkos and Stavros is the disappointing **Cedar Valley.** It's short, unexciting, and easy to miss—not worth much of a side trip. The area is famous as the home of the *moufflon,* a mountain goat found only in Cyrpus, but the animals are extremely reticent and rarely seen. **Kambos Company** buses, located across from the KEMEK station in Nicosia, go to Kykkos once a day except on weekends. From there, try hitching to Stavros tis Psokas. The Cyprus Tourism Organization publishes a large, helpful map of the central part of the mountain range which includes most of the sights and villages listed above. It's always available at the Pano Platres tourist office, and usually at the offices in Nicosia and Limassol, as well.

Northern Cyprus

If you speak to Cypriots living in the southern part of the island, they'll sadly admit that some of the most beautiful parts of their tiny homeland are in the northern 40% of Cyprus, occupied by the Turkish army since the summer of 1974. If you arrived in one of the southern cities, it is virtually impossible to cross over to the Turkish side of the island in order to spend a few days or proceed to Turkey. But if you don't have a Greek last name, you can visit the Turkish quarter for a day, provided that you return on the same day by 6:30pm. If you are late (a few minutes is all right), you will not be allowed to return to Cyprus. This prohibition is officially based on the following logic: all but a few of the hotels in the north existing before the 1974 war were owned by Greek Cypriots, so by spending the night in them you are using stolen property and thus breaking Cypriot law. If you don't return, the hassles will be enormous. The Cypriots are in general very understanding and hesitant to make visitors feel unwelcome, but if you violate the curfew you could face arrest and prosecution.

The only place in Cyprus where it is possible to cross the border is at the **Ledra Palace Hotel** (now occupied by the United Nations), just outside the walls on the western side of Nicosia. To get to the border, which opens at 8am, from Eleftheria Sq., follow the walls of the old city along Stassinos, Homer, Egypt, and Marcos Drakos Avenues. At UN Square, take the right fork. The Cypriot border police will record your passport number and confiscate any overnight luggage until you return. The front of the building, pockmarked with bullet holes, sandbagged, and barricaded with barbed wire, serves as a grim reminder of the recent and turbulent past.

Two hundred yards down the road is the Turkish checkpoint, where your passport number will again be recorded. The Turkish border guard will insist that you spend the day in Turkish Nicosia, claiming that Kyrenia or any other areas of the island are too far away and require at least an overnight visit. If you want to visit other parts of the island, you should fill out a visa application for a later date. When you cross over to the Turkish side a second time, the visa should be waiting for you. (The visa process takes 48 hours.) Visitors have been known to go beyond Nicosia without a visa, but this is *not* recommended. The border is closed on weekends and on Islamic holidays, so plan accordingly. If you have landed on the Turkish side of Cyprus, it is impossible to visit southern Cyprus. Turkish Cyprus uses the Turkish lire, although some places will accept Cypriot currency. Don't purchase any gifts while you're on the Turkish side. Though the Cypriot border agents are reluctant to enforce the dictum, it is technically forbidden to bring anything back. Finally, don't rent a car in southern Cyprus with the intention of taking it to Turkish Cyprus—the Turks have been known to impound them.

Turkish Nicosia (Lefkoşa)

As soon as you pass within the walls of Turkish Nicosia, you'll notice a change in the atmosphere: the buildings look a little older, the shops have more of a cluttered look to them, and people on the street will probably pay more attention to you. Toward the center of the old town, near the city market and the Selimiye Mosque, you'll notice the similarities with the Greek side—the food, the English-speaking locals—but you'll also be struck by the old-worldliness of the busy streets, filled with bicyclists and horse-drawn fruit and vegetable wagons.

To get to the **bank,** take your first left as you leave the Turkish checkpoint (or turn right if you've just been to the visa office). To get to the heart of the old city, take your first right as you leave the border, another right onto Tanzimat St. once you pass the walls of the old city, and then a left onto Müftü Ziyai St. On the right, you'll pass the small, simple **Arabahmet Mosque,** built in the early seventeenth century. Up ahead in the distance you'll be able to see the twin minarets of the Selimiye Mosque, and if you continue in this direction, you'll pass through most of the city's shopping district. On the left, you'll pass

Kyrenia Ave., which leads to **Atatürk Square,** and its Venetian column, taken from Salamis as a symbol of Venetian rule on the island. This is the main square on the Turkish side of the city, containing a Post Office, shared taxis to Kyrenia and Famagusta, a few travel agencies, and an English bookstore (Rustem's, just south of the square at 22-24 Kyrenia Ave.). The road continuing to Selimiye runs roughly parallel to the Green Line. If you look to your right down any given side street, you'll see murals depicting Turkish infantrymen in patriotic scenes.

One block before the mosque you'll pass **Asmaalti Street,** which leads to the **Buyuk Khan** (take the first left) and the **Kumarcilar Khani** (straight ahead), lodgings once used by Anatolian merchants and two of the city's most notable examples of Turkish architecture. The Kumarcilar Khani, the smaller of the two inns, is open in the morning and serves as a surrogate tourist office (the official one is several kilometers out of town), distributing helpful information on Nicosia and the rest of the Turkish quarter. Unfortunately, the map of the city they provide is virtually useless. The Buyuk Khan was closed for restoration in 1983 but should reopen in 1984.

The monumental **Selimiye Mosque,** formerly the St. Sophia Cathedral, is decidedly the most impressive building in Turkish Nicosia, with its ribbed vaulted archways, flying buttresses, and ornate carvings. Built between 1208 and 1326 in the French Gothic style, this cathedral was the place where the kings of Cyprus were crowned. It was converted into a mosque in the sixteenth century under Ottoman rule and has since declined due to benign neglect. If you can find Mustafa Biyikli, the caretaker, he'll give you a friendly, detailed tour of the place in English (a few hundred lire will suffice for the tour). A dirt-cheap covered **market** can be found next to the mosque.

Two museums worth visiting are the **Cyprus Turkish Ethnographic Museum** on Kyrenia Street (open Mon.-Fri. 8:30am-2pm; admission 20TL) and the **Museum of Barbarism,** outside the walls northeast of town—it's the Turkish answer to the Museum of National Struggle. For information and directions inquire at the Kumarcilar Khani.

To visit the city's lesser sights, you must ask for a guide at the Kumarcilar Khani. Regular opening times are impractical, since there are so few tourists. The guide simply unlocks doors for you, and you pay only the regular 20-40TL admission fees.

Kyrenia (Girne)

Kyrenia, or "Girne" in Turkish, may be the most appealing harbor town on the island. The newer part of the city, dominated by the luxury Dome Hotel, is not so memorable, but the old port nearby retains an idyllic setting, with the Kyrenia Castle at one end and unobtrusive cafes and stone buildings of different colors surrounding the rest of the harbor.

The **Kyrenia Castle,** believed to have been built by the Byzantines in the seventh century A.D., has winding passages and stairways to explore. Its large interior courtyard is occasionally used for summer theater productions, and several rooms on the eastern side have been converted into a **shipwreck museum.** Just a few amphora remain, but part of the hull of a 2300-year-old vessel remains relatively intact. Both the castle and the museum are open every day 8am-1pm and 2:30-6pm; admission to each 35TL. Also on the harbor is a modest **Folk Art Museum** (open Mon.-Fri. 8am-1pm and 4-6pm; admission 35TL). Sometimes it closes at odd hours for no apparent reason.

Buses for Kyrenia leave from the parking lot outside and to the left of the Kyrenia Gate in Nicosia. More convenient and comfortable are the minibuses that leave every fifteen minutes from the Tufan Turizm sign on Kyrenia Ave. at the southern end of the Ethnographical Museum (60TL one way).

Eight miles from Kyrenia is **St. Hilarion Castle,** the most impressive of the three fortresses situated high in the Kyrenia range—the other two being **Buffavento** and **Kantara Castles.** St. Hilarion, now in ruins, owes its construction first to the monks, then to the Byzantines, and finally to the Lusignans. As recently as 1974, the Turkish Army utilized its location at the top of jagged cliffs as an observation post; it forever offers a scenic overlook for the northern coast and the Kyrenia range. The castle is open from 8am-6pm, accessible by bus or *dolmuş* (service taxi). Take the St. Hilarion turn-off on the Nicosia-Kyrenia road, five miles south of Kyrenia, and then walk or try to catch a lift the remaining three miles.

Bellapais Abbey, four miles southeast of Kyrenia, is an exceptional cluster of buildings in various states of preservation. Built originally by monks of the Order of St. Augustine in the late twelfth century, the hillside sanctuary offers a commanding view of the surrounding countryside. The fourteenth-century central courtyard with its elegant arcades, the large empty church to the south (closed to visitors) and the nearly flawless refectory on the north side suggest some of the Abbey's prosperity in earlier days. The Abbey is open every day 9am-1:30pm and 2:30-6pm; admission 35TL. Be sure to ask for the small pamphlet (free) describing the site. There is infrequent bus service to Bellapais from Kyrenia, or take a taxi for 450TL each way, no charge for waiting.

Famagusta (Gazi Magusa)

Forty kilometers east of Nicosia, Famagusta is uniformly regarded as the most enchanting city in Cyprus. Greek Cypriots will invariably describe it as the most sorely missed possession on their troubled island. The ancient walled city contains a treasure-trove of lovely churches and age-old tombs, while the new city is oddly punctuated by brand new Turkish monuments, war-scarred buildings, and craters left by fallen shells. A map of the old city is essential—be sure to pick one up at the Kumarcilar Khani in Nicosia.

To get to Famagusta from Nicosia, take a **Lozan** bus from the office inside and to the east of Kyrenia Gate (approximately every hour on the hour until 5pm; 110TL one way). If you wish to visit both cities in one day, **Kombos** taxis leave from Cumhuriyet St. in Kyrenia, but try to book a few hours in advance (230TL one way).

If you're coming from Turkey and thus will be spending your time in the Turkish quarter, ferries travel to both Kyrenia and Famagusta. The *Ertürk* leaves for Kyrenia from Taşucu on Tues., Thurs., and Sat. at 9:30am (2500TL one way, deck class for students). A Mersin-Famagusta boat operates year round (3280TL, cabins only, no student discount).

WESTERN COAST OF TURKEY

$1 U.S. = 250TL   **1 lira (TL) = $.004**

What is a chapter on the western coast of Turkey doing in a guide book to Greece? What does Turkey have to do with Greece? More than you might think. Most Americans visit the Aegean and roam from one crowded island to the next, unaware that the Turkish Coast offers most of what they look for in Greece: superb archeological sites, remote beaches, and idyllic coastline scenery. If you can afford to travel in Greece, you can easily afford Turkey: restaurants and accommodations are often two to four times cheaper. If Turkey sounds too far away to fit into your itinerary, take a closer look at your map. Practically kissing the Turkish Coast, several Greek islands—Lesvos, Chios, Samos, Patmos, Kos, Simi, Rhodes, and Kastelorizo—are only one or two miles away. All but two of them have frequent boats to Turkey. The history and geography of the Turkish Coast and the Greek islands immediately adjoining it are deeply and intricately related; most of the islands were part of Turkey until 1912.

A few misconceptions have tended to prevent tourists from crossing over to Turkey. Westerners sometimes associate Turkey with the Arab countries of the Middle East, assuming that all of the violence, crime, and Muslim extremism often attributed to the latter countries apply to Turkey as well. As far as the western coast of Turkey is concerned, nothing could be further from the truth. The bus system is efficient and clean, foreign languages are widely and eagerly spoken, and the Turkish people are for the most part embarrasingly hospitable and scrupulously honest. Since a great deal of Greek cuisine derives from Turkish cooking, food in Turkey resembles that of Greece; often a wider selection is available. The only real obstacle to a visit from Greece to the Turkish Coast is the exorbitant cost of the ferries that make the short crossing. But the cheaper cost of living and traveling in Turkey should more than make up for the expense incurred.

To and From Turkey

The most reliable connections from Greece to Turkey are from Samos and Rhodes. The boats from Chios, Lesvos, and Kastelorizo run only in summer and their frequency depends upon local tourist demand. Turkish boats go year round, daily in summer, from Kos, but the local authorities do their best to conceal this fact. The details on all of these boats are listed below according to Greek island. From Athens, there are daily flights to Izmir and daily trains to Istanbul. If you have a Eurail or InterRail pass, the cheapest (and the slowest) approach is to take the train to Istanbul, and then a bus to the coast. Buses in Turkey are so cheap that this method entails a considerable savings. (A bus from Istanbul to Kuşadasi, for example, is only $6, whereas a boat (indirect) from Athens costs $42.)

From Samos Town: In summer, at least two boats a day travel to Kuşadasi. The *Samos Express* goes Sun., Mon., and Tues. at 8am. The *Stella* goes daily at 8am. A Turkish boat sails daily at 5pm. In the off-season, three boats a week make the trip. All boats cost $25 one way, $30 round trip; 10% student discount, 20% group discount (over 16 people). Two-hour trip. The travel agencies along the waterfront all sell tickets. Turn in passports the night before.

377

From Pythagoria (on Samos): The *Samos Express* goes Thurs. and Sat. to Kuşadasi. Same prices as from Samos Town. Summer only.

From Rhodes: In summer, three boats daily (except Sun.) travel to Marmaris. Off-season, four or five boats weekly. Departure times are never fixed until the day before. The harbor police and the NTOG generally avoid providing information on the boats. For departure schedule (go the day before), tickets, and to turn in your passport (night before), go to the **Turkish Maritime Lines Office**, 15 N. Plastira St. (tel. 23 39 5 or 24 29 4). One flight up, across from the shopping arcade next to the Hotel Spartalis. Open 9:30am-noon, 6-8pm. One-way fare is 1500dr. Three-hour trip.

From Kos: Only Turkish boats travel to Bodrum. Everyone will tell you they don't exist. There is no official schedule because of the strained relations. Contact Mr. Politis, on the third floor above the restaurant to the right of the Customs Office, at the corner of the block. He will arrange tickets, customs, and baggage. In summer the boats run daily. In the off-season, usually Mon., Wed., and Fri. Departures are supposed to be 12:30pm, but are often closer to 3pm. When the ferry arrives (the only boat flying a Turkish flag), Politis will organize the boarding. In 1983, the fare was 1400dr one way.

From Chios: From July 15 to Sept. 15, a ferry runs three times a week to nearby Cesme; from June 1 two times weekly; once a week in May and last half of Sept. Fare 1500dr one way, 2200dr round trip with open return; you must leave passport with travel agent one day in advance.

From Lesvos: Boats to Ayvalik leave three or four times a week May-Oct.: Schedule varies. 2½ hour trip; fare 1500dr one way, 2500dr round trip.

From Kastelorizo: Local fishing boats will take you to Kaş. The trip takes only a half-hour (two nautical miles) and costs around 500dr per person. It is also relatively easy to hitch a ride on a yacht from here to Kaş.

From Cyprus: Boats three times a week to Taşucu and Mersin. Every Tues. a boat goes from Famagusta to Fethiye and Kuşadasi.

From Ancona, Italy: Departs every Sat. at 8pm for Izmir. One-way deck-class fare $100. Contact Alfredo Fritelli, Piazza S. Maria 2, Ancona, P.O. Box 263 for tickets in Ancona.

Turkish Maritime Lines: A relaxing way to tour the coast. Consider an Aegean and Mediterranean cruise. About every two weeks from June through September, the *Karadeniz* leaves Istanbul for a variety of Aegean and Mediterranean ports. Not a regular ferry service, the comfortable ship sails only at night, giving you a full day in each port. From Istanbul, you should buy tickets at least a week in advance; there are usually spaces on the return journey to Istanbul. On the lower classes, fares are incredibly cheap—the higher classes have compulsory meals and are prohibitively expensive. C-class involves 2-4 bed cabins, D-class 8-10 bed cabins and E-class 40-bed dormitories in the bowels of the ship (strictly for the impoverished). The boat docks at Kuşadasi, Bodrum, Fethiye, and Antalya, among other places, and it is possible to buy a ticket between any two points on the itinerary. Despite what the brochure says, there's no deck-class fare, although if you have a sleeping bag, the deck is the coolest place to sleep. This ship includes ice-cold water fountains, several restaurants, lounges, and plenty of friendly Turkish tourists.

Transportation routes, rates, and discounts within and to Turkey are currently in a state of flux. For up-to-date information, write to the **Turkish Tourist and Information Office,** 821 United Nations Plaza, New York, NY

10017. They'll send you boat, train, and plane schedules. **Turkish Airlines (THY)** has regular service to Turkey from European and Middle Eastern cities, and offers discounts of 60% on international and 10% on domestic flights to students holding an ISIC and under 27 years of age. In Istanbul, they're at 200 Cumhuriyet Cad. Elmadag (tel. 146 20 61).

If you have a railpass, take the train as far as Alexandroupolis (Greece) and ride the bus from there (Eurail and InterRail not valid in Turkey). If you hitch to Turkey, try to make Istanbul in one ride from Kavala (Greece), as the road is terrible and traffic minimal. Also, make sure that the driver's car is not stamped into your passport as your own. If it is, the owner can make a mountain of money selling his car illegally in Turkey, and you'll be buried in an avalanche of red tape trying to leave the country without it.

Getting Around

Getting around Turkey is a budget traveler's dream. There are frequent and direct buses between all sizeable cities—all are Mercedes Benzes and incredibly cheap. They are run by private companies, but all prices are fixed by the government. You will need to go from booth to booth to piece together a complete schedule: one bus company will not divulge departure times of other companies. Exchanging your ticket can be difficult. For long trips, there are always overnight buses; request a window seat in the middle of the bus, away from the driver's radio and behind the overhead window. For a frequent run you'll have to buy a seat an hour in advance. For a less frequent trip, buy the ticket the day before. You can reserve a seat by phone. Restaurant stops along the way will delay arrival.

Despite the low fares, trains within Turkey are no bargain. They are extremely slow and comfort is minimal except in first- and second-class *couchettes*.

Extensive shared taxi service *(dolmuş)* follow fixed routes between small towns. They leave as soon as they fill up *(dolmuş* means stuffed) and are almost as cheap as buses. Best of all, you can get on and off anywhere you like—salvation for the weary hitchhiker.

Hitching in Turkey is easy and interesting. If you're hitching between towns, locals invariably offer rides. For long distances between major cities, truckers are your best bet. If you're asked to pay for the ride, offer half of what the trip costs by bus. The hitching signal is a waving hand.

Orientation and Practical Information

Money: Turkey's inflation rate now stands at 25%, so expect substantial price increases from those listed in this book.

As we go to press, the black market exchange rate is only slightly better than the official rate—and definitely not worth the risk. The government has cracked down on the black market; you need your bank receipts to change back your Turkish money at the border and sometimes to buy boat or train tickets (the ticket price will double if you cannot produce a receipt when they check). Always be sure to have enough money. Even in large cities, banks are open only Mon.-Fri. till 5pm, and close for lunch from noon to 1 or 1:30pm. Turkey has no 24-hour currency exchanges at train stations, although in major tourist areas, there are places to change money on weekends.

If you're coming from Greece, change your drachmas before arriving. The select banks that accept drachmas invariably exchange them at an absurd rate. It is hard to get change for bills of 1000TL or more at museum entrances and cheap restaurants. If you're in desperate need of money, don't try to have it wired to Turkey. It will take several weeks at the least, and you'll probably have to take all or most in lira. If you do have money sent, no bank will give you more than half of your money in hard currency—more likely only a third. They'll insist that they have no foreign dollars, so you'll have to insist that you've done this before and that they do. Remember that American Express offices are not banks, so you can't have money wired or money orders cashed there.

Drugs: *Avoid drugs in Turkey.* The horror stories of lengthy prison sentences and dealer-informers are true. Embassies are generally helpless in such cases. The minimum sentence for even the smallest quantity is sixteen months, and nothing compares with a Turkish prison. Turkish law also provides for "guilt by association"; those in the company of the person caught are subject to prosecution. And they mean it.

Language: In the major coastal resorts, everyone speaks some of everything. Inland, some people speak English in the big cities, but they are few and far between in the provinces. French, pantomime, and especially German are often helpful. Buy a phrase book, such as Berlitz' *Turkish for Travelers*, and keep a pen and pad handy for addresses, phrases, or numbers. Keep in mind that when a Turk raises his chin and shuts his eyes he means "no," and when he waves his hand up and down, he means "come."

You've probably never heard anything quite like the Turkish language—there is nothing quite like it. A branch of the Ural-Altaic group, it does not belong to the Indo-European family of languages. Technically, it is a relative of Finnish, Hungarian, and Mongolian, but it has also been influenced by the classical Arabic of the Qur'an. Nevertheless, you can learn a few words of Turkish without too much difficulty, and appreciative smiles will reward your efforts everywhere you go. Here are the most basic expressions: Thank you: *teşekkur ederim;* hello: *merhaba;* good evening: *iyi akşamlar.* "Good bye" is a little more complicated—the departing guest says *allaha ismarladik* and the host responds *gülegüle.* If you speak German, Langenscheidt's has an excellent book on Turkish for beginners.

Tourist Offices and Hotels: Throughout the Turkish Coast, you'll find well-organized tourist offices where some English is usually spoken. They can help you find accommodations. It's best to see several places before deciding, as cleanliness varies widely (a proprietor should gladly show you a few rooms). If posted prices seem exorbitant, look disappointed and politely bargain. Make sure your hotel has water before paying, and be prepared for water breakdowns. Avoid rooms facing the street—nearby cafes and discos blast sleep-banishing music late into the night. If traveling in winter, check the heating first. Camping is a cheap alternative, and very popular among Turks. Although sites are cramped, they are the only safe alternative. Sometimes the best place to obtain a hot shower is at the local campground.

Sights: Museums, archeological sights, and monuments in Turkey are generally open from 9am-5pm; many are closed on Mon. or Tues. Most cost 60TL per person. There are no student discounts, but Wed. and weekends are half-price days at some places. To bring in cameras, you must pay another 100TL, unless you smuggle them by the ticket-taker. Cinemas and concerts sometimes offer half-price tickets to students.

Mail and Telephones: Unfortunately, mail to or from North America takes two to three weeks. Post Offices (known as PTTs) are usually open Mon.-Fri. 8:30am-noon and 1-5:30pm. A town's central post office *(merkez postanesi)* is often open Mon.-Sat. 8am-midnight; Sun. 9am-7pm. In big cities the post office is open 24 hours. Poste Restante should be addressed to the *Merkez Postanesi.* Be sure to check under both your first and your last name for mail. Also, specify *Uçak Ile* (air mail) when requesting stamps, and write it on your mail (or just ask for aerogrammes). Telephone calls, including international calls, can be placed at the central post office, but expect to wait two hours for a call to get through to the U.S. from anywhere but Istanbul or Ankara. Costs are upwards of 500TL for three minutes. Telegram charges are about 70TL per word.

Amenities: There are washing facilities at every mosque. Toilet paper (you should always carry your own supply) and other toiletries are cheap and readily available. An exception is tampons, which you should bring.

The Rest of Turkey: For more information on parts of Turkey not covered in the following chapter, consult the section on Turkey in *Let's Go: Europe*.

Women

> *In some places I have seen women who put a piece of cloth over their heads to hide their faces, and who turn their backs or huddle on the ground when a man passes by. What is the meaning of this behavior? Gentlemen, can the mothers and daughters of a civilized nation adopt this strange manner, this barbarous posture? It is a spectacle that makes the nation an object of ridicule. It must be remedied at once.*
>
> —Mustafa Kemayal Atatürk

Atatürk's "at once" has not yet arrived for the majority of Turkish women. However, the larger resorts on the western coastline represent some of the most progressive and Westernized sectors of the country; this is reflected in the relative emancipation of the female population. Nonetheless, especially in small towns, men and women tend to socialize separately, men at çay shops and women at home. Women are on the same legal and political footing as men in western Turkey, but ancient traditions fade slowly. Although nothing prevents a woman from entering a mosque, the force of tradition and an unwritten law decree that a mosque is a public place: a place where only men congregate.

As a foreign woman, you will be free to spend time with men and women wherever you please—but expect a few eyebrows to be raised in local cafes and to attract attention if you go about unaccompanied, particularly at night. If you've heard warnings about Turkish men, they probably won't apply to the Western Coast. Shorts can easily be worn in Kuşadasi, Bodrum, Marmaris, and Kaş, the four major resorts—and, of course, around any beach. Elsewhere, particularly in smaller villages, you may wish to cover your knees, not so much for safety as to avoid offending the locals. If you decide to do any nude sunbathing you will become an object of attention; try to pick a very secluded spot. Women unaccompanied by a male should be especially cautious and follow a few basic rules, mostly dictated by common sense. Don't hitchhike, and anticipate spending a little more on accommodations. If you wish to visit mosques, carry a scarf to slip on. Do not go out alone at night outside main tourist areas.

Despite the need for these precautions, the Turkish Coast is not a difficult place for women to travel. In general, a woman traveling about the country is accorded a great deal of respect. You will rarely have to stand on a bus or be crowded in a dolmuş, and can expect to be treated in a polite and discreet fashion.

Life on the Turkish Coast

It is difficult to imagine a people more friendly and welcoming than the Turks. Once you leave the major resorts along the coast, their warmth and generosity will often astound you. People may shower you with small gifts—cigarettes, glasses of tea, freshly picked fruit—and eagerly inquire after your impressions of Turkey, your travel plans, and your health in some mixture of German, French, and English. The first reaction of most Western visitors to this surge of hospitality is to view it with suspicion. However, except for a few hustlers in heavily-touristed towns such as Kuşadasi, the hospitality is usually genuine. You may wish to carry a few packs of American cigarettes with you since they are a highly-valued status symbol and provide an appropriate way of reciprocating favors. They are available in the duty-free shops on the ports of Kuşadasi and Marmaris. Beyond that, especially in the countryside, all you can do is face the onslaught of Turkish hospitality. Succumb, relax, and enjoy.

Food

Turkish cuisine is generally fresh, cheap, and painstakingly prepared. And Turkey is one of the few places left in the Mediterranean where eating inexpensively still entitles the budget traveler to sample a great variety of dishes. In selecting food at a restaurant, it's customary to go to the kitchen yourself and take a look before choosing. Try *tarhana çorbasi,* a tomato-yogurt soup; *erişteli corba,* a tomato-based noodle soup; different varieties of *pilav* (rice, sometimes served with a light sauce); and *pilaki,* navy beans in a tomato sauce, often with pieces of meat added; *manti,* small ravioli covered with a yogurt and peanut oil sauce, sprinkled with red pepper (a specialty of Bodrum); and last but not least, *muçver,* a delicious experience involving breaded zucchini spiced and deep-fried (you don't have to like zucchini to love it).

Most famous, however, and very popular in Turkey, are the *dolma,* or stuffed vegetables, served hot or cold. They're usually filled with chopped meat, rice, onions, and seasoning. The common varieties are *biber dolmasi* (stuffed peppers); *domates dolmasi* (stuffed tomatoes); and *patlican dolmasi* (stuffed eggplant). *Imam bayildi* is eggplant filled with onions, parsley, and tomatoes and served cold. Salads composed of the freshest vegetables, available anywhere along the coast, include *çoban salatasi* (cucumber and tomato salad) and *karişik salata*—both can be very spicy. Turkish yogurt is a little sweeter than Greek yogurt along the Aegean Coast, but along the Mediterranean Coast it is quite bitter. Available everywhere *zeytin* (olives) are terrific.

Anywhere you go, you'll find barbecue joints, specializing in *döner kebab* (slices cut from a leg of lamb roasting on a spit) and *şiş kebab* (skewered chunks of lamb). In the coastal resorts the favorite is *balik kebab,* or more affectionately, fish kebab (skewered cubes of fish roasted with lemons, tomatoes, and green peppers). Naturally, along the coast the speciality of most restaurants is seafood. Unfortunately, it is usually quite expensive. Along the Aegean coast, however, *kalamari* (squid) can be eaten for a reasonable price; along the Mediterranean Coast, particularly around Kaş, the best buy is *sokor*—a very tasty and inexpensive regional fish.

Be sure to try a *menemem,* a delicious kind of loose omelette with tomatoes and onions. *Pide* is a distant Turkish relative of pizza—flat bread served with your choice of eggs, meat, tomatoes, cheese, or spices. Or try *köfte,* a spicy member of the meatball family—it comes either skewered and roasted or served in a tomato broth, with potatoes and vegetables.

For dessert, an endless selection of pastries—*baklava* (a flaky pastry jammed with nuts and soaked in honey), *kadaif* (a shredded wheat dough filled with nuts and sugar), and *halva* (a sesame seed and honey mush) are the most popular choices. Of course, there is always Turkish taffee. Most restaurants also serve some sort of fresh fruit or melon. *Lale* (pudding) or *sutak* (rice pudding) are both excellent. Most Turks draw out their evening meals interminably (beginning at 7pm and ending around 11pm). Those with strong stomachs throw down a few glasses of *raki* (a licorice-flavored liqueur) and stagger home.

It is difficult to spend a day in Turkey without pausing at a *çay* shop and ordering a glass of *çay* (a small tea) or *duvle çay* (a large tea). Ironically, *kahve* (Turkish coffee) drunk so widely throughout Greece and the Middle East, is difficult to procure and expensive, due to the high import tax on coffee. Nevertheless, you'll soon learn to adjust to a heavy diet of tea (it is grown along the Black Sea Coast and is always delicious). For snacking, try *börek* (layers of cheese and light dough). Bottled drinks include excellent *meyve suyu* (fruit juice); *meyveli gazoz* (Turkish soda), which some find too sweet; *ayran* (a very popular mixture of yogurt and milk); *soda* (soda water); *su* (good old bottled mineral water); and *maden suyu* (carbonated mineral water). *Bira* (beer) is very popular: *Efes-pilsen* and *Tekelbeyaz* are light, while *Tekel siyah* is dark—and all are pretty good at around 80-100TL. Turkey has a sizeable domestic wine crop and all the coastal resorts are well stocked with the stuff.

Holidays and Festivals

Everything closes on the national holidays: April 22 and 23, May 19, August 30, and October 29. During the month-long Islamic holiday *Ramadan*, pious Muslims will not eat, drink, smoke, or travel between dawn and sunset. You'd hardly notice it in the coastal resort towns, but in smaller towns and inland only one or two restaurants may be open during the day. It's a lot easier to get hotel rooms during this period, even at the resorts. Large celebrations mark the holiday's conclusion, known as *Bayram;* it becomes practically impossible to get bus and train tickets and hotel rooms. They've all been booked weeks in advance. The feast of *Bayram* lasts three days. Ramadan will last from early June to early July in 1984.

The spring and summer months are the time for festivals along the western coast. In the last week of April, the **Spring Festival** is held in Manisa. **May Day**, the feast of spring, is also celebrated by the Turks. It marks the beginning of a month of festivities along the coast. The first of these, beginning May 1, is the **festival of Ephesus.** A series of theater, music, and folklore festivals are all held in the remains of ancient Greek theaters. Next come the festivals of *Silifke, Marmaris,* and *Bergama.* In June, the one-week **Trojan Horse Festival** is held at Çanakkale. On the 29th of June the **feast day of St. Peter** is honored at Antakya by ceremonies in the grotto of St. Peter. On the 15th of August, the **Assumption** is celebrated near Selçuk in the House of the Virgin Mary. From August 20 to September 10, a huge international fair, the largest commercial event of the Near East, is held in Izmir.

Islamic Architecture

Most of the monuments discussed in the following chapter were built during ancient Greek and Roman times. Most of Turkey's finest Islamic architectural treasures lie farther inland and beyond the scope of our coverage. However, every village throughout the Turkish Coast has at least one or two mosques. Non-Muslims are permitted to visit any place of worship in Turkey, although you will find that you are less welcome at some. The Turkish word for mosque is *cami* (or *camii*); the *cami* serves as the Muslim place of study and worship. The older mosques represent the finest achievements of Turkish art and architecture. You'll notice two styles: the more Oriental, Syrian-influenced buildings, with many columns in the interior supporting a low-ceilinged simple structure; and the great Ottoman mosques—symmetrical, lofty structures with great domes and sometimes elaborate tile decoration and stained glass. In both types, look for the *mihrab* (prayer niche) in the center of the east wall pointing towards Mecca and the *minbar* (pulpit). Sometimes these are lavishly carved, tiled, or otherwise adorned. In larger cities, you may also see a *turbe* (mausoleum) or *medrase* (Koranic school).

History

In ancient times, the western coast of Turkey was very much a part of the Greek world. Its fate was inextricably entangled with that of the whole of Hellenic civilization. Paralleling the destiny of other parts of Greece, the coast was conquered by invading Persians in the sixth century B.C.; two centuries later the colossal war machine of Alexander the Great followed the Persians. Under Alexander's reign, great metropolises began to spring up along the coast. The climax of their prosperity was reached during the period from the second century B.C. onwards when the coastline was the commercial and political core of the Roman province of Asia Minor. Subsequently, under the rule of the emperor at Constantinople, the ports along the coast continued to thrive, constituting an integral part of Byzantium.

With the arrival of the Turks the ports along the coast began to diminish in importance as cities in the north and east became the major commercial centers. From then on, the history of the coast became tied to that of the Turkish nation as a whole.

The Seljuk Turks originally hailed from Mongolia. They were a restless people, and over the course of the first millenium A.D. they gradually migrated westwards, achieving notoriety for their prowess in battle along the way. In the eleventh century A.D., they began to settle in the plains of central Anatolia, the region that was eventually to become the heartland of their permanent home. It was not until the advent of the Ottoman dynasty of sultans, several centuries later, that Turkish dominion over the entire Near East flourished. With the accession of Mehmet II, an enthusiastic patron of the arts and a great modernizer, the Turkish Empire began to assume the contours of a major world power. Mehmet II overpowered Byzantium and marched into the city of Constantinople in 1453. Five years later he declared the city, newly dubbed Istanbul, to be the capital of the rapidly-swelling Ottoman Empire. Under the reign of Suleymein the Magnificent (1520-66), the Empire grew until the sultan's dominion stretched from Algeria through North Africa and the Near East to Iraq, and all the way around the Black Sea, encompassing the Balkan countries as well. The Crusaders managed to maintain a tenuous grip on the southern Aegean Coast, including Bodrum, Marmaris, and certain other Middle Eastern ports. In 1522, however, they were finally expurgated from the region.

The subsequent centuries witnessed the gradual decline of the Ottoman Empire. Attempts at modernizing the Empire and placing checks on the rampant corruption that marred its existence were doomed to failure. The final death blow came with the disastrous political blunder of allying the Empire with Germany in World War I.

Politics

> *The movement of the Turks through the centuries always maintained a straight course. We have always marched from the East to the West.*
>
> —Mustafa Kemayal Atatürk, First President of the Republic of Turkey, 1923-38.

Atatürk wanted his country to continue marching boldly in the westerly direction as he had planned, but Turkey has proven too firmly bound to age-old traditions to whole-heartedly adopt the modern secular culture of the West. At the crossroads of two continents, Turkey is a curious and exciting blend of the Oriental and the Occidental. This fact is reflected in every facet of Turkish life.

Atatürk ("Father of the Turks") was a general in World War I, a hero who led the victory at Gallipoli. He almost single-handedly carved the Turkish state out of the collapsed Ottoman Empire. Everywhere you go along the Turkish Coast a statue of Atatürk greets you in the town square. His portrait peers down at you from every public office, and the main street of most large cities is named Atatürk Caddesi. Although Atatürk is genuinely loved and admired by a great many Turks, the ubiquity of his face and figure is rooted in the contemporary political situation as well. The massive propaganda effort by the present government to keep Atatürk's popularity alive is an effective way to generate sympathy and tolerance for its own policies.

On October 29, 1923, the Republic of Turkey was proclaimed and Atatürk was elected its first president. During the next fifteen years, he succeeded in transforming the shattered remnants of the decaying Ottoman Empire into the foundations of a vital modern nation. Equating modernization with rapid westernization and secularization, he abolished the Caliphate, outlawed Muslim tribunals, and changed the alphabet from Arabic to Roman. Naturally, these sweeping measures met with the greatest resistance from the religious orthodoxy. Atatürk even forbade the *meuzzins* (prayer callers) to sing their prayers in the classical Arabic of the Qur'an, decreeing that they could only be recited in modern Turkish. Since his death in 1938, there has been some backlash and a relaxation of his reforms. And since World War II, the country has been struggling with its two-party system of democracy. Recent governments have been faced with the task of maintaining restraints on an explosive situation while facing strong opposition from both flanks—orthodox Muslim extremists on the right and determined Marxists on the left. These factions shoulder the guilt for a staggering amount of cold-blooded violence in the course of the past several decades. On three occasions the military has taken power after deciding the civilian government was incompetent to rule the country. The last takeover was in September, 1980, after politically-related street killings had reached a national average of forty per week. Most Turks seem to welcome the stability that has resulted from the military government's harsh measures, which have almost completely eradicated the terrorist violence. One direct consequence of these measures seems to be the marked increase in tourism over the last three years. Along with the political "undesirables," most of the hustlers have been cleared out of the major tourist areas by severe police crackdowns. Do not be surprised to find that many of the Turks in the coastal resorts whose livelihood depends upon tourism are disturbingly enthusiastic about some of the present government's brutal policies. And don't be surprised that many people would rather discuss anything other than domestic politics.

In order to revive the struggling economy, the government has levied hefty taxes on all foreign imports. Anything not produced on Turkish soil—coffee, whiskey, cameras, vehicles, blue jeans, etc.—can easily be sold on the street for at least double its value.

Literature

Several supplementary books may be worthwhile for longer visits: try *Ancient Cities of Western Anatolia* and *Historic Treasures of Turkey*. Hachette's

Blue Guide is dull but thorough. For related pleasure reading, pick up a biography of Atatürk or Homer's *Iliad;* both make perfect traveling companions.

The Aegean Coast

An ominous warning is beginning to spread among tourists throughout the Greek Isles: Beware the Turkish Aegean Coast. Once you begin to explore the crystal clear waters of this handsome, winding coastline and the magnificent archeological wealth of sumptuous Hellenistic cities, you'll soon find there is no turning back. It's like a bottle of *raki,* the local liquorice-flavored liqueur—after even a small taste, it is impossible to stop until you're completely intoxicated. But rumor has it that a few disciplined visitors are able to proceed without fear of succumbing to the region's lure. Apparently, the risk is considerably less if one is completely unmoved by the spectacle of vast, deserted beaches and stunning examples of well-preserved ancient Greek and Roman architecture. However, those of you who are not immune to such temptations—be forewarned! The danger is especially immediate if you happen to find yourself on one of the following Greek islands: Lesvos, Chios, Samos, or Kos. You're just a couple of hours away from splendid beaches around Çesme, Kuşadasi, and Bodrum; and only a few more minutes from the extensive Hellenistic ruins at Pergammon, Ephesus, Priene, Miletus, Didyma, Aphrodisias, and Hieropolis—to mention only the finest of the innumerable archeological sites.

You may be wondering why the most superb remnants of Greek civilization are to be found in Turkey. During the early stages of the classical Greek era, the ports along the Ionian coast of Asia Minor formed the fringe of Hellenic civilization, serving as the outposts for trade with the Orient. Beginning with the rule of Alexander the Great, the ports became the focal points of commerce along the major trade routes across the ancient world. These ports continued to grow in size and accumulate wealth while the rest of Greek civilization declined. As the Greek city-states on the mainland continued to quarrel with one another, and were subsequently plundered by the Romans, the commercial and cultural center of ancient Greece gradually shifted to the long column of Asian coastal cities and to the neighboring islands.

The Aegean Coast of Asia Minor also played a crucial role in the historical development of Western culture. The thriving trade with the East in goods and spices led to an unpredecented appreciation of new customs and ideas through exposure to other civilizations, cultures, and languages. The result of this vast cultural and intellectual exchange proved to be as enduring as it was fertile. For not only was this coastline the world's first international marketplace, it was also a cradle of Western philosophy, mathematics, and science. This was where the seeds of Hellenic, and hence modern European, civilization were first cultivated—particularly in the teachings of Heraclitus of Ephesus and in the works of the Ionian School of Miletus, led by Thales, Anaximander, Anaximenes, and Anaxagoras. The thriving metropolises of the Asia Minor Coast also played a pivotal role in the second major revolution in Western culture. The Apostle Paul came here to preach the newly revealed teachings of Christianity and the good news rapidly spread up and down the coast. The new religion eventually gave birth to the Byzantine Empire when in 330 A.D. the Roman Emperor Constantine proclaimed Christianity the official state religion and christened its capital Constantinople (the present-day city of Istanbul).

Although Islam later replaced Christianity as the dominant religion along the Aegean Coast, Christian pilgrims still converge here to visit the seven churches of Asia Minor, referred to in Revelations 2-7.

The Aegean Coast of Turkey has ceased to be the lively and populous region it was in ancient times. The sea has receded, leaving the remains of the ancient ports peacefully stranded some seven or eight kilometers inland. Today, the shores are dotted with tranquil villages and lined with dramatic coastal scenery, interrupted by only one large city (Izmir) and a handful of resorts, all easily accessible from Greece.

Kuşadasi

If you're looking for cheap hotels, secluded beaches, inexpensive crafts, and genuine Turkish atmosphere, then the port of Kuşadasi, only two hours by ferry from Samos, is not the best place to go, for you can do better on all of these counts almost anywhere else along the Turkish coast. Nevertheless, Kuşadasi is a pleasant place to stay. It's a comfortable and ideally situated base from which you can take a week's worth of daytrips to see beautiful natural scenery and explore a host of fascinating archeological sites. A national park, a beautiful lake, the bizarre rock formations at Pamukkale, and the ancient ruins at Ephesus, Selçuk, Priene, Miletus, Didyma, Aphrodisias, and Hieropolis are each near enough for a single-day excursion from Kuşadasi.

Kuşadasi, or "bird island," takes its name from the small island crowned by a Selçuk fortress guarding the mouth of the harbor. Although birds are no longer in abundance here, Kuşadasi retains in some respects the characteristics of an island. Surrounded by breathtaking coastline and unspoiled countryside, Kuşadasi flaunts its identity as the area's only major resort without the slightest trace of embarrassment. It boasts souvenir shops and travel agencies with that unselfconscious pride peculiar to a country that has only just been discovered by the tourist industry. In this regard, the port's active nightlife and gaudy bazaars make Kuşadasi a rather uncharacteristic gateway to Turkey. But the generosity and hospitality of its townspeople are representative. Even here, in one of the most commercial Turkish resorts, the tourist trappings prove to be an easily penetrable facade beyond which you'll discover smoke-filled cafes, winding peaceful alleyways, and plenty of small-town atmosphere.

Practical Information

Most visitors in Kuşadasi arrive by boat. The harbor master, duty free shop, fish market, passport police, and customs are all in the port area. There is no way around paying the port tax, but it is cheapest in dollars ($7); in most other currencies, most notably drachmas, it comes to about two dollars more. Once you clear the customs area, you'll face the **Tourist Office**, which distributes a free map of the town, but ask for a *Turquoise Tours* brochure (it contains a slightly better map). Just beyond the tourist office loom the turreted walls of an ancient Seljuk *caravanserai,* now the home of **Kervanseray Hotel,** run by the Club Med. One block in from the water stands Kuşadasi's other ancient structure, the **watchtower,** which now serves as a police station. The one-block strip between the two ancient monuments is the main tourist drag: **Teyyare Caddesi.** Here you'll find most of the travel agencies, banks, tourist shops, etc. If you bear slightly left and continue past the watchtower, you'll be walking along **Kahramanlar Caddesi,** Kuşadasi's less expensive commercial strip. On your left will be the **bus station** (*Otobüs Garaji*). On the streets that intersect the watchtower and run parallel to the waterfront, **Saglik Caddesi** and **Aslanlar Caddesi,** you can do your grocery shopping. Although they are few and far between, Kuşadasi does have a handful of hustlers. Avoid anyone who is a little too eager to accompany you.

Tourist Office: in the port. Each staff member speaks either French, German, or English. Often more than one visit is advisable, since both the language ability and the quality of the staff vary greatly. Complete listings of accommodations, campgrounds, bus schedules and just about everything else are available. Open daily in summer (Apr. 1-Dec. 1) 7:30am-8pm; winter (Dec. 1-Apr. 1) 8:30am-noon and 1:30-5:30pm.

Post Office: halfway up Teyyare Caddesi. Services open Mon.-Fri. 8:30am-noon and 1:30-6pm, Sat. 8:30am-noon, closed Sun. Also houses telegraph and two long-distance telephones which are open 24 hours a day. Stamps available 24 hours.

Dolmuş: in the front half of the bus station. Every 30 minutes to either Selçuk (90TL) or Söke (100TL)—just buy a ticket from the appropriate window. Both run from about 7am until 8pm. Less frequent runs to other neighboring villages, especially Davutlar.

Buses: back half of the bus station. The main companies are Elbirilik (tel. 15 05), Pamukkale (tel. 21 26), Aydin (tel. 22 76), and Köseoğlu (tel. 25 38). To **Izmir:** Elbirilik runs nine times a day. To **Istanbul:** Pumakkale goes at 8:45am, 7pm, and 9pm (1400TL). To **Bodrum:** take a dolmuş to Söke from where there are frequent connections (300TL). To **Marmaris:** take a bus to Aydin and change there for a direct connection. To **Nazilli** or **Denizli:** Pamukkale and Köseoğlu each have a few direct buses a day (500TL), but there are frequent connections from Selçuk (400TL).

Taxis: Murat Taksi, in front of the bus station (tel. 14 74), is perhaps the best company. 4000TL to hire a taxi for half a day. Maximum load is five passengers and at 800TL per person is a good deal for elaborate excursions.

Ferry to Samos: The ferry fares are fixed by the government at a 25% higher rate on the Turkish side. One way to Samos $25, round trip $30. Turkish boats leave in summer daily at 8am, returning at 5pm. In summer, Greek boats return to Samos 5pm daily. If you buy a round-trip ticket either way, you must return on a boat of the same nationality. In the off-season, there are three boats a week.

Travel Agencies: They're all about the same. Perhaps the most reliable is **Turquoise Tours,** in the Grand Bazaar, 10/1 Yali Caddesi (tel. 13 59). Most agencies offer guided tours at the following rates: Ephesus $8; Priene, Miletus, and Didyma $14 (and an additional $3 for lunch); Pamukkale and Aphrodisias $12.

Police *(Polis)*: in the watchtower (tel. 10 22). Headquarters: Hükümet Caddesi (tel. 13 82).

Hospital *(Hastahaneler)*: on the waterfront at the northern edge of town (tel. 16 14).

Private Doctor: Dr. Şenol Şenyilmaz. His office is across from the watchtower on Teyyare Caddesi (tel. 14 70). Home tel. 15 65.

Pharmacy: next door to the above on Teyyare Caddesi; the sign reads *Eczane*.

Boat Rentals: Kuşadasi-Turizm Seyahat Acentasi (tel. 12 82), in the marina, on the northern edge of the waterfront. They rent sailboats, motorboats, and yachts on either a day or a weekly basis.

Car Rental: Turquoise Tours is the Avis representative. However, **Gino Tours** (tel. 24 50), on Teyyare Caddesi, is slightly cheaper: Renault 12TS with 27TL per kilometer rate costs 2700TL per day and 16,200TL per week; the unlimited mileage rate is 21,000TL for three days, 7000TL for each additional day, or 42,000TL per week. Add to all rates another 700TL daily for insurance and 10% tax.

Foreign Newspapers: *International Herald Tribune, Time* and *Newsweek* are all available at the **Ali Baba** shop, directly behind the Kervanseray Hotel, as are other English and continental papers. Also consider buying a good map to Turkey while you have the chance.

Accommodations

If you've just come from Greece, you'll find accommodations cheap here; by Turkish standards, they're comparatively expensive. Finding a room is never a problem, however. Pensions offer the cheapest lodging, but they can fill up in the high season. Two of the most inexpensive ones, charging between 600-700TL for a double, are right in a row on Aslanlar Caddesi: **Pension Su** (tel. 14 53) is at #13, while **Safak** (tel. 17 64) is at #25. The **Akan Pension** (tel. 12 35), across from Hotel Neptun (see below), is very clean and only 675TL for a double, but only Turkish is spoken. The **Kayati** (tel. 28 37) is a shade more expensive and less hygienic, but convenient; follow the signs from the bus station.

Even in high season, Kuşadasi's hotels have plenty of room. The cheapest are the third class ones, officially priced as follows: singles 875TL, doubles 1375TL, triples 1800TL with about an additional 200TL for a room with private shower, and 250TL per person for breakfast. The best third class hotels are:

Hotel Neptun: Bezirgin Sok (tel. 15 40). Walk down Alslanlar Caddesi and turn right at Pension Rose, or climb up the steps just beyond the Shell station and before the Ural Restaurant on the waterfront. Leaves the competition in the dust. Run by Hildegard Pischke, an hospitable retired German nurse who has brought revolutionarily meticulous standards of hygiene to the Turkish hotel industry. Everything is shiny and reshined daily. Upper floors feature breathtaking views. Hot showers at no extra charge from late afternoon until sundown. Breakfast 250TL or a heavy German breakfast 300TL per person. Only German spoken. Official rates (absolutely no reductions) except that there is no 200TL surcharge for the private bathrooms adjoining all rooms.

Hotel Atlantik, 17 Teyyare Cadesi (tel. 10 39). The second best, and the more convenient choice; comparatively clean rooms. English spoken. Can fill up. Prices usually reduced to 500TL per person.

Hotel Ölmez, at the end of Teyyare Caddesi (tel. 21 07), just down the street from the Atlantik with slightly more modest rooms. Only Turkish spoken but help can be fetched. Also may chip their prices down to 500TL per person.

Hotel Demir Oğlu, Kahramanlar Caddesi (tel. 10 35), next to the bus station. Very friendly; English spoken. No hot water; no breakfast; your basic Turkish hotel. 500TL per person.

Pension Renk: Liman Caddesi (tel. 12 42). Take the steps up from the Shell gas station on the waterfront. Hip management with lots of funky music—popular with young people. Great view from the terrace, but a bit overpriced. Modest rooms with mandatory breakfast. Some rooms are better than others; be choosy. Singles 800TL, doubles 1500TL, triples 2000TL.

Camping: The best campgrounds are 2-3km south of town on the coastal road to Izmir by the beach. Take the Selçuk dolmuş or walk. Spartan **Cennet Camping** (tel. 15 00) is the first and cheapest of them: 125TL per person, 60TL per child and per tentsite. Adjacent **Diana Mocamp** (tel. 14 57) is a shade nicer and more expensive: 150TL per person, 75TL per child and per tentsite. Both of the above are open June 15-Sept. 1. **Önder Camping** (tel. 24 13) has the longest season and is by far the nicest, the safest, and the most expensive: 185TL per person, 100TL per child and per tentsite, 60TL per vehicle, 200TL for breakfast.

Food

Avoid the pricey places along the harbor and on Teyyare Caddesi. Also beware of the following racket: friendly local fellow invites you to sit down with him—a few drinks and one meal later, he disappears and you're left holding an outrageous bill. Liquor is expensive when ordered in restaurants. Otherwise, prices are reasonable and the food quite good, particularly along Kahramanlar Caddesi.

Duyar Restaurant, Kahramanlar Caddesi, directly across from the bus station. A bit noisy, but one of the best deals in town. Generous portions of *köfte* with potatoes, goulash, *dolma,* and other entrees for 145TL. Side orders of rice 75TL. Delicious *baklava* 100TL.

ALP Döner Kebab, at the end of Teyyare Caddesi, facing the watchtower. Popular with locals, specializes in meat. *Şiş kebab, köfte, döner kebab,* or *biftek* for 140TL. Large orders of *döner kebab* with tomato, yogurt sauce, and pita for 250TL. Quiet dining area upstairs.

Konya Pide Salonu, 65 Kahramanlar Caddesi, up from the bus station, specializes in *pide*. Simple meals, but it's hard to beat dinner for two for 80¢. Regular pide 85TL per serving; with cheese, meat, and egg 100TL per serving.

Bunes Kebab, to your right as you face the Kervanseray Hotel, offers rather small but very tasty portions of *şiş kebab* or *köfte* for 140TL, side order of rice 60TL.

Sights and Entertainment

Connected by a slender causeway, Kuşadasi's only substantial tourist attraction is its picturesque namesake, **Bird Island**—a tiny fortified islet, graced from within by some cozily cushioned cafes, blessed from without by a perimeter of excellent rocks to swim from, and capped off on top with a fine view of the port.

You'll soon realize that between the numerous cruise ships and the ferries from Samos, Kuşadasi is all a great many visitors will ever see of Turkey. Despite the overblown prices, shopping tends to be the favorite pastime here. If you are planning on seeing more of Turkey, be informed that the Grand Bazaar and Teyyare Caddesi are some of the most expensive places in the country. Nonetheless, as the shopkeepers will never tire of reminding you, it doesn't cost anything just to look and sip the endless glasses of tea they will offer you. The second favorite pastime among visitors is to spend all day basking on the ample beaches that line the coast in either direction. **Kadinlar Plaji,** the main beach, lies 3km beyond Bird Island—taxis run passengers on a collective basis from the taxi stand next to the Kervanseray Hotel for 50TL per person. Kadinlar's restaurants are a bit steep, but reasonable beachside rooms are available at **Ertürk Pension** (tel. 18 51): doubles are 1500TL, including breakfast. The other nearby beach lies to the south, 3km down the road to Izmir. Ask the Selçuk dolmuş to let you off at the Tusan Hotel. A 5km climb farther down the coast will be rewarded by an endless stretch of deserted beach. Across from the Tusan Hotel, several of the campgrounds have tennis courts. **Önder Camping** rents equipment for 200TL per person per hour. In town, the **gaming room,** just past the Shell station and behind the Ural Restaurant, has ping-pong, foosball, and billiard tables. Farther down the waterfront are Kuşadasi's most popular discos.

Near Kuşadasi

Aside from its wealth of archeological treasures, the surrounding country-side offers two scenic excursions to a nearby National Park and a beautiful lake.

Kalamanki National Park, known to local Turks as the **Milli Park,** 30km south of Kuşadasi, is an unspoiled expanse of woodlands, glistening water-falls, cliffs, and deserted beaches. Unfortunately, it is not accessible by public transportation. If you have wheels, take the turn-off marked Milli Park on the road to Kadinlar Beach. Otherwise, dolmuş leave from the Kuşadasi bus station to **Davutlar,** 20km to the south; they also leave about four mornings a week directly to **Güzel Çamli,** which is only a 5km walk from the park. Since the park is completely uninhabited, hitching tends to be best on weekends when Turkish families go for picnics. If you're in a group, you might consider taking a taxi—the ride one way is 1500TL; half-day rental is 4000TL.

The other way to get far off the beaten track and enjoy a taste of paradise is to head for **Lake Bafe** (*Bafe Gölü* in Turkish), a blissfully serene lake punc-tuated by a handful of little islets and surrounded by a series of hills and a mountain, rising up from the water. Beginning about 15km south of Söke, the road to Bodrum wraps all the way around the western edge of the lake. Heading south, at the end of the first turn-off on your left, by the BP gas station, you'll find **Göl Camping and Restaurant** and **Turgut Motel and Camp-ing;** at the next turn-off you'll find **Gerinin Camping and Restaurant.** As visitors tend to be rather infrequent, the rates mostly depend upon your will-ingness to bargain. To get to Bafe Gölü, ask at either the Pamukkale or Aydin bus company offices in Söke to have the driver of the bus to Bodrum let you off, or just take a taxi from Söke.

Ephesus (Efes)

The best preserved, most extensive, and most exciting remains of an ancient Greek city are at Ephesus, only 1.5km from Selçuk and 17km from Kuşadasi. Even if you're planning on visiting the Turkish Coast for only a single day, you should follow the swarms of tourists who cross over from Samos and make a beeline for the ruins. If you're on Samos, you should not miss the opportunity to see this magnificent archeological site.

Practical Information

Large signs on the travel agencies on Samos and in Kuşadasi insist that guided tours of Ephesus are "highly recommended"—we highly recommend you avoid them. First of all, the tours are a bit pricey: most agencies in Kuşadasi charge $8; they're $6 if you arrange in advance on Samos at **Samos Tours** (tel. 27 71 5 or 27 73 8). Secondly, they go too quickly; the ruins extend across an area of over two thousand acres, most of which the guides simply rush you by in the course of a couple of hours. Here's how to do it yourself in three easy steps.

The first step is optional. Consider procuring a good guidebook to Ephesus—the souvenir shops in Kuşadasi are overflowing with a wide selec-tion. The *NET Guide to Ephesus* by Şadan Gökovali, though translated with an unfortunate degree of grammatical creativity, appears to be the best value for your money at 500TL. It has a large and useful map (the ruins are largely unmarked). Step two is to bring a waterbottle. Most of the time you'll be stumbling around in the heat at least a kilometer from the nearest refreshment stand. Step three is getting there. Head for the Kuşadasi bus station, hop the dolmuş to Selçuk, and tell the driver you want off at Ephesus (90TL). He'll deposit you at the turn-off for the site. The main entrance, where you pay admission, is a 1km walk, but the actual ruins start just a few yards from the road to Selçuk. Open in summer daily 8:30am-7:30pm, in winter slightly shorter hours; admission 60TL per person, 100TL per camera. You can check your camera at the admission booth. Next to the entrance are toilets (10TL per shot), a post office, a police station, some overpriced restaurants, and an expensive motel. For either food or lodgings proceed to Selçuk or Kuşadasi.

Depending upon the extent of your enthusiasm and endurance, a tour of the site can take up to eight hours or longer. If you wish to return to Kuşadasi, it is advisable to catch a dolmuş from Selçuk, since they're usually full when they pass the turn-off for Ephesus. Hitching along the Selçuk-Kuşadasi road is usually excellent. From May 1-6 the annual **Festival of Ephesus** features theater, music, and folklore events performed in the antique theater.

History

It is difficult to appreciate the ruins at Ephesus fully without some knowledge of their historical significance. Once the second largest city of the Roman Empire, site of the greatest of the seven wonders of the ancient world, and one of the holiest shrines of Christianity, Ephesus' past is as illustrious as it is checkered. Its strategic coastal location at the edge of the Western world enabled Ephesus to become one of the most prosperous cities of its day. The city was the home of the world's first bank, and capital of the Roman provinces of Asia.

The origins of Ephesus are shrouded in myth. Legend has it that the city was founded in a manner prescribed by the Delphic Oracle. The Oracle delivered its advice in typically enigmatic fashion: the appropriate site, it foretold, would be disclosed by a fish and a wild boar. Eventually, the day came when the meaning of this mysterious message became clear. The prophecy was fulfilled when a fish leapt from the flames over which it was being cooked, setting fire to the neighboring brush, thus startling a wild boar, which was slaughtered on the spot where the city of Ephesus was built. History testifies that the Oracle's advice left something to be desired, however, for the city's location had to be changed several times due to the continual recession of the harbor waters. Today, the ruins of the ancient port lie 10km inland from the coast. The shifting of the sea prompted the relocation of an entire city—an arduous task which naturally met with some resistance. Lysimachos, general of Alexander the Great, was once compelled to close off all of the city's sewage facilities in order to secure the cooperation of the townspeople.

This reluctance to move was partially due to the Ephesians' desire to remain near the colossal **Temple of Artemis.** This dazzling structure was described by Pausanias, the author of the first and most celebrated travel guide to ancient Greece, as the "most wondrous of the seven ancient wonders" and as "the most beautiful work ever created by humankind." The first major structure ever to be built entirely out of marble and the largest edifice in the ancient Greek world, the Temple of Artemis was the glory of Ephesus and unrivalled among temples in Asia Minor. What is most remarkable is that this massive monument was built twice. Burnt down by a madman in 356 B.C., the temple was completely reconstructed to its original dimensions under the leadership of Alexander the Great. The offerings and donations of hundreds of thousands of pilgrims each year enabled the temple to grow so wealthy that it could issue travelers checks and letters of credit, thus becoming the world's first bank. Today, little remains of the magnificent structure; it was sacked by plundering Goths in the third century A.D., and more recently by the voracious British School of Archeology (check the British Museum in London). Nonetheless, a great deal remains of the sprawling city that grew up around the temple.

Ephesus reached its zenith under Roman rule when, as the capital of the Province of Asia, its inhabitants numbered over a quarter of million, making it the world's most populous city after Alexandria. Most of the ruins that one sees today date from this period. The founders of Christianity recognized the significance of such a metropolis. St. Paul arrived in 50 A.D. and converted a small group of Ephesians to the new religion, so Ephesus became the spiritual center where the Christian faith blossomed and from which it spread throughout the Roman empire. Ephesus' importance to Christians stems from several events. Both the Virgin Mary and St. John the Theologian spent their last years here, and the city's name provides a title for one of the books of the New Testament (Ephesians). As the site of the tomb of St. John and the first basilica, Ephesus was the first city to attract Christian pilgrims; the Christian shrines at Selçuk continue to do so.

Heraclitus, Ephesus' most famous native son, once remarked that one can never step into the same river twice, in order to dramatize the central teaching of his philosophy—the ephemeral and transient nature of life. The fruits of his wisdom eventually caught up with his native city. As the neighboring river Cayster emptied into the Aegean, it choked the harbor with silt, transforming it into marshy swampland. By the sixth century A.D., the recession of the sea had sealed the fate of the city. The swamps became infested with malaria and triggered a tremendous epidemic, resulting in over 200,000 deaths, as the entire population of Ephesus was either driven out or laid to waste.

Sights

If you're not on a guided tour, you will approach the ruins from the road between Kuşadasi and Selçuk. Your first glimpse of the site will therefore be the remains from the outskirts of the ancient city. The most important of these is the **Vedius Gymnasium,** to your left as you proceed down the road to the main entrance. The Gymnasium is one of the best preserved buildings at Ephesus, since its walls remain largely intact. Wander briefly through the large spacious chambers before continuing to the entrance. Large classes were held in most of these rooms, for a Roman *gymnasium* was roughly equivalent to an American high school. The Vedius Gymnasium also contains the remains of a gymnasium for athletic events as well as some adjoining baths. Farther on, one can also make out the contours of what must have been an enormous **stadium.**

Once you pass through the main entrance, you won't be able to resist charging to the center of the site and looking straight down the **Arcadian Street,** a magnificent and beautifully-preserved colonnaded marble avenue. The avenue originally served as the ancient counterpart to the present-day tourist drag in Kuşadasi. It was lined with shops and extended to the harbor, where visitors disembarked and trading ships docked, laden with cargo from the Orient. Now the street eventually degenerates into a small marsh, but a great many of the original columns have survived and a stroll down its length gives one a sense of the original grandeur of ancient Ephesus. Once you reach the far end of the avenue, turn around and admire the marvelous view of the **Grand Theater,** one of the finest examples of its kind. Perhaps the most awe-inspiring remant of ancient Ephesus, the theater, with its seating capacity of 24,000, dominates the entire site from an elevated setting, carved into the side of Mt. Pion. The acoustics of the theater are remarkable. Even at a whisper, voices from the stage reach the topmost row. Over the centuries, the size of the theater was gradually enlarged in order to accommodate the expanding population of the city. The top commands a fine panorama of the surrounding valley. As you take your leave of the theater, to your left you'll find the **Commercial Agora**—the main plaza of the city. This spacious colonnaded square once housed one of the most sumptuous marketplaces of ancient times. The four circumscribing rows of majestic Roman columns clearly demarcate the Agora's original proportions. Bordering the Agora is the slightly elevated **Marble Road,** the best-preserved street of Ephesus and originally part of the city's sacred main thoroughfare that led all the way to the Temple of Artemis. Strewn with a variety of architectural fragments, some with striking bas-reliefs, the road leads past the Agora to the **Library of Celsus.** This library has been almost entirely reconstructed by Viennese archeologists, but in a sensitive and tasteful fashion. The elaborately carved marble facade of the library presents an indication of the dazzling luxury of ancient Ephesus. The Austrians couldn't resist leaving their thumbprint, so the beautiful reconstruction is marred by the bold inscriptions in the marble interior, in both German and Turkish, in which they immodestly assume full credit for the present state of the structure. In its heyday, the library's collection was considered the third most important in the world, excelled only by those in Alexandria and Pergammon. Stand under the central columns and look straight up to view the ornate, double-storied facade ceilings. The facade is constructed with a false perspective: the outer columns are slightly shorter than the inner ones in order to create an illusion of greater distance. Beyond the library and the Commercial Agora lie various fragments of the **Harbor Baths** and the **Harbor Gymnasium.**

After the library, the Marble Road leads into **Curetes Street,** which also formed part of the Sacred Way, and climbs uphill to the other significant remains. Situated across from the library at the corner of the Marble Road and Curetes Street, the remains of the brothel cover a significant area, and contain a pleasure parlor, ancient public lavatories, and baths. The famous statue of Priapus, the prodigiously endowed god of sex, was, appropriately enough, discovered during excavations of the brothel. It's now in the Selçuk Museum. Relief of a slightly less lascivious variety is still available here today in the form of a deliciously cool **water fountain** concealed just inside the side entrance to the brothel from Curetes Street. If you leave the brothel from the water fountain, you'll face the **Byzantine Fountain,** which provided the original outlet for the waters of the natural well, and whose limestone blocks originally constituted part of a momumental Christian tomb. Continuing up the hill, the left side of the road is dominated by the imposing ruins of the **Temple of Hadrian,** whose intricately carved facade was recently renovated and remains in excellent condition. Friezes depicting the founding of Ephesus and the figure of Artemis, the goddess of fertility, adorn the temple's marble doorway. Beyond the temple and adjoining the rear of the brothel you'll find the **Baths of Scholastikia,** named after a wealthy Christian woman who leveled several important buildings in the fifth century A.D. in order to restore and extend the city's bath complex. Her headless statue still remains *in situ.* Across the street from the Temple of Hadrian begin the so-called Houses on the Slope which extend up the hill. These are the largest dwellings yet to be unearthed at Ephesus; they once housed the wealthiest and most prominent families of the city. Their interiors are covered with superbly preserved wall frescoes and mosaic floors. In 1983, this portion of the site was undergoing extensive restoration and the majority of it was closed to tourists.

Farther up the hill, to your left along Curetes Street after the temple, you'll find the ruins of the exquisite **Fountain of Trajan.** The present reconstruction of the fountain consists of various fragments excavated at this location piled up in a piecemeal fashion to simulate the original structure. The colossal statue of the emperor Trajan that once stood before the fountain has been completely destroyed, except for its base, which has been restored to its original position. Trajan's two royal feet and a globe symbolized the emperor's dominion over the entire world. The series of statue bases that line the following stretch of

Curetes Street once displayed the figures and busts of a variety of famous Ephesians. Upon reaching the hilltop where the road divides, turn around and notice the vista overlooking the site and the surrounding countryside. If you continue from here to the right, you'll come to the scanty remains of **Domitian Square,** the site of the first temple of Ephesus to be dedicated to a Roman emperor. Still farther up, you'll find the equally scanty remains of the **State Agora.** It was in this corner of town that political affairs were negotiated and resolved—hence the proximity of the **Odeon,** just across the way. A small, well-preserved amphitheater with a seating capacity of 1400, it served as a council chamber and lecture hall. Today, the Sacred Way culminates in an alternative admission booth to the site and a refreshment stand. Farther up the road, outside of the main site, lie the surviving fragments of the **East Gymnasium.** Only regular taxis run along this road. In order to catch a dolmuş, you have to walk back through the site to the main road between Kuşadasi and Selçuk.

Selçuk

The quiet village of Selçuk's main claim to fame is its proximity to the ruins of Ephesus. The village boasts three important attractions of its own: the **Ephesus Archeological Museum,** and two famous Christian shrines—the **Basilica of St. John** and the **House of the Virgin Mary.** Each is related to the history of Ephesus in one way or another.

Practical Information and Accommodations

It's easy to find your way in Selçuk, because the town is so small. The tourist office, smack in the center of the village, has everything else around it: behind is the Ephesus Museum; next door the **hospital;** and across the street the **bus station,** where the Kuşadasi dolmuş leaves every 30 minutes from 7am until 8pm. The **Tourist Office** (open daily in summer 8:30am-7:30pm; in winter 9am-6pm) provides a little map of the town and a complete list of pensions. The best **public rest rooms** around and a place to check your pack are both to be found in the Ephesus Museum. Disengage yourself from anyone who "just wants to practice English"—Selçuk does have a couple of clumsy hustlers.

Since the whole village curls up and goes to sleep after sunset, the main reason for spending the night here is to be near the ruins bright and early the next morning. But with Kuşadasi only a short ride away, even that reason is not particularly compelling. In summer, Selçuk's six little pensions tend to fill up, but with a little looking you can almost always find a bed. The four best pensions all offer clean rooms for 400TL per person. The **Pension Baykal,** 22 Kuşadasi Caddesi (tel. 13 5), next door to the Ephesus Museum, also offers hot showers for 100TL, and breakfast for 175 TL. The manager is friendly and speaks some English, but the rooms are cramped and afford little privacy. The alternatives are slightly more spacious, but often don't have hot water. To get to **Pension Akbulut** (tel. 13 9), 4 Atatürk Caddesi Spor Sahasi 2nd Sokak (behind the hospital), from the tourist office, take the first right off the main drag in the direction of Aydin. The second right will take you to **Pension Sentop** (tel. 27 5), Spor Sahasi 3rd Sokak. The **Pension Uyaroğlu** is at 7/A Atatürk Mah. Kubilay Sok (tel. 28 7). If the pensions are full, there is always a vacancy at the cheapest of Selçuk's three hotels, the **Günes Hotel,** on the main street, by the turn-off for the St. John Basilica. 500TL per person, and the rooms are less than immaculate.

Sights

Selçuk's most popular attraction is the tastefully laid-out **Ephesus Museum.** The exhibits feature the highlights of over a century's worth of excavation at Ephesus. Its most famous pieces are both rather suggestive: two beautiful **statues of Artemis,** the goddess of fertility, easily identified by her multitude of breasts; and the even more arresting **statue of Priapus,** the well-equipped deity of sex. Also of note are the fragments from the Temple of Artemis; a fresco **portrait of Socrates** found at the Houses of the Slope; and a fine collection of ancient coins. Open daily 9am-6:30pm; admission 60TL per person, 100TL per camera. Across from the tourist office, near the Ephesus Museum, is the tiny **Museum of Turkish Baths.**

If you head from Selçuk towards the ruins at Ephesus, the first turn-off to your right leads to most of the village's other monuments. First you'll come to the fourteenth-century **Isa Bey Mosque,** an imposing rectangular edifice and the oldest surviving mosque in Turkey with a central courtyard. A portion of the mosque is still used for worship, while the rest contains an impressive array of Ottoman tombstones. Some of the marble used to build the mosque was taken from the nearby remains of the Temple of Artemis. Climb the minaret for a breathtaking view. Farther up the hill, you'll come to **Persecution Gate,** a colossal structure which was once the southernmost entrance to ancient Ephesus and now serves as the entrance to the basilica and the rooftop site of numerous storks' nests. Beyond the archway sprawls the **Basilica of St. John,** containing the tomb of St. John the Theologian, author of one of the books of the Gospel and the Book of Revelations; the tomb is housed in the small wooden chapel. One of Christianity's most sacred shrines, the basilica is primarily of interest from an architectural point of view for its marble columns and mosaic floors. The road that leads uphill to the right as you face the basilica brings you to **Selçuk Castle**—its crenellated walls endow the village skyline with a medieval aura.

Selçuk's most famous attraction is also its least impressive—the scanty remains of the once glorious **Temple of Artemis.** The second turn-off to the right on the road to Ephesus leads to the temple's original site. The fragments of the great altar and its columns excavated here have been shipped to museums in Vienna and London.

Meryemana

Seven kilometers outside of Selçuk lies Turkey's most important destination for Christian pilgrims, Meryemana—or more colloquially, the **House of the Virgin Mary.** From an historical point of view, the authenticity of the site is hardly indisputable. But it's reputed to be the location of the house where Christ's mother spent the last years of her life. According to the Bible, the Virgin Mary lived in Ephesus for the latter part of her life, although it does not actually specify that she died here. In the early nineteenth century, a devout German nun, who had never set eyes upon Ephesus, was said to have seen the house of the Holy Virgin in a vision. No one took her very seriously at the time, so she wrote a book discussing the plan and location of the house in detail. After her death, excavations around Ephesus unearthed a first-century A.D. stone cottage that perfectly fit the details of her description. Ever since, the site has been popular among Christian pilgrims who come to pay their respects to the Virgin Mary. A tasteful chapel has been erected over the ancient remains. Thousands of pilgrims converge here annually on August 15, when the Assumption is celebrated and the Archbishop of Izmir performs a Mass.

Priene, Miletus, and Didyma

Priene, Miletus, and Didyma, three of Turkey's finest archeological sites, lie in a single neat row conveniently within range of a daytrip from Kuşadasi. The remains of each of these three cities are unique: Priene perches on the scenic slopes of Mt. Mycale, Miletus boasts a formidable amphitheater, and Didyma's superbly preserved ruins represent the largest Greek religious structure to survive to the present day.

Practical Information and Transportation

With an early start and a modicum of efficiency, all three sites can be visited from Kuşadasi in a single day. You may prefer to break up your tour of the ruins into two separate daytrips. The best strategy is to make a short excursion to Priene and a long one to Miletus and Didyma. It is possible to take a single-day organized tour of all three sites from Kuşadasi (or more expensively from Bodrum) for $14 per person, plus an optional $3 charge for lunch. Another hassle-free option is to rent a taxi from Kuşadasi for 4000TL for a half-day. For a group of five people, this alternative is not unreasonable, since to visit all three sites from Kuşadasi through a series of dolmuş rides usually costs about 650TL per person. The drawback to the taxi is that a half-day tour of all three sites requires more hurrying than you might wish.

To do it on your own, first take a dolmuş or a bus to Söke from Kuşadasi (the 20km ride costs 100TL). Depending on how you come, the dolmuş from Kuşadasi will let you off at the edge of town and the private bus companies will deposit you down the street in front of their offices. To get to the Söke dolmuş station, walk into town from where the dolmuş dropped you off and take your first right. From the bus office, walk towards Kuşadasi and take a left, then cross the bridge and take the first left. From here dolmuş run until about 8pm to Priene and to Didyma: just take the appropriately marked dolmuş. Getting to Miletus by public transportation is a bit trickier: the dolmuş to Didyma goes through the village of **Akköy**; from there it is a 4km walk north to Miletus along the road to Priene. The ruins are on your right just by the road. During the summer months, the best way to see all three sites in a day is to go to Priene by dolmuş early in the morning and hitch a ride with tourists to the other sites. Contrary to what most guidebooks say, the direct road between Priene and Miletus is open and newly paved—although in 1983 it was not yet usually serviced by dolmuş. In order to get from Priene to the other sites by dolmuş, you must go back to Söke and change there.

All the sites are open from 8am-8pm in summer and from sunrise to sunset in winter; admission 60TL per person, and 100TL per camera. Priene and Miletus both have adjoining cafes; Didyma has two restaurants; and in Söke, next door to the Pamukkale bus company office, **Öz Gaziantep** serves good *döner kebab* for 150TL.

Priene

Nestled on the slopes of Mt. Mycale, high above the surrounding plains, Priene's spectacular locale at the foot of a jagged rock cliff imbues the ruins with a peculiarly magical quality. Once a major commercial port, Priene stands out as the oldest surviving example of a Hellenic metropolis in which the streets were laid out in a checkerboard fashion, intersecting at right angles.

The dolmuş drops you off by a cafe and a souvenir shop. To reach the site, follow the road that climbs straight up the slope, forking off to the right of the direct road to Miletus and Didyma. Your first encounter with the site will be the massive ancient **city walls** that circumscribe the ruined metropolis constructed upon a series of terraces along the slope of the mountain. From the main entrance a path conducts you to what was once the main avenue of ancient Priene. To your right will be the unmistakable **Bouleterion,** or Senate House, a well-preserved and elegant square auditorium. With a seating capacity of approximately 640 people, the Bouleterion was reserved as a council chamber for the highest elected officials of the community, and indicates the parliamentary political practices of ancient Hellenic city-states. The interior chamber was originally adorned with a huge marble altar of which only the foundations remain.

Larger congregations convened just up the hill at the **theater,** one of the handsomest structures at Priene. With a capacity of only about 5000 spectators and encompassed by a grove of pine trees, the theater's intimate, peaceful atmosphere contrasts strikingly with the barren rock face of Mt. Mycale rising up dramatically in the background. The front row of the theater retains its five thrones of honor with their dignified bases, carved in the shape of lion's feet. The square holes bored into the sides of the thrones were used to support a canopy which protected their noble occupants from the afternoon sun. On the left side of the stage are the remnants of a water-clock that was used to enforce the time limit for debates and orations delivered by politicians.

Continuing along the upper terrace, there is no mistaking Priene's most prominent edifice: the **Temple of Athena,** occupying the ruined city's highest point. Designed by Pytheos, the architect who designed the Mausoleum of Halicarnassus (one of the ancient world's seven wonders), the temple's front steps and interior floor remain largely intact. Although only the foundation of the great altar remains visible since the rest has been removed to the Istanbul Museum, five fluted columns, running the length of the northernmost edge, have been resurrected. They evoke the grandeur of the original structure's proportions. The temple was revered as the paradigm of classic architecture, upon which all subsequent Ionic monuments were based. The Goddess herself could hardly have disapproved of the temple's spectacular location.

Descend from the ruins of the temple to the terraces below to visit the extensive remnants of the private houses of Priene, among the best-preserved examples of Ionian domestic architecture in existence. Heading back towards the entrance, you'll pass through the spacious **Agora,** and to your right, the third-century B.C. **Temple of Olympic Zeus** (more of which can be seen in the British Museum). If you have no car, the most prudent course of action is to befriend some visitors touring the site who happen to be more fortunate in this regard, and beg a ride to Miletus.

Miletus

Now landlocked by arid plains, it is hard to believe that Miletus was once seated upon a slender tongue of land and surrounded by four separate harbors. The city was destroyed and resettled more than once due to its strategic coastal location. The city's fate paralleled that of its Ionian confederate, Ephesus: the silting over of its harbor and waters by neighboring rivers caused the decline of this once sprawling metropolis and respected intellectual center. For centuries Miletus stood at the forefront of the major commercial and cultural developments of Western civilization. In the fifth century B.C., the Milesian alphabet was adopted as the standard form of Greek writing; Miletus was the first Greek city to coin its own money; and it was the headquarters of the Ionian school of philosophers, who helped to lay the foundations of mathematics and the natural sciences. The city's tradition of leadership, however, eventually resulted in disaster. In 499 B.C., Miletus headed an unsuccessful Ionian revolt against the Persian army. The Persians retaliated by wiping out the entire population of the city. The men were all massacred and the women and children sold into slavery.

The main attraction of the present-day site is the fantastic **Theater,** clearly visible from the Priene-Didyma highway. Remarkably well-preserved, with a seating capacity of over 15,000 people, the theater dates from Hellenistic times though most of the visible structure is of Roman construction. The theater was originally positioned right at the water's edge overlooking the boats docked at the harbor. The lower stories are completely intact, and the front row contains two surviving marble columns flanking the central seat of honor. Behind the spectator seats, the main stairways still lead up to the upper tiers through massive stone archways. Although the uppermost levels have deteriorated somewhat they offer a splendid overview of the rest of the site.

Unfortunately, the remaining portions of Miletus are flooded marshland during much of the year. In late summer, it's often possible to tour the rest of the ruins without too much discomfort. The most notable monuments are the **Ionic Stoa** (to the right of the theater as you enter the site) which is presently under restoration; the **gymnasium** next to it; and farther on, the well-preserved **Faustina Baths** (behind and to the left of the theater). The baths were erected by Faustina, wife of the Roman emperor Marcus Aurelius. By the entrance is the small **Archeological Museum** with finds from the site. The peculiar dome-shaped structure, to the right of the road leading to the ruins, is the **Mosque of Ilyas Bey**—although the minaret is now missing, the interior of the fifteenth-century Islamic shrine is exquisitely decorated.

Didyma

The sanctuary at Didyma ranked as the third largest sacred structure in the ancient Hellenic world after its gargantuan neighbors to the north, the Temple of Artemis at Ephesus and the Temple of Hera on Samos. Since virtually nothing remains of either of the latter two buildings, today the sanctuary at Didyma stands alone as the best surviving example of these colossal temples. Indeed, it is hard to imagine how any of this seemingly indestructible edifice could have failed to survive. It was built to last—many of its individual marble slabs weigh over a metric ton each. Even those least enthusiastic about ancient ruins cannot fail to be impressed by the shrine's mammoth proportions. Ancient Didyma was not a residential community, but rather the site of a sacred sanctuary dedicated to Apollo and an Oracle which was almost as esteemed as the one at Delphi. The fame and wealth of Didyma was primarily due to the Oracle's popularity. It attracted pilgrims from every part of ancient Greece and citizens of nearby Miletus and Priene visited regularly during the various annual religious festivals. The sacred road which ran from Miletus to Didyma culminated in the gates of the ancient temple, presently the site of souvenir shops and restaurants, and the final stretch was lined on both sides with statues (now in the British Museum).

Entering at the main gate, you will pass an enormous Corinthian capital which once crowned one of the colossal columns surrounding the temple. As you first enter, you will also notice a charming marble **Persian lion;** and to your right a striking bas-relief of a giant **Medusa head**—a fragment of an ornate frieze that originally ran all around the exterior of the temple. The full magnitude of the temple is only apparent once you climb the thirteen steps up the stairway to the main facade. All that remains of most of the gigantic columns are the bases and lower sections. Ten columns originally stood across the front of the facade and twenty-five columns along the sides of the temple, each of them 2.5 meters in diameter and nearly twenty meters high. As the two columns which have been restored to their original height demonstrate, the proportions of the original edifice were monstrous. To get a full sense of the temple's scale, stand directly under the two full columns and gaze upwards. Despite their size, the tapered and fluted shafts of these columns possess a remarkably degree of delicacy. The third surviving full column remains unfluted, an indication that construction of the temple was never completed. The present sanctuary was begun during the second and first centuries B.C., and work continued until the second century A.D. But the original plans proved too ambitious and were never brought to fruition. Most of the columns in the inner row are undecorated and date back to the second century B.C., while those belonging to the outer colonnade are adorned with ornate Roman carvings. The original temple possessed one hundred twenty of these mammoth supports. The single pillar holding up the left-hand side of the main doorway and still in place today is the largest monolith known to have been used in antiquity, weighing seventy tons. How did the Greeks manage to transport such cumbersome chunks of marble? They constructed long shafts of stone leading to the temple site, greased them over with soap, and then slid the building materials over the lubricated surface.

Two marble tunnels stretch from the facade to the **inner sanctuary** of the temple. Its walk once rose to over 25 meters in height. Today the inner courtyard contains some fragments of the frieze that once adorned the uppermost portion of these walls. In the southeast corner of the courtyard are traces of a **sacred fountain,** as well as the foundations of a *naiskos*—a tiny temple which housed a venerated bronze statue of Apollo. The temple appears to have been erected before the larger edifice was begun (in about 300 B.C.) and also served as the site of the Oracle. Only priests and priestesses of the sanctuary were permitted to enter the *naiskos*. Those who came to hear the oracle's pronouncements were required to await the delivery of a written message. The news was received in a waiting room located at the temple's far end, at the top of the staircase of 24 steps which still remains today. Ascend the stairs for a stunning view of the entire sanctuary from above.

The small modern resort of **Didim** nearby offers some inexpensive pensions and miles of deserted beaches.

Euromos

One of the best-preserved ancient temples of Asia Minor lies just south of the turn-off for Didyma, along the main road from Söke to Bodrum. Although the remains of the ancient city of Euromos are easily visible from the highway, they are seldom visited by tourists. They lie just south of Lake Bafe, near the tiny village of Selimiye. If you're driving by car you won't be able to resist stopping. Otherwise, you can ask the bus driver to let you off, though you may have difficulty getting a bus to pick you up again. The main attraction is the **Temple of Zeus,** constructed during the reign of Emperor Hadrian, which still retains sixteen of its original seventeen Corinthian columns.

Pamukkale (Hieropolis)

The Roman spa of Hieropolis was known throughout Asia Minor for its natural thermal springs. Today the place goes under the Turkish name of Pamukkale and remains a popular tourist resort. The Turkish name literally means "cotton castle," and refers to the dazzling chalk white cliffs upon which the resort is built. The extraordinary surface of the cliffs was shaped over the course of millenia by the gradual accumulation of calcium oxide resources deposited by a local stream. Dripping slowly down the massive face of the mountainside, the water forms multiple semi-circular terraces, the edges of which spill over into dramatic chalk-white petrified cascades of stalactites, thus creating a series of thermal wading pools. A sheer drop from the terraces leads to the surrounding valley and the small modern village of Pamukkale far below. Aside from boasting one of Turkey's most fascinating geological formations, Pamukkale also features one of the country's most significant archeological sites. Scattered about the top of the cliffs lie the extensive ruins of the Roman city of Hieropolis, particularly famous for the magnificently preserved amphitheater.

Transportation and Accommodations

None of Turkey's private bus companies have direct buses to Pamukkale (including the Pamukkale bus company!). However, there are frequent dolmuş and mini-buses that run back and forth between Pamukkale and the bustling regional capital of Denizli (50TL), which has excellent bus connections to all major Turkish cities. Less expensive and less comfortable—except perhaps for overnight *couchettes*—direct train connections also exist from Izmir and Istanbul to Denizli. The dolmuş and mini-buses to Pamukkale leave from directly in front of the Denizli bus station—about a mile from the train station. If you're coming from the Aegean Coast, buses run up twice an hour between Izmir and Denizli via Selçuk. It is possible to visit Pamukkale as a long daytrip from Kuşadasi: the Pamukkale bus company has a direct bus from Kuşadasi to Denizli leaving at 7:30am and arriving at noon (500TL). To return from Denizli, catch the 4:30pm bus bound from Izmir (400TL) and you will be able to get off at Selçuk in time to catch the last dolmuş back to Kuşadasi (90TL).

Finding accommodations at Pamukkale presents no difficulty. The motels in the tourist complex are all expensive, but the tiny village which lies in the valley beneath the tourist area has several very pleasant pensions all of which charge 500-600TL per person. From the wading pools on the cliff's edge, a long track leads down to the village. The proprietor of the **Anatolia Pension** also drives a taxi and will be delighted to take you down to the village free of charge if you're interested in staying in his pension. Just wait at the sign that reads "Anatolia Pension" by the dolmuş stop. If the pensions should all be full, there is always room at the **Hotel Konak Sade**, on the highway at the bottom of the hill, which has rooms for 600TL per person. Sometimes they let backpackers sleep on the carpeted floors for 250TL per person. Either the Hotel Konak Sade or **Ali's Camping** will let you use their campgrounds for 250TL per person.

Sights

Pamukkale, still coveted today for the healing powers of its thermal springs, will prove a particularly appealing destination if you're missing the comforts of a hot bath. The warm water springs forth from the ground filled with oxygen bubbles, like an endless supply of overheated soda. Not surprisingly, Pamukkale's natural amenities have not failed to attract the tourist industry. Three large motels have sprouted up amongst the thermal springs and ancient ruins, and on weekends local Turks flock to the waters of the milky white mountaintop. It is not hard to see why—all of the terraced wading pools command excellent views of the valley below. There are actually two different series of terraces located on either side of the main highway to Denizli. Elegant broad shallow pools, gradually increasing in depth as one progresses down the slope, are located in front of the Tusan Motel, the one nearest to the highway. The deepest, most intricately shaped and most popular terraces are situated directly behind the nameless restaurant/cafe facing the main parking lot. In the deepest of the pools, it is possible to submerge yourself fully while absorbing the superb panorama.

For a different taste of Pamukkale's thermal springs, take a plunge into the **Sacred Fountain,** once revered by ancient Romans and now housed within the tacky Motel Turizm, up the hill toward the amphitheater. Supplied by a steady flow of naturally heated mineral water from a neighboring stream, a dip in this ancient pond is the closest most of us will ever come to bathing in a fountain of warm Perrier. The pond is also a paradise for archeology buffs, for it has been filled with a variety of ruins from ancient Hieropolis that are easily visible in the remarkably clean water and are delightful to snorkel around. Changing rooms adjoin the pond; a swim costs 100TL per person. A less exotic bathing alternative is the complex of swimming pools located within the grounds of the Tusan Motel. Admission 150TL for two hours; lockers 200TL; and you can borrow a swimsuit for a 50TL deposit.

Between the motels stand the huge vaulted archways of their ancient counterpart, the **Hieropolis City Baths.** The visible portions of this first-century structure are all that remains of what was once one of Asia Minor's greatest ancient tourist industries. The springs of Hieropolis were particularly popular with vacationing Romans. After a cataclysmic earthquake leveled the spa in 17 A.D., Hieropolis was promptly rebuilt, reaching the zenith of its prosperity during the second and third centuries A.D. The city baths were particularly renowned for ther glossy marble interior. Today the interior has been converted into a pleasant **archeological museum** containing some fine Roman statues sculpted by artists of the famous school at neighboring Aphrodisias.

Dominating the scene from is elevated perch, carved into the side of the mountain, the huge **Grand Theater** is unquestionably the most imposing remnant of ancient Hieropolis. A hike up to the theater is a must. Almost all of the seating area for 25,000 spectators is completely intact and the variety of ornately sculpted decorative elements adorning the facade and stage area are very well preserved. Be sure to proceed with caution since the theater is still under excavation and portions of the structure are somewhat unstable. Above and behind the theater lies one of the largest surviving examples of its kind from antiquity: the **Necropolis** of Hieropolis, comprising over twelve hundred tombs and sarcophagi. Among these lies the **Martyrium,** an octagonal edifice dating from the fifth century A.D., believed to have been erected upon the site where St. Philip was martyred in 80 A.D. To reach the Necropolis follow the road up past the theater.

Aphrodisias

With increasing numbers of visitors every year, Aphrodisias is rapidly joining the ranks of Turkey's other famous archeological sites. Excavations are still in progress and the consensus among experts is that a great deal remains to be uncovered. The ruins of a vast ancient metropolis are gradually coming to light. The highlights of the presently excavated ruins include a beautifully preserved Roman stadium and equally well-preserved odeon, as well as a temple, an agora, a palace and some thermal baths. 165km from Kuşadasi and 110km from Pamukkale, the ruins can easily be reached on a daytrip from either city.

The remains of Aphrodisias adjoin the modern village of **Karaçasu,** serviced by five direct buses a day from Izmir running via the towns of Selçuk and Nazilli, 42km north of Karaçasu. To reach Aphrodisias from Kuşadasi, take a dolmuş to Selçuk and then a bus. The first direct bus from Selçuk to Karaçasu leaves at 10:30am and the first direct bus back goes at 3pm. Since the bus ride alone takes three hours each way, that does not leave much time for sightseeing. To get an earlier start, take one of the frequent buses from Selçuk to Nazilli, and from the Nazilli bus station you can easily get a dolmuş or bus to

Karaçasu. If you don't mind being rushed along, Kuşadasi travel agencies offer a package single-day tour to Pamukkale and Aphrodisias for $12 per person. If you're coming from Pamukkale, there are no direct buses from Denizli to Karaçasu; you've got to go all the way to Nazilli and change there. Admission to the site is 60TL per person and 100TL per camera. Rooms can be let at Karaçasu for 400TL per person, but there is not much to do once you've seen the ruins.

Named after Aphrodite, the goddess of beauty and love, the ancient city of Aphrodisias devoted itself, appropriately enough, to the higher arts. Before King Attalos III died in 133 B.C., he bequeathed the city of Pergammon to the hated Romans. All of the finest artists living in Pergammon and other parts of the kingdom promptly fled to Aphrodisias and founded a school of sculpture and plastic arts which brought the city great fame. Crafted from the fine white and bluish-grey marble of nearby quarries, the handsomest statues in the Roman Empire were often marked with the signature of the celebrated Aphrodisian school. The home of the great medical scientist Xenocrates, Aphrodisias was an important intellectual as well as artistic center of Asia Minor.

Aphrodisias' artistic heritage is evident from the present-day ruins of the city. Although only a portion of its spiral-fluted Corinthian colonnade remains, the **Temple of Aphrodite** is particularly elegant. Dating from the first century A.D., the temple originally housed a famous statue of Aphrodite; so far only copies of the original have been unearthed. With its extraordinary blue marble stage, the **odeon,** just to the south, was originally used by the elected officials of the city as a council chamber. The seven columns standing nearby were resurrected as part of a building christened by archeologists as the **Bishop's Palace,** due to the large number of religious artifacts and statues unearthed on its premises. Across from the odeon, the **Agora** shows severe signs of deterioration, while the theater's well-preserved stage, orchestra pit, and seating area remain relatively unscathed. Next to the theater stands the marble forecourt of **Hadrian's Bath,** which includes a sauna chamber, frigidarium, and changing rooms. The high point of a visit to Aphrodisias, however, is to be found across the road: the best preserved ancient **stadium** ever to have been excavated. With an enormous seating capacity of 30,000, even the marble blocks in the central arena which once marked the starting line for foot races are still in place.

The North Coast

Accessible during the summer months from the Greek islands of Lesvos and Chios, the northern stretch of Aegean coastline above Kuşadasi is not nearly as exciting or beautiful as the region to the south. But it does feature a smattering of charming little fishing ports and four famous archeological sites: Troy, Pergammon, Sardis, and Magnesia. The first of these is vastly overpublicized, but the second is not—the ruins at **Pergammon** are fabulous. If you're on Lesvos, don't hesitate to take a boat over to the Turkish port of **Ayvalik,** only 18km from the ruins. If you're coming to Chios, the boat runs daily in summer and will deposit you at the resort of **Çesme,** dominated by a fifteenth-century fortress and popular among Turks for its thermal spas. Çesme has a small town beach, but the prices are lower, the tourists fewer, and the beaches nicer to the north at **Foça.** Frequent buses run from Foça and Çesme to the metropolitan sprawl of **Izmir,** Turkey's third largest city with almost two million inhabitants. Despite its immense size, the city has little to offer besides a prodigious number of foreign NATO military personnel, a decent **archeological museum** situated within the wooded **Kultur Parki,** and some ridiculously overrated ruins of the ancient port of Smyrna. Most visitors to Izmir are seized by an irresistible inclination to confine their tour of the urban area to the city's extremely efficient bus station, which has frequent connections to just about anywhere in Turkey. If you're on Chios and only contemplating a short excursion to the shores of Turkey, consider visiting one of the archeological sites at Sardis and Magnesia, each a short, comfortable bus ride from Izmir.

Sardis and Magnesia

Both Sardis and Magnesia are easily reached from Izmir. The former is the farther and more worthwhile excursion—take any of the frequent Izmir-Ankara buses and ask the driver to let you off at the tiny village of **Sart Moustafa,** 103km from Izmir. The ruins are next to the village, and are being excavated by an American team of archeologists from Harvard and Cornell Universities who are usually willing to answer visitors' questions. The ruins of Magnesia that are interesting to tourists are of the ancient city of **Magnesia ad Sipylus,** thus named to distinguish the city from an earlier neighboring city also named Magnesia, originally located near the present-day village of Selçuk. Of the latter, practically nothing remains, so don't be misled by some of the sloppily compiled tourist literature. To reach the former site, take any bus bound for the pleasant city of Manisa. The ruins lie just before the city off the Izmir-Manisa highway, 34km from Izmir. Admission to the ruins at either Sardis or Magnesia is 60TL per person and 100TL per camera. Either site can be visited as an ambitious daytrip from Kuşadasi.

Once one of the wealthiest of the metropolises of ancient Greece, **Sardis** was the first city in the world to mint its own coins. This is hardly surprising, since Sardis was also the home of King Croesus, who was famous for being the richest man in the world. Like so many wealthy individuals, Croesus' greed eventually proved to be his own undoing. He consulted the Oracle at Delphi and was informed that if he crossed the river Halys, he would destroy an entire empire. He promptly proceeded to march his troops across the river, was defeated at the hands of the Persian army, then realized that the empire the Oracle had in mind was his own. This was only the first of a series of imprudent military campaigns that gradually depleted the treasury of Sardis. Under the reign of Alexander the Great, however, funds were invested in the construction of one of the largest Ionic temples of ancient times. Only a few columns of the once splendid **Temple of Artemis** now remain, but their scrolled capitals are exquisitely crafted. Today, the structure of primary interest at Sardis is the recently restored **Synagogue,** a handsome edifice dating from the second century A.D., with elegant mosaic floors and spiral-fluted columns adorning its facade.

Situated at the foot of Mt. Sipylus, **Magnesia** suddenly became the capital of the crumbling Byzantine Empire during the thirteenth century. Reflecting the city's role in history as the refuge for a fleeing emperor, most of the remains at Magnesia are fortifications, including a large thirteenth-century **citadel.** Only a portion of the area's charm is to be discovered among the ancient ruins, however. A cable car leads up to the summit of **Mt. Sipylus** for a fine panorama of the surrounding countryside, while the neighboring city of **Manisa** offers several interesting Islamic monuments. In the center of town you'll find two noteworthy mosques: **Muradiye Cami,** built by the celebrated Ottoman archietct Sinan in the sixteenth century; **Ulu Cami** (or Main Mosque) featuring Corinthian columns pilfered from ancient Roman structures; and a neighboring **Archeological Museum** housed in a sixteenth-century religious structure.

Pergammon and Troy

The ruins of ancient Pergammon neighbor the pleasant modern city of **Bergama,** easily accessible from the island of Lesvos in summer via the port of Dikili, and accessible all year round by buses from Izmir or Bursa. Just up the main street from the bus station is the **Park Hotel.** All the backpackers stay here and it is not hard to see why: it's cheap (doubles 800TL), clean, friendly, and even has sit-down toilets. Bergama is located about halfway between Bodrum and Istanbul, making it a good place to break up a journey north and spend the night. Travelers moving on to Istanbul should definitely consider stopping off for a day at **Bursa,** the home of some of Turkey's most beautiful mosques. (For more information on Istanbul and Bursa consult the chapter on Turkey in *Let's Go: Europe.*)

In ancient times Pergammon was most famous for its library, which contained over 200,000 volumes. It was the second largest in the ancient world after that in Alexandria. Little remains of it today as it was plundered by Marc Antony in the first century A.D., and its collection presented to Cleopatra shortly after her own library burned down. Equally little remains of the renowned **Altar of Zeus,** considered by many to be the finest artistic achievement of the Hellenistic era. Today it forms the centerpiece of the celebrated Pergammon Museum in East Berlin. Fortunately, the 30,000 acres of ruins were just too large to move. Most notable is the mammoth **amphitheater,** capable of seating 50,000 spectators. It was built by the Roman emperor Caracella after he was healed by the famous physician Galen, the father of modern medicine, whose **Asclepion,** or medical center, had its headquarters at Pergammon. An impressive portion of the Asclepion remains, including a marble colonnade, various healing rooms, and a well-preserved theatre. Scattered about also are the remains of a huge gymnasium, several temples, the lavishly frescoed House of Attalus, and a large Roman circus.

The ruins of ancient **Troy** (or **Truva**) are unquestionably the Aegean Coast's most overrated tourist attraction. Nonetheless, their powerful appeal is easy to understand. Not only Troy's legendary associations, but even its original archeological discovery contains the elements of epic romance. It all began when Heinrich Schliemann, a German millionaire turned amateur archeologist, became convinced that the Homeric myths were not mere myths and set out to prove his point. In what seemed like an insane scheme, he staked out the most promising location along the Turkish coast and paid local workers to begin excavating upon the spot. To the astonishment of the academic world he succeeded, thereby revolutionizing the field of archeology and laying the strategy for his subsequent discoveries of Mycenae and Knossos. Naturally, this heart-warming story manages to attract busloads of tourists to the site of ancient Troy. The only snag is that although Schliemann may have found ancient Troy, he did not find much of it. Frankly, there is not a whole lot to look at here. The one exception is an amazingly tacky wooden reconstruction of the **Trojan Horse,** no doubt erected expressly in order to provide dissatisfied tourists with a target for their hungry cameras. Admittedly, classics buffs who know the *Iliad* by heart will probably be stirred by the place, as long as their imaginations are fertile enough to supplement the scanty remains with images of Homeric heroes such as Priam, Hector, Agamemnon, Ajax, and Achilles. Nine different cultural layers have been excavated at Troy and dubbed Troy I through Troy IX for easy reference. Troy I dates from 3200 B.C., Troy II is the earliest known example of a planned city, while Troy VIIA is believed by some to be the city of Homer's *Iliad.*

Thirteen kilometers to the north is **Çanakkale,** the best place near Troy to

spend the night and the main transportation hub for the immediate region. The
Aegean Coast's northernmost resort, Çanakkale faces the narrowest point of
the Dardanelles Straits. Boats run from here to the Turkish island of **Imroz**.
Across the Straits on the European side lies the modern city **Gelibolu**, more
familiar to students of World War I as Gallipoli. The most scenic stretch of the
North Coast lies just south of Troy. Near the village of **Behremkale**, 69km
south of Troy, the ruins of ancient **Assos** boast a sixth-century B.C. Temple of
Athena and a good view of the northern edge of the isle of Lesvos. Around the
corner from Assos, a good road hugs the coast of the Gulf of Edremit, passing
through several tiny resorts, the nicest of which is **Ayvalik**, a small fishing
village with a picturesque harbor. Dolmuş run along the coast. Just 35km south
of Ayvalik is **Dikili**, where the boats from Lesvos occasionally dock.

Bodrum

One of the prettiest resorts in Turkey, with picturesque harbors on both
sides of an archetypal medieval castle, Bodrum is the favorite summer hangout
of Turkey's intellectuals and artists. Most of Bodrum's visitors come regularly
and are Turkish, so the town has all the advantages of a beautiful Aegean
resort without having sold its soul to the pocketbooks of foreign guests. Everything in Bodrum seems to shine and there's a reason for this: every wall visible
from the waterfront is freshly whitewashed in accordance with the law.

Whether you reach Bodrum by boat from Kos or by bus from Marmaris or
Izmir, the approach to the city is breathtaking. The port is ensconced in the
serpentine coastline of the sprawling **Bodrum Peninsula**, a sun-worshipper's
paradise brimming with beaches, secluded coves, and uninhabited islands, all
easily accessible by fishing boat from the main port. And Bodrum is not without its own archeological attraction: the **Mausoleum of Halicarnassus**, one of
the ancient world's seven wonders.

Orientation and Practical Information

Streets in Bodrum are often very poorly marked. Orient yourself with respect to the **Kale**, the centrally located castle from which most of the town's
main streets emanate. The castle divides the waterfront into two long semi-
circular coves along both of which you'll find most of the action. The *liman*
(harbor) is almost completely enclosed by two long slender breakwaters and
forms the older and more picturesque half, while along the more polished and
recently developed cove you'll find the highest concentration of pensions and
restaurants. The main thoroughfare along the waterfront keeps changing its
name. Starting from the castle and moving along the enclosed harbor, it begins
as **Karantina Caddesi**, becomes **Belideyi Meydani** after the mosque, then **Ney-
zan Tevfik** along most of the harbor, and ends at the marina as **Yat Limani**
(yacht harbor). Going the other way from the castle, first it is **Kasaphane
Caddesi**, then **Kumbahçe Mahellesi** until close to the water it becomes the main
commecial drag of **Cumhuriyet Caddesi**, ending by the large Halikarnas Hotel
as **Paşa Tarlasi**. **Turgut Reis Caddesi**, the long street one block in from the
harbor, leads to the main road, to **Gümbet Beach** (3km), and to points along the
peninsula. Extending inland from the entrance to the castle, **Kale Caddesi** is
the narrow, partially covered alley which is Bodrum's main shopping strip. It
then becomes **Çevat Şakir Caddesi**, bordering the parking lot of the bus station,
where all buses, taxis, and dolmuş leave.

Tourist Office: next to the entrance to the castle. Half the staff is incompetent and
uninformed. The better people are usually around in the morning. They have

complete accommodations listings and a lousy map. Better maps are available in the bookstore. They may help you find a room if you're having difficulty. Open daily from June 15-Sept. 15 8am-8pm; during the rest of the year 8:30am-noon and 1:30-7pm.

Post Office: Çevat Şakir Cad., next to the bus station.

International telephones: next to the entrance to the castle. In summer, expect to wait in line.

Boats to Knidos: Wonderful trip to ruins on Datça Peninsula. Both Karya Tours and Eti Seyahata sell tickets. Once a week from June 15-Sept. 15. $12.50 per person. Leave 7:30am and return 8pm.

Buses: Pamukkale and Aydin are the main companies. Several buses a day to Marmaris, Izmir, or Istanbul, but in summer book a day ahead. For Kuşadasi, take a bus to Söke and then a dolmuş. Bus company offices are next to the bus station, and Pamukkale has an office on Belideyi Meydani.

Dolmuş: from the bus station to anywhere on the peninsula. In summer, hourly departures to major destinations such as Torba or Turgut Reis. Lesser destinations several times daily. In high season, fares are double the normal cost. To Gümbet, outfitted jeeps run as frequently as collective taxis (50TL per person) from the parking lot.

Boats to Kos: There are two different companies—the first is cheaper, the second has more reliable departures. **Merhaba Tours:** on the waterfront, next to the castle, has boats three times weekly in summer. One way $13, round trip $24. **Duru Tours** at 15 Karantina Cad. (tel. 41 3). In summer their boat, the *Duru Kos,* sails daily, one way $17, round trip $30. In the off-season, boat departures fluctuate with demand (usually two or three times a week). All boats leave at 10am and return at 6pm.

Turkish Maritime Lines: Their cruise boats connect Bodrum with every major port between Mersin and Istanbul and pass through in each direction two or three times a month in summer. The place for tickets is **Eti Seyahata,** Kasaphane Cad. Fares to Istanbul are C-class 8500TL, D-class 6000TL, 10% discount for students.

Karya Tours 13 Karantina Caddesi (tel. 36 5). The most organized and efficient travel agency in town. Ask for Sevinç Gökbel (tel. 75 9); she speaks English and is very helpful. Their cheapest boats are $170 in low season and $200 in high season per day including crew.

Police: next to the castle, as are the **Customs Police** and the **Harbor Master.**

Hospital: Turgut Reis Cad., past the ruins of the mausoleum.

Pharmacy *(Eczane):* on Kale Cad., across from the bookstore.

Doctor: Tuncel Ziylan. His office is on Belediye Meydani.

Markets: Big fruit and vegetable affair on Thursday and Friday mornings, next to the bus station. Nearby **Milas** has large markets, including local crafts, every Tuesday morning.

Boat Rentals: The most popular way to tour the peninsula. Get together a large group of people and look for agencies that advertise *Mavi Yolculuk* ("Blue Road"). The most reliable though not the cheapest agency is Karya Tours.

Car Rentals: Karya Tours is also the Avis representative. Rates start at 2900TL per day plus 29TL per kilometer, not including insurance and 10% tax.

Bookstore: Ozalit Bookstore, in the basement of the Belideyi Mosque, at the end of Kale Caddesi. Good maps of Bodrum town and peninsula (100TL), some good guides to Turkey, and recent issues of *Time* and *Newsweek*.

Foreign Newspapers: On the waterfront, across from the bookstore. *International Herald Tribune* (200TL), various European papers, and the *Turkish Daily News*.

Work Opportunities: The **Institute of Underwater Archeology,** located inside the castle, needs skilled volunteers of all sorts to do anything from carpentry to art restoration. Talk to the president, Don Fry, a charismatic American professor from Texas A & M University.

Accommodations

During the summer months, water can be a scarce commodity here. Pensions are generally the way to go, since hotels are not abundant and tend to be overpriced. The two exceptions to this rule, **Ege Oteli** and **Emil Oteli,** tend to fill up quickly (both are next to the bus station and charge 500TL per person). During the peak season finding a room can be a challenge and may call for the Grand Search (see below).

Belmi Pension, off Neyzen Tevfik Cad; follow the blue sign. Very clean rooms, quiet location, nice outdoor tables. The only catch is that on summer evenings their plumbing may leave you high and dry. Otherwise, one of the best deals at 500TL per person. The **Pension Kaptanin** next door charges the same for nice rooms or may let you sleep on the roof for less.

Aile Pension, Firkateyn Sokak off of Neyzen Tavfik. Very clean, very quiet. Usually has space due to its obscure location. Doubles 1000TL, triples 1200TL.

Merhaba Pansiyon, 3 Akasia Sokak. At the end of the waterfront, just before the Hotel Halikarnas, turn left and follow the sign. The proprietor, Mehmet Atav, speaks English and is very hospitable, if somewhat lecherous. Every room has a private shower. Singles 600TL, doubles 1000TL, triples 1250TL.

Deniz Pension, Neyzen Tevfik Cad., across from the waterfront mosque. Rooms are not very impressive. Very pleasant terraces overlooking the harbor where you can have breakfast for as little as 150TL per person. Doubles listed at 1600TL, but they'll chip them down to 1200TL if business is slack. Next door, **Pension Oya** has clean doubles for 1000TL, but rooms are small. Make sure you get one with windows.

Rockbottom Pensions: The following are not the cleanest, but they are the cheapest at 400TL per body: **Yilmaz** and **Yali** are both on Neyzen Tevfik Cad., while **Metin, Ali Baba,** and **Titez** are all along Türk Kusuyu Cad. Take the left-hand fork off of Çevat Şakir Cad.

The Grand Search: We know the problem—it's peak season and you are really stuck. Along Kumbahçe Mah and Cumhuriyet Cad. is a long chain of pensions, the cheapest of which charge 1000TL for doubles and 1250 for triples. Starting from the castle, the four cheap ones on Kumbahçe are **Şoray, Durak, Dadas,** and **Arci;** and the five on Cumhuriyet are **Gökova, Aşkin, Kemer, Gözen,** and **Genç.** Good luck!

Camping: Most of the campgrounds are 3km away on Gümbet Beach. They all charge 250-300TL per person and 100-150TL per tent. If it rains, **Baba Kamping** also arranges rooms to let for 750-800TL per person, including breakfast. In town, there's one campground, but it's not very nice: **Yuvam Kamping,** off Neyzen Tevfik Cad., 150TL per person.

Food

Bodrum is a gastronomic paradise with restaurants to satisfy budgets of every size. The following are the best places for inexpensive eating:

Sokkali Ali Doksan Restaurant, 15 Kale Cad., affectionately known to locals as the **Köfte-çi.** A bit hectic, but the most popular lunch place and it's no mystery why. Good, quick, cheap food! Come between noon and 2pm before they start running out of dishes. Be aggressive about claiming a free seat or you'll wait all day.

Nazilli Pide Salonu, at the mouth of Cumhuriyet Cad. Good inexpensive *pide* for 85TL regular; 100TL with meat, cheese and eggs.

Turgut Reis Lokantasi, across from the above. Very good food and low prices. Try the excellent *manti* (ravioli in yogurt sauce) for 85TL or the steaming hot *sahan köfte* (meatballs in a tomato sauce and green pepper stew) for 125TL.

Kardeşler Restaurant, next to the bus station. The place to fill up for very little. Heavy meat dishes 150TL, *dolma* 100TL, side orders of *pilav* 75TL.

Do your splurging at Bodrum. The port is famous throughout Turkey for its fish restaurants. The following three are excellent without being unreasonably expensive.

Hey Yarum Hey, off of Cumhuriyet Cad. Excellent view of the castle from tables romantically situated right on the beach. Delicious seafood. *Kalamari* 550TL, fish kebab 600TL. Finish off the evening in a decadent fashion across the street, with superb Turkish desserts at the **Samaryolu Pastanasi.**

Körfez Garden Restaurant, Neyzen Tevfik Cad. The oldest restaurant in town; it has survived for a reason. If you don't mind garlic, don't miss their heavenly, if somewhat rich, yogurt and spinach appetizer. Delicious fish kebab for 600TL, *kalamari* 650TL.

Orhan's No. 7, so called because it is at #7 Eski Banka Sokak, off of Kale Cad. In summer, the interior dining room is often reserved for private parties, but you can usually eat at their outdoor tables. The appetizers are wonderful at 100-150TL each. Try the *muçver* (tastefully seasoned deep-fried squash), delicious cheesy shrimp *güveç* (stew) for 450TL, or fresh steamed shrimp for 100TL per shrimp. Octopus 600TL.

Sights

Dominating Bodrum from its strategic waterfront position stands the **Kale,** reputed to be the world's best-preserved Crusader castle. It was constructed by the notorious Order of the Knights of St. John during the fifteenth and sixteenth centuries A.D. When the knights were forced to retreat from the Holy Land in 1291 A.D., they relocated their headquarters on the nearby island of Rhodes; they arrived in Bodrum in 1402 A.D. and immediately began construction of the castle, finally completing it in 1513. The castle towers were built by knights of different nations and four of them are accordingly known as the English, German, French, and Italian towers. In addition, there exists the squat yet handsome Harbor Tower and a sinister-looking battlement appropriately christened the Snake Tower. Despite its immense proportions and extensive crenellated fortifications, only ten years after its completion the knights were compelled to surrender the castle. In 1523 they were overpowered by the great Ottoman general Suleymein the Magnificent and eventually forced to retreat again, this time to Malta where their Order exists to this day. The castle houses Bodrum's **Museum of Underwater Archeology,** a fascinating collection of ancient shipwreck remains recently excavated by the Institute of Underwater Archeology from sites along the surrounding Turkish coastline. The institute, the only one of its kind in the world, is affiliated with Texas A & M University and partially funded by National Geographic Magazine, and has been the subject of several documentary films. Several more wrecks were recently sighted along the coast; their excavation awaits the funds necessary for the extremely costly endeavor of submerging an entire archeological team.

A Byzantine chapel in the central courtyard of the castle houses the **Bronze Age Hall,** containing finds from a 1200 B.C. shipwreck, including the ship's lamp, weights, and scrap bronze that was in transit to Cyprus. Huge jars found on board date from as far back as 1600 B.C. and show Cretan influences, strongly indicating the existence of a trade route between ancient Crete and the Asia Minor coast. The archeological significance of an ancient shipwreck is evident here: it is like discovering a time-capsule where one can rest assured that all the artifacts date from a single historical moment. Scattered in every corner of the museum are thousands of ancient **amphoras** (antiquity's answer to giant tin cans) which have been adopted by the souvenir shops as the tourist symbol of Bodrum. The amphoras were among the cargo of a fourth-century A.D. shipwreck and a seventh-century A.D. vessel. The latter was so well preserved that the entire hull of the ship could be reconstructed. Don't miss the small room exhibiting the exquisite **glassware** salvaged from the eleventh-century A.D. *Serçe Limani* wreck, the oldest known example of a ship constructed along modern lines. Not usually on display to the public without special permission, the bulk of the ship's cargo, several tons of shattered Islamic glassware, forms what is undoubtedly the world's largest jigsaw puzzle: presently it is being painstakingly pieced together in the English Tower. Other highlights of the museum include a fine collection of **Mycenean pottery** (1400-1200 B.C.) and several of the **Ottoman cannons** originally used to defend the castle. Open in summer (June 15-Sept. 15) 8am-noon and 3-7pm, otherwise 8:30am-noon and 3-5:30pm; admission 60TL per person, 100TL per camera.

The ruins of ancient **Halicarnassus,** site of one of the seven wonders of the ancient world, are Bodrum's better known if less picturesque attraction. Often remembered as the home of the historian Herodotus, by the fourth century B.C. Halicarnassus had become one of the mightiest ports on the Aegean Coast under the leadership of King Mausoleus, a Persian who imposed ruthlessly strict laws upon the city. For example, he enforced a decree calling for the punishment of any man with long hair. During his reign, work began on his tomb and it was finally completed in 353 B.C. after his death. It was subsequently declared one of the world's seven wonders and provided the etymological roots of the modern word "mausoleum." The structure consisted of a rectangular foundation and stone pedestal upon which the sepulchral chamber rested, surrounded by 36 Ionic columns. The mausoleum was covered with a gigantic pyramidal roof, crowned by a statue of Mausoleus driving a chariot drawn by four horses. Towering to a height of fifty meters, the colossal edifice was clearly visible from long distances at sea. The frieze which once adorned the lower pediment was removed first by the Crusaders to decorate their castle, then by the English to the British Museum in London. A plaster copy of it now stands at the site. (Admission free; located on Turgut Reis Cad.; follow the signs from Neyzen Tevfik up Tepecik Hamam Sokak.) A small **museum** adjoins the site and is due to open in 1984.

Nightlife

There's lots of it. Perhaps the most telling indication of the relative sophistication of Bodrum's clientele is the existence of alternatives to the usual blaring disco scene, particularly in the shape of pleasant pubs for just relaxing and listening to music.

Emin Findikoğlu 3, 94 Cumhuriyet Cad. Highbrow and mellow. Popular with the Istanbul intelligentsia. Live jazz from 11pm-2am, occasionally featuring some of Turkey's finest jazz artists. Beer 450TL, western style pizza 150-200TL.

Jazz Club, Neyzen Tevfik Cad., next door to Pension Deniz. Less sophisticated and expensive than the above. A laid-back cafe/bar with recorded jazz music.

Cafe Hadigari Bar, 28 Kasaphane Cad. They specialize in recordings of soft rock with an occasional jazz interlude. Where the hip crowd hangs out.

Han Restaurant/Bar, 29 Kale Cad., in a medieval *caravanserai*. Several nights a week they have live Turkish music. Expensive food; stick to drinks.

Restaurant/Bar Den, Neyzen Tevfik Cad., a decent fish restaurant that often turns into a wild nightspot on summer evenings with live music and traditional dancing into the wee hours.

Near Bodrum

Most summertime visitors to Bodrum spend their days basking on **Gümbet Beach,** 3km by road from the bus station and easily accessible by dolmuş. You can try your hand at windsurfing for 1000TL per hour; no extra charge for a teacher; or explore less inhabited coves with a rowboat for 200TL per hour or 1000TL per day. Resist the temptation to swim by uncrowded portions of the beach. Parts of the shoreline are infested with sea urchins (if you're windsurfing it's a good idea to wear something on your feet). Most of the hotels along the beach are expensive. The one exception is the **Ege Motel,** with doubles for 950 TL, triples for 1170TL. Around the next large cove from Gümbet is the slightly less crowded beach at **Bitez,** easily accessible by dolmuş or boat from Bodrum.

The main source of Bodrum's popularity among Turkish tourists derives from its strategic location at the head of the enchanting **Bodrum Peninsula,** which is dotted with charming villages, inexpensive seafood restaurants, sandy beaches, and breathtaking scenery. It is the ideal area for a peaceful vacation of swimming, sunshine, and relaxing dinners by the shore. Almost every village has inexpensive accommodations. It is impossible to single out any one spot on the peninsula in particular. Much of the region's charm lies in the fact that its summertime visitors disperse themselves all along the coastline. The southern edge of the peninsula has the best beaches and is more popular, though the rugged and less touristed northern half is not without its charms. *Dolmuş motorlari* (collective boat-taxis) service the entire southern coast of the peninsula and all of the neighboring islands. You might begin by trying one of the day tours offered by the *dolmuş motorlari* that leave every morning at 11am, returning between 5-7pm, from along the harbor by Neyzen Tevfik or from in front of the castle. Most of the day tours stop off at **Ada Island,** the beaches at **Capa Tatil, Kargi, Bağla,** and **Karaincir,** and the village of **Akyarlar.** Fare is usually 500TL per person. During the summer, boats also leave at least three times a week from in front of the castle to tranquil **Orak Island,** an excellent place to get away from it all. A less remote and more popular daytrip is the voyage across to **Karaada Island,** which offers both beaches and natural springs. Boats leave at 10am or 11am from the front of the castle for 300TL per person. The prices and departure times are the same to the beach at **Baradakçi,** recently becoming a very popular trip.

For longer stays on the peninsula, head inland by dolmuş. The most accessible point, **Turgut Reis,** is an 18km trip from Bodrum (off-season 70TL; high season 140TL). It's the closest thing in the area to a tourist center, with plenty of waterfront and oodles of accommodations. The cheapest rooms here are 650TL for a double and 900TL for a triple in high season at any of the following pensions: **Sefa, Pekdemir, Aytekin,** or **Aslan.** The most popular spot with Europeans, **Gümüşlük,** at the far western end of the peninsula, also makes an excellent daytrip from Bodrum. The Turkish name means "silver-like" and the waters off the small beach do seem to shine uncannily. Near the beach lie the ruins of ancient **Myndos,** once a stronghold of the Persian Empire, which consists of a chunky nine-foot-thick fortified wall and a Roman basilica. Also by the beach, the **Syphos** and **Mindos** pensions each charge 850TL per night for a double and 1150TL for a triple. Down the coast towards Turgut Reis, **Çesel Kamping** charges 150TL per person. In high season three or four dolmuş a day leave directly for Gümüşlük from Bodrum; in the off-season, they leave only once a day. **Gölköy,** 13km from Bodrum, is the best spot on the north coast to enjoy fresh fish from a table overlooking the water. Just step into the restaurant and point to what you want; most entrees are around 500TL. The **Başkent Pension** offers the least expensive beds, with doubles for 1370TL and triples 1775TL (including breakfast). Closer to Bodrum, just off the road to Milas, the village of **Torba** nestles within a small cove at the foot of some large hills with a pleasant stretch of beach and several pensions for 400TL per person.

Among Turkish students the most popular way to spend time along the Bodrum Peninsula is to travel down the so-called **Mavi Yolculuk,** or the "Blue Road," since the most spectacular stretches of coastline are only accessible by boat. The only catch is that it takes a large group of people (8-15) to make it a financially reasonable undertaking ($12-20 per day). Don't pass up an opportunity to tag along; otherwise, talk to people and organize your own contingent. Most of the travel agencies rent boats—just look for the large signs saying *Mavi Yolculuk.* Rentals include a crew who do all the sailing and most of the cooking and cleaning up, though a little help is always appreciated.

The Mediterranean Coast

Extending from Marmaris to Kaş, the western half of Turkey's Mediterranean Coast, opposite the Greek islands of Rhodes and Kastelorizo, offers everything from lively resorts to long expanses of unexplored and sometimes virtually inaccessible beaches. The most scenic stretch runs from **Fethiye** to **Kaş,** featuring rugged, spectacular, and remarkably unspoiled coastline. Beyond Kaş the coast between Antalya and Alanya becomes far more touristy, less beautiful, and more difficult to reach from Greece.

During the first and second millenia B.C., the area around Fethiye and Kaş formed the Kingdom of Lycia. The Lycian culture placed a heavy emphasis on the significance of burial rites and funerary monuments. Plenty of evidence of the Lycian preoccupation with death still remains today. Carved into the cliffsides all along the coast are numerous Lycian rock tombs, while almost everywhere you look—in the middle of city streets, littered around the countryside, and even perched on off-shore islands—you'll see countless ancient Lycian sarcophagi. The sites of a number of Lycian cities also punctuate the coast. Most significant among these are the ruins of **Xanthos** (see near Fethiye section).

The best boat connection between the Greek islands and Turkey's Mediterranean shores is the ferry between Rhodes and **Marmaris,** which leaves daily in summer. Unfortunately, Marmaris is one of the coastline's most developed and least attractive resorts. Allow enough time to explore farther east. Distances on the maps are deceiving: beyond Fethiye the road winds through tortuous mountain terrain and becomes as slow as it is scenic. If you are at all sensitive to carsickness, reserve seats in advance towards the front of the bus. The only other quasi-official boat connection is between Kastelorizo and Kaş. However, it hardly constitutes a reliable connection. Since Kastelorizo and Kaş are only a half-hour apart, in summer it is sometimes possible to hitch a ride on a yacht. Boats also run between Turkish Cyprus and the ports of **Taşucu** (hydrofoil) and **Mersin** (ferry). From Greek Cyprus you can only take advantage of these boats if you can find some way to smuggle your baggage across the border in Nicosia. This is done frequently in the off-season before security is tightened up. Travel from these ports to Greek Cyprus is impossible. (For more information on travel between Turkey and Greek Cyprus, consult the Northern Cyprus section.) Antalya has an international airport with remarkably inexpensive domestic flights to major Turkish cities. The quickest inexpensive way to get from the Mediterranean Coast to Istanbul is to take a direct bus from Antalya (1300TL, 12-14 hours).

Accommodations along the western segment of the Mediterranean Coast are, for the most part, relatively inexpensive, and excellent cheap seafood restaurants abound. Water can sometimes become a problem, since during the summer months the smaller communities, most notably Kalkan and Kaş, often suffer shortages. In order to ration the water supply between June and August the regional government occasionally shuts off all water in certain towns from 7am until 6pm. Water shut-offs are always announced by local authorities in advance. They can occur for several consecutive days. Don't let this deter you. Once you adjust to a schedule of doing all your washing in the evening, the limited availability of water ceases to be a major inconvenience.

Marmaris

Located where Turkey's Aegean and Mediterranean coastlines meet, Marmaris' natural setting could not be more picturesque. Wooded mountains along the coast and on neighboring islands rise straight up from the sea, encircling the harbor's deep blue waters with a verdant backdrop. Unfortunately, the waterfront of the port is unappealing and suffers visibly from the mushrooming tourist industry. Even more unfortunately, Marmaris' overdeveloped shoreline promenade is all that most of the many visitors who come via the daily ferry from Rhodes ever see of Turkey. Marmaris may be one of the least attractive corners of Turkey's coastline, but some of its most beautiful scenery is only hours away. With dramatic vistas and secluded beaches in every direction, the only good reason to linger in Marmaris is to catch one of the dolmuş boats from the harbor that depart every morning for the unspoiled islets and nearby beaches.

Orientation and Practical Information

If you're in Marmaris you're probably there in connection with the ferry to Rhodes. Conveniently enough, the whole downtown area is stretched along the port. You're never more than three blocks from the sea in Marmaris since the whole town is one long sprawl of hotels, restaurants, and cafes hugging the shoreline. The most commercialized section of town is just before the fortress, consisting of several blocks of souvenir shops. On the other side of the fortress is Marmaris' most pleasant neighborhood, the **Old City,** flanked on one side by the main port where the ferry from Rhodes docks, and on the other by a delightful little marina. **Kordon Caddesi** runs along the main waterfront, becoming **Atatürk Caddesi** where the road bends towards the main beach. The shopping bazaar by the fortress consists of **Iskele Sokak** and **Yeni Garşi,** extending back from the waterfront and terminating in **Oto Tamir,** which eventually becomes **Datça Road** as it leads off up the hill.

Tourist Office: Kordon Cad., across from the main ferry dock. English spoken. They provide maps and suggestions for excursions, and sometimes help locate a room during the high season. Open June-Sept. 8am-8pm; otherwise 8:30am-noon, 1-5:30pm.

Post Office: half a block in from the waterfront on Fevzi Paja Cad., the second street after the shopping bazaar. **International telephones** next door.

Bus Station: Atatürk Cad., by the bend in the waterfront. Buses to Izmir run fifteen times daily (500TL); six time daily to Ankara (1400TL) via Denizli; six times daily to Datça (300TL); twice daily to Fethiye (500TL); three times daily to Bodrum (500TL).

Boat to Rhodes: In summer, daily departures from the pier in front of the tourist office at 8:30am; in the off-season two or three boats a week. Two-hour journey. One way 3000TL, single-day round trip 5000TL (no student discounts). Charge for car or motorcycles is 15TL per kilogram. Tickets are available at **Yeşil Marmaris Travel Agency,** 37 Kordon Cad. (tel. 22 90 or 22 91). Open in summer 7:30am-9:30pm, winter 8am-7pm. There are also two other agencies, each with its own boat. If you're not careful it is easy to miss your boat. Passports are required the night before you leave.

Police: corner of Kordon and Fevzi Paja Cad.

Hospital: on the road to Datça, 1.5km from town.

Private Doctor: Doktor Ahmet Kuyzu, Kordon Cad. across from the Atatürk statue (tel. 47 0).

Public Restrooms: in the tourist office (free) and on the beach (10TL).

Car Rental: Hertz on Iskele Sok., across from the tourist office. With 30TL per kilometer charge: 3000TL daily rate. 18,000TL weekly, 72,000 monthly. Unlimited mileage: 7500TL daily, 7000TL daily if more than a week. Insurance and tax not included in fees.

Laundry Service: Ship Chandler, located on the marina waterfront, behind the castle. Quite expensive—jeans and button shirts 150TL, T-shirts 75TL, small articles 25TL per item.

Accommodations

Cheap, clean rooms are hard to find here. Generally the two adjectives are mutually exclusive and choosing a room requires opting for one or the other. In the center of town in summer, you usually can't do better than 500TL per person. If you walk towards the wooden footbridge that leads to the National Park at the edge of town, however, doubles in private homes cost 800TL or less. Sometimes buses conveniently let you off at the parking lot at this edge of town.

Acar Hotel, 32 Kordon Cad. (tel. 11 17). The best of the second-class hotels in town. Moderately clean rooms, some with balconies overlooking the harbor. Singles 700TL, doubles 1400TL, triples 2000TL. Breakfast 250TL.

Imbat Hotel, Iskele Sok. (tel. 14 13). Not very clean, but the cheapest hotel beds in town. Officially, the rates are the same as above, but they'll usually shave them down to 400TL per person.

Hotel Pina (tel. 10 53) and **Hotel Kapitan** (tel. 12 51), right next to each other on Kordon Cad. in front of the castle. They're the cheapest of the first-class hotels. For those who opt for clean over cheap. Both feature rooms with terraces overlooking the port with outdoor tables. Rates include a mandatory 300TL per person breakfast. Doubles 2200TL, triples 3150TL. In the off-season, they can be bargained down.

Gökce Pensiyon, at the far end of the marina (tel 17 14). The most picturesque location available at 500TL per person. In summer, they're often full, but can arrange rooms with neighbors for the same charge.

Okşan Pension, before the footbridge to the park. They charge 400TL per person, as do many of the families in the neighborhood. Just walk around with a backpack and you'll be taken in hand. The family just before the Okşan runs an unofficial pension. 400TL per person with access to washing machine and refrigerator.

Pension Suat, conveniently near the beach. You'll see their sign by the gaming room on Atatürk Cad. Very basic rooms; pleasant outdoor common area with cafe. 500TL per person.

Food

If you're coming from Greece, most restaurants in Marmaris may seem inexpensive, but if you're coming from elsewhere in Turkey they will not. Here are some exceptions, cheap by any standards.

Acar Kafeterya, Kordon Cad., across from the statue of Atatürk. Excellent *pide* with any combination of meat, cheese, or egg for 100-130TL.

Hasanin Yeri Karaca Lokantasi, 15 Yeri Garşi. Mediocre food, but its Marmaris' cheapest restaurant. *Köfte* with potatoes or other meat entrees 125TL, rice 50TL. Around the corner, **Ayyildiz Lokantasi** is the place for barbecued meat. *Şiş, döner,* or *köfte* for 175TL.

Tilla Restaurant, Atatürk Cad., across from the beach. Tasty and reasonably priced. *Köfte* 200TL, *dolma* 100TL, spinach and yogurt salad 100TL.

The provisions stores along the marina sell canned goods for people planning on doing some serious sailing.

Sights

Marmaris itself has little to offer besides a large town beach and the walk of a **fortress** built in 1522 by Suleymein the Magnificent as a military base for his successful campaign against the Crusaders of Rhodes. The alleyways hugging the castle walk form the oldest and most picturesque section of the city. Only 1.5km away, **Günnücek National Park** features a small beach and picnic tables set against a verdant forest containing some rare frankincense trees. To reach the park, follow the coastal road past the marina and out of town, across the small wooden footbridge.

The best beaches and scenery around Marmaris are only accessible by boat. Lush green shrubbery covers the grey rocks of the coast like a velvet blanket, contrasting beautifully with the blue waters of the Bay of Marmaris. Servicing the Bay, *dolmuş motorlari* boats depart from the harbor along Kordon Caddesi every morning for a variety of destinations. The best way to start is to take a full day tour for 500TL; boats depart between 10 and 11am, returning around 7-7:30pm. The tours differ somewhat and the drivers are casual regarding the itineraries. The single most popular destination is beautiful **Turunç Beach,** across the bay from Marmaris. Since electricity was installed in 1979, the beach has become increasingly popular with Turkish vacationers and is gradually becoming commercialized. Flanking Turunç to the north and to the south respectively are Gölenye Springs, where the waters are reputed to cure intestinal ailments of all kinds, and the less crowded **Kumlu Beach,** near the scanty remains of an old fortress. Both are convenient by boat. Most of the mouth of the Bay of Marmaris is sealed off by the heavily wooded **Nimara Peninsula,** along the far end of which are the fluorescent phosphorous caves by **Alkoya Point**—a favorite destination for Marmaris' excursion boats. Sandwiched between the peninsula and the mainland is the tiny uninhabited island of Keçi, which offers a nice view of the surrounding coastline.

Near Marmaris

Two noteworthy archeological sites lie on either side of Marmaris: to the west at the tip of the **Datça Peninsula** are the ruins of the ancient city of **Knidos;** to the east near the town of Köyceğiz are the remains of **Caunos.** Knidos involves at least a two-day excursion from Marmaris. Caunos can be seen in a daytrip.

Knidos was one of the artistic and intellectual centers of the ancient Hellenic world. It was the home of Sostratos, the famous architect who designed the lighthouse at Alexandria (one of the seven wonders of the world), and the astronomer Eudoxus, who first calculated the circumference of the earth. The city was most renowned in antiquity for its statue of the goddess Aphrodite. As one of the first female nudes to be sculpted in ancient Greece, the work scandalized Hellenic society, which had until that time confined itself to the naked male form. Nothing remains of the statue, but the contours of the ancient metropolis can still be discerned. The most notable remains are the well-preserved city walls, the temples dedicated to Dionysus and Demeter, and some medieval fortified structures. Much of the charm of the ruins at Knidos comes from their scenic, remote location. Best reached by boat from either Marmaris or Bodrum (see Bodrum section), the site is worth visiting for the breathtaking approach by sea to the deserted ruins, surrounded by splashing waves. From Marmaris, a bus takes you three-quarters of the way to the village of **Datça** (80km), a small coastal resort located half-way down the peninsula of the same name. From here you have the option of proceeding to Knidos either by hiring a jeep via dirt road (30km), or by chartering a boat. The latter is only a feasible option in summer and even then the cost depends on how many tourists at Datça are interested in the venture. Once in Datça you may find yourself with little inclination to leave the peninsula. Rooms are plentiful here for about 400TL per person. Unspoiled by tourism, the surrounding coastline offers rugged scenery and a host of secluded beaches.

The ruins of ancient **Caunos** can be visited either as a daytrip from Marmaris or on the way to or from Fethiye. If you're coming by bus, disembark at **Köyceğiz,** about an hour from Marmaris on the main route to Fethiye (250TL), and hire a taxi; or get off just past Köyceğiz at the turn-off for Caunos and try to hitch a ride (probably with tourists). The ruins lie by a small river which connects **Lake Köyceğiz** to the sea at what is considered to be the point where the Aegean and the Mediterranean officially meet. You can stay in Köyceğiz in the **Hotel Kent,** next door to the bus station, for 400TL per person. Follow the signs from the main street. However, a more pleasant place to lodge in the area is the peaceful lakeside fishing village of **Dalyan.** It is the closest community to the ruins, has a quiet beach, and very few tourists. Occasional dolmuş run to Dalyan from Köyceğiz and from Ortaca (the place to get off if you're coming from Fethiye). The Turkish word **dalyan** means "fishery" and the local fishermen thrive by simply casting their nets in the river and hauling up the underwater traffic between the lake and the sea. In ancient times, when a steady and ample supply of fish counted for more in the world economy, this strategic location allowed ancient Caunos to grow into a wealthy metropolis. Almost all of the ruins presently standing are of Roman construction—a large theater capable of seating 20,000, some well preserved baths, a water reservoir, and a finely decorated basilica. Carved into a cliffside high above the site are the most important pre-Roman remains: the so-called **Graves of Caunos,** some Lycian rock tombs dating from the fourth century B.C.

Fethiye

The small modern port of Fethiye is probably not the pristine coastal village you have been looking for. Most vacationers are in search of something more picturesque than the tumble of concrete buildings that line Fethiye's dusty streets. The town has expanded unattractively away from the harbor, leaving the beachless waterfront surprisingly lifeless. Nonetheless, Fethiye boasts some striking Lycian rock tombs and remains a popular base for excursions, particularly to the fabulous lagoon at Ölü Deniz, only 14km away.

Practical Information and Accommodations

The **Tourist Office** is on the waterfront across from the large pier where the cruise ships dock. They speak a little of everything, provide maps (100TL), arrange boat trips, and have listings of pensions. Open May 1-Sept. 1, 8am-8pm; rest of the year 8am-noon and 1-5:30pm. **Atatürk Caddesi,** the main avenue running parallel to the harbor, has banks, pharmacies, and most of the town's major shops. In rapid succession follow the **police, post office,** and **hospital,** a few blocks down from the tourist office. The only English-language newspaper in town is available at the shop at 15 Atatürk Cad., which sells *The Wall Street Journal* for some mysterious reason. For a tasty and inexpensive meal, pull up a seat at the busy **Iç Ki Siz Lokanta,** just down the street off of Atatürk Cad. Alcohol is not served since the establishment is run by a devout Muslim. The **bus station** is at the edge of town off Çarsi Caddesi, by the main road out of town. Buses depart four times daily to Kalkan and Kaş. There are only a few direct buses each morning to Marmaris. However, you can take any one of the frequent buses to Izmir, ask to get off at **Gökova,** and catch a bus or a dolmuş from there to Marmaris without difficulty.

Fethiye is exploding with inexpensive pensions. Since the supply far exceeds the demand, cheap rooms are effortlessly found. But unless you need to catch an early morning bus or boat, don't spend the night in town. A more scenic setting and comfortable bungalows are available at the campgrounds on any of the nearby beaches at Ölü Deniz, Çaliş, or Günlük Bay (see below). If you do wish to spend the night, the official price is 450TL per person and can usually be bargained down. The cleanest of the conveniently located pensions are along the waterfront past the tourist office on Karagözler Mah., each charging 400-450TL per person: **Çim** (tel. 16 39), **Telmesos** (tel. 10 42), **Deniz** tel. 17 53), and **Özcan** (tel. 21 40).

Sights

Some of Turkey's best preserved Lycian rock tombs are carved into the face of the cliff directly overlooking Fethiye. Originally part of the ancient city of

Telmessos, the fronts of the most striking tombs are carved into the forms of Greek temple facades, complete with pediments, porticoes, and cornices. Connected to the road by several flights of steps, the most impressive tomb is the **Temple of Amyntas,** which takes its name from a fourth-century B.C. inscription on the left-hand column that reads: "This is the tomb of Amyntas, son of Hermapias." You can enter the other tombs as well, though they require a bit of clambering around the rocks. From the tombs you can see the remains of a medieval **citadel,** as well as several of the islands sprinkled about the Bay of Fethiye. In town, next to the hospital, is an **archeological museum** containing Lycian artifacts. It has been closed for renovation and is scheduled to reopen in 1984.

Fethiye's main beach, **Çaliş,** only 5km away, is a relatively uncrowded crescent of sand extending over two miles. In summer (June-Sept.) a little municipal vehicle runs every hour from the harbor (25TL), supplemented by year-round dolmuş service (50TL). Boats run from here to the beaches on the off-shore isle of **Sövalye.** Slightly farther on lie the even less inhabited beaches at **Günlük Bay** and **Katranci Bay;** either one can be reached by dolmuş (100TL) or by any of the frequent buses to Izmir. **Dirlik Kamp** and **Seketer Kamp** at Çaliş and **Mokamp Ruzi** at Günlük Bay have a variety of facilities from tent sites to bungalows, including full pension. Their rates are approximately the same as at the campgrounds at Ölü Deniz (see below). You can camp unofficially at Katranci in the picnic area—a beautiful spot surrounded by pines overlooking a handsome rocky cove.

Near Fethiye

Excursion boats leave the harbor at Fethiye for a variety of destinations. Some just provide transport to nearby beaches for 200TL. The most popular daytrip is the so-called **Twelve Island Tour** (600TL), which hops from one to the next of the twelve principal members of the archipelago scattered about the Bay of Fethiye. Several of the islands have small beaches and the boats pause to allow time for swimming and exploration. The most worthwhile of the excursions offered in the Bay of Fethiye is to the island of **Lydia,** which possesses some of Turkey's finest Lycian rock tombs. Boats run according to demand and the price varies depending on the number of passengers on board. If the boat runs full (24 people), the fare is about 600TL per person. To keep the fare down you may have to interest some other tourists in coming along. The trip takes 3½ hours each way.

A more popular daytrip is to the ruins of the ancient city of **Xanthos,** 60km from Fethiye along the road to Kalkan. Xanthos was the capital of the ancient Kingdom of Lycia, founded in the second millenium B.C. by a fiercely independent tribe renowned for its courage in battle. The kingdom and its capital city perished in a remarkable fashion. In 545 B.C., when the Xanthians realized they would be overpowered by the Persian army, they gathered all the women, children, and valuables of the community upon their acropolis and set them afire. The male population then marched into battle and fought until all were dead. Under Roman rule, Xanthos emerged again as an important center. The second-century A.D. **Theater** and **City Agora** that you see today are of Roman origin. Several important Lycian structures have been excavated as well. Most notable is the funerary **Monument of the Harpies,** a sixth-century B.C. monolithic column rising to a height of five meters. A celebrated frieze depicting the Harpies, mythological winds of destruction which could be summoned to destroy invading armies, decorated the original funeral chamber. The original frieze now stands in the British Museum; what you see today at Xanthos is a plaster copy. Adjoining the monument stands the **Xanthian Obelisk.** Its upper section has been removed so that philologists around the world can puzzle over its long inscription in the hitherto undeciphered Lycian language. A series of Lycian **rock tombs** are carved into the hillside, complete with pillars, pediments, and decorative friezes. To get to Xanthos, take any bus running between Fethiye and Kalkan or Kaş and get off at the village of **Kinik** (Fethiye-Kinik: 1½ hours, 150TL; Kalkan-Kinik: one hour, 100TL). The ruins are visible from the highway. Admission to the site is 60TL per person and 100TL per camera.

Ölü Deniz

You can see posters of the almost completely enclosed lagoon at Ölü Deniz, surrounded by spectacular wooded mountains, in almost every Turkish hotel or tourist office. What you don't see in the posters are the vacationers' campsites filled with European tourists. The spot is an archetypal Shangri-La fantasy of endless sandy beach and turquoise water. If you're in search of traditional Turkish culture, this is not the place to come. But if you're just interested in enjoying the sun and surf of the Mediterranean at its most stunningly beautiful, you'll find Ölü Deniz the most inviting slice of Turkey's western coast. The main spread of beach is long enough (3km) and remote enough (14km from Fethiye) to have remained remarkably unspoiled by the annual invasion of European tourists. The usual seaside cluster of ice cream stands, souvenir shops, and gaudily decorated restaurants is totally absent, replaced by a string of well-contained campgrounds, replete with bungalows, hot showers, and cafeterias.

Ölü Deniz can prove a comparatively expensive retreat by Turkish standards, and the first of its several hidden costs confronts the visitor immediately: getting there. From Fethiye the most common and convenient form of transportation is the taxi, but they run for a flat rate of 200TL per person one way in either direction. In the summer, dolmuş (100TL) also run three or four times a day between Fethiye and Ölü Deniz, but finding one often involves a great deal of waiting around. If you are not in a hurry, during the high season you might consider trying to hitch a ride.

Accommodations and Food

Except for one expensive hotel there are only tent sites and bungalows at Ölü Deniz. It is simply a matter of exploring which of the three cheapest campgrounds will give you the best value for the money. Prices listed below are approximate since they are subject to negotiation during the off-season. Generally speaking, Deniz Camping tends to have the most priceworthy rates, while Sun Camping tends to be the rock-bottom cheapest. The local taxis from Fethiye are paid on a percentage basis to drive prospective customers deep into a campsite, delivering them into the welcoming hands of the eager campground proprietors. Insist upon looking around before committing yourself. Don't believe what the employees of one campground tell you about their neighbors. Derya Camping is the most notorious for making deals with taxi drivers to get you into their campground.

Deniz Camping: The best of the inexpensive campgrounds. They have the nicest bungalows, and tend to be the best bet during the off-season when they cut their rates. But in July and August, you have to be on full board to stay (1400TL per person). Off-season per person: bungalows 300TL without sheets, 500TL with sheets, 1200TL with sheets and full board. Tents 150TL. They're the best for hot water, officially from 11am-8pm, but often around the clock. Cooking, facilities, library, and laundry area. English spoken. Lunch, dinner 500TL. Late afternoon volleyball matches.

Sun Camping, located at the far end of the main beach. Off-season: singles for 300TL, with breakfast 500TL, half pension 800TL, full pension 1100TL. Tents 150TL. High season (July and August) rates are slightly higher depending upon the rate of business. Tends to be the cheapest place in high season. Hot water 4-9pm.

Derya Camping: The bungalows here are the least attractive, but it's the cheapest place to pitch your own tent at 100TL per site. All rates include breakfast. During the low-season, cramped bungalows are 400TL per person, larger bungalows 600TL, with private toilet and shower 800TL. Tent rentals 400TL, including breakfast. High season (July and August) full board per person: tent rentals 700TL, cramped bungalows 900TL, with private toilet and shower 1100TL. Hot water. English spoken. Lunch 300TL, dinner 400TL. Ping-pong table.

Motel Çetin: Clean spacious bungalows. A cut above the competition, but also a bit more expensive: high-season rates (June-Sept.) are singles 600TL, with breakfast 800TL, full pension 2000TL per person.

Motel Meri, overlooking the lagoon. Fabulous view. The only place where you can sleep in a hotel room, but you pay handsomely for the privilege. Rates per person: 2800TL without and 3100TL with breakfast during high season (June-Sept.). 20% less during the off-season. All prices subject to 15% service charge.

Eating inexpensively at Ölü Deniz is a challenge. Most people eat at the campground cafeterias where the food is overpriced, overcooked, and under-spiced. In addition, drinking water presents some hidden costs. The tap water along the main beach is not potable. (This becomes an issue when summer temperatures are as high as 110 degrees Fahrenheit.) It is possible to buy bottled water; or fill a canteen at either Fethiye or the springs at the secluded beach. For food, Deniz Camping is best; they also have an expensive grocery store. On the road to Fethiye, next to the Motel Çetin, are two expensive *kebab* restaurants. **Coşkin Kebab** is slightly better; *döner kebab* is 900TL per kilo; 600TL buys a sizeable dinner for two. If possible, arrange a meal at the house of the farmer directly behind Derya Camping. Reservations for dinner are accepted until the early afternoon of the same day. He also grows and sells fresh vegetables and other groceries for less than the campground stores charge. The best strategy, however, is to stock up with groceries at Fethiye. All the campgrounds have cooking facilities.

Sights

The primary attraction is not difficult to find—the main beach is a mammoth sweep of uncrowded sand, climaxing at its western tip in the tranquil crystal-line circle of the **lagoon,** from which Ölü Deniz derives both its name and a great deal of its fame. The waters of the lagoon are almost completely en-closed, surrounded by a band of handsome mountains, with a gentle white sand bar piercing the mouth of its turquoise surface. Picnic tables and a re-freshment stand are located nearby. Admission to the lagoon area is 30TL per person. At the eastern edge of the main beach a dirt road leads to a more secluded beach which has been converted into a picnic area. Admission is 30TL per person. Next to the beach are showers and a spring with potable water. The sand is finer here, and the relative privacy has given rise to some nudist activity. The coastline below the road is magnificent.

Two favorite excursions from Ölü Deniz are to the nearby remains of Greek Christian communities which were compelled to evacuate by the local Muslim population. The more extensive of the pair is **Karaköy,** 10km away and at present only accessible by a dirt road. Taxis from Fethiye or Ölü Deniz charge

2000TL for the trip. However, an asphalt road is being put in and the fares should go down soon. The more popular destination is tiny **Aya Nikola Island.** The swimming here is great, as is the fantastic view of the coast and the remains of a Byzantine basilica. Deniz, Derya, and Sun Camping all organize boat trips there for 500-600TL. Consult the posters on their bulletin boards for details. Usually, the fare includes a packed lunch which is a rip-off. If you can convince them to dispense with it, you may be able to go for as little as 350TL. Deniz Camping also organizes some longer boat trips, but they are usually quite expensive (5000-10,000TL). Ask to talk to Captain Bob.

Kalkan

Kalkan is the quintessential Turkish fishing village. Its enchanting harbor is enclosed by a graceful stone breakwater, surrounded by a delightful huddle of austere stone houses with handsome wooden balconies. This picture-perfect scene is punctuated by the slender white needlepoint of the village mosque's minaret. But, thankfully, the village has gone unappreciated by photographers, and tourist brochures have paid little attention to its lovely waterfront. So Kalkan remains remarkably unaffected by the tourist traffic along the Mediterranean Coast, and usually all of the summertime vacationers here are Turkish. On the main road between Fethiye (2½ hours, 250TL) and Kaş (¾ hour, 100TL), all buses running between the two ports stop at Kalkan. It is also often not too difficult to catch a ride with the local traffic between Kalkan and Kaş.

Kalkan does not have a tourist office. The **Post Office** is by the bus stop at the top of the village. Bus tickets must be bought on the bus; it is impossible to make reservations here as the bus companies have no offices at Kalkan. Accommodations here are not as cheap as one might anticipate. Rooms in any one of the handful of pensions go for about 450TL per person. Several pensions are strung along in a row comprising the village's main waterfront stretch—the **Akin, Kin, Ay,** and **Patara.** All of them are clean and comfortable. The last of these is not recommended for female guests as one member of the staff is rather forceful in expressing his affections. One level farther down, strung along the harbor in a parallel line, are the four main restaurants. **Restaurant Deniz** has particularly fine seafood.

The main beach, just past the town below the road to Kaş, is small and pebbly. Next to the beach, delicious fresh spring water flows from the rocks. A short climb farther on brings you to another smaller (and usually completely deserted) pebble beach with still waters, perfect for relaxing in the water while sunbathing. About 3km along the road to Kaş, a very steep climb beneath a small metal bridge, lies the lovely little sandy beach of **Kaputaş.** The best beaches are along the coast between Kalkan and Fethiye. Near the ancient ruins of **Letoon,** 10km through tomato fields from the main road, is an excellent beach that stretches for miles. To the west, 17km from Kalkan, is the beach at **Patara,** near the ruins of the ancient Lycian city of the same name. Unfortunately, there is no public transportation to Patara or Letoon and taxis charge 800-1000TL for the trip. The fare is not unreasonable for a group of five passengers, however. One of the most scenic stretches of highway in Turkey runs from Kalkan to Kaş, hugging the coast every inch of the way, with wonderful views of off-shore islands.

Kaş

The amiable fishing village of Kaş, tucked at the base of a ruggedly handsome mountain and surrounded on three sides by the brilliant turquoise sheen of the Mediterranean, can cast an irresistable spell over its visitors. It is not hard to see why. With few tourists, inexpensive accommodations and restaurants, genuine hospitality, and miles of wonderful serpentine coastline, Kaş is one of the Mediterranean Coast's most seductive retreats. For most visitors, it is love at first sight. The approach to Kaş by road from either direction is enchanting, winding by calm glittering inlets dotted with deserted patches of pebble beach. An uninhabited peninsula extends from one side of the town's delightful harbor, curving round to create a calm lagoon edged with rocks, ideal for swimming. For some visitors, the love affair begins only with closer acquaintance. At first, they climb off the bus and scratch their heads. Why do people rave about Kaş so much? What is there to do here? Why nothing, of course, except waste an afternoon, sip tea by the waterfront and laugh at the harbor's ridiculously crooked lighthouse; explore the mountainous countryside with its panoramic views of the coast; or just seek out a secluded cove, admire the fish through the remarkably clear water, and soak in the sun.

Orientation and Practical Information

Most of the town's activity centers around the small harbor front along the main street, **Cumhuriyet Caddesi**. At the small waterfront mosque, the street changes its name to **Hajtanc Caddesi** and leads down the peninsula, while **Elmali Caddesi** branches off to the right and becomes the road to Kalkan. By the statue of Atatürk on Cumhuriyet Cad., **Çukurbag Caddesi** leads up the hill.

Tourist Office: Cumhuriyet Cad. (tel. 23 8). Not especially helpful and only some members of the staff speak English. Open daily in summer (April 21-Sept. 30) 8am-8pm; off-season 8am-noon and 1:30-6:30pm.

Currency Exchange: Kaş' only bank is sandwiched between the post office and the bus station.

Post Office: Çukurbag Cad., one block from the waterfront. Open 8am-midnight. Telegrams and long-distance telephones open 24 hours.

Bus Station: one block up from Cumhuriyet Cad. Aydin and Pamukkale offices are at the back end of the parking lot. Akdeniz company employees, at the front end, try to monopolize the business. Buses four times a day to Izmir, Fethiye, and Kalkan. To Marmaris take the Izmir bus and get off at Gökova. Buses five times a day to Antalya, Kemer, and Demre.

Police: Cumhuriyet Cad. (tel. 24), just beyond the tourist office.

Hospital: on Hajtanc Cad. (tel. 18 5), 500 meters after the mosque, just before the campground.

Pharmacy: Hajtanc Cad., just beyond the mosque.

Accommodations

Accommodations are remarkably inexpensive here. Most pensions charge 350TL per person. In the off-season, rates can be bargained down easily. If you can convince someone to let you sleep on a roof, terrace, or garden, it usually costs 100TL.

Andifli Motel, Hajtanc Cad (tel. 42). A little more expensive than the rest, but worth it. Wonderful spotless rooms, some with balconies overlooking the sea. Hot water on the first floor. Small beach in front. 450TL per person.

Can Pansiyon, upstairs and behind the Eris Restaurant (tel. 26). Clean, comfortable rooms with terraces overlooking the harbor. Kitchen facilities and hot water. 350TL per person.

Kismet Pansiyon, located behind the Eris Restaurant (tel. 83). Run by Joseph, the hospitable French-speaking proprietor of the restaurant. Clean rooms 350TL per person. But, if there is room, you can sleep in one of the beds on the roof for 100TL.

Gürsoy Hotel, Çukurbag Cad. (tel. 38). Not the Ritz, but the cheapest place in town. Friendly chaotic dormitory atmosphere; a bit noisy. Very basic rooms. Official rates are 350TL per person, but generally rooms go for 250TL per person. In high season, singles are 300TL. If you want a room with a door that locks, you have to ask for it. All the hot water you want, but you have to heat up the wood stove yourself.

Kaş Camping, Hajtanc Cad. (tel. 50), past the hospital. Fantastic seaside location, but very mediocre facilities. Tent sites are rocky and steep. 200TL per tent, 100TL per person. Bungalows: singles 550TL, doubles 900TL, extra bed 300TL. Breakfast 100TL. Bungalows with full board: singles 1150TL, doubles 2100TL, triples 3000TL. Sleeping bag rentals 100TL each.

Food

The fruit and vegetable **market** is at the bus station. The best **bakery** is on Çukurbag Cad.—delicious fresh *pide* for 50TL. Restaurant prices are fixed by the local government, so the only choice is in the quality of the food, atmosphere, and service. *Dolma,* goulash, and other precooked dishes cost 100TL. *Şiş kebab* and *köfte* and other barbecued meat or liver dishes are 150TL. Fish ranges from 200-1200TL; the cheapest kind is *sokor.*

Derya Restaurant, on the covered alley that runs from the bus station to Cumhuriyet Cad. Limited variety, but excellent *şiş, köfte,* and other barbecued dishes. *Sokor* 200TL. Excellent *mucver* for 100TL.

Eris Restaurant, next to the tourist office. Tablecloths, music, fancier atmosphere than the competition, and the largest variety of food. The quality of the food is variable. Good *dolma,* good desserts.

Eva Kent Restaurant, next to the bus station. Specializes in *şiş kebab* and *köfte.* Good yogurt and spinach salad for 100TL.

Sights

The main beach of Kaş is neither large nor sandy, but it is beautifully situated and usually uncrowded. Unfortunately, it is about to be developed for tourism. Showers, sunshades, etc., are in the plans. As of 1983, there were only large straw mats provided for the convenience of sunbathers. The beach is a fifteen-minute walk along the dirt road off of Cumhuriyet Cad., past the police station. Swimming can be somewhat difficult here due to the rockiness of the shore. Better swimming, warmer water, and breathtaking scenery await you in the opposite direction from Kaş, following Hajtanc Cad. along the peninsula. On the way you'll pass some picturesque ruins—the lovely little **Hellenistic Theater.** The only ancient structure in Kaş to survive nearly intact, the theater overlooks the sea from a solitary elevated perch, commanding an excellent view of the Greek island of Kastelorizo. Climb to the topmost level to admire the landscape and test the excellent acoustics.

Continuing along the peninsula, beyond Kaş Camping, you'll come upon the calmly shimmering waters of the inlet formed by the peninsula. Baked to a warm temperature during the summer months and stocked with a myriad of exotic fish, the peaceful lagoon is good for swimming or snorkeling. After a twenty-minute walk from town, the road dips down and meets the water at an ideal spot for off-shore swimming. Or climb down from the road and pick a spot of your own, but beware of the sea urchins inhabiting the rocks just off-shore. Farther on, the coast is virtually deserted except for a handful of nudists attracted by the extreme privacy of the area. Women should pick their spot carefully here: when the local fishing boats discover a female sunbathing nude, they head back to town and promptly return with a full load of spectators.

If you are interested in a more active form of sightseeing, a trail leads from town up to the summit of the neighboring mountain. The one-hour hike is rewarded by the finest view available of Kaş and the surrounding coast, as well as a variety of impressive **Lycian rock tombs** carved into the jagged rock faces of the neighboring cliffs. Between June and September, a 6-7am departure will enable you to avoid the full brunt of the summer sun.

Near Kaş

The area around Kaş offers four good excursions: one trip overland to the ruins at Demre, and three worthwhile daytrips via the local excursion boats to some Lycian remains, nearby sea caves, and a Greek island.

The farming community of **Demre,** an hour's bus ride (200TL) east of Kaş on the road to Antalya, sits on a smooth, fertile plain sandwiched between the mountains and the sea. The town itself is dusty, unattractive, and not overly friendly, but several interesting attractions lie nearby—the ruins of the ancient city of **Myra,** an enormous beach, and, conveniently located by the bus stop, the **Tomb of St. Nicholas,** housed in a well-preserved fourth-century Byzantine **basilica.** The good saint is better known to Turks as Baba Noel and to Americans as Santa Claus, and has become famous throughout the world for his annual gift-bearing expeditions. Contrary to popular belief, he never resided in the North Pole. He was born in the fourth century A.D. in Patara, became bishop of Myra, and was eventually martyred. In 1087 thieves plundered his tomb, escaping to Bari, Italy with his bones. Today, the burial chapel in the basilica still houses the marble **sarcophagus** that originally contained the remains of the saint—intact, except for the gaping hole inflicted on it by his Italian kidnappers. The entrance to the basilica is covered with faded frescoes of the saints dating from the fourth century. Nicholas himself is pictured in the lower niche immediately to your right as you enter.

The ancient remains of **Myra,** 3km inland from Demre, feature some important **Lycian rock tombs** and the remains of a **Roman theater.** The local taxis charge an exorbitant 1000TL to take you to the ruins and back, or you can hike or hitch the 3km yourself. Hitching is a good strategy for reaching the huge expanse of beach. Local taxis charge 400TL for the 5km ride. You can stay in town at either the **Myra Pension** (behind #1 Müze Cad.) or the **Palmiye Pansiyon** (follow the signs) for 350TL per person.

The most popular attraction around Kaş is the boat excursion to nearby **Kekova,** a partially submerged Lycian city about 3½ hours east by boat. Give your name to the tourist office the day before; meet the captain of the boat on the harbor the following morning at 8:30am. During the summer (June 15-Sept. 1) the price is fixed at 1000TL per person. During the off-season you should be able to find someone who will take you for 500TL if you look around. It's an all-day trip (9am-9pm). First you'll visit some Byzantine ruins, then Kekova, then two nearby fishing villages, one lying under a cliff honeycombed with Lycian tombs and a hill crowned with a half-ruined castle, and both surrounded by a dozen or so huge Lycian sarcophagi. The actual remains of the Lycian city at Kekova aren't especially scintillating, but when you can explore the ruins with a snorkel in amazingly clear water, who's to complain? Wear a bathing suit under your clothes. You might want to take some food since the restaurant where the boat stops has only eggs and fish, both overpriced. Don't let them make you feel obliged to eat there; climb above, enjoy a picnic, and admire the view. Some of the boat drivers tend to rush the trip, but take your time and make sure you see everything. In windy weather, the little boats sometimes can't make it back, in which case you'll have to spend the night at Kekova.

The cost of boat trips to other destinations depends upon the number of people interested. In the summer (June 15-Sept. 1) boats cost 10,000TL, and in the off-season 5000-8000TL per day. Maximum capacity is 10-12 passengers. In summer it is usually not too difficult to find other tourists who wish to share a boat. One possible destination is the **Blue Caves,** Turkey's largest sea caves and the home of the Mediterranean's only colony of seals. Or you can visit the Greek island of **Kastelorizo** (or **Megisti**), known to Turks as **Meis Ada.** Only two miles (a half-hour by boat) from the harbor and clearly visible, the mountainous island is one of the smallest and the most isolated of the Dodecanese group (see Kastelorizo section). The Turks in Kaş will tell you that the Greeks only permit you to stay for three or four hours if you come on a Turkish boat. If you want to enter Greece, or just save money, hitch a ride from any yacht leaving the harbor. If you just want to leave Turkey in order to renew your visa, it can be done on the island. If you stay in Kaş a while, your pension proprietor may arrange a boat for you (Joseph of the Kismet Pension occasionally does this). Two boats a week connect Kastelorizo with Rhodes.

Beyond Kaş

Though less convenient to Greece, the coast east of Kaş has a great deal to offer. After Demre, the next significant bus stop is the lovely little resort of **Kemer,** with good beaches and seafood restaurants. The coastline between Antalya and Alanya is the most heavily touristed in Turkey; four superb Hellenistic and Roman archeological sites are to be found at Perge, Termessos, Aspendos, and Side. This portion of the coast is flatter and less scenic than to the west, and in July and August, temperatures usually exceed 100 degrees Fahrenheit. The stretch of coast beyond Alanya is less accessible, but the scenery improves and the coastline is less crowded. The easternmost sector between Silifke and Antakya is relatively undeveloped. Due to the lack of famous sights and the unbearable summer heat, the only visitors here are generally going to or coming from Taşucu and Mersin where the boats to Cyprus dock.

Antalya, a rough, seven-hour bus ride from Kaş or Konya, is a large, dull city with a few historical sights, some caves, and two mediocre beaches. The main reason to come here is as a step-off point for the ruined Roman cities to the east. There are several cheap hotels near the bus station for about 250TL a person, showers usually 75-100TL extra. Considering the heat (104° average in summer), you might consider splurging on a room with a private bath. At Kazim Özalp Cad., #122 (on the left as you walk into town) is the **Kervan Oteli** (tel. 12044), with very clean rooms with private shower baths—singles 850TL, doubles 1500TL, triples 2000TL—you can sit and soak all day. For the best view of the harbor, stay at the **Ertan Pension** (tel. 15535), #9 Uzuqarsi Sokak (go straight at the clock tower). Singles 600TL, doubles 1100TL, triples 1200TL (rooms with private shower-bath about 200TL more).

To get to the **Tourist Office,** walk down Kazim Özalp until you come to the intersection with the clock tower, turn right onto Cumhuriyet Cad. and it is about ten minutes on the left. In summer open Mon.-Fri. 8am-7pm, Sat. and Sun. 9am-6pm (tel. 11747). Two hundred meters down the same street, after it becomes K. Evren Bulvari, you'll find the official **Turkish Maritime Lines Agent** on the right.

Much farther down the same road (take a *dolmuş* for 25TL) is the **Archeological Museum,** containing finds from excavations in the area (open 8am-noon and 1:30-5:30pm, closed Mon.). Don't miss the museum if you're going to see the ruins. The harbor serving Turkish Maritime Lines is a long 10km down the road. Take a *dolmuş* marked "Liman" from any of the *dolmuş* stops along K. Evren Bulvari (35TL). They run frequently until 8:30pm.

East of Antalya stretches what was the Roman province of **Pamphylia;** there are several important and only partially excavated sites in the area. A guidebook is very helpful when visiting the ruins. The local publication, *Pamphylia: An Archeological Guide,* (500TL) is more informative and better translated than most books of this genre. It includes plans of the sites, so you'll know what you're looking at. At **Perge** (16km from Antalya), the theater with its beautiful marble reliefs, the stadium, and the long colonnaded avenue are all in good condition and give a vivid sense of what the city was like during its heyday in the second and third centuries A.D. (Open 8:30am-6pm, admission 40TL, students 20TL, cameras 100TL.) To get here from Antalya take a *dolmuş* to Aksu from the central *dolmuş* station, then walk 1km.

Much more impressive are the ruins at **Aspendos** 49km from Antalya. The huge (15,000-20,000 person) theater is one of the best preserved in the world—even the stage has remained almost completely intact. To get to the turn-off from Antalya, take the Manavgat *dolmuş* 5km past the village of Serik. From the turn-off, the ruins are another 4km; there are no *dolmuş* (taxis are extremely rare). It can be thumbed, but you'll have to wait a while. Bring a hat and plenty of water. Aspendos has the same hours and admission fee as Perge. It is possible to visit both Aspendos and Perge as a long daytrip from Antalya. Start early, and go to Aspendos first; Perge is on the way back.

Side is on a point where the beaches and the ruins are right next to each other—considering the summer heat, this is a feature not to be sneezed at. Unfortunately, the town is the favorite vacation destination from Ankara. Although best visited as a daytrip in summer, if you choose to stay in Side, the street between the bus station and the beach is lined with pensions (800TL for doubles)—the probability of finding a room is directly proportional to its distance from the beach. Near the beginning of the street, off to the left, the pension **Ankara** is overpriced considering the level of comfort, but it often has space—doubles 800TL, beds on the roof 400TL. Further down, on an alleyway off to the right, the **Grup** pension (German spoken) is much nicer (450TL per person) but is usually full in summer. About two hundredyards to the east stretches the best beach in Side (you'll have to walk to the end to avoid the crowds), and the ideal place to sack out. As in the rest of Turkey, however, you should not attempt this alone—and watch valuables *closely.* You can wash off the salt in the outdoor shower at the Micro Pisco.

You'll have no problem finding the ruins; particularly outstanding is the second century A.D. **theater,** with a splendid view from the top. The sites are labeled, and a small archeological museum houses the finds in what were once Roman baths. (Open 9am-noon and 1-5:30pm, closed Mon. in winter). 40TL, students 20TL, cameras 100TL.

There are a few direct buses daily to Side (100TL) from Antalya and Alanya; otherwise take one of the buses running between Antalya and Alanya (about once an hour) and have them let you off at the turn-off near Manavgat. From here it's an easy *dolmuş* ride (50TL for the remaining 3km).

Alanya, an hour east of Manavgat and two hours from Antalya, is an unabashed resort town, teeming with tourist shops and hotels. Fortunately, the most developed area is along the beaches somewhat out of town; the center is still charming, fringed by lush parks right along the water. Alanya lies at the base of a large promontory, dominated by the walls of the thirteenth-century **Alaaddin Castle.** Buses run to Antalya every two hours (300TL).

Buses stop along the main coastal road; walk east past the PT then take the next right into town. The **Plaj Hotel** is found right where the end of the east beach meets the promontory. Large, clean rooms, many with balconies; singles 500TL, doubles 900TL, triples 1200TL. For a cheaper place, follow the street to your left as you step out and up along the promontory. The **Yayla Palas** is simple but very clean and cheap; 400TL per person includes use of shower. In both places, rooms overlooking the bustling street are interesting, but noisy until the music stops at midnight-1am. On the same street as the Yayla, further out towards the dock is the **Tourist Office,** open daily 8am-5pm (French and some English spoken; gives out a map of the town). There's **camping** at **Yeni International Motel,** on the far east end of town; across the street from the beach, it costs 140TL per peson, 120TL for a tent, 100TL for a car.

The restaurants along the water are atmospheric, but dinners can quickly add up to 1000TL per person. Less expensive restaurants can be found back in town. The small **Alanya Museum** (open 8:30am-noon, 1:30-6:30pm; 20TL) houses collections of Hellenistic, Roman, and Turkish coins and ceramics, some old carpets, and a bold bronze statuette of Herakles from the second century A.D.

Antony gave the region east of Alanya, ancient Cilicia, to Cleopatra as a wedding present. Today, *dolmuş* service connects Alanya with Gazipaşa, the next town east. There's nothing to detain you here, so get a *dolmuş* to **Anamur,** which has a magnificent castle above its two beaches. **Silifke,** 100km from Anamur, has a Crusader castle, and from nearby Taşucu you can get to Girne on Cyprus for 300TL.

Mersin is a large, modern port which offers little to the tourist except some Neolithic ruins to the north and three weekday boats to Cyprus (Mağusa). **Adana,** 68km farther southeast, is more interesting than Mersin and offers fine mosques; if you're heading east you might want to stop here. **Antakya** is the last major city before the Syrian border. The Biblical Antioch, it was the site of St. Paul's first proselytizing among the Gentiles.

A Final Note

The history of *Let's Go* is as motley as the crew that produces it and the styles that go into its far-from-seamless prose. Older now than most of the current staff members, *Let's Go* began in 1960 as a pamphlet issued to passengers on a student charter flight. It featured a comprehensive four-page section on France. The 1968 edition included a section on "The Traveling Girl" and suggested that the reader take underwear to Europe. Over the years, *Let's Go* has expanded from a single book on Western Europe to nine books, covering all of Europe and the United States as well as parts of Asia and North Africa. Those original four pages on France have ballooned into a four-hundred-page regional guide, and a tenth book, on Mexico, is well into production.

Of the fifty-odd Harvard students who compile the guide, thirty are traveling researchers, masters of ferry-boat and picnic-table prose. These harried correspondents scribble out manuscripts while dashing across counties, countries, and occasionally continents. Editors select researchers every March from a pool of over one hundred applicants on the basis of solo travel experience, linguistic flair, and *chutzpah*.

In 1983, one bout with a Greek surgeon, two automobile accidents, three con jobs, four tropical diseases, and five counts of grand larceny brightened the lives of the *Let's Go* researchers while the editorial staff sequestered itself in a remote basement office. In the space of three month four tropical diseases, and five counts of grand larceny brightened the lives of the *Let's Go* researchers while the editorial staff sequestered itself in a remote basement office. In the space of three months, some thirty thousand pages of manuscript (nearly twenty thousand of which were legible) flooded the underground headquarters. A platoon of ardent editors and intrepid typists reduced this imposing mass to about twelve thousand pages of text.

Labor Day travelers on the People Express flights between Boston and New York may encounter an exhausted courier clutching an over-large suitcase, headed for the Flatiron Building.

INDEX

A
AAA see American Automobile Association
Advanced Booking Excursion Fare (APEX) 29
Aegina 222-4
Aegina Town 222-3
Afissos 133
Afsendiou (Kos) 293
Agia Galini 324
Agia Roumeli 336, 338
Agia Triada 321-2
Agio Nikolaos 106
Agios Ioanis 132
Agios Nikolaos (Crete) 344-6
Air travel: to Greece 28-9, to Cyprus 354, to Turkish Coast 379
Akrotiri (Crete) 334
Akrotiri (Santorini) 198
Alanya 426-7
Alexandroupolis 167
Aliens Bureau (Athens) 16, 41
Alonissos 214-6
Alphabet, Greek 27
American Automobile Association (AAA) 18, 21
American Express (AMEX) 17-8, 21
American Hellenic Chamber of Commerce 41
Amnissos 319-20
Amorgos 189-90
Andritsena 98
Andros 176-7
Anogia 320
Antalya 425
Antiparos 182-3
APEX see Advanced Booking Excursion Fare
Aphrodisias 402-3
Apollo Coast 66-7
Apolon (Naxos) 187
Arachova 122
Archeological Institute of America 42
Architecture: Greek 46-7, Islamic 383-4
Areopolis 113-4
Argos 79-81
Argostoli (Cephalonia) 245-6
Arkadi Monastery (Crete) 328
Art 46-7
Arvi 349
Asclepion (Kos) 292-3
Aspendos 426
Assini 85
Astipalea 303-4

ATHENS 53-67
Athens 53-64: orientation 53-4, practical information 55-6, accommodations 56-8, food 59-60, sights 60-3, nightlife 63-4

B
BankAmerica travelers checks 18
Barclay's travelers checks 18
Batis 166
Beach Blanket Bingo Meets Frankenstein see Matala
Bergama 405
Boats see Ferry travel
Bodrum 406-11
Brauron 69
Buses: international 30, domestic Greece 35-6, Cyprus 354, Turkish Coast 379
Business hours: Greece 34, Cyprus 356

C
Cameras 22
Camping: Greece 40, Cyprus 356-7, Turkish Coast 380
Canadian Universities Travel Service see Travel CUTS
Çanakkale 405-6
Cape Sounion 66
Cars 38-39
Caunos 416-7
Cephalonia 245-8
Chalki (Naxos) 187
Chalkis 125
Charter flights 28-9
Chersonissos 340-1
Chios 260-3
Chios Town 261-2
Chora (Patmos) 301-2
Chora Sfakion 337
Chorio (Kalymnos) 297
CIEE see Council on International Educational Exchange
Citicorp travelers checks 18
Cold damp dark, the 115
College Year in Athens, Inc. 42-3
Consulates 14-5
Corfu 231-42
Corfu Town 232-9
Corinth, Ancient 74-5
Corinth, New 72-4

Council on International Educational Exchange (CIEE) 13, 17, 21, 28, 29
CRETE 309-52
Curium 361
Currency and Exchange: Greece 34, Cyprus 356, Turkish Coast 379-80
Customs 16
CYCLADES 169-204
CYPRUS 353-76
Cyprus Tourism Organization 356
CYTA 356

D
Daphni 68
Datça 416
Deak-Perera 18
Delos 173-5
Delphi 119-22
Delphic Oracle 120
Demre 424
Diafani (Karpathos) 307
Didyma 399-400
Dikteon Cave (Crete) 343-4
Dimitsana 99
Disabled travelers 25
DODECANESE 271-308
Dodoni 145
Dolmuş see Service taxis: Turkish Coast
Drakia 133
Drugs: Greece 24, Turkish Coast 380

E
Edessa 149-50
Educational Travel Centre (ETC) 14
Electricity 22
Elefsina 68-9
ELPA see Greek Automobile and Touring Club
Embassies 14
Ephesus 391-5
Epidavros 85-6
ETC see Educational Travel Centre
Euboea see Evia
Euromos 400
Evia (Euboea) 125-8

F
Falassarna 340
Famagusta 376
Federation of International Youth Travel Organization (FIYTO) 17, 31, 33

429